Principles of Network and System Administration

Second Edition

Principles of Network and System Administration

Second Edition

Mark Burgess
Oslo University College, Norway

John Wiley & Sons, Ltd

Other Wiley Editorial Offices

John Wiley & Sons Inc., 111 River Street, Hoboken, NJ 07030, USA

Jossey-Bass, 989 Market Street, San Francisco, CA 94103-1741, USA

Wiley-VCH Verlag GmbH, Boschstr. 12, D-69469 Weinheim, Germany

John Wiley & Sons Australia Ltd, 33 Park Road, Milton, Queensland 4064, Australia

John Wiley & Sons (Asia) Pte Ltd, 2 Clementi Loop #02-01, Jin Xing Distripark, Singapore 129809

John Wiley & Sons (Canada) Ltd, 22 Worcester Road, Etobicoke, Ontario M9W 1L1

Wiley also publishes its books in a variety of electronic formats. Some content that appears
in print may not be available in electronic books.

Library of Congress Cataloging-in-Publication Data

Burgess, Mark, 1966–
    Principles of network and system administration / Mark Burgess. – 2nd ed.
        p. cm.
    ISBN 0–470–86807–4 (Paper : alk. paper)
1. Computer networks – Management.   2. Computer systems.   I. Title.
    TK5105.5.B863 2003
    005.4´3 – dc22

                                                                        2003019766

British Library Cataloguing in Publication Data

A catalogue record for this book is available from the British Library

ISBN-10: 0–470–86807–4 (pbk.)   ISBN-13: 978-0-470-86807-2 (pbk.)

Typeset in 10/12pt Bookman by Laserwords Private Limited, Chennai, India
Printed and bound in Great Britain by Biddles Ltd, King's Lynn, Norfolk
This book is printed on acid-free paper responsibly manufactured from sustainable forestry,
in which at least two trees are planted for each one used for paper production.

Contents

Preface to second edition

This book grew originally out of a one-semester course in Network and System Administration which has now run successfully for six years at Oslo College, Norway. This first course is an introductory course and involves about thirty percent theory and seventy percent practical work [40]; it assumes knowledge equivalent to a typical college course on Operating Systems as well as some basic computer skills. The purpose of this book was to provide a mixture of theory and practice for a such course in system administration; to extract those principles and ideas of system administration which do not change on a day-to-day basis; and to present them in a defensible manner [188].

In writing the second edition, I have not only corrected shortcomings and anachronisms in the original edition, but have attempted to compile a textbook that goes beyond a single introductory course, and paints a larger picture. This has been a very difficult task, and my book is very imperfect. It attempts to strike a balance between completeness and selective tasting to satisfy the needs of a student with a limited budget. It cannot hope to cover everything that a system administrator ought to know, but it can provide a beginning. The resulting book forms a sufficient basis for two or more courses at university level, assuming a previous knowledge of operating systems. Indeed, this book is now the hub of our Masters Degree in Network and System Administration at Oslo University College. It makes contact with more traditional areas of computer science and engineering, and provides an overview of material that will help to bind other more specific works into a coherent whole. Although it covers material sufficient for more than one course, it did not seem appropriate to divide the book into smaller parts, as it also functions as an initial reference work for the field.

On a personal note, I never want to write a book like this again! Maintaining this book is far harder than maintaining computers – and I can't do it with cfengine. The possibility for error and anachronism is enormous and the amount of work to compile, maintain and generalize these concepts huge. To assemble the book, I have reviewed the research work of many authors, most of which has centered around the USENIX organization and its many groundbreaking conferences. In spite of a desire for completeness, I have resisted the temptation to include every possible detail and fact which might be useful in the practical world. Several excellent books already exist, which cover this need, and I see no reason to compete with them (see the recommended reading list). I have therefore limited myself to examples of each which are either practical or illustrative. If any operating systems have been unfairly brought into focus, I hope it is only the Free operating systems such as GNU/Linux and the BSD's, from which no one other than their users will benefit.

For the new edition, I must add my thanks to several individuals. I am most grateful to Steven Jenkins and Nick Christenson for both thorough, heroic readings and razor-sharp critiques of the almost finished manuscript. Steve VanDevender and Æleen Frisch also provided helpful comments and corrections. Thanks to Jonathan Laventhol for interesting discussions about company policy in the UK and for providing me with real-world examples, and the permission to adapt and reproduce them here. Thanks to Hal Miller and Lee Damon for permission to reproduce their versions of the SAGE code of ethics. Part of the section on SNMP is based on Jürgen Schönwälder's excellent writings; I'm grateful to him for allowing me the indulgence, and for reading the result. Rob Apthorpe also allowed me to base the discussion of fault trees on his LISA paper that I whipped and beat him for a year earlier. I have benefited from my lunch discussions with Kyrre Begnum and Assi Gueye.

From the original edition, I offer my special thanks to Tina Darmohray for her comments and encouragement, as well as for allowing me to adapt some firewall examples from her excellent notes. Russ Harvey of the University of California, Riverside also made very positive and useful criticisms of the early materials. Special thanks to Per Steinar Iversen for making detailed comments and constructive criticisms on the manuscript from his near-infinite reservoir of technical expertise. Thanks also to David Kuncicky, Sigmund Straumsnes and Kjetil Sahlberg for their careful readings and suggestions for improvement. Any remaining errors must be entirely someone else's fault (but I haven't figured out who I can blame yet). Thanks to Knut Borge of USIT, University of Oslo, for moderating the course on which this book is based and for teaching me many important things over the years; also to Tore Øfsdahl and Harald Hofsæter, our system administrators at Oslo College who constantly help me in often intangible ways. Sigmund generated the graphs which appear in this volume. In addition to them, Runar Jørgensen and Hårek Haugerud commented on the manuscript. Ketil Danielsen has provided me with both tips and encouragement. Thanks to Greg Smith of the NASA Ames Research Center for performance tips and to Steve Traugott for discussions on infrastructure. I'm grateful to Cami Edwards of USENIX for making copies of old LISA proceedings available from the archives. I was shocked to discover just how true is the panel debate: why do we keep reinventing the wheel? I should also like to thank all of the students at Oslo University College who have attended my lectures and have inspired me to do better than I might otherwise have done. Finally, all credit to the SAGE/USENIX association for their unsurpassed work in spreading state of the art knowledge about computing systems of all sizes and shapes.

Mark Burgess
Oslo University College

Chapter 1

Introduction

1.1 What is network and system administration?

Network and system administration is a branch of *engineering* that concerns the operational management of human–computer systems. It is unusual as an engineering discipline in that it addresses both the technology of computer systems and the users of the technology on an equal basis. It is about putting together a network of computers (workstations, PCs and supercomputers), getting them running and then *keeping* them running in spite of the activities of *users* who tend to cause the systems to fail.

A system administrator works for users, so that they can use the system to produce work. However, a system administrator should not just cater for one or two selfish needs, but also work for the benefit of a whole community. Today, that community is a global community of machines and organizations, which spans every niche of human society and culture, thanks to the Internet. It is often a difficult balancing act to determine the best policy, which accounts for the different needs of everyone with a stake in a system. Once a computer is attached to the Internet, we have to consider the consequences of being directly connected to all the other computers in the world.

In the future, improvements in technology might render system administration a somewhat easier task – one of pure resource administration – but, today, system administration is not just an administrative job, it is an extremely demanding engineer's job. It's about hardware, software, user support, diagnosis, repair and prevention. System administrators need to know a bit of everything: the skills are technical, administrative and socio-psychological.

The terms *network administration* and *system administration* exist separately and are used both variously and inconsistently by industry and by academics. System administration is the term used traditionally by mainframe and Unix engineers to describe the management of computers whether they are coupled by a network or not. To this community, network administration means the management of network infrastructure devices (routers and switches). The world of personal computers (PCs) has no tradition of managing individual computers and their subsystems, and thus does not speak of system administration, *per se.*

To this community, network administration is the management of PCs in a network. In this book, we shall take the first view, since this is more precise.

Network and system administration are increasingly challenging. The complexity of computer systems is increasing all the time. Even a single PC today, running Windows NT, and attached to a network, approaches the level of complexity that mainframe computers had ten years ago. We are now forced to think *systems* not just computers.

1.2   Applying technology in an environment

A key task of network and system administration is to build hardware configurations, another is to configure software systems. Both of these tasks are performed for users. Each of these tasks presents its own challenges, but neither can be viewed in isolation.

Hardware has to conform to the constraints of the physical world; it requires power, a temperate (usually indoor) climate, and a conformance to basic standards in order to work systematically. The type of hardware limits the kind of software that can run on it. Software requires hardware, a basic operating system infrastructure and a conformance to certain standards, but is not necessarily limited by physical concerns as long as it has hardware to run on.

Modern software, in the context of a global network, needs to inter-operate and survive the possible hostilities of incompatible or inhospitable competitors. Today the complexity of multiple software systems sharing a common Internet space reaches almost the level of the biological. In older days, it was normal to find proprietary solutions, whose strategy was to lock users into one company's products. Today that strategy is less dominant, and even untenable, thanks to networking. Today, there is not only a physical environment but a technological one, with a diversity that is constantly changing. Part of the challenge is to knit apparently disparate pieces of this community into a harmonious whole.

We apply technology in such an environment for a purpose (running a business or other practice), and that purpose guides our actions and decisions, but it is usually insufficient to provide all the answers. Software creates abstractions that change the basic world view of administrators. The software domain .com does not have any fixed geographical location, but neither do the domains .uk or .no. Machines belonging to these software domains can be located anywhere in the world. It is not uncommon to find foreign embassies with domain names inside their country of origin, despite being located around the world. We are thus forced to think globally.

The global view, presented to us by information technology means that we have to think penetratingly about the systems that are deployed. The extensive filaments of our inter-networked systems are exposed to attack, both accidental and malicious in a competitive jungle. Ignore the environment and one exposes oneself to unnecessary risk.

1.3   The human role in systems

For humans, the task of system administration is a balancing act. It requires patience, understanding, knowledge and experience. It is like working in the casualty ward of a hospital. Administrators need to be the doctor, the psychologist, and – when instruments fail – the mechanic. We need to work with the limited resources we have, be inventive in a crisis, and know a lot of general facts and figures about the way computers work. We need to recognize that the answers are not always written down for us to copy, that machines do not always behave the way we think they should. We need to remain calm and attentive, and learn a dozen new things a year.

Computing systems require the very best of organizational skills and the most professional of attitudes. To start down the road of system administration, we need to know many *facts* and build confidence though experience – but we also need to know our limitations in order to avoid the careless mistakes which are all too easily provoked.

1.4   Ethical issues

Because computer systems are human–computer communities, there are ethical considerations involved in their administration. Even if certain decisions can be made objectively, e.g. for maximizing productivity or minimizing cost, one must have a policy for the use and management of computers and their users. Some decisions have to be made to protect the rights of individuals. A system administrator has many responsibilities and constraints to consider. Ethically, the first responsibility must be to the greater network community, and then to the users of our system. An administrator's job is to make users' lives bearable and to empower them in the production of real work.

1.5   Is system administration a discipline?

Is system administration a science? Is computer science a science? The same question has been asked of many disciplines. We can answer the question in like mind here. Unlike physics, chemistry or biology, system administration is lacking in a systematic body of experimental data which would give its rules and principles an empirical rigor. However, that is not to say that system administration cannot be made to follow this scientific form. Indeed, there is good reason to suppose that the task is easier in the administration of systems than in fields like software engineering, where one cannot easily separate human subjective concerns from an objective empiricism.

System administration practices, world-wide, vary from the haphazard to the state of the art. There is a variety of reasons for this. The global computer community has grown considerably, operating systems have become increasingly complex, but the number of system administrators has not grown in proportion. In the past, system administration has been a job which has not been carried out by dedicated professionals, but rather by interested computer users, as a necessary chore in getting their work done. The focus on making computers easy to use has distracted many vendors from the belief that their computers should also be easy to manage. It is only over the gradual course of time that this has changed, though even today, system administrators are a barely visible race, until something goes wrong.

The need for a formal discipline in system administration has been recognized for some time, though it has sometimes been met with trepidation by many corners of the Internet community, perhaps because the spirit of free cooperation which is enjoyed by system administrators could easily be shattered by too pompous an academic framework. Nonetheless, there are academics and software engineers working on system administration, and it is quite common for system administrators to spawn from a scientific education.

Academic concerns aside, the majority of computer systems lie in the private sector, and the Internet is only amplifying this tendency. In order to be good at system administration, a certain amount of dedication is required, with both theoretical and practical skills. For a serious professional, system administration is a career in engineering. There is now an appreciable market for consulting services in security and automation of system administrative tasks. Not only is system administration a fascinating and varied line of work, it can also be lucrative.

1.6   The challenges of system administration

System administration is not just about installing operating systems. It is about planning and designing an efficient *community* of computers so that real *users* will be able to get their jobs done. That means:

- Designing a network which is logical and efficient.

- Deploying large numbers of machines which can be easily upgraded later.

- Deciding what services are needed.

- Planning and implementing adequate security.

- Providing a comfortable environment for users.

- Developing ways of fixing errors and problems which occur.

- Keeping track of and understanding how to use the enormous amount of knowledge which increases every year.

Some system administrators are responsible for both the hardware of the network and the computers which it connects, i.e. the cables as well as the computers. Some are only responsible for the computers. Either way, an understanding of how data flow from machine to machine is essential as well as an understanding of how each machine affects every other.

In all countries outside the United States, there are issues of internationalization, or tailoring the input/output hardware and software to local language. Internationalization support in computing involves three issues:

- Choice of keyboard: e.g. British, German, Norwegian, Thai etc.

- Fonts: Roman, Cyrillic, Greek, Persian etc.

- Translation of program text messages.

Inexperienced computer users usually want to be able to use computers in their own language. Experienced computer users, particularly programmers, often prefer the American versions of keyboards and software in order to avoid the awkward placement of commonly used characters on non-US keyboards.

1.7 Common practice and good practice

In a rational world, every choice needs a reason, even if that reason is an arbitrary choice. That does not undermine the need for a book of this kind, but it cautions us about accepting advice on trust. This is just the scientific method at work: informed scepticism and constant reappraisal.

If this book does nothing else, it should encourage a critical approach to network and system engineering. One can spend a career hearing advice from many different sources and not all of it will be good advice. The best generic advice anyone can give in life is: think for yourself; pay attention to experts but don't automatically believe anyone.

In the system administration world, it is common to speak of 'best practice'. A scientific mind is immediately suspicious of such a claim. In what sense is a practice best? When and for whom? How should one evaluate such a claim. This is one of the things we wish to consider in this book.

Clearly, it is always a good idea to see what others have done in the past, but history has no automatic authority. There are three reasons why ideas catch on and 'everyone does it':

- Someone did it once, the idea was copied without thinking and no one has thought about it since. Now everyone does it because everyone else does it.

- Experts have thought a lot about it and it really is the best solution.

- An arbitrary choice had to be made and now it is a matter of convention.

For example, in the British Isles it is a good idea to drive on the left-hand side of the road. That's because someone started doing so and now everyone does it – but it's not just a fad: lives actually depend on this. The choice has its roots in history and in the dominance of right-handed sword-wielding carriage drivers and highwaymen but, for whatever reason, the opposite convention now dominates in other parts of the world and, in Britain, the convention is now mainly preserved by the difficulty of changing. This is not ideal, but it is reasonable.

Some common practices, however, are bizarre but adequate. For instance, in parts of Europe the emergency services Fire, Police and Ambulance have three different numbers (110, 112 and 113) instead of one simple number like 911 (America) or, even simpler, 999 (UK). The numbers are very difficult to remember; they are not even a sequence. Change would be preferable.

Other practices are simply a result of blind obedience to poorly formulated rules. In public buildings there is a rule that doors should always open outwards from a room. The idea is that in the case of fire, when people panic, doors should 'go with the flow'. This makes eminent sense where large numbers of people are involved. Unfortunately the building designers of my College have taken this literally and done the same thing with every door, even office doors in narrow corridors. When there is a fire (actually all the time), we open our doors into the faces of passers-by (the fleeing masses), injuring them and breaking their noses. The rule could perhaps be reviewed.

In operating systems, many conventions have arisen, e.g. the conventions for naming the 'correct' directory for installing system executables, like daemons, the permissions required for particular files and programs and even the use of particular software; e.g. originally Unix programs were thrown casually in usr/bin or etc; nowadays sbin or libexec are used by different schools of thought, all of which can be discussed.

As a system administrator one has the power to make radical decisions about systems. Readers are encouraged to make logical choices rather than obedient ones.

1.8   Bugs and emergent phenomena

Operating systems and programs are full of bugs and emergent features that were not planned or designed for. Learning to tolerate bugs is a matter of survival for system administrators; one has to be creative and work around these bugs. They may come from:

- Poor quality control in software or procedures.

- Problems in operating systems and their subsystems.

- Unfortunate clashes between incompatible software, i.e. one software package interferes with the operation of another.

- Inexplicable phenomena, cosmic rays, viruses and other attacks.

A system administrator must be prepared to live with and work around these uncertainties, no matter what the reason for their existence. Not all problems can be fixed at source, much as one would prefer this to be the case.

1.9   The meta principles of system administration

Many of the principles in this book derive from a single overriding issue: they address the *predictability* of a system. The term system clearly implies an operation that is *systematic*, or predictable – but, unlike simple mechanical systems, like say a clock, computers interact with humans in a complex cycle of feedback, where uncertainty can enter at many levels. That makes human–computer systems difficult to predict, unless we somehow fix the boundaries of what is allowed, as a matter of policy.

Principle 1 (Policy is the foundation). *System administration begins with a policy – a decision about what we want and what should be, in relation to what we can afford.*

Policy speaks of what we wish to accomplish with the system, and what we are willing to tolerate of behavior within it. It must refer to both the component parts and to the environment with which the system interacts. If we cannot secure predictability, then we cannot expect long-term conformance with a policy.

> **Principle 2 (Predictability).** *The highest level aim in system administration is to work towards a predictable system. Predictability has limits. It is the basis of reliability, hence trust and therefore security.*

Policy and predictability are intertwined. What makes system administration difficult is that it involves a kind of 'search' problem. It is the hunt for a stable region in the landscape of all policies, i.e. those policies that can lead to stable and predictable behavior. In choosing policy, one might easily promote a regime of cascading failure, of increasing unpredictability, that degenerates into chaos. Avoiding these regimes is what makes system administration difficult.

As networks of computers and people grow, their interactions become increasingly complex and they become *non-deterministic*, i.e. not predictable in terms of any manageable number of variables. We therefore face another challenge that is posed by inevitable growth:

> **Principle 3 (Scalability).** *Scalable systems are those that grow in accordance with policy; i.e. they continue to function predictably, even as they increase in size.*

These meta-themes will recur throughout this book. The important point to understand about predictability is that it has limits. Human–computer systems are too complex and have too many interactions and dependencies to be deterministic. When we speak of predictability, it must always be within a margin of error. If this were not the case, system administration would not be difficult.

1.10 Knowledge is a jigsaw puzzle

Factual knowledge, in the world of the system administrator, is almost a disposable commodity – we use it and we throw it away, as it goes out of date. Then we need to find newer, more up-to-date knowledge to replace it. This is a continual process; the turn-around time is short, the loop endless, the mental agility required demanding. Such a process could easily splay into chaos or lapse into apathy. A robust discipline is required to maintain an island of logic, order and stability in a sea of turbulent change.

This book is about the aims and principles involved in maintaining that process – i.e. it is about the core of knowledge and ideas that remain constant throughout the turnover. It is supplemented with some practical, example recipes and advice. When you master this book you will come to understand why no single book will ever cover every aspect of the problem – you need a dozen others as well.[1] True knowledge begins with understanding, and understanding is a jigsaw puzzle

---

[1]Later you might want to look at some of the better how-to books such as those in the recommended reading list, refs. [223, 123, 122, 211].

you will be solving for the rest of your life. The first pieces are always the hardest to lay correctly.

1.11   To the student

To study this subject, we need to cultivate a way of thinking which embodies a basic scientific humility and some core principles:

- Independence, or self-sufficiency in learning. We cannot always ask someone for the right answer to every question.

- Systematic and tidy work practices.

- An altruistic view of the system. Users come first: collectively and only then individually.[2]

- Balancing a fatalistic view (the inevitability of errors) with a determination to gain firmer control of the system.

Some counter-productive practices could be avoided:

- The belief that there exists a right answer to every problem.

- Getting fraught and upset when things do not work the way we expect.

- Expecting that every problem has a beginning, a middle and an end (some problems are chronic and cannot be solved without impractical restructuring).

We can begin with a checklist:

- Look for answers in manuals and newsgroups.

- Use controlled trial and error to locate problems.

- Consider all the information; listen to people who tell you that there is a problem. It might be true, even if you can't see it yourself.

- Write down experiences in an A–Z so that you learn how to solve the same problem again in the future.

- Take responsibility for your actions. Be prepared for accidents. They are going to happen and they will be your fault. You will have to fix them.

- Remember tedious jobs like vacuum cleaning the hardware once a year.

- After learning about something new, always pose the question: *how does this apply to me?*

---

[2]The needs of the many outweigh the needs of the few (or the one)...

American English is the language of the net. System administrators need it to be able to read documentation, to be able to communicate with others and to ask questions on the Internet. Some sites have even written software tools for training novice administrators. See for instance, ref. [278]. Information can be found from many sources:

- Printed manuals

- Unix manual pages (man and apropos and info commands)

- The World Wide Web

- RFCs (Requests for comment), available on the web

- Newsgroups and discussions

- Papers from the SAGE/Usenix LISA conferences [22]

- More specialized books

A supplement to this book, with a collection of useful recipes and facts, is provided as a resource for system administrators at http://www.iu.hio.no/SystemAdmin. More detailed online course materials relating to the Oslo University Colleges Masters Degree are available at http://www.iu.hio.no/teaching/materials.

1.12 Some road-maps

This book contains many overlapping themes. If you are browsing through the book with a specific aim, the following road-maps might help you to shorten your journey.

1. Resource management: Chapters 2, 4, 5, 6, 7, 8, 9

2. Human management: Chapters 3, 5, 8, 11

3. IP networking: Chapters 2, 3, 6, 8, 10, 11, 12

4. System analysis: Chapters 3, 6, 8, 13

5. Security: Chapters 3, 5, 6, 7, 8, 11, 12

Much of the thinking behind the security policy recommendations in ISO 17799 permeate the book.

Exercises

Self-test objectives

1. What kinds of issues does system administration cover?

2. Is system administration management or engineering?

3. Why does the physical environment play a role in system administration?

4. Describe why ethics and human values are important.

5. Is system administration a science? Why/why not?

6. State the top-most principles that guide network and system administrators.

Problems

As a practical, hands-on subject, network and system administration exercises are heavily dependent on what equipment is available to students. Course instructors should therefore use the exercises in this book as templates for customizing their own exercises rather than viewing them as literal instructions.

1. Browse through this whole book from start to finish. Browsing information is a skill you will use a lot as a system administrator. Try to get an overall impression of what the book contains and how it is laid out.

2. List what you think are the important tasks and responsibilities of a system administrator. You will have the opportunity to compare this with your impressions once we reach the end of the book.

3. Locate other books and information sources which will help you. These might take the form of books (such as the recommended reading list at the end of this book) or newsgroups, or web sites.

4. Buy an A–Z notebook for systemizing the facts and knowledge that you pick up along the way.

5. What is an RFC? Locate a list of RFCs on a WWW or FTP server.

Chapter 2

System components

In this chapter we assemble the components of a human–computer community, so as to prepare the way for a discussion of their management.

2.1 What is 'the system'?

In system administration, the word *system* is used to refer both to the operating system of a computer and often, collectively the set of all computers that cooperate in a network. If we look at computer systems analytically, we would speak more precisely about *human–computer systems*:

> **Definition 1 (human–computer system).** *An organized collaboration between humans and computers to solve a problem or provide a service. Although computers are deterministic, humans are non-deterministic, so human–computer systems are non-deterministic.*

For the machine part, one speaks of operating systems that govern the operation of computers. The term *operating system* has no rigorously accepted definition. Today, it is often thought of as the collection of all programs bundled with a computer, combining both in a kernel of basic services and utilities for users; some prefer to use the term more restrictively (see below).

2.1.1 Network infrastructure

There are three main components in a human–computer system (see figure 2.1):

- *Humans*: who use and run the fixed infrastructure, and cause most problems.

- *Host computers*: computer devices that run software. These might be in a fixed location, or mobile devices.

- *Network hardware*: This covers a variety of specialized devices including the following key components:

– dedicated computing devices that direct traffic around the Internet. Routers talk at the IP address level, or 'layer 3',[1] simplistically speaking.

– *Switches*: fixed hardware devices that direct traffic around local area networks. Switches talk at the level of Ethernet or 'layer 2' protocols, in common parlance.

– *Cables*: There are many types of cable that interconnect devices: fiber-optic cables, twisted pair cables, null-modem cables etc.

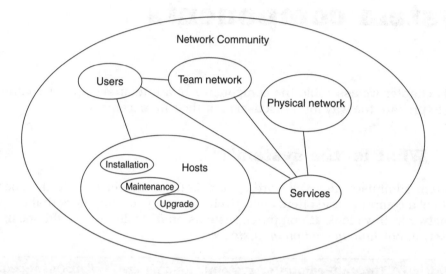

Figure 2.1: Some of the key dependencies in system administration. The sum of these elements forms a networked community, bound by human ties and cable ties. Services depend on a physical network, on hosts and users, both as consumers of the resources and as teams of administrators that maintain them.

2.1.2 Computers

All contemporary computers in common use are based on the Eckert–Mauchly–von Neumann architecture [235], sketched in figure 2.2. Each computer has a clock which drives a *central processor unit* (CPU), a *random access memory* (RAM) and an array of other devices, such as disk drives. In order to make these parts work together, the CPU is designed to run programs which can read and write to hardware devices. The most important program is the *operating system kernel*. On top of this are software layers that provide working abstractions for programmers and users. These consist of files, processes and services. Part of 'the system' refers to the network devices that carry messages from computer to computer, including the cables themselves. Finally, the system refers to all of these parts and levels working together.

---

[1]Layer 3 refers loosely to the OSI model described in section 2.6.1.

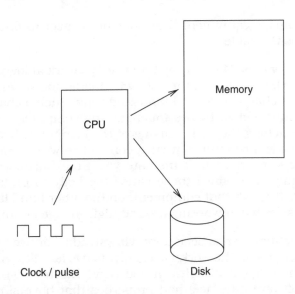

Figure 2.2: The basic elements of the von Neumann architecture.

2.2 Handling hardware

To be a system administrator it is important to have a basic appreciation of the frailties and procedures surrounding hardware. In our increasingly virtual world of films and computer simulations, basic common-sense facts about the laws of physics are becoming less and less familiar to us, and people treat fragile equipment with an almost casual disregard.

All electronic equipment should be treated as highly fragile and easily damaged, regardless of how sturdy it is. Today we are far too blasé towards electronic equipment.

- Never insert or remove power cords from equipment without ensuring that it is switched off.

- Take care when inserting multi-pin connectors that the pins are oriented the right way up and that no pins are bent on insertion.

Moreover:

- *Read instructions:* When dealing with hardware, one should always look for and *read* instructions in a manual. It is foolish to make assumptions about expensive purchases. Instructions are there for a reason.

- *Interfaces and connectors:* Hardware is often connected to an interface by a cable or connector. Obtaining the correct cable is of vital importance. Many manufacturers use cables which look similar, superficially, but which actually are different. An incorrect cable can result in damage to an interface. Modem cables in particular can damage a computer or modem if they are incorrectly wired, since some computers supply power through these cables which can damage equipment that does not expect to find a power supply coming across the cable.

- *Handling components:* Modern day CMOS chips work at low voltages (typically 5 volts or lower). Standing on the floor with insulating shoes, you can pick up a static electric charge of several thousand volts. Such a charge can instantly destroy computer chips. Before touching any computer components, earth yourself by touching the metal casing of the computer. If you are installing equipment inside a computer, wear a conductive wrist strap. Avoid wearing rubber sandals or shoes that insulate you from Earth when dealing with open-case equipment, since these cause the body to build up charge that can discharge through that equipment; on the other hand it is a good idea to wear rubber soles when working around high voltage or current sources.

- *Disks:* Disk technology has been improving steadily for two decades. The most common disk types, in the workplace, fall into two families: ATA (formerly IDE) and SCSI. The original IDE (Integrated Drive Electronics) and SCSI (Small Computer Software Interface) had properties that have since evolved faster than the prejudices about them. ATA disks are now generally cheaper than SCSI disks (due to volume sales) and excel at sequential access, but SCSI disks have traditionally been more efficient at handling multiple accesses due to a multitasking bus design, and are therefore better in multitasking systems, where random access is important. However, filesystem design also plays an important role in determining the perceived performance of each; i.e. how operating systems utilize buses during updates is at least as important as bus performance itself. Interesting comparisons show that IDE technology has caught up with the head start that SCSI disks once had [322] for many purposes, but not all.

  SCSI [208] comes in several varieties: SCSI 1, SCSI 2, wide SCSI, fast-wide etc. The difference has to do with the width of the data-bus and the number of disks which can be attached to each controller. There are presently three SCSI standards: SCSI-1, SCSI-2 and SCSI-3. The SCSI-2 standard defines also wide, fast and fast/wide SCSI. Each SCSI disk has its own address (or number) which must be set by changing a setting on the disk-cabinet or by changing jumper settings inside the cabinet. Newer disks have programmable identities. Disk chain buses must be terminated with a proper terminating connector. Newer disks often contain automatic termination mechanisms integrated into the hardware. The devices on the SCSI bus talk to the computer through a controller. On modern PCs the SCSI controller is usually connected to the PCI bus either as an on-board solution on motherboards or as a separate card in a PCI slot. Other buses are also used as the carrier of the SCSI protocol, like FireWire (IEEE 1394) and USB. The SCSI standard also supports removable media devices (CD-ROM, CD-R, Zip drives), video frame grabbers, scanners and tape streamers (DAT, DLT).

- *Memory:* Memory chips are sold on small pluggable boards. They are sold in different sizes and with different speeds. A computer has a number of slots where they can be installed. When buying and installing RAM, remember

- The physical size of memory plugins is important. Not all of them fit into all sockets.

- Memory is sold in units with different capacities and data rates. One must find out what size can be used in a system. In many cases one may not mix different types.

- There are various incompatible kinds of RAM that work in different ways. Error correcting RAM, for instance, is tolerant to error from external noise sources like cosmic rays and other ultra short wave disturbances. It is recommended for important servers, where stability is paramount.

- On some computers one must fill up RAM slots in a particular order, otherwise the system will not be able to find them.

Another aspect of hardware is the extent to which weather and environment are important for operation.

- *Lightning:* strikes can destroy fragile equipment. No fuse will protect hardware from a lightning strike. Transistors and CMOS chips burn out much faster than any fuse. Electronic spike protectors can help here, but nothing will protect against a direct strike.

- *Power:* failure can cause disk damage and loss of data. A UPS (uninterruptible power supply) can help.

- *Heat:* Blazing summer heat or a poorly placed heater can cause systems to overheat and suddenly black out. One should not let the ambient temperature near a computer rise much above 25 degrees Centigrade. Clearly some equipment can tolerate heat better than other equipment. Bear in mind that metals expand significantly, so moving parts like disks will be worst affected by heat. Increased temperature also increases noise levels that can reduce network capacities by a fraction of a percent. While this might not sound like much, a fraction of a percent of a Giga-bit cable is a lot of capacity. Heat can cause RAM to operate unpredictably and disks to misread/miswrite. Good ventilation is essential for computers and screens to avoid electrical faults.

- *Cold:* Sudden changes from hot to cold are just as bad. They can cause unpredictable changes in electrical properties of chips and cause systems to crash. In the long term, these changes could lead to cracks in the circuit boards and irreparable chip damage.

- *Humidity:* In times of very cold weather and very dry heat, the humidity falls to very low levels. At these times, the amount of static electricity builds up to quite high levels without dissipating. This can be a risk to electronic circuitry. Humans pick up charge just by walking around, which can destroy fragile circuitry. Paper sticks together causing paper crashes in laser printers. Too much humidity can lead to condensation and short circuits.

2.3 Operating systems

An operating system has a number of key elements: (i) a *technical layer of software* for driving the hardware of the computer, like disk drives, the keyboard and the screen; (ii) a *filesystem* which provides a way of organizing files logically, and (iii) a simple *user interface* which enables users to run their own programs and to manipulate their files in a simple way.

Of central importance to an operating system is a core software system or *kernel* which is responsible for allocating and sharing the resources of the system between several running programs or *processes*. It is supplemented by a number of supporting *services* (paging, RPC, FTP, WWW etc.) which either assist the kernel or extend its resource sharing to the network domain. The operating system can be responsible for sharing the resources of a single computer, but increasingly we are seeing *distributed operating systems* in which execution of programs and sharing of resources happens without regard for hardware boundaries; or *network operating systems* in which a central server adds functionality to relatively dumb workstations. Sometimes programs which do not affect the job of sharing resources are called *user programs*.

In short, a computer system is composed of many subsystems, some of which are *software systems* and some of which are *hardware systems*. The operating system runs interactive programs for humans, *services* for local and distributed users and support programs which work together to provide the infrastructure which enables machine resources to be shared between many processes. Some operating systems also provide text editors, compilers, debuggers and a variety of other tools. Since the operating system (OS) is in charge of a computer, all requests to use its resources and devices need to go through the OS kernel. An OS therefore provides *legal entry points* into its code for performing basic operations like writing to devices.

For an operating system to be managed consistently it has to be possible to prevent its destruction by restricting the privileges of its users. Different operating systems vary in their provisions for restricting privilege. In operating systems where any user can change any file, there is little or no possibility of gaining true control over the system. Any accident or whim on the part of a user can make uncontrollable changes.

Today it important to distinguish between a user interface and an operating system. A windowing system is a *graphical user interface* (GUI); an operating system shares resources and provides functionality. This issue has been confused by the arrival of the operating systems collectively called Windows, which include a graphical user interface. In principle, an operating system can have any number of different windowing interfaces, one for every taste.

Operating systems may be classified both by how many tasks they can perform 'simultaneously' and by how many users can be using the system 'simultaneously'. That is: *single-user* or *multi-user* and *single-tasking* or *multitasking*. A multi-user system must clearly be multitasking. The table below shows some examples.

OS	Users	Tasks	Processors
MS/PC DOS	S	S	1
Windows 3x	S	QM	1
Macintosh System 7.*	S	QM	1
Windows 95/98/ME	S	M*	1
AmigaDOS	S	M	1
Unix-like	M	M	n
VMS	M	M	n
NT-like	S/M	M	n
Windows 2000/XP	M	M	n
OS390 (zOS)	M	M	n

The first of these (MS/PC DOS/Windows 3x) are single-user, single-task systems which build on a ROM-based library of basic input–output functions called the BIOS. Windows also includes a windowing library. These are system calls which write to the screen or to disk etc. Although all the operating systems can service *interrupts*, and therefore simulate the appearance of multitasking in some situations, the DOS environment cannot be thought of as a multitasking system in any sense. Only a single user application can be open at any time. Note that Windows 3x is not really a separate operating system from DOS; it is a user interface to DOS.

The Macintosh System 7 could be classified as single-user quasi-multitasking (QM). Apple's new Mac OS X has a Unix-like emulator running on top of a Mach kernel. That means that it is possible to run several user applications simultaneously. A window manager can simulate the appearance of several programs running simultaneously, but this relies on each program obeying specific rules in order to achieve the illusion. Prior to Mac OS X, the MacIntosh was not a true multitasking system; if one program crashed, the whole system would crash. Similarly, Windows 9x purported to be pre-emptive multitasking but many program crashes would also crash the entire system.

Windows NT is now a family of operating systems from Microsoft (including Windows 2000 and XP), based, in part, on the old VAX/VMS kernel from the Digital Equipment Corporation and the Windows 32 API. It has virtual memory and multi-threaded support for several processors. NT has a built-in object model and security framework which is amongst the most modern in use. Windows NT has been reincarnated now in the guise of Windows 2000 and XP, which adopt many of the successful features of the Novell system, such as consistent directory services. Later versions of Windows NT and Windows 2000 (a security and kernel enhanced version of NT) allow true multitasking and multiple logins also through a terminal server. Windows 2000 thus has comparable functionality to Unix in this respect.

IBM S/370, S/390 mainframe and AS/400 mini-computers are widely used in banks and large concerns for high level processing. These are fully multitasking systems of high calibre, supporting virtual machine architectures. These mainframe computers are now referred to as the IBM z-series computers, and the operating system is z/OS. Z/OS has a virtual hosting manager that can support multiple concurrent operating systems. Z-series computers have enjoyed a revival with the advent of GNU/Linux. IBM has reported running many thousands of concurrent Linux virtual kernels on their mainframe computers.

Unix is arguably the most important operating system today, both for its widespread use and its historical importance. We shall frequently refer to Unix-like operating systems below. 'Unix' (insofar as it is correct to call it that now) comes in many forms, developed by different manufacturers and enthusiasts. Originally designed at AT&T, Unix split into two camps early on: BSD (Berkeley Software Distribution) and System V (or System 5) (AT&T license). The BSD version was developed as a research project at the University of California Berkeley (UCB). Many of the networking and user-friendly features originate from these modifications. With time, these two versions have been merged back together and most systems are now a mixture of both worlds. Historically BSD Unix has been most prevalent in universities, while System 5 has been dominant in business environments. In the 1990s Sun Microsystems and Hewlett Packard started a move towards System V, keeping only the most important features of the BSD system, but later suppressed the visible System V aspects in favor of BSD again. Today, the differences are few, thanks to a de-facto standardization. A standardization committee for Unix called POSIX, formed by the major vendors and independent user groups, has done much to bring compatibility to the Unix world. Here are some common versions of Unix.

Unix-like OS	Manufacturer	Type
BSD	Univ. California Berkeley	BSD
SunOS (Solaris 1)	Sun Microsystems	BSD/Sys V
Solaris(2)	Sun Microsystems	Sys V/BSD
Tru64	DEC/Compaq/HP	BSD/Sys V
HPUX	Hewlett Packard	Sys V
AIX	IBM	Sys V / BSD
IRIX	Silicon Graphics	Sys V
GNU/Linux	GPL Free Software	Posix (Sys V/BSD)
MacOS X	Apple	BSD/Sys V
Unixware	Novell	Sys V

Note that multiple mergers have now stirred this mixture: Ultrix, OSF/1 and Digital Unix were products of DEC before the Compaq merger, Tru64 was what Compaq renamed Digital Unix after the merger, and now it is called HP Tru64 Unix.

The original BSD source code is now available to the public and the GNU/Linux source code is free (and open source) software. Unix is one of the most portable operating systems available today. It runs on everything from palm-computers to supercomputers. It is particularly good at managing large database applications and can run on systems with hundreds of processors. Most Unix-like operating systems support symmetric multi-threaded processing and all support simultaneous logins by multiple users.

2.3.1 Multi-user operating systems

The purpose of a multi-user operating system is to allow multiple users to share the resources of a single host. In order to do this, it is necessary to protect users from one another by giving them a unique identity or *user name* and a private login area, i.e. by restricting their privilege. In short, we need to simulate a virtual workstation for each individual user, with private files and private processes.

2.3.2 The legacy of insecure operating systems

The home computer revolution was an important development which spread cheap computing power to a large part of the world. As with all rapid commercial developments, the focus in developing home operating systems was on immediate functionality, not on planning for the future. The home computer revolution preceded the network revolution by a number of years and home computer operating systems did not address security issues. Operating systems developed during this period include Windows, MacIntosh, DOS, Amiga-DOS. All of these systems are completely insecure: they place *no limits* on what a determined user can do.

Fortunately these systems will slowly be replaced by operating systems which were designed with resource sharing (including networking) in mind. Still, there is a large number of insecure computers in use and many of them are now connected to networks. This should be a major concern for a system administrator. In an age where one is forced to take security extremely seriously, leaving insecure systems where they can be accessed physically or by the network is a potentially dangerous situation. Such machines should not be allowed to hold important data and they should not be allowed any privileged access to network services. We shall return to this issue in the chapter on security.

2.3.3 Securable operating systems

To distinguish them from insecure operating systems we shall refer to operating systems like Unix and NT as *securable* operating systems. This should not give the impression that Unix and NT are secure: by its nature, security is not an achievable goal, but an aspiration that includes accepted levels of risk (see section 11.4). Nevertheless, these operating systems do have the mechanisms which make a basic level of preventative security possible.

A fundamental prerequisite for security is the ability to restrict access to certain system resources. The main reason why DOS, Windows 9x and the MacIntosh are so susceptible to virus attacks is because any user can change the operating system's files. Properly configured and bug-free Unix/NT systems are theoretically immune to such attacks, if privilege is not abused, because ordinary users do not have the privileges required to change system files.[2] Unfortunately the key phrases *properly configured* and *bug-free* highlight the flaw in this dream.

In order to restrict access to the system we require a notion of *ownership* and *permission*. Ordinary users should not have access to the hardware devices of a secure operating system's files, only their own files, for then they will not be able do anything to compromise the security of the system. System administrators need access to the whole system in order to watch over it, make backups and keep it running. Secure operating systems thus need a privileged account which can be used by the system administrator when he/she is required to make changes to the system.

2.3.4 Shells or command interpreters

Today it is common for operating systems to provide graphical window systems for all kinds of tasks. These are often poorly suited to system administration because they only allow us to choose between pre-programmed operations which the program designers foresaw when they wrote the program. Most operating systems provide an alternative command line user interface which has some form of interpreted language, thus allowing users to express what they want with more freedom and precision. Windows proprietary shells are rudimentary; Unix shells are rich in complexity and some of them are available for installation on Windows. Shells can be used to write simple programs called *scripts* or *batch files* which often simplify repetitive administrative tasks.

2.3.5 Logs and audits

Operating system kernels share resources and offer services. They can be asked to keep lists of transactions which have taken place so that one can later go back and see exactly what happened at a given time. This is called logging or auditing.

Full system auditing involves logging every single operation that the computer performs. This consumes vast amounts of disk space and CPU time and is generally inadvisable unless one has a specific reason to audit the system. Part of auditing used to be called system accounting from the days when computer accounts really were accounts for real money. In the mainframe days, users would pay for system time in dollars and thus accounting was important since it showed who owed what [133], but this practice remains mainly on large super-computing installations today and 'computing farms'.

Auditing has become an issue again in connection with security. Organizations have become afraid of break-ins from system crackers and want to be able to trace the activities of the system in order to be able to look back and find out the identity of a cracker. The other side of the coin is that system accounting is so resource consuming that the loss of performance might be more important to an organization than the threat of intrusion.

---

[2]Not all viruses have to change system files, it is also possible to infect programs directly in memory if process security is weak.

For some organizations auditing is important, however. One use for auditing is so-called *non-repudiation*, or non-denial. If everything on a system is logged, then users cannot back away and claim that they did not do something: it's all there in the log. Non-repudiation is a security feature which encourages users to be responsible for their actions.

2.3.6 Privileged accounts

Operating systems that restrict user privileges need an account which can be used to configure and maintain the system. Such an account must have access to the whole system, without regard for restrictions. It is therefore called a privileged account.

In Unix the privileged account is called *root*, also referred to colloquially as the super-user. In Windows, the *Administrator* account is similar to Unix's root, except that the administrator does not have automatic access to everything as does root. Instead he/she must be first granted access to an object. However the Administrator always has the right to grant themself access to a resource so in practice this feature just adds an extra level of caution. These accounts place virtually no restriction on what the account holder can do. In a sense, they provide the privileged user with a skeleton key, a universal pass to any part of the system.

Administrator and root accounts should never be used for normal work: they wield far too much power. This is one of the hardest things to drill into novices, particularly those who have grown up using insecure operating systems. Such users are used to being able to do whatever they please. To use the privileged account as a normal user account would be to make the systems as insecure as the insecure systems we have mentioned above.

> **Principle 4 (Minimum privilege).** *Restriction of unnecessary privilege protects a system from accidental and malicious damage, infection by viruses and prevents users from concealing their actions with false identities. It is desirable to restrict users' privileges for the greater good of everyone on the network.*

Inexperienced users sometimes aspire to gain administrator/root privileges as a mark of status. This can generate the myth that the purpose of this account is to gain power over others. In fact the opposite is true: privileged accounts exist precisely because one does *not* want to have too much power, except in exceptional circumstances. The corollary to our principle is this:

Corollary to principle (Minimum privilege). *No one should use a privileged root or Administrator account as a user account. To do so is to place the system in jeopardy. Privilege should be exercised only when absolutely necessary.*

One of the major threats to Internet security has been the fact that everyone can now be root/Administrator on their own host. Many security mechanisms associated with trusted ports, TCP/IP spoofing etc. are now broken, since all of the security of these systems lies in the outdated assumption that ordinary users will not have privileged access to network hardware and the kernel. Various schemes for providing limited privilege through special shells, combined with the

setuid mechanism in Unix, have been described. See refs. [152, 64]. See also the
amusing discussion by Simmons on use and abuse of the superuser account in
ref. [286] and an administration scheme where local users have privileges on their
own hosts [91].

2.3.7 Comparing Unix-like and Windows computers

The two most popular classes of operating system today are Unix-like operating
systems (i.e. those which are either derived from or inspired by System V or BSD)
and Microsoft Windows NT-like operating systems. We shall only discuss Windows
NT and later derivatives of the Windows family, in a network context. For the sake
of placing the generalities in this book in a clearer context, it is useful to compare
'Unix' with Windows.

The file and directory structures of Unix and Windows are rather different, but
it is natural that both systems have the same basic elements.

Unix-like OS	Windows
chmod	CACLS
chown	CACLS
chgrp	*No direct equivalent*
emacs	*Wordpad* or emacs in GNU tools
kill	kill command in Resource Kit
ifconfig	ipconfig
lpq	lpq
lpr	lpr
mkfs/newfs	format and label
mount	net use
netstat	netstat
nslookup	nslookup
ps	pstat in Resource Kit
route	route
setenv	set
su	su in resource kit
tar	tar command in Cygnus tools
traceroute	tracer

Table 2.1: Comparison of Unix and Windows shell commands.

Unix-like operating systems are many and varied, but they are basically similar in concept. It is not the purpose of this book to catalogue the complete zoological inventory of the 'Unix' world; our aim is to speak primarily of generalities which rise above such distinctions. Nonetheless, we shall occasionally need to distinguish the special features of these operating systems, and at least distinguish them from Windows. This should not detract from the fact that Windows has adopted much from the Unix cultural heritage, even though superficial attempts to hide this (e.g. renaming / with \ in filenames, changing the names of some commands etc.) might obscure the fact.

Windows NT, 2000, XP are multitasking operating systems from Microsoft which allow users to log in to a console or *workstation*. The consoles may be joined together in a network with common resources shared by an NT *domain*. An NT host is either a network server or a personal workstation. The basic Windows distribution contains only a few tools which can be used for network administration. The Resource Kit is an extra package of documentation and unsupported software which nonetheless provides many essential tools. Other tools can be obtained free of charge from the network.

Windows did not have a remote shell login feature like Unix at the outset. One may now obtain a Terminal Server which gives Windows telnet-like functionality. This adds an important possibility: that of direct remote administration. The

Unix-like OS	Windows
/usr	%SystemRoot% usually points to C:\WinNT
/bin or /usr/bin	%SystemRoot%\System32
/dev	%SystemRoot%\System32\Drivers
/etc	%SystemRoot%\System32\Config
/etc/fstab	No equivalent
/etc/group	%SystemRoot%\System32\Config\SAM* (binary)
/etc/passwd	%SystemRoot\%\System32\Config\SAM* (binary)
/etc/resolv.conf	%SystemRoot%\System32\DNS*
/tmp	C:\Temp
/var/spool	%SystemRoot%\System32\Spool

Table 2.2: Comparison of Unix and Windows directories and files.

free Perl Win32 package and related tools provides tools for solving a number of problems with NT from a script viewpoint.

Although we are ignoring many important operating systems by comparing just two main players, a comparison of Unix-like operating systems with NT covers most of the important differences. The latest offerings from the MacIntosh world, for instance, are based on emulation of BSD 4.4 Unix and MacOS on a Mach kernel, with features designed to compete with NT. IBM's z-series operating

Unix-like OS	Windows
Standard libraries	WIN32 API
Unix libraries	Posix compatibility library
Symbolic/hard Links	Hard links (short cuts)
Processes	Processes
Threads	Threads
Long filenames	Long filenames on NTFS
Mount disk on directory	Mount drive A: B: etc
endl is LF	endl is CR LF
UID (User ID)	SID (Subject ID)
groups	groups
ACLs (non standard)	ACLs
Permission bits	(Only in ACLs or with Cygwin)
Shared libraries	DLL's
Environment variables	Environment variables
Daemons/services/init	Service control manager
DNS/DHCP/bootp (free)	DNS/DHCP (NT server)
X windows	X windows
Various window managers	Windows GUI
System admin GUI (non-standard)	System Admin GUI (Standard)
cfengine	cfengine as of 1.5.0
Any client-server model	Central server model
rsh	limited implementation in server
Free software	Some free software
Perl	Perl + WIN32 module
Scripts	Scripts
Shells	DOS Command window
Primitive security	Primitive security
Dot files for configuration	System registry
Pipes with comm1 | comm2	Combinations comm1 | comm2
Configuration by text/ascii files	Config by binary database

Table 2.3: Comparison of Unix and Windows software concepts.

system for mainframes has experienced a revival of interest since the GNU/Linux system was ported to run on its virtual engine.

Unix is important, not only for its endurance as the sturdy workhorse of the network, but also for its cultural significance. It has influenced so many other operating systems (including Windows) that further comparisons would be largely redundant. Let us note briefly then, for the record, the basic correspondences between Unix-like operating systems and Windows. Many basic commands are very similar. Tables 2.1, 2.2 and 2.3 give some comparisons between Unix and Windows concepts.

Note: there are differences in nomenclature. What Windows refers to as pipes[3] in its internal documentation is not what Unix refers to as pipes in its internal documentation.

A major problem for Windows has been the need for compatibility with DOS, through Windows 9x to NT. Since both DOS and Windows 9x are insecurable systems, this has led to conflicts of interest. Unix vendors have tried to keep step with Microsoft's impressive user interface work, in spite of the poor public image of Unix (often the result of private dominance wars between different Unix vendors) but the specially designed hardware platforms built by Unix vendors have had a hard time competing with inferior but cheaper technology from the PC world.

2.4 Filesystems

Files and filesystems are at the very heart of what system administration is about. Almost every task in host administration or network configuration involves making changes to files. We need to acquire a basic understanding of the principles of filesystems, so what better way than to examine some of the most important filesystems in use today. Specifically what we are interested in is the user interfaces to common filesystems, not the technical details which are rather fickle. We could, for instance, mention the fact that old filesystems were only 32 bit addressable and therefore supported a maximum partition size of 2GB or 4GB, depending on their implementation details, or that newer filesystems are 64 bit addressable and therefore have essentially no storage limits. We could mention the fact that Unix uses an index node system of block addressing, while DOS uses a tabular lookup system: the list goes on. These technical details are of only passing interest since they change at an alarming pace. What is more constant is the user functionality of the filesystems: how they allow file access to be restricted to groups of users, and what commands are necessary to manage this.

2.4.1 Unix file model

Unix has a hierarchical filesystem, which makes use of directories and subdirectories to form a tree. All file systems on Unix-like operating systems are based on a system of *index nodes*, or *inodes*, in which every file has an index entry stored in a special part of the filesystem. The inodes contain an extensible system of pointers

---

[3]Ceci n'est pas une pipe!

to the actual disk blocks which are associated with the file. The inode contains essential information needed to locate a file on the disk.

The top or start of the Unix file tree is called the root filesystem or '/'. Although the details of where common files are located differ for different versions of Unix, some basic features are the same.

The file hierarchy

The main subdirectories of the root directory together with the most important file are shown below. Their contents are as follows.

- /bin Executable (binary) programs. On most systems this is a separate directory to /usr/bin. In SunOS, this is a pointer (link) to /usr/bin.

- /etc Miscellaneous programs and configuration files. This directory has become very messy over the history of Unix and has become a dumping ground for almost anything. Recent versions of Unix have begun to tidy up this directory by creating subdirectories /etc/mail, /etc/inet etc.

- /usr This contains the main meat of Unix. This is where application software lives, together with all of the basic libraries used by the OS.

- /usr/bin More executables from the OS.

- /usr/sbin Executables that are mainly of interest to system administrators.

- /usr/local This is where users' custom software is normally added.

- /sbin A special area for (often statically linked) system binaries. They are placed here to distinguish commands used solely by the system administrator from user commands, and so that they lie on the system root partition, where they are guaranteed to be accessible during booting.

- /sys This holds the configuration data which go to build the system kernel. (See below.)

- /export Network servers only use this. This contains the disk space set aside for client machines which do not have their own disks. It is like a 'virtual disk' for diskless clients.

- /dev and /devices A place where all the 'logical devices' are collected. These are called 'device nodes' in Unix and are created by mknod. Logical devices are Unix's official entry points for writing to devices. For instance, /dev/console is a route to the system console, while /dev/kmem is a route for reading kernel memory. Device nodes enable devices to be treated as though they were files.

- /home (Called *users* on some systems.) Each user has a separate login directory where files can be kept. These are normally stored under /home by some convention decided by the system administrator.

- /root On newer Unix-like systems, root has been given a home-directory which is no longer the root of the filesystem '/'. The name root then loses its logic.

- /var System V and mixed systems have a separate directory for spooling. Under old BSD systems, /usr/spool contains spool queues and system data. /var/spool and /var/adm etc. are used for holding queues and system log files.

Every Unix directory contains two 'virtual' directories marked by a single dot and two dots.

```
ls -a
.      ..
```

The single dot represents the directory one is already in (the current directory). The double dots mean the directory one level up the tree from the current location. Thus, if one writes

```
cd /usr/share
cd ..
```

the final directory is /usr. The single dot is very useful in C programming if one wishes to read 'the current directory'. Since this is always called '.' there is no need to keep track of what the current directory really is. '.' and '..' are hard links to the current and parent directories, respectively.

Symbolic links

A symbolic link is a pointer or an alias to another file. The command

```
ln -s fromfile /other/directory/tolink
```

makes the file fromfile appear to exist at /other/directory/tolink simultaneously. The file is not copied, it merely appears to be a part of the file tree in two places. Symbolic links can be made to both files and directories.

A symbolic link is just a small file that does not appear explicitly to the user, and which contains the name of the real file one is interested in. Unlike Windows's short-cuts, symbolic links cannot be seen to be files with a text editor; they are handled specially at the level of the operating system. Application programs can choose whether they want to treat a symbolic link as a separate file object, or simply as an alias to the file it points to. If we remove the file a symbolic link points to, the link remains – it just points to a non-existent file.

Hard links

A *hard link* is a duplicate directory reference to an *inode* in the filesystem. It is in every way equivalent to the original file reference. If a file is pointed to by a number of hard links, it cannot be removed until all of the links are removed. If a file has n hard links, all of them must be removed before the file can be removed.

The number of hard links to a file is stored in the filesystem *index node* for the file. A hard link is created with the `ln` command, without the `-s` option. Hard links are, in all current Unix-like operating systems, limited to aliasing files on the same filesystem. Although the POSIX standard specifies the possibility of making hard links across disk partitions with separate filesystems, this has presented an insurmountable technical difficulty because it would require inodes to have a global numbering scheme across all disk partitions. This would be an inefficient overhead for an additional functionality of dubious utility, so currently this has been ignored by filesystem designers.

File access control

In order to restrict privilege to files on the system, and create the illusion of a virtual host for every logged-on user, Unix records information about *who* creates files and also who is allowed to access them later. Unix makes no policy on what names files should have: a file can have any name, as long as it does not contain illegal characters such as forward-slash. A file's contents are classified by so-called *magic numbers* which are 16 or 32 bit codes kept at the start of a file and defined in the magic number file for the system. Magic numbers tell the system what application a file type belongs to, or how it should be interpreted (see the Unix command `file`). This is in contrast to systems like Windows, where file extensions (e.g. `.EXE`) are used to identify file contents. Under Unix, file extensions (e.g. `.c`) are only discretionary.

Each user has a unique *username* or *loginname* together with a unique *user id* or *uid*. The user id is a number, whereas the login name is a text string – otherwise the two express the same information. A file belongs to user A if it is *owned* by user A. User A then decides whether or not other users can read, write or execute the file by setting the *protection bits* or the *permission* of the file using the command `chmod`.

In addition to user identities, there are groups of users. The idea of a group is that several named users might want to be able to read and work on a file, without other users being able to access it. Every user is a member of at least one group, called the *login group* and each group has both a textual name and a number (*group id*). The *uid* and *gid* of each user is recorded in the file `/etc/passwd` (see chapter 6). Membership of other groups is recorded in the file `/etc/group` or on some systems `/etc/logingroup`.

The following output is from the command `ls -lag` executed on a SunOS type machine.

```
lrwxrwxrwx  1 root   wheel         7 Jun  1  1993 bin -> usr/bin
-r--r--r--  1 root   bin      103512 Jun  1  1993 boot
drwxr-sr-x  2 bin    staff     11264 May 11 17:00 dev
drwxr-sr-x 10 bin    staff      2560 Jul  8 02:06 etc
drwxr-sr-x  8 root   wheel       512 Jun  1  1993 export
drwx------  2 root   daemon      512 Sep 26  1993 home
-rwxr-xr-x  1 root   wheel    249079 Jun  1  1993 kadb
lrwxrwxrwx  1 root   wheel         7 Jun  1  1993 lib -> usr/lib
```

```
drwxr-xr-x  2 root   wheel      8192 Jun  1  1993 lost+found
drwxr-sr-x  2 bin    staff       512 Jul 23  1992 mnt
dr-xr-xr-x  1 root   wheel       512 May 11 17:00 net
drwxr-sr-x  2 root   wheel       512 Jun  1  1993 pcfs
drwxr-sr-x  2 bin    staff       512 Jun  1  1993 sbin
lrwxrwxrwx  1 root   wheel        13 Jun  1  1993 sys->kvm/sys
drwxrwxrwx  6 root   wheel       732 Jul  8 19:23 tmp
drwxr-xr-x 27 root   wheel      1024 Jun 14  1993 usr
drwxr-sr-x 10 bin    staff       512 Jul 23  1992 var
-rwxr-xr-x  1 root   daemon  2182656 Jun  4  1993 vmunix
```

The first column is a textual representation of the protection bits for each file. Column two is the number of hard links to the file, for regular files, or the number of objects contained in a subdirectory. The third and fourth columns are the user name and group name and the remainder show the file size in bytes and the creation date. Notice that the directories /bin and /sys are symbolic links to other directories.

There are sixteen protection bits for a Unix file, but only twelve of them can be changed by users. These twelve are split into four groups of three. Each three-bit number corresponds to one *octal* number.

The leading four invisible bits give information about the type of file: is the file a *plain file*, a *directory* or a *link* etc. In the output from ls this is represented by a single character: -, d or l.

The next three bits set the so-called *s-bits* and *t-bit* which are explained below.

The remaining three groups of three bits set flags which indicate whether a file can be read r, written to w or executed x by (i) the user who created them, (ii) the other users who are in the group the file is marked with, and (iii) any user at all.

For example, the permission

```
Type Owner Group Anyone
  d   rwx   r-x   ---
```

tells us that the file is a directory, which can be read and written to by the owner, can be read by others in its group, but not by anyone else.

Note about directories. It is impossible to cd *to a directory unless the* x *bit is set. That is, directories must be 'executable' in order to be accessible.*

Here are some examples of the relationship between binary, octal and the textual representation of file modes.

```
Binary  Octal   Text

 001      1      --x
 010      2      -w-
 100      4      r--
 110      6      rw-
 101      5      r-x
  -      644     rw-r--r--
```

It is well worth becoming familiar with the octal number representation of these permissions, since they are widely used in literature.

chmod

The chmod command changes the permission or *mode* of a file. Only the owner of the file or the superuser can change the permission. Here are some examples of its use. Try them.

```
# make write-able for everyone
chmod a+w myfile

# add the user (owner) 'execute' flag for directory
chmod u+x mydir/

# open all files for everyone
chmod 755 *

# set the s-bit on my-dir's group
chmod g+s mydir/

# descend recursively into directory opening all files
chmod -R a+r dir
```

New file objects: umask

When a new file is created, the operating system must decide what default protection bits to set on that file. The variable umask decides this. umask is normally set by each user in his or her .cshrc file (see next chapter). For example

```
umask 077    # safe
umask 022    # liberal
```

umask only removes bits, it never sets bits which were not already set in 666. For instance

umask	Permission
077	600 (plain)
077	700 (dir)
022	644 (plain)
022	755 (dir)

Making programs executable

A Unix program is normally executed by typing its pathname. If the x execute bit is not set on the file, this will generate a 'permission denied' error. This protects the system from interpreting nonsense files as programs. To make a program executable for someone, you must therefore ensure that they can execute the file, using a command like

```
chmod u+x  filename
```

This command would set execute permissions for the owner of the file;

```
chmod ug+x  filename
```

would set execute permissions for the owner and for any users in the same group as the file. Note that script programs must also be readable in order to be executable, since the shell has to interpret them by reading.

chown and chgrp

These two commands change the ownership and the group ownership of a file. For example:

```
chown mark ~mark/testfile
chgrp www  ~mark/www/tmp/cgi.out
```

In newer implementations of `chown`, we can change both owner and group attributes simultaneously, by using a dot notation:

```
chown mark.www ~mark/www/tmp/cgi.out
```

Only the superuser can change the ownership of a file. This is to prevent users from being able to defeat quota mechanisms. (On some systems, which do not implement quotas, ordinary users can give a file away to another user but not get it back again.) The same applies to group ownership.

Making a group

The superuser creates groups by editing the file `/etc/group`. Normally users other than root cannot define their own groups. This is a historical weakness in Unix, and one which no one seems to be in a hurry to change. It is possible to 'hack' a solution to this which allows users to create their own groups. The format of the group file is:

```
 group-name:: group-number: comma-separated-list-of-users
```

The Unix group mechanism is very convenient, but poorly conceived. ACLs go some way to redressing its shortcomings (see below) but at an enormous price, in terms of computer resources. The group mechanism is fast and efficient, but clumsy for users.

s-bit and t-bit (sticky bit)

Apart from the read, write and execute file attributes, Unix has three other flags. The s- and t- bits have special uses. They are set as follows:

Name	Octal form	Text form
Setuid bit	chmod 4000 *file*	chmod u+s *file*
Setgid bit	chmod 2000 *file*	chmod g+s *file*
Sticky bit	chmod 1000 *file*	chmod +t *file*

The effect of these bits differs for plain files and directories and also differs between
different versions of Unix. Check particularly the manual page man sticky on
each system. The following is common behavior.

For executable files, the setuid bit tells Unix that *regardless of who runs the
program* it should be executed with the permissions and rights of the owner of the
file. This is often used to allow normal users limited access to root privileges. A
setuid-root program is executed as root for any user. The setgid bit sets the group
execution rights of the program in a similar way.

In BSD Unix, if the setgid bit is set on a directory then any new files created
in that directory assume the group ownership of the parent directory and not
the login group of the user who created the file. This is standard policy under
System V.

A directory for which the sticky bit is set restricts the deletion of files within
it. A file or directory inside a directory with the t-bit set can only be deleted or
renamed by its owner or the superuser. This is useful for directories like the mail
spool area and /tmp which must be writable to by everyone, but should not allow
a user to delete another user's files.

Access control lists

ACLs, or access control lists are a modern replacement for file modes and permissions. With access control lists we can specify precisely the access rights to
files for each user individually. Although ACLs are functionally superior to the old
Unix group ownership model, experience shows that they are too complicated for
most users in practice. Also, the overhead of reading and evaluating ACLs places
a large performance burden on a system.

Previously the only way to grant access to a file to a known list of users, was to
make a group of those users, and use the group attribute of the file. With ACLs this
is no longer necessary. ACLs are both a blessing and a nightmare. They provide a
functionality which has long been missing from operating systems, and yet they are
often confusing and even hopelessly difficult to understand in some filesystems.
One reason for this is when filesystems attempt to maintain compatibility with
older protection models (e.g. Unix/Posix permissions and ACLs, as in Solaris). The
complex interactions between creation masks for Unix permissions and inherited
properties of ACLs make ACL behavior non-intuitive. Trying to obtain the desired
set of permissions on a file can be like a flirtation with the forces of mysticism.
This is partly due to the nature of the library interfaces and partly due to poor or
non-existent documentation.

ACLs existed in several operating systems prior to Unix, but were introduced to
Unix in the DOMAIN OS by Apollo, and were later adapted by Novell, HP and other
vendors. A POSIX standard for ACLs has been drafted, but as of today there is
no adopted standard for ACLs and each vendor has a different set of incompatible
commands and data-structures. Sun Microsystems' Solaris implementation for
NFS3 is based on the POSIX draft and includes ACLs. We shall follow Solaris ACLs
in this section. GNU/Linux and the BSD operating systems do not have ACLs at
all. If we grant access to a file which is shared on the network to a machine which
doesn't support ACLs, they are ignored. This limits their usefulness in most cases.

ACLs are literally lists of access rights. Each file has a list of data structures with pairs of names and permissions:

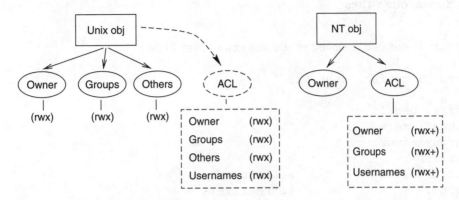

Figure 2.3: The standard permission model for file objects in Unix and Windows.

An ACL is specified by saying what permissions we would like to grant and which user or group of users the permissions should apply to. An ACL can grant access or deny access to a specific user. Because of the amount of time required to check all the permissions in an ACL, ACLs slow down file search operations. Under Solaris, the commands to read and write ACLs have the cumbersome names

- getfacl *file* Examine the ACLs for a file.

- setfacl *file* -s *permission* Set ACL entries for a file, replacing the entire list.

- setfacl *file* -m *permission* Set ACL entries for a file, adding to an existing list.

For example, if we create a new file, it ends up with a default ACL which is based upon the Unix umask value and any ACL masks which are set for the parent directory. Suppose umask is 077, and no directory ACLs are set, giving minimal rights to others:

```
mercury% touch testfile

mercury% getfacl testfile

# file: testfile
# owner: mark
# group: iugroup
user::rw-
group::---              #effective:---
mask:---
other:---
```

This tells us that a new file is created with read/write permission for the owner (mark) of the file, and no other rights are granted. To open the file for a specific user demos, one writes

```
mercury% setfacl -m user:demos:rw- testfile

mercury% getfacl testfile

# file: testfile
# owner: mark
# group: iugroup
user::rw-
user:demos:rw-            #effective:---
group::---                #effective:---
mask:---
other:---
```

To open a file for reading by a group iugroup, except for one user called robot, one would write:

```
mercury% setfacl -m group:iugroup:r--,user:robot:--- testfile

mercury% getfacl testfile

# file: testfile
# owner: mark
# group: iugroup
user::rw-
user:robot:---            #effective:---
user:demos:rw-            #effective:---
group::---                #effective:---
group:iugroup:r--         #effective:---
mask:---
other:---
```

Notice that this is accomplished by saying that the group has read permission whilst the specific user should have no permissions.

2.4.2   Windows file model

The Windows operating system supports a variety of legacy filesystems for backward compatibility with DOS and Windows 9x. These older filesystems are insecure, in the sense that they have no mechanisms for restricting access to files. The filesystem NTFS was introduced with NT in order to solve this problem. The filesystem has gone through a number of revisions and no doubt will go through many more before it reaches constancy.

NTFS, like the Unix file system, is a hierarchical file system with files and directories. Each file or directory has an owner, but no group membership. Files do not have a set of default permission bits, as does Unix; instead they all have full-blooded ACLs, which assign a set of permission bits to a specific user. NTFS ACLs are similar to other access control list models, in filesystems such as the AFS and DCE/DFS. They have all of the flexibility and all of the confusions which accompany ACLs, such as inheritance of attributes from parent directories and creation masks. The NTFS file system is indexed by a master file table, which serves an analogous function to Unix's inodes, though the details are somewhat different.

Filesystem layout

Drawing on its DOS legacy, Windows treats different disk partitions as independent floppy disks, labelled by a letter of the alphabet:

```
A: B: C: D: ...
```

For historical reasons, drive `A:` is normally the diskette station, while drive `C:` is the primary hard disk partition. Other drive names are assigned at random, but often `H:` is reserved for partitions containing users' home directories. Unlike Unix, different devices are not sewn seamlessly into a unified file tree, though this will probably change in a future release of Windows. Originally, DOS chose to deviate from its Unix heritage by changing the subdirectory separator from / to \. Moreover, since each device is treated as a separate entity, there is a root directory on every disk partition:

```
A:  B:  C:  ...
```

and one has a notion of *current working drive*, as well as *current working directory*. These distinctions often cause confusion amongst users who work with both Unix and Windows.

The layout of the Windows filesystem has changed through the different versions, in an effort to improve the structure. This description relates to NT 4.0. The system root is usually stored in `C:\WinNT` and is generally referred to by the system environment variable `%SystemRoot%`.

- `C:\I386` This directory contains binary code and data for the Windows operating system. This should normally be left alone.

- `C:\Program Files` This is Windows's official location for new software. Program packages which you buy should install themselves in subdirectories of this directory. More often than not they choose their own locations, however, often with a distressing lack of discipline.

- `C:\Temp` Temporary scratch space, like Unix's /tmp.

- `C:\WinNT` This is the root directory for the Windows system. This is mainly for operating system files, so you should not place new files under this directory yourself unless you really know what you are doing. Some software packages might install themselves here.

- C:\WinNT\config Configuration information for programs. These are generally binary files so the contents of Windows configuration files is not very interesting.

- C:\WinNT\system32 This is the so-called system root. This is where most system applications and data-files are kept.

File extensions

Whereas files can go by any name in Unix, Microsoft operating systems have always used the concept of file extensions to identify special file types. For example:

file.EXE	An executable program
file.DOC	Word document
file.JPG	Graphic file format

Links and shortcuts

Like Unix, Windows also has ways of aliasing files in the filesystem. Windows has hard links, or duplicate entries in the master file table, allowing one to associate several names with a given file. This is not a pointer to a file, but an alternative entry point to the same file. Although the filesystem structure of NTFS is different from the Unix filesystem, the idea is the same. Hard links are created from the POSIX compatibility subsystem, using the traditional Unix command name ln. As with Unix, hard links can only be made to files on the same disk partition. Most users will not use these hard links, however.

Windows also has short cuts. A *short cut* is a small file which contains the name of another file, like a short script. It is normally used for aliasing scripts or programs. Unlike Unix's symbolic links, short cuts are not handled transparently by the operating system, they are actual files which can be opened with a text editor. They must be read and dealt with at the application level. Short cuts can be given any name, but they always have the file extension .LNK. This suffix is not visible in the graphical user interface. They are created from the graphical user interface by right-clicking on the item one wishes to obtain a pointer to.

Unix compatibility packages like Cygwin32 use short cuts to emulate symbolic links. However, since short cuts work at the application level, what one package does with a short cut is not guaranteed to apply to other software, so the usefulness of short cuts is limited.

Access control lists

Windows files and directories have the following attributes. Access control lists are composed of access control entries (ACEs) which consist of these.

Permission bit	Files	Directories
R (Read)	See file contents	See directory contents
W (Write)	Modify file contents	Modify directory contents
X (Execute)	Executable program	Can cd to directory
D (Delete)	Deletable	Deletable
P (Permission)	Permissions changeable	Permissions changeable
O (Ownership)	Ownership changeable	Ownership changeable

The read, write and execute flags have the same functions as their counterparts in Unix. The execute flag is always set on .EXE files. The additional flags allow configurable behavior, where behavior is standardized in Unix. The delete flag determines whether or not a particular user has permission to delete an object (note that a user which has write access to the file can destroy its contents independently of this). The permission and ownership flags likewise determine whether or not a specified user can take ownership or modify the permissions on a file.

Access control lists, or Access control entries are set and checked with either the Windows Explorer program (File/Properties/Security/Permissions menu) or the cacls command. This command works in more or less the same way as the POSIX setfacl command, but with different switches. The switches are

/G	Grant access to user.
/E	Edit ACE instead of replacing.
/T	Act on all files and subdirectories.
/R	Revoke (remove) access rights to a user.
/D	Deny access rights to a given user.

For example:

```
hybrid> CACLS testfile
C:\home\mark\testfile BUILTIN\Administrators:F
                      Everyone:C
                      MT AUTHORITY\SYSTEM:F

hybrid> CACLS testfile /G ds:F

Are you sure(Y/N)?

hybrid> CACLS testfile
C:\home\mark\testfile HYBRID\ds:F
```

In this example the original ACL consisted of three entries. We then replace it with a single entry for user ds on the local machine HYBRID, granting full rights.

The result is shown in the last line. If, instead of replacing the ACE, we want to supplement it, we write

```
hybrid> CACLS testfile /E /G mark:R
{\var wait for 30 seconds}
Are you sure(Y/N)?

hybrid> CACLS testfile
C:\home\mark\testfile HYBRID\ds:F
                      HYBRID\mark:R
```

New files: inheritance

Although the technical details of the NTFS and its masking schemes are not well documented, we can note a few things about the inheritance of permissions. In the absence of any ACL settings on a parent directory, a new file is created, granting all rights to all users. If the parent directory has an ACL, then a new file inherits that ACL at the time of its creation. When a file is moved, it keeps its NTFS permissions, but when a file is copied, the copy behaves like a new file, inheriting the attributes of its new location.

2.4.3   Network filesystem models

Unix and Windows have two of the most prevalent filesystem interfaces, apart from DOS itself (which has only a trivial interface), but they are both stunted in their development. In recent years, filesystem designers have returned to an old idea which dates back to a project from Newcastle University, called the Newcastle Connection, an experimental distributed filesystem which could link together many computers seamlessly into a single file tree [35]. To walk around the disk resources of the entire network, one simply used cd to change directory within a global file tree.

This idea of distributed filesystems was partially adopted by Sun Microsystems in developing their Network File System (NFS) for Unix-like operating systems. This is a distributed filesystem, for mainly local area networks. The use of open standards and a willingness to allow other vendors to use the technology quickly made NFS a de-facto standard in the Unix world, overtaking alternatives like RFS. However, owing to vendor disagreement, the Network File System has been limited to the lowest common denominator Unix filesystem-model. Vendor-specific improvements are available, but these do not work in a heterogeneous environment and thus NFS is relatively featureless, by comparison with the functionality available on local disk filesystems. In spite of this, there is no denying that NFS has been very effective, as is testified by the huge number of sites which use it unconditionally.

Other filesystems that are gaining in popularity include the Andrew File System (AFS), since it was released as an OpenAFS version. AFS became popular in institutions such as high energy physics laboratories that needed to share large

Flag	Rights acquired by named user, group, other in ACL
r	Ability of open and read a file or directory contents.
w	Ability to open and write to a file or to add files to a directory.
x	Ability to execute files as programs or enter directories.
d	Ability to erase (delete) a file or directory.
c	Ability to modify file attributes including rename.
i	Ability to add files to a directory.

Table 2.4: DFS permissions. New files inherit the initial object ACL of their parent directory. These flags can be applied to named lists of users, or groups or others, in the Unix sense.

amounts of experimental data with colleagues all over the world. The local network domain model of NFS was not sufficient for this task. AFS has an Access Control List (ACL) model, thus improving on Unix file security. A further improvement came with the Distributed Computing Environment (DCE) filesystem DFS, that provided further enhancements and a sanitized ACL model (see table 2.5).

AFS and DFS have been embraced widely in this context, allowing collaborators in Japan, Europe and the United States to be connected simply by changing directory to a new country, organization and site (see section 3.8.7). These filesystems also employ Access Control Lists, based on, but not limited by, the Unix permission model (see table 2.4). AFS now has an OpenAFS implementation.

Note that the DCE/DFS filesystem is not related to Windows's DFS filesystem, though the idea is similar.

As we can see, many of these file systems have drawn on the pioneering ideas of experimental filesystems. Today, most filesystems work in a similar way, with Unix lagging behind in sophistication, but not in functionality. Ironically, for all the flexibility that ACLs offer, they have proved to be confusing and difficult to understand and the extra functionality they provide is dwarfed by the feeling of dread which they instill in administrators and users alike. On systems with only ACLs, file permissions tend to be set inappropriately more often than on Unix-like systems. Unix's simpler approach, while basically old and simplistic, is a more palatable and manageable alternative for all but the most sophisticated users.

Another major filesystem, in a similar vein, is the Novell Netware filesystem. This is an interesting filesystem which can also create a seamless file tree called the Novell Directory Service (NDS) within an organization. Here files

Flag	Rights acquired by named user, group in ACL
r	Ability of open and read a file or directory contents.
l	Lookup within a directory.
w	Ability to open and write to a file.
i	Ability to insert files in directories.
d	Ability to erase (delete) a file or directory.
a	Ability to modify file attributes including rename.
k	Lock files.

Table 2.5: AFS permissions. These flags can be applied to named lists of users, or groups but not 'others'. Four shorthand forms also exist `write=rlidwk`, `read=rl`, `all=rlidwka`, and `none` removes an entry.

have an owner and an Access Control List, which can grant or restrict access to named users or groups. The Windows model was presumably inspired by this. The Netware idea is not unlike NFS or DFS in attempting to integrate organizations' disks into a communal file tree, but the user interface is superior, since it is not limited by compatibility issues. However Netware forces a particular object-oriented interpretation of the network onto disks, whereas NFS does not care about the file tree structure of hosts which incorporate shared filesystems. With NFS, hosts do not have to subscribe to a global vision of shared network resources, they simply take what they want and maintain their own private file tree: each host could be kept quite different. Oddly enough, Windows did not embrace the model of seamless sharing, choosing instead to mount drives on the old DOS drive letters `A:`, `B:` etc, though it is likely that such seamless integration will come in a future version. Novell too has to deal with this antiquity, since it serves primarily Windows based machines.

While Solaris' NFS does support its own brand of Access Control Lists, NFS cannot be used to provide inter-platform ACL functionality. Netware does support its own state of the art filesystem attributes, based on the usual object inheritance model of directories as containers for smaller containers. Each file has an owner and an ACL (see table 2.6).

The Common Internet File System (CIFS), based on Microsoft's Server Message Block (SMB) protocols sets is yet another popular way of sharing files. Windows software and Unix's Samba software bind together hosts using this form of Remote Procedure Call (see section 9.10).

Flag	Rights acquired by named user in ACL
S	Supervisor rights grant all rights to a file, directory and all subdirectories.
R	Ability of open and read a file or directory contents.
W	Ability to open and write to a file or to add files to a directory.
C	Ability to create new files and undelete old ones, or create new directories.
E	Ability to erase (delete) a file or directory.
M	Ability to modify file attributes including rename.
F	Ability to see files within a directory when viewing contents.
A	Ability to change access rights on file or directory, including granting others access rights. Also change inheritance masks for directories.

Table 2.6: Netware 5 permissions. New file objects inherit the default permissions of their container, minus any flags in the Inherited Rights Filter/Mask (IRF). Permissions can be applied to named users or groups.

2.4.4 Unix and Windows sharing

Filesystems can be shared across a network by any of the methods we have discussed above. We can briefly note here the correspondence of commands and methods for achieving network sharing.

With AFS and DCE/DFS, used mainly on Unix-like hosts, the security model is such that a computer becomes part of a cell or domain. Within such a cell, disk partitions are referred to as volumes. These can be replicated and shared with other computers. AFS cells on other server hosts can be attached to client hosts using the afsd program. A local cell can be published to the rest of the AFS speaking network by adding its attributes to a database. The resulting seamless file tree is visible under /afs. The visibility of files in this model is controlled by the Access Control Lists.

Unix-like hosts use NFS to share filesystems, by running the daemons (e.g. `rpc.mountd` and `rpc.nfsd`). Filesystems are made available for sharing by adding them to the file `/etc/exports`, on most systems, or confusingly to `/etc/dfs/dfstab` on SVR4 based Unix. The syntax in these files is particular to the flavor of the Unix-like operating system one is using. With some operating systems, using `/etc/exports`, it is necessary to run the command `exportfs -a` to make the contents of the export file visible to the daemons which control access. On SVR4 systems, like Solaris, there is a command called `share` for exporting filesystems, and the file `/etc/dfs/dfstab` is just a shell script containing a lot of `share` commands, e.g.

```
allhosts=nomad:vger:nomad.domain.country:vger.domain.country
```

```
share -F nfs -o rw=$allhosts  /site/server/local
```

Here the command `shareall` is the equivalent for exporting all filesystems in this file. It simply runs a shell script containing all such commands. The example above makes the directory tree `/iu/server/local` available to the hosts nomad and vger. Note that due to different name services implementations and their various behaviors, it is often necessary to use both the unqualified and fully qualified names of hosts when sharing.

On the client or receiving end, we attach a shared filesystem to a host by 'mounting' it. NFS filesystems are mounted in exactly the same way as they mount a local disk, i.e. with the `mount` command, e.g.

```
mkdir -p /site/server/local
mount server:/site/server/local /site/server/local
```

Here we create a directory on which to mount a foreign filesystem and then mount it on a directory which has the same name as the original on the server. The original name and the new name do not have to be the same, but there is a point to this which we shall return to later. Assuming that the server-host granted us the right to mount the filesystem on our host, we now have access to the remote filesystem, as though it were a local disk. The only exception is the superuser root, who is granted the access rights of a user called nobody. The point of this is that the administrator on the client host is not necessarily the administrator on the server host, and has no obvious right to every users' files there. This mapping can be overridden if convenience outweighs the minor security it adds.

Windows filesystems on a server are shared, either using the GUI, or by executing the command

```
net share alias=F:\filetree
```

On the client side, the file tree can then be 'mounted' by executing the command

```
net use X: \\serverhost\alias
```

This attaches the remote file tree, referenced by the alias, to Windows drive `X:`. One of the logistical difficulties with the Windows drive model is that drive associations are not constant, but might change when new hardware is detected. Drive associations can be made to persist by adding a flag

```
net use X: \\serverhost\alias /persistent:yes
```

to the mount command. This is not a perfect solution, but it works.

2.5 Processes and job control

On a multitasking computer, all work on a running program is performed by an abstraction called a *process*. This is a collection of resources such as file handles, allocated memory, program code and CPU registers that is associated with a specific running program. A cursory overview of various operating system models for running programs follows. On modern operating systems, processes can contain many concurrent threads which share program resources.

2.5.1 The Unix process model

Unix starts new processes by copying old ones. Users start processes from a *shell* command line interface program or by clicking on icons in a window manager. Every Unix process has a process ID (PID) which can be used to refer to it, suspend it or kill it entirely.

A background process is started from a shell using the special character & at the end of the command line.

```
find / -name '*lib*' -print >& output   &
```

The final & at the end of this line means that the job will be run in the background. Note that this will not be confused with the redirection operator >& since it must be the last non-whitespace character of the command. The command above looks for any files in the system containing the string 'lib' and writes the list of files to a file called 'output'.

If we want to see what processes are running, we can use the ps command. ps without any arguments lists your current processes, i.e. all processes owned by the user identity you logged in with that are connected to the shell you are currently using. ps takes many options, for instance ps auxg will list all user processes in detail on BSD-like systems, while ps -efl will provide a similar, if not entirely compatible, listing on System V-like systems. Some Unix-like systems support both the BSD and System V flags to the ps command.

Processes can be stopped and started, or killed once and for all. The kill command does this and more. In fact, it sends generalized signals to running processes, not only the kill signal. There are two versions of the kill command. One of them is built into the C-shell and the other is not. If you use the C-shell then you will never care about the difference unless the process table is full. We shall nonetheless mention the special features of the C-shell built-ins below. The kill command takes a number called a *signal* as an argument and another number called the *process identifier* or *PID* for short. Kill send signals to processes. Some of these are fatal and some are for information only. The two commands

```
kill -15 127
kill 127
```

are identical. They both send signal 15 to PID 127. This is the normal *termination* signal and it is often enough to stop any process from running.

Programs can choose to ignore certain signals by trapping signals with a special handler. One signal they cannot ignore is signal 9.

```
kill -9  127
```

is a sure way of killing PID 127. Even though the process dies, it may not be removed from the kernel's process table if it has a parent (see next section).

2.5.2   Child processes and zombies

When we start a process, the new process becomes a *child* of the original. If one of the children starts a new process then it will be a child of the child (a grandchild). Processes therefore form *hierarchies*. Several children can have a common *parent*. All Unix user-processes are children of the initial process init, with process ID 1.

If we kill a parent, then (unless the child has detached itself from the parent) all of its children die too. If a child dies, the parent is not affected. Sometimes when a child is killed, it does not die but becomes *defunct* or a *zombie* process. This means that the child has a parent which is *waiting* for it to finish. If the parent has not yet been informed that the child has died, because it has been suspended itself for instance, then the dead child is not completely removed from the kernel's process table. When the parent wakes up and receives the message that the child has terminated (and its exit status), the process entry for the dead child can be removed.

Most Unix processes go through a zombie state, but most terminate so quickly that they cannot be seen. A few hang around and use up valuable process slots, which can be a problem. It is not possible to kill a zombie process, since it is already dead. The only way to remove a zombie is to either reactivate the process which is waiting for it, or to kill that process. Persistent zombie processes are usually caused by software bugs.

2.5.3   The Windows process model

Like Unix, processes under Windows/NT can live in the foreground or in the background, though unlike Unix, Windows does not fork processes by replicating existing ones. A background process can be started with

```
start /B
```

In order to kill the process it is necessary to purchase the Resource kit which contains a kill command. A background process detaches itself from a login session and can continue to run even when the user is logged out.

Generally speaking, Windows and Novell abhor processes. Threads are the preferred method for multitasking. This means that additional functionality is often implemented as modules to existing software, rather than as independent objects.

The shutdown of the whole system is normally performed from the Windows menu. Any logged on user can shut down a host. Background processes die when this happens and updates from an administrator could fail to be applied. A number of `shutdown` commands also exists for shutting down local or remote systems; some of these are commercial third-party software.

2.5.4 Environment variables

Environment variables are text-string variables which can be set in any process [294]. Normally they are set by users in shell environments in order to communicate user preferences or configuration information to software. In the C-shell, they are set with the command

```
setenv VARIABLE value
```

and are not to be confused with C-shell's local (non-inherited) variables which are created with `set variable=value`. In the original Bourne shell they are set by

```
VARIABLE=value
export VARIABLE
```

The `export` command is needed to make the variable global, i.e. to make it inheritable by child processes. In newer Bourne shells like `ksh` and `bash`, one can simply write

```
export VARIABLE=value
```

The values of these variables are later referred to using the dollar symbol:

```
echo $VARIABLE
```

When a process spawns a child process, the child inherits the environment variables of its parent. Environment variables are an important way of transmitting preference information between processes.

On Windows systems environment variables are set in the DOS prompt interface by

```
set VARIABLE=value
```

Try not to confuse this with the C-shell's `set` command. Environment variables in Windows are later dereferenced using the percent prefix and suffix:

```
echo %%VARIABLE%%
```

2.6   Networks

The network is the largest physical appendage to our computer systems, but it is also the least conspicuous, often hidden behind walls and in locked switching rooms, or passing invisibly through us as electromagnetic radiation. To most users, the network is a piece of magic which they have abruptly learned to take for granted, and yet, without it, modern computing practices would be impossible.

A network is a number of pathways for communication between two or more hosts. Networking is increasingly important, as computers are used more and more as devices for media access rather than for computation. Networking raises issues for system management at many levels, from its deployment to its configuration and usage. We begin here, simply, by identifying the main components involved in this important subsystem.

The most simplistic way to ensure communication between N hosts would be to stretch a private cable between every pair of hosts on a network. This would require a cat's cradle of N network interfaces and $N - 1$ cables per host, i.e. $N(N - 1)/2$ links in total, which would be quite unmanageable and equally expensive. The challenge of networking is therefore to provide some kind of shared cable which is attached to several hosts simultaneously by means of a single *network interface*. Some studies in setting up physical infrastructure have been reported in refs. [196, 271]; see also discussion of load [209, 90] in Wide Area Networks [210].

2.6.1   The OSI model

The International Standards Organization (ISO) has defined a model for describing communications across a network, called the OSI model, for *Open Systems Interconnect (reference model)*. This model is a generalized abstraction of how network communication can be and is implemented. The model does not fit every network technology perfectly, but it is widely used to discuss and refer to the layers of technology involved in networking, thus we begin by recapping this model. The OSI model describes seven layers of abstraction.

Layer	Name	Example
7	Application layer	Program protocol commands
6	Presentation layer	XDR or user routines
5	Session layer	RPC / sockets
4	Transport layer	TCP or UDP
3	Network layer	IP Internet protocol
2	Data link layer	Ethernet protocol
1	Physical layer	Cables, interfaces

At the lowest level, the sending of data between two machines takes place by manipulating voltages along wires. This means we need a device driver for the signaler, and something to receive the data at the other end – a way of converting the signals into bytes; then we need a way of structuring the data so that they make sense. Each of these elements is achieved by a different level of abstraction.

1. *Physical layer.* This is the sending a signal along a wire, amplifying it if it gets weak, removing noise etc. If the type of cable changes (we might want to reflect signals off a satellite or use fiber optics) we need to convert one kind of signal into another. Each type of transmission might have its own accepted ways of sending data (i.e. protocols).

2. *Data link layer.* This is a layer of checking which makes sure that what was sent from one end of a cable to the other actually arrived. This is sometimes called *handshaking*. The Ethernet protocol is layer 2, as is Token Ring. This level is labelled by Media Access Control (MAC) addresses.

3. *Network layer.* This is the layer of software which recognizes structure in the network. It establishes global identity and handles the delivery of data by manipulating the physical layer. The network layer needs to know something about addresses – i.e. where the data are going, since data might flow along many cables and connections to arrive where they are going. Layer 3 is the layer at which IP addresses enter.

4. *Transport layer.* We shall concentrate on this layer for much of what follows. The transport layer builds 'packets' or 'datagrams' so that the network layer knows what is data and how to get the data to their destination. Because many machines could be talking on the same network all at the same time, data are broken up into short 'bursts'. Only one machine can talk over a cable at a time so we must have *sharing*. It is easy to share if the signals are sent in short bursts. This is analogous to the sharing of CPU time by use of time-slices. TCP and UDP protocols are encoded at this layer.

5. *Session layer.* This is the part of a host's operating system which helps a user program to set up a connection. This is typically done with *sockets* or the RPC.

6. *Presentation layer.* How are the data to be sent by the sender and interpreted by the receiver, so that there is no doubt about their contents? This is the role played by the external data representation (XDR) in the RPC system.

7. *Application layer.* The program which wants to send data has its own protocol layer, typically a command language encoding (e.g. GET, PUT in FTP or HTTP).

These layers are not always so cleanly cut. Today, networking technologies at all levels are mixing them up: routers and switches are merging layers 2 and 3, and routers that prioritize traffic need to know what application is being transported, so that the information can be fed into layers 2 and 3 in order to provide guarantees on performance (so-called Quality of Service). As always, the advantage of using a layered structure is that we can change the details of the lower layers without having to change the higher layers. Layers 1 to 4 are those which involve the transport of data across a network. We could change all of these without doing serious damage to the upper layers – thus as new technology arrives, we can improve network communication without having to rewrite software. That is precisely what is happening with new technologies such as IPv6 and MPLS.

2.6.2 Cables and interface technologies

Different vendors have invested in different networking technologies, with different Media Access Control (MAC) specifications. Most Unix systems use some form of Ethernet interface. IBM systems have employed Token Ring networking technology very successfully for their mainframes and AS/400 systems; they now support Ethernet also on their RS/6000 systems. Now most manufacturers provide solutions for both technologies, though Ethernet is undoubtedly popular for local area networks.

- *Bus/Ethernet approach:* Ethernet technology was developed by Xerox, Intel and DEC in 1976, at the Palo Alto Research Center (PARC) [103]. In the Ethernet bus approach, every host is connected to a common cable or bus. Only one host can be using a given network cable at a given instant. It is like a conference telephone call: what goes out onto a network reaches all hosts on that network (more or less) simultaneously, so everyone has to share the line by waiting for a suitable moment to say something. Ethernet is defined in the IEEE 802.3 standard documents. An Ethernet network is available to any host at any time, provided the line isn't busy. This is called CSMA/CD, or Carrier Sense Multiple Access/Collision Detect. A collision occurs when two hosts attempt to send signals simultaneously. CSMA/CD means that if a card has something to send, it will listen until no other card is transmitting, then start transmitting and listen if no other card starts transmitting at the same time. If another card began transmitting it will stop, wait for a random interval and try again. The original Ethernet, with a capacity of 10 megabits per second, could carry packets of 1518 bytes.

  Today, Ethernet is progressing in leaps and bounds. Switched Ethernet running on twisted pair cables can deliver up to 100 megabits per second (100BaseT, fast Ethernet). Gigabit Ethernets are already common. The main limitation of Ethernet networks is the presence of collisions. When many hosts are talking, performance degrades quickly due to time wasted by hosts waiting to get a word in. In order to avoid collisions, packet sizes are limited. With a large number of small packets, it is easier to share the time between more hosts. Ethernet interfaces are assigned a unique MAC address when they are built. The initial numbers of the address identify each manufacturer uniquely. Full-duplex connections at 100MB are possible with fast Ethernets on dedicated cables where collisions cannot occur.

- *Token Ring/FDDI approach:* In the token ring approach [253], hosts are coupled to hubs or nodes each of which has two network interfaces and the hosts are connected in a uni-directional ring. The token ring is described in IEEE 802.5. The token ring is a deterministic protocol; if Ethernet embraces chaos, then the token ring demands order. No matter when a host wishes to transmit, it must wait for a passing token, in a specified time-slot. If a signal (token) arrives, a host can append something to the signal. If nothing is appended, the token is passed on to the next host which has the opportunity to do the same. Similarly, if the signal arriving at one of the interfaces is for the host itself then it is read. If it is not intended for the host itself, the signal is forwarded to the next host where the same applies. A common token ring based interface in use today is the optical FDDI (Fiber distributed data interface). Token rings can pass 16 megabits per second, with packet sizes of 18 kilobytes. The larger packet sizes are possible since there is no risk of collisions.

Like Ethernet interfaces, token ring interfaces are manufactured with a uniquely assigned MAC address.

- *Frame Relay* is an alternative layer 2 packet-switching protocol for connecting devices on a Wide Area Network (WAN) or backbone. It is used for point-to-point connections, but is capable of basic switching, like ATM, so it can create virtual point-to-point circuits, where several switches might be involved (see chapter 10). Frame relay is popular because it is relatively inexpensive. However, it is also being replaced in some areas by faster technologies, such as ATM. Frame relay has the advantage of being widely supported, and is better suited than ATM for data-only, medium-speed (56/64 Kbps, T1): the ratio of header size to frame size is typically much smaller than the overhead ratio for ATM.

- *ATM*, Asynchronous Transfer Mode technology [23], is a high capacity, deterministic, transmission technology developed by telephone companies in order to exploit existing copper telephone networks. ATM is a layer 2–3 hybrid technology. ATM is believed to be able to reach much higher transfer rates than Ethernet, since it disallows collisions and is optimized for switching. Its expense, combined with the increasing performance of fast Ethernet, has made ATM most attractive for high speed Internet backbones and Wide Area Networks, though some local area networks have been implemented as proof of principle.

Even with the bus approach, any host can be connected to several independent network segments if it has a network interface for each network it is attached to. Each network interface then has a separate network address; thus a host which is connected to several networks will have a different address on each network. A device which is coupled to several networks and which forwards data from one network to another is called a *router*.

Network signals are carried by a variety of means. These days copper cables are being replaced by fiber-optic glass transmission for long-distance communication and even radio links. In local area networks it is still usually copper cables which carry the signals. These cables usually carry Ethernet protocols over twisted pair (telephone-like) cables. Twisted pair lines are sometimes referred to as 10baseT, 100baseT etc. The numbers indicate the capacity of the line, 'base' indicates that the cable is used in a *baseband* system and the 'T' stands for twisted-pair. Each

host has a single cable connecting it to a *multi-way repeater* or *hub*. Fiber-optic
cables (FDDI, SONET, SDH) have varying appearances.

2.6.3 Connectivity

Network cables are joined together by hardware which makes sure that messages
are transmitted from cable to segment in the right direction to reach their destinations. A host which is coupled to several network segments and which forwards
data from one network to another is called a *router*. Routers not only forward data
but they prevent the spread of network messages which other network segments
do not need to know about. This limits the number of hosts which are sharing
any given cable segment, and thus limits the traffic which any given host sees.
Routers can also filter unwanted traffic for security purposes [77]. A router knows
which destination addresses lie on which of the networks it is connected to and it
does not let message traffic spread onto irrelevant cables.

A *bridge* is a hardware device which acts like a filter on busy networks. A bridge
works like a 'mini-router' and separates two segments of the same cable. A bridge
knows which incoming cables do *not* offer a destination address and prevents
traffic from spreading to this part of a cable. A bridge is used to isolate traffic
on busy sections of a network or conversely to splice networks together. It is a
primitive kind of switch.

A *repeater* is an amplifier that strengthens the network signal over long
stretches of cable. A *multi-port repeater* also called a *hub* does the same thing
and also splits one cable into N sub-cables for convenience. Hubs are common in
twisted pair networks where it is necessary to fan a cable out into a star pattern
from the hub to send one cable to each host.

A *switch* is a hub which can direct a message from one host cable directly to the
intended host by routing the signal directly. The advantage with this is that other
machines do not have to see the traffic between two hosts. Each pair of hosts has
a virtual private cable. Switched networks are not immune to spies, net-sniffing or
network listening devices, but they make it more difficult for the casual browser
to see traffic that does not concern them. A switch performs many of the tasks of
a router and vice versa. The difference is that a switch works at layer 2 of the OSI
model (i.e. with MAC addresses), whereas a router works at layer 3 (IP addresses).
A switch cannot route data on a world-wide basis.

When learning about a new network one should obtain a plan of the physical
setup. If we have done our homework, then we will know where all of these boxes
are on the network.

Note that, while it is common to refer to routing and switching as 'layer 3'
and 'layer 2' in loose parlance, sticklers for correctness will find this is somewhat
ill-defined. These labels mix up the OSI model with the IP model. However, since
they roughly coincide at layers 2 and 3, we can identify layer 2 as 'Ethernets'
(or equivalent) and layer 3 as the IP-addressable transport layer. Modern rout-
ing/switching equipment is not so easily placed into either of these categories,
however; network junction devices typically contain modules for both types of
communication.

2.6.4 LANs, WANs and VLANs

In the 1980s and 1990s, most networks consisted of a hierarchy of routers, joined into a Wide Area Network (WAN). Each Local Area Network (or local community, such as a business or university) would have its own gateway router, connecting it to the rest of the world. The purpose of a router was two-fold:

- To forward traffic meant for remote locations along a suitable route, so that it would arrive at the right address.

- To prevent purely local traffic from leaking out of the local network and causing unnecessary congestion.

When an electrical signal passes along a cable it is like a light being switched on in a room. The picture of a network transmission as a stream of bytes travelling along a cable, like cars in a train, is often misleading.[4] In local area networks, the distances are often so short that transmission is almost instantaneous and each bit fills an entire cable segment; though this depends on the data rate. Every bit, every 1 or 0, is a signal (a voltage or light pulse) on a cable which fills a space, the size of a wavelength, at about two-thirds of the speed of light in a vacuum – so, on short segments, this is often the entire cable. It is like sending Morse code with a lighthouse. Every part of the network sees the signal, but only the addressed recipient normally bothers to read it.

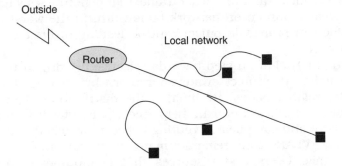

Figure 2.4: Traffic control with a router. Routers forward traffic that needs to leave a local network, and shield the external world from local traffic.

A router isolates one part of a network from another, both logically and physically.[5] It will only forward the signal if the signal needs to travel along another segment to reach its destination address (see figure 2.4). The router is able to make this determination based on information about the topology of the network. This is an important function in the network: if every signal, sent by

---

[4]In conventional encoding schemes, a single bit is represented by one wavelength of the base-frequency clock rate. Thus, the wave equation tells us the distance required to encode a bit: it is the wavelength $\lambda = c/f$, where f is the frequency or transmission rate and $c \sim 2 \times 10^8 \mathrm{ms}^{-1}$. Thus, at Ethernet rates (10Mbs), a single bit is of the order of ten metres. At Giga-bit rates, a bit is only a few centimetres.

[5]Some types of switch or bridge can also isolate networks physically, to the extent that they split up collision zones, but not all.

every computer, travelled along every cable in the world, communication would be impossible. Thus routers are essential to the scalability of networks as well as to the direction of traffic.

This simple model of network communications worked adequately for several years, but as the demands on networks increased, the load on routers became intolerable. There was therefore the need for a different architecture. This was provided by *switches*. Switches are topologically similar to routers, in that they act as a junction (often in star-formation) for several cables. The difference is that the switch knows nothing of the IP addresses or network segments joined to it. It routes and shields traffic by MAC address alone. This is cheaper and faster and can shield routers from purely local traffic, allowing them to concentrate on traffic to and from external sites.

Like routers, switches prevent traffic from leaking along cables that it does not need to traverse; however, traditional switches segment only unicast, or node-to-node, traffic. Unlike routers, they do not normally limit broadcast traffic (packets that are addressed to all the nodes within the same IP network locale) or multicast traffic (packets that are distributed to a group of nodes). However, switch technology is advancing rapidly (see below). As switched networks have become more common, routers have continued to exist within the network, but they have been pushed toward the periphery of IP junctions.

As networks grow and traffic increases, one is forced to segment networks into more and more switched subnets to meet increasing performance demands. With these changes, broadcast and multicast traffic, that penetrates switch boundaries, has placed a greater burden on network bandwidth. In the worst case scenario, broadcast traffic can propagate out of control, leading to *broadcast storms* that paralyze a network.

VLANs (virtual LANs) are a step towards selective filtering at the switch level. They allow switches to protect swamped routers by offering different groups, or channels for related nodes. By limiting the distribution of broadcast, multicast and unicast traffic, they can help free up bandwidth, and reduce the need for expensive and complicated routing between switched networks, without involving routers. VLANs thus reinstate many of the advantages of routing-free LANs, but cheaply. Users and resources that communicate most frequently with each other can be grouped into common VLANs, regardless of physical location.

2.6.5 Protocols and encapsulation

Information transactions take place by agreed standards or *protocols*. Protocols exist to make sure that transmitted data are understood by the receiver in the way that the sender intended. On a network, protocols are required to make sure that data are understood, not only by the receiver, but by all the network hardware which carry them between source and destination. The data are wrapped up in envelope information which contains the address of the destination. Each transmission layer in the protocol stack (protocol hierarchy) is prefixed with some header information which contains the destination address and other data which identify it. The Ethernet protocol also has a trailer, see figure 2.5.

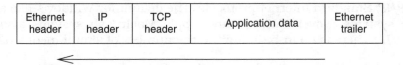

Ethernet header	IP header	TCP header	Application data	Ethernet trailer

Figure 2.5: Protocol encapsulation.

Wrapping data inside envelope information is called *encapsulation* and it is important to understand the basics of these mechanisms. Network attacks make clever use of the features and flaws in these protocols and system administrators need to understand them in order to protect systems.

The Internet Family of protocols has been the basis of Unix networking for thirty years, since it was implemented as part of the Berkeley Software Distribution (BSD) Unix. The hierarchy is shown in figure 2.6.

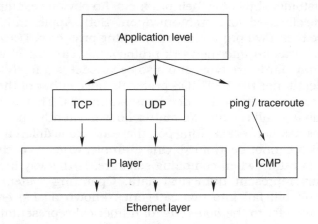

Figure 2.6: The Internet protocol hierarchy.

The transmission control protocol (TCP) is for reliable connection-oriented transfer. The user datagram protocol (UDP) is a rather cheaper connection-less service and the Internet control message protocol (ICMP) is used to transmit error messages and routing information for TCP/IP. These protocols have an address structure which is hierarchical and *routable*, which means that IP addresses can find their way from any host in the world to any other so long as they are connected. The Ethernet protocol does not know much more about the world than the cable it is attached to.

Windows supports at least three network protocols, running on top of Ethernet.

- *NETBEUI:* NETBIOS Extended User Interface, Microsoft's own network protocol. This was designed for small networks and is not routable. It has a maximum limit of 20 simultaneous users and is thus hardly usable.

- *NWLink/IPX:* Novell/Xerox's IPX/SPX protocol suite. Routable. Maximum limit of 400 simultaneous users.

- *TCP/IP:* Standard Internet protocols. The default for Windows-like and Unix-like systems. Novell Netware and Apple MacIntosh systems also support TCP/IP. There is no in-built limit to the number of simultaneous users.

Novell's Netware PC server software is based mainly on the IPX suite running on Ethernet hardware; MacIntosh networks have used their own proprietary Appletalk which will run on Ethernet or token ring hardware, but this is now being exchanged for TCP/IP. All platforms are converging on the use of TCP/IP for its open standard and its generality.

2.6.6 Data formats

There are many problems which arise in networking when hardware and software from different manufacturers have to exist and work together. Some of the largest computer companies have tried to use this to their advantage on many occasions in order to make customers buy only their products. An obvious example is the choice of network protocols used for communication. Both Apple and Microsoft have tried to introduce their own proprietary networking protocols. TCP/IP has won the contest because it was an *inter*-network protocol (i.e. capable of working on and joining together any hardware type) and also because it is a freely open standard. Neither the Appletalk nor the NETBIOS protocols have either of these features.

This illustrates how networking demands standards. That is not to say that some problems do not still remain. No matter how insistently one attempts to fuse operating systems in a network melting pot, there are basic differences in hardware and software which cannot be avoided. One example, which is occasionally visible to system administrators when compiling software, is the way in which different operating systems represent numerical data. Operating systems (actually the hardware they run on) fall into two categories known as *big endian* and *little endian*. The names refer to the *byte-order* of numerical representations.

The names indicate how large integers (which require say 32 bits or more) are stored in memory. Little endian systems store the least significant byte first, while big endian systems store the most significant byte first. For example, the representation of the number 34,677,374 has either of the forms shown in figure 2.7. Obviously if one is transferring data from one host to another, both

Big endian

2	17	34	126

Little endian

126	34	17	2

Figure 2.7: Byte ordering sometimes has to be specified when compiling software. The representation of the number 34,677,374 has either of these forms.

hosts have to agree on the data representation otherwise there would be disastrous consequences. This means that there has to be a common standard of *network byte ordering.* For example, Solaris (SPARC hardware) uses network byte ordering (big endian), while Windows or Unix-like operating systems on Intel hardware use the opposite (little endian). Intel systems have to convert their data format every time ordered data are transmitted over the network.

2.7 IPv4 networks

TCP/IP networking is so important to networked hosts that we shall return to it several times during the course of this book. Its significance is cultural, historical and practical, but the first item in our agenda is to understand its logistic structure.

2.7.1 IP addresses

Every network interface on the Internet needs to have a unique number which is called its address. IP addresses are organized hierarchically so that they can be searched for by router networks. Without such a structure, it would be impossible to find a host unless it were part of the same cable segment. At present the Internet protocol is at version 4 and this address consists of four bytes, or 32 bits. In the future this will be extended, in a new version of the Internet protocol IPv6, to allow more IP addresses since we are rapidly using up the available addresses. The addresses will also be structured differently. The form of an IP address in IPv4 is

```
aaa.bbb.ccc.mmm
```

Some IP addresses represent networks, whereas others represent individual interfaces on hosts and routers. Normally an IP address represents a host attached to a network.

In every IPv4 address there are 32 bits. One uses these bits in different ways: one could imagine using all 32 bits for host addresses and keep every host on the same enormous cable, without any routers (this would be physically impossible in practice), or we could use all 32 bits for network addresses and have only one host per network (i.e. a router for every host). Both these extremes are silly; we are trying to save resources by sharing a cable between convenient groups of hosts, but shield other hosts from irrelevant traffic. What we want instead is to group hosts into clusters so as to restrict traffic to localized areas.

Networks were grouped *historically* into three classes called class A, class B and class C networks, in order to simplify traffic routing (see chapter 10). Class D and E networks are also now defined, but these are not used for regular traffic. This rigid distinction between different types of network addresses has proved to be a costly mistake for the IPv4 protocol. Amongst other things, it means that only about two percent of the actual number of IP addresses can actually be used with this scheme. So-called *classless* addresses (CIDR) were introduced in the 1990s to patch the problem of the classed addressing, but not all deployed devices and protocol versions were able to understand the new classless addresses, so classed addressing will survive in books and legacy networks for some time.

The difference between class A, B and C networks lies in which bits of the IP addresses refer to the network itself and which bits refer to actual hosts within a network. Note that the details in these sections are subject to rapid change, so readers should check the latest details on the web.

Class A legacy networks

IP addresses from 1.0.0.0 to 127.255.255.255 are *class A* networks. Originally only 11.0.0.0 to 126.255.255.255 were used, but this is likely to change as the need for IPv4 address space becomes more desperate. In a class A network, the first byte is a network part and the last three bytes are the host address (see figure 2.8). This allows 126 possible networks (since network 127 is reserved for the loopback service). The number of hosts per class A network is 256^3 minus reserved host addresses on the network. Since this is a ludicrously large number, none of the owners of class A networks are able to use all of their host addresses. Class A networks are no longer issued (as class A networks), they are all assigned, and all the free addresses are now having to be reclaimed using CIDR. Class A networks were intended for very large organizations (the U.S. government, Hewlett Packard, IBM) and are only practical with the use of a netmask which divides up the large network into manageable subnets. The default subnet mask is 255.0.0.0.

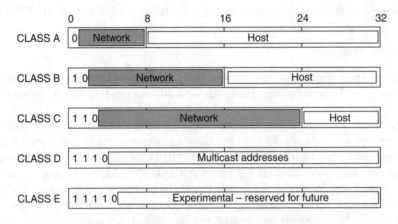

Figure 2.8: Bit view of the 32 bit IPv4 addresses.

Class B legacy networks

IP addresses from 128.0.0.0 to 191.255.0.0 are *class B* networks. There are 16,384 such networks. The first two bytes are the network part and the last two bytes are the host part. This gives a maximum of 256^2 minus reserved host addresses, or 65,534 hosts per network. Class B networks are typically given to large institutions such as universities and Internet providers, or to institutions such as Sun Microsystems, Microsoft and Novell. All the class B addresses have now been allocated to their parent organizations, but many of these lease out these addresses to third parties. The default subnet mask is 255.255.0.0.

Class C legacy networks

IP addresses from `192.0.0.0` to `223.255.255.0` are *class C* networks. There are 2,097,152 such networks. Here the first three bytes are network addresses and the last byte is the host part. This gives a maximum of 254 hosts per network. The default subnet mask is `255.255.255.0`. Class C networks are the most numerous and there are still a few left to be allocated, though they are disappearing with alarming rapidity.

Class D (multicast) addresses

Multicast networks form what is called the MBONE, or multicast backbone. These include addresses from `224.0.0.0` to `239.255.255.0`. These addresses are not normally used for sending data to individual hosts, but rather for routing data to multiple destinations. Multicast is like a restricted broadcast. Hosts can 'tune in' to multicast channels by subscribing to MBONE services.

Class E (Experimental) addresses

Addresses `240.0.0.0` to `255.255.255.255` are unused and are considered experimental, though this may change as IPv4 addresses are depleted.

Other addresses

Some IP addresses are reserved for a special purpose. They do not necessarily refer to hosts or networks.

```
0.0.0.0           Default route
0.*.*.*           Not used
127.0.0.1         Loopback address
127.*.*.*         Loopback network
*.*.*.0           Network addresses (or old broadcast)
*.*.*.255         Broadcast addresses
*.*.*.1           Router or gateway (conventionally)
224.*.*.*         Multicast addresses
```

RFC 1918 defines private addresses that are not routed

```
10.0.0.0        - 10.255.255.255    (10/8 prefix)
172.16.0.0      - 172.31.255.255    (172.16/12 prefix)
192.168.0.0     - 192.168.255.255   (192.168/16 prefix)
```

and as of July 2001

```
169.254.0.0     - 169.254.255.255   (192.254/16 prefix)
```

The network

```
192.0.2.0       - 192.0.2.255
```

is reserved by RFC 1166 to be the domain `example.org` for testing and example (as in this book).

Note that older networks used the network address itself for broadcasting. This practice has largely been abandoned however. The default route is a default destination for outgoing packets on a subnet and is usually made equal to the router address.

The *loopback address* is an address which every host uses to refer to itself internally. It points straight back to the host. It is a kind of internal pseudo-address which allows programs to use network protocols to address local services without anything being transmitted on an actual network.

The zeroth address of any network is reserved to mean the network itself, and the 255th (or on older networks sometimes the zeroth) is used for the broadcast address. Some Internet addresses are reserved for a special purpose. These include *network addresses* (usually xxx.yyy.zzz.0), *broadcast addresses* (usually xxx.yyy.zzz.255, but in older networks it was xxx.yyy.zzz.0) and *multicast addresses* (usually 224.xxx.yyy.zzz).

2.7.2 Subnets and broadcasts

What we refer to as a network might consist of very many separate cable systems, coupled together by routers and switches. One problem with very large networks is that *broadcast messages* (i.e. messages which are sent to every host) create traffic which can slow a busy network. In most cases broadcast messages only need to be sent to a subset of hosts which have some logical or administrative relationship, but unless something is done a broadcast message will by definition be transmitted to all hosts on the network. What is needed then is a method of assigning groups of IP addresses to specific cables and limiting broadcasts to hosts belonging to the group, i.e. breaking up the larger community into more manageable units. The purpose of subnets is to divide up networks into regions which naturally belong together and to isolate regions which are independent. This reduces the propagation of useless traffic, and it allows us to *delegate* and distribute responsibility for local concerns.

This logical partitioning can be achieved by dividing hosts up, through routers, into subnets. Each network can be divided into *subnets* by using a *netmask*. Each address consists of two parts: a *network address* and a *host address*. A system variable called the *netmask* decides how IP addresses are interpreted locally. The netmask decides the boundary between how many bits of the IP address will be kept for hosts and how many will be kept for the network location name. There is thus a trade-off between the number of allowed domains and the number of hosts which can be coupled to each subnet. Subnets are usually separated by routers, so the question is, how many machines do we want on one side of a router?

The netmask is most easily interpreted as a binary number. When looking at the netmask, we have to ask which bits are ones and which are zeros? The bits which are *ones* decide which bits can be used to specify the subnets within the domain. The bits which are zeros decide which are hostnames on each subnet. The local network administrator decides how the netmask is to be used.

The host part of an IP address can be divided up into two parts by moving the boundary between network and host part. The netmask is a variable which contains zeros and ones. Every one represents a network bit and every zero represents a host bit. By changing the value of the netmask, we can trade many hosts per network for many subnets with fewer hosts. A subnet mask can be used to separate hosts which also lie on the same physical network, thereby forcing them to communicate through the router.

2.7.3 Netmask examples

The most common subnet mask is 255.255.255.0. This forces a separation where three bytes represent a network address and one byte is reserved for hosts. For example, consider the class B network 128.39.0.0. With a netmask of 255.255.255.0 everywhere on this network, we divide it up into 255 separate subnets, each of which has room for 254 hosts (256 minus the network address, minus the broadcast address):

```
128.39.0.0
128.39.1.0
128.39.2.0
128.39.3.0
128.39.4.0
. . .
```

We might find, however, that 254 hosts per subnet is too few. For instance, if a large number of client hosts contact a single server, then there is no reason to route traffic from some clients simply because the subnet was too small. We can therefore double the number of hosts by moving the bit pattern of the netmask one place to the left (see figure 2.9). Then we have a netmask of 255.255.254.0. This has the effect of pairing the addresses in the previous example. If this netmask were now used throughout the class B network, we would have single subnets formed as follows:

```
128.39.0.0
128.39.1.0

128.39.2.0
128.39.3.0

128.39.4.0
128.39.5.0
. . .
```

Each of these subnets now contains 510 hosts ($256 \times 2 - 2$), with two addresses reserved: one for the network and one for broadcasts. Similarly, if we moved the netmask again one place to the left, we would multiply by two again, and group the addresses in fours: i.e. netmask 255.255.252.0:

```
128.39.0.0
128.39.1.0
```

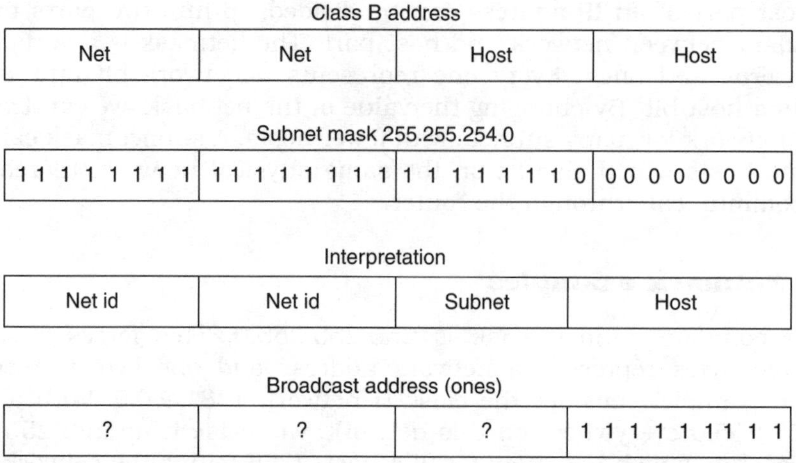

Class B address

Net	Net	Host	Host

Subnet mask 255.255.254.0

1 1 1 1 1 1 1 1	1 1 1 1 1 1 1 1	1 1 1 1 1 1 1 0	0 0 0 0 0 0 0 0

Interpretation

Net id	Net id	Subnet	Host

Broadcast address (ones)

?	?	?	1 1 1 1 1 1 1 1

Figure 2.9: Example of how the subnet mask can be used to double up the number of hosts per subnet by pairing host parts. The boundary between host and subnet parts of the address is moved one bit to the left, doubling the number of hosts on the subnets which have this mask.

```
128.39.2.0
128.39.3.0

128.39.4.0
128.39.5.0
128.39.6.0
128.39.7.0
...
```

It is not usually necessary for every host on an entire class B network to share the same subnet mask, though certain types of hardware could place restrictions upon the allowed freedom (e.g. multi-homed hosts). It is only necessary that all hosts within a self-contained group share the same mask. For instance, the first four groups could have netmask 255.255.252.0, the two following could have mask 255.255.254.0, the next two could have separately 255.255.255.0 and 255.255.255.0 and then the next four could have 255.255.252.0 again. This would make a pattern like this:

```
128.39.0.0    (255.255.252.0)
128.39.1.0
128.39.2.0
128.39.3.0

128.39.4.0    (255.255.254.0)
128.39.5.0

128.39.6.0    (255.255.255.0)

128.39.7.0    (255.255.255.0)
```

```
128.39.8.0    (255.255.252.0)
128.39.9.0
128.39.10.0
128.39.11.0
...
```

2.7.4   Interface settings

The IP address of a host is set in the network interface. The Unix command `ifconfig` (interface-configuration) or the Windows command `ipconfig` are used to set this. Normally the address is set at boot time by a shell script executed as part of the `rc` startup files. These files are often constructed automatically during the system installation procedure. The `ifconfig` command is also used to set the broadcast address and netmask for the subnet. Each system interface has a name. Here are the network interface names commonly used by different Unix types.

```
Sun             le0 / hme0
DEC ultrix      ln0
DEC OSF/1       ln0
HPUX            lan0
AIX             en0
GNU/Linux       eth0
IRIX            ec0
FreeBSD         ep0
Solarisx86      dnet0
```

Look at the manual entry for the system for the `ifconfig` command, which sets the Internet address, netmask and broadcast address. Here is an example on a SUN system with a Lance-Ethernet interface.

```
ifconfig le0 192.0.2.10 up netmask 255.255.255.0 broadcast 192.0.2.255
```

Normally we do not need to use this command directly, since it should be in the startup-files for the system, from the time the system was installed. However we might be working in single-user mode or trying to solve some special problem. A system might have been incorrectly configured.

2.7.5   Default route

Unless a host operates as a router in some capacity, it only requires a minimal routing configuration. Each host must define a *default route* which is a destination to which outgoing packets will be sent for processing when they do not belong to the subnet. This is the address of the router or gateway on the same network segment. It is set by a command like this:

```
route add default  my-gateway-address 1
```

The syntax varies slightly between systems. On GNU/Linux systems one writes:

```
/sbin/route add default gw  my-gateway-address metric 1
```

The default route can be checked using the `netstat -r` command. The result should just be a few lines like this:

```
Kernel IP routing table
Destination      Gateway     Genmask           Flags Metric Ref Use  Iface
localnet         *           255.255.255.0     U     0      0    932 eth0
loopback         *           255.0.0.0         U     0      0     38 lo
default          my-gw       0.0.0.0           UG    1      0   1534 eth0
```

where `my-gw` is the address of the local gateway (usually subnet address 1).

If this default route is not set, a host will not know where to send packets and will therefore attempt to build a table of routes, using a different entry for every outgoing address. This consumes memory rapidly and leads to great inefficiency. In the worst case the host might not have contact with anywhere outside its subnet at all.

As of Solaris 9, one obtains a nice overview of both IPv4 and IPv6 protocols:

```
Routing Table: IPv4
  Destination           Gateway              Flags  Ref    Use    Interface
-------------------   -------------------   -----  -----  ------  ---------
128.39.89.0           128.39.89.4           U      1         8   le0
224.0.0.0             128.39.89.4           U      1         0   le0
default               128.39.89.1           UG     1        67
127.0.0.1             127.0.0.1             UH     1         0   lo0

Routing Table: IPv6
  Destination/Mask      Gateway                       Flags Ref Use   If
-------------------   -------------------------    ----- --- --- -----
2001:700:700:3::/64   2001:700:700:3:a00:20ff:fe85:bb11 U 1    0 le0:1
fe80::/10             fe80::a00:20ff:fe85:bb11      U         1   0 le0
ff00::/8              fe80::a00:20ff:fe85:bb11      U         1   0 le0
default               fe80::2a0:c9ff:fe28:2489      UG        1   0 le0
::1                   ::1                           UH        1   9 lo0
```

See section 2.9 for a discussion of IPv6.

2.7.6 ARP/RARP

The Address Resolution Protocol (ARP) is a name service directory for translating from IP address to hardware, Media Access Control (MAC) address (e.g. Ethernet address). The ARP service is mirrored by a reverse lookup ARP service (RARP). RARP takes a hardware address and turns it into an IP address.

Ethernet MAC addresses are required when forwarding traffic from one device to another, on the same subnet. While it is the IP addresses that contain the structure of the Internet and permit routing, it is the hardware address to which one must deliver packets in the final instance; because IP addresses are encapsulated in Ethernet packets.

Hardware addresses are cached by each host on the network so that repeated calls to the service ARP translation service are not required. Addresses are checked later however, so that if an address from a host claiming to have a certain IP address originates from an incorrect hardware address (i.e. the packet does not agree with the information in the cache) then this is detected and a warning can be issued to the effect that two devices are trying to use the same IP address. ARP sends out packets on a local network asking the question 'Who has IP address xxx.yyy.zzz.mmm?' The host concerned replies with its hardware address.

For hosts which know their own IP address at boot-time these services only serve as confirmations of identity. Diskless clients (which have no place to store their IP address) do not have this information when they are first switched on and need to ask for it. All they know originally is the unique hardware (Ethernet) address which is burned into their network interface. In order to bring up and configure an Internet interface they must first use RARP to find out their IP addresses from a RARP server. Services like BOOTP or DHCP are used for this. Also the Unix file /etc/ethers and rarpd can be used. The ARP protocol has no authentication mechanism, and it is therefore easily poisoned with incorrect data. This can be used by malicious parties to reroute packets to a different destination.

2.8 Address space in IPv4

As we have seen, the current implementation of the Internet protocol has a number of problems. The model of *classed* Internet addresses was connected to the design of early routing protocols. This has proved to be a poor design decision, leading to a sparse usage of the available addresses.

It is straightforward to calculate that, because of the structure of the IP addresses, divided into class A, B and C networks, something under two percent of the possible addresses can actually be used in practice. A survey from *Unix Review* in March 1998 showed that, of the total numbers of addresses, these are already allocated:

```
               Max possible   Percent allocated
Class A            127         100%
Class B          16382          62%
Class C        2097150          36%
```

Of course, this does not mean that all of the allocated addresses are in active use. After all, what organization has 65,535 hosts? In fact the survey showed that under two percent of these addresses were actually in use. This is an enormous wastage of IP addresses. Amongst the class C networks, where smaller companies would like address space, the available addresses are being used up quickly, but amongst the class A networks, the addresses will probably never be used. A new addressing structure is therefore required to solve this problem. Three solutions have been devised.

2.8.1 Classless addresses (CIDR)

CIDR stands for Classless Inter-Domain Routing and is documented in RFCs 1517, 1518, 1519, and 1520. CIDR was introduced as an interim measure to combat the problems of IP address allocation as well as that of routing table overflow. It is also the strategy of choice for IPv6 addressing. The name refers to inter-domain routing because it provides not only an addressing solution, but also an improved model for routing packets, by defining *routing domains* (distinct from logical domains of the Domain Name Service).

The IPv4 address space has two problems:

- It is running out of address space, because many addresses are bound up in classes that make them unusable, with the class A,B,C scheme of IP addresses.

- Global routing tables are becoming too large, making routing slow and memory intensive.

In the early 1990s, the limit of routing table size was believed to be somewhere in the order of 100,000 routes. Beyond this, the time it would take for lookup would be longer than TCP/IP timeouts, and the Internet would fail to function. In fact we have already passed this mark [30], but the problem would have been much worse had it not been for classless addressing.

The solution to this problem was a straightforward extension of the idea used in subnetting: to allow the possibility to aggregate or join together smaller networks into larger ones, while at the same time being able to address individual elements within these conglomerates (see table 2.7).

Broadcast flood	Routing table flood
Local Area Net	Wide Area Net
Subnet mask	CIDR mask
Subnet address	Aggregate network address
Host address	Autonomous system number
(computer)	(Routing domain)

Table 2.7: Analogy between subnetting of hosts and super-netting of routing domains.

The classless IPv4 addresses are identical in concept to addresses and subnet masks. The main change is in notation. A 'slash' form is used to represent the number of network bits, instead of another address. This is more compact. For example, the network:

$$192.0.2.0 \ , \ 255.255.255.0 \rightarrow 192.0.2.0/24$$

The number of bits that are '1' in the netmask are simply written after the slash. This notation works across any class of address. It respects only power-of-two (bit) boundaries. Thus CIDR addresses no longer refer to any class of network, only a range of addresses. In order to make this work, new routing protocols were required (such as BGP-4) that did not rely on the simplifications inherent in the classed address scheme.

Address class	IP prefix	Network bits	Hosts bits
Class A	1–126	8 bits	24 bits
Class B	128–191	16 bits	16 bits
Class C	192–224	24 bits	8 bits

Table 2.8: Summary of network classes, and numbers of bits used.

CIDR mask	Equiv. class C	Host addresses
/27	1/8th	32
/26	1/4th	64
/25	1/2	128
/24	1	256
/23	2	512
/22	4	1,024
/21	8	2,048
/20	16	4,096
/19	32	8,192
/18	64	16,384
/17	128	32,768
/16	256 = 1 class B	65,536
/15	512	131,072
/14	1,024	262,144
/13	2,048	524,288

Table 2.9: Examples of bit usage in generalized classless addresses.

Table 2.8 shows the bit usage of the original IPv4 address classes, and table 2.9 shows how the concept of network part and host part is generalized by the classless addressing scheme. Notice how, at this stage, this is nothing more than a change of notation. The importance of the change, however, lies in the ability to combine or aggregate addresses with a common prefix. Routing authorities that support CIDR are hierarchically organized. Each bit boundary that distinguishes a different network must be responsible for its own administration, so that the level above can simply refer to all its IP sub-ranges in one table entry.

2.8.2 Routing domains or Autonomous Systems

Having made a more general split between the network part and host part of an IP address, one can associate a general network prefix with all the hosts in a block of addresses, provided one refers to a block by a bit-boundary. It is now easier to make a generalized hierarchy of 'containers within containers', making each organization responsible for its own internal routing.

An Autonomous System (AS) (sometimes called a routing domain) is a set of routers under a single administrative umbrella, that is responsible for its own internal routing, but which needs to exchange data along *exterior* or *border* routes between itself and other autonomous systems. Within the AS, interior routing protocols are used; between ASs, border protocols are used, e.g. the Border Gateway Protocol (version 4 supports CIDR) (see figure 2.10).

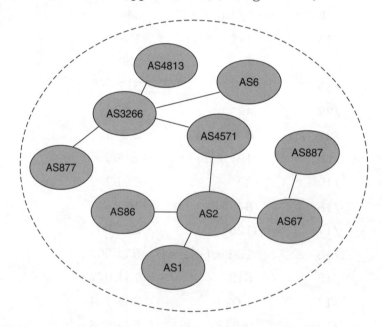

Figure 2.10: The Internet is made up of top-level autonomous systems. These are not necessarily related to the 'Top Level Domains', like .com and .net.

In routing tables, CIDR address boundaries are used to represent aggregated containers, i.e. the largest container that contains all of the hosts one is interested in. In general, this aggregate address boundary will also contain more than one is interested in, so there must be a way of restricting traffic to parts within the aggregate address. As with subnetting of hosts, the routers within the aggregate container only pay attention to data if they are addressed to them, using an 'Autonomous System Number' (ASN). The ASN of a routing domain is analogous to a 'host' address on a Local Area Network, and it requires that each border router knows its ASN identity.

Currently, blocks of addresses are assigned to the large Internet Service Providers (ISPs) who then allocate portions of their address blocks to their customers. These customers, who are often smaller ISPs themselves, then distribute portions of their address block to their customers. Because of the bit-structure in the top-level global routing tables all these different networks and hosts can be represented by the single Internet route entry for the largest container. In this way, the growth in the number of routing table entries at each level in the network hierarchy has been significantly reduced.

In the past, one would get a Class A, B or C address assignment directly from the appropriate Internet Registry (i.e. the InterNIC). Under this scenario, one 'owned' the address and could continue to use it even in the event of changing Internet Service Providers (ISPs). However, this would break the CIDR scheme that allows route aggregation. Thus the new model for address assignments is to obtain them from a 'greater' ISP in the hierarchy of which the system is a part.

At the time of writing, the global routing tables have approximately 120,000 entries. There are 22,000 assigned Autonomous Systems, of which about half are active.

2.8.3 Network Address Translation

In order to provide a 'quick fix' for organizations that required only partial connectivity, Network Address Translation (NAT) was introduced by a number of router manufacturers [331]. In a NAT, a network is represented to the outside world by a single official IP address; it shields the remainder of its networked machines on a private network that (hopefully) uses non-routable addresses (usually 10.x.x.x). When one of these hosts on the private network attempts to contact an address on the Internet, the Network Address Translator creates the illusion that the request comes from the single representative address. The return data are, in turn, routed back to the particular host 'as if by magic' (see figure 2.11). NAT makes associations of this form:

```
(private IP, private port) <-> (public IP, public port)
```

It is important that the outside world (i.e. the true Internet) should not be able to see the private addresses behind a NAT. Using a private address in a public IP address is not just bad manners, it could quickly spoil routing protocols and preclude us from being able to send to the real owners of those addresses. NATs are often used in conjunction with a firewall.

Network address translation is a quick and cheap solution to giving many computers access to the Internet, but it has many problems. The most serious, perhaps, is that it breaks certain IP security mechanisms that rely on IP addresses, because IP addresses are essentially spoofed. Thus some network services will not run through a NAT, because the data stream looks as though it has been forged. Indeed, it has.

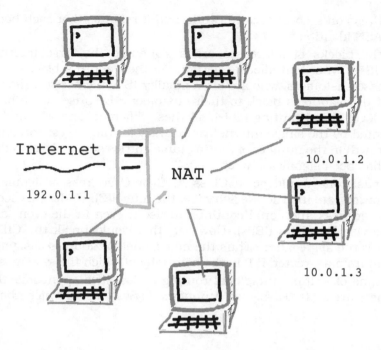

Figure 2.11: Network address translation masquerades many private addresses as a single IP address.

2.9   IPv6 networks

We have already mentioned the problems with IPv4 in connection with address allocation and routing. Other problems with IPv4 are that it is too easy to take control of a connection by guessing sequence numbers. Moreover there is no native support for encryption, Quality of Service guarantees or for mobile computing. All of these things are increasingly important, in a congested virtual community.

In an attempt to address these problems, the Internet Engineering Task Force (IETF) put together a workgroup to design a new protocol. Several suggestions were put forward, some of which attempted to bring the IP model closer to the OSI reference model (see table 2.10), however these suggestions were abandoned in favor of a simple approach that eliminated obsolete elements of IPv4 and extended addresses from 32 to 128 bits. The new IPv6 proposal was adopted for its inclusion of issues like Quality of Service (QoS) and mobility. With 128 bit addresses, even with a certain inefficiency of allocation, it is estimated that there will be enough IPv6 addresses to support a density of more than 10,000 IP addresses per square meter which ought to be enough for every toaster and wristwatch on the planet and beyond. The port space of IPv6 is shared with IPv4.

2.9.1   IPv6 addresses

Stepping up from 32 bits to 128 bits presents problems of representation for IPv6 addresses. If they were coded in the usual denary 'dotted' octet form, used by

0–3	Never used in a working version
4	The Internet as we know it
5	Stream protocol –ST –(never an IPng)
6	SIP → SIPP (Simple Internet protocol plus) → IPv6
7	IPv7 → TP/IX → CATNIP (died)
8	Pip (later joined SIP)
9	TUBA (died)
10–15	Not in use

Table 2.10: A history of projects for IP protocol development.

IPv4, addresses would be impossibly long and cumbersome. Thus a hexadecimal notation was adopted, together with some rules for abbreviation. Each pair of hexadecimal digits codes one byte, or eight bits, so addresses are 32 hexadecimal characters long, or eight blocks of 4 hex-numbers: e.g.

```
2001:0700:0700:0004:0290:27ff:fe93:6723
```

The addresses are prefixed in a classless fashion, like CIDR addresses, making them hierarchically delegable. The groups of four hexadecimal numbers are separated by a colon ':' -- to look like a 'big dot'. The empty colon set '::' stands for a string of 0 bits, or ':0000:'. Similarly, trailing zeros can be omitted.

Here is an example address:

```
2001:700:700:4:290:27ff:fe93:6723
**************          ++
```

The starred part is a delegated IP-series, given by an Internet addressing authority or service provider. The '++' numbers are usually 'ff' or some other padding. The remaining numbers are taken from the MAC (Media Access Control), e.g. Ethernet address of the network interface. This can be seen with:

```
host$ ifconfig -a


eth0      Link encap:Ethernet  HWaddr 00:90:27:93:67:23
          inet addr:128.39.74.16  Bcast:128.39.75.255  Mask:255.255.254.0
          inet6 addr: fe80::290:27ff:fe93:6723/10 Scope:Link
          inet6 addr: 2001:700:700:4:290:27ff:fe93:6723/64 Scope:Global
...
```

Thus, once a prefix has been provided by a local gateway, every host knows its global address at once – no manual address allocation is required. A host can have several IPv6 addresses however. Others can be assigned according to some procedure. A version of the dynamic host control protocol (DHCPv6) has been put forward for this purpose.

2.9.2   Address allocation

The IETF has designated the address range 2000::/3 to be global unicast address space that IANA may allocate to the Regional Internet Registries (RIR)s (see figure 2.12). IANA has allocated initial ranges of global unicast IPv6 address space from the 2001::/16 address block to the existing RIRs. The subsequent allocations of the 2000::/3 unicast address space are made by Regional Internet Authorities (RIRs), with their own allocation policies. End sites will generally be given /48, /64 or /128 assignments.

Type	IPv4	IPv6
Multicast addresses	class D	FF01: - FF0F:
Link local address	N/A	FE80:/10
Unicast address	class A,B,C	2000:/3
Loopback address	127.0.0.1	::1
Unspecified address	0.0.0.0	::0
Mapped IPv4 address	192.0.2.14	::ffff:192.0.2.14

Table 2.11: Some important IPv4 and IPv6 addresses compared.

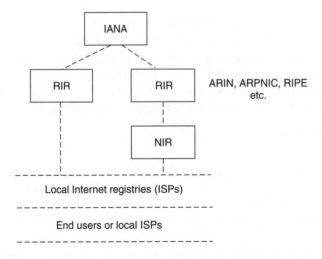

Figure 2.12: The hierarchy of Internet address delegation. IANA (Internet Assigned Numbers Authority) leads the administration of the Internet at the topmost level, and delegates authority to regional Internet registries (RIR) such as INTERNIC (US), APNIC (Asia-Pacific) and RIPE NCC (Europe). These, in turn, delegate to countries and thence to ISPs.

2.9.3   Autoconfiguration and neighbor discovery

With huge networks and unwieldy addresses, an important aspect of IPv6 is autoconfiguration, including neighbor discovery protocols.

When an IPv4 host joins a local area network, it uses the ARP protocol to bind its IP address to its Ethernet MAC address. The Address Resolution Protocol (ARP), documented in RFC 826, is used to do this. It has also been adapted for other media, such as FDDI. ARP works by broadcasting a packet to all hosts on the local network. The packet contains the IP address the sender is interested in communicating with. Most hosts ignore the packet. The target machine, recognizing that the IP address in the packet matches its own, returns an answer.

To reduce the number of address resolution requests, a client (host, router or switch) normally caches resolved addresses for a short interval of time. The ARP cache is of a finite size, and would become full of incomplete and obsolete entries for computers that are not in use if it was allowed to grow without check; thus, it is periodically flushed of all entries. This deletes unused entries and frees space in the cache. It also removes any unsuccessful attempts to contact computers which are not currently running. Since it has no authentication mechanisms, the ARP cache can be poisoned by attackers allowing data to be redirected to the wrong receiver.

In IPv6, ARP is supplanted by a message-passing protocol for neighbor discovery that uses the IPv6 mechanisms on the link-level addresses. A new host can thus automatically discover a local IPv6 gateway to find a route to the outside world. A default route assignment does not normally require a manual assignment. When a gateway is found, a 'scope global' address is automatically assigned to the interface, based on the MAC address of the host, allowing routable communication. The same IPv6 address can be configured on several interfaces. If a gateway is not found, a host can still contact other IPv6 enabled hosts on the same VLAN using the 'link local' address that is configured at start up.

2.9.4   Mobile computing

IPv6 includes support for mobile routing. If a computing device belonging to a particular routing domain finds itself connected via a different routing environment, it first attempts to connect to its home router and establish a forwarding address. This allows packets sent to its fixed IP address to be forwarded to the new location, as well as establishing a direct route for all self-initiated communication. The forwarding addresses are called 'care of' (i.e. c/o) addresses.

Exercises

Self-test objectives

1. Describe the main hardware components in a human–computer system.

2. What rules of thumb would you use for handling the different hardware components.

3. What effect does temperature have on computer systems?

4. What is the function of an operating system? (Hint: how do you define an operating system?)

5. Why is it important to distinguish between single and multiuser operating systems?

6. What is meant by a securable operating system?

7. What is meant by a shell?

8. What is the role of a privileged account? Do non-securable operating systems have such accounts?

9. Summarize the similarities between Unix and Windows.

10. What do the DOS/Windows drive letters A:, B:, etc. correspond to in Unix-like operating systems?

11. What is an Access Control List?

12. How are files shared between users in Unix/Windows?

13. How are files shared between computers in Unix/Windows?

14. What is meant by a process or task?

15. How are processes started and stopped?

16. Name and describe the layers of the OSI model.

17. Describe the main local area networking technologies and how they differ.

18. What are the following?: i) repeater, ii) hub, iii) switch, iv) bridge, v) router.

19. How is a network packet from a single host computer prevented from spreading randomly all over the planet? How is such a packet still able to reach a specified location on the other side of the planet?

20. What does it mean to say that a computer is big-endian?

21. What is an IP address and what does it look like?

22. Do class A,B,C IP addresses have any meaning today?

23. What IPv4 addresses are reserved and why?

24. What is a loopback address?

25. What is meant by a broadcast address?

26. Describe the purpose of a subnet and its netmask.

27. What is a default route?

28. What are ARP and RARP? Are they needed in IPv6? Why/why not?

29. Explain the concept of an Autonomous System.

30. What is meant by Network Address Translation, and what is its main purpose?

31. Describe how IPv6 addresses differ from IPv4 addresses.

32. Can IPv6 completely replace IPv4?

Problems

1. Compare and contrast Windows with Unix-like operating systems. If you need a refresher about Unix, consider the online textbook at Oslo University College [40].

2. Under what circumstances is it desirable to use a graphical user interface (GUI), and when is it better to use a command language to address a computer? (If you answer *never* to either of these, you are not thinking hard enough.)

3. The purpose of this exercise is to make yourself familiar with a few Unix tools which you will need to use to analyze networks later. Remember that the aim of this course is to make you self-sufficient, not to force feed you information. This exercise assumes that you have access to a Unix-like operating system.

   (a) Use the `ssh` command to log onto a host in your domain.

   (b) Use the command `uname` with all of its options to find out what type of host it is.

   (c) Familiarize yourself with the commands `df`, `nslookup`, `mount`, `finger` `.clients` (GNU finger). What do these commands do and how can you use them?

   (d) Start the program `nslookup`. This starts a special shell. Assuming that your local domain is called domain.country, try typing

   ```
   > ls domain.country
   ```

   If you get an error, you should ask your administrator why. The ability to list a domain's contents can be restricted for security reasons. Then try this and explain what you find:

   ```
   > set q=any
   > domain.country
   ```

   (e) The `nslookup` command is now deprecated, according to some Unices, and is replaced with `dig` and `host`. Use the dig command to look up host names:

   ```
   dig www.gnu.org
   dig -x 199.232.41.10
   ```

Now do the same using the host command with IPv4 and IPv6

```
host nexus.iu.hio.no
nexus.iu.hio.no has address 128.39.89.10

host -t aaaa nexus.iu.hio.no
nexus.iu.hio.no has AAAA address
2001:700:700:3:a00:20ff:fe9b:dd4a

host -n 2001:700:700:3:a00:20ff:fe9b:dd4a
a.4.d.d.b.9.e.f.f.f.0.2.0.0.a.0.3.0.0.0.0.0.7.0.0.0.7.0.
1.0.0.2.ip6.int domain name pointer nexus.iu.hio.no.
```

4. Review the principal components in a computer. Are there any differences between an electronic calculator and a PC? Which parts of a computer require maintenance?

5. Deconstruct and recontruct a PC from basic components. Make sure that it works. Document the process as you go, so that you could build another computer from scratch.

6. Review the concept of *virtual memory*. If you do not have access to a textbook on operating systems, see my online textbook [40]. What is swapping and what is paging? Why is paging to a file less efficient than paging to a raw partition?

7. Explain how a filesystem solves the problem of storing and retrieving files from a storage medium, such as a disk. Explain how files can be identified as entities on the magnetic surface. Finally, explain how the concept of a filesystem can hide the details of the storage medium, and allow abstractions like network disk sharing.

8. Locate the important log files on your most important operating systems. How do you access them, and what information do they contain? You will need this bird's eye view of the system error messages when things go wrong. (Hint: there are log files for system messages, services like WWW and FTP and for mail traffic. Try using `tail -f logfile` on Unix-like hosts to follow the changes in a log file. If you don't know what it does, look it up in the manual pages.)

9. Explain what an access control list is. Compare the functionality of the Unix file permission model with that of access control lists. Given that ACLs take up space and have many entries, what problems do you foresee in administering file security using ACLs?

10. Explain why the following are invalid IPv4 host addresses:
    (a) `10.1.0.0`
    (b) `10.1.0.255`
    (c) `0.12.16.89`
    (d) `255.9.56.45`
    (e) `192.34.255.255`

Chapter 3

Networked communities

System administration is not just about machines and individuals, it is about communities. There is the local community of users on multi-user machines; then there is the local area network community of machines at a site. Finally, there is the global community of all machines and networks in the world.

We cannot learn anything about a community of networked computer systems without knowing where all the machines are, both physically and in the network, what their purposes are, and how they interrelate to one another. Normally we do not start out by building a network of computers from nothing, rather we inherit an existing network, serviceable or not; thus the first step is to acquaint ourselves with the system at hand.

The aim of this chapter is to learn how to navigate network systems using standard tools, and place each piece of the puzzle into the context of the whole.

3.1   Communities and enterprises

The basic principle of communities is:

Principle 5 (Communities). *What one member of a cooperative community does affects every other member and vice versa. Each member of the community therefore has a responsibility to consider the well-being of the other members of the community.*

When this principle is ignored, it leads to conflict. One attempts to preserve the stability of a community by making *rules*, *laws* or *policies*. The main difference between these is only our opinion of their severity: rules and laws do not exist because there are fundamental rights and wrongs, they exist because there is a need to summarize the consensus of opinion in a community group. A social rule thus has two purposes:

- To provide a widely accepted set of conventions that simplify decisions, avoiding the need to think through things from first principles every time.

- To document the will of the community for reference.

Rules can never cover every eventuality. They are convenient approximations to reality that summarize common situations. An idealist might hope that rules would never be used as a substitute for thought, however this is just how they are used in practice. Rules simplify the judgment process for common usage, to avoid constant re-evaluation (and perhaps constant change).

We can apply this central axiom for the user community of a multiuser host:

Corollary to principle (Multiuser communities). *A multiuser computer system does not belong to any one user. All users must share the common resources of the system. What one user does affects all other users and vice versa. Each user has a responsibility to consider the effect of his/her actions on all the other users.*

and also for the world-wide network community:

Corollary to principle (Network communities). *A computer that is plugged into the network is no longer just our own. It is part of a society of machines which shares resources and communicates with the whole. What that machine does affects other machines. What other machines do affects that machine.*

The ethical issues associated with connection to the network are not trivial, just as it is not trivial to be a user in a multiuser system, or a member of a civil community. Administrators are, in practice, responsible for their organization's conduct to the entire rest of the Internet, by ensuring conformance with policy. This great responsibility should be borne wisely.

3.2   Policy blueprints

By placing a human–computer system into an environment that it has no direct control over, we open it up to many risks and random influences. If we hope to maintain a predictable system, it is important to find a way to relate to and make sense of these external factors. Moreover, if we wish to maintain a predictable system, then we need to know how to recognize it: what should the system look like and how should it behave? The tool for accomplishing this is policy.

> **Definition 2 (Policy).** *Policy is a statement of aims and wishes that is codified, as far as possible, into a formal blueprint for infrastructure and a schema of responses (contingencies) for possible events.*

A policy's aim is to maintain order in the face of the chaos that might be unleashed upon it–either from the environment that it does not control, or from a lack of control of its own component parts. Any system can spiral out of control if it is not held in check. By translating hopes and wishes into concrete rules and regimens, we build a model for what a predictable system should look like.

- A blueprint of infrastructure.
- Production targets (resource availability).
- Restriction of behavior (limiting authority, access).
- Stimulus–response checklists (maintenance).

A policy determines only an approximate state for a human–computer system – not a state in the sense of a static or frozen configuration, but rather a dynamical equilibrium or point of balance. Human–computer systems are not deterministic, but the aim of policy is to limit the unpredictable part of their behavior to the level of background noise.

3.3 System uniformity

The opportunity to standardize parts of a system is an enticing prospect that can potentially lead to great simplification; but that is not the full story. Given the chance to choose the hardware and software at a site, one can choose a balance between two extreme strategies: to standardize as far as possible, or to vary as much as possible. Curiously, it is not necessarily true that standardization will always increase predictability. That would be true in a static system – but in a real life, dynamical system we have to live with the background noise caused by the parts that we do not control.

Strategically, trying 'every which way', i.e. every possible variation on a theme, can pay off in terms of productivity. Moreover, a varied system is less vulnerable to a single type of failure. Thus, if we look at the predictability of *productivity*, a certain level of variation can be an advantage. However, we must find an appropriate balance between these two principles:

> **Principle 6 (Uniformity).** *A uniform configuration minimizes the number of differences and exceptions one has to take into account later, and increases the static predictability of the system. This applies to hardware and software alike.*

> **Principle 7 (Variety).** *A variety of configurations avoids 'putting all eggs in one basket'. If some components are poor, then at least not all will be poor. A strategy of variation is a way of minimizing possible loss.*

It is wise for system administrators to spend time picking out reliable hardware and software. The more different kinds of system we have, the more difficult the problem of installing and maintaining them, but if we are uncertain of what is best, we might choose to apply a random sample in order to average out a potential loss. Ideally perhaps, one should spend a little time researching the previous experiences of others in order to find a 'best choice' and then standardize to a large degree.

PC hardware is often a melange of random parts from different manufacturers. Much work can be saved by standardizing graphics and network interfaces, disk sizes, mice and any other devices that need to be configured. This means not only that hosts will be easier to configure and maintain, but also that it will be easier to buy extra parts or cannibalize systems for parts later. On the other hand, automated agents like cfengine can make the task of maintaining a variety of options a manageable task.

With software, the same principle applies: a uniform software base is easier to install and maintain than one in which special software needs to be configured in special ways. Fewer methods are available for handling the *differences* between systems; most administration practices are based on standardization. However, dependence on one software package could be risky for an organization. There is clearly a complex discussion around these issues.

3.4   User behavior: socio-anthropology

Most branches of computer science deal primarily with software systems and algorithms. System administration is made more difficult by the fact that it deals with communities and is therefore strongly affected by what human beings do. In short, a large part of system administration can be characterized as sociology or anthropology.

A newly installed machine does not usually require attention until it is first used, but as soon as a user starts running programs and storing data, the reliability and efficiency of the system are tested. This is where the challenge of system administration lies.

The load on computers and on networks is a social phenomenon: it peaks in response to patterns of human behavior. For example, at universities and colleges network traffic usually peaks during lunch breaks, when students rush to the terminal rooms to surf on the web or to read E-mail. In industry the reverse can be true, as workers flee the slavery of their computers for a breath of fresh air (or polluted air). In order to understand the behavior of the network, the load placed on servers and the availability of resources, we have to take into account the users' patterns of behavior (see figure 3.1).

3.5   Clients, servers and delegation

At the heart of all cooperation in a community is a system of *centralization* and *delegation*. No program or entity can do everything alone, nor is everyone expected to do so. It makes sense for certain groups to specialize in performing certain jobs. That is the function of a society and good management.

> **Principle 8 (Delegation I).** *Leave experts to do their jobs. Assigning responsibility for a task to a body which specializes in that task is a more efficient use of resources.*

If we need to find out telephone numbers, we invent the directory enquiry service: we give a special body a specific job. They do the phone-number research (once and for everyone) and have the responsibility for dealing out the information on request. If we need a medical service, we train doctors in the specialized knowledge and trust them with the responsibility. That is much more efficient than expecting every individual to have to research phone numbers by themselves, or to study medicine personally. The advantage with a *service* is that one avoids repeating work unnecessarily and one creates special agents with an aptitude for their task. In database theory, this process is called *normalization* of the system.

The principle of specialization also applies in system administration. Indeed, in recent years the number of client-server systems has grown enormously, because

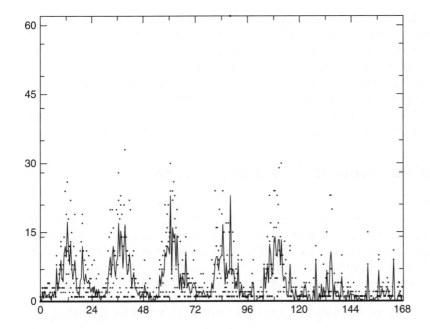

Figure 3.1: E-mail traffic at Oslo College measured over the course of many weeks. The plot shows the weekly average from Monday to Sunday. Over each 24 hour period, there is a daily peak showing users' working hours, and during the week, there is a peak around midweek, and little activity during the weekends.

of possibilities offered by networking. Not only can we give a special daemon on one host a special job, but we can say that that daemon will do the job for every other host on the network also. As long as the load placed on the network does not lead to a bottleneck, this is a very efficient centralization of resources. Clearly, the client-server model is an extended way of sharing resources. In that sense it is like a distributed generalization of the kernel.[1]

The client-server nomenclature has been confused by history. A server is not a host, but a program or process which runs on a host. A client is any process which requires the services of a server. In Unix-like systems, servers are called daemons. In Windows they are just called services. Unfortunately, it is common to refer to the host on which a server process runs as being a server. This causes all sorts of confusion.

The name 'server' was usurped, early on, for a very specific client-server relationship. A server is often regarded as a large machine which performs some difficult and intensive task for the clients (an array of workstations). This prejudice comes from the early days when many PC-workstations were chained together in a network to a single PC which acted as file-server, and printer server, sharing a disk and printer with all of the machines. The reason for this architecture, at the time, was that the operating system of that epoch MS-DOS was not capable of

---

[1]In reality, there are many levels at which the client-server model applies. For example, many system calls can be regarded as client-server interactions, where the client is any program and the server is the kernel.

multitasking, and thus the best solution one could make was to use a new PC for each new task. This legacy of one-machine, one-user, one-purpose, still pervades newer PC operating system philosophy. Meanwhile, Unix and later experimental operating systems have continued a general policy of 'any machine, any job', as part of the vision of *distributed operating systems*. There are many reasons for choosing one strategy or the other, so we shall return to this issue.

In fact a server-host can be anything from a Cray to a laptop. As long as there is a process which executes a certain service, the host is a server-host.

3.6 Host identities and name services

Whenever computers are coupled together, there is a need for each to have an individual and unique identity. This need has been recognized many times, by different system developers, and the result is that today's computer systems can have many different names which identify them in different contexts. The outcome is confusion. For Internet-enabled machines, the IP address of the host is usually sufficient for most purposes. A host can have all of the following:

- *Host ID:* Circuit board identity number. Often used in software licensing.

- *Install name:* Configured at installation time. This is often compiled into the kernel, or placed in a file like /etc/hostname. Solaris adds to the multiplicity by also maintaining the install name in /etc/hostname.le0 or an equivalent file for the appropriate network interface, together with several files in /etc/net/*/hosts.

- *Application level name:* Any name used by application software when talking to other hosts.

- *Local file mapping:* Originally the Unix /etc/hosts file was used to map IP addresses to names and vice versa. Other systems have similar local files, to avoid looking up on network services.

- *Network Information Service:* A local area network database service developed by Sun Microsystems. This was originally called Yellow Pages and many of its components still bear the 'yp' prefix.

- *Network level address(es):* Each network interface can be configured with an IP address. This number converts into a text name through a name service.

- *Link level address(es):* Each network interface (Ethernet/FDDI etc.) has a hardware address burned into it at the factory, also called its MAC address, or media access control address. Some services (e.g. RARP) will turn this into a name or an IP address through a secondary naming service like DNS.

- *DNS name(s):* The name returned by a domain name server (DNS/BIND) based on an IP address key.

- *WINS name(s):* The name returned by a WINS server (Microsoft's name server) based on an IP address. WINS was deprecated as of Windows 2000.

Different hardware and software systems use these different identities in different ways. The host ID and network level addresses simply exist. They are unique and nothing can be done about them, short of changing the hardware. For the most part they can be ignored by a system administrator. The network level MAC address is used by the network transport system for end-point data delivery, but this is not something which need concern most system administrators. The network hardware takes care of itself.

At boot-time, each host needs to obtain a unique identity. In today's networks that means a unique IP address per interface and an associated name for convenience or to bind the multiple IP addresses together. The purpose of this identity is to uniquely identify the host amongst all of the others on the world-wide network. Although every network interface has a unique Ethernet address or token ring address, these addresses do not fall into a hardware-independent hierarchical structure. In other words Ethernet addresses cannot be used to route messages from one side of the planet to the other in a simple way. In order to make that happen, a system like TCP/IP is required. At boot-time then each host needs to obtain an Internet identity. It has two choices:

- Ask for an address to be provided from a list of free addresses. (DHCP or BOOTP protocols)

- Always use the same IP address, stored on its system configuration files. (Requires correct information on the disk)

The first of these possibilities is sometimes useful for terminal rooms containing large numbers of identical machines. In that case, the specific IP address is unimportant as long as it is unique. The second of these is the preferred choice for any host which has special functions, particularly hosts which provide network services. Network services should always be at a well-known, static location.

From the IP address a name can be automatically attached to the host through an Internet *naming service*. There are several services which can perform this conversion. DNS, NIS and WINS are the three prevalent ones. DNS is the superior service, based on a world-wide database; it can determine hostname to IP address mappings for any host in the world. NIS (Unix) and WINS (Windows) are local network services which are essentially redundant as name services. They continue to exist because of other functions which they can perform.

As far as any host on a TCP/IP network is concerned, a host is its IP address and any names associated with that address. Any names which are used internally by the kernel, or externally, are quite irrelevant. The difficulty with having so many names, quite apart from any confusion which humans experience, is that naming conflicts can cause internal problems. This is an operating system dependent problem but, as a general rule, if we are forced to use more than one naming service, we must be careful to ensure complete consistency between them.

The only world-wide service in common use today is DNS (the Domain Name Service) whose common implementation is called BIND (Berkeley Internet Name Domain). This associates IP addresses with a list of names. Every host in the DNS has a *canonical name*, or official name, and any number of *aliases*. For instance, a host which runs several important services might have the canonical name

```
mother.domain.country
```

and aliases,

```
www.domain.country
ftp.domain.country
```

DNS binds a local network to the world-wide Internet in several important ways. It makes it possible for data belonging to organizations to be spread across the surface of the planet (or beyond) at any location, and yet still maintain a transparent naming structure. E-mail services use the DNS to route mail.

WINS (Windows Internet Name Service) was a proprietary system built by Microsoft for Windows. Since any local host can register data in this service, it was insecure and is therefore inadvisable in any trusted network. WINS has now been replaced by DNS as of Windows 2000.

Under Windows, each system has an alphanumeric name which is chosen during the installation. A domain server will provide an SID (security ID) for the name which helps prevent spoofing. When Windows boots it broadcasts the name across the network to see whether it is already in use. If the name is in use, the user of the workstation is prompted for a new name.

The security of a name service is of paramount importance, since so many other services rely on name services to establish identity. If one can subvert a name service, hosts can be tricked into trusting foreign hosts and security crumbles.

3.7 Common network sharing models

During the 1970s it was realized that expensive computer hardware could be used most cost-efficiently (by the maximum number of people) if it was available *remotely*, i.e. if one could communicate with the computer from a distant location and gain access to its resources. Inter-system communication became possible, in stages, through the use of modems and UUCP batch transfer and later through real-time wide area networks.

The large mainframe computers which served sometimes hundreds of users were painfully slow for interactive tasks, although they were efficient at batch processing. As hardware became cheaper many institutions moved towards a model of smaller computers coupled to file-servers and printers by a network. This solution was relatively cheap but had problems of its own. At this time the demise of the mainframe was predicted. Today, however, mainframe computers are very much alive for computationally intensive tasks, while the small networked workstation provides access to a world of resources via the Internet.

Dealing with networks is one of the most important aspects of system administration today. The network is our greatest asset and our greatest threat. In order to be a system administrator it is necessary to understand how and *why* networks are implemented, using a world-wide protocol: the Internet protocol family.

Without getting too heavily bogged down in details which do not concern us at an elementary level, we shall explore these themes throughout the remainder of this book.

3.7.1 Constraints on infrastructure

Different operating systems support different ideas about how network services should be used. We are not always free to use the hardware resources as we would like. Operating system technologies restrict the kind of infrastructures it is possible to build in practice (see figure 3.2).

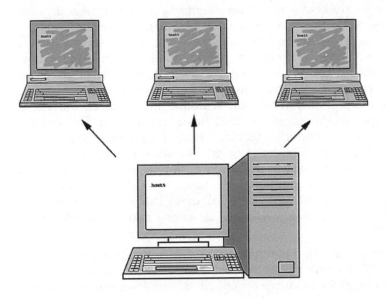

Figure 3.2: Some network infrastructure models single out a special server-host, which is used to consolidate network services and resources. Such a centralization has many administrative advantages, but it concentrates load and can create a bottleneck.

- *Unix:* Much, if not all, of Unix's success can be attributed to the astonishing freedom which is granted to its users and administrators. Without a doubt, Unix-like operating systems are the most configurable and adaptable ever created. This has kept Unix at the forefront of new technology but has also created a class of operating systems rather like disorganized piles of treasure in Aladdin's cave.

  Unix-like operating systems are not tied to any specific model for utilizing network resources, though vendors sometimes introduce specific technologies for sharing, which favor a particular kind of model. (This is almost viewed as a treasonable offence and is usually quickly rejected in favor of software which offers greater freedom.) Unix lets us decide how we want the network to look. Any Unix system can perform any function, as server, client or both. A Unix network is fully distributed; there is no requirement about centralization of resources, but central models are commonly used. Unix contains troves of tools for making many hosts work together and share resources, but each host can also be configured as a stand-alone system. Each host either has a fixed IP address, or can be assigned one dynamically at boot-time by a service such as *BOOTP* or *DHCP*.

- *Windows:* Windows networks are built around a specific model. There are two types of Windows system with separate software licenses: *workstations* and *servers*. Windows can work as a stand-alone system or as a workstation, integrated into a system of network services. Windows revolves around a model in which programs are run on a local workstation, but where network services and resources are kept and run on a centralized server. IP addresses may be fixed or may be assigned automatically by a network service such as *BOOTP* or *DHCP*. Several Windows servers can coexist. Each server serves a logical group of hosts, users and services called a *domain*. Domains are now merged into an Active Directory model that provides a logical directory structure for network services. Client machines subscribe to as many domains as they wish, or have permission to join. Windows supports two kinds of organizational groups: *workgroups* in which hosts share a simple peer-to-peer network, perhaps with Windows 9x machines, and *domains* which have a central authority through a domain server. Domains provide a common framework including user-ids (SIDs in Windows language), passwords and user profiles. Domains have a common user-database and a common security policy. Any host which subscribes to a domain inherits the users and the security policy of the domain. Windows domains can be simulated by Unix-like hosts [198].

  Windows 2000 is a reincarnation of Windows NT 4.0. It redresses many of the shortcomings of the NT domain model by moving towards Novell-like directory services as its new model for resource organization. It allows remote services such as terminal login, which was only introduced as an afterthought in NT.

- *Novell Netware:* The Novell Netware software [127] has been through several major versions, each of which has been significantly different. To begin with Netware was little more than a disk and printer server for small PC networks. It found wide acceptance due to its broad support of different network interface technologies. Today, Netware version 5 is a fully distributed, object-oriented remote procedure service. Novell Netware is not an operating system, per se. It is a network service for PCs which adds file storage, printing and other network services on top of the basic operating system: Windows, DOS, MacIntosh or GNU/Linux. The network protocol for local traffic is IPX; this is lighter than IP and is an inter-networking protocol, but it is not a world-wide protocol, thus Novell-run PCs still need IP configurable interfaces to talk to the world. Each PC can have a fixed or dynamically allocated IP address, with a BOOTP or DHCP broadcast request. In Netware 5, several Novell file-servers can coexist to provide a seamless Network Directory Service (NDS), an object-based service model. All services run on these servers, which support a form of modular thread-based multitasking. Novell services are not distributed arbitrarily amongst the PCs it serves, as is more common with Unix: they require one or more special dedicated machines to work on behalf of users' PCs, more like Windows. The client machines must run Netware client software in order to communicate transparently with the servers. Although the nomenclature is different to that of Windows domains and Directory Services, all the same functionality and more is available in the Novell software.

- *MacIntosh:* Each MacIntosh is an independent system. Simple services like `ftp` can be run in a limited way from a normal machine. Macintosh once used its own network protocol called Apple-talk which is incompatible with IP and IPX. Apple-talk servers allowed networking and disk sharing. Recently MacIntosh have released a new operating system based on emulation of Unix and old-style MacIntosh. This uses TCP/IP and NetInfo for directory services. The Mac OS Server X provides a powerful server based on Mach kernel technology and BSD Unix, to rival Novell's Netware and Windows.

3.7.2 User preference storage

Software packages often allow users to store preferences about the way that software should look and behave. Such data are stored in some kind of information repository. Another issue for networked systems is where software preference data should be stored for users. There are two possibilities here which correspond approximately to the Unix approach and the Windows approach.

- *Windows/Mac/Personal:* Under earlier Windows and MacIntosh systems, each user was assumed to have his or her own personal workstation which would not normally be used by other users. Current Windows versions allow logins by multiple users. Configuration data or preferences which the user selects are stored locally on the system disk in a location provided by the operating system. Later versions of Windows (NT, 2000, XP etc.) solve these problems by maintaining *user profiles* which are stored on the domain server in a \profiles subdirectory of the system-root. These data are copied into the local workstation when a user logs on to a domain server.

- *Unix/Shared:* Under Unix, each user sets up personal preferences in his or her personal *dot files* which are stored in private user space. More general global preferences are stored in a directory of the administrator's choice. Traditionally this has been the directory /etc.

The difficulties associated with having a fixed location for the configuration information which lies in the system files are several. In any single-user operating system, one user can overwrite another user's preferences simply by changing them since the system is not capable of telling the difference between users. This is a fundamental problem which indicates that single-user operating systems are basically unsuited to a shared environment. For a multi-user, networked world, the following points must be considered:

- When the operating system is reinstalled, configuration information can easily be lost or overwritten if they are stored in an operating system directory.

- In a distributed environment, where users might not sit at the same physical workstation day after day, the user's personal configuration data will not follow him or her from machine to machine.

On a Unix system, it is easy to specify the locations of configuration files in software and these can then be kept separate from operating system files, e.g. on a different disk partition so that they are immune to accidental deletion by system reinstallation. The main problem with Unix is the lack of any uniformity of approach. In the future, there might be a semblance of uniformity. RFC 2244 and RFC 2245 describe the Application Configuration Access Protocol which describes a centralized user application configuration database.

3.8   Local network orientation and analysis

A network community is an organism, working through the orchestrated cooperation of many parts. We need to understand its operation carefully in order to make it work well. The choices we make about the system can make it easy to understand, or difficult to understand, efficient or inefficient. This is the challenge of community planning.

Within a local area network, a top-down approach is useful for understanding host interrelationships. We therefore begin at the local network level, i.e. at the level of the collective society of machines.

In most daily situations, one starts with a network already in place, i.e. we do not have to build one from scratch. For an administrator, it is important to know what hardware one has to work with and where everything is to be found; how it is organized (or not) and so on.

> **Principle 9 (Resource map).** *A resource map of a site aids the* predictability *of the system by allowing an administrator to learn about the parts of the system, understand interrelationships and prepare a contingency plan for expected problems with the specific elements.*

Here is a checklist:

- How does the network physically fit together? (What is its topology?)

- How many different subnets does the network have?

- What are their network addresses?

- Find the router addresses (and the default routes) on each segment.

- What is the netmask?

- What hardware is there in the network? (Hosts, printers etc.)

- Which function does each host/machine have on the network?

- Where are the key network services located?

Some hardware can be efficiently identified and queried using SNMP technology. Most newer network hardware supports some kind of querying using SNMP protocols (see section 6.4.1). This is a form of network communication which talks directly to the device and extracts its hardware profile. Without SNMP, identifying hardware automatically is problematical. One author has proposed using the Unix log service syslogd to track hardware configurations [250]. An overview of network services can sometimes be obtained using port-scanning software, such as nmap, though this should be agreed in advance to avoid misunderstandings. Many network intrusion attempts begin with port scans; these can make security conscious administrators nervous.

Of course, when automated methods fail, one can always resort to a visual inspection. In any event, an organization needs some kind of *inventory list* for the purpose of insurance or theft, if not merely for good housekeeping. A rough overview of all this information needs to be assembled in system administrators' minds, in order to understand the challenge ahead.

Having thought about the network in its entirety, we can drop down a level and begin to think about individual host machines. We need to know hosts both from the viewpoint of hardware and software.

- What kind of machines are on the network? What are their names and addresses and where are they? Do they have disks. How big? How much memory do they have? If they are PCs, which screen cards do they have?

- How many CPUs do the hosts have?

- What operating systems are running on the network? MS-DOS, Novell, Windows or Unix? (If so which Unix? GNU/Linux, Solaris, HPUX?)

- What kind of network cables are used?

- Where are hubs/repeaters/the router or other network control boxes located? Who is responsible for maintaining them?

- What is the hierarchy of responsibility?

There is information about the local environment:

- What is the local timezone?

- What broadcast address convention is used? 255 or the older 0?

- Find the key servers on these networks.

  - Where are the network disks located? Which machine are they attached to?

  - Which name service is in use (DNS, NIS or NIS plus)?

  - Where is the inevitable WWW/HTTP service? Who is running pirate servers?

Finding and recording this information is an important learning process, and the information gathered will prove invaluable for the task ahead. Of course, the information will change as time goes by. Networks are not static; they grow and evolve with time, so we must remain vigilant in pursuit of the moving target.

3.8.1 Network naming orientation

Familiarizing oneself with an organization's network involves analyzing the network's hosts and all of their interrelationships. It is especially important to know who is responsible for maintaining different parts of the network. It might be us or it might be someone else. We need to know whom to contact when something is going wrong over which we have no control ourselves. The most obvious way to view an organization is by its logical structure. This is usually reflected in the names of different machines and domains. Whom do we call if the Internet connection is broken? What service contracts exist on hardware, what upgrade possibilities are there on software? What system is in use for making backups? How does one obtain a backup should the need arise? In short, it is essential to know where to begin in solving any problem which might arise, and whom to call if the responsibility for a problem lies with someone else.

The Internet is permeated by a *naming scheme* which, naturally, is used to describe organizational groupings of Internet addresses. We can learn a lot by inspecting the name data for an organization. Indeed, many organizations now see this as a potential security hazard and conceal their naming strategies from outsiders. The Domain Name Service (DNS) is the Internet's primary naming service. It not only allows us to name hosts, but also whole organizations, placing many different IP addresses under a common umbrella. The DNS is thus a hierarchical organization of machine names and addresses. Organizations are represented by *domains* and a domain is maintained either by or on behalf of each organization. Global domains are divided into countries, or groupings like .com and .org, and *sub-domains* are set up within larger domains, so that a useful name can be associated with the function of the organization. To analyze our own network, we begin by asking: who runs the DNS domain above ours?

For our organizational enquiry, we need an overview of the hosts which make up our organization. A host list can be obtained from the DNS using nslookup/dig or Nslookup etc. (unless that privilege has been revoked by the DNS administrator, see section 9.5.3). If there are Unix systems on the network, one can learn a lot without physical effort by logging onto each machine and using the uname command to find out what OS is being used:

```
sunshine% uname -a
SunOS nexus 5.9 Generic_112233-04 sun4u sparc


gnu% uname -a
Linux gnu 2.4.10-4GB #1 Fri Sep 28 17:20:21 GMT 2001 i686 unknown
```

This tells us that host nexus is a SunOS kernel version 5.9 (colloquially known as Solaris 2.9) system with a sun4u series processor, and that host gnu is a GNU/Linux system kernel version 2.4.10. If the uname command doesn't exist, then the operating system is an old dinosaur from BSD 4.3 days and we have to find out what it is by different means. Try the commands arch and mach.

Knowing the operating system of a host is not sufficient. We also need to know what kind of resources the host has to offer the network, so that we can later plan the distribution of services. Thus we need to dig deeper:

- How much memory does a host have? (Most systems print this when they boot. Sometimes the information can be coaxed out of the system in other ways.) What disks and other devices are in use?

- Use `locate` and `find` and `which` and `whereis` to find important directories and software. How is the software laid out?

- What software directories exist? `/usr/local/bin`, `/local/bin`?

- Do the Unix systems have a C compiler installed? This is often needed for installing software. Finding out information about other operating systems, such as Windows, which we cannot log onto is a tedious process. It must be performed by manual inspection, but the results are important nonetheless.

3.8.2 Using `nslookup` and `dig`

The `nslookup` program is for querying the Domain Name Service (DNS). On Unix it has now been officially deprecated and replaced by a new program, `dig` or `host`, in the source implementations of the BIND software. On Windows one has `Nslookup`. It is still in widespread use, however, both in Unix and Windows milieux. Moreover, IPv6 lookup does not work in all implementations of `nslookup`. The name service provides a mapping or relationship between Internet numbers and Internet names, and contains useful information about domains: both our own and others. The first thing we need to know is the domain name. This is the suffix part of the Internet name for the network. For instance, suppose our domain is called `example.org`. Hosts in this domain have names like `hostname.example.org`.

If you don't know your DNS domain name, it can probably be found by looking at the file `/etc/resolv.conf` on Unix hosts. For instance:

```
gnu% more /etc/resolv.conf
domain example.org
nameserver 192.0.2.10
nameserver 192.0.2.17
nameserver 192.0.2.244
```

Also most Unix systems have a command called `domainname`. This prints the name of the local Network Information Service (NIS) domain which is not the same thing as the DNS domain name (though, in practice, many sites would use the same name for both). Do not confuse the output of this command with the DNS domain name.

Once you know the domain name, you can find out the hosts which are registered in your domain by running the name service lookup program `nslookup`, or `dig`.

```
gnu% nslookup
Default Server:  mother.example.org
Address:  192.0.2.10
>
```

nslookup always prints the name and the address of the server from which it obtains its information. Then you get a new prompt > for typing commands. Typing help provides a list of the commands which nslookup understands.

Hostname/IP lookup

Type the name of a host or Internet (IP) address and nslookup returns the equivalent translation. For example:

```
host% nslookup
Default Server:  mother.example.org
Address:  192.0.2.10

> www.gnu.org
Server:  mother.example.org
Address:  192.0.2.10

Name: www.gnu.org
Address:  206.126.32.23


>  192.0.2.238
Server:  mother.example.org
Address:  192.0.2.10

Name:   dax.example.org
Address:  192.0.2.238
```

In this example we look up the Internet address of the host called www.gnu.org and the name of the host which has Internet address 192.0.2.238. In both cases the default server is the name server mother.example.org which has Internet address 192.0.2.10.

Note that the default server is the first server listed in the file /etc/resolv.conf which answers queries on starting nslookup. Using dig, we write the following to find IPv4 A records:

```
host% dig -t a www.gnu.org

; <<>> DiG 9.2.1 <<>> -t a www.gnu.org
;; global options:  printcmd
;; Got answer:
;; ->>HEADER<<- opcode: QUERY, status: NOERROR, id: 33680
;; flags: qr rd ra; QUERY: 1, ANSWER: 1, AUTHORITY: 5, ADDITIONAL: 5

;; QUESTION SECTION:
;www.gnu.org.                    IN A

;; ANSWER SECTION:
www.gnu.org.            86376   IN A         199.232.41.10
```

```
;; AUTHORITY SECTION:
gnu.org.                    86388    IN NS     nic.cent.net.
gnu.org.                    86388    IN NS     ns1.gnu.org.
gnu.org.                    86388    IN NS     ns2.gnu.org.
gnu.org.                    86388    IN NS     ns2.cent.net.
gnu.org.                    86388    IN NS     ns3.gnu.org.

;; ADDITIONAL SECTION:
nic.cent.net.               101919   IN A      140.186.1.4
ns1.gnu.org.                118216   IN A      199.232.76.162
ns2.gnu.org.                118216   IN A      195.68.21.199
ns2.cent.net.               101919   IN A      140.186.1.14
ns3.gnu.org.                118216   IN A      209.115.72.62

;; Query time: 5 msec
;; SERVER: 127.0.0.1#53(127.0.0.1)
;; WHEN: Fri Sep  6 13:21:28 2002
;; MSG SIZE  rcvd: 223
```

The '-t' argument specifies the type of record to be looked up when using the hostname as an argument. Thus, to look up IPv6 'AAAA' records, we write

```
host% dig -t aaaa daneel.iu.hio.no

; <<>> DiG 9.2.1 <<>> -t aaaa daneel.iu.hio.no
;; global options:  printcmd
;; Got answer:
;; ->>HEADER<<- opcode: QUERY, status: NOERROR, id: 61573

;; QUESTION SECTION:
;daneel.iu.hio.no.              IN AAAA

;; ANSWER SECTION:
daneel.iu.hio.no.      14400   IN AAAA 2001:700:700:3:290:27ff:fea2:477b

;; AUTHORITY SECTION:
iu.hio.no.             14400   IN NS   cube.iu.hio.no.
iu.hio.no.             14400   IN NS   nexus.iu.hio.no.

;; ADDITIONAL SECTION:
dns.hio.no.            5582    IN A    158.36.161.3
dns.hio.no.            86038   IN AAAA 2001:700:700:1::3
cube.iu.hio.no.        14400   IN A    128.39.74.16
cube.iu.hio.no.        14400   IN AAAA 2001:700:700:4:290:27ff:fe93:6723
nexus.iu.hio.no.       14400   IN A    128.39.89.10
quetzalcoatal.iu.hio.no. 14400 IN A    128.39.89.26

;; Query time: 6 msec
;; SERVER: 127.0.0.1#53(127.0.0.1)
;; WHEN: Fri Sep  6 13:23:09 2002
;; MSG SIZE  rcvd: 292
```

Similarly, IPv4 reverse lookup is performed with:

```
dig -x 192.0.1.3
```

As to what works with IPv6 – this is a study in confusion. To date the only method that seems to work on newer versions of BIND is

```
host -n 2001:700:700:4:290:27ff:fe93:6723
```

There has been disagreement about the name of the reverse lookup domain for IPv6. As of January 2003, it has finally been decided that it will be called ip6.arpa, but some resolvers still try to look up ip6.int. This can cause all manner of confusion (see section 9.5.9). Try this:

```
host$ host -n 2001:700:700:3:0:0:0:1
1.0.0.0.0.0.0.0.0.0.0.0.0.0.0.0.3.0.0.0.0.0.7.0.0.0.7.0.1.0.0.2.ip6.int
domain name pointer ip6-gw.p52.hio.no.
host$ host -t PTR 1....3.0.0.0.0.7.0.0.0.7.0.1.0.0.2.ip6.arpa
1.0.0.0.0.0.0.0.0.0.0.0.0.0.0.0.3.0.0.0.0.0.7.0.0.0.7.0.1.0.0.2.ip6.arpa
domain name pointer ip6-gw.p52.hio.no.
host$ host -t PTR 1....3.0.0.0.0.7.0.0.0.7.0.1.0.0.2.ip6.int
1.0.0.0.0.0.0.0.0.0.0.0.0.0.0.0.3.0.0.0.0.0.7.0.0.0.7.0.1.0.0.2.ip6.int
domain name pointer ip6-gw.p52.hio.no.
```

Note that these horrendous lines are too wide for the page of the book, so in reverse 'nibble' format, one must type all of the '.0.0's between the 1 and the 3 above.

Special information

The domain name service identifies certain special hosts which perform services like the name service itself and mail-handlers (called mail exchangers). These servers are identified by special records so that people outside of a given domain can find out about them. After all, the mail service in one domain needs to know how to send mail to a neighboring domain. It also needs to know how to find out the names and addresses of hosts for which it does not keep information personally.

We can use nslookup to extract this information by setting the 'query type' of a request. For instance, to find out about the mail exchangers in a domain we write

```
> set q=mx
>   domain name
```

For example

```
> set q=mx
> otherdomain.org
Server:  mother.example.org
Address:  192.0.2.10
```

```
Non-authoritative answer:
otherdomain.org preference = 0,
mail exchanger = mercury.otherdomain.org

Authoritative answers can be found from:
otherdomain.org        nameserver = mercury.otherdomain.org
otherdomain.org        nameserver = delilah.otherdomain.org
mercury.otherdomain.org  internet address = 158.36.85.10
   delilah.otherdomain.org  internet address = 129.241.1.99
```

Or

```
 dig -t mx otherdomain.org
```

Here we see that the only mail server for `otherdomain.org` is `mercury.otherdomain.org`.

Another example, is to obtain information about the nameservers in a domain. This will allow us to find out information about hosts which is not contained in our local database. To get this, we set the query-type to `ns`.

```
> set q=ns
> otherdomain.org
Server:  mother.example.org
Address:  192.0.2.10

Non-authoritative answer:
otherdomain.org    nameserver = delilah.otherdomain.org
otherdomain.org        nameserver = mercury.otherdomain.org

Authoritative answers can be found from:
delilah.otherdomain.org  internet address = 192.0.2.78
mercury.otherdomain.org  internet address = 192.0.2.80
>
```

Here we see that there are two authoritative nameservers for this domain called `delilah.otherdomain.org` and `mercury.otherdomain.org`.

Finally, other lookup criteria are provided. For instance, if we set the query type to 'any', we get a summary of all this information.

Listing hosts belonging to a domain

To list every registered Internet address and hostname for a given domain one can use the `ls` command inside `nslookup`. For instance

```
> ls example.org
[mother.example.org]
example.org.                        server = mother.example.org
example.org.                        server = mercury.otherdomain.org
pc61                                192.0.2.61
```

```
pc59                                     192.0.2.59
pc59                                     192.0.2.59
pc196                                    192.0.2.196
  etc...
```

Newer nameservers can restrict access to prevent others from obtaining this list all in one go, since it is now considered a potential security hazard. First the nameservers are listed and then the host names and corresponding IP addresses are listed.

If we try to look up hosts in a domain for which the default nameserver has no information, we get an error message. For example, suppose we try to list the names of the hosts in the domain over ours:

```
> ls otherdomain.org
[mother.example.org]
*** Can't list domain otherdomain.org: Query refused
>
```

This does not mean that it is not possible to get information about other domains, only that we cannot find out information about other domains from the local server. See section 3.8.1.

Changing to a different server

If we know the name of a server which contains authoritative information for a domain, we can tell `nslookup` to use that server instead. That way it might be possible to list the hosts in a remote domain and find out detailed information about it. At the very least, it is possible to find out about key records, like nameservers and mail exchangers (MX). To change the server we simply type

```
> server  new-server
```

Once this is done we use `ls` to list the names.

```
> server ns.college.edu
Default Server:  ns.college.edu
Address:  192.0.2.10

> ls college.edu

 (listing ..)
```

Another advantage to using the server which is directly responsible for the DNS data, is that we obtain extra information about the domain, namely a contact address for the person responsible for administrating the domain. For example:

```
> server ns.college.edu
Default Server:  ns.college.edu
Address:  192.0.2.10
```

```
> college.edu
Server:  ns.college.edu
Address:  192.0.2.10

college.edu        preference = 0, mail exchanger = ns.college.edu
college.edu        nameserver = ns.college.edu
college.edu
     origin = ns.college.edu
     mail addr = postmaster.ns.college.edu
     serial = 1996120503
     refresh = 3600 (1 hour)
     retry   = 900 (15 mins)
     expire  = 604800 (7 days)
     minimum ttl = 86400 (1 day)
college.edu            nameserver = ns.college.edu
ns.college.edu         internet address = 192.0.2.10
```

This is probably more information than we are interested in, but it does tell us that we can address queries and problems concerning this domain to `postmaster@ns.college.edu`. (Note that DNS does not use the @ symbol for 'at' in these data.)

3.8.3 Contacting other domain administrators

Sometimes we need to contact other domains, perhaps because we believe there is a problem with their system, or perhaps because an unpleasant user from another domain is being a nuisance and we want to ask the administrators there to put that person through a long and painful death. We now know how to obtain one contact address using `nslookup`. Another good bet is to mail the one address which every domain should have: postmaster@domain. Various unofficial standards (RFC 2142) also encourage sites to have the following mail addresses which one can try:

```
webmaster
www
ftp
abuse
info
security
hostmaster
```

Apart from these sources, there is little one can do to determine who is responsible for a domain. A number of domains are registered with another network database service called the *whois* service. In some cases it is possible to obtain information this way. For example:

```
host% whois moneywurld.com
   Financial Connections, Inc (MONEYWURLD-COM)
```

```
2508 5th Ave, #104
Mars, MA 98121

Domain Name: MONEYWURLD.COM

Administrative Contact, Technical Contact, Zone Contact:
   Willumz, Bob  (BW747)  willy@MONEYWURLD.COM
   206 269 0846

Record last updated on 13-Oct-96.
Record created on 26-Oct-95.

Domain servers in listed order:

NSH.WORLDHELP.NET              206.81.217.6
NSS.MONEYWURLD.COM             205.227.174.9
```

```
The InterNIC Registration Services Host contains ONLY Internet Info
(Networks, ASN's, Domains, and POC's).
Please use the whois server at nic.ddn.mil for MILNET Information.
```

3.8.4   Ping and traceroute

The most basic tools for testing network connectivity are `ping` and `traceroute` (`tracert` on Windows). These tools determine network connectivity, host availability and overall latency. The `ping` command sends the network equivalent of a sonar ping to a remote interface:

```
host$ ping www.gnu.org
www.gnu.org is alive
```

The command returns with a simple message to say whether or not the interface is up, i.e. whether the host is online or not. The `-s` flag causes packets to be sent at regular intervals, with sequence numbers and latency timings visible. This is useful for gauging transit times and network line capacity:

```
host$ ping -s www.gnu.org
 PING www.gnu.org (199.232.41.10) from 80.111.2.134 : 56(84) bytes of data.
64 bytes from www.gnu.org (199.232.41.10): seq=1 ttl=236 t=225.569 ms
64 bytes from www.gnu.org (199.232.41.10): seq=2 ttl=236 t=153.235 ms
```

Pings on free Unix-like operating systems behave like `ping -s` on older systems, i.e. it defaults into periodic transmission mode.

The `traceroute` command sends UDP packets to the destination, with stepwise incremental 'time to live' fields, which then provoke a 'time out' error at each router in turn, thus mapping out the route taken. Hosts that are attached to the same subnet do not normally pass through a router, thus there is a single hop which is directly to the destination address by unicast:

```
host$ /usr/sbin/traceroute pax.example.org
traceroute to pax.example.org (128.39.89.4), 30 hops max,
40 byte packets
 1 pax.example.org (128.39.89.4) 0.682 ms 0.414 ms 0.402 ms
```

A host on a neighboring subnet must pass through a router or 'gateway' (usually denoted 'gw'):

```
host$ /usr/sbin/traceroute cube
traceroute to cube.example.org (128.39.74.16), 30 hops max,
40 byte packets
 1 org-gw.example.org (128.39.89.1) 1.473 ms 0.932 ms 0.829 ms
 2 cube.example.org (128.39.74.16) 0.647 ms 0.508 ms 0.699 ms
```

More distant hosts require several hops to reach their destinations:

```
host$ /usr/sbin/traceroute www.neighbour.org
traceroute to www.neighbour.org (129.240.148.31), 30 hops max,
40 byte packets
 1 org-gw.example.org (128.39.89.1) 1.248 ms 0.906 ms 1.576 ms
 2 pil52-gw.example.org (158.36.84.21) 0.804 ms 0.744 ms 0.969 ms
 3 oslo-gw1.other.org (128.39.0.73) 0.829 ms 1.596 ms 0.883 ms
 4 128.39.3.94 (128.39.3.94) 1.192 ms 1.188 ms 1.230 ms
 5 www.neighbour.org (129.240.148.31) 1.049 ms 1.975 ms 0.907 ms
```

Timings in milliseconds show the round time for this node.

Choosing a distant host shows how complex routes can be. This example from Oslo to Boston illustrates the point:

```
host$ /usr/sbin/traceroute www.gnu.org
traceroute to www.gnu.org (199.232.41.10), 30 hops max,
40 byte packets
 1 gw-s14h1.upc.chello.no (212.186.239.1) 25 ms 21 ms 24 ms
 2 osl-rb-04-fe-2-0.upc.no (62.179.128.1) 26 ms 25 ms 24 ms
 3 osl-rb-01-ge-1-1.upc.no (62.179.128.233) 21 ms 19 ms 38 ms
 4 no-osl-rd-03-ge-5-0-0.chlo.com (213.46.177.88) 22 ms 19 ms 24 ms
 5 no-osl-rd-05-fe-1-1-0.chlo.com (213.46.177.17) 24 ms 22 ms 22 ms
 6 se-sto-rc-01-pos-1-0.chlok.com (213.46.177.5) 39 ms 32 ms 36 ms
 7 213.242.69.5 (213.242.69.5) 33 ms 33 ms 29 ms
 8 ae0-12.mpls2.Stockholm1.Level3.net (213.242.68.18) 29 ms 32 ms
 9 so-3.London1.Level3.net (212.187.128.57) 64 ms 66 ms 66 ms
10 so-1.NewYork1.Level3.net (212.187.128.153) 133 ms 132 ms 132 ms
11 gigaeth5-0.core1.NewYork1.Level3.net (64.159.17.37) 132 ms 131 ms
12 * ewr-brdr-01.inet.qwest.net (63.211.54.102) 133 ms 135 ms
13 ewr-core-01.inet.qwest.net (205.171.17.125) 133 ms 134 ms 134 ms
14 dca-core-03.inet.qwest.net (205.171.5.17) 137 ms 139 ms 141 ms
15 dcx-edge-01.inet.qwest.net (205.171.9.162) 141 ms 140 ms 145 ms
16 res1-br1-g0-0-0.gnaps.net (65.123.21.202) 143 ms 142 ms *
17 qcy1-ar1-g1-0.gnaps.net (199.232.131.1) 151 ms 151 ms 154 ms
18 * www.gnu.org (199.232.41.10) 154 ms 154 ms
```

IPv6 addresses are gradually becoming incorporated into these tools:

```
host$ ping -s -A inet6 2001:700:700:3:290:27ff:fea2:477b
PING 2001:700:700:3:290:27ff:fea2:477b: 56 data bytes
64 bytes from 2001:700:700:3:290:27ff:fea2:477b: seq=0. t=1. ms
64 bytes from 2001:700:700:3:290:27ff:fea2:477b: seq=1. t=1. ms
```

3.8.5 Netcat

Netcat is described as the 'Swiss army knife' of network utilities. It is a multi-purpose client-server peer program that reads and writes data across network connections, using TCP or UDP protocols. It is described as a 'feature-rich network debugging and exploration tool'. Netcat, or nc, can be used to send or receive network connections. Suppose, for instance we want to find out whether a Web server is working:

```
host$ echo -e "GET http://www.cfengine.org HTTP/1.0\n\n" |
nc www.cfengine.org 80 | head -20

HTTP/1.1 200 OK
Date: Wed, 02 Oct 2002 14:08:33 GMT
Server: Apache/1.3.26 (Unix) PHP/4.2.2 mod_ssl/2.8.10 OpenSSL/0.9.6d
X-Powered-By: PHP/4.2.2
Connection: close
Content-Type: text/html

<!DOCTYPE HTML PUBLIC "-//W3C//DTD HTML 4.0 Transitional//EN">
<html>
<head>
 <title>Cfengine - config for Unix and Windows</title>
 <link rel="stylesheet" href="cfengine.css">
</head>
```

Netcat is somewhat like telnet, but it solves several problems such as the ability to interrupt and timeout connections.

3.8.6 Locating services

Existing network services have to be analyzed, so that we know where we are starting from, and new networks need to be planned or extended. If the obligatory school frog dissections never appealed, then one can at least take comfort in the fact that dissecting the network organism is, if nothing else, a cleaner operation. Starting with the knowledge we have already gained about host types and operating systems, we must now identify all of the services which are running on all of the hosts.

Location can be performed by a visual inspection of the process tables, or from configuration files. There are tools for port scanning networks in order to locate services, e.g. the nmap program. We should be careful about using these however, since port scans normally signify a network intrusion attempt, so others might misconstrue. If a network is well run, local administrators will know what services are running on which hosts. The information we gather is then open to scrutiny. Our aim is to arrange for the machines in the network to work together optimally, so we begin by thinking:

- How to choose the right hardware for the right job.

- Which hosts should be servers and for which services?

- How to make disks available to the network.

- How to share tasks between machines.

- How clock/time synchronization will work.

What roles do the hosts play now? How might this be improved in the future? Is everything already working satisfactorily or do we need to rewire our frog? In the ideal universe, we would always have unlimited resources for every task, but when reality bites, some kind of compromise is usually needed.

The efficiency of a network can be improved greatly by planning carefully how key networks services are organized, particularly file-servers and name services, which form the basic infrastructure of a network. Here is a partial checklist:

- Which hosts keep the physical disks for disk servers? It makes sense to keep all file-services, which use those disks, on that same host. If the source data are on host A, then we run all file services for those data on host A, otherwise data will first have to be copied from A to B, over the network, in order to be served back over the network to host C, i.e. there will be an unnecessary doubling of traffic.

- Normally we shall want to use a powerful system for the servers which provide key disk and WWW services, since these are at the heart of network infrastructure. Other hosts depend on these. However, if resources are limited we might need to reserve the fastest host for running some especially heavy software. This has to be a site-dependent calculation.

- File-servers always benefit from a large amount of RAM. This is a cheap form of optimization which allows caching. Fast network interfaces and hard-disks are also amongst the most effective optimizations one can invest in. If you are going to buy RAM and fast disks, don't give it all away for users' selfish workstations, treat the server-host to the biggest share.

- If we can, it helps to separate users' home directories over several disks and keep problem disk-users on a partition for themselves, away from honest users.

- Shall we consolidate many services on one host, or distribute them across many? The first possibility is easier to administer, but the second might be more efficient and less prone to host crashes.

- Any binary or software servers we set up to share software are individual to each operating system type we maintain. A Sun machine cannot run software compiled on a GNU/Linux host etc.

- Dependency can be a source of many insidious problems. Try not to create deadlocks whereby host A needs host B and host B needs host A. This is a particularly common mistake with NFS filesystem mounts. It can cause a hanging loop.

- If high availability is an issue, will one server per service be enough? Do we need a backup server? Backup name service servers (DNS, NIS, WINS) could be considered a must. Without a name service, a network is paralyzed.

There is no textbook solution to these issues. There are only recipes and recommendations based on trial and error experience. If we want our frog to win the high-jump, we need to strike the balance between concentrating muscle in key areas, and spreading the load evenly. We are unlikely to get everything just right, first time around, so it is important to construct a solid system, at the same time as anticipating future change.

> **Principle 10 (Adaptability).** *Optimal structure and performance are usually found only with experience of changing local needs. The need for system revision will always come. Make network solutions which are adaptable.*

3.8.7   Uniform resource locators (URLs)

URLs became well known, as a concept, in connection with the World Wide Web. The principle of referring to resources by a standardized name format can be adopted here too. Each operating system has a model for laying out its files in a standard pattern, but user files and local additions are usually left unspecified. Choosing a sound layout for data can make the difference between an incomprehensible chaos and a neat orderly structure. An orderly structure is useful not only for the users of the system, but also when making backups. Some of the issues are:

- Disk partitions are associated with drives or directory trees when connected to operating systems. These need names.

- Naming schemes for files and disks are operating system dependent.

- The name of a partition should reflect its function or contents.

- In a network the name of a partition ought to be a URL, i.e. contain the name of the host.

- It is good practice to consolidate file storage into a few special locations rather than spreading it out all over the network. Moreover, a basic principle in cataloging resources is:

> **Principle 11 (One name for one object I).** *Each unique resource requires a unique name, which labels it and describes its function.*

with the corollary:

Corollary to principle (Aliases). *Sometimes it is advantageous to use aliases or pointers to unique objects so that a generic name can point to a specific resource. The number of aliases should be kept to a minimum, to avoid confusion.*

Data kept on many machines can be difficult to manage, compared with data collected on a few dedicated file-servers. Also, insecure operating systems offer files on a local disk no protection.

The URL model of file naming has several advantages. It means that one always knows the host-provider and function of a network resource. Also it falls nicely into a hierarchical directory pattern. For example, a simple but effective scheme is to use a three-level mount-point for adding disks: each user disk is mapped onto a directory with a name of the form

`/site/host/content`

(see figure 3.3). This scheme is adequate even for large organizations and can be extended in obvious ways. Others prefer to build up names around services, e.g.

`/nfs/host/content`

One objection to the naming scheme above is that the use of the server name ties a resource to a particular server host, and thus makes it difficult to move resources around. Technologies like amd (automount), AFS, DFS (the Open Group's), and Dfs (Microsoft's) help address this issue and can make the filesystem based on a logical layout rather than an actual physical location. On the other hand, location independence can always be secured with aliases (symbolic) or with truly distributed filesystems. Moving actual resources is always a relatively non-trivial operation, and a naming scheme like that above yields clarity for a minimum of work.

In DOS-derived operating systems one does not have the freedom to 'mount' network filesystems into the structure of the local disk; network disks always

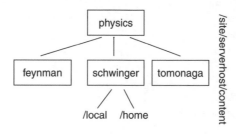

Figure 3.3: A universal naming scheme (URL) for network resources makes distributed data comprehensible.

become a special 'drive', like H: or I: etc. It is difficult to make a consistent view of the disk resources with this system, however future Windows systems will have seamless integration and one can already use filesystems like the DFS on NT which do support this model.

Within an organization a URL structure provides a global naming scheme, like those used in true network filesystems like AFS and DFS. These use the name of the host on which a resource is physically located to provide a point of reference. This is also an excellent way of labelling backups of partitions since it is then immediately clear where the data belong. A few rules of thumb allow this naming scheme to live painlessly alongside traditional Unix naming schemes.

- When mounting a remote filesystem on a host, the client and server directories should always have exactly the same name, to avoid confusion and problems later [221].

- The name of every filesystem mount-point should be unique and tell us something meaningful about where it is located and what its function is.

- For tradition, one can invoke the corollary and use an alias to provide a generic reference point for specific resources. For instance, names like /usr/local can be used to point to more accurate designations like /site/ host/local. On different clients, the alias /usr/local might point to a filesystem on a single server, or to filesystems on many servers. The purpose of an alias is to hide this detail, while the purpose of the filesystem designation is to identify it. This satisfies all needs and is consistent.

- It doesn't matter whether software compiles the path names of special directories into software as long as we follow the points above.

For example, the following scheme was introduced at Oslo at the University and later copied at the College. The first link in the mount-point is the department of the organization or, in our case, the university faculty which the host belongs to; the second link is the name of the host to which the disk is physically connected, and the third and final link is a name which reflects the contents of the partition. Some examples:

```
/site/hostname/content

/research/grumpy/local
/research/happy/home1
/research/happy/home2

/sales/slimy/home1

/physics/einstein/data
/biology/pauling/genome-db
```

The point of introducing this scheme was two-fold:

- To instantly be able to identify the server on which the disk resource physically resided.

- To instantly be able to identify the correct locations of files on backup tapes, without any special labelling of the tapes (see section 12.3.3).

System administrators are well known for strong opinions, and many practicing system administrators will strongly disagree with this practice. However, one should have an excellent reason to ignore a systematic approach.

3.8.8   Choosing server-hosts

Choosing the best host for a service is an issue with several themes. The main principles have to do with efficiency and security and can be summarized by the following questions.

- Does traffic have to cross subnet boundaries?

- Do we avoid unnecessary network traffic?

- Have we placed insecure services on unimportant hosts?

Service requests made to servers on different subnets have to be routed. This takes time and uses up switching opportunities which might be important on a heavily loaded network. Some services (like DNS) can be mirrored on each subnet, while others cannot be mirrored in any simple fashion. Unnecessary network traffic can be reduced by eliminating unnecessary dependencies of one service on another.

Example 1. *Suppose we are setting up a file-server (WWW or FTP). The data which these servers will serve to clients lie on a disk which is physically attached to some host. If we place the file-server on a host which does not have direct physical access to the disks, then we must first use another network service (e.g. NFS) as a proxy in order to get the data from the host with the disk attached. Had we placed the file-server directly on the host with the disk, the intermediate step would have been unnecessary and we could approximately halve the amount of network traffic.*

We can codify this advice as a principle: avoid making one service reliant on another.

Principle 12 (Inter-dependency). *The more dependent a service is, the more vulnerable it is to failure. With fewer dependencies, there are fewer possible failure modes, and therefore predictability and reliability are increased.*

Some services are already reliant on others, by virtue of their design. For example, most services are reliant on the DNS.

3.8.9   Distributed filesystems and mirroring

The purpose of a network is to share resources amongst many hosts. Making files available to all hosts from a common source is one of the most important issues in setting up a network community. There are three types of data which we have to consider separately:

- Users' home directories.

- Software or binary data (architecture specific).

- Other common data (architecture unspecific).

Since users normally have network accounts which permit them to log onto any host in the network, user data clearly have to be made available to all hosts. The same is not true of software, however. Software only needs to be shared between hosts running comparable operating systems. A Windows program will not run under GNU/Linux (even though they share a common processor and machine code), nor will an SCO Unix program run under Free BSD. It does not make sense to share binary filesystems between hosts, unless they share a common architecture. Finally, sharable data, such as manual information or architecture independent databases, can be shared between any hosts which specifically require access to them.

How are network data shared? There are two strategies:

- Use of a shared filesystem (e.g. NFS, AFS or Novell Netware).

- Remote disk mirroring.

Using a network filesystem is always possible, and it is a relatively cheap solution, since it means that we can minimize the amount of disk space required to store data, by concentrating the data on just a few servers. The main disadvantage with use of a network filesystem is that network access rates are usually much slower than disk access rates, because the network is slow compared with disks, and a server has to talk to many clients concurrently, introducing *contention* or competition for resources. Even with the aggressive caching schemes used by some network filesystems, there is usually a noticeable difference in loading files from the network and loading files locally.

Bearing in mind the principles of the previous section, we would like to minimize load on the network if possible. A certain amount of network traffic can be avoided by mirroring software rather than sharing with a network filesystem. Mirroring means copying every file from a source filesystem to a remote filesystem. This can be done during the night when traffic is low and, since software does not change often, it does not generate much traffic for upgrades after the initial copy. Mirroring is cheap on network traffic, even during the night, During the daytime, when users are accessing the files, they collect them from the mirrors. This is both faster and requires no network bandwidth at all.

Mirroring cannot apply to users' files since they change too often, while users are logged onto the system, but it applies very well to software. If we have disk space to spare, then mirroring software partitions can relieve the load of sharing. There are various options for disk mirroring. On Unix hosts we have `rdist`, `rsync` and `cfengine`; variations on these have also been discussed [264, 309, 117, 98]. The use of `rdist` can no longer be recommended (see section 6.5.6) for security reasons. Cfengine can also be used on Windows. Network filesystems can be used for mirroring, employing only standard local copy commands; filesystems are first mounted and then regular copy commands are used to transfer the data as if they were local files.

The benefits of mirroring can be considerable, but it is seldom practical to give every workstation a mirror of software. A reasonable compromise is to have a group of file-servers, synchronized by mirroring from a central source. One would expect to have at least one file-server per subnet, to avoid router traffic, money permitting.

Exercises

Self-test objectives

1. What is the main principle at work in any cooperative enterprise, such as a network or community with limited resources?

2. Explain the role of policy in a community.

3. Are rules meant for humans comparable to rules meant for machines? Explain.

4. Describe the social community structures in a human–computer system.

5. What consequences result from placing a computer in an environment that is controlled by external parties?

6. What are the pros and cons of making a network completely uniform in the choice of hardware and software?

7. Explain how patterns of user behavior have a direct and measurable effect on a computer system.

8. Explain the pros and cons of centralization versus delegation in a system.

9. List the different identifiers that label a computer.

10. How does a computer know its IP address?

11. How does a computer know its Ethernet address?

12. What is a MAC address?

13. What is the service that relates Internet Domain Names to IP addresses?

14. What is the service that relates IP addresses to MAC addresses?

15. Describe alternative models for organizing network resources.

16. What is meant by a 'server host' and how is it different from a 'server'?

17. How are user preferences stored on Unix and Windows?

18. How would you go about mapping out an existing Local Area Network to find out how it worked?

19. Name the most common network services that most Local Area Networks implement.

20. Why is it important to know what software and hardware is running across a network that you are responsible for?

21. What is usually meant by a 'resolver'?

22. What tools can you use to find out the IP address of a host?

23. What tools can you use to find out the IPv6 address of a host?

24. How would you find out the domain that a given IP address belongs to?

25. How would you find out the domain that a given IPv6 address belongs to?

26. How would you get in touch with the Network or System Administrator who was responsible for a particular IP address?

27. Explain what the `ping` program does.

28. Explain what the Unix program `traceroute` and Windows program `tracert` do.

29. How would you go about trying to locate the World Wide Web server of a network that you were not familiar with? (Would the same method work for other services like E-mail or FTP?)

30. Why is computer clock sychronization important? How can this be achieved?

31. What is meant by a Uniform Resource Locator (URL) and how can this be used to create a systematic naming scheme for network resources?

32. What is meant by dependency amongst computers and services? What are the pros and cons of dependency?

Problems

1. Use the `ping` and `ping6` commands to ping different IP addresses on your network (note that these differ somewhat on different platforms – the examples here are from GNU/Linux). Try pinging the addresses repeatedly with a large packet size (9064 bytes):

   ```
   ping -s 9064 192.0.2.4
   ```

2. What are the advantages and disadvantages of making access to network disks transparent to users? Discuss this in relation to the reliability of hosts.

3. What is meant by a name service? Name two widely used name services that contain IP addresses and one that contains Ethernet addresses.

4. What is the Domain Name Service? How do hosts depend on this service? Suppose that the data in the DNS could be corrupted. Explain how this could be a security risk.

5. In what way is using a name service better than using static host tables? In what way is it worse?

6. Draw a diagram of the physical topology of your local network, showing routers, switches, cables and other hardware.

7. Determine all of the subnets that comprise your local network. (If there are many, consider just the closest ones to your department.) What is the netmask on these subnets? (You only need to determine the subnet mask on a representative host from each subnet, since all hosts must agree on this choice. Hint. try `ifconfig -a`.)

8. If the network xxx.yyy.74.mmm has subnet mask 255.255.254.0, what can you say about the subnet mask for the addresses on xxx.yyy.75.mmm? (Hint: how many hosts are allowed on the subnet?) Which IP addresses does the subnet consist of?

9. If the network xxx.yyy.74.mmm has subnet mask 255.255.255.0, what can you say about the subnet mask for the addresses on xxx.yyy.75.mmm?

10. Using `dig` or `nslookup`, determine the answers to the following questions:

    (a) What is the IP address of the host `www.gnu.org`?

    (b) What are names of the nameservers for the domain `gnu.org`?

    (c) Are `ftp.iu.hio.no` and `www.iu.hio.no` two different hosts?

    (d) What is name of the mail exchanger for the domain `iu.hio.no`?

11. The purpose of this problem is to make you think about the consequences of cloning all hosts in a network, so that they are all alike. The principles apply equally well to other societies. Try not to get embroiled in politics, concentrate on practicalities rather than ideologies.

    (a) Discuss the pros and cons of uniformity. In a society, when is it advantageous for everyone in a group to have equal access to resources? In what sense are they equal? What special characteristics will always be different, i.e. why are two persons never completely equal? (e.g. their names are different)

    (b) When is it advantageous for some members of a community to have more resources and more power than others? You might like to consider what real power is. For instance, would you say that garbage disposal workers and water engineers have power in a society? What does this tell you about the organization of privilege within a human–computer system?

    (c) What is meant by delegation. How is delegation important to cooperation?

    (d) What is meant by dependency? How does delegation lead to dependency? Can you foresee any problems with this, for network efficiency?

    (e) What is meant by a network service? What issues can you identify that should be considered when deploying a new network service?

(f) Discuss each of the above points in connection with computers in a network.

12. Design a universal naming scheme for directories, for your site. Think about what types of operating system you have and how the resources will be shared; this will affect your choices. How will you decide drive names on Windows hosts?

13. What are ARP and RARP? Why can't we use Ethernet addresses instead of IP addresses to send data from one side of the planet to the other? Could IP addresses eliminate Ethernet addresses? Why do we need both these addresses?

14. At some sites, it was common practice to use remote mirroring to synchronize the system disks or filesystems of hosts, where compiled software had been mixed in with the operating system's own files. This solves the problem of making manual changes to one host, and keeping other hosts the same as the source machine. Discuss whether this practice is advisable, with respect to upgrades of the operating system.

15. Discuss the pros and cons of the following advice. Place all file-servers which serve the same data on a common host, e.g. WWW, FTP and network file systems serving user files. Place them on the host which physically has the disks attached. This will save an unnecessary doubling of network traffic and will speed up services. A fast host with a lot of memory and perhaps several CPUs should be used for this. Explain how the optimal answer depends on the hardware one has available.

16. Prepare a sample of what you consider to be the main elements of a system policy. Swap your answers with classmates and review each other's answers.

Chapter 4

Host management

The foregoing chapters have explored the basics of how hosts need to function within a network community; we are now sufficiently prepared to turn our attention to the role of the individual host within such a network. It should be clear from the previous chapter that it would be a mistake to think of the host as being the fundamental object in the human–computer system. If we focus on too small a part of the entire system initially, time and effort can be wasted configuring hosts in a way that does not take into account the cooperative aspects of the network. That would be a recipe for failure and only a prelude to later reinstallation.

4.1   Global view, local action

Life can be made easy or difficult by the decisions made at the outset of host installation. Should we:

- Follow the OS designer's recommended setup? (Often this is insufficient for our purpose)

- Create our own setup?

- Make all machines alike?

- Make all machines different?

Most vendors will only provide immediate support for individual hosts or, in the best case, clusters of hosts manufactured by them. They will almost never address the issue of total network solutions, without additional cost, so their recommendations often fall notably short of the recommendable in a real network. We have to be aware of the big picture when installing and configuring hosts.

4.2   Physical considerations of server room

Critical hardware needs to be protected from accidental and malicious damage. An organization's very livelihood could be at stake from a lack of protection of its basic hardware. Not all organizations have the luxury of choosing ideal conditions for their equipment, but all organizations could dedicate a room or two to server equipment. Any server room should have, at the very least, a lockable door, probably cooling or ventilation equipment to prevent the temperature from rising above about 20 degrees Celsius and some kind of anti-theft protection.

Remember that backup tapes should never be stored in the same room as the hosts they contain data from, and duplicate servers are best placed in different physical locations so that natural disasters or physical attacks (fire, bombs etc.) will not wipe out all equipment at the same time.

Internet Service Providers (ISP) and Web hosting companies, who rely on 100 percent uptime for their customers, need a quite different level of security. Any company with a significant amount of computing equipment should consider a secure environment for their hardware, where the level of security is matched with the expected threat. In some countries, bombs or armed robbery are not uncommon, for instance. With high capital costs involved, physical security is imperative.

An ISP should consider obscuring the nature of its business to avoid terrorist attack, by placing it in an inauspicious location without outer markings. Security registration should be required for all workers and visitors, with camera recorded registration and security guards. Visitors should present photo-ID and be prevented from bringing anything into the building; they should be accompanied at all times. Within the server area:

- A reliable (uninterruptable) power supply is needed for essential equipment.

- Single points of failure, e.g. network cables, should be avoided.

- Hot standby equipment should be available for minimal loss of uptime in case of failure.

- Replaceable hard disks should be considered[1] with RAID protection for continuity.

- Protection from natural disasters like fire and floods, and heating failure in cold countries should be secured. Note that most countries have regulations about fire control. A server room should be in its own 'fire cell', i.e. it should be isolated by doorways and ventilation systems from neighboring areas to prevent the spread of fire.

- Important computing equipment can be placed in a Faraday cage to prevent the leakage of electromagnetic radiation, or to protect it from electromagnetic pulses (EMP), e.g. from nuclear explosions or other weaponry.

- Access to cabling should be easy in case of error, and for extensibility.

- Humans should not be able to touch equipment. No carpeting or linoleum that causes a build up of static electricity should be allowed near delicate equipment. Antistatic carpet tiles can be purchased quite cheaply.

---

[1]On a recent visit to an Internet search engine's host site, I was told that vibration in large racks of plugin disks often causes disks to vibrate loose from their sockets, meaning that the most common repair was pushing a disk back in and rebooting the host.

- Humidity should also be kept at reasonable levels: too high and condensation can form on components causing short circuits and damage; too low and static electricity can build up causing sparks and spikes of current. Static electricity is especially a problem around laser printers that run hot and expel moisture. Static electricity causes paper jams, as pages stick together in low moisture environments.

In a large server room, one can easily lose equipment, or lose one's way! Equipment should be marked, tagged and mapped out. It should be monitored and kept secure. If several companies share the floor space of the server room, they probably require lockable cabinets or partitioned areas to protect their interests from the prying hands of competitors.

4.3 Computer startup and shutdown

The two most fundamental operations which one can perform on a host are to start it up and to shut it down. With any kind of mechanical device with moving parts, there has to be a procedure for shutting it down. One does not shut down any machine in the middle of a crucial operation, whether it be a washing machine in the middle of a program, an aircraft in mid-flight, or a computer writing to its disk.

With a multitasking operating system, the problem is that it is never possible to predict when the system will be performing a crucial operation in the background. For this simple reason, every multitasking operating system provides a procedure for shutting down safely. A safe shutdown avoids damage to disks by mechanical interruption, but it also synchronizes hardware and memory caches, making sure that no operation is left incomplete.

4.3.1 Booting Unix

Normally it is sufficient to switch on the power to boot a Unix-like host. Sometimes you might have to type 'boot' or 'b' to get it going. Unix systems can boot in several different modes or *run levels*. The most common modes are called multi-user mode and single-user mode. On different kinds of Unix, these might translate into run-levels with different numbers, but there is no consensus. In single-user mode no external logins are permitted. The purpose of single-user mode is to allow the system administrator access to the system without fear of interference from other users. It is used for installing disks or when repairing filesystems, where the presence of other users on the system would cause problems.

The Unix boot procedure is controlled entirely by the `init` program; `init` reads a configuration file called `/etc/inittab`. On older BSD Unices, a file called `/etc/rc` meaning 'run commands' and subsidiary files like `rc.local` was then called to start all services. These files were no more than shell scripts. In the System V approach, a directory called (something like) `/etc/rc.d` is used to keep one script per service. `/etc/inittab` defines a number of run-levels, and starts scripts depending on what run-level you choose. The idea behind `inittab` is to make Unix installable in packages, where each package can be started or configured by a separate script. Which packages get started depends on the run-level you choose.

The default form for booting is to boot in multi-user mode. We have to find out how to boot in single-user mode on our system, in case we need to repair a disk at some point. Here are some examples.

Under SunOS and Solaris, one interrupts the normal booting process by typing stop a, where stop represents the 'stop key' on the left-hand side of the keyboard. If you do this, you should always give the `sync` command to synchronize disk caches and minimize filesystem damage.

```
Stop a

ok? sync
ok? boot -s
```

If the system does not boot right away, you might see the line

```
type b) boot, c) continue or n) new command
```

In this case, you should type

```
b -s
```

in order to boot in single-user mode. Under the GNU/Linux operating system, using the LILO OR GRUB boot system, we interrupt the normal boot sequence by pressing the SHIFT key when the LILO prompt appears. This should cause the system to stop at the prompt:

```
Boot:
```

To boot, we must normally specify the name of a kernel file, normally `linux`. To boot in single-user mode, we then type

```
Boot: linux single
```

Or at the LILO prompt, it is possible to type '?' in order to see a list of kernels. There appears to be a bug in some versions of GNU/Linux so that this does not have the desired effect. In some cases one is prompted for a run-level. The correct run-level should be determined from the file `/etc/inittab`. It is normally called S or 1 or even 1S.

Once in single-user mode, we can always return to multi-user mode just by exiting the single-user login.

4.3.2   Shutting down Unix

Anyone can start a Unix-like system, but we have to be an administrator or 'superuser' to shut one down correctly. Of course, one could just pull the plug, but this can ruin the disk filesystem. Even when no users are touching a keyboard anywhere, a Unix system can be writing something to the disk – if we pull the plug, we might interrupt a crucial write-operation which destroys the disk contents. The correct way to shut down a Unix system is to run one of the following programs.

- `halt`: Stops the system immediately and without warning. All processes are killed with the TERM-inate signal 15 and disks are synchronized.

- `reboot`: As `halt`, but the system reboots in the default manner immediately.

- `shutdown`: This program is the recommended way of shutting down the system. It is just a friendly user-interface to the other programs, but it warns the users of the system about the impending shutdown and allows them to finish what they are doing before the system goes down.

Here are some examples of the `shutdown` command. The first is from BSD Unix:

```
shutdown -h +3 "System halting in three minutes, please log out"

shutdown -r +4 "System rebooting in four minutes"
```

The `-h` option implies that the system will halt and not reboot automatically. The `-r` option implies that the system will reboot automatically. The times are specified in minutes.

System V Unix R4 (e.g. Solaris) has a different syntax which is based on its system of run-levels. The shutdown command allows one to switch run-levels in a very general way. One of the run-levels is the 'not running' or 'halt' run-level. To halt the system, we have to call this.

```
shutdown -i 5 -g 120 "Powering down os...."
```

The `-i 5` option tells SVR4 to go to run-level 5, which is the power-off state. Run-level 0 would also suffice here. The `-g 120` option tells `shutdown` to wait for a grace-period of 120 seconds before shutting down. Note that Solaris also provides a BSD version of shutdown in `/usr/ucb`.

Never assume that the run-levels on one system are the same as those on another.

4.3.3 Booting and shutting down Windows

Booting and shutting down Windows is a trivial matter. To boot the system, it is simply a matter of switching on the power. To shut it down, one chooses shutdown from the Start Menu.

There is no direct equivalent of single-user mode for Windows, though 'secure mode' is sometimes invoked, in which only the essential device drivers are loaded, if some problem is suspected. To switch off network access on a Windows server so that disk maintenance can be performed, one must normally perform a reboot and connect new hardware while the host is down. Filesystem checks are performed automatically if errors are detected. The plug'n'play style automation of Windows removes the need for manual work on filesystems, but it also limits flexibility.

The Windows boot procedure on a PC begins with the BIOS, or PC hardware. This performs a memory check and looks for a boot-able disk. A boot-able disk is one which contains a master boot record (MBR). Normally the BIOS is configured to check the floppy drive `A:` first and then the hard-disk `C:` for a boot block. The boot block is located in the first sector of the boot-able drive. It identifies which partition is to be used to continue with the boot procedure. On each primary partition of a boot-able disk, there is a boot program which 'knows' how to load the operating system it finds there. Windows has a menu-driven boot manager program which makes it possible for several OSs to coexist on different partitions.

Once the disk partition containing Windows has been located, the program NTLDR is called to load the kernel. The file BOOT.INI configures the defaults for the boot manager. After the initial boot, a program is run which attempts to automatically detect new hardware and verify old hardware. Finally the kernel is loaded and Windows starts properly.

4.4 Configuring and personalizing workstations

Permanent, read–write storage changed PCs from expensive ping-pong games into tools for work as well as pleasure. Today, disk space is so cheap that it is not uncommon for even personal workstations to have several hundreds of gigabytes of local storage.

Flaunting wealth is the sport of the modern computer owner: more disk, more memory, better graphics. Why? Because it's there. This is the game of free enterprise, encouraged by the availability of home computers and personal workstations. Not so many years before such things existed, however, computers only existed as large multiuser systems, where hundreds of users shared a few kilobytes of memory and a processor no more powerful than a now arthritic PC. Rational resource sharing was not just desirable, it was the only way to bring computing to ordinary users. In a network, we have these two conflicting interests in the balance.

4.4.1 Personal workstations or 'networkstations'?

Today we are spoiled, often with more resources than we know what to do with. Disk space is a valuable resource which can be used for many purposes. It would be an ugly waste to allow huge areas of disk to go unused, simply because small disks are no longer manufactured; but, at the same time, we should not simply allow anyone to use disk space as they please, just because it is there.

Operating systems which have grown out of home computers (Windows and MacIntosh) take the view that, whatever is left over of disk resources is for the local owner to do with as he or she pleases. This is symptomatic of the idea that one computer belongs to one user. In the world of the network, this is an inflexible model. Users move around organizations; they ought not to be forced to take their hardware with them as they move. Allowing users to personalize workstations is thus a questionable idea in a network environment.

Network sharing allows us to make disk space available to all hosts on a network, e.g. with NFS, Netware or DFS. This allows us to make disk space available to all hosts. There are positives and negatives with sharing, however. If sharing was a universal panacea, we would not have local disks: everything would be shared by the network. This approach has been tried: diskless workstations, network computers and X-terminals have all flirted with the idea of keeping all disk resources in one place and using the network for sharing. Such systems have been a failure: they perform badly, are usually more expensive than an off-the-shelf PC, and they simply waste a different resource: network bandwidth. Some files are better placed on a local disk: namely the files which are needed often, such as the operating system and temporary scratch files, created in the processing of large amounts of data.

In organizing disk space, we can make the best use of resources, and separate:

- Space for the operating system.

- Space which can be shared and made available for all hosts.

- Space which can be used to optimize local work, e.g. temporary scratch space, space which can be used to optimize local performance (avoid slow networking).

- Space which can be used to make distributed backups, for multiple redundancy.

These independent areas of use need to be separated from one another, by partitioning disks.

4.4.2 Partitioning

Disks can be divided up into partitions. Partitions physically divide the disk surface into separate areas which do not overlap. The main difference between two partitions on one disk and two separate disks is that partitions can only be accessed one at a time, whereas multiple disks can be accessed in parallel.

Disks are partitioned so that files with separate purposes cannot be allowed to spill over into one another's space. Partitioning a disk allows us to reserve a fixed amount of space for a particular purpose, safe in the knowledge that nothing else will encroach on that space. For example, it makes sense to place the operating system on a separate partition, and user data on another partition. If these two independent areas shared common space, the activities of users could quickly choke the operating system by using up all of its workspace.

In partitioning a system, we have in mind the issues described in the previous section and try to size partitions appropriately for the tasks they will fulfill. Here are some practical points to consider when partitioning disks:

- Size partitions appropriately for the jobs they will perform. Bear in mind that operating system upgrades are almost always bigger than previous versions, and that there is a general tendency for everything to grow.

- Bear in mind that RISC (e.g. Sun Sparc) compiled code is much larger than CISC compiled code (e.g. software on an Intel architecture), so software will take up more space on a RISC system.

- Consider how backups of the partitions will be made. It might save many complications if disk partitions are small enough to be backed up in one go with a single tape, or other backup device.

Choosing partitions optimally requires both experience and forethought. Thumb-rules for sizing partitions change constantly, in response to changing RAM requirements and operating system sizes, disk prices etc. In the early 1990s many sites adopted diskless or partially diskless solutions [11], thus centraliz-ing disk resources. In today's climate of ever cheaper disk space, there are few limitations left.

Disk partitioning is performed with a special program. On PC hardware, this is called `fdisk` or `cfdisk`. On Solaris systems the program is called, confusingly, `format`. To repartition a disk, we first edit the partition tables. Then we have to write the changes to the disk itself. This is called *labelling* the disk. Both of these tasks are performed from the partitioning programs. It is important to make sure manually that partitions do not overlap. The partitioning programs do not normally help us here. If partitions overlap, data will be destroyed and the system will sooner or later get into deep trouble, as it assumes that the overlapping area can be used legitimately for two separate purposes.

Partitions are labelled with logical device names in Unix. As one comes to expect, these are different in every flavor of Unix. The general pattern is that of a separate device node for each partition, in the `/dev` directory, e.g. `/etc/sd1a`, `/etc/sd1b`, `/dev/dsk/c0t0d0s0` etc. The meaning of these names is described in section 4.5.

The introduction of meta-devices and logical volumes in many operating sys-tems allows one to ignore disk partitions to a certain extent. Logical volumes provide seamless integration of disks and partitions into a large virtual disk which can be organized without worrying about partition boundaries. This is not always desirable, however. Sometimes partitions exist for protection, rather than merely for necessity.

4.4.3 Formatting and building filesystems

Disk formatting is a way of organizing and finding a way around the surface of a disk. It is a little bit like painting parking spaces in a car park. We could make a car park in a field of grass, but everything would get rapidly disorganized. If we paint fixed spaces and number them, then it is much easier to organize and reuse space, since people park in an orderly fashion and leave spaces of a standard, reusable size. On a disk surface, it makes sense to divide up the available space into sectors or blocks. The way in which different operating systems choose to do this differs, and thus one kind of formatting is incompatible with another.

The nomenclature of formatting is confused by differing cultures and technolo-gies. Modern hard disks have intelligent controllers which can map out the disk surface independently of the operating system which is controlling them. This means that there is a kind of factory formatting which is inherent to the type of disk. For instance, a SCSI disk surface is divided up into *sectors*. An operating system using a SCSI disk then groups these sectors into new units called *blocks* which are a more convenient size to work with, for the operating system. With the analogy above, it is a little like making a car park for trucks by grouping parking spaces for cars. It also involves a new set of labels. This regrouping and labelling procedure is called *formatting* in PC culture and is called *making a filesystem* in Unix culture.[2] Making a filesystem also involves setting up an infrastructure for creating and naming files and directories. A filesystem is not just a labelling scheme, it also provides functionality.

If a filesystem becomes damaged, it is possible to lose data. Usually filesystem checking programs called disk doctors, e.g. the Unix program `fsck` (filesystem check), can be used to repair the operating system's map of a disk. In Unix filesystems, data which lose their labelling get placed for human inspection in a special directory which is found on every partition, called `lost+found`.

The filesystem creation programs for different operating systems go by various names. For instance, on a Sun host running SunOS/Solaris, we would create a filesystem on the zeroth partition of disk 0, controller zero with a command like this to the raw device:

```
newfs -m 0 /dev/rdsk/c0t0d0s0
```

The `newfs` command is a friendly front-end to the `mkfs` program. The option `-m 0`, used here, tells the filesystem creation program to reserve zero bytes of special space on the partition. The default behavior is to reserve ten percent of the total partition size, which ordinary users cannot write to. This is an old mechanism for preventing filesystems from becoming too full. On today's disks, ten percent of a partition size can be many files indeed, and if we partition our cheap, modern disks correctly, there is no reason not to allow users to fill them up completely. This partition is then made available to the system by mounting it. This can either be performed manually:

```
mount /dev/dsk/c0t0d0s0 /mountpoint/directory
```

or by placing it in the filesystem table `/etc/vfstab`.

GNU/Linux systems have the `mkfs` command, e.g.

```
mkfs /dev/hda1
```

The filesystems are registered in the file `/etc/fstab`. Other Unix variants register disks in equivalent files with different names, e.g. HPUX in `/etc/checklist` (prior to 10.x) and AIX in `/etc/filesystems`.

On Windows systems, disks are detected automatically and partitions are assigned to different logical drive names. Drive letters `C:` to `Z:` are used for non-floppy disk devices. Windows assigns drive letters based on what hardware it finds at boot-time. Primary partitions are named first, then each secondary partition is assigned a drive letter. The `format` program is used to generate a filesystem on a drive. The command

```
format /fs:ntfs /v:spare F:
```

would create an NTFS filesystem on drive `F:` and give it a volume label 'spare'. The older, insecure filesystem FAT can also be chosen, however this is not recommended. The GUI can also be used to partition and format inactive disks.

---

[2]Sometimes Unix administrators speak about reformatting a SCSI disk. This is misleading. There is no reformatting at the SCSI level; the process referred to here amounts to an error-correcting scan, in which the intelligent disk controller re-evaluates what parts of the disk surface are undamaged and can be written to. All disks contain unusable areas which have to be avoided.

4.4.4   Swap space

In Windows operating systems, virtual memory uses filesystem space for saving data to disk. In Unix-like operating systems, a preferred method is to use a whole, unformatted partition for virtual memory storage.

A virtual memory partition is traditionally called the swap partition, though few modern Unix-like systems 'swap' out whole processes, in the traditional sense. The swap partition is now used for *paging*. It is virtual memory scratch space, and uses direct disk access to address the partition. No filesystem is needed, because no functionality in terms of files and directories is needed for the paging system.

The amount of available RAM in modern systems has grown enormously in relation to the programs being run. Ten years ago, a good rule of thumb was to allocate a partition twice the size of the total amount of RAM for paging. On heavily used login servers, this would not be enough. Today, it is difficult to give any firm guidelines, since paging is far less of a problem due to extra RAM, and there is less uniformity in host usage.

4.4.5   Filesystem layout

We have no choice about the layout of the software and support files which are installed on a host as part of 'the operating system'. This is decided by the system designers and cannot easily be changed. Software installation, user registration and network integration all make changes to this initial state, however. Such additions to the system are under the control of the system administrator and it is important to structure these changes according to logical and practical principles which we shall consider below.

A working computer system has several facets:

- The operating system software distribution,

- Third party software,

- Users' files,

- Information databases,

- Temporary scratch space.

These are logically separate because:

- They have different functions,

- They are maintained by different sources,

- They change at different rates,

- A different policy of backup is required for each.

Most operating systems have hierarchical file systems with directories and subdirectories. This is a powerful tool for organizing data. Disks can also be divided up into partitions. Another issue in sizing partitions is how you plan to make a backup of those partitions. To make a backup you need to copy all the data to some other location, traditionally tape. The capacity of different kinds of tape varies quite a bit, as does the software for performing backups.

The point of directories and partitions is to separate files so as not to mix together things which are logically separate. There are many things which we might wish to keep separate: for example,

- User home directories

- Development work

- Commercial software

- Free software

- Local scripts and databases.

One of the challenges of system design is in finding an appropriate directory structure for all data which are not part of the operating system, i.e. all those files which are locally maintained.

Principle 13 (Separation I). *Data which are separate from the operating system should be kept in a separate directory tree, preferably on a separate disk partition. If they are mixed with the operating system file tree it makes reinstallation or upgrade of the operating system unnecessarily difficult.*

The essence of this is that it makes no sense to mix logically separate file trees. For instance, users' home directories should never be on a common partition with the operating system. Indeed, filesystems which grow with a life of their own should never be allowed to consume so much space as to throttle the normal operation of the machine.

These days there are few reasons for dividing the files of the operating system distribution into several partitions (e.g. /, /usr). Disks are large enough to install the whole operating system distribution on a single independent disk or partition. If you have done a good job of separating your own modifications from the system distribution, then there is no sense in making a backup of the operating system distribution itself, since it is trivial to reinstall from source (CD-ROM or ftp file base). Some administrators like to keep /var on a separate partition, since it contains files which vary with time, and should therefore be backed up.

Operating systems often have a special place for installed software. Regrettably they often break the above rule and mix software with the operating system's file tree. Under Unix-like operating systems, the place for installed third party software is traditionally /usr/local, or simply /opt. Fortunately under Unix, separate disk partitions can be woven anywhere into the file tree on a directory boundary, so this is not a practical problem as long as everything lies under a common directory. In Windows, software is often installed in the same directory as the operating system itself; also Windows does not support partition mixing in the same way as Unix so the reinstallation of Windows usually means reinstallation of all the software as well.

Data which are installed or created locally are not subject to any constraints, however; they may be installed anywhere. One can therefore find a naming scheme which gives the system logical clarity. This benefits users and management issues. Again we may use directories for this purpose. Operating systems which descended from DOS also have the concept of drive numbers like A:, B:, C: etc. These are assigned to different disk partitions. Some Unix operating systems have virtual file systems which allow one to add disks transparently without ever reaching a practical limit. Users never see partition boundaries. This has both advantages and disadvantages since small partitions are a cheap way to contain groups of misbehaving users, without resorting to disk quotas.

4.4.6   Object orientation: separation of independent issues

The computing community is currently riding a wave of affection for object orientation as a paradigm in computer languages and programming methods. Object orientation in programming languages is usually presented as a fusion of two independent ideas: classification of data types and access control based on scope. The principle from which this model has emerged is simpler than this, however: it is simply the observation that information can be understood and organized most efficiently if *logically independent* items are kept separate.[3] This simple idea is a powerful discipline, but like most disciplines it requires a strong will on the part of a system administrator in order to avoid a decline into chaos. We can restate the earlier principle about operating system separation now more generally:

> **Principle 14 (Separation II).** *Data which are logically separate belong in separate directory trees, perhaps on separate filesystems.*

The basic filesystem objects, in order of global to increasingly local, are *disk partition*, *directory* and *file*. As system administrators, we are not usually responsible for the contents of files, but we do have some power to decide their organization by placing them in carefully labelled directories, within partitions. Partitions are useful because they can be dumped (backed-up to tape, for instance) as independent units. Directories are good because they hide and group related files into units.

Many institutions make backups of the whole operating system partition because they do not have a system for separating the files which they have modified, or configured specially. The number of actual files one needs to keep is usually small. For example

- The password and group databases

- Kernel configuration

- Files in /etc like services, default configurations files

- Special startup scripts.

---

[3]It is sometimes claimed that object orientation mimics the way humans think. This, of course, has no foundation in the cognitive sciences. A more careful formulation would be that object orientation mimics the way in which humans organize and administrate. That has nothing to do with the mechanisms by which thoughts emerge in the brain.

It is easy to make a copy of these few files in a location which is independent of the locations where the files actually need to reside, according to the rules of the operating system.

A good solution to this issue is to make *master copies* of files like /etc/group, /etc/services, /etc/sendmail.cf etc., in a special directory which is separate from the OS distribution. For example, you might choose to collect all of these in a directory such as /local/custom and to use a script, or cfengine to make copies of these master files in the actual locations required by the operating system. The advantages to this approach are

- RCS version control of changes is easy to implement

- Automatic backup and separation

- Ease of distribution to other hosts.

The exception to this rule must be the password database /etc/passwd which is actually altered by an operating system program /bin/passwd rather than the system administrator. In that case the script would copy from the system partition to the custom directory.

Keeping a separate disk partition for software that you install from third parties makes clear sense. It means that you will not have to reinstall that software later when you upgrade your operating system. The question then arises as to how such software should be organized within a separate partition.

Traditionally, third party software has been installed in a directory under /usr/local or simply /local. Software packages are then dissected into libraries, binaries and supporting files which are installed under /local/lib, /local/bin and /local/etc, to mention just a few examples. This keeps third party software separate from operating system software, but there is no separation of the third party software. Another solution would be to install one software package per directory under /local.

4.5 Installing a Unix disk

Adding a new disk or device to a Unix-like host involves some planning. The first concern is what type of hard-disk. There are several types of disk interface used for communicating with hard-disks.

- *ATA/IDE disks:* ATA devices have suffered from a number of limitations in data capacity and number of disks per controller. However, most of these barriers have been broken with new addressing systems and programming techniques. Both parallel (old ribbon cables) and serial interfaces now exist.

- *SCSI disks:* The SCSI interface can be used for devices other than disks too. It is better than IDE at multitasking. The original SCSI interface was limited to 7 devices in total per interface. Wide SCSI can deal with 14 disks. See also the notes in chapter 2.

- *IEEE 1394 disks:* Implementations include Sony's iLink and Apple Computer's FireWire brandnames. These disks use a superior technology (some claim) but have found limited acceptance due to their expense.

In order to connect a new disk to a Unix host, we have to power down the system. Here is a typical checklist for adding a SCSI disk to a Unix system.

- Power down the computer.

- Connect disk and terminate SCSI chain with proper terminator.

- Set the SCSI id of the disk so that it does not coincide with any other disks. On Solaris hosts, SCSI id 6 of controller zero is typically reserved for the primary CD-ROM drive.

- On SUN machines one can use the ROM command `probe-scsi` from the monitor (or `probe-scsi-all`, if there are several disk interfaces) to probe the system for disks, This shows which disks are found on the bus. It can be useful for trouble-shooting bad connections, or accidentally overlapping disk IDs etc.

- Partition and label the disk. Update the defect list.

- Edit the `/etc/fstab` filesystem table or equivalent to mount the disk. See also next section.

4.5.1 `mount` **and** `umount`

To make a disk partition appear as part of the file tree it has to be *mounted*. We say that a particular filesystem is *mounted on* a directory or *mountpoint*. The command `mount` mounts filesystems defined in the filesystem table file. This is a file which holds data for mount to read.

The filesystem table has different names on different implementations of Unix.

Solaris 1 (SunOS)	/etc/fstab
Solaris 2	/etc/vfstab
HPUX	/etc/checklist or /etc/fstab
AIX	/etc/filesystems
IRIX	/etc/fstab
ULTRIX	/etc/fstab
OSF1	/etc/fstab
GNU/Linux	/etc/fstab

These files also have different syntax on different machines, which can be found in the manual pages. The syntax of the command is

```
mount filesystem directory type (options)
```

There are two main types of filesystem – a disk filesystem (called ufs, hfs etc.) (which means a physical disk) and the *NFS* network filesystem. If we mount a 4.2 filesystem it means that it is, by definition, a local disk on our system and is described by some logical device name like /dev/something. If we mount an NFS filesystem, we must specify the name of the filesystem and the name of the host to which the physical disk is attached.

Here are some examples, using the SunOS filesystem list above:

```
mount -a              # mount all in fstab
mount -at nfs         # mount all in fstab which are type nfs
mount -at 4.2         # mount all in fstab which are type 4.2
mount /var/spool/mail # mount only this fs with options given in fstab
```

(The -t option does not work on all Unix implementations.) Of course, we can type the commands manually too, if there is no entry in the filesystem table. For example, to mount an nfs filesystem on machine 'wigner' called /site/wigner/local so that it appears in our filesystem at /mounted/wigner, we would write

```
mount wigner:/site/wigner/local /mounted/wigner
```

The directory /mounted/wigner must exist for this to work. If it contains files, then these files will no longer be visible when the filesystem is mounted on top of it, but they are not destroyed. Indeed, if we then unmount using

```
umount /mounted/wigner
```

(the spelling umount is correct) then the files will reappear again. Some implementations of NFS allow filesystems to be merged at the same mount point, so that the user sees a mixture of all the filesystems mounted at the same point.

4.5.2 Disk partition device names

The convention for naming disk devices in BSD and system 5 Unix differs. Let us take SCSI disks as an example. Under BSD, the SCSI disks have names according to the following scheme:

/dev/sd0a	First partition of disk 0 of the standard disk controller. This is normally the root file system /.
/dev/sd0b	Second partition of disk 0 on the standard disk controller. This is normally used for the swap area.
/dev/sd1c	Third partition of disk 1 on the standard disk controller. This partition is usually reserved to span the entire disk, as a reminder of how large the disk is.

System 5 Unix employs a more complex, but also more general naming scheme. Here is an example from Solaris 2:

`/dev/dsk/c0t3d0s0`	Disk controller 0, target (disk) 3, device 0, segment (partition) 0
`/dev/dsk/c1t1d0s4`	Disk controller 1, target (disk) 1, device 0, segment (partition) 4

Not all systems distinguish between target and device. On many systems you will find only `t` or `d` but not both.

4.6   Installation of the operating system

The installation process is one of the most destructive things we can do to a computer. Everything on the disk will disappear during the installation process. One should therefore have a plan for restoring the information if it should turn out that reinstallation was in error.

Today, installing a new machine is a simple affair. The operating system comes on some removable medium (like a CD or DVD) that is inserted into the player and booted. One then answers a few questions and the installation is done.

Operating systems are now large so they are split up into packages. One is expected to choose whether to install everything that is available or just certain packages. Most operating systems provide a package installation program which helps this process.

In order to answer the questions about installing a new host, information must be collected and some choices made:

- We must decide a name for each machine.

- We need an unused Internet address for each.

- We must decide how much virtual memory (swap) space to allocate.

- We need to know the local netmask and domain name.

- We need to know the local timezone.

We might need to know whether a Network Information Service (NIS) or Windows domain controller is used on the local network; if so, how to attach the new host to this service. When we have this information, we are ready to begin.

4.6.1   Solaris

Solaris can be installed in a number of ways. The simplest is from CD-ROM. At the boot prompt, we simply type

```
? boot cdrom
```

This starts a graphical user interface which leads one through the steps of the installation from disk partitioning to operating system installation. The procedure is well described in the accompanying documentation, indeed it is quite intuitive, so we needn't belabor the point here. The installation procedure proceeds through the standard list of questions, in this order:

- Preferred language and keyboard type.

- Name of host.

- Net interfaces and IP addresses.

- Subscribe to NIS or NIS plus domain, or not.

- Subnet mask.

- Timezone.

- Choose upgrade or install from scratch.

Solaris installation addresses an important issue, namely that of customization and integration. As part of the installation procedure, Solaris provides a service called Jumpstart, which allows hosts to execute specialized scripts which customize the installation. In principle, the automation of hosts can be completely automated using Jumpstart. Customization is extremely important for integrating hosts into a local network. As we have seen, vendor standard models are almost never adequate in real networks. By making it possible to adapt the installation procedure to local requirements, Solaris makes a great contribution to automatic network configuration.

Installation from CD-ROM assumes that every host has a CD-ROM from which to install the operating system. This is not always the case, so operating systems also enable hosts with CD-ROM players to act as network servers for their CD-ROMs, thus allowing the operating system to be installed directly from the network.

4.6.2 GNU/Linux

Installing GNU/Linux is simply a case of inserting a CD-ROM and booting from it, then following the instructions. However, GNU/Linux is not one, but a family of operating systems. There are many distributions, maintained by different organizations and they are installed in different ways. Usually one balances ease of installation with flexibility of choice.

What makes GNU/Linux installation unique amongst operating system installations is the sheer size of the program base. Since every piece of free software is bundled, there are literally hundreds of packages to choose from. This presents GNU/Linux distributors with a dilemma. To make installation as simple as possible, package maintainers make software self-installing with some kind of default configuration. This applies to user programs and to operating system services. Here lies the problem: installing network services which we don't intend to use presents a security risk to a host. A service which is installed is a way into the system. A service which we are not even aware of could be a huge risk. If we install everything, then, we are faced with uncertainty in knowing what the operating system actually consists of, i.e. what we are getting ourselves into.

As with most operating systems, GNU/Linux installations assume that you are setting up a stand-alone PC which is yours to own and do with as you please. Although GNU/Linux is a multiuser system, it is treated as a single-user system. Little thought is given to the effect of installing services like news servers and web servers. The scripts which are bundled for adding user accounts also treat the host as a little microcosm, placing users in /home and software in /usr/local. To make a network workstation out of GNU/Linux, we need to override many of its idiosyncrasies.

4.6.3 Windows

The installation of Windows[4] is similar to both of the above. One inserts a CD-ROM and boots. Here it is preferable to begin with an already partitioned hard-drive (the installation program is somewhat ambiguous with regard to partitions). On rebooting, we are asked whether we wish to install Windows anew, or repair an existing installation. This is rather like the GNU/Linux rescue disk. Next we choose the filesystem type for Windows to be installed on, either DOS or NTFS. There is clearly only one choice: installing on a DOS partition would be irresponsible with regard to security. Choose NTFS.

Windows reboots several times during the installation procedure, though this has improved somewhat in recent versions. The first time around, it converts its default DOS partition into NTFS and reboots again. Then the remainder of the installation proceeds with a graphical user interface. There are several installation models for Windows workstations, including regular, laptop, minimum and custom. Having chosen one of these, one is asked to enter a license key for the operating system. The installation procedure asks us whether we wish to use DHCP to configure the host with an IP address dynamically, or whether a static IP address will be set. After various other questions, the host reboots and we can log in as Administrator.

Windows service packs are patch releases which contain important upgrades. These are refreshingly trivial to install on an already-running Windows system. One simply inserts them into the CD-ROM drive and up pops the Explorer program with instructions and descriptions of contents. Clicking on the install link starts the upgrade. After a service pack upgrade, Windows reboots predictably and then we are done. Changes in configuration require one to reinstall service packs, however.

4.6.4 Dual boot

There are many advantages to having both Windows and GNU/Linux (plus any other operating systems you might like) on the same PC. This is now easily

---

[4]Since Windows 9x is largely history, and NT changes names (NT, 2000, XP, ...) faster than a speeding bullet, I have chosen to refer to 'Windows' meaning modern NT-based Windows, and largely ignore the older versions in this book.

achieved with the installation procedures provided by these two operating systems. It means, however, that we need to be able to choose the operating system from a menu at boot time. The boot-manager GRUB that is now part of GNU/Linux distributions performs this tasks very well, so one scarcely needs to think about this issue anymore. Note, however, that it is highly advisable to install Windows before installing GNU/Linux, since the latter tends to have more respect for the former than vice versa! GNU/Linux can preserve an existing Windows partition, and even repartition the disk appropriately.

4.6.5 Configuring name service lookup

Name service lookup must be configured in order for a system to be able to look up hostnames and Internet addresses. On Windows systems, one configures a list of name servers by going to the menu for TCP/IP network configuration. On Unix hosts there are often graphical tools for doing this too. However, automation requires a non-interactive approach, for scalability, so we consider the low-level approach to this. The most important file in this connection is /etc/resolv.conf. Ancient IRIX systems seem to have placed this file in /usr/etc/resolv.conf. This old location is obsolete. Without the resolver configuration file, a host will often stop dead whilst trying, in vain, to look up Internet addresses. Hosts which use NIS or NIS plus might be able to look up local names; names can also be registered manually in /etc/hosts. The most important features of this file are the definition of the domain-name and a list of nameservers which can perform the address translation service. These nameservers must be listed as IP numerical addresses. The format of the file is as shown.

```
domain domain.country
nameserver 192.0.2.10
nameserver 158.36.85.10
nameserver 129.241.1.99
```

Some prefer to use the search directive in place of the domain directive, since it is more general and allows several domains to be searched in special circumstances:

```
search domain.country
nameserver 192.0.2.10
nameserver 192.0.2.85
nameserver 192.0.2.99
```

The default is to search the local domain, so these are equivalent unless several domains are to be searched. On the host which is itself a nameserver, the first nameserver should be listed as the loopback address, so as to avoid sending traffic out onto the network when none is required:

```
search domain.country
nameserver 127.0.0.1
nameserver 192.0.2.10
nameserver 192.0.2.99
```

DNS has several competitor services. A trivial mapping of hostnames to IP addresses is performed by the /etc/hosts database, and this file can be shared using NIS or NIS plus. Windows had the WINS service, though this is now deprecated. Modern Unix-like systems allow us to choose the order in which these competing services are given priority when looking up hostname data. Unfortunately there is no standard way of configuring this. GNU/Linux and public domain resolver packages for old SunOS (resolv+) use a file called /etc/hosts.conf. The format of this file is

```
order hosts,bind,nis
multi on
```

This example tells the lookup routines to look in the /etc/hosts file first, then to query DNS/BIND and then finally to look at NIS. The resolver routines quit after the first match they find, they do not query all three databases every time. Solaris, and now also some GNU/Linux distributions, use a file called /etc/nsswitch.conf which is a general configuration for all database services, not just the hostname service.

```
#               files,nis,nisplus,dns

passwd:         files
group:          files
hosts:          files dns
ipnodes:        files dns
networks:       files
protocols:      files
rpc:            files
ethers:         files
netmasks:       files
bootparams:     files
```

Note that Solaris has 'ipnodes' which is used for name lookup in the new IPv6 compatible lookup routines. If DNS is not added here, Solaris does not find IPv6 addresses registered in DNS.

4.6.6 Diskless clients

Diskless workstations are, as per the name, workstations which have no disk at all. They are now rare, but with the increase of network speeds, they are being discussed again in new guises such as 'thin clients'.

Diskless workstations know absolutely nothing other than the MAC address of their network interface (Ethernet address). In earlier times, when disks were expensive, diskless workstations were seen as a cheap option. Diskless clients require disk space on a server-host in order to function, i.e. some other host which does have a disk, needs to be a disk server for the diskless clients. Most vendors supply a script for creating diskless workstations. This script is run on the server-host.

When a diskless system is switched on for the first time, it has no files and knows nothing about itself except the Ethernet address on its network card. It proceeds by sending a RARP (reverse address resolution protocol) or BOOTP or DHCP request out onto the local subnet in the hope that a server (`in.rarpd`) will respond by telling it its Internet address. The server hosts must be running two services: `rpc.bootparamd` and `tftpd`, the trivial file transfer program. This is another reason for arguing against diskless clients: these services are rather insecure and could be a security risk for the server host. A call to the `rpc.bootparamd` daemon transfers data about where the diskless station can find a server, and what its swap-area and root directory are called in the file tree of this server. The root directory and swap file are mounted using the NFS. The diskless client loads its kernel from its root directory and thereafter everything proceeds as normal. Diskless workstations swap to files rather than partitions. The command `mkfile` is used to create a fixed-size file for swapping.

4.6.7 Dual-homed host

A host with two network interfaces, both of which are coupled to a network, is called a dual-homed host. Dual-homed hosts are important in building *firewalls* for network security. A host with two network interfaces can be configured to automatically forward packets between the networks (act as a bridge) or to block such forwarding. The latter is normal in a firewall configuration, where it is left to proxy software to forward packets only after some form of inspection procedure. Most vendor operating systems will configure dual-network interfaces automatically, with forwarding switched off. Briefly here is a GNU/Linux setup for two network interfaces.

1. Compile a new kernel with support for both types of interface, unless both are of the same type.

2. Change the lilo configuration to detect both interfaces, if necessary, by adding:

   ```
   append="ether=0,0,eth0 ether=0,0,eth1"
   ```

   to `/etc/lilo.conf`.

3. The new interface can be assigned an IP address in the file `/etc/init.d/network`.

One must then decide how the IP addresses are to be registered in the DNS service. Will the host have the same name on both interfaces, or will it have a different name? Packet routing on dual-homed hosts has been discussed in ref. [272].

4.6.8 Cloning systems

We are almost never interested in installing every machine separately. A system administrator usually has to install ten, twenty or even a hundred machines at a

time. He or she would also like them to be as far as possible the same, so that
users will always know what to expect. This might sound like a straightforward
problem, but it is not. There are several approaches.

- A few Unix-like operating systems provide a solution to this using package
  templates so that the installation procedure becomes standardized.

- The hard disks of one machine can be physically copied and then the
  hostname and IP address can be edited afterwards.

- All software can be placed on one host and shared using NFS, or another
  shared filesystem.

Each of these approaches has its attractions. The NFS/shared filesystem approach
is without doubt the least amount of work, since it involves installing the software
only once, but it is also the slowest in operation for users.

As an example of the first, here is how Debian GNU/Linux tackles this problem
using the Debian package system:

```
Install one system

  dpkg --get-selections > file

On the remaining machines type

  dpkg --set-selections < file

Run install packages program.
```

Alternatively, one can install a single package with:

```
dpkg -i package.deb
```

This method has now been superceded by an extremely elegant package system
using the apt-get command. Installation of a package is completely transparent
as to source and dependencies:

```
host# apt-get install bison
Reading Package Lists... Done
Building Dependency Tree... Done
The following NEW packages will be installed:
  bison
0 packages upgraded, 1 newly installed, 0 to remove and 110 not upgraded.
Need to get 387kB of archives. After unpacking 669kB will be used.
Get:1 http://sunsite.uio.no stable/main bison 1:1.35-3 [387kB]
Fetched 387kB in 0s (644kB/s)
Selecting previously deselected package bison.
(Reading database ... 10771 files and directories currently installed.)
Unpacking bison (from .../bison_1%3a1.35-3_i386.deb) ...
Setting up bison (1.35-3) ...
```

In RedHat Linux, a similar mechanism looks like this:

```
rpm -ivh package.rpm
```

Disks can be mirrored directly, using some kind of cloning program. For instance, the Unix tape archive program (tar) can be used to copy the entire directory tree of one host. In order to make this work, we first have to perform a basic installation of the OS, with zero packages and then copy over all remaining files which constitutes the packages we require. In the case of the Debian system above, there is no advantage to doing this, since the package installation mechanism can do the same job more cleanly. For example, with a GNU/Linux distribution:

```
tar --exclude /proc --exclude /lib/libc.so.5.4.23 \
    --exclude /etc/hostname --exclude /etc/hosts -c -v \
    -f host-imprint.tar /
```

Note that several files must be excluded from the dump. The file `/lib/libc.so. 5.4.23` is the C library; if we try to write this file back from backup, the destination computer will crash immediately. `/etc/hostname` and `/etc/hosts` contains definitions of the hostname of the destination computer, and must be left unchanged. Once a minimal installation has been performed on the destination host, we can access the tar file and unpack it to install the image:

```
(cd / ; tar xfp /mnt/dump/my-machine.tar; lilo)
```

Afterwards, we have to install the boot sector, with the `lilo` command. The cloning of Unix systems has been discussed in refs. [297, 339].

Note that Windows systems cannot be cloned without special software (e.g. Norton Ghost or PowerQuest Drive Image). There are fundamental technical reasons for this. One is the fact that many host parameters are configured in the impenetrable *system registry*. Unless all of the hardware and software details of every host are the same, this will fail with an inconsistency. Another reason is that users are registered in a binary database with security IDs which can have different numerical values on each host. Finally domain registration cannot be cloned. A host must register manually with its domain server. Novell Zenworks contains a cloning solution that ties NDS objects to disk images.

4.7 Software installation

Most standard operating system installations will not leave us in possession of an immediately usable system. We also need to install third party software in order to get useful work out of the host. Software installation is a similar problem to that of operating system installation. However, third party software originates from a different source than the operating system; it is often bound by license agreements and it needs to be distributed around the network. Some software has to be compiled from source. We therefore need a thoughtful strategy for dealing with software. Specialized schemes for software installation were discussed in refs. [85, 199] and a POSIX draft was discussed in ref. [18], though this idea has not been developed into a true standard. Instead, de-facto and proprietary standards have emerged.

4.7.1   Free and proprietary software

Unlike most other popular operating systems, Unix grew up around people who wrote their own software rather than relying on off-the-shelf products. The Internet now contains gigabytes of software for Unix systems which cost nothing. Traditionally, only large companies like the oil industry and newspapers could afford off-the-shelf software for Unix.

There are therefore two kinds of software installation: the installation of software from binaries and the installation of software from source. Commercial software is usually installed from a CD by running an installation program and following the instructions carefully; the only decision we need to make is where we want to install the software. Free software and open source software usually come in source form and must therefore be compiled. Unix programmers have gone to great lengths to make this process as simple as possible for system administrators.

4.7.2   Structuring software

The first step in installing software is to decide where we want to keep it. We could, naturally, locate software anywhere we like, but consider the following:

- Software should be separated from the operating system's installed files, so that the OS can be reinstalled or upgraded without ruining a software installation.

- Unix-like operating systems have a naming convention. Compiled software can be collected in a special area, with a `bin` directory and a `lib` directory so that binaries and libraries conform to the usual Unix conventions. This makes the system consistent and easy to understand. It also keeps the program search `PATH` variable simple.

- Home-grown files and programs which are special to our own particular site can be kept separate from files which could be used anywhere. That way, we define clearly the validity of the files and we see who is responsible for maintaining them.

The directory traditionally chosen for installed software is called `/usr/local`. One then makes subdirectories `/usr/local/bin` and `/usr/local/lib` and so on [147]. Unix has a de-facto naming standard for directories which we should try to stick to as far as reason permits, so that others will understand how our system is built up.

- `bin` Binaries or executables for normal user programs.

- `sbin` Binaries or executables for programs which only system administrators require. Those files in `/sbin` are often statically linked to avoid problems with libraries which lie on unmounted disks during system booting.

- `lib` Libraries and support files for special software.

- `etc` Configuration files.

- share Files which might be shared by several programs or hosts. For instance, databases or help-information; other common resources.

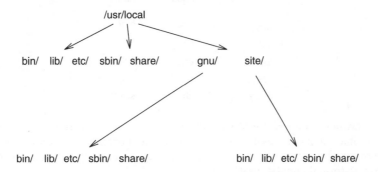

Figure 4.1: One way of structuring local software. There are plenty of things to criticize here. For instance, is it necessary to place this under the traditional /usr/local tree? Should GNU software be underneath /usr/local? Is it even necessary or desirable to formally distinguish GNU software from other software?

One suggestion for structuring installed software on a Unix-like host is shown in figure 4.1. Another is shown in figure 4.2. Here we divide these into three categories: regular installed software, GNU software (i.e. free software) and site-software. The division is fairly arbitrary. The reason for this is as follows:

- /usr/local is the traditional place for software which does not belong to the OS. We could keep everything here, but we will end up installing a lot of software after a while, so it is useful to create two other sub-categories.

- GNU software, written by and for the Free Software Foundation, forms a self-contained set of tools which replace many of the older Unix equivalents, like ls and cp. GNU software has its own system of installation and set of standards. GNU will also eventually become an operating system in its own right. Since these files are maintained by one source it makes sense to keep them separate. This also allows us to place GNU utilities ahead of others in a user's command PATH.

- Site-specific software includes programs and data which we build locally to replace the software or data which follows with the operating system. It also includes special data like the database of aliases for E-mail and the DNS tables for our site. Since it is special to our site, created and maintained by our site, we should keep it separate so that it can be backed up often and separately.

A similar scheme to this was described in refs. [201, 70, 328, 260], in a system called *Depot*. In the Depot system, software is installed under a file node called /depot which replaces /usr/local. In the depot scheme, separate directories are maintained for different machine architectures under a single file tree. This has the advantage of allowing every host to mount the same filesystem, but the disadvantage of making the single filesystem very large. Software is installed in

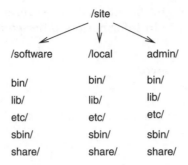

Figure 4.2: Another, more rational way of structuring local software. Here we drop the affectation of placing local modifications under the operating system's /usr tree and separate it completely. Symbolic links can be used to alias /usr/local to one of these directories for historical consistency.

a package-like format under the depot tree and is linked in to local hosts with symbolic links. A variation on this idea from the University of Edinburgh was described in ref. [10], and another from the University of Waterloo uses a file tree /software to similar ends in ref. [273]. In the Soft environment [109], software installation and user environment configuration are dealt with in a combined abstraction.

4.7.3 GNU software example

Let us now illustrate the GNU method of installing software which has become widely accepted. This applies to any type of Unix, and to Windows if one has a Unix compatibility kit, such as Cygwin or UWIN. To begin compiling software, one should always start by looking for a file called README or INSTALL. This tells us what we have to do to compile and install the software. In most cases, it is only necessary to type a couple of commands, as in the following example. When installing GNU software, we are expected to give the name of a *prefix* for installing the package. The prefix in the above cases is /usr/local for ordinary software, /usr/local/gnu for GNU software and /usr/local/site for site-specific software. Most software installation scripts place files under bin and lib automatically. The steps are as follows.

1. Make sure we are working as a regular, unprivileged user. The software installation procedure might do something which we do not agree with. It is best to work with as few privileges as possible until we are sure.

2. Collect the software package by ftp from a site like ftp.uu.net or ftp.funet.fi etc. Use a program like ncftp for painless anonymous login.

3. Unpack the file using tar zxf *software*.tar.gz, if using GNU tar, or gunzip *software*.tar.gz; tar xf software.tar if not.

4. Enter the directory which is unpacked, cd *software*.

5. Type: `configure --prefix=/usr/local/gnu`. This checks the state of our local operating system and other installed software and configures the software to work correctly there.

6. Type: `make`.

7. If all goes well, type `make -n install`. This indicates what the make program will install and where. If we have any doubts, this allows us to make changes or abort the procedure without causing any damage.

8. Finally, switch to privileged root/Administrator mode with the `su` command and type `make install`. This should be enough to install the software. Note, however, that this step is a security vulnerability. If one blindly executes commands with privilege, one can be tricked into installing back-doors and Trojan horses, see chapter 11.

9. Some installation scripts leave files with the wrong permissions so that ordinary users cannot access the files. We might have to check that the files have a mode like 555 so that normal users can access them. This is in spite of the fact that installation programs attempt to set the correct permissions [287].

Today this procedure should be more or less the same for just about any software pick up. Older software packages sometimes provide only Makefiles which you must customize yourself. Some X11-based windowing software requires you to use the `xmkmf` X-make-makefiles command instead of configure. You should always look at the README file.

4.7.4 Proprietary software example

If we are installing proprietary software, we will have received a copy of the program on a CD-ROM, together with licensing information, i.e. a code which activates the program. The steps are somewhat different.

1. To install from CD-ROM we must start work with root/Administrator privileges, so the authenticity of the CD-ROM should be certain.

2. Insert the CD-ROM into the drive. Depending on the operating system, the CD-ROM might be mounted automatically or not. Check this using the `mount` command with no arguments, on a Unix-like system. If the CD-ROM has not been mounted, then, for standard CD-ROM formats, the following will normally suffice:

```
mkdir /cdrom              if necessary
mount /dev/cdrom /cdrom
```

For some manufacturers, or on older operating systems, we might have to specify the type of filesystem on the CD-ROM. Check the installation instructions.

3. On a Windows system a clickable icon appears to start the installation program. On a Unix-like system we need to look for an installation script

```
cd /cdrom/ cd-name
less README
./install-script
```

4. Follow the instructions.

Some proprietary software requires the use of a license server, such as lmgrd. This is installed automatically, and we are required only to edit a configuration file with a license key which is provided, in order to complete the installation. Note however, that if we are running multiple licensed products on a host, it is not uncommon that these require different and partly incompatible license servers which interfere with one another. If possible, one should keep to only one license server per subnet.

4.7.5 Installing shared libraries

Systems which use shared libraries or shared objects sometimes need to be reconfigured when new libraries are added to the system. This is because the names of the libraries are cached to provide fast access. The system will not look for a library if it is not in the cache file.

- SunOS (prior to Solaris 2): After adding a new library, one must run the command ldconfig lib-directory. The file /etc/ld.so.cache is updated.

- GNU/Linux: New library directories are added to the file /etc/ld.so.conf. Then one runs the command ldconfig. The file /etc/ld.so.cache is updated.

4.7.6 Configuration security

In the preceding sections we have looked at some examples and suggestions for dealing with software installation. Let us now take a step back from the details to analyze the principles underlying these.

The first is a principle which we shall return to many times in this book. It is one of the key principles in computer science, and we shall be repeating it with slightly different words again and again.

> **Principle 15 (Separation III).** *Independent systems should not interfere with one another, or be confused with one another. Keep them in separate storage areas.*

The reason is clear: if we mix up files which do not belong together, we lose track of them. They become obscured by a lack of structure. They vanish into anonymity. The reason why all modern computer systems have directories for grouping files, is precisely so that we do not have to mix up all files in one place. This was discussed in section 4.4.5. The application to software installation is clear: we should not ever consider installing software in /usr/bin or /bin or /lib or /etc or any directory which is controlled by the system designers. To do so is like lying down in the middle of a freeway and waiting for a new operating system or upgrade to roll over us. If we mix local modifications with operating system files, we lose track of the differences in the system, others will not be able to see what we have done. All our hard work will be for nothing when a new system is installed.

> **Suggestion 1 (Vigilance).** *Be on the lookout for software which is configured, by default, to install itself on top of the operating system. Always check the destination using* make -n install *before actually committing to an installation. Programs which are replacements for standard operating system components often break the principle of separation.[a]*
>
> ---
>
> [a]Software originating in BSD Unix is often an offender, since it is designed to be a part of BSD Unix, rather than an add-on, e.g. sendmail and BIND.

The second important point above is that we should never work with root privileges unless we have to. Even when we are compiling software from source, we should not start the compilation with superuser privileges. The reason is clear: why should we trust the source of the program? What if someone has placed a command in the build instructions to destroy the system, plant a virus or open a back-door to intrusion? As long as we work with low privilege then we are protected, to a degree, from problems like this. Programs will not be able to do direct and pervasive damage, but they might still be able to plant Trojan horses that will come into effect when privileged access is acquired.

> **Principle 16 (Limited privilege).** *No process or file should be given more privileges than it needs to do its job. To do so is a security hazard.*

Another use for this principle arises when we come to configure certain types of software. When a user executes a software package, it normally gets executed with the user privileges of that user. There are two exceptions to this:

- *Services which are run by the system:* Daemons which carry out essential services for users or for the system itself, run with a user ID which is independent of who is logged on to the system. Often, such daemons are started as root or the Administrator when the system boots. In many cases, the daemons do not need these privileges and will function quite happily with ordinary user privileges after changing the permissions of a few files. This is a much safer strategy than allowing them to run with full access. For example, the httpd daemon for the WWW service uses this approach. In recent years, bugs in many programs which run with root privileges have been exploited to give intruders access to the system. If software is run with a non-privileged user ID, this is not possible.

- *Unix setuid programs:* Unix has a mechanism by which special privilege can be given to a user for a short time, while a program is being executed. Software which is installed with the Unix setuid bit set, and which is owned by root, runs with root's special privileges. Some software producers install software with this bit set with no respect for the privilege it affords. Most programs which are setuid root do not need to be. A good example of this is the Common Desktop Environment (a multi-vendor desktop environment used on Unix systems). In a recent release, almost every program was installed setuid root. Within only a short time, a list of reports about users exploiting bugs to gain control of these systems appeared. In the next release, none of the programs were setuid root.

All software servers which are started by the system at boot time are started with root/Administrator privileges, but daemons which do not require these privileges can relinquish them by giving up their special privileges and running as a special user. This approach is used by the Apache WWW server and by MySQL for instance. These are examples of software which encourage us to create special user IDs for server processes. To do this, we create a special user in the password database, with no login rights (this just reserves a UID). In the above cases, these are usually called www and mysql. The software allows us to specify these user IDs so that the process owner is switched right after starting the program. If the software itself does not permit this, we can always force a daemon to be started with lower privilege using:

```
su -c 'command' user
```

The management tool cfengine can also be used to do this. Note however that Unix server processes which run on reserved (privileged) ports 1–1023 have to be started with root privileges in order to bind to their sockets.

On the topic of root privilege, a related security issue has to do with programs which write to temporary files.

Principle 17 (Temporary files). *Temporary files or sockets which are opened by any program, should not be placed in any publicly writable directory like* /tmp. *This opens the possibility of race conditions and symbolic link attacks. If possible, configure them to write to a private directory.*

Users are always more devious than software writers. A common mistake in programming is to write to a file which ordinary users can create, using a privileged process. If a user is allowed to create a file object with the same name, then he or she can direct a privileged program to write to a different file instead, simply by creating a symbolic or hard link to the other file. This could be used to overwrite the password file or the kernel, or the files of another user. Software writers can avoid this problem by simply unlinking the file they wish to write to first, but that still leaves a window of opportunity after unlinking the file and before opening the new file for writing, during which a malicious user could replace the link (remember that the system time-shares). The lesson is to avoid making privileged programs write to directories which are not private, if possible.

Before closing this section, a comment is in order. Throughout this chapter, and others, we have been advocating a policy of building the best possible, most logical system by tailoring software to our own environment. Altering absurd software defaults, customizing names and locations of files and changing user identities is no problem as long as everyone who uses and maintains the system is aware of this. If a new administrator started work and, unwittingly, reverted to those software defaults, then the system would break.

Principle 18 (Flagging customization). *Customizations and deviations from standards should be made conspicuous to users and administrators. This makes the system easier to understand both for ourselves and our successors.*

4.7.7 When compilation fails

Today, software producers who distribute their source code are able to configure it automatically to work with most operating systems. Compilation usually proceeds without incident. Occasionally though, an error will occur which causes the compilation to halt. There are a few things we can try to remedy this:

- A previous configuration might have been left lying around, try

```
make clean
make distclean
```

  and start again, from the beginning.

- Make sure that the software does not depend on the presence of another package, or library. Install any dependencies, missing libraries and try again.

- Errors at the linking stage about missing functions are usually due to missing or un-locatable libraries. Check that the

```
LD_LIBRARY_PATH
```

  variable includes all relevant library locations. Are any other environment variables required to configure the software?

- Sometimes an extra library needs to be added to the Makefile. To find out whether a library contains a function, we can use the following C-shell trick:

```
host% cd /lib
host% foreach lib ( lib* )
> echo Checking $lib ----------------------
> nm $lib | grep function
>end
```

- Carefully try to patch the source code to make the code compile.

- Check in news groups whether others have experienced the same problem.

- Contact the author of the program.

4.7.8   Upgrading software

Some software (especially free software) gets updated very often. We could easily spend an entire life just chasing the latest versions of favorite software packages. Avoid this.

- It is a waste of time.

- Sometimes new versions contain more bugs than the old one, and an even-newer-version is just around the corner.

- Users will not thank us for changing things all the time. Stability is a virtue. Everyone likes time to get used to the system before change strikes.

A plan is needed for testing new versions of software. Package systems for software make this process easier, since one can allow several versions of software to coexist, or roll back to earlier versions if problems are discovered with newer versions.

4.8   Kernel customization

The operating system kernel is that most important part of the system which drives the hardware of the machine and shares it between multiple processes. If the kernel does not work well, the system as a whole will not work well. The main reason for making changes to the kernel is to fix bugs and to upgrade system software, such as support for new hardware; performance gains can also be achieved however, if one is patient. We shall return to the issue of performance again in section 8.11. Kernel configuration varies widely between operating systems. Some systems require kernel modification for every miniscule change, while others live quite happily with the same kernel unless major changes are made to the hardware of the host.

Many operating system kernels are monolithic, statically compiled programs which are specially built for each host, but static programs are inflexible and the current trend is to replace them with software configurable systems which can be manipulated without the need to recompile the kernel. System V Unix has blazed the trail of adaptable, configurable kernels, in its quest to build an operating system which will scale from laptops to mainframes. It introduces kernel modules which can be loaded on demand. By loading parts of the kernel only when required, one reduces the size of the resident kernel memory image, which can save memory. This policy also makes upgrades of the different modules independent of the main kernel software, which makes patching and reconfiguration simpler. SVR4 Unix and its derivatives, like Solaris and Unixware, are testimony to the flexibility of SVR4.

Windows has also taken a modular view to kernel design. Configuration of the Windows kernel also does not require a recompilation, only the choice of a number of parameters, accessed through the system editor in the Performance Monitor, followed by a reboot. GNU/Linux switched from a static, monolithic kernel to a modular design quite quickly. The Linux kernel strikes a balance between static compilation and modular loading. This balances the convenience of modules with the increased speed of having statically compiled code forever in memory. Typically, heavily used kernel modules are compiled in statically, while infrequently used modules are accessed on demand.

Solaris

Neither Solaris nor Windows require or permit kernel recompilation in order to make changes. In Solaris, for instance, one edits configuration files and reboots for an auto-reconfiguration. First we edit the file /etc/system to change kernel parameters, then reboot with the command

```
reboot -- -r
```

which reconfigures the system automatically. There is also a large number of system parameters which can be configured on the fly (at run time) using the ndd command.

GNU/Linux

The Linux kernel is subject to more frequent revision than many other systems, owing to the pace of its development. It must be recompiled when new changes are to be included, or when an optimized kernel is required. Many GNU/Linux distributions are distributed with older kernels, while newer kernels offer significant performance gains, particularly in kernel-intensive applications like NFS, so there is a practical reason to upgrade the kernel.

The compilation of a new kernel is a straightforward but time-consuming, process. The standard published procedure for installing and configuring a new kernel is as follows. New kernel distributions are obtained from any mirror of the Linux kernel site [176]. First we back up the old kernel, unpack the kernel sources into the operating system's files (see the note below) and alias the kernel revision to /usr/src/linux. Note that the bash shell is required for kernel compilation.

```
$ cp /boot/vmlinuz /boot/vmlinux.old
$ cd /usr/src
$ tar zxf /local/site/src/linux-2.2.9.tar.gz
$ ln -s linux-2.2.9 linux
```

There are often patches to be collected and applied to the sources. For each patch file:

```
$ zcat /local/site/src/patchX.gz | patch -p0
```

Then we make sure that we are building for the correct architecture (Linux now runs on several types of processor).

```
$ cd /usr/include
$ rm -rf asm linux scsi
$ ln -s /usr/src/linux/include/asm-i386 asm
$ ln -s /usr/src/linux/include/linux linux
$ ln -s /usr/src/linux/include/scsi scsi
```

Next we prepare the configuration:

```
$ cd /usr/src/linux
$ make mrproper
```

The command `make config` can now be used to set kernel parameters. More user-friendly windows-based programs `make xconfig` or `make menuconfig` are also available, though the former does require one to run X11 applications as root, which is a potential security faux pas. The customization procedure has defaults which one can fall back on. The choices are `Y` to include an option statically in the kernel, `N` to not include and `M` to include as module support. The capitalized option indicates the default. Although there are defaults, it is important to think carefully about the kind of hardware we are using. For instance, is SCSI support required? One of the questions prompts us to specify the type of processor, for optimization:

```
Processor type (386, 486, Pentium, PPro) [386]
```

The default, in square brackets, is for generic 386, but Pentium machines will benefit from optimizations if we choose correctly. If we are compiling on hosts without CD-ROMs and tape drives, there is no need to include support for these, unless we plan to copy this compiled kernel to other hosts which *do* have these.

After completing the long configuration sequence, we build the kernel:

```
# make dep
# make clean
# make bzImage
```

and move it into place:

```
# mv arch/i386/boot/zImage /boot/vmlinuz-2.2.9
# ln -s /boot/vmlinuz-2.2.9 /boot/vmlinuz
# make modules
# make modules-install
```

The last step allows us to keep track of which version is running, while still having the standard kernel name.

To alter kernel parameters on the fly, Linux uses a number of writable pseud- ofiles under `/proc/sys`, e.g.

```
echo 1 >/proc/sys/vm/overcommit_memory
cat /proc/sys/vm/overcommit_memory
```

This can be used to tune values or switch features.

`lilo` **and Grub**

After copying a kernel loader into place, we have to update the boot blocks on the system disk so that a boot program can be located before there is an operating kernel which can interpret the filesystem. This applies to any operating system, e.g. SunOS has the `installboot` program. After installing a new kernel in GNU/Linux, we update the boot records on the system disk by running the lilo program. The new loader program is called by simply typing lilo. This reads a default configuration file /etc/lilo.conf and writes loader data to the Master Boot Record (MBR). One can also write to the primary Linux partition, in case something should go wrong:

```
lilo -b /dev/hda1
```

so that we can still boot, even if another operating system should destroy the boot block. A new and superior boot loader called Grub is now gaining popularity in commercial Linux distributions.

Logistics of kernel customization

The standard procedure for installing a new kernel breaks a basic principle: don't mess with the operating system distribution, as this will just be overwritten by later upgrades. It also potentially breaks the principle of reproducibility: the choices and parameters which we choose for one host do not necessarily apply for others. It seems as though kernel configuration is doomed to lead us down the slippery path of making irreproducible, manual changes to every host.

We should always bear in mind that what we do for one host must usually be repeated for many others. If it were necessary to recompile and configure a new kernel on every host individually, it would simply never happen. It would be a project for eternity.

The situation with a kernel is not as bad as it seems, however. Although, in the case of GNU/Linux, we collect kernel upgrades from the net as though it were third party software, it is rightfully a part of the operating system. The kernel is maintained by the same source as the kernel in the distribution, i.e. we are not in danger of losing anything more serious than a configuration file if we upgrade later. However, reproducibility across hosts is a more serious concern. We do not want to repeat the job of kernel compilation on every single host. Ideally, we would like to compile once and then distribute to similar hosts. Kernels can be compiled, cloned and distributed to different hosts provided they have a common hardware base (this comes back to the principle of uniformity). Life is made easier if we can standardize kernels; in order to do this we must first have standardized hardware. The modular design of newer kernels means that we also need to upgrade the modules in /lib/modules to the receiving hosts. This is a logistic problem which requires some experimentation in order to find a viable solution for a local site.

These days it is not usually *necessary* to build custom kernels. The default kernels supplied with most OSs are good enough for most purposes. Performance enhancements are obtainable, however, particularly on busy servers. See section 8.11 for more hints.

Exercises

Self-test objectives

1. List the considerations needed in creating a server room.

2. How can static electricity cause problems for computers and printers?

3. What are the procedures for shutting down computers safely at your site?

4. How do startup and shutdown procedures differ between Unix and Windows?

5. What is the point of partitioning disk drives?

6. Can a disk partition exceed the size of a hard-disk?

7. How do different Unix-like operating systems refer to disk partitions?

8. How does Windows refer to disk partitions?

9. What is meant by 'creating a new filesystem' on a disk partition in Unix?

10. What is meant by formatting a disk in Unix and Windows (hint: they do not mean the same)?

11. What different filesystems are in use on Windows hosts? What are the pros and cons of each?

12. What is the rationale behind the principle of (data) Separation I?

13. How does object orientation, as a strategy, apply to system administration?

14. How is a new disk attached to a Unix-like host?

15. List the different ways to install an operating system on a new computer from a source.

16. What is meant by a thin client?

17. What is meant by a dual-homed host?

18. What is meant by host cloning? Explain how you would go about cloning a Unix-like and Windows host.

19. What is meant by a software package?

20. What is meant by free, open source and proprietary software? List some pros and cons of each of these.

21. Describe a checklist or strategy for familiarizing yourself with the layout of a new operating system file hierarchy.

22. Describe how to install Unix software from source files.

23. Describe how you would go about installing software provided on a CD-ROM or DVD.

24. What is meant by a shared library or DLL?

25. Explain the principle of limited privilege.

26. What is meant by kernel customization and when is it necessary?

Problems

1. If you have a PC to spare, install a GNU/Linux distribution, e.g. Debian, or a commercial distribution. Consider carefully how you will partition the disk. Can you imagine repeating this procedure for one hundred hosts?

2. Install Windows (NT, 2000, XP etc). You will probably want to repeat the procedure several times to learn the pitfalls. Consider carefully how you will partition the disk. Can you imagine repeating this procedure for 100 hosts?

3. If space permits, install GNU/Linux and Windows together on the same host. Think carefully, once again, about partitioning.

4. For both of the above installations, design a directory layout for local files. Discuss how you will separate operating system files from locally installed files. What will be the effect of upgrading or reinstalling the operating system at a later time? How does partitioning of the disk help here?

5. Imagine the situation in which you install every independent software package in a directory of its own. Write a script which builds and updates the PATH variable for users automatically, so that the software will be accessible from a command shell.

6. Describe what is meant by a URL or universal naming scheme for files. Consider the location of software within a directory tree: some software packages compile the names of important files into software binaries. Explain why the use of a universal naming scheme guarantees that the software will always be able to find the files even when mounted on a different host, and conversely why cross mounting a directory under a different name on a different host is doomed to break the software.

7. Upgrade the kernel on your GNU/Linux installation. Collect the kernel from ref. [176].

8. Determine your Unix/Windows current patch level. Search the web for more recent patches. Which do you need? Is it always right to patch a system?

9. Comment on how your installation procedure could be duplicated if you had not one, but one hundred machines to install.

10. Make a checklist for standardizing hosts: what criteria should you use to ensure standardization? Give some thought to the matter of quality assurance. How can your checklist help here? We shall be returning to this issue in chapter 8.

11. Make a scaling checklist for your system policy.

12. Suppose your installed host is a mission-critical system. Estimate the time it would take you to get your host up and running again in case of complete failure. What strategy could you use to reduce the time the service was out of action?

13. Given the choice between compiling a critical piece of software yourself, or installing it as a software package from your vendor or operating system provider, which would you choose? Explain the issues surrounding this choice and the criteria you would use to make the decision.

Chapter 5

User management

Without users, there would be few challenges in system administration. Users are both the reason that computers exist and their greatest threat. The role of the computer, as a tool, has changed extensively throughout history. From John von Neumann's vision of the computer as a device for predicting the weather, to a calculator for atomic weapons, to a desktop typewriter, to a means of global communication, computers have changed the world and have reinvented themselves in the process. System administrators must cater to all needs, and ensure the stability and security of the system.

5.1 Issues

User management is about interfacing humans to computers. This brings to light a number of issues:

- Accounting: registering new users and deleting old ones.

- Comfort and convenience.

- Support services.

- Ethical issues.

- Trust management and security.

Some of these (account registration) are technological, while others (support services) are human issues. Comfort and convenience lies somewhere in between. User management is important because the system exists to be used by human beings, and they are both friend and enemy.

5.2 User registration

One of the first issues on a new host is to issue accounts for users. Surprisingly this is an area where operating system designers provide virtually no help. The tools provided by operating systems for this task are, at best, primitive and are

rarely suitable for the task without considerable modification. For small organizations, user registration is a relatively simple matter. Users can be registered at
a centralized location by the system manager, and made available to all of the
hosts in the network by some sharing mechanism, such as a login server, distributed authentication service or by direct copying of the data. There are various
mechanisms for doing this, and we shall return to them below.

For larger organizations, with many departments, user registration is much
more complicated. The need for centralization is often in conflict with the need
for delegation of responsibility. It is convenient for autonomous departments to
be able to register their own users, but it is also important for all users to be
registered under the umbrella of the organization, to ensure unique identities for
the users and flexibility of access to different parts of the organization. What is
needed is a solution which allows local system managers to be able to register new
users in a global user database. User account administration has been discussed
many times, see refs. [1, 299, 78, 190, 163, 195, 73, 216]. The special problems
of each institution and work environment are reflected in these works.

PC server systems like NT and Netware have an apparent advantage in this
respect. By forcing a particular administration model onto the hosts in a network,
they can provide straightforward delegation of user registration to anyone with
domain credentials. Registration of single users under NT can be performed
remotely from a workstation, using the

```
net user   username password /ADD   /domain
```

command. While most Unix-like systems do not provide such a ready-made tool,
many solutions have been created by third parties. The price one pays for such
convenience is an implicit *trust relationship* between the hosts. Assigning new user
accounts is a security issue, thus to grant the right of a remote user to add new
accounts requires us to trust the user with access to that facility.

It is rather sad that no acceptable, standardized user registration methods
have been widely adopted. This must be regarded as one of the unsolved problems
of system administration. Part of the problem is that the requirements of each
organization are rather different. Many Unix-like systems provide shell scripts or
user interfaces for installing new users, but most of these scripts are useless,
because they follow a model of system layout which is inadequate for a network
environment, or for an organization's special needs.

5.2.1   Local and network accounts

Most organizations need a system for centralizing passwords, so that each user will
have the same password on each host on the network. In fixed model computing
environments such as NT or Novell Netware, where a login or domain server is
used, this is a simple matter. In larger organizations with many departments or
sub-domains it is more difficult [82, 306, 315].

Both Unix and NT support the creation of accounts locally on a single host, or
'globally' within a network domain. With a local account, a user has permission
to use only the local host. With a network account, the user can use any host
which belongs to a network *domain*. Local accounts are configured on the local

host itself. Unix registers local users by added them to the files /etc/passwd and /etc/shadow. In NT the Security Accounts Manager (SAM) is used to add local accounts to a given workstation.

For network accounts, Unix-like systems have widely adopted Sun Microsystems' Network Information Service (NIS), formerly called Yellow Pages or simply YP, though this is likely to be superceded and replaced by the more widely accepted standard LDAP in the next few years. The NIS-plus service was later introduced to address a number of weaknesses in NIS, but this has not been widely adopted. NIS is reasonably effective at sharing passwords, but it has security implications: encrypted passwords are distributed in the old password format, clearly visible, making a mockery of shadow password files. NIS users have to be registered locally as users on the master NIS server; there is no provision for remote registration, or for delegation of responsibility. Variations on the NIS theme have been discussed in refs. [75, 252, 146]. NT uses its model of domain servers, rather like a NIS, but including a registration mechanism. A user in the SAM of a primary domain controller is registered within that domain and has an account on any host which subscribes to that domain. An approach to user accounts based on SQL databases was discussed in ref. [20].

An NT domain server involves not only shared databases but also shared administrative policies and shared security models. A host can subscribe to one or more domains and one domain can be associated with one another by a trust relationship. When one NT domain 'trusts' another, then accounts and groups defined in the *trusted* domain can be used in the *trusting* domain. NIS is indiscriminating in this respect. It is purely an authentication mechanism, implying no side-effects by the login procedure.

Other models of network computing include Kerberos and the Open Software Foundation's Distributed Computing Environment (DCE). The former is a service brokering system with a common authentication service (see section 12.4.6). The latter is a distributed user environment which can be used to provide a seamless world-wide distributed network domain. The DCE has been ported to both Unix and NT and requires a special login authentication after normal login to Unix/NT.

To summarize, rationalized user registration is a virtually unsupported problem in most operating systems. The needs of different organizations are varied and no successful solution to the problem has been devised and subsequently adopted as a standard. Networks are so common now that we have to think of the network first. Whether it happens today or tomorrow, at any given site, users will be moving around from host to host. They will need access to system resources wherever they are. It follows that they need distributed accounts. In creating a local solution, we have to bear in mind some basic constraints.

> **Principle 19 (Distributed accounts).** *Users move around from host to host, share data and collaborate. They need easy access to data and workstations all over an organization.*

Standardizing usernames across all platforms simplifies both the logistics of user management and opens the way for cross-platform compatibility. User names

longer than eight characters can cause problems with Unix-like systems and
FTP services. Users normally expect to be able to use the same password to log
onto any host and have access to the same data, except for hosts with special
purposes.

> **Suggestion 2 (Passwords).** *Give users a common username on all hosts, of no
> more than eight characters. Give them a common password on all hosts, unless
> there is a special reason not to do so. Some users never change their passwords
> unless forced to, and some users never even log in, so it is important to assign
> good passwords initially. Never assign a simple password and assume that it
> will be changed.*

Perl scripts are excellent ways of making user installation scripts which are
tailored to local needs. See ref. [211] for an excellent discussion of this on NT.
Interactive programs are almost useless since users are seldom installed one by
one. At universities hundreds of students are registered at the same time. No
system administrator would type in all the names by hand. More likely they would
be input from some administrative list generated by the admissions department.
The format of that list is not a universal standard, so no off-the-shelf software
package is going to help here.

Sites which run special environments, such as the Andrew File System (AFS),
the Distributed Computing Environment (DCE), Athena or Kerberos, often require
extra authentication servers and registration procedures [83, 315].

5.2.2   Unix accounts

To add a new user to a Unix-like host we have to:

- Find a unique username, user-id (uid) number and password for the new
  user.

- Update the system database of user accounts, e.g. add a line to the file
  /etc/passwd for Unix (or on the centralized password server of a network)
  for the new user.

- Create a login directory (home directory) for the user.

- Choose a shell for the user (if appropriate).

- Copy some configuration files like .cshrc or .profile into the new user's
  directory, or update the system registry.

Because every site is different, user registration requires different tools and
techniques in almost every case. For example: where should users' home directories be located? GNU/Linux has an adduser script which assumes that the
user will be installed on the local machine under /home/user, but many users
belong to a network and their disk space lies physically on a different host which
is mounted by NFS.

Unix developers have created three different password file formats which
increase the awkwardness of distributing passwords. The traditional password

file format is the following:

```
mark:Ax7Wc1Kd8ujo2:123:456:Mark Burgess:/home/mark:/bin/tcsh
```

The first field is a unique username (up to eight characters) for the user. The second is an encrypted form of the user's password; then comes the user-id (a unique number which represents the user and is equivalent to the username) and the default group-id (a unique number which represents the default group of users to which this user belongs). The fifth field is the so-called GECOS field, which is usually just the full name of the user. On some systems, comma-separated entries may be given for full name, office, extension and home phone number. The sixth field is the home directory for the user (the root directory for the user's private virtual machine). Finally the seventh field is the user's default shell. This is the command interpreter which is started when the user logs in.

Newer Unix-like systems make use of *shadow password files*, which conceal the encrypted form of the password for ordinary users. The format of the password file is then the same as above, except that the second password field contains only an 'x', e.g.:

```
mark:x:123:456:Mark Burgess:/home/mark:/bin/tcsh
```

There is then a corresponding line in /etc/shadow with the form

```
mark:Ax7Wc1Kd8ujo2:6445::::::
```

or with an MD5 password hash, on some systems. The shadow file is not readable by ordinary users. It contains many blank fields which are reserved for the special purpose of password aging and other expiry mechanisms. See the manual page for 'shadow' for a description of the fields. The only number present by default is the time at which the password was last changed, measured in the number of days since 1. Jan. 1970.

The third form of password file is used by the BSD 4.4 derived operating systems.

```
mark:Ax7Wc1Kd8ujo2:3232:25::0:0:Mark Burgess:/home/mark:/bin/tcsh
```

It has extra fields, which are not normally used. These systems also have an optimization: in addition to the master password file base, they have a compiled binary database for rapid lookup. Administrators edit the file /etc/master.password and then run the pwd_mkdb command to compile the database which is actually used for lookups. This generates text and binary versions of the password database.

Entries might have to be added to the group membership file /etc/group, E-mail system and quota database, depending on local requirements.

5.2.3 Windows accounts

Single Windows accounts are added with the command

```
net user  username password /ADD  /domain
```

or using the GUI. Windows does not provide any assistance for mass registration of users. The additional Resource Kit package contains tools which allow lists of users to be registered from a standard file format, with `addusers.exe`, but only at additional cost.

Windows users begin in the root directory by default. It is customary to create a `\users` directory for home directories. Network users conventionally have their home directory on the domain server mapped to the drive `H:`. There is only a single choice of shell (command interpreter) for NT, so this is not specified in the user registration procedure. Several possibilities exist for creating user profiles and access policies, depending on the management model used.

5.2.4 Groups of users

Both Unix and NT allow users to belong to multiple groups. A group is an association of usernames which can be referred to collectively by a single name. File and process permissions can be granted to a group of users. Groups are defined statically by the system administrator.

On Unix-like systems they are defined in the `/etc/group` file, like this:

```
users::100:user1,mark,user2,user3
```

The name of the group, in this case, is `users`, with group-id 100 and members user1, mark, user2 and user3. The second, empty field provides space for a password, but this facility is seldom used. A number of default groups are defined by the system, for instance

```
root::0:root
other::1:
bin::2:root,bin,daemon
```

The names and numbers of system groups vary with different flavors of Unix. The root group has superuser privileges.

Unix groups can be created for users or for software which runs under a special user-id. In addition to the names listed in the group file, a group also accrues users from the default group membership in field four of `/etc/passwd`. Thus, if the group file had the groups:

```
users::100:
msql::36:
ftp::99:
www::500:www
www-data::501:www,toreo,mark,geirs,sigmunds,mysql,ulfu,magnem
privwww::502:
```

and every user in `/etc/passwd` had the default group 100, then the `users` group would still contain every registered user on the system. By way of contrast, the group `ftp` contains no members at all, and is to be used only by a process which the system assigns that group identity, whereas `www-data` contains a specific named list and no others as long as all users have the default group 100.

NT also allows the creation of groups. Groups are created by command, rather than by file editing, using:

```
net group  groupname /ADD
```

Users may then be added with the syntax,

```
net group  groupname username1 username2... /ADD
```

They can also be edited with the GUI on a local host. NT distinguishes global groups (consisting only of domain registered users) from local groups, which may also contain locally registered users. Some standard groups are defined by the system, e.g.

```
Administrators
Users
Guest
```

The Administrators group has privileged access to the system.

5.3   Account policy

Most organizations need a strict policy for assigning accounts and opening the system for users. Users *are* the foremost danger to a computing system, so the responsibility of owning an account should not be dealt out lightly. There are many ways in which accounts can be abused. Users can misuse accounts for villainous purposes and they can abuse the terms on which the account was issued, wasting resources on personal endeavors. For example, in Norway, where education is essentially free, students have been known to undergo semester registration simply to have an account, giving them essentially free access to the Internet and a place to host their web sites.

Policy rules are required for guiding user behavior, and also for making system rules clear.

Experience indicates that simple rules are always preferable, though this is so far unsubstantiated by any specific studies. A complex and highly specific rule, that is understood only by its author, may seem smart, but most users will immediately write it off as being nonsense. Such a rule is ill advised because it is opaque. The reason for the rule is not clear to all parties, and thus it is unlikely to be respected.

> **Principle 20 (Simplest is best).** *Simple rules make system behavior easy to understand. Users tolerate rules if they understand them and this tends to increase their behavioral predictability.*

What should an account policy contain?

1. Rules about what users are allowed/not allowed to do.

2. Specifications of what mandatory enforcement users can expect, e.g. tidying of garbage files.

Any account policy should contain a clause about weak passwords. If weak passwords are discovered, it must be understood by users that their account can be closed immediately. Users need to understand that this is a necessary security initiative. Closing Unix accounts can be achieved simply by changing their default shell in /etc/passwd to a script such as

```
#!/bin/sh

echo "/local/bin/blocked.passwd was run" | mail sysadm
/usr/bin/last -10   | mail sysadm

message='
Your account has been closed because your password was found to
be vulnerable to attack. To reopen your account, visit the
admin office, carrying some form of personal identification.
'
echo "$message"

sleep 10
exit 0
```

Although this does not prevent them from doing simple things on an X-windows console running a login manager, like xdm, it does prevent them from logging in remotely, and it gets their attention. A more secure method is to simply replace their encrypted password with NP or *, which prevents them from being authenticated.

It is occasionally tempting to create guest accounts for visitors and transient users. NT has a ready-made guest account, which is not disabled by default on some versions of NT. Guest accounts are a bad idea, because they can be used long after a visitor has gone, they usually have weak or non-existent passwords and therefore are an open invitation to attack the system. Shared accounts are also a bad idea, since they are inherently more fragile from a security perspective, though the use of shared Unix accounts, in which users could not log in as a shared user, are described in ref. [32]. This is similar to the ability in Unix to set a password on a group.

5.4 Login environment

When a new user logs in for the first time, he or she expects the new account to work straight away. Printing should work, programs should work and there should be no strange error messages about files not being found or programs not existing. Most users want to start up a window environment. If users will be able to log on to many different kinds of operating system, we have to balance the desire to make systems look alike, with the need to distinguish between different environments. Users need to understand the nature of their work environment at all times in order to avoid hapless errors. The creation of default login environments has been discussed in refs. [288, 15, 326] though these are now somewhat out of date.

5.4.1 Unix environment

Unix and its descendents have always been about the ability to customize. Everything in Unix is configurable, and advanced users like to play around; many create their own setups, but many users simply want basics. The use of multitudinous 'dot' files for setting defaults in Unix has led to its being criticized for a lack of user-friendliness. Various attempts have been made to provide interfaces which simplify the task of editing these configuration files [125, 99], though the real problem is not so much the fact that one has to edit files, as the fact that every file has its own syntax. A system administrator has to ensure that everything works properly with acceptable defaults, right from the start. Here is a simple checklist for configuring a user environment. Gradually, the appearance of newer and better user interfaces like KDE and GNOME is removing the need for users to edit their own window configuration files.

- `.cshrc` If the default shell for users is a C-shell or derivative, then we need to supply a default 'read commands' file for this shell. This should set a path which searches for commands, a terminal type and any environment variables that a local system requires.

- `.profile` or `.bashrc` If the default shell is a Bourne-again shell like `bash` or `ksh`, then we need to supply this file to set a `PATH` variable, terminal type and environment variables that the system requires.

- `.xsession` This file is read by the Unix `xdm` login service. It specifies what windows and what window manager will be used when the X-windows system is started. The file is a shell script which should begin by setting up applications in the background (with a `&` symbol after them) and end up `exec`-ing a window manager in the foreground. If the window manager is called as a background process, the script will be able to exit immediately and users will be logged out immediately. Some systems use the file called `.xinitrc` though this file is officially obsolete. The official way to start the X11 window system is through the `xdm` program, which provides a login prompt window. GNU/Linux seems to have revived the use of the obsolete command `startx` which starts the X-windows system from a tty-shell. The older `startx` system used the `.xinitrc` file, whereas `xdm` uses `.xsession`. Most GNU/Linuxes hack this so that one only needs a `.xsession` file.

- `.mwmrc` This file configures the default menus etc. for the `mwm` window manager and the Common Desktop Environment (CDE) window manager, IIRC

A shell setup should define a terminal type, a default prompt and appropriate environment variables, especially a command path.

> **Suggestion 3 (Environment).** *It should always be clear to users which host they are using and what operating system they are working with. Default environments should be kept simple, both in appearance (prompts etc.) and in functionality (specially programmed keys etc.). Simple environments are easy to understand.*

We need to aim a default environment at an average user and ensure that basic operating system functions work unambiguously. The visual clarity of a work environment is particularly important. In a windowing environment, this is usually not a problem. Command shells require some extra thought, however. A command shell can, in principle, be opened on any Unix-like host. A user with many windows open, each with a shell running on a different host, could easily become confused. Suppose we wish to copy a newer version of a file on one host to a repository on another host. If we mix the hosts up, we could risk over-writing the new version with an old version, instead of the other way around.

> **Suggestion 4 (Clear prompts).** *Try to give users a command prompt which includes the name of the host they are working on. This is important, since different hosts might have different operating systems, or different files. Including the current directory in the prompt, like DOS, is not always a good idea. It uses up half the width of the terminal and can seem confusing. If users want the name of the current directory in the prompt, let them choose that. Don't assign it as a default.*

Some systems offer global shell configuration files which are read for every user. These files are usually located in /etc or /etc/default. The idea of a global default file has attractive features in principle, but it is problematic in practice. The problem has to do with the separation of local modifications from the operating system, and also the standardization of defaults across all hosts. These files could be distributed from a central source to every host, but a better approach is to simply place an equivalent defaults file on the same distributed filesystems which contain users' home directories. This is easily achieved by simply ignoring the global defaults, and giving every user a default shell configuration file which reads a site-dependent file instead.

> **Suggestion 5 (Unix shell defaults).** *Avoid host-wide files for shell setup in /etc. They are mixed up in the operating system distribution and changes here will be lost at upgrade time. Use an overridable include strategy in the user's own shell setup to read in global defaults. Do not link a file on a different filesystem to these in case this causes problems during system boot-up.*

Here is an example of a configuration file for the C-shell, which would be installed for all users in their home directories:

```
#
# cshrc file (for tcsh)
#

source ../.setupfiles/cshrc-global

#
# Place own definitions below
#
```

```
alias f  finger
alias ed emacs
```

Note that we use the `source` directive to read in a file of global C-shell definitions which we have copied into place from a central repository for all important system master files. Notice also that, by copying this onto the same filesystem as the home directory itself (the directory over the user's home directory), we make sure that the file is always NFS exported to all hosts together with the home directory. This allows us to change the global setup for everyone at the same time, or separately for different classes of user on different partitions. For each separate home partition, we could have a different set of defaults. This is probably not recommended however, unless users are distinguished in some important way.

One of the functions of a local shell configuration is to set up a command path and a library path for software. Since the command path is searched in order, we can override operating system commands with local solutions, simply by placing site-dependent binaries at the start of the path. GNU file utilities and binary utilities can also be placed ahead of operating system standard utilities. They are often more standard and more functional.

5.4.2 Example shell configuration

Here is an example shell configuration for the `tcsh`.

```
#!/bin/csh -f
##############################################################
#
# C Shell startup file
# System Wide Version.
#
##############################################################

umask 077  # default privacy on new files

setenv HOSTTYPE `uname`

##############################################################

switch ($HOSTTYPE)

  case SunOS:
     set path = (                 \
                /local/site/bin    \
                /local/kde/bin     \
                /local/gnu/bin     \
                /usr/ccs/bin       \
                /local/jdk1.1.6/bin \
                /local/bin         \
                /local/qt/bin      \
                /usr/ucb           \
                /bin               \
                /usr/bin           \
                /usr/openwin/bin   \
                .                  \
                )
           breaksw

  case Linux:
     set path  = (                \
                /local/site/bin    \
                /local/bin         \
```

```
                   /local/jdk1.1.6/bin  \
                   /local/bin/X11       \
                   /local/qt/bin        \
                   /local/kde/bin       \
                   /local/gnu/bin       \
                   /local/bin/X11       \
                   /usr/bin/X11         \
                   /usr/bin             \
                   /bin                 \
                   .                    \
                   )
              breaksw

endsw

##############################################################################

  #
  #   set TERM for "at" batches in non-interactive shells
  #   tcsh wants to write something to stdout, but I
  #   can't see what => term has to be set even though its
  #   irrelevant )
  #

if (! $?TERM) setenv TERM vt100;
if (! $?term) set term = vt100;
if (! $?prompt) exit 0;

  #
  # End for non-interactive shells (batch etc.)
  #

setenv TERM vt100  # Many shell types do not work
set term = $TERM   # This is a safe default, omit it if you dare

##############################################################################
# set
##############################################################################

set history=100 savehist=100
set prompt = "`hostname`% "
set prompt2 = "%m %h> "
set fignore = (.o \~ .BAK .out \%)

##############################################################################
# Common Environment
##############################################################################

setenv EDITOR      emacs
setenv ESHELL      tcsh
setenv NNTPSERVER  nntp-server.domain.country
setenv QTDIR       /usr/local/qt
setenv CLASSPATH   /usr/local/jdk1.1.6/lib/classes.zip:.
setenv JAVA_HOME   /usr/local/jdk1.1.6
setenv MYSQL       /usr/local/bin/mysql

##############################################################################
# platform specific environment (overrides common)
##############################################################################

switch ($HOSTTYPE)

   #############

   case SunOS*:
   case solaris:
      setenv LD_LIBRARY_PATH /usr/openwin/lib:/local/lib/X11:\
/local/gnu/lib:/usr/dt/lib:/local/qt/lib:/local/lib:/usr/local/kde/lib

      setenv LPATH /usr/lib:/local/lib:
```

```
        if ( $?DISPLAY || $TERM == "sun" ) then
            setenv MOTIFHOME /usr/dt
            setenv X11HOME /usr/openwin
            setenv FONTPATH  /usr/openwin/lib/X11/fonts:\
/usr/openwin/lib/locale/iso_8859_5/X11/fonts:\
/usr/openwin/share/src/fonts:/usr/openwin/lib/X11/fonts:\
/local/sdt/sdt/fonts/SDT3/X11

            setenv OPENWINHOME /usr/openwin
            setenv XKEYSYMDB /local/site/X11/XKeysymDB
            setenv XAPPLRESDIR /usr/openwin/lib/X11/app-defaults
            setenv GS_FONTPATH /local/share/ghostscript/fonts
            setenv GS_LIB_PATH /local/share/ghostscript/4.03
            endif

            setenv MANPATH /local/gnu/man:/usr/man:/local/man:\
/usr/openwin/share/man

        limit coredumpsize 0
        breaksw

    #############

    case Linux:
    case i486:
            setenv MANPATH /local/man:/local/site/man:/local/man:\
/usr/man:/usr/man:/usr/man/preformat:/usr/X11/man
            setenv XAPPLRESDIR /local/site/X11/app-defaults:\
/var/X11R6/lib/app-defaults
            stty erase '^?' intr '^C' kill '^U' susp '^Z'
            setenv LD_LIBRARY_PATH /usr/X11R6/lib:/local/lib:\
/local/qt/lib:/local/kde/lib
            setenv XNLSPATH /usr/X11R6/lib/X11/nls
        breaksw
endsw


#############################################################################
# aliases
#############################################################################

alias del        'rm -i '
alias dir        'ls -lg \!* | less -E'
alias .          'echo $cwd'
alias f finger
alias h history
alias go a.out
alias cd.. cd ..
alias grant setfacl
alias cacls getfacl
alias rlogin ssh
alias rsh ssh

#############################################################################
#
# Check message of the day
#
#############################################################################

  # Not always necessary

if ( -f /etc/motd ) then
    /bin/cat /etc/motd
endif

#############################################################################
#
# Check whether user has a vacation file
#
#############################################################################
```

```
if ( -f ~/.forward ) then

    if ( "`grep vacation ~/.forward`" != "" ) then

        echo '*********************************************************'
        echo '            YOU ARE RUNNING THE vacation SERVICE          '
        echo '             RUN vacation AGAIN TO CANCEL IT !            '
        echo '*********************************************************'

    endif

endif
```

5.4.3 The privileged account's or superuser's environment

What kind of user environment should the superuser have? As we know, a privileged account has potentially dangerous consequences for the system. From this account, we have the power to destroy the system, or sabotage it. In short, the superuser's account should be configured to avoid as many casual mistakes as possible.

There is no harm in giving Unix's root account an intelligent shell like tcsh or bash provided that shell is physically stored on the root partition. When a Unix system boots, only the root partition is mounted. If we reference a shell which is not available, we can render the host unbootable.

The superuser's PATH variable should never include '.', i.e. the current directory. This is because it opens the system to a type of security vulnerability that can lead to accidental execution of the wrong command. For instance, suppose an ordinary user left a file called ls in the /tmp directory, and suppose the root account had the path

```
setenv PATH .:/bin:/usr/bin
```

If the superuser does the following

```
host# cd /tmp
host# ls
```

then, because the path search looks in the current directory first, it would find and execute the program which had been left by the user. That program then gets executed with root privileges and could be used to give the user concerned permanent privileged access to the system, for instance by installing a special account for the user which has root privileges. It should be clear that this is a security hazard.

A common mistake that is frequently perpetrated by inexperienced administrators, and which is actually encouraged by some operating systems, is to run X11 applications with root privileges. Root should never run X11 or any other complex applications. There are just too many uncertainties involved. There are so many applications for X11 which come from different sources. There could be a Trojan horse in any one of them. If possible, root should only use a few trusted application programs.

The privileged user should never log in directly (unless the system is in single user mode or on the console). On Unix, one should log in as a user and su to root.

This keeps a record of who is root at any time, and is more secure in the sense of having fewer points of attack.

The privileged user should have a minimal environment, should not read or reply to its own E-mail (this should be sent to a system administration group), and should never log in over an unencrypted channel.

5.5 User support services

All users require help at some time or another. The fact that normal users are not *privileged users* means that they must occasionally rely on a superuser to clean up a mess, or fix a problem which is beyond their control. If we are to distinguish between privileged and non-privileged users, we cannot deny users this service.

5.5.1 Support policy

The amount of support that one offers users is a matter of policy. One has the choice between supporting users directly, and investing time in making them self-sufficient. Which of these two strategies pays most dividends depends on the nature of the problem. In almost all cases both strategies are needed. Thus one looks for a mixture of the following:

- Training users.

- Helping users.

- Documenting and providing the answers to frequently asked questions.

The proportion of time spent on each must be chosen as policy.

System administrators' time is usually in short supply, though increased automation is steadily freeing us to concentrate on higher level problems, like support. The ability to support a system depends on its size in relation to the available resource personnel. Supporting hardware and software means fixing errors, upgrading and perhaps providing tuition or telephone help-desks. E-mail help-desks such as Rust, Gnats, Nearnet, Netlog, PTS, QueueMH can assist in the organization of support services, but they are mainly task-tracking tools. Sometimes hosts and software packages are labelled *unsupported* in order to emphasize to users that they are on their own if they insist on using those facilities.

One of the challenges system administrators sometimes have to endure on coming to a new site, where chaos reigns, is the transition from anarchy to a smaller set of supported platforms and software. See for instance, refs. [226, 182]. This can be a tough problem, since users always prefer freedom to restriction. Support services need to be carefully considered and tailored to each local environment.

A recent development in user assistance is the Virtual Network Computing model from AT&T [24]. This is a way to allow a remote user duplicate access to a graphical user interface. Thus an administrator can log onto an existing user session and have dual controls, allowing users to be nurse-maided through difficulties online.

5.5.2 Checklist

The provision of a service to users suggests the need for quality controls. This goes back to the central principle of predictability in management: a controlled and verified result allows one to have confidence in the effectiveness of the procedure and thus the long-term stability of the human–computer system. We shall return to the issue of quality control in a more formal setting in section 8.12.1.

Checklists are a useful algorithmic aid to securing predictable results. The basic checklist for user services is this:

1. Read the user request properly.

2. Do you understand the request?

3. Is the request in line with policy?

4. Are you competent to deal with the request?

5. Schedule the request (rapid response mitigates frustration).

Limoncelli has defined a model to promote standardization of user assistance, in what he calls the Nine Step Model [197]. This is a way of regularizing the interaction between user and help-desk in order to promote predictability in the process and quality control of the result (see table 5.1).

Greeting
1. Greeting 'How may I help you?'
Problem identification
2. Identify problem
3. Refine and express the problem
4. Verify the problem
Correction
5. Propose solutions
6. Select solution
7. Execution
Verification
8. Self-check
9. User-check

Table 5.1: The nine steps in Limoncelli's model of user assistance. The all-important greeting should not be forgotten as one launches into a technical procedure.

The Nine Step Model is actually a straightforward example of a development cycle: problem identification, solution, verification. It is not unlike procedures one might use in software engineering to create a computer program. The main difference is an attention to the social graces: users appreciate being noticed and taken seriously (hence the greeting), and they also appreciate an explanation of what is going on during the assistance. Some administrators are good at talking users through their logical analysis, while others tend to keep their thoughts to themselves. Human users generally appreciate being included in the procedures.

5.6 Controlling user resources

Every system has a mixture of passive and active users.

Passive users utilize the system often minimally, quietly accepting the choices which have been made for them. They seldom place great demands on the system. They do not follow the development of the system with any zeal and they are often not even aware of what files they have. They seldom make demands other than when things go wrong. Passive users can be a security risk, because they are not aware of their actions.

Active users, on the other hand, follow every detail of system development. They frequently find every error in the system and contact system administrators frequently, demanding upgrades of their favorite programs. Active users can be of great help to a system administrator, because they test out problems and report them actively. They are an important part of the system administration team, or community, and can also go a long way to helping the passive users. An important point about active users, however, is that they are not authorized staff.

> **Principle 21 (Active users).** *Active users need to understand that, while their skills are appreciated, they do not decide system policy: they must obey it. Even in a democracy, rules are determined by process and then obeyed by everyone.*

Skilled administrators need to be social engineers, placating active user wishes and keeping them in the loop, without bowing to their every whim. Individual skill amongst users does not necessarily carry with it responsibility to the whole system. System administrators have a responsibility to find a balance which addresses users' needs but which keeps the system stable and functional. If we upgrade software too often, users will be annoyed. New versions of software function differently and this can hinder people in their work. If we do not upgrade often enough, we can also hinder work by restricting possibilities.

5.6.1 Resource consumption

Disks fill up at an alarming rate. Users almost never throw away files unless they have to. If one is lucky enough to have only very experienced and extremely friendly users on the system, then one can try asking them nicely to tidy up their files. Most administrators do not have this luxury however. Most users never think about the trouble they might cause others by keeping lots of junk around. After all, multi-user systems and network servers are designed to give every user the impression that they have their own private machine. Of course, some users are problematical by nature.

> **Suggestion 6 (Problem users).** *Keep a separate partition for problem users' home directories, or enforce strict quotas on them.*

No matter what we do to fight the fire, users still keep feeding the flames. To keep hosts working it is necessary to remove files, not just add them. Quotas limit the amount of disk space users can have access to, but this does not solve the real problem. The real problem is that in the course of using a computer many files are created as temporary data but are never deleted afterwards. The solution is to delete them.

- Some files are temporary by definition. For example, the byproducts of compilation, `*.o` files, files which can easily be regenerated from source like TeX `*.dvi` files, cache files in `.netscape/` loaded in by Netscape's browser program etc.

- Some files can be defined as temporary as a matter of policy. For example, files which users collect for personal pleasure like `*.mp3`, video formats and pornography.

When a Unix program crashes, the kernel dumps its image to disk in a file called `core`. These files crop up all over the place and have no useful purpose for most users.[1] To most users they are just fluff on the upholstery and should be removed. A lot of free disk space can be reclaimed by deleting these files. Many users will not delete them themselves, however, because they do not even understand why they are there.

Disk quotas mean that users have a hard limit to the number of bytes they are allowed to use on the disk. They are an example of a more general concept known as system accounting whereby you can control the resources used by any user, whether they be the number of printed pages sent to the printer or the number of bytes written to the disk. Disk quotas have advantages and disadvantages.

- The advantage is that users really cannot exceed their limits. There is no way around this.

- Disk quotas are very restrictive and when a user exceeds their limit they often do not understand what has happened. Usually users do not even get a message unless they are logging in. Quotas also prevent users from creating large temporary files which can be a problem when compiling programs. They carry with them a system overhead, which makes everything run a little slower.

In some environments, the idea of deleting a user's files is too much to contemplate. In a company or research laboratory, one might want to be extremely careful in

---

[1]In some instances, core files have been used by malicious users to obtain secret information about the system that was held in memory prior to the crash.

such a practice. In other cases, like schools and universities, this is pure necessity. Deciding whether to delete files automatically must be a policy decision. It might be deemed totalitarian to delete files without asking. On the other hand, this is often the only way to ever clear anything up. Many users will be happy if they do not have to think about the problem themselves. A tidy policy, rather than a quota policy, gives users a greater illusion of freedom, which is good for system morale. We must naturally be careful never to delete files which cannot be regenerated or re-acquired if necessary. File tidying was first suggested by Zwicky in ref. [336], within a framework of quotas. See also refs. [134, 55].

Example 2. *A useful strategy is to delete files one is not sure about only if they have not been* accessed *for a certain period of time, say a week. This allows users to use files freely as long as they need to, but prevents them from keeping the files around for ever. Cfengine can be used to perform this task.*

For example a simple cfengine program would look like:

```
control:

  actionsequence = ( tidy )

  mountpattern = ( /site/host )
  homepattern = ( home? )

 #
 # 3 days minimum, remember weekends
 #

tidy:

      home                pattern=core   recurse=inf age=0
      home                pattern=a.out recurse=inf age=3
      home                pattern=*%     recurse=inf age=3
      home                pattern=*~     recurse=inf age=3
      home                pattern=*.o    recurse=inf age=1
      home                pattern=*.aux recurse=inf age=3
      home                pattern=*.mp3 recurse=inf age=14

      home/Desktop/Trash   pattern=*      recurse=inf age=14
      home/.netscape/cache pattern=*      recurse=inf age=0
```

This script iterates automatically over all users' home directories, and recurses into them, deleting files if the time since they were last accessed exceeds the time limits specified.

Care should always be taken in searching for and deleting patterns containing 'core'. Some operating systems keep directories called core, while others have files called `core.h`. As long as the files are plain files with an exact name match, one is usually safe.

5.6.2 Quotas and limits in general

In a shared environment, all users share the same machine resources. If one user is selfish that affects all of the other users. Given the opportunity, users will consume all of the disk space and all of the memory and CPU cycles somehow, whether through greed or simply through inexperience. Thus it is in the interests of the *user community* to limit the ability of users to spoil things for other users.

One way of protecting operating systems from users and from faulty software is to place quotas on the amount of system resources which they are allowed.

- *Disk quotas:* Place fixed limits on the amount of disk space which can be used per user. The advantage of this is that the user cannot use more storage than this limit; the disadvantage is that many software systems need to generate/cache large temporary files (e.g. compilers, or web browsers) and a fixed limit means that these systems will fail to work as a user approaches his/her quota.

- *CPU time limit:* Some faulty software packages leave processes running which consume valuable CPU cycles to no purpose. Users of multiuser computer systems occasionally steal CPU time by running huge programs which make the system unusable for others. The C-shell `limit cputime` function can be globally configured to help prevent accidents.

- *Policy decisions:* Users collect garbage. To limit the amount of it, one can specify a system policy which includes items of the form: 'Users may not have mp3, wav, mpeg etc. files on the system for more than one day'.

Quotas have an unpleasant effect on system morale, since they restrict personal freedom. They should probably only be used as a last resort. There are other ways of controlling the build-up of garbage.

> **Principle 22 (Freedom).** *Quotas, limits and restrictions tend to antagonize users. Users place a high value on personal freedom. Restrictions should be minimized or made inconspicuous to avoid a backlash. Workaround solutions which avoid rigid limits are preferable, if possible.*

5.6.3 Killing old processes

Processes sometimes do not get terminated when they should. There are several reasons for this. Sometimes users forget to log out, sometimes poorly written terminal software does not properly kill its processes when a user logs out. Sometimes background programs simply crash or go into loops from which they never return. One way to clean up processes in a work environment is to look for user processes which have run for more than a day. (Note that the assumption here is that everyone is supposed to log out each day and then log in again the next day – that is not always the case.) Cfengine can also be used to clean up old processes. Cfengine's processes commands are used to match processes in the process table (which can be seen by running `ps ax` on Unix).

5.6.4 Moving users

When disk partitions become full, it is necessary to move users from old partitions to new ones.[2] Moving users is a straightforward operation, but it should be done with some caution. A user who is being moved should not be logged in while the move is taking place, or files could be copied incorrectly. We begin by looking for an appropriate user, perhaps one who has used a particularly large amount of disk space.

Example 3. *On Unix-like systems we have all the tools we require:*

```
cd /site/host/home-old
du -s *
```

Having chosen a user, with username user, *we copy the directory to its new location,*

```
tar cf - user | (cd /site/host/home-new; tar xpvf - )
```

edit the new location in the password file,

```
emacs /etc/passwd
```

and finally remove the old data:

```
rm -r user
```

Users need to be informed about the move: we have to remember that they might hard-code the names of their home directories in scripts and programs, e.g. CGI-scripts. Also, the user's account must be closed by altering their login shell, for instance, before the files are moved.

5.6.5 Deleting old users

Users who leave an organization eventually need to be deleted from the system. For the sake of certainty, it is often advisable to keep old accounts for a time in case the user actually returns, or wishes to transfer data to a new location. Whether or not this is acceptable must be a question of policy. Clearly it would be unacceptable for company secrets to be transferred to a new location. Before deleting a user completely, a backup of the data can be made for safe-keeping. Then we have to remove the following:

- Account entry from the password database.

- Personal files.

- E-mail and voice mail and mailing lists.

- Removal from groups and lists (e.g. mailing lists).

- Removal of cron and batch tasks.

- Revocation of smartcards and electronic ID codes.

---

[2]Some systems might be equipped with virtual volume managers which provide the illusion of infinitely large partitions, but not everyone can afford this luxury.

5.7   Online user services

There are many instances of using the World Wide Web to provide online registration of data, for instance, as colleges and universities modernize, they are increasingly looking for ways to make use of information technology to simplify the administration of examinations. This presents a somewhat different set of logistical problems than with traditional examinations. It requires users to be managed in a potentially different way for part of the time – during the examination.

In this section, we shall consider the specific example of online examinations, for the sake of concreteness. The idea can be generalized or adapted to apply to other services (see exercises).

We are interested in achieving a number of goals with an online system:

- To cope with large numbers of users (e.g. students),

- To allow more general examination methods (continuous assessment etc.),

- To prevent unnecessary copying, or 'cheating', amongst the students,

- To move the bulk of the burden from grading work to pedagogical design,

- To provide an online (distributed) solution, which solves the most pressing security problems adequately.

These are significant challenges at present, since current online technologies are not well standardized in a way that is ideally suited to this task. Until some dedicated software is available for this purpose, it is a task for system administration to make interim solutions possible.

5.7.1   Security perspective

Security is the discipline of protecting *interests* and things of *value*. Student evaluation is a security problem at several levels. Security spans a number of issues: reliability, integrity, privacy, authenticity and – the heart of every security problem – how far one is willing to *trust* the parts of a system.

Figure 5.1 shows the beginnings of a (potentially very large) 'cause tree' for traditional examination failure; it illustrates a point which many teachers take for granted about the evaluation of students – namely, that any system in which points are awarded, or students receive some kind of reward (payoff), is subject to attack by malicious or incidental factors. Let us mention a few of the ways in which the tenets of security apply to the evaluation process.

- **Trust:** The fundamental issue in any security system is where one places one's trust; it is about deciding what is an acceptable risk. For example, staff might trust students never to cheat. If that is the case, security is very simple. On the other hand, staff might only trust students not to cheat in a supervised room (with an exam invigilator present). Conversely, students might not trust the course teacher to grade their papers correctly, or to give them a fair hearing; in that case, a quality control protocol can be implemented to offer a level of security to the students.

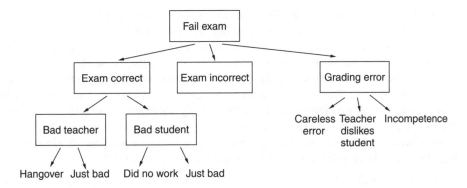

Figure 5.1: A partial cause tree for examination failure.

In each case, what we are willing to trust guides the security measures which need to be implemented. At no point is any system infallible. If one assumes that students and staff are hostile partners, the worst case would be that both sides would engage in an arms race, each trying to outsmart the other. In practice, only a small fraction of staff and students behaves in this manner, but nevertheless, this is a problem which must be taken seriously, at some level.

- **Reliability:** The reliability of the examination procedure must be secured against both malicious exploitation and accidental error. In an alternative evaluation scheme, it is natural to eliminate humans from the grading process as far as possible. If a machine can be made to perform the grading, then clearly the only source of error would be a systematic error, perhaps from an error in programming of the system itself. Such an error would not prejudice any one student, and could be corrected in time.

- **Integrity:** Integrity concerns the ability to transmit information, or intent, without alteration or error. Integrity of evaluation information applies both to the problems posed to students and in the collection of their replies. With Web-based technologies, this can be a problem unless students are using standardized browsers and operating systems. The disturbing lack of standardization in browser technology means that not all data can be rendered in any browser. Moreover, early Netscape browsers crash often, and Internet Explorer fails to show HTTPS secured pages a significant percentage of the time with an unspecific 'Page cannot be shown' error.

- **Authenticity and identity:** Students need to trust the authenticity of the exam paper, or the problems they are to answer. It would be unacceptable for a malicious party to replace the actual exam with a fake exam, or an exam to which the students already had the written solutions. Similarly, the examiners need to know that the student whose name is on the resulting work, actually did that work. Copying from one another without learning is one way in which students can attack examination and evaluation systems, and undermine the purpose of the educational establishment.

Correctly identifying the author of an examination paper is a subtle task. In the security sense, one can visually inspect the student ID of a student who shows up for an examination (though ID can be forged). Similarly, one can forge electronic credentials relatively easily. In spite of the dangers to themselves, students regularly swap passwords and loan accounts to their classmates. Thus, when an assignment is submitted without physical supervision (e.g. electronically), there is no guarantee that the person whose name is registered by the receiver is the author of the work. In a written examination, students regularly memorize passages and methods written by others – it just requires a little more concentration to achieve.

The act of confirming one's identity by use of a secret password or other means is called *authentication*.

• **Privacy:** Finally, can the process of evaluation be conducted with sufficient respect for individual privacy? The teacher's privacy is needed to prevent students from cheating by finding the solutions or by gaining knowledge of the problems in advance, and the student's privacy is needed to prevent their identities from compromising the objectivity (reliability) of the process.

Discussing student evaluation in terms of information security is perhaps an unusual point of view, but it is not one to be dismissed lightly. The validity of the university's conclusions about a student's performance is precisely what is at stake, both for its reputation and for society at large.

5.7.2 Reconfiguring hosts for electronic exams

Imperial College in London has devised an administrative scheme called Lexis for conducting examinations using specially secured computers [330]. The college chose the GNU/Linux operating system for this purpose and used a separate run-level to configure hosts at startup in a secure environment.

Lexis was designed specifically with programming examinations in mind. It seeks to provide a familiar lab-like environment during exams, with all resources necessary to complete the exam, including a secure environment and means of collecting exam answers. Students should have no access to unauthorized data, no access to other users on the network, and not be distracted by other users or signals from the network.

A similar approach has been examined at Oslo University College, using cfengine to reconfigure computers temporarily.

5.7.3 User identification

At a university, students come and go and login names can be reused over time. This has potential consequences for the long-term storage and identification of student results online. The use of student numbers or personal identification numbers has been used here in Oslo, since these are unique even over long periods of time.

How should students and their answers be identified during the examination? The use of usernames and passwords to authenticate users seemed to be the best compromise. The use of digital signatures might also be considered; however, digital signing is deemed too complicated for non-computer science users – even computer science students who were studying security found signatures to be confusing. Also, there is a significant administrative overhead involved in setting up and maintaining signatures in a student environment, where login names and accounts are frequently appearing and disappearing.

The issue of confirming student identity online is called authentication. It works by challenging the user to provide knowledge of some password or private secret which they would not normally divulge to anyone else. This is the most difficult and pressing issue in online services. Students are not afraid to swap passwords to college accounts, because they often have private accounts elsewhere (Hotmail or home accounts etc.), and thus regard their college accounts as 'disposable'. As long as students are not afraid to lend their secrets to others, there will be no unique way of identifying them, and thus of being certain that they are responsible for their own grades.

5.8 User well-being

Because computer systems are communities, populated by real people, there are issues in system administration which are directly connected with users' well-being. Contented users work well and treat the system well; disgruntled users cause trouble for the system and for their neighbors. This is not to say that system administrators are (or should be) responsible for the psychological well-being of all the system's users, but there are some simple precautions which the system staff can observe in order to promote the smooth running of the community. In some countries, an organization might be sued by a user who believed he or she had not been sufficiently looked after.

5.8.1 Health

Frequent computer users are not usually aware of how they can be damaging their own health. Unlike cigarettes, computers do not have a government health warning. Whether or not this is an issue for system administrators is open for discussion, but often the system administrator is the only person who thinks about the users and the hardware they use. Certainly every administrator needs to look after his/her own health and, along the way, it is natural to think of the health of others. Fortunately it is not difficult to avoid the worst problems.

- *Eyes* should be protected, We only have one pair and they must last our entire lives. Ironically, users who wear glasses (not contact lenses) suffer less from computer usage, because their eyes are partially protected from the radiation from the screen.

  A computer screen works by shooting charged electrons at a phosphorescent surface. If one touches the screen one notices that it is charged with static electricity. The effect of this is to charge dust particles and throw them out into users' faces. This can cause irritation to the eyes over long periods. Solution: wear glasses or obtain an anti-static screen with an earth wire which counteracts this problem.

Another major cause of eye strain is reflection. If there is a light source behind a user, it will reflect in the screen and the eyes will be distracted by the reflection. The image on the screen lies on the screen surface, any reflected images lie behind the screen (as far behind the screen as the source is in front of the screen). This confuses the eyes into focusing back and forth between the reflection and the image. The result is eye strain. The solution is to (i) eliminate all light sources which can cause reflections, (ii) obtain an anti-reflective screen cover. This can be combined with an anti-static screen. The best solution today, however, is to purchase only good LCD flat screens; these have sharp clear pictures, low radiation and are usually coated in anti-glare plastic. They are a giant leap forward in screen technology.

Prolonged eye strain can lead to problems reading and focusing. It can lead to headaches and neck ache from squinting.

- *Back*: The back (spine) is one of the most complex and important parts of the body. It supports the upper body and head, and is attached to the brain (where applicable). The upper body is held up by muscles in the stomach and lower back. If these muscles are relaxed by slouching for long periods, unnecessary strain is placed on muscles and bones which were not meant to bear the weight of the body.

  To avoid back problems, users should (i) sit in a good chair, (ii) sit upright, using those all-important flat tummy muscles and lower back muscles to support the upper body. They should not sit in a draft. Cold air blowing across the back and neck causes stiffness and tension.

- *Mouse strain*: Mouse strain is a strain in the tendons of the finger and forearm, which spreads to the shoulder and back and can be quite painful. It comes from using the mouse too much. The symptoms can be lessened by making sure that users do not sit too far away from the desk where the mouse lies and by having a support for the mouse forearm. The ultimate solution is simple: don't use the mouse. Use of the keyboard is far less hazardous. Learning keyboard shortcuts is good for prolonged work.

- *Pregnancy and cancer*: Some studies recommend that pregnant women wear protective aprons when sitting in front of computer screens. It is unclear whether this has any real purpose, since any radiation from the screen would be easily stopped by normal clothing.

- *Generally*: Users should not sit for long periods without taking a break. Looking away from the screen (to a far away object) at regular intervals relaxes the eyes. Walking around exercises the back and relaxes the shoulders. Use of anti-static, anti-reflective screens is recommended.

5.8.2 Dealing with users: etiquette

Although even the most stoical administrator's convictions might occasionally be called into question, system administration is a social service and it is important to remain calm and reasonable. Users frequently believe that the system administrator has nothing better to do than to answer every question and execute every whim and fancy. Dealing with users is not a small task. In ref. [172], user-friendly administrators are likened to user-friendly software!

5.8.3 Cultural and age groups

Today, network communities, linked by an ever-increasing number of Internet Service Providers, consist of all cultures and age groups. It is a basic fact of life that different groups have different attitudes and concerns and that they behave differently towards one another and amongst themselves. In the anonymous world of electronic communication, age is not usually apparent except through behavior. While as pre-teenagers we tend to be careful and polite, as teenagers we are often rude and arrogant. The same applies to different cultures.

The art of communication between groups is a difficult one. The way in which age groups use computers, reflects their interests and attitudes and we have to consider this in relation to the rules and policies for use of a computer system.

One must separate recreational use from professional use and consider to what extent recreational use could damage an organization professionally. It is not uncommon to see employees sign their E-mail with a phrase of the form

The opinions expressed here are purely my own, and should not be identified in any way with my employer.

Indeed, some companies insist on such a message. This is one way of clarifying the point, but it might not be sufficient. If a user expresses radical or discomforting opinions about something publicly, this could color others' views of the organization which the individual works for. It might not be fair, but it is unavoidable. System policy has to take into account the human differences between age groups. Whatever seems to be acceptable behavior for one group in a community can be unacceptable for another.

5.9 Ethical conduct of administrators and users

No system involving human beings is complete without a consideration of human social anthropology. Humans meet in consensus, and oppose one another in competition. Our beliefs are based on complex historical and cultural factors and span everything from lifestyle, gender, religious beliefs, cultural norms, justice, autonomy, democracy, privacy and the list goes on.

We believe that we know the difference between right and wrong, and those beliefs influence our use of policy as a tool. However, complete consensus between everyone in a society is impossible to achieve, moreover our sense of responsibility is not always as well developed as our sense of righteousness, and thus there is a need for reminders and the enforcement of ethical decisions.

5.9.1   Compliance with laws and social norms

The basis of any stable community is a 'pact' of common beliefs and ethical principles. These are usually codified into 'policy' and even formalized even further into 'law'. Human–computer communities are usually described as being 'virtual' milieux, which tends to suggest that we do not fully believe in their reality. So far, few laws have been codified to regulate our behavior in these realms. Nevertheless, our strong dependence on technology means that real harm can come to us as a result of anti-social behavior. Thus, in the absence of strict laws, determined by society at large, network communities can easily become unruly places that fail to work in a way that is conducive to their purpose.

Given the temptation to exceed the boundaries of common sense and courtesy, humans excel at challenging every assumption that we might make about behavior. Experience shows that regulations and their enforcement are necessary parts of any interpersonal system. Administrators have a natural position of power in this community model, and this brings with it great responsibility.

5.9.2   Responsibility to others

A system administrator wields great power. He or she has the means to read everyone's mail, change anyone's files, to start and kill anyone's processes. This power can easily be abused and that temptation could be great. Nevertheless, administrators are sometimes required to involve themselves in others' affairs, to help out or even settle conflicts of interest.

The ethical integrity of a system administrator is clearly an important issue. Administrators for top secret government organizations and administrators for small businesses have the same responsibilities towards their users and their organizations. One has only to look at the governing institutions around the world to see that power corrupts. Few individuals, however good their intentions, are immune to the temptations of such power at one time or other. As with governments, it is perhaps a case of those who wish for power are least suited to deal with it.

Administrators 'watch over' backups, E-mail, private communications and they have access to everyone's files. While it is almost never necessary to look at a user's private files, it is possible at any time and users do not usually consider the fact that their files are available to other individuals in this way. Users need to be able to trust the system and its administrator.

As an administrator, one needs to consider:

- What kind of rules can you fairly impose on users?

- What responsibilities do you have to the rest of the network community, i.e. the rest of the world?

- Censoring of information or views.

- Restriction of personal freedom.

- Taking sides in personal disputes.

- Extreme views (some institutions have policies about this).

- Unlawful behavior.

- Jeopardizing user security.

A system administrator should avoid taking sides in ethical, moral, religious or political debates, in the role of system administrator; personal views should be kept separate from professional views, or the temptation to abuse privileges could become irresistable. However, the extent to which this is possible depends strongly on the individual and organizations have to be aware of this. Some organizations dictate policy for their employees. This is also an issue to be cautious with: if a policy is too loose it can lead to laziness and unprofessional behavior; if it is too paranoid or restrictive it can lead to bad feelings in the organization. Historically, unhappy employees have been responsible for the largest computer crimes. For references see [104, 105].

There is a temptation for an administrator to think that the system exists primarily for him or her and that the users are simply a nuisance to the smooth running of things; if network service is interrupted, or if a silly mistake is made which leads to damage in the course of an administrator's work, that is okay: the users should accept these mistakes because they were made whilst trying to improve the system. When wielding such power there is always the chance that such arrogance will build up. Some simple rules of thumb are useful; examples of these are provided in the codes of ethics in section 5.9.4.

5.9.3 Propaganda and misinformation

Computers lie with flawless equanimity; to the inexperienced user they always tell the truth. A computer has a perceived authority which makes it a very powerful tool for abuse. An ill-thought out remark in a login message, or a deliberate attempt to steer users with propaganda can have equally insidious results. One might argue that this is no worse than our eager reliance on television and media, and indeed this is true. Information warfare plays on our vulnerabilities to authority symbols, and it is on the rise.

In the Paramount film *The Wrath of Khan*, a questioning lieutenant Saavik queries Spock about his use of a verbal code to mislead the enemy: 'You lied?' she says. Spock replies: 'I exaggerated.' Although the scene is amusing, it highlights another way in which computers can convince us of incorrect information. A sufficient exaggeration might also be enough to convince us of a lie. Information can always be presented misleadingly. Where do we draw the line? Software which is incorrectly configured and delivers incorrect information is perhaps the worst example. For example, an early version of Mathematica (a tool for mathematical manipulation) gave an incorrect answer for the derivative of a well-known function. It would have been easy to have simply used this answer, knowing that Mathematica performs many complex manipulations flawlessly. Fortunately the main users of Mathematica, at the time, were scientists, who are a naturally sceptical breed and so the error was discovered. In a CD-ROM encyclopedia, a Norwegian right-wing political party was listed as a neo-Nazi organization. This was an unfair exaggeration of the truth, with potentially damaging consequences abroad, had this party ever been elected to government. The fact that the information was on a CD-ROM containing a body of essentially correct information would tend to convince readers of its general truth.

The book you are reading, by virtue of being in print, also has an authority and the power to mislead. If it were written, 'the correct way to do X is Y', it might appear that that was the only correct solution to the problem. That might be true, but it might also only be my flawed opinion. That is one of the reasons why the emphasis of this book is on becoming independent and thinking for oneself. To summarize: most users look up to computers in awe; for that reason, the computer is an authority symbol with a great potential for abuse. System administrators need to be on the look out for problems like this, which can damage credibility and manipulate users.

> **Principle 23 (Perceived authority).** *Computers have a perceived authority. Administrators need to be on the look out for abuses of that authority, whether by accident or by design.*

5.9.4   The SAGE code of ethics

The System Administrator's Guild has developed its own professional guidelines for system administrators. We cite them here for reference. The original draft of this document was written by Hal Miller, and the revised draft by Lee Damon.

Original draft

Background: Computers, and particularly networked systems, have become as necessary a part of life as the telephone. The functionality they bring to home and office environments is now taken for granted as a part of daily life. As the world moves toward becoming a paperless society, the information stored and handled in the computing environment becomes more critical to that lifestyle. Proper operation, support and integrity of computing assets is regarded as being as important as that of the telephone system in most countries today.

System administrators, under any title and whether or not they are members of a professional organization, are relied upon to ensure proper operation, support and protection of those computing assets. Unlike most previous technological advances, any problem with a computer system may negatively impact millions of people world-wide, thus such protection is more crucial than equivalent roles within other technologies. The ever-increasing reliance upon computers in all parts of society has led to system administrators having access to more information, particularly information of critical importance to the users, thus increasing the impact that any mis-step may have.

The scope of the system administrator's responsibilities is wide. Users rely upon the advice, planning, maintenance and repair tasks performed, whether pro-actively or reactively performed. System administrators are expected to have a good understanding of what is available in the vendor world, and what the user community may require in the foreseeable future.

With such responsibilities upon the shoulders of these individuals, it is important that all computer users and system administrators understand the norms and principles to be applied to the task. A code of ethics supplies these norms and principles as canons of general concepts. Such a code must be applied by individuals, guided by their professional judgment, within the confines of the environment and situation in which they may be.

The code sets forth commitments, responsibilities and requirements of members of the system administration profession within the computing community. As used within this document, the word 'users' applies not only to those computer-utilizing members of that computing community who call upon system administrators for support, but also to those system administrators, and even to management personnel who may not actually be using a computer.

This Code of Ethics has as its purposes the following:

- to provide a set of codified guidelines for ethical directions that system administrators must pursue;

- to act as a reference for construction of local site acceptable use policies;

- to enhance the professionalism and image of the Guild and of its individual members by promoting ethical behavior;

- to act as an 'industry standard' reference of behavior in difficult situations, as well as in common ones;

- to establish a baseline for addressing more complex issues.

This Code is not:

- a set of enforceable laws;

- an enumeration of procedures;

- proposed responses to situations;

- all-encompassing;

- an enumeration of sanctions and punishments.

1. **Canon 1**

   The integrity of a system administrator must be beyond reproach.

   A system administrator may come into contact with privileged information on a regular basis and thus has a duty to the owners of such information to both keep confidential and to protect the confidentiality of all such information.

   Protecting the integrity of information includes ensuring that neither system administrators nor unauthorized users unnecessarily access, make any changes to, or divulge data not belonging to them. It includes all appropriate effort, in accordance with industry-accepted practices, by the system administrator to enforce security measures to protect the computers and the data contained on them.

System administrators must uphold the law and policies as established for the systems and networks they manage, and make all efforts to require the same adherence from their users. Where the law is not clear, or appears to be in conflict with their ethical standards, system administrators must exercise sound judgment, and are also obliged to take steps to have the law upgraded or corrected as is possible within their jurisdiction.

2. **Canon 2**

A system administrator shall not unnecessarily infringe upon the rights of users.

System administrators shall not act with, nor tolerate from others, discrimination between authorized users based on any commonly recognized grounds (e.g., age, gender, religion etc.), except where such discrimination (e.g. with respect to unauthorized users as a class) is a necessary part of their job, and then only to the extent that such treatment is required in dealing with the issue at hand.

System administrators will not exercise their special powers to access any private information other than when necessary to their role as system managers, and then only to the degree necessary to perform that role, while remaining within established site policies. Regardless of how it was obtained, system administrators will maintain the confidentiality of all private information.

3. **Canon 3**

Communications of system administrators with all whom they may come in contact shall be kept to the highest standards of professional behavior.

System administrators must keep users informed about computing matters that might affect them, such as conditions of acceptable use, sharing and availability of common resources, maintenance of security, occurrence of system monitoring, and any applicable legal obligations. It is incumbent upon the system administrator to ensure that such information is presented in a manner calculated to ensure user awareness and understanding.

Honesty and timeliness are keys to ensuring accurate communication to users. A system administrator shall, when advice is sought, give it impartially, accompanied by any necessary statement of the limitations of personal knowledge or bias. Any potential conflicts of interest must be fully and immediately declared.

4. **Canon 4**

The continuance of professional education is critical to maintaining currency as a system administrator.

Since technology in computing continues to make significant strides, a system administrator must take an appropriate level of action to update and enhance personal technical knowledge. Reading, study, acquiring training, and sharing knowledge and experience are requirements to maintaining currency and ensuring the customer base of the advantages and security of advances in the field.

5. **Canon 5**

   A system administrator must maintain an exemplary work ethic.

   System administrators must be tireless in their effort to maintain high levels of quality in their work. Day to day operation in the field of system administration requires significant energy and resiliency. The system administrator is placed in a position of such significant impact upon the business of the organization that the required level of trust can only be maintained by exemplary behavior.

6. **Canon 6**

   At all times, system administrators must display professionalism in the performance of their duties.

   All manner of behavior must reflect highly upon the profession as a whole. Dealing with recalcitrant users, upper management, vendors or other system administrators calls for the utmost patience and care to ensure that mutual respect is never at risk.

   Actions that enhance the image of the profession are encouraged. Actions that enlarge the understanding of the social and legal issues in computing are part of the role. System administrators are obliged to assist the community at large in areas that are fundamental to the advancement and integrity of local, national and international computing resources.

New draft

As a member of the international community of systems administrators, I will be guided by the following principles:

1. **Fair treatment**

   I will treat everyone fairly. I will not discriminate against anyone on grounds such as age, disability, gender, sexual orientation, religion, race, national origin, or any other non-business related issue.

2. **Privacy**

   I will only access private information on computer systems when it is necessary in the course of my duties. I will maintain and protect the confidentiality of any information to which I may have access, regardless of the method by which I came into knowledge of it. I acknowledge and will follow all relevant laws governing information privacy.

3. **Communication**

   I will keep users informed about computing matters that may affect them – such as conditions of acceptable use, sharing of common resources, maintenance of security, occurrence of system monitoring, and any relevant legal obligations.

4. **System integrity**

   I will strive to ensure the integrity of the systems for which I have responsibility, using all appropriate means – such as regularly maintaining software and hardware; analyzing levels of system performance and activity; and, as far as possible, preventing unauthorized use or access.

5. **Cooperation**

   I will cooperate with and support my fellow computing professionals. I acknowledge the community responsibility that is fundamental to the integrity of local, national, and international network and computing resources.

6. **Honesty**

   I will be honest about my competence and will seek help when necessary. When my professional advice is sought, I will be impartial. I will avoid conflicts of interest; if they do arise I will declare them and recuse (sic) myself if necessary.

7. **Education**

   I will continue to update and enhance my technical knowledge and other work-related skills through training, study, and the sharing of information and experiences with my fellow professionals. I will help others improve their skills and understanding where my skills and experience allow me to do so.

8. **Social responsibility**

   I will continue to enlarge my understanding of the social and legal issues relating to computing environments. When appropriate, I will communicate that understanding to others and encourage the writing and adoption of policies and laws about computer systems consistent with these ethical principles.

9. **Quality**

   I will be honest about the occurrence and impact of mistakes, and where possible and appropriate I will attempt to correct them.

   I will strive to achieve and maintain a safe, healthy, and productive workplace.

10. **Ethical responsibility**

    I will lead by example, maintaining a consistently high ethical standard and degree of professionalism in the performance of all my duties.

5.9.5 Responsibility for actions and conflicts of interest

How responsible are we for our actions and inactions? Everyone in a position of responsibility for others walks a fine ethical line. The problem is that a society binds everyone together in a tight web of responsibility. We are so used to such a web that we often ignore the subtle responsibilities like politeness and consideration for others, and focus on 'larger' issues where quantities of greater value are at stake.

Users tend to think locally, but the power of the Internet is to allow them to act globally. Bad behavior on the net is rather like tourists who travel to other countries and behave badly, without regard for local customs. Users are not used to the idea of being 'so close' to other cultures and policies. Guidelines for usage of the system need to encompass these issues, so that users are forced to face up to their responsibilities.

> **Principle 24 (Conflicts of interest).** *The network reduces the logical distance to regions where different rules and policies apply. If neighbors do not respect each others' customs and policies, conflict (even information warfare) can be the result.*

If a single user decides to harass another domain, with different customs, then it becomes the system administrator's problem, because he or she is the first point of contact for the domain. System administrators have to mediate in such conflicts and avoid escalation that could lead to information warfare (spamming, denial of service attacks etc.) or even real-world litigation against individuals or organizations. Normally, an organization giving a user access to the network is responsible for that user's behavior.

Responsibility for actions also has implications for system administrators directly. For example, are we responsible for deploying unsafe systems even if we do not know that they are unsafe? Are we responsible for bad software? Is it our responsibility to know? Is it even possible to know everything? As with all ethical issues, there is no fixed line in the sand for deciding these issues.

The responsibility for giving careless advice is rather easier to evaluate, since it is a matter of negligence. One can always adopt quality assurance mechanisms, e.g. seek peer review of decisions, ensure proper and achievable goals, have a backup plan and adequate documentation.

Even knowing the answer, there is the issue of how it is implemented. Is it ethical to wait before fixing a problem? (Under what circumstances?) Is it ethical of users to insist on immediate action, even if it means a system administrator working unreasonable hours?

5.9.6 Harassment

Organizations are responsible for their users, just as countries are responsible for their citizens. This also applies in cyberspace. An information medium, like the Internet, is a perfect opportunity for harassing people.

> **Principle 25 (Harassment).** *Abuse of a public resource or space may be viewed as harassment by others sharing it. Abuse of one user's personal freedom to others' detriment is an attack against their personal freedoms.*

Example 4. *Is spam mail a harassment or a right to freedom of speech? Dealing with spam mail costs real money in time and disk space. Is poster advertising harassment on the streets or a freedom of speech?*

Harassment can also touch on issues like gender, beliefs, sexual persuasion and any other attribute that can be used to target a group. Liability for libelous materials is a potential problem for anyone that is responsible for individuals, since a certain fraction of users will not obey policy for whatever reason.

The question of how to deal with harassment is equally tricky. Normally one prefers law enforcement to be sanctioned by society at large, i.e. we prefer police forces to vigilante groups and gang-warfare. However, consider what E-mail has done to the world. It has removed virtually every cultural barrier for communication. It belongs to no country, and cannot be controlled by anyone. In that instance, there is no official body capable of enforcing or even legislating on E-mail realistically.

Example 5. *The Realtime Black Hole List (RBL) is a database of known E-mail abusers that was created essentially by an Internet vigilante group that was tired of dealing with spam. Known spammers were entered into a database that is accessible to everyone. Mail programs are thus able to check for known spammers before accepting mail from them. While this idea seems to work and might even be necessary, it flies in the face of conventional civic practice in many countries, to allow a random group to set up such a service, however well-intentioned the service may be. See http://www.mail-abuse.org.*

Clearly, the Internet distorts many of our ideas about law-making and enforcement.

5.9.7 Privacy in an open network

As the information age opens its sluices and pours information over us in every imaginable form, by every imaginable medium, carving ourselves a quiet space for private thoughts is becoming the central challenge for this new age. The right to privacy has long been an issue in societies around the world, but the vast connectivity coupled to light-speed resources for manipulating data present us with ways for invading privacy that we have never seen the like of before.

- Software manufacturers have begun to include spy-software that monitors user behavior and reports it to interested parties: advertising companies, law enforcement agencies etc.

- Have you ever read the license agreements that you click 'accept' to, when installing software? Some of these contain acceptance clauses that allow software manufacturers to do almost anything to your computer.

- Companies (e.g. search engines) now exist that make a living from data mining – i.e. finding out behavioral information from computer log files. Is this harassment? That depends very much on one's point of view.

- In recent years, several research organizations and groups have used the freedom of the Internet to map out the Internet using programs like ping and traceroute. This allows them to see how the logical connections are made, but it also allows them to see what machines are up and down. This is a form of surveillance.

Example 6. *In the military actions on Kosovo and the former Yugoslavia, scientists were able to follow the progress of the war simply by pinging the infrastructure machines of the Yugoslavian networks. In that way, they were able to extract information about them and their repair activities/capabilities simply by running a program from their office in the US.*

Clearly, there are information warfare issues associated with the lack of privacy of the Internet, or indeed any public medium that couples large numbers of people together. Is it ethical to ping someone? Is it ethical to use the process list commands in operating systems to see what other users are doing?

Example 7. *Mobile technologies rely on protocols that need to understand the location of an individual in relation to transmitters and receivers. Given that the transmitters have a fixed location, it is possible (at least in principle) to use the very technology that makes freedom of movement possible, to trace and map out a user's motion. Who should have access to this information? What is a system administrator's role in protecting user privacy here?*

Where does one draw the line on the ethical usage of these materials?

5.9.8   User surveillance

The dilemma of policing any society is that, in order to catch criminals, one has to look for them among the innocent. Offenders do not identify themselves with T-shirts or special hairstyles, so the eye of scrutiny is doomed to fall on the innocent most of the time.

One of the tools in maintaining order, whether it be local policy, national or international law, is thus surveillance. It has been argued that the emergence of a virtual society (cyberspace) leaves regular police forces ill-equipped to detect crime that is committed there. Similarly, local administrators often feel the need to scan public resources (disks and networks) for transgressions of policy or law.

Some governments (particularly the EU and the US government) have tried to push through legislation giving greater powers for conducting surveillance. They have developed ways of cracking personal encryption. At the time of writing, there are rumours of an FBI Trojan horse called Magic-Lantern that is used to obtain PGP and other encryption keys from a computer, thus giving law enforcement the power to listen in on private conversations. In the real world, such wire-tapping requires judicial approval. In cyberspace, everyone creates their own universe and the law is neither clear nor easily enforceable.

The tragic events of 11th September 2001, surrounding the destruction of the World Trade Center in New York, have allowed governments to argue strongly for surveillance in the name of anti-terrorism. This seems, on the one hand, to be a reasonable idea. However, large quantities of data are already monitored by governments. The question is: if the existing data could not be effectively used to avoid terrorist attacks from happening, how will even more data do so in the future? Many believe it will not, and that our privacy will be invaded and some people will get a very good profile of who we are talking to and for how long, who we have exchanged E-mails with etc. Such information could be used for corrupt purposes.

Richard Stallman of the Free Software Foundation expresses it more sharply: 'When the government records where you go, and who you talk with, and what you read, privacy has been essentially abolished.'

The EU Parliament decided, contrary to the basic statement of the directive about data protection, and the recommendations of the committee for civil rights in the European Parliament, to say 'yes' to data retention by Internet service providers without evidence. Thus the member countries are empowered to enact national laws about retention of digital network data, in open disregard of the EU Directive on data protection.

- Should ISPs record surveillance data, IP addresses, E-mail message IDs etc?

- Who should have access to this?

Europol wishlist

In the European Union, police forces have published a list of information they would like to have access to, from Internet service providers and telecommunications companies. If they have their way, this will present a great burden in real cost of delivering computing services to these companies.

1. Network

   (NAS) Access logs specific to authentication and authorization servers such as TACACS+ (Terminal Access Controller Access Control System) or RADIUS (Remote Authentication Dial in User Service) used to control access to IP routers or network access servers

   Member States comments:

   A Minimum List

   - Date and time of connection of client to server
   - User-id and password
   - Assigned IP address NAS Network
   - Attached storage IP address
   - Number of bytes transmitted and received
   - Caller Line identification (CLI)

   B Optional List

   - User's credit card number / bank account for the subscription payment

2. E-mail servers

   SMTP (Simple Mail Transfer Protocol) Member States comments:

   Minimum List

   - Date and time of connection of client to server
   - IP address of sending computer

- Message ID (msgid)
- Sender (login@domain)
- Receiver (login@domain)
- Status indicator

POP (Post Office Protocol) log or IMAP (Internet Message Access Protocol) log

Member States comments:

Minimum List

- Date and time of connection of client to server
- IP address of client connected to server
- User-id
- In some cases identifying information of E-mail retrieved

3. File upload and download servers

FTP (File Transfer Protocol) log

Member States comments:

A Minimum List

- Date and time of connection of client to server
- IP source address
- User-id and password
- Path and filename of data object uploaded or downloaded

B Optional List

- Web servers
- HTTP (HyperText Transfer Protocol) log

Member States comments:

A Minimum List

- Date and time of connection of client to server
- IP source address
- Operation (i.e. GET command)
- Path of the operation (to retrieve HTML page or image file)
- Those companies which are offering their servers to accommodate web pages should retain details of the users who insert these web pages (date, time, IP, UserID etc.)

B Optional List

- 'Last visited page'
- Response codes

5.9.9 Digital cameras

Face recognition is now possible with a high level of accuracy. If cameras are attached to computers and they can be accessed by anybody, then anybody can watch you.

5.10   Computer usage policy

Let us formulate a generic policy for computer users, the like of which one might expect company employees to agree to. By making this generic, we consider all kinds of issues, not all of which are appropriate for every environment.

A user's behavior reflects on the organization that houses him or her. Computer systems are uniforms and flags for companies (as well as for public services). It is therefore generally considered an organization's right to expect its users to comply with certain guidelines of behavior.

Information Technology Policy Documents are becoming more widely used. Their practice has to be recommended, if only to make it clear to everyone involved what is considered acceptable behavior. Such documents could save organizations real money in law-suits. The policy should include:

- What all parties should do in case of dismissal

- What all parties should do in case of security breach

- What are users' responsibilities to their organization?

- What are the organization's responsibilities to their users?

The policy has to take special care to address the risks of using insecure operating systems (Windows 95, 98, ME and Macintosh versions prior to MacOSX), since these machines are trivially compromised by careless use.

5.10.1   Example IT policy document for a company

1. *Why do we need a policy?*

   As our dependence on technology increases, so do the risks and opportunities for misuse. We are increasingly vulnerable to threats from outside and inside the organization, both due to carelessness and malice.

   From our clients' viewpoint: we need to be perceived as competent and professional in our ability to conduct our business electronically.

   From our company's perspective: we need to maximize the benefits and reduce the risks of using information technology and protect company assets (including reputation).

   From your viewpoint: we need to protect your interests as an individual in a community, and reduce the risk of your liability for legal damages.

   These policy guidelines must be adhered to at all times to ensure that all users behave in a professional, legal and ethical manner. Failure to

do so may result in disciplinary action, including dismissal and legal action.

2. *The network*

   For the purpose of this policy, we define 'the network' to mean the company computer and telephone network, including all of its hardware and software.

   The use of the network is not private. The company retains the right to monitor the use of the network by any user, within the boundaries of national law. All users are obliged to use company resources in a professional, ethical and lawful manner.

   Material that is fraudulent, harassing or offensive, profane, obscene, intimidating, defamatory, misleading or otherwise unlawful or inappropriate may not be displayed, stored or transmitted using the network, by any means, or in any form (including SMS).

3. *Security*

   Any hardware or software that is deemed a security risk may be disconnected or de-installed at any time, by the system administrator.

   User accounts are set up, managed and maintained by the system administrators.

   Users accessing the network must have authorization by access-rights, password or by permission of the owner of the information.

   Users must take reasonable precautions to prevent unauthorized access to the network. This includes leaving equipment unattended for extended periods while logged on.

   Users must not attempt to gain unauthorized access to restricted information.

   Passwords are provided to help prevent unauthorized access to restricted areas of the network. Users must not log on to any system using another user's password or account without their express permission.

   Under no circumstances should any user reveal his/her password to anyone else, even by consent.

   Users have a responsibility to safeguard passwords. They must not be written down on paper, stored unprotected online, or be located in readable form anywhere near a network terminal.

4. *Copyright*

   Copyright is a statutory property right which protects an author's interest in his or her work. The right exists as soon as the work is created and continues to exist for the lifetime of the author and beyond, during which time the owner of the copyright may bring actions for infringement.

   International copyright law protects a copyright owner's interest by preventing others from unlawfully exploiting the work that is protected. There are no registration requirements for the legal existence of copyright. Copyright subsists in most materials that are found on the Internet, including imagery and databases.

Copyright is infringed when a copyright work is copied without the consent of the copyright owner. Downloading information from any source constitutes copying. Unauthorized copy-cut-pasting from any text, graphical or media source may be in breach of copyright, as may copying, distributing or even installing software.

Many information sites express legal terms by which materials may be used. Users should refer to those terms and conditions before downloading any materials.

5. *Data protection (e.g. UK)*

   Any person using a computer may be a *data processor*. Every individual is responsible for maintaining confidentiality of data by preventing unauthorized disclosure.

   Personal data are legally defined as data that relate to a living individual who can be identified from those data, or from those and other data in possession of the data user. The use of personal data is governed by law (e.g. the UK Data Protection Act 1998).

   The act lays out the following principles of data protection:

   - Personal data shall be processed fairly and lawfully and such processing must comply with at least one of a set of specified conditions.
   - Personal data shall be obtained only for one or more specified and lawful purposes, and shall not be processed in any manner incompatible with that purpose or those purposes.
   - Personal data shall be adequate, relevant and not excessive in relation to the purpose or purposes for which they are processed.
   - Personal data shall be accurate and, where necessary, up to date.
   - Personal data processed for any purpose or purposes shall not be kept for longer than is necessary for that purpose or those purposes.
   - Personal data shall be processed in accordance with the rights of data subjects under the Act.
   - Appropriate technical and organizational measures shall be taken against unauthorized or unlawful processing of personal data and against accidental loss or destruction of, or damage to, personal data.
   - Personal data shall not be transferred to a country or territory outside the European Economic Area unless that country or territory ensures an adequate level of protection for the rights and freedoms of data subjects in relation to the processing of personal data.

   The rules concerning the processing of personal data are complex. If in any doubt as to their interpretation, users should consult legal advice.

6. *E-mail and SMS*

   All electronic messages created and stored on the network are the property of the company and are not private. The company retains the right to access any user's E-mail if it has reasonable grounds to do so.

The company E-mail system may be used for reasonable personal use, provided it does not interfere with normal business activities or work, and does not breach any company policy.

Users should be aware that:

- E-mail is a popular and successful vehicle for the distribution of computer viruses.
- Normal E-mail carries the same level of privacy as a postcard.
- E-mail is legally recognized as publishing and is easily recirculated.
- Users should take care to ensure that they are not breaching any copyright or compromising confidentiality of either the company or its clients or suppliers by sending, forwarding or copying an E-mail or attachment.
- Nothing libelous, harassing, discriminatory or unlawful should be written as part of any message.

E-mail is often written informally. Users should apply the same care and attention as in writing a conventional business correspondence, including ensuring accurate addressing.

Users must not participate in chain or junk E-mail activities (spam); mass E-mailing should be avoided whenever possible.

E-mail attachments provide a useful means of delivering files to other users. However, careful consideration should be paid to ensure that the recipient can read and make use of the data.

- Not all file types are readable by all computers.
- Many sites have a maximum acceptable file size for E-mail.
- The recipient must have suitable software installed in order to display a file.

In order to prevent the spread of viruses, users should not attempt to open any attachment from an unknown or unexpected source. Certain file types may be blocked by mail-filtering software.

Users must not disguise themselves or falsify their identity in any message.

Where provided, users must ensure that company disclaimers are included when sending E-mail.

7. *The World Wide Web*

Access to the World Wide Web is provided for business purposes. The World Wide Web may be accessed for limited personal use provided that such use does not interfere with normal business practice or work, and that personal use complies with all aspects of this policy.

The company may monitor individual use, including visits to specific web sites.

Access may only be sought using an approved browser, which is installed on the user's computer by the system administrator.

The World Wide Web is uncontrolled and unregulated. Users should therefore be aware that there is no guarantee that any information found there is accurate, legal or factual.

Software may only be downloaded by an authorized system administrator.

8. *Transactions*

   Any commercial transaction made electronically must adhere to standard ordering policy.

   The company will not accept liability for any commercial transaction which has not been subject to the appropriate approval.

   The company will not accept liability for any personal transaction.

9. *Hardware and software*

   The company provides computer, telecommunications equipment and software for business purposes. It is the responsibility of the system administrator to select, provide and maintain computer equipment in accordance with the work required.

   Users must not connect unauthorized equipment to the network, use software that has not been provided or installed by the company, or attempt to alter the settings of any software that compromise security or reliability. No attempt should be made to alter the software or hardware, copy or distribute software, or download software, including screen-savers.

   Installations and upgrades may only be performed by an authorized system administrator.

10. *Surveillance*

    Digital cameras or audio input devices must not be connected to any computer that is not specifically authorized to have one. Users must not bring any possible surveillance device into an area where the company's private assets, intellectual or otherwise, are developed or stored. Employees must not disclose any such information to persons or transmit it to any machine or information storage device not authorized to receive it.

11. *Usage*

    The company reserves the right to view any data stored on the network.

    Users may not store personal files on the network. Any personal files can be deleted at any time.

    The network is provided to enable

    - Authorized users to store and retrieve work
    - Authorized users to share/exchange assets
    - Backup and recovery
    - Security and confidentiality of work.

All users must store files in the appropriate areas of the network. Users who create files on mobile devices should transfer their data to the appropriate area on the network as soon as possible.

12. *Management*

    Managers must ensure that they are fully aware of any potential risks when assessing requests by users for permission to:

    - Download files from the Internet
    - Access additional areas of the network.

    Managers may not request any action by any system administrator which could result in a breach of any of the company policies.

5.10.2 Example IT procedure following a breach of policy

IT policy ought to contain instructions as to how users will be dealt with when they breach policy. There are many ways of dealing with users, with varying degrees of tolerance: reprimand, dismissal, loss of privilege etc. Clear guidelines are important for professional conduct, so that all users are treated either equally, or at least *predictably*.

5.10.3 When an employee leaves the company

A fixed policy for dismissing a member of staff can be useful when the employee was harmful to the organization. An organization can avoid harmful lawsuits by users who feel that they have been treated unfairly, by asking them to sign an acceptance of the procedure. The issue of dismissal was discussed in ref. [254].

Users typically have to be granted access to disparate systems with their own authentication mechanisms, e.g. Windows, Unix, key-cards, routers, modems, database passwords. These must all be removed to prevent a user from being able to change data after their dismissal.

A clear procedure is important for both parties:

- To protect an organization from a disgruntled employee's actions.

- To protect the former employee from accusations about what he or she did after their dismissal that they might not be responsible for.

It is therefore important to have a clear checklist for the sake of security.

- Change combination locks.

- Change door keys.

- Surrender laptops and mobile devices.

- Remove all authentication privileges.

- Remove all pending jobs in `at` or `cron` that could be logic bombs.

> **Principle 26 (Predictable failure of humans).** *All systems fail eventually, but they should fail predictably. Where humans are involved, we must have checklists and guidelines that protect the remainder of the system from the failure.*

Human failures can be mitigated by adherence to quality assurance schemes, such as ISO 9000 (see section 8.12.1).

Exercises

Self-test objectives

1. List the main issues in user management.

2. Where are passwords stored in Unix-like and Windows computers?

3. What does it mean that passwords are not stored in 'clear text'?

4. What is meant by a distributed account?

5. What special considerations are required for distributed accounts?

6. What is meant by a user shell?

7. What mechanisms exist for users to share files in Unix? What are the limitations of the Unix model for file sharing between users? What is a potential practical advantage of the Unix model?

8. What mechanisms are available for users to share files on Windows computers?

9. What is meant by an account policy?

10. Explain the justification for the argument 'simplest is best'.

11. What considerations should be taken into account in designing a login environment for users? Does this list depend on whether the account is a distributed account or not?

12. Why is it not a good idea to log onto a computer with root or Administrator privileges unless absolutely necessary?

13. What is meant by 'support services'?

14. List the main elements of user support.

15. What is the nine-step approach to user support?

16. What are active and passive users?

17. What is meant by a user quota, and what is it used for?

18. What are the pros and cons of the use of disk quotas?

19. What is meant by garbage collection of user files?

20. Why is it important to be able to identify users by their username? What role does a password play in identifying users?

21. What are the main health risks in the use of computers?

22. List the main areas in which ethics play a role in the management of computers.

23. What is meant by a computer usage policy? Why could such a policy be essential for the security of a company or organization?

24. What kinds of behavior can be regarded as harassment in the context of computer usage?

25. Which routine maintenance activities might be regarded as user-surveillance or breaches of privacy?

Problems

1. What issues are associated with the installation of a new user account? Discuss this with a group of classmates and try to turn your considerations into a policy checklist.

2. Imagine that it is the start of the university semester and a hundred new students require an account. Write an `adduser` script which uses the filesystem layout that you have planned for your host to install home-directories for the users and to register them in the password database. The script should be able to install the accounts from a list of users provided by the university registration service.

   Start either by modifying an existing script (e.g. GNU/Linux has an adduser package) or from scratch. Remember that installing a new user implies the installation of enough configuration to make the account work satisfactorily at once, e.g. Unix dot files.

3. One of the central problems in account management is the distribution of passwords. If we are unable (or unwilling) to use a password distribution system like NIS, passwords have to be copied from host to host. Assume that user home-directories are shared amongst all hosts. Write a script which takes the password file on one host and converts it into all of the different file formats used by different Unix-like OSs, ready for distribution.

4. Consider the example of online services in section 5.7. Adapt this example to create a model for online purchasing of documents or support services. Explain how user security is provided and how system security is assured.

5. Write a script to monitor the amount of disk space used by each user and warn about users that exceed a fixed quota.

6. Consider the terminal room at your organization. Review its layout critically. Does the lighting cause reflection in the screens, leading to eye strain? How is the seating? Is the room too warm or too cold? How could the room be redesigned to make work conditions better for its users?

7. Describe the available support services for users at your site. Could these be improved? What would it cost to improve support services (can you estimate the number of man-hours, for instance) to achieve the level of support which you would like?

8. Analyze and comment on the example shell configuration in section 5.4.2. Rewrite the shell configuration in bash.

9. Discuss the following: Human beings are not moral creatures, we are creatures of habit. Thus law and policy enforcement is about making ethical choices habitual ones.

10. Discuss the following: Two or three generations of users have now grown up with computers in their homes, but these computers were private machines which were not, until recently, attached to a network. In short, users have grown up thinking that what they do with their computers is nobody's business but their own. That is not a good attitude in a network community.

Chapter 6

Models of network and system administration

Understanding human–computer systems requires an ability to see relationships between seemingly distinct parts of a system. Many failures and security violations result from the neglect of interrelationships within such systems. To model the management of a complete system, we need to understand the complete causal web.

> **Principle 27 (System interaction).** *Systems involve layers of interacting (cooperating and competing) components that interdepend on one another. Just as communities are intertwined with their environments, so systems are complex ecological webs of cause and effect. Ignoring the dependencies within a system will lead to false assumptions and systemic errors of management.*

Individual parts underpin a system by fulfilling their niche in the whole, but the function carried out by the total system does not necessarily depend on a unique arrangement of components working together – it is often possible to find another solution with the resources available at any given moment. The flexibility to solve a problem in different ways gives one a kind of guarantee as to the likelihood of a system working, even with random failures.

> **Principle 28 (Adaptability).** *An adaptable system is desirable since it can cope with the unexpected. When one's original assumptions about a system fail, they can be changed. Adaptable systems thus contribute to predictability in change or recovery from failure.*

In a human–computer system, we must think of both the human and the computer aspects of organization. Until recently, computer systems were organized either by inspired local ingenuity or through an inflexible prescription, dictated by a vendor. Standardizing bodies like the Internet Engineering Task Force (IETF) and International Standards Organization (ISO) have attempted to design models for the management of systems [59, 205]; unfortunately, these models have often proved to be rather short-sighted in anticipating the magnitude and complexity of the tasks facing system administrators and are largely oriented on device monitoring. Typically, they have followed the singular paradigm of placing humans in the driving seat over the increasingly vast arrays of computing machinery. This kind of micro-management is not a scalable or flexible strategy however. Management needs to step back from involving itself in too much detail.

> **Principle 29 (System management's role).** *The role of management is to secure conditions necessary for a system's components to be able to carry out their function. It is not to direct and monitor (control) every detail of a system.*

This principle applies both to the machines in a network, and to the organization of people using them and maintaining them. If a system is fundamentally flawed, no amount of management will make it work. First we design a system that functions, then we discuss the management of its attributes. This has several themes:

- Resource management: consumables and reusables.

- Scheduling (time management, queues).

- Strategy.

More recently, the emphasis has moved away from *management* (especially of devices) as a paradigm for running computer systems, more towards *regulation*. This is clearly consistent with the principle above: the parts within a system require a certain freedom to fulfill their role, without the constant interference of a manager; management's role, instead, moves up a level – to secure the conditions under which the parts can be autonomous and yet still work together.

In this chapter we consider the issues surrounding functioning systems and their management. These include:

- The structuring of organizational information in directories.

- The deployment of services for managing structural information.

- The construction of basic computing and management infrastructure.

- The scalability of management models.

- Handling inter-operability between the parts of a system.

- The division of resources between the parts of the system.

6.1   Information models and directory services

One way of binding together an organization is through a structured information model – a database of its personnel, assets and services [181]. The X.500 standard [167] defines:

> **Definition 3 (Directory service).** *A collection of open systems that cooperate to hold a logical database of information about a set of objects in the real world. A directory service is a generalized name service.*

Directory services should not be confused with directories in filesystems, though they have many structural similarities.

- Directories are organized in a structured fashion, often hierarchically (tree structure), employing an object-oriented model.

- Directory services employ a common schema for what can and must be stored about a particular object, so as to promote inter-operability.

- A fine grained access control is provided for information, allowing access per record.

- Access is optimized for lookup, not for transactional update of information. A directory is not a read–write database, in the normal sense, but rather a database used for read-only transactions. It is maintained and updated by a separate administrative process rather than by regular usage.

Directory services are often referred to using the terms *White Pages* and *Yellow Pages* that describe how a directory is used. If one starts with a lookup key for a specific resource, then this is called White Pages lookup – like finding a number in a telephone book. If one does not know exactly what one is looking for, but needs a list of possible categories to match, such as in browsing for users or services, then the service is referred to as Yellow Pages.

An implementation of yellow pages called Yellow Pages or YP was famously introduced into Unix by Sun Microsystems and later renamed the Network Information Services (NIS) in the 1980s due to trademark issues with British Telecom (BT); they were used for storing common data about users and user groups.

6.1.1 X.500 information model

In the 1970s, attempts were made to standardize computing and telecommunications technologies. One such standard that emerged was the OSI (Open Systems Interconnect) model (ISO 7498), which defined a seven-layered model for data communication, described in section 2.6.1. In 1988, ISO 9594 was defined, creating a standard for directories called X.500. *Data Communications Network Directory, Recommendations X.500–X.521* emerged in 1990, though it is still referred to as X.500. X.500 is defined in terms of another standard, the Abstract Syntax Notation (ASN.1), which is used to define formatted protocols in several software systems, including SNMP and Internet Explorer.

X.500 specifies a Directory Access Protocol (DAP) for addressing a hierarchical directory, with powerful search functionality. Since DAP is an application layer protocol, it requires the whole OSI management model stack of protocols in order to operate. This required more resources than were available in many small environments, thus a lightweight alternative was desirable that could run just with the regular TCP/IP infrastructure. LDAP was thus defined and implemented in a number of draft standards. The current version is LDAP v3, defined in RFC 2251–2256. LDAP is an Internet open standard and is designed to be inter-operable between various operating systems and computers. It employs better security than previous open standards (like NIS). It is therefore gradually replacing, or being integrated with, vendor specific systems including the Novell Directory Service (NDS) and the Microsoft Active Directory (AD).

Entries in a directory are name-value pairs called *attributes* of the directory. There might be multiple values associated with a name, thus attributes are said to be either single-value or multi-valued. Each attribute has a syntax, or format, that defines a set of sub-attributes describing the type of information that can be stored in the direction schema. An attribute definition includes *matching rules* that govern how matches should be made. It is possible to require equality or substring matches, as well as rules specifying the order of attribute matching in a search. Some attributes are mandatory, others are optional.

Objects in the real world can usually be classified into categories that fit into an object hierarchy. Sub-classes of a class can be defined, that inherit all mandatory and optional attributes of their parent class. The 'top' class is the root of the object class hierarchy. All other classes are derived from it, either directly or through inheritance. Thus every data entry has at least one object class. Three types of object class exist:

- *Abstract*: these form the upper levels of the object class hierarchy; their entries can only be populated if they are inherited by at least one structural object class. They are meant to be 'inherited from' rather than used directly, but they do contain some fields of data, e.g. 'top', 'Country', 'Device' 'Organizational-Person', 'Security-Object' etc.

- *Structural*: these represent the 'meat' of an object class, used for making actual entries. Examples of these are 'person' and 'organization'. The object class to which an entry pertains is declared in an 'objectClass' attribute, e.g. 'Computer' and 'Configuration'.

- *Auxiliary*: this is for defining special-case attributes that can be added to specific entries. Attributes may be introduced, as a requirement, to just a subset of entries in order to provide additional hints, e.g. both a person and an organization could have a web page or a telephone number, but need not.

One special object class is *alias*, which contains no data but merely points to another class. Important object classes are defined in RFC 2256.

All of the entries in an X.500 directory are arranged hierarchically, forming a Directory Information Tree (DIT). Thus a directory is similar to a filesystem in structure. Each entry is identified by its *Distinguished Name* (DN), which is a hierarchical designation based on inheritance. This is an entries 'coordinates' within the tree. It is composed by joining a Relative Distinguished Name (RDN) with those of all its parents, back to the top class. An RDN consists of an assignment of an attribute name to a value, e.g.

```
cn=''Mark Burgess''
```

X.500 originally followed a naming scheme based in geographical regions, but has since moved towards a naming scheme based on the virtual geography of the Domain Name Service (DNS). To map a DNS name to a Distinguished Name, one uses the 'dc' attribute, e.g. for the domain name of Oslo University College (hio.no)

```
dc=hio,dc=no
```

Hierarchical directory services are well suited to being distributed or delegated to several hosts. A Directory Information Tree is partitioned into smaller regions, each of which is a connected subtree, which does not overlap with other subtree partitions (see figure 6.1). This allows a number of cooperating authorities within an organization to maintain the data more rationally, and allows – at least in principle – the formation of a global directory, analogous to DNS. Availability and redundancy can be increased by running *replication services*, giving a backup or fail-over functionality. A master server within each partition keeps master records and these are replicated on slave systems. Some commercial implementations (e.g. NDS) allow multi-master servers.

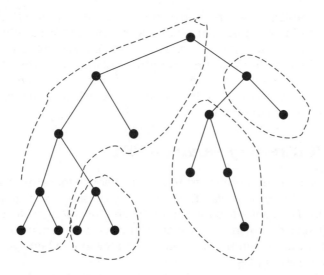

Figure 6.1: The partitioning of a distributed directory. Each dotted area is handled by a separate server.

The software that queries directories is usually built into application software.

Definition 4 (Directory User Agent (DUA)). *A program or subsystem that queries a directory service on behalf of a user.*

For example, the name resolver library in Unix supports the system call 'gethostbyname', which is a system call delegating a query to the hostname directory. The 'name server switch' is used in Unix to select a policy for querying a variety of competing directory services (see section 4.6.5), as are Pluggable Authentication Modules (PAM).

6.1.2 Unix legacy directories

Before networking became commonplace, Unix hosts stored directory information in the /etc file directory, in files such as /etc/passwd, /etc/services and so on. In the 1980s this was extended by a network service that could bind hosts together with a common directory for all hosts in a Local Area Network. Sun Microsystems, who introduced the service, called it 'YP' or Yellow Pages, but later had to change the name to the Network Information Service (NIS) due to a trademarking conflict with British Telecom (BT). The original NIS directory was very popular, but was both primitive, non-hierarchical and lacked an effective security model and was thus replaced by 'NIS+' which was able to add strong authentication to queries, and allow modernized and more flexible schema. NIS+ never really caught on, and it is now being replaced by an open standard LDAP.

6.1.3 OpenLDAP

The OpenLDAP implementation is the reference implementation for Unix-like systems. Directory information can be accessed through a variety of agents, and can be added to the Unix name server list via nsswitch.conf and Pluggable Authentication Modules (PAM). The strength of LDAP is its versatility and inter-operability with all operating systems. Its disadvantage is its somewhat arbitrary and ugly syntactical structure, and its vulnerability to loss of network connectivity. See section 7.12.2 for more details.

6.1.4 Novell Directory Service – NDS

Novell Netware is sometimes referred to as a Network Operating System (NOS) by PC administrators, because it was the 'add on' software that was needed to complete the aging MSDOS software for the network sharing age. Novell Netware was originally a centralized sharing service that allowed a regiment of PCs to connect to a common disk and a common printer, thus allowing expensive hardware to be shared amongst desktop PCs.

As PCs have become more network-able, Netware has developed into a sophisticated directory-based server suite. The Novell directory keeps information about all devices and users within its domain: users, groups, print queues, disk volumes and network services. In 1997, LDAP was integrated into the Novell software, making it LDAP compatible and allowing cross-integration with Unix based hosts. In an attempt to regain market share, lost to Microsoft and Samba (a free software alternative for sharing Unix filesystems with Windows hosts, amongst other things), Novell has launched its eDirectory at the core of Directory Enabled Net Infrastructure Model (DENIM), that purports to run on Netware, Windows, Solaris, Tru64 and Linux. Perhaps more than any other system, Novell Netware adopted a consistent distributed physical organization of its devices and software objects in its directory model. In Novell, a directory does not merely assist the organization: the organization *is* a directory that directly implements the information model of the organization.

6.1.5 Active Directory – AD

Early versions of Windows were limited by a flat host infrastructure model that made it difficult to organize and administer Windows hosts rationally by an information model. Active Directory is the directory service introduced with and integrated into Windows 2000. It replaces the Domain model used in NT4, and is based on concepts from X.500. It is LDAP compatible. In the original Windows network software, naming was based around proprietary software such as WINS. Windows has increasingly embraced open standards like DNS, and has chosen the DNS naming model for LDAP integration.

The smallest LDAP partition area in Active Directory is called a *domain* to provide a point of departure for NT4 users. The Active Directory is still being developed. Early versions did not support replication, and required dedicated multiple server hosts to support multiple domains. This has since been fixed.

The schema in Active Directory differ slightly from the X.500 information model. Auxiliary classes do not exist as independent classes, rather they are incorporated into structural classes. As a result, auxiliary classes cannot be searched for, and cannot be added dynamically or independently. Other differences include the fact that all RDNs must be single valued and that matching rules are not published for inspection by agents; searching rules are hidden.

6.2 System infrastructure organization

As we have already mentioned in section 3.1, a network is a community of cooperating and competing components. A system administrator has to choose the components and assign them their roles on the basis of the job which is intended for the computer system. There are two aspects of this to consider: the machine aspect and the human aspect. The machine aspect relates to the use of computing machinery to achieve a functional infrastructure; the human aspect is about the way people are deployed to build and maintain that infrastructure.

Identifying the purpose of a computer system is the first step to building a successful one. Choosing hardware and software is the next. If we are only interested in word-processing, we do not buy a supercomputer. On the other hand, if we are interested in high volume distributed database access, we do not buy a laptop running Windows. There is always a balance to be achieved, a right place to spend money and right place to save money. For instance, since the CPU of most computers is idle some ninety percent of the time, simply waiting for input, money spent on fast processors is often wasted; conversely, the greatest speed gains are usually to be made in extra RAM memory, so money spent on RAM is usually well spent. Of course, it is not always possible to choose the hardware we have to work with. Sometimes we inherit a less than ideal situation and have to make the best of it. This also requires ingenuity and careful planning.

6.2.1 Team work and communication

The process of communication is essential in any information system. System administration is no different; we see essential bi-directional communications taking place in a variety of forms:

- Between computer programs and their data,

- Between computers and devices,

- Between collaborating humans (in teams),

- Between clients and servers,

- Between computer users and computer systems,

- Between policy decision-makers and policy enforcers,

- Between computers and the environment (spilled coffee).

These communications are constantly being intruded upon by environmental noise. Errors in this communication process can occur in two ways:

- Information is distorted, inserted or omitted, by faulty communication, or by external interference,

- Information is interpreted incorrectly; symbols are incorrectly identified, due to imprecision or external interference (see figure 6.2).

For example, suppose one begins with the simplest case of a stand-alone computer, with no users, executing a program in isolation. The computer is not communicating with any external agents, but *internally* there is a fetch–execute cycle, causing data to be read from and written to memory, with a CPU performing manipulations along the way. The transmission of data, to and from the memory, is subject to errors, which are caused by electrical spikes, cosmic rays, thermal noise and all kinds of other effects.

Suppose now that an administrator sends a configuration message to a host, or even to a single computer program. Such a message takes place by some agreed form of coding: a protocol of some kind, e.g. a user interface, or a message format. Such a configuration message might be distorted by errors in communication, by software errors, by random typing errors. The system itself might change during the implementation of the instructions, due to the actions of unknown parties, working covertly. These are all issues which contribute uncertainty into the configuration process and, unless corrected, lead to a 'sickness' of the system, i.e. a deviation from its intended function.

Consider a straightforward example: the application of a patch to some programming code. Programs which patch bugs in computer code only work reliably if they are not confused by external (environmental) alterations performed outside the scope of their jurisdiction. If a line break is edited in the code, in advance, this can be enough to cause a patch to fail, because the semantic content of the file was distorted by the coding change (noise). One reason why computer systems have been vulnerable to this kind of environmental noise, traditionally, is that error correcting protocols of sufficient flexibility have not been available for making system changes. Protocols, such as SNMP or proprietary change mechanisms, do not yet incorporate feedback checking of the higher level protocols over extended periods of time.

Humans working in teams can lead to an efficient delegation of tasks, but also an inconsistent handling of tasks – i.e. a source of noise. At each level of computer operation, one finds messages being communicated between different parties. System administration is a meta-program, executed by a mixture of humans and machines, which concerns the evolution and maintenance of distributed computer systems. It involves:

- Configuring systems within policy guidelines,

- Keeping machines running within policy guidelines,

- Keeping user activity within policy guidelines.

Quality control procedures can help to prevent teams from going astray.

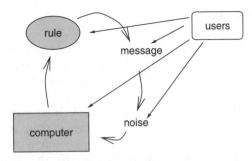

Figure 6.2: A development loop, showing the development of a computer system in time, according to a set of rules. Users can influence the computer both through altering the rules, altering the conditions under which the rules apply, and by directly touching the computer and altering its configuration.

6.2.2 Homogeneity

Assuming that we can choose hardware, we should weigh the convenience of keeping to a single type of hardware and operating system (e.g. just PCs with NT) against the possible advantages of choosing the absolutely best hardware for the job. Product manufacturers (vendors) always want to sell a solution based on their own products, so they cannot be trusted to evaluate an organization's needs objectively. For many issues, keeping to one type of computer is more important than what the type of computer is.

> **Principle 30 (Homogeneity/Uniformity I).** *System homogeneity or uniformity means that all hosts appear to be essentially the same. This makes hosts predictable for users and manageable for administrators. It allows for reuse of hardware in an emergency.*

If we have a dozen machines of the same type, we can establish a standard routine for running them and for using them. If one fails, we can replace it with another.

A disadvantage with uniformity is that there are sometimes large performance gains to be made by choosing special machinery for a particular application. For instance, a high availability server requires multiple, fast processors, lots of memory and high bandwidth interfaces for disk and network. In short it has to be a top quality machine; a word-processor does not. Purchasing such a machine might complicate host management slightly. Tools exist to help integrate hosts with special functions painlessly.

Having chosen the necessary hardware and software, we have to address the function of each host within the community, i.e. the *delegation* of specialized tasks called *services* to particular hosts, and also the competition between users and hosts for resources, both local and distributed. In order for all of this to work with some measure of equilibrium, it has to be carefully planned and orchestrated.

6.2.3   Load balancing

In the deployment of machinery, there are two opposing philosophies: one machine, one job, and the consolidated approach. In the first case, we buy a new host for each new task on the network. For instance, there is a mail server and a printer server and a disk server, and so on. This approach was originally used in PC networks running DOS, because each host was only capable of running one program at a time. That does not mean that it is redundant today: the distributed approach still has the advantage of spreading the load of service across several hosts. This is useful if the hosts are also workstations which are used interactively by users, as they might be in small groups with few resources. Making the transition from a mainframe to a distributed solution was discussed in a case study in ref. [308].

On the whole, modern computer systems have more than enough resources to run several services simultaneously, so the judgment about consolidation or distribution has to be made on a case-by-case basis, using an analytical evaluation. Indeed, a lot of unnecessary network traffic can be avoided by placing all file services (disk, web and FTP) on the same host, see chapter 9. It does not necessarily make sense to keep data on one host and serve them from another, since the data first have to be sent from the disk to the server and then from the server to the client, resulting in twice the amount of network traffic.

The consolidated approach to services is to place them all on just a few server-hosts. This can plausibly lead to better security in some cases, though perhaps greater vulnerability to failure, since it means that we can exclude users from the server itself and let the machine perform its task.

Today most PC network architectures make this simple by placing all of the burden of services on specialized machines which they call 'servers' (i.e. server-hosts). PC server-hosts are not meant to be used by users themselves: they stand apart from workstations. With Unix-based networks, we have complete freedom to run services wherever we like. There is no principal difference between a workstation and a server-host. This allows for a rational distribution of load.

Of course, it is not just machine duties which need to be balanced throughout the network, there is also the issue of human tasks, such as user registration, operating system upgrades, hardware repairs and so on. This is all made simpler if there is a team of humans, based on the principle of delegation.

> **Principle 31 (Delegation II).** *For large numbers of hosts, distributed over several locations, a policy of delegating responsibility to local administrators with closer knowledge of the hosts' patterns of usage minimizes the distance between administrative center and zone of responsibility. Zones of responsibility allow local experts to do their jobs.*

This suggestion is borne out by the model scalability arguments in section 6.3.

It is important to understand the function of a host in a network. For small groups in large organizations, there is nothing more annoying than to have central administrators mess around with a host which they do not understand. They will make inappropriate changes and decisions.

Zones of responsibility have as much to do with human limitations as with network structure. Human psychologists have shown that each of us has the ability to relate to no more than around 150 people. There is no reason to suppose that this limitation does not also apply to other objects which we assemble into our work environment. If we have 4000 hosts which are identical, then that need not be a psychological burden to a single administrator, but if those 4000 consist of 200 different groups of hosts, where each group has its own special properties, then this would be an unmanageable burden for a single person to cope with. Even with special software, a system administrator needs to understand how a local milieu uses its computers, in order to avoid making decisions which work against that milieu.

6.2.4 Mobile and ad hoc networks

Not all situations can be planned for in advance. If we suppose that system design can be fully determined in advance of its deployment, then we are assuming that systems remain in the same configuration for all time. This is clearly not the case. One must therefore allow for the possibility of random events that change the conditions under which a system operates. One example of this is the introduction of mobile devices and humans. Mobility and partial connectivity of hosts and users is an increasingly important issue in system administration and it needs to be built into models of administration.

An 'ad hoc' network (AHN) is defined to be a networked collection of mobile objects, each of which has the possibility to transmit information. The union of those hosts forms an arbitrary graph that changes with time. The nodes, which include humans and devices, are free to move randomly thus the network topology may change rapidly and unpredictably. Clearly, ad hoc networks are important in a mobile computing environment, where hosts are partially or intermittently connected to other hosts, but they are also important in describing the high level associations between parts of a system. Who is in contact with whom? Which ways do information flow?

While there has been some discussion of decentralized network management using mobile agents [333], the problem of mobile nodes (and so strongly time-varying topology) has received little attention. However, we will argue below that ad hoc networks provide a useful framework for discussing the problems surrounding configuration management in all network types, both fixed and mobile. This should not be confused with the notion of 'ad hoc management' [204], which concerns randomly motivated and scheduled checks of the hosts.

6.2.5 Peer-to-peer services

Another phenomenon that has received attention in recent years is the idea of peered networks, i.e. not hierarchical structures in which there are levels of authority, but networks in which each user has equal authority.

The emergence of network file sharing applications, such as Napster and Gnutella, has focused attention on an architecture known as peer-to-peer, whose aim is to provide world-wide access to information via a highly decentralized network of 'peers'. An important challenge to providing a fully distributed information sharing system is the design of scalable algorithmic solutions. Algorithms such as those for routing and searching peer-to-peer networks are typically implemented in the form of an application-level protocol.

> **Definition 5 (Peer-to-peer application).** *A peer-to-peer network application is one in which each node, at its own option, participates in or abstains from exchanging data with other nodes, over a communications channel.*

Peer-to-peer has a deeper significance than communication. It is about the demotion of a central authority, in response to the political wishes of those participating in the network. This is clearly an issue directly analogous to the policies used for configuration management. In large organizations, i.e. large networks, we see a frequent dichotomy of interest:

- At the high level, one has specialized individuals who can paint policy in broad strokes, dealing with global issues such as software versions, common security issues, organizational resource management, and so on. Such issues can be made by software producers, system managers and network managers.

- At the local level, users are more specialized and have particular needs, which large-scale managers cannot address. Centralized control is therefore only a partial strategy for success. It must be supplemented by local know-how, in response to local environmental issues. Managers at the level of centralized control have no knowledge of the needs of specialized groups, such as the physics department of a university, or the research department of a company. In terms of configuration policy, what is needed is the ability to accept the advice of higher authorities, but to disregard it where it fails to meet the needs of the local environment. This kind of authority delegation is not well catered for by SNMP-like models. Policy-based management attempts to rectify some of these issues [86].

What we find then is that there is another kind of networking going on: a social network, superimposed onto the technological one. The needs of small clusters of users override the broader strokes painted by wide-area management.

This is the need for a scaled approach to system management [47].

6.3 Network administration models

The management of clusters of systems leads to the concept of *logistic networks*. Here it is not the physical connectivity that is central to the deployment, but rather the associative relationships and channels of communication. Here, we follow the discussion in ref. [53].

Central management 'star' model

The traditional (idealized) model of host configuration is based on the idea of remote management (e.g. using SNMP). Here one has a central manager who decides and implements policy from a single location, and all networks and hosts are considered to be completely reliable. The manager must monitor the whole network, using bi-directional communication. This leads to an $N : 1$ ratio of clients to manager (see figure 6.3). This first model is an idealized case in which there is no unreliability in any component of the system. It serves as a point of reference.

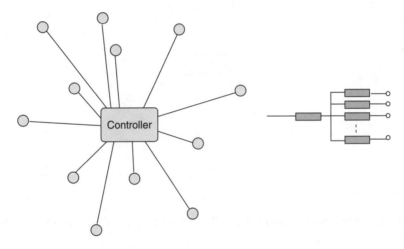

Figure 6.3: Model 1: the star network. A central manager maintains bi-directional communication with all clients. The links are perfectly reliable, and all enforcement responsibility lies with the central controller.

The topology on the left-hand side of figure 6.3 is equivalent to that on the right-hand side. The request service capacity of the controller is thus:

$$I_{\text{controller}} = I_1 + I_2 + \cdots + I_N. \tag{6.1}$$

The controller current cannot exceed its capacity, which we denote by C_S. We assume that the controller puts out the flow of repair instructions at its full capacity; this gives the simple maximum estimate

$$I_{\text{repair}} = \frac{C_S}{N}. \tag{6.2}$$

The total current is limited only by the bottleneck of queued messages at the controller, thus the throughput per node is only $1/N$ of the total capacity. This highlights the clear disadvantage of centralized control, namely the bottleneck in communication with the controller.

Models 1 and 2: Star model in intermittently connected environment

The previous model was an idealization, and was mainly of interest for its simplicity. Realistic centralized management must take into account the unreliability of the environment (see figure 6.4).

In an environment with partially reliable links, a remote communication model bears the risk of not reaching every host. If hosts hear policy, they must accept and comply; if not, they fall behind in the schedule of configuration. Monitoring in distributed systems has been discussed in ref. [3].

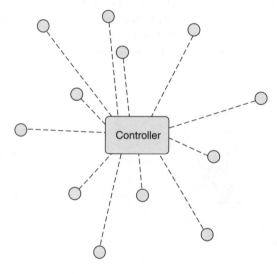

Figure 6.4: Model 2: a star model with built-in unreliability. Enforcement is central as in Model 1.

The capacity of the central manager C_S is now shared between the average number of hosts $\langle N \rangle$ that is available. The result is much the same as for Model 1, the completely reliable star. This is because there is an implicit assumption that the controller was clever enough to find (with negligible overhead) those hosts that are available at any given time, and so to only attempt to communicate with them – no latencies or other probabilities of unavailability were included.

This model then fails (perhaps surprisingly), on average, at the same threshold value for N as does Model 1. If the hunt for available nodes places a non-negligible burden on the controller capacity, then it fails at a lower threshold.

Model 3: Mesh topology with centralized policy and local enforcement

The serialization of tasks in the previous models forces configuration 'requests' to queue up on the central controller. Rather than enforcing policy by issuing every instruction from the central source, it makes sense to download a summary of the policy to each host and empower the host itself to enforce it.

There is still a centrally determined policy for every host, but now each host carries the responsibility of configuring itself. There are thus two issues: i) the update of the policy and ii) the enforcement of the policy. A pull model for updating policy is advantageous here, because every host then has the option to obtain updates at a time convenient to itself, avoiding confluence contentions (clients might not even be switched on or connected to a mobile network when the controller decides to send its information); moreover, if it fails to obtain the update, it can retry until it succeeds. We ask policy to contain a self-referential rule for updating itself.

The distinction made here between communication and enforcement is important because it implies distinct types of failure, and two distinct failure metrics: i) distance of the locally understood policy from the latest version, and ii) distance of the host configuration from the ideal policy configuration. In other words: i) communication failure, and ii) enforcement failure.

In this model, the host no longer has to share any bandwidth with its peers, unless it is updating its copy of the policy, and perhaps not even then, since policy is enforced locally and updates can be scheduled to avoid contention. The load on the controller is also much smaller in this model, because the model does not rely on the controller for every operation, only for a copy of its cache-able policy. The nodes can cooperate in diffusing policy updates via flooding.[1] (See figure 6.5.)

The worst case – in which the hosts compete for bandwidth, and do not use flooding – is still an improvement over the two previous models, since the rate at which updates of policy are required is much less than the traffic generated by the constant to and fro of the much more specific messages in the star models. However, note that this can be further improved upon by allowing flooding of updates: the authorized policy instruction can be available from any number of redundant sources, even though the copies originate from a central location. In this case, the model truly scales without limit.

There is one caveat to this encouraging result. If the (meshed) network of hosts is truly an ad hoc network of mobile nodes, employing wireless links, then connections are not feasible beyond a given physical range r. In other words, there are no long-range links: no links whose range can grow with the size of the network. As a result of this, if the AHN grows large (at fixed node density), the path length (in hops) between any node and the controller scales as a constant times $\sqrt{N}$. This growth in path length limits the effective throughput capacity between node and controller, in a way analogous to the internode capacity. The latter scales as $1/\sqrt{N}$ [137, 193]. Hence, for sufficiently large N, the controller and AHN will fail collectively to convey updates to the net. This failure will occur at a threshold value defined by

$$I_{\text{fail}}(ii) = I_{\text{update}} - \frac{C_S}{c\sqrt{N_{\text{thresh}}}} = 0, \tag{6.3}$$

where c is a constant. The maximal network size N_{thresh} is in this case proportional to $\left(\frac{C_S}{I_{\text{update}}}\right)^2$, still considerably larger than for Models 1 and 2.

---

[1]Note, flooding in the low-level sense of a datagram multicast is not necessarily required, but the effective dissemination of the policy around the network is an application-layer flood.

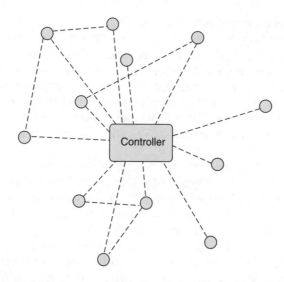

Figure 6.5: Model 3 mesh topology. Nodes can learn the centrally-mandated policy from other nodes as well as from the controller. Since the mesh topology does not assure direct connection to the controller, each node is responsible for its own policy enforcement.

Model 4: Mesh topology, partial host autonomy and local enforcement

As a variation on the previous model, we can begin to take seriously the idea of allowing hosts to decide their own policy, instead of being dictated to. In this model, hosts can choose not to receive policy from a central authority, if it conflicts with local interests. Hosts can make their own policy, which could be in conflict or in concert with neighbors. (See figure 6.6.)

Communication thus takes the role of conveying 'suggestions' from the central authority, in the form of the latest version of the policy. For instance, the central authority might suggest a new version of widely-used software, but the local authority might delay the upgrade due to compatibility problems with local hardware. Local enforcement is now employed by each node to hold to its chosen policy P_i. Thus communication and enforcement use distinct channels (as with Model 3); the difference is that each node has its own target policy P_i which it must enforce.

Thus the communications and enforcement challenges faced by Model 4 are the same (in terms of scaling properties) as for Model 3. Hence this model can in principle work to arbitrarily large N.

Model 4 is the model used by cfengine [41, 49]. The largest current clusters sharing a common policy are known to be of the order 10^4 hosts, but this could soon be of the order 10^6, with the proliferation of mobile and embedded devices.

Model 5: Mesh, with partial autonomy and hierarchical coalition

An embellishment of Model 4 is to allow local groups of hosts to form policy coalitions that serve to their advantage. Such groups of hosts might belong to one

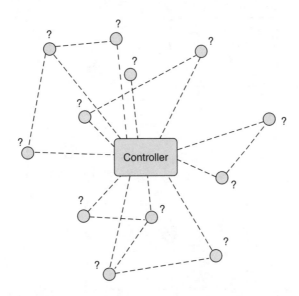

Figure 6.6: Model 4. As in Model 3, except the hosts can choose to disregard or replace aspects of policy at their option. Question marks indicate a freedom of hosts to choose.

department of an organization, or to a project team, or even to a group of friends in a mobile network (see figure 6.7).

Once groups form, it is natural to allow sub-groups and thence a generalized hierarchy of policy refinement through specialized social groups.

If policies are public then the scaling argument of Model 3 still applies since any host could cache any policy; but now a complete policy must be assembled from several sources. One can thus imagine using this model to distribute policy so as to avoid contention in bottlenecks, since load is automatically spread over multiple servers. In effect, by delegating local policy (and keeping a minimal central policy) the central source is protected from maximal loading. Specifically, if there are S sub-controllers (and a single-layer hierarchy), then the effective update capacity is multiplied by S. Hence the threshold N_{thresh} is multiplied (with respect to that for Model 3) by the same factor.

This model could be implemented using cfengine, with some creative scripting.

Model 6: Mesh, with partial autonomy and inter-peer policy exchange

The final step in increasing autonomy is the free exchange of information between arbitrary hosts. Hosts can now offer one another information, policy or source materials in accordance with an appropriate trust model. In doing so, impromptu coalitions and collaborations wax and wane, driven by both human interests and possibly machine learning. A peer-to-peer policy mechanism of this type invites trepidation amongst those versed in control mechanisms, but it is really no more than a distributed genetic algorithm. With appropriate constraints it could be made to lead to sensible convergent behavior, or to catastrophically unstable behavior (see figure 6.8).

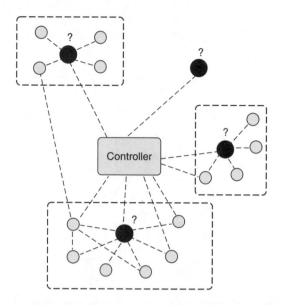

Figure 6.7: Model 5. Communication over a mesh topology, with policy choice made hierarchically. Sub-controllers (dark nodes) edit policy as received from the central controller, and pass the result to members of the local group (as indicated by dashed boxes). Question marks indicate the freedom of the controllers to edit policy from above.

One example of such a collaborative network that has led to positive results is the Open Source Community. The lesson of Open Source Software is that it leads to a rapid evolution. A similar rapid evolution of policy could also be the result from such exchanges. Probably policies would need to be weighted according to an appropriate fitness landscape. They could include things like shared security fixes, best practices, code revisions, new software, and so on.

Until this exchange nears a suitable stationary point, policy updates could be much more rapid than for the previous models. This could potentially dominate configuration management behavior.

Note that this model has no center. Hence it is, by design, scale-free: all significant interactions are local. Therefore, in principle, if the model can be made to work at small system size, then it will also work at any larger size.

In practice, this model is subject to potentially large transients, even when it is on its way to stable, convergent behavior. These transients would likely grow with the size of the network. Here we have confined ourselves to long-time behavior for large N – hence we assume that the system can get beyond such transients, and so find the stable regime.

Finally, we note that we have only assessed the goodness of a given model according to its success in communicating and enforcing policy. When policy is centrally determined, this is an adequate measure of goodness. However, for those cases in which nodes can choose policy, one would also like to evaluate the goodness of the resulting choices. We do not address this important issue here. We note however that Model 6, of all the models presented here, has the greatest freedom to explore the space of possible policies. Hence an

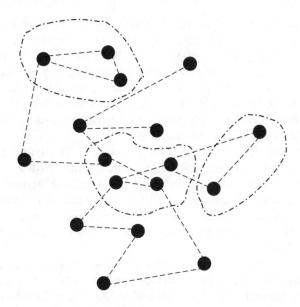

Figure 6.8: Model 6. Free exchange of policies in a peer-to-peer fashion; all nodes have choice (dark). Nodes can form spontaneous, transient coalitions, as indicated by the dashed cells. All nodes can choose; question marks are suppressed.

outstanding and extremely nontrivial question for this peer-to-peer model of configuration management is: can such a system find 'better' policies than centralized systems?

In short, this model has no immediate scaling problems with respect to communication and enforcement. Open questions include the scaling behavior of transients, and the ability of this completely decentralized model to find good policy.

6.4 Network management technologies

The ability to read information about the performance of network hardware via the network itself is an attractive idea. Suppose we could look at a router on the second floor of a building half a mile away and immediately see the load statistics, or the number of rejected packets it has seen; or perhaps the status of all printers on a subnet. That would be useful diagnostic information. Similar information could be obtained about software systems on any host.

6.4.1 SNMP network management

The Simple Network Management Protocol (SNMP) is a protocol designed to do just this [59, 268, 269]. SNMP was spawned in 1987 as a Simple Gateway Monitoring Protocol, but was quickly extended and became a standard for network monitoring. SNMP was designed to be small and simple enough to be able to run on even minor pieces of network technology like bridges and printers. The model of configuration management is particularly suited to non-interactive devices like printers and static network infrastructure that require an essentially static configuration over long periods of time. SNMP has since been extended, with less success, to some aspects of host management such as workstations and PC network server configuration; however, the static model of configuration is less appropriate here since users are constantly perturbing servers in unpredictable ways and, combined with the unimpressive security record of early versions, this has discouraged its use for host management.

SNMP now exists in three versions (see figure 6.9). The traditional SNMP architecture is based on two entities: managers and agents. SNMP managers execute management applications, while SNMP agents mediate access to management variables. These variables hold simple typed values and are arranged into groups of scalars of single-valued variables or into conceptual tables of multi-valued variables. The set of all variables on a managed system is called the Management Information Base (MIB).[2]

SNMP has often been criticized for the weak security of its agents, which are configured by default with a clear text password of 'public'. Version 3 of the SNMP protocol was finally agreed on and published in December 2002 in order to address these problems, using strong encryption methods. If or when this version becomes widespread, SNMP will be as secure as any other network service.

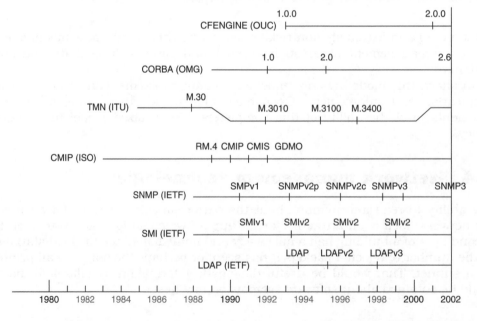

Figure 6.9: A historical perspective of some network management technologies.

SNMP supports three operations on devices: *read*, *write* and *notify* (through 'traps'). The management console can read and modify the variables stored on a device (see section 7.10) and issue notifications of special events. SNMP access is

---

[2]The term MIBs is sometimes used to refer to the collection of variables on a box and, in other contexts, to the SMI module defining the semantics, data types and names of variables.

mediated by a server process on each hardware node (the agent), which normally communicates by UDP/IP on ports 161 and 162. Modern operating systems often run SNMP daemons or services which advertise their status to an SNMP-capable manager. The services are protected by a rather weak password which is called the *community string*.

Because SNMP is basically a 'peek–poke' protocol for simple values, its success depends crucially on the ability of the Management Information Bases or MIBs to correctly characterize the state of devices, and how the agents translate MIB values into real actions. For monitoring workload (e.g. load statistics on network interfaces, or out-of-paper signals on a printer), this model is clearly quite good. Indeed, even host-based tools (ps, top, netstat etc.) use this approach for querying resource tables on more complex systems. Moreover, in the case of dumb network devices, whose behavior is essentially fixed by a few parameters or lists of them (printers, switches etc.), this model even meets the challenge of configuration reasonably well.

The notify functionality is implemented by 'traps' or events that can be configured in the SNMP agent. Each event type is defined by the SNMP software of the device being managed, e.g. Cisco routers have general traps, such as:

```
coldStart
linkDown
linkUp
authenticationFailure
egpNeighborLoss
reload
tcpConnectionClose
ciscoConfigManEvent
```

that are triggered by interface changes and management events.

The variables that exist in an MIB are formally defined in so-called MIB modules (RFC 1213) that are written in a language called the Structure of Management Information (SMI). The SMI provides a generic and extensible name-space for identifying MIB variables. Due to a lack of higher level data structuring facilities, MIB modules often appear as a patchwork of individual variable definitions rather than a class structure in Java or other object-oriented languages. An SNMP request specifies the information it wants to read/write by giving the name of an instance of the variable to read or write in a request. This name is assigned in the formal MIB module. There are standard MIB modules for address translation tables, TCP/IP statistics and so on. These have default parameters that can be altered by SNMP: system name, location and human contact; interface state (up/down), hardware and IP address, IP state (forwarding gateway/not) IP TTL, IP next HOP address, IP route age and mask, TCP state, neighbor state, SNMP trap enabling, and so on.

Although SNMP works fairly well for monitoring clusters of static devices, its success in managing hosts, including workstations and servers, is more questionable. Even disregarding the scalability problems noted in section 6.3, the MIB model is very difficult to tailor to hosts where users are interacting with the system constantly. Hosts are no longer basically predictable devices with approximately constant state; their state changes dynamically in response to user interaction, and in response to the services they perform. The SNMP management philosophy, i.e. of communicating with an agent for reading and writing, is only effective when the rate of change of state of a device is slow, i.e. when the device changes only at about the same rate as the rate of change of policy itself. Moreover, the complexity of operations that can be carried out by a dumb SNMP agent, based only on MIB 'push button' instructions and a bilateral communication with a management interface, is limited. Thus, in practice, SNMP can only be used to detect problems, not to repair them. This is not so much a problem in the model, but in the manner in which it is implemented. If SNMP agents contained on-board intelligence, then the communication model could be retained. One is then into the territory of more intelligent agent systems like cfengine and PIKT.

Despite the shortcomings of SNMP for host operations, many operating systems do define their own MIBs for the collection of system performance data and even for essential configuration parameters. Some commercial network management systems like Hewlett Packard's OpenView work by reading and writing MIBs using SNMP client-server technology. Most Unix variants, Novell and NT now also support SNMP. Their MIBs can be used even to collect information such as the names of users who are logged on. This information is not particularly relevant to the problem of resource management and can even be considered a security risk, thus many remain sceptical about the use of SNMP on hosts.

In 1997, SNMPv3 was put forward in order to provide stronger security, particularly in the authentication of the manager–agent connection. This has helped to allay some of the fears in using SNMP where it is appropriate, but it does not make the task of tailoring the MIB model easier.

SNMP seems to be increasing in popularity for monitoring network hardware (routers and switches etc.), but like any public information database, it can also be abused by network attackers. SNMP is a prime target for abuse and some sites choose to disable SNMP services altogether on hosts, using it only for monitoring network transport hardware.

Suggestion 7 (SNMP containment). *Sites should filter SNMP packets to and from external networks to avoid illegal access of these services by intruders.*

6.4.2   OSI, TMN and others

SNMP has many competitors. The International Telecommunications Union (ITU) has defined the Telecommunications Management Network (TMN) standards for managing telecommunications networks [205]. It is an alternative scheme designed for telecommunications networks and has a strong relationship with the OSI Management Model known as the Common Management Information Protocol (CMIP). Common Object Request Broker Architecture (CORBA) is now being adopted as the middle-ware for TMN. The Distributed Management Task Force (DMTF) developed the Desktop Management Interface (DMI) until 1998. Moreover, central to several configuration management schemes is LDAP, the lightweight directory service (see section 9.8). Recently, a rival IETF group began work on a competing system to SNMP called COPS-PR [101].

These systems all use an abstraction based on the concept of 'managed objects'. A different approach is used by systems like cfengine [41] and PIKT [231], which use descriptive languages to describe the attributes of many objects at the same time, and agents to enforce the rules.

The ISO 7498 Open System Interconnect (OSI) Model consists of a large number of documents describing different aspects of network communication and management.[3] Amongst these is the basic conceptual model for management of networked computers. It consists of these issues:

- Configuration management

- Fault management

- Performance management

- Security management

- Accounting management.

Configuration management is taken to include issues such as change control, hardware inventory mapping, software inventories and customization of systems. Fault management includes events, alarms, problem identification, troubleshooting, diagnosis and fault logging. Performance covers capacity planning, availability, response times, accuracy and throughput. Security discusses policy, authorization, exceptions, logging etc. Finally, accounting includes asset management, cost controls and payment for services.

The OSI Management Model is rather general and difficult to disagree with, but it does not specify many details either. Its interpretation has often been somewhat literal in systems like TMN and SNMP.

6.4.3 Java Management Extension (JMX)

Java Management Extension (JMX) is Java's answer to dealing with managed objects. The paradigm of monitoring and changing object contents is absorbed into Java's model of enterprise management. Its aim is to allow the management of new and legacy systems alike. The basic idea of JMX is not very different to that of SNMP, but the transport mechanisms are integrated into Java's extensive middleware framework.

MX defines a standard instrumentation model, called MBeans, for use in Java programs and by Java management applications. JMX also specifies a set of complementary services that work with MBean instrumentation to monitor and manage Java-based applications. These services range from simple monitors and timers to a powerful relation service that can be used to create user-defined associations between MBeans in named roles and a mechanism for dynamically loading new instrumentation and services at run time.

---

[3]These documents must be purchased from the ISO web site.

6.4.4 Jini and UPnP: management-free networks

Jini is a Java derivative technology that is aimed at self-configuring ad hoc networks. It is middle-ware that provides application programming interfaces (API) and networking protocols for discovery and configuration of devices that have only partial or intermittent connectivity. A similar project is Microsoft's Universal Plug'n'Play (UPnP), a peer-to-peer initiative that uses existing standards like TCP/IP, HTTP and XML to perform a similar function. The aim of these technologies is to eliminate the need for system administrators, by making devices configure themselves.

In a traditional fixed infrastructure network, many services rely on the existence of the fixed infrastructure. If a host is removed or a new host is added to the network, a manual reconfiguration is often necessary. Jini and UPnP aim to remove the need for this manual reconfiguration by providing negotiation protocols that make computing devices much more 'plug'n'play'. They are designed to accept all kinds of devices, including mobile computing platforms and home appliances. These technologies are hailed as the way forward towards *pervasive computing*, i.e. a future in which embedded networked computers are in appliances, walls, even clothes.

A Jini environment is a distributed environment. It requires a certain level of infrastructure in order to work, but it also provides redundancy and fail-over capabilities. Each device coupled to a network advertises its interfaces and services to the network, including information about who is allowed to communicate with it. Devices are represented as Java objects. Each device provides a set of services resulting in a *federation*. Two services of special interest are *lookup* and *discovery* services, which are responsible for allowing new devices to join an existing ad hoc federation.

No central authority controls this federation of devices. Jini is peer-to-peer in the sense that each device can act as a client or a server depending on whether it is providing or requesting a service. Services could be anything from file-transfer to querying temperature sensors in a building. In order to handle failures of infrastructure, Jini only leases a resource to a client for a fixed amount of time. After the term has expired, the client must renew the lease to continue using the service. The lease expires for all users if a service goes down. A device may then attempt to contact a different service provider if one is available, by looking for one in the published list of services.

The Java Naming and Directory Interface (JNDI) is the front-end to object naming and directory services on the network. It works in concert with other J2EE (Java 2 Enterprise Edition) components to organize and locate services. JNDI provides Java-enabled applications with a unified interface in an enterprise environment (see section 9.12).

In other distributed computing models, such as CORBA, DCOM, or even Unix RPC services, the functioning of services relies on client-server 'stubs' or protocol interfaces that handle the communication standards. These need to be in place before a device can communicate with other devices. Jini makes use of Web services and Java code portability to allow such a stub to be downloaded through a generic download mechanism. The only requirement is that all devices need to run their own Java Virtual Machine. Devices that do not have a Java virtual machine can be adapted with 'surrogate' devices. A surrogate device is like a 'ghost' of the actual device, kept on a fixed infrastructure host. This acts as a mediator between the actual device and a Jini interface.

These auto-configuration protocols will make future computing device configuration less of a headache for system administrators, and will allow us to take advantage of short-range wireless network communication protocols like Bluetooth. Of course, they do not really remove the need for a system administrator, but they push the need for administration up a layer of abstraction. Administrators will no longer need to fiddle with device drivers on individual hosts; rather, they will be tasked to maintain the Java infrastructure, including setting up the appropriate bindings within JNDI, and similar directory services. This is a simpler and more rational approach to device management.

6.5 Creating infrastructure

Until recently, little attention was given to analyzing methodologies for the construction of efficient and stable networks from the ground up, although some case studies for large-scale installations were made [170, 112, 289, 60, 215, 179, 129, 276, 149, 212, 164, 107]. One interesting exception is a discussion of human roles and delegation in network management in refs. [207, 135]. With the explosion in numbers of hosts combined in networks, several authors have begun to address the problem of defining an infrastructure model which is stable, reproducible and robust to accidents and upgrades [41, 108, 305, 44].

The term 'bootstrapping an infrastructure' was coined by Traugott and Huddleston in ref. [305] and nicely summarizes the basic intent. Both Evard [108] and Traugott and Huddleston have analyzed practical case studies of system infrastructures both for large networks (4000 hosts) and for small networks (as few as 3 hosts). Interestingly, Evard's conclusions, although researched independently of Burgess [39, 41, 55, 42, 43], clearly vindicate the theoretical model used in constructing the tool cfengine.

6.5.1 Principles of stable infrastructure

The principles on which we would like to build an infrastructure are straightforward, and build upon the idea of predictability under load.

> **Principle 32 (Scalability).** *Any model of system infrastructure must be able to scale efficiently to large numbers of hosts (and perhaps subnets, depending on the local netmask).*

A model which does not scale efficiently with numbers of hosts is likely to fail quickly, as networks tend to expand rapidly beyond expectations.

> **Principle 33 (Reliability).** *Any model of system infrastructure must have reliability as one of its chief goals. Down-time can often be measured in real money.*

Reliability is not just about the initial quality of hardware and software, but also about the need for preventative maintenance.

Corollary to principle (Redundancy). *Reliability is safeguarded by redundancy, or backup services running in parallel, ready to take over at a moment's notice [285].*

Although redundancy does not prevent problems, it aids swift recovery. Barber has discussed improved server availability through redundancy [26]. High availability clusters and mainframes are often used for this problem. Gomberg et al. have compared scalable software installation methods on Unix and NT [132]. A refinement of the principle of homogeneity can be stated here, in its rightful place:

> **Principle 34 (Homogeneity/Uniformity II).** *A model in which all hosts are basically similar is i) easier to understand conceptually both for users and administrators, ii) cheaper to implement and maintain, and iii) easier to repair and adapt in the event of failure.*

and finally:

Corollary to principle (Reproducibility). *Avoid improvising system modifications, on the fly, which are not reproducible. It is easy to forget what was done and this will make the functioning of the system difficult to understand and predict, for you and for others.*

The issue of *convergence* towards a stable state is central here (see section 6.7). Basically, convergence means that a system should always get closer to an ideal configuration, rather than farther away from it. This signals the need for continual maintenance of the system. The convergence idea will return several times throughout the book.

6.5.2 Virtual machine model

Traugott and Huddleston [305] have eloquently argued that one should think of a networked system not so much as a loose association of hosts, but rather as a large virtual machine composed of associated organs. It is a small step from viewing a multitasking operating system as a collaboration between many specialized processes, to viewing the entire network as a distributed collaboration between specialized processes on different hosts. There is little or no difference in principle between an internal communication bus and an external communication bus. This would seem to suggest that the idea of peer association, described in section 6.3, is to be abandoned, but that need not be the case: there are several levels at which one can interpret the models in section 6.3. One must first specify what a node is. What Traugott and Huddleston observe is that it makes sense to treat tightly collaborating clusters as a unit.

Many sites adopt specific policies and guidelines in order to create this seamless virtual environment [58] by limiting the magnitude of the task. Institutions with a history of managing large numbers of hosts have a tradition of either adapting imperfect software to their requirements or creating their own. Tools such as make, which have been used to jury-rig configuration schemes [305] can now be replaced by more specific tools like cfengine [41, 55]. As with all things, getting started is the hard part.

6.5.3 Creating uniformity through automation

Simple, robust infrastructure is created by planning a system which is easy to understand and maintain. If we want hosts to have the same software and facilities, creating a general uniformity, we need to employ automation to keep track of changes [154, 41, 55]. To begin, we must formulate the needs of and potential threats to system availability. That means planning resources, as in the foregoing sections, and planning the actual motions required to implement and maintain the system. If we can formalize those needs by writing them in the form of a policy, program or script, then half the battle is already won, and we have automatic reproducibility.

> **Principle 35 (Abstraction generalizes).** *Expressing tasks in an operating system independent language reduces time spent debugging, promotes homogeneity and avoids unnecessary repetition.*

A script implies reproducibility, since it can be rerun on any host. The only obstacle to this is that not all script languages work on all systems.

> **Suggestion 8 (Platform independent languages).** *Use languages and tools which are independent of operating system peculiarities, e.g.* cfengine, Perl, python. *More importantly, use the right tool for the right job.*

Perl is particularly useful, since it runs on most platforms and is about as operating system independent as it is possible to be. The disadvantage of Perl is that it is a low-level programming language, which requires us to code with a level of detail which can obscure the purpose of the code. Cfengine was invented to address this problem. The cfengine is a very high-level interface to system administration. It is also platform independent, and runs on most systems. Its advantage is that it hides the low-level details of programming, allowing us to focus on the structural decisions. We shall discuss this further below.

6.5.4 Revision control

One approach to the configuration of hosts is to have a standard set of files in a file-base which can be simply copied into place. Several administration tools have been built on this principle, e.g. Host Factory [110]. The Revision Control System (RCS), designed by Tichy [302], was created as a repository for files, where changes could be traced through a number of evolving versions. RCS was introduced as a tool for programmers, to track bug fixes and improvements through a string of versions. The CVS system is an extended front-end to this system. System configuration is a similar problem, since it involves modifying the contents of many key files. Many administrators have made use of the revision control systems to keep track of configuration file changes, though little has been written about it. PC management with RCS has been discussed by Rudorfer [261]. Revision control is a useful way of keeping track of text-file changes, but it does not help us with other aspects of system maintenance, such as file permissions, process management or garbage collection.

6.5.5   Software synchronization

In section 3.8.9 we discussed the distribution of data amongst a network community. This technique can be used to maintain a level of uniformity in the software used around the network. Software synchronization has been discussed in refs. [27, 147, 282]. Distribution by package mechanisms were pioneered by Hewlett Packard [256] with the install program. For some software packages Hewlett Packard use cfengine as a software installation tool [55]. Distribution by placement on network filesystems like the AFS has been discussed in [183].

6.5.6   Push models and pull models

Revision control does not address the issue of uniformity unless the contents of the file-base can be distributed to many different hosts. There are two types of distribution mechanism, which are generally referred to as *push* and *pull* models of distribution.

- *Push:* The push model is epitomized by the `rdist` program. Pushing files from a central location to a number of hosts is a way of forcing a file to be written to a group of hosts. The central repository decides when changes are to be sent, and the hosts which receive the files have no choice about receiving them [203]. In other words, control over all of the hosts is forced by the central repository. The advantage of this approach is that it can be made efficient. A push model is more easily optimized than a pull approach. The disadvantage of a push model is that hosts have no freedom to decide their own fate. A push model forces all hosts to open themselves to a central will. This could be a security hazard. In particular, `rdist` requires a host to grant not just file access, but full complete privilege to the distributing host. Another problem with push models is the need to maintain a list of all the hosts to which data will be pushed. For large numbers of hosts, this can become unwieldy.

- *Pull:* The pull model is represented by `cfengine` and `rsync`. With a pull model, each host decides to collect files from a central repository, of its own volition. The advantage of this approach is that there is no need to open a host to control from outside, other than the trust implied by accepting configuration files from the distributing host. This has significant security advantages. It was recommended as a model of centralized system administration in refs. [265, 55, 305]. The main disadvantage to this method is that optimization is harder. `rsync` addresses this problem by using an ingenious algorithm for transmitting only file changes, and thus achieves a significant compression of data, while `cfengine` uses multi-threading to increase server availability.

6.5.7   Reliability

One of the aims of building a sturdy infrastructure is to cope with the results of failure. Failure can encompass hardware and software. It includes downtime due to physical error (power, net cables and CPUs) and also downtime due to software crashes. The net result of any failure is loss of service. Our only defence against actual failure is parallelism, or redundancy. When one component fails, another can be ready to take over. Often it is possible to *prevent failure* with pro-active maintenance (see the next chapter for more on this issue). For instance, it is possible to vacuum clean hosts to prevent electrical short-circuits. It is also possible to perform garbage collection which can prevent software error. System monitors (e.g. cfengine) can ensure that crashed processes get restarted, thus minimizing loss. Reliability is clearly a multifaceted topic. We shall return to discuss reliability more quantitatively in section 13.5.10.

Component failure can be avoided by parallelism, or redundancy. One way to think about this is to think of a computer system as providing a service which is characterized by a flow of information. If we consider figure 6.10, it is clear that a flow of service can continue when servers work in parallel, even if one or more of them fails. In figure 6.11 it is clear that systems which are dependent on other systems are coupled in series and a failure prevents the flow of service. Of course, servers do not really work in parallel. The normal situation is to employ a *fail-over* capability. This means that we provide a backup service. If the main service fails, we replace it with a backup server. The backup server is not normally used however. Only in a few cases can one find examples of load-sharing by switching between (de-multiplexing) services on different hosts. Network Address Translation can be used for this purpose (see figure 2.11).

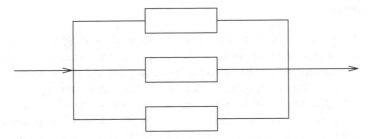

Figure 6.10: System components in parallel, implies redundancy.

Figure 6.11: System components in series, implies dependency.

6.6 System maintenance models

Models of system maintenance have evolved by distilling locally acquired experience from many sites. In latter years, attempts have been made to build software systems which apply certain principles to the problem of management. Network management has, to some extent, been likened to the process of software development in the System Administration Maturity Model, by Kubicki [187]. This work was an important step in formalizing system administration. Later, a formalization was introduced by describing system administration in terms of automatable primitives.

- Unix administrators have run background scripts to perform system checks and maintenance for many years. Such scripts (often called *sanity checking* scripts) run daily or hourly and make sure that each system is properly configured, perform garbage cleaning and report any serious problems to an administrator. In an immunological model, the aim is to minimize the involvement of a human being as far as possible.

- Windows can be both easier and harder to administrate than Unix. It can be easier because the centralized model of having a domain server running all the network services, means that all configuration information can be left in one place (on the server), and that each workstation can be made (at least to a limited degree) to configure itself from the server's files. It is harder to administer because the tools provided for system administration tasks work mainly by the GUI (*graphical user interface*) and this is not a suitable tool for addressing the issues of hundreds of hosts.

Several generalized approaches to the management of computers in a network have emerged.

6.6.1 Reboot

With the rapid expansion of networks, the number of local networks has outgrown the number of experienced technicians. The result is that there are many administrators who are not skilled in the systems they are forced to manage. A disturbing but common belief, which originated in the 1980s microcomputer era, is that problems with a computer can be fixed by simply rebooting the operating system. Since home computer systems tend to crash with alarming regularity, this is a habit which has been acquired from painful experience. One learns nothing from this procedure, however, and the same strategy can cause problems for machines that are part of a larger system. Just because a terminal hangs, it does not mean that the host is not working at something important.

Although rebooting or powering down can appear to solve the immediate obstacle, and in some few cases might be the only course of action, one stands also to lose data that might be salvaged, and perhaps interrupt the interaction of the machine with remote hosts. Rebooting a multi-user system is dangerous since users might be logged in from remote locations and could lose data and service.

6.6.2 Manual administration

The default approach to system management is to allow qualified humans to do everything by hand. This approach suffers from a lack of scalability. It suffers from human flaws and a lack of intrinsic documentation. Humans are not well-disciplined at documenting their work, or their intended configurations. There are also issues concerned with communication and work in a team, which can interfere with the smooth running of systems. When two manual administrators have a difference of opinion, there can be contention. The relevance of interpersonal skills in system administration teamwork was considered in ref. [168] and a cooperative shell environment for helping to discipline work habits was considered in ref. [2].

6.6.3 Central control

Another approach to system administration is the use of control systems, in the manner of the star model. Tivoli, HP OpenView and Sun Solstice are examples of these. In the control approach, the system administrator follows the state of the network by defining error conditions to look for. A process on each host reports errors as they occur to the administrator. In this way the administrator has an overview of every problem on the network from his/her single location and can either fix the problems by hand as they occur (if the system supports remote login), or distribute scripts and antidotes which provide a partial automation of the process. The disadvantage with this system is that a human administrator usually has to start the repair procedures by hand and this creates a bottleneck: all the alarms go to one place to be dealt with serially. With this approach, the amount of work required to run the system increases roughly linearly with the number of hosts on the network.

6.6.4 Immunology (self-maintenance)

A relatively new approach to system management which is growing in popularity is the idea of equipping networked operating systems with a simple immune system. By analogy with the human body, an immune system is an automatic system that every host possesses which attempts to deal with emergencies. An immune system is the Fire, Police and Paramedic services as well as the garbage collection agencies. In an immune system, every host is responsible for automatically repairing its own problems, without crying warnings about what is going on to a human. This avoids a serial bottleneck created by a human administrator. The time spent on implementing and running this model is independent of the number of hosts on the network.

6.7 Competition, immunity and convergence

All collective systems (including all biological phenomena) are moderated and stabilized by a cooperative principle of *feedback regulation*. This regulating principle is sometimes called the prey–predator scenario, or a game, because it is about *competition* between different parts of a system. When one part of the system starts to grow out of control, it tends to favor the production of an antidote which keeps that part in check. Similarly, the antidote cannot exist without the original system, so it cannot go so far as to destroy the original system, since it destroys itself in the process. A balance is therefore found between the original part of the system and its antidote. The classical example of a prey–predator model is that of populations of foxes and rabbits. If the number of rabbits increases suddenly, then foxes feed well and grow in numbers, eating more rabbits, thus stabilizing the numbers. If rabbits grow scarce, then foxes die and thus an equilibrium is maintained. Another example of this type of behavior is to be found in the body's own repair and maintenance systems. The name 'immunity' is borrowed from the idea that systems of biological complexity are able to repair themselves in such a way as to maintain an equilibrium called *health*. The relative immunity of, for instance, the human body to damage and disease is due to a continual equilibrium between death, cleanup and renewal. Immunity from disease is usually attributed to an *immune system*, which is comprised of cells which fight invading organisms, though it has become clear over the years that the phenomenon of immunity is a function of many cooperating systems throughout the entire human organism, and that disease does not distinguish between *self* and *non-self* (body and invader) as was previously thought. In the immunity model, we apply this principle to the problem of system maintenance.

The immunity model is about self-sufficient maintenance and is of central importance to all scalable approaches to network management, since it is the only model which scales trivially with the number of networked hosts. The idea behind immunity is to automate host maintenance in such a way as to give each host responsibility for its own configuration. A level of automation is introduced to every host, in such as way as to bring each host into an *ideal state*. What we mean by an ideal state is not fixed: it depends on local system policy, but the central idea of the immunity model is to keep hosts as close to their ideal state as possible.

The immunity model has its origins in the work of John von Neumann, the architect of modern computer systems. He was the first person to recognize the analogy between living organisms and computers [313, 314], and clearly understood the conceptual implications of computing machines which could repair and maintain themselves, as early as 1948.

Automatic systems maintenance has been an exercise in tool-building for many years. The practice of automating basic maintenance procedures has been commonplace in the Unix world, see section 7.8.1. Following von Neumann's insights, the first theoretical work on this topic, addressing the need for convergence, appears in refs. [41, 55]. The biological analogy between computers and human immune systems has been used to inspire models for the detection of viruses, principally in insecure operating systems. This was first discussed in 1994 by Kephart of IBM in ref. [175] and later expanded upon by Forrest et al. [118, 291, 121, 119, 156, 290, 317, 155, 94, 120, 238, 93]. The analogy between system administration and immunology was discussed independently by Burgess in [43, 44], in the wider context of general system maintenance. References [44, 42] also discuss how computer systems can be thought of as statistical mechanical systems, drawing on a wide body of knowledge from theoretical physics. Interestingly, ref. [44] and ref. [291], which appeared slightly earlier, point out many of the same ideas independently, both speculating freely on the lessons learned from human immunology, though the latter authors do not seem to appreciate the wider validity of their work to system maintenance.

The idea of immunity requires a notion of convergence. *Convergence* means that maintenance work (the counter-force or antidote) tends to bring a host to a state of *equilibrium*, i.e. a stable state, which is the state we would actually like the system to be in. The more maintenance that is performed, the closer we approach the ideal state of the system. When the ideal state is reached, maintenance work stops, or at least has no further effect. The reason for calling this the immunity model is that this is precisely the way that biological maintenance works. As long as there is damage or the system is threatened, a counter-force is mobilized, followed by a garbage collection and a repair team. There is a direct analogy between medicine and computer maintenance. Computer maintenance is just somewhat simpler.

Critics of the convergence approach to system administration argue that systems should be controlled absolutely and not allowed to simply meander into a stable state. Traugott has argued that many users are not disciplined enough to make convergence adequate for ensuring predictability, and that hosts should be managed absolutely by wiping out hosts that deviate from specification and rebuilding them step by step. This approach is called congruence rather than convergence [304]. Convergence proponents retort that convergence by ensuring sequences of commuting atomic operations is the only reliable way to achieve a guaranteeable state.

6.8 Policy and configuration automation

The idea of being able to automate the configuration from a high-level policy was the idea behind cfengine. Prior to cfengine, several authors had explored the possibilities for automation and abstraction without combining all the elements into an integrated framework [138, 114, 154, 14]; most of these were too specific or too low level to be generally useful.

Cfengine and PIKT [231] are system administration tools consisting of two elements: a language and a configuration engine. Together these are used to instruct and enable all hosts on a network about how to configure and maintain themselves. Rather than being a cloning mechanism, cfengine takes a broader view of system configuration, enabling host configurations to be built from scratch on *classes* of host.

Cfengine is about defining the way we want all the hosts on our network to be configured, and having them do the work themselves. PIKT is similar, but allows a mixture of declarative and imperative programming to define host policy. These and other tools are for automation and for definition. Because they include language for describing system configuration at a high level, they can also be used to express system policy in formal terms. The correct way to use cfengine is therefore to specify and automate system policy in terms of concrete actions. See section 7.11.

What make declarative languages different from scripting languages is the high level at which they operate. Rather than allowing complete programming generality, they usually provide a set of *intelligent primitives* for configuring and maintaining systems. An important feature of cfengine primitives is that they satisfy, as far as possible, the principle of convergence (see section 6.7). This means that a policy expressed by a cfengine program can easily be made to embody a convergent behavior. As a system inevitably drifts from its ideal state, a cfengine policy brings it back to that ideal state. When it reaches that state, cfengine becomes quiescent and does no more.

Policy-based administration works from a central configuration, maintained from one location. That central configuration describes the entire network by referring to classes and types of host. Many abstraction mechanisms are provided for mapping out the networks. The work of configuration and maintenance is performed by each host separately. Each host is thus given responsibility for its own state and the work of configuration is completely distributed. This means that a cfengine or PIKT policy, for instance, scales trivially with the number of hosts, or put another way, the addition of extra hosts does not affect the ability of other hosts to maintain themselves. Traffic on servers increases at most linearly with the number of hosts and the network is relied upon as little as possible. This is not true of network-based control models, for instance, where network resource consumption increases at least in proportion to the total number of hosts, and is completely reliant on network integrity (see section 6.3).

6.9   Integrating multiple OSs

Combining radically different operating systems in a network environment is a challenge both to users and administrators. Each operating system services a specific function well, and if we are to allow users to move from operating system to operating system with access to their personal data, we need to balance the convenience of availability with the caution of differentiation. It ought to be clear to users where they are, and what system they are using, to avoid unfortunate mistakes. Combining different Unix-like systems is challenge enough, but adding Windows hosts or MacIntosh technology to a primarily Unix-based network, or vice versa, requires careful planning [37]. Integrating radically different network technologies is not worth the effort unless there is some particular need. It is always possible to move data between two hosts using the universally supported FTP protocol. But do we need to have open file sharing or software compatibility?

6.9.1   Compatible naming

Different operating systems use quite different naming schemes for objects. Until the late 1990s, Unix names could not be represented in MSDOS unless they were no longer than eight characters. Some operating systems did not allow spaces in filenames. Some assign and reserve special meanings for characters. The Internet URL naming scheme has created its own naming scheme for objects, which takes into account the service or communications channel used to access the object:

```
Channel://Object-name
```

File names are often, but not always, hierarchical. Windows introduced the notion of 'drives', for instance: A:, B:, C: and so on. The Internet Protocol family uses a hierarchical naming scheme encoded into IP addresses. The general problem of naming objects in distributed systems has great importance to being able to locate resources and express their locations. See ref. [71] for a discussion of this, for example.

Names can play a fundamental role in how we choose to integrate resources within a system. They address both cultural and practical issues.

6.9.2 Filesystem sharing

Sharing of filesystems between different operating systems can be useful in a variety of circumstances. File-servers, which host and share users' files, need to be fast, stable and capable machines. Workstations for end-users, on the other hand, are chosen for quite different reasons. They might be chosen to run some particular software, or on economic ground, or perhaps for user-friendliness. The MacIntosh has always been a favorite workstation for multi-media applications. It is often the preferred platform for music and graphical applications. Windows operating systems are cheap and have a wide and successful software base.

There are other reasons for wanting to keep an inhomogeneous (heterogeneous) network. An organization might need a mainframe or vector processor for intensive computation, whose disks need to be available to workstations for collecting data. There might be legacy systems waiting to be replaced with new machinery, which we have to accommodate in order to run old software, or development groups supporting software across multiple platforms. There are a dozen reasons for integration.

What about solutions? Most solutions to the file-sharing problem are software based. Client and server software is available for implementing network-sharing protocols across platform boundaries. For example, client software for the Unix NFS filesystem has been implemented for both Windows (PCNFS) and MacIntosh system 7/8/9. This enables Windows and MacIntosh workstations to use Unix-like hosts as file and printer servers, in much the same way as Windows servers or Novell Netware servers provide those services. These services are adequate for insecure operating systems, since there is no need to map file permissions across foreign filesystems. Windows is more of a problem, however. Windows ACLs cannot be represented in a simple fashion on a Unix filesystem.

The converse, that of making Unix files available to PCs, has the reverse problem. While NT is capable of representing Unix file permissions, Windows 9x and the MacIntosh are not. Insecure operating systems are always a risk in network sharing. The Samba software is a free software package which implements Unix file semantics in terms of the Windows SMB (Server Message Block) protocols.

Netware provides an NT client called NDS (Network Directory Services) for NT which allows NT domain servers to understand the Novell object directory model. Clearly, there is already filesystem compatibility between PC servers. Conversely, NT provides Netware clients and other server products can be purchased to provide access to AS/400 mainframes. Both Novell and NT provide MacIntosh clients, and MacIntosh products can also talk to NT and Unix servers. GNU/Linux has made a valiant attempt to link up with most existing sharing protocols on Unix, PCs and Apple hosts.

Mechanisms clearly exist to implement cross-platform sharing. The main question is, how easy are these systems to implement and maintain? Are they worth the cost in time and money?

6.9.3   User IDs and passwords

If we intend to implement sharing across such different operating systems as Unix and Windows, we need to have common usernames on both systems. Cross-platform user authentication is usually based on the understanding that username text can be mapped across operating systems. Clearly numerical Unix user IDs and Windows security IDs cannot map meaningfully between systems without some glue to match them: that glue is the username. To achieve sharing, then, we must standardize usernames. Unix-like systems often require usernames to be no more than eight characters, so this is a good limit to keep to if Unix-like operating systems are involved or might become involved.

> **Principle 36 (One name for one object II).** *Each user should have the same unique name on every host. Multiple names lead to confusion and mistaken identity. A unique username makes it clear which user is responsible for which actions.*

Common passwords across multiple platforms is much harder than disk sharing, and it is a much more questionable practice (see below).

6.9.4   User authentication

Making passwords work across different operating systems is often a pernicious problem in a scheme for complete integration. The password mechanisms for Unix and Windows are completely different and basically incompatible. The new Mac OS Server X is based on BSD4.4 emulation, so its integration with other Unix-like operation systems should be relatively painless. Windows, however, remains the odd-one-out. Whether or not it is correct to merge the password files of two separate operating systems is a matter for policy. The user bases of one operating system are often different from the user bases of another. From a security perspective, making access easy is not always the right thing to do.

Passwords are incompatible between Windows and Unix for two reasons: NT passwords can be longer than Unix passwords and the form of encryption used to store them is different. The encryption mechanisms which are used to store passwords are one-way transformations, so it is not possible to convert one into the other. There is no escaping the fact that these systems are basically incompatible.

A fairly recent development is the invention of Pluggable Authentication Modules (PAM) in Solaris, and their subsequent adopting in other flavors of Unix. The PAM mechanism is an indirection mechanism for exchanging or supplementing authentication mechanisms, for users and for network services, simply by adding modules to a configuration file /etc/pam.conf.

Instead of being prompted for a Unix password on login, users are connected to one or more password modules. Each module prompts for a password and grants security credentials if the password is correctly received. Thus, for instance, users could be immediately prompted for a Unix password, a Kerberos password and a DCE password on login, thus removing the necessity for a manual login to these extra systems later. PAM also supports the idea of mapped passwords, so that a single strong password can be used to trigger the automatic login to several stacked modules, each with its own private password stored in a PAM database.

This is a very exciting possibility, mitigated only by a conspicuous lack of documentation about how to write modules for PAM. PAM could clearly help in the integration of Unix with Windows if a module for Windows-style authentication could be written for Unix.

6.10 A model checklist

A model of system administration that encompasses cooperation and delegation must pass some basic tests.

- What technologies are supported by the model?

- What human practices are supported by the model?

- Will the model survive a reinstallation or upgrade of the major hardware at our site?

- Will the model survive a reinstallation or upgrade of the major software at our site?

- Will the network and its productivity survive the loss of any component?

- Do any of the solutions or choices compromise security or open any back-doors?

- What is more important: user freedom or system well-being (convenience or security)?

- Do users understand their responsibilities with regard to the network? (Do they need to be educated as part of the model?)

- Have we observed all moral and technical responsibilities with respect to the larger network?

- Is the system easy to understand for users and for system administrators?

- Does the system function predictably and fail predictably?

If it fails one of these tests, one could easily find oneself starting again in a year or so.

Exercises

Self-test objectives

1. What are the objectives of computer management?

2. What is the difference (if any) between management and regulation?

3. What is meant by an information model? What information needs to be modeled in a human–computer system?

4. What is a directory service?

5. What is meant by White Pages and Yellow Pages?

6. Describe the X.500 information model.

7. What are current popular implementations of directory services and how do they differ?

8. What is the main problem with Sun Microsystem's Network Information Service (NIS) today?

9. What is meant by system infrastructure?

10. Argue for and against homogeneity of hardware and software in a computer network.

11. What is meant by load balancing?

12. What is an ad hoc network?

13. What is meant by a peer-to-peer network?

14. Explain why a peer-to-peer network *is* a client-server technology, in spite of what is sometimes claimed.

15. Explain what is meant by the star model of network management.

16. Describe the ability of the star model to cope with large numbers of machines.

17. How does intermittent connectivity (e.g. mobile communications) affect the ability of the star model to cope with large numbers of devices?

18. What is meant by a hierarchical topology?

19. What is meant by a mesh topology?

20. Describe the SNMP management model.

21. What is an MIB?

22. Describe the Jini system of device management. How does it differ from SNMP?

23. What are the main principles of stable infrastructure?

24. Explain the virtual machine model of human–computer networks.

25. What role does revision control play in system administration?

26. What is meant by a push model of host management? What is meant by a pull model?

27. Describe the OSI model for network management.

28. What is TMN?

29. What does convergence mean in the context of system administration?

30. Describe the issues in integrating multiple operating systems.

Problems

1. Discuss why system homogeneity is a desirable feature of network infrastructure models. How does homogeneity simplify the issues of configuration and maintenance? What limits have to be placed on homogeneity, i.e. why can't hosts all be exactly identical?

2. Draw an information hierarchy for your company, college or university. Use it to draw up a schema for building a directory service.

3. Explain what is meant by Traugott and Huddleston's virtual machine view of the network. Compare this view of a computer system with that of a living organism, formed from many cooperating organs.

4. Compare the file system naming conventions in Windows and Unix. How are devices named? How are they referred to? Are there any basic incompatibilities between Unix and Windows names today?

5. Explain what is meant by the term *convergence* in configuration management. What are the advantages of convergence? Are there any disadvantages?

6. What is a directory service? What is the difference between a directory service and a name service?

7. Discuss how a directory service can bind together an organization.

8. In an administrative environment, it is often important to have the ability to *undo* changes which have been made. Discuss how you might implement a version control scheme for your system in which you could roll out and then roll back a system to a previous state. Describe how you would implement a scheme using

   (a) A convergent policy declaration (e.g. cfengine).
   (b) An imperative specification of steps (e.g. make and Perl).

9. Explain the difference between a *push* model and a *pull* model of system administration. What are the security implications of these and how well do they allow for delegation of responsibility in the network?

10. Discuss what special problems have to be solved in a heterogeneous network, i.e. one composed of many different operating systems.

11. Evaluate the cfengine language primitives: are these natural and sufficient for writing a policy that maintains any operating system? If not, what extra primitives are needed?

12. What are the advantages of a central point of control and configuration in network management? What are the disadvantages?

13. Suppose you have at your disposal four Unix workstations, all of the same type. One of them has twice the amount of memory. What would you use for DNS? Which would be a web server? Which would be an NFS server? Explain your reasoning.

14. These days, network communities consist of many PCs with large disks that utilize their space very poorly. Discuss a strategy for putting this spare disk capacity to use, e.g. as a possible backup medium. Consider both the practical and security aspects of your plan.

15. Formulate a plan for delegation of tasks within a system administration team. Create an information model that tries to prevent members of a team from interfering with one another, but at the same time gives no one administrator too much power or responsibility. If one of the team falls ill, will the team continue to function? Is the same true if a new member comes into the group? What personal considerations are important?

Chapter 7

Configuration and maintenance

We are now faced with two overlapping issues: how to make a computer system operate in the way we have intended, and how to keep it in that state over a period of time. Configuration management is the administration of *state* in hosts or network hardware. Host state is configured by a variety of methods:

- Configuration text file

- XML file

- Database format (registry)

- Transmitted protocol (ASN.1).

Configuration and maintenance are clearly related issues. Maintenance is simply configuration in the face of creeping decay. All systems tend to decay into chaos with time. There are many reasons for this decline, from deep theoretical reasons about thermodynamics, to the more intuitive notions above wear and tear. To put it briefly, it is clear that the number of ways in which a system can be in order is far fewer than the number of ways in which a system can be in a state of disorder, thus statistically any random change in the system will move it into disorder, rather than the other way around. We can even elevate this to a principle to emphasize its inevitability:

> **Principle 37 (Disorder).** *Systems tend to a state of disorder unless a disciplined policy is maintained, because they are exposed to random noise through contact with users.*

Whether by creeping laziness or through undisciplined cooperation in a team [242, 270, 340, 106], poor communication or whatever, the system *will* degenerate as small errors and changes drive it forward. That degeneration can be counteracted by repair work which either removes or mitigates the errors.

> **Principle 38 (Equilibrium).** *Deviation from a system's ideal state can be smoothed out by a counteractive response. If these two effects are in balance, the system will stay in equilibrium.*

Equilibrium is a 'fixed point' of the system behavior. System administration is about finding such fixed points and using them to develop policy. The time scales over which errors occur and which repairs are made are clearly important. If we correct the system too slowly, it will run away from us; there is thus an inherent potential for instability in computer networks.

7.1 System configuration policy

So far our analysis of networks has been about mapping out which machines performed what function on the network (see chapter 3 and section 3.8.6). Another side of network setup is the policies, practices and procedures which are used to make changes to or to maintain the system as a whole, i.e. what humans decide as part of the system administration process.

System administration is often a collaborative effort between several administrators. It is therefore important to have agreed policies for working so that everyone knows how to respond to 'situations' which can arise, without working against one another. A system policy also has the role of summarizing the attitudes of an organization to its members and its surroundings and often embodies security issues. As Howell cites from Pogo [161], '*We have met the enemy, and he is us!*' A system policy should contain the issues we have been discussing in the foregoing chapters. There are issues to be addressed at each level: network level, host level, user level.

> **Principle 39 (Policy).** *A clear expression of goals and responses prepares a site for future trouble and documents intent and procedure. Policy should be a protocol for achieving system predictability.*

It is crucial that everyone agrees on policy matters. Although a policy can easily be an example of blind rule-making, it is also a form of communication. A policy documents acceptable behavior, but it should also document what response is appropriate in a crisis. Only then are we assured of an orchestrated response to a problem, free of conflicts and disagreements. What is important is that the document does not simply become an exercise in bureaucracy, but is a living guide to the *practice* of network community administration. A system policy can include some or all of the following:

- *Organization:* What responsibility will the organization take for its users' actions? What responsibility will the organization take for the users' safety. Who is responsible for what? Has the organization upheld its responsibilities to the wider network community? Measures to prevent damage to others and from others.

- *Users:* Allowing and forbidding certain types of software. Rigid control over space (quotas) or allow freedom, but police the system with controls. Choice of default configuration. A response to software piracy. A response to anti-social behavior and harassment of others (spamming, obnoxious news postings etc.). Are users allowed to play games, if so when? Are users allowed to chat online? Are users allowed to download files such as MP3 or pornography? Policy on sharing of accounts (i.e. preferably not). Policy on use of IRC robots and other automatic processes which collect large amounts of data off-line. Policy on garbage collection when disks become full: what files can legitimately be deleted?

- *Network:* Will the network be segmented, with different access policies on different subnets? Will a firewall be used? What ports will be open on which subnets, and which will be blocked at the router? What services will be run?

- *Mail:* Limit the size of incoming and outgoing mail. Spam filtering. Virus controls.

- *WWW:* Allowing or forbidding user CGI scripts. Guidelines for allowed content of web pages. Policy regarding advertising on web pages. Load restrictions: what to do if certain pages generate too much traffic. Policy on plagiarism and illegal use of imagery.

- *Printing:* How many pages can be printed? Is printing of personal documents allowed? Should there be a limit to the number of pages which can be printed at one time (large documents hold up the print queue)?

- *Security:* Physical security of hosts. Backup schedule. Who is allowed to be master of their own hosts? Can arbitrary users mount other users' home directories or mailboxes with NFS on their private PCs (this means that they have automatic access to everyone's personal files)? What access controls should be used on files? Password policy (aging, how often should passwords change) and policy on closing accounts which have been compromised.

- *Privacy:* Is encryption allowed? What tools will be provided for private communication?

See also the discussion of policy as a system administration tool in refs. [341, 140].

7.2 Methods: controlling causes and symptoms

Component-based software development is a central theme in modern design, and it has almost exclusively followed the path of trading control over algorithmic detail for limited freedoms through configurable parameters to standardized 'methods'. Sun Microsystems' Java technology and Microsoft's .NET are two recent developments that exemplify this trend. The need for *configuration* is thus a feature of all modern software systems, and what was previously an issue of programming a sequence of imperative logic, is now an issue of administrating a few basic choices. Thus programming is increasingly turning into system administration.

As we move ever more towards standardized methods and algorithms, the process of programming becomes increasingly one of administering the few remaining choices, as configuration options.

Example 4. *In Java-related technologies, there is a vast library of standardized methods for performing every kind of operation, from basic algorithms for hashing or encryption, to graphics, to database access. Low-level details are withheld from programmers, e.g. explicit database queries in SQL are replaced by standardized methods that hide the implementation details, and offer parameters for customizing usage. The issue is no longer one of creativity with basic imperative logic, but one of combining standardized blocks and materials into a usable scheme, more like an interior designer.*

Software engineers seldom think of the process of configuring components as a system administration issue, because 'system administration' is commonly assumed to apply only to the low-level infrastructure such as hardware and software installation. Nevertheless, it is important to understand the equivalence of these issues, because many flaws in software systems are provoked and exploited because software engineers make naive assumptions about infrastructure. Similarly, software engineers seldom think carefully about how software will be configured in practice across large installation bases. System administrators are thus left to improvise the best from a bad lot.

Clearly, there is a trade-off between detailed control and increasing standardization.

Principle 40 (Standardized methods offer predictability). *Replacing direct low-level control with configurable high-level interfaces increases standardization and thus predictability. If the methods are implemented correctly, this improves quality control; if they are flawed, it becomes a systematic error, but with only a single point of failure and repair.*

This trade-off is always a dilemma in the policy-making and government of both man and machine. There are ethical issues here also. By adopting standardized methods, one removes freedom of choice from the end user, or programmer; it is an authoritarian strategy that some users find disturbing, because it assumes that a high-level, standard authority knows better than a low-level technician, which is seldom true in a knowledge-based society; but it also has clear benefits of simplification to offer. There is economy in standardization, and – correctly implemented – a standard can find great leverage in the experiences of experts. Great power requires great responsibility, however, and should not be wielded in an inflexible way.

Example 5. *The control of basic infrastructure can be a huge responsibility. We have seen examples of this in the dominance of the Windows operating systems. The ease with which viruses propagate, for instance, is a direct result of the permissiveness of the operating system infrastructure. The lack of control administrators have over the basic methods prevents them from effectively solving the problem of viruses, except by installing counter-virus software.*

In this case, standardization to an unsatisfactory state leads to strategies for relieving symptoms rather than curing them at source. We can elevate this to a principle.

> **Principle 41 (Symptoms and cause).** *Inadequate control over infrastructure demands a strategy of short-term symptom relief in lieu of a more permanent reparation at source.*

Although it is preferable to fix problems at source, it is not always possible to do so. There will always be a need to distinguish between short-term patches and long-term patches, since the rate of software correction is much less than the rate at which errors are discovered.

7.3 Change management

The opposite side of the coin in configuration and maintenance is the management of significant changes, e.g. upgrades, redesign and replacement. Can such things be done without disruption to service? Does this idea contradict the idea of convergence referred to in section 6.7? Planning changes of infrastructure can be dealt with using two general strategies:

- Deconstruction followed by reconstruction.

- Change of policy description followed by convergence to a new state.

We might call these 'change' and 'organic growth' respectively. Traugott and Huddleston introduced the idea of infrastructure management in ref. [305] to describe the construction of systems from the bottom up. Traugott has later argued that this infrastructure needs to be maintained in much the same way as building it in the first place. Change management then becomes a reconstruction of infrastructure. An ideologically 'convergent' approach (typified by cfengine) would be to try to gradually change aspects of policy and allow the system to converge towards the state associated with the change.

To date, no study has been performed to compare these two approaches for major changes. Clearly, the larger the magnitude of a change, the closer these two approaches must become. The amount of work required to perform large changes through differential adjustment grows significantly with the magnitude of the change. At some point, the benefit of adjustment rather than reconstruction becomes ambiguous. Many system administrators will doubtless feel more comfortable with starting from scratch when large changes need to be made as a matter of convenience.

Why would people go over to the new, if the old still works? When making changes, one must not forget the issue of service provision and reliability. Temporary redundancy of service is a sensible precaution in a mission-critical environment. If something should go wrong during a change, service must continue. Securing predictability during a change is a tricky business, because the conditions under which a system is performing its function are changing. Change management can thus be viewed as a problem in risk or fault management. We return to this viewpoint in section 8.8.

7.4 Declarative languages

The idea that standardization can be achieved by providing only configuration parameters to predefined methods naturally leads us into the area of declarative languages, such as `make` or Prolog.

An imperative programming language, such as C or Perl, is a traditional specification of the steps required to build an algorithm that alters the state of the system from some initial state to a final one. The key feature is that the programmer must specify the route taken to get from initial to final state. With a declarative language, one does not say *how* to get from initial to final state, but rather what the final state should be. The language itself uses its battery of standard methods then to evaluate a solution to the problem. The result is an extremely economical form of expression, stripped of details that are usually irrelevant to the language user.

Cfengine is one specialized language for the purpose of configuration management [38, 41, 55] that has features in common with Prolog [79]. A declaration takes the form:

```
circumstances:

   declarative actions   new resulting circumstances
```

Thus when a certain set of circumstances arises, the declared actions are evaluated, leading possibly to new follow-up circumstances, with other rules to be evaluated. Rules are evaluated in an unspecified order, using an unspecified schedule.

The Unix tool `make` is similar to this, but it evaluates its dependencies both imperatively and recursively:

```
circumstances:  prior dependent circumstances

   imperative actions
```

With `make`, users have to specify the details of how to get from the initial to the final state using a secondary language; `make` is only a host framework for other language interpreters. Cfengine, on the other hand, has expert knowledge in the form of standard methods with special properties (see section 7.11).

7.5 Policy configuration and its ethical usage

The move towards systems built from standard configurable methods has another aspect that is somewhat darker. Although we shall not exaggerate its importance, it has long-term implications that are worthy of consideration by all system designers.

The removal of control from end users can mean a removal of the detailed knowledge required to run a system. This is a 'dumbing down' of the task of system administration. Such a prolonged dumbing down can result in a loss of the expertise required to diagnose and run the system. In turn this implies a polarization into those who 'can' and those who 'can't'. Will pilots one day lose the ability to fly jet-airliners? If so, what will happen when the technology fails? Will we one day end up slaves to a technology we no longer understand?

On the other hand, this process of absorbing common knowledge into standardized methods has been going on throughout history. It is nothing more than the abstraction of common wisdom into law or policy, i.e. by codifying it into a set of rules. Once an algorithm for solving a problem passes a certain threshold of maturity, it makes sense to remove it from the realm of constant doubt by formalizing it as policy. This involves a saving in time and effort. We no longer have to question what is well known. Naturally, this does not exempt us from re-evaluating that policy in the future, in new and unexpected circumstances. Indeed, the scientific method begs us to question all common wisdom in the light of all new circumstances.

The danger of codifying rules is that users lose their influence at each stage. If the purpose of the system is to serve users, then policy-making has the added responsibility to be for the greater good of a network community.

7.6 Common assumptions: clock synchronization

All software systems assume the existence of a certain reliable infrastructure. Often, it is the lack of such a reliable infrastructure that leads to security breaches and failures in software.

One of the most fundamental tasks in a network is to keep the clocks on all hosts synchronized. Many security and maintenance issues depend on clocks being synchronized correctly. Clock reliability varies enormously. The clocks on cheap PC hardware tend to drift very quickly, whereas clocks on more expensive workstations are often rather better at keeping time. This is therefore a particular problem for cheap PC networks.

One option for most Unix-like systems is the rdate command, which sets the local clock according to the clock of another host. The rdate is absent from some operating system distributions. It can be simulated by a script:

```
#!/bin/sh
#
# Fake rdate script for linux - requires ssh access on server
#

echo Trying time server

DATE=`/bin/su -c '/usr/bin/ssh time-server date'  remote-user`

echo Setting date string...

/bin/date --set="$DATE"
```

A more reliable way of keeping clocks synchronized, which works both for Unix and for Windows, is to use the NTP protocol, or network time protocol. A time-server is used for this purpose. The network time protocol daemon xntpd is used to synchronize clocks from a reliable time-server. Two configuration files are needed to set up this service on a Unix-like host: `/etc/ntp.conf` and `/etc/ntp.drift`. `/etc/ntp.conf` looks something like this, where the IP address is that of the master time-server, whose clock we trust:

```
driftfile /etc/ntp.drift
authdelay 0.000047
server 128.39.89.10
```

The `/etc/ntp.drift` file must exist, but its contents are undetermined. Commercial, free and open source NTP clients are available for virtually all operating systems [67].

7.7 Human–computer job scheduling

Scheduling of work, both human and automatic, can play an important role in the smooth functioning of a human–computer system. If repairs come too late, unnecessary problems can be caused. If repairs are scheduled too often, it can be wasteful and detract from other tasks. The ability for an administration system to execute jobs at predetermined times lies at the heart of keeping control over a changing, dynamic system.

7.7.1 The Unix `cron` service

Unix has a time daemon called `cron`: its chronometer. Cron reads a configuration file called a `crontab` file which contains a list of shell-commands to execute at regular time intervals. On modern Unix-like systems, every user may create and edit a crontab file using the command

```
crontab -e
```

This command starts a text editor allowing the file to be edited. The contents of a user's crontab file may be listed at any time with the command `crontab -l`. The format of a crontab file is a number of lines of the form

```
minutes  hours  day  month  weekday  Shellcommand
 0-59    0-23   1-31  1-12   Mon-Sun
```

An asterisk or star * may be used as a wildcard, indicating 'any'. For example:

```
# Run script every weekday morning Mon-Fri at 3:15 am:

15 3 * * Mon-Fri /usr/local/bin/script
```

A typical root crontab file looks like this:

```
#
# The root crontab
#
0 2 * * 0,4 /etc/cron.d/logchecker
```

```
5 4 * * 6   /usr/lib/newsyslog
0 0 * * *   /usr/local/bin/cfwrap /usr/local/bin/cfdaily
30 * * * *  /usr/local/bin/cfwrap /usr/local/bin/cfhourly
```

The first line is executed at 2:00 a.m. on Sundays and Wednesdays, the second at 4:05 on Saturdays; the third is executed every night at 00:00 hours and the final line is executed one per hour on each half-hour.

In old BSD 4.3 Unix, it was only possible for the system administrator to edit the crontab file. In fact there was only a single crontab file for all users, called `/usr/lib/crontab` or `/etc/crontab`. This contained an extra field, namely the username under which the command was to be executed. This type of crontab file is largely obsolete now, but may still be found on some older BSD 4.3 derivatives.

```
0,15,30,45 * * * * root /usr/lib/atrun
00 4 * * *          root /bin/sh /usr/local/sbin/daily   2>&1 | mail root
30 3 * * 6          root /bin/sh /usr/local/sbin/weekly  2>&1 | mail root
30 5 1 * *          root /bin/sh /usr/local/sbin/monthly 2>&1 | mail root
```

A related service under Unix, is the `at` command. This executes specific batch processes once only at a specific time. The `at` command does not use a configuration file, but a command interface. On some Unix-like systems, `at` is merely a front-end which is handled by a `cron`-scheduled program called `atrun`.

> **Suggestion 9 (Cron management).** *Maintaining cron files on every host individually is awkward. We can use cfengine as a front-end to cron, to give us a global view of the task list (see section 7.11.5).*

7.7.2 Windows schedule service

The Windows scheduling service is similar to `cron`. By default, only the Administrator has access to the scheduling service. All jobs started by the scheduling service are executed with the same user rights as the user who runs the service itself (normally the Administrator). Some commercial replacements for the schedule service exist, but these naturally add extra cost to the system.

When the scheduling service is running, the `at` command provides a user interface for managing the queue of tasks to execute. The scheduling service is coordinated for all hosts in a domain by the domain server, so the hostname on which a batch job is to run can be an argument to the scheduling command.

To schedule a new job to be executed either once or many times in the future, we write:

```
at host time command
```

The host argument is optional and refers to the host's Windows name, not its DNS name (hopefully the two coincide, up to a domain name). The time argument is written in the form `3:00 pm` or `15:00` etc. It may be followed by a qualifier which specifies the day, date and/or how many times the job is to be scheduled. The qualifier is a comma-separated list of days or dates. `/next` means execute once for each date or day in the following list. `/every` means execute every time one of the items in the following list matches. For example:

```
at 3:00pm /next Friday,13 C:\\site\host\local\myscript
```

would execute myscript at 15:00 hours on the first Friday following the date
on which the command was typed in, and then again on the first 13th of the
month following the date at which the command was typed in. It does not mean
execute on the first coming Friday 13th. The items in the list are not combined
logically with AND as one might be tempted to believe. The at command without
any arguments lists the active jobs, like its Unix counterpart. Here one finds that
each job has its own identity number. This can be used to cancel the job with a
command of the form:

```
at   ID /delete
```

7.7.3 Scheduling strategies

Scheduling is a way of parsing a tree of tasks in as efficient a manner as possible. The techniques for scheduling are well known from parallel processing and
operating system design. We follow the discussion in ref. [56], where it is argued
that, in the absence of optimal knowledge, random scheduling is an efficient way
of covering a task schedule. This was investigated further in ref. [263].

Considerable effort has been invested in the analysis and design of protocols
for enabling distributed system administration. Amongst these are control and
monitoring protocols, such as the Simple Network Management Protocol (SNMP)
[333, 230], and the higher level, abstract languages for policy-based management
[138, 12, 41, 86]. These languages address the issues of what is to be done if a
system is found to be in a particular state, or has received a particular signal.
They offer varying levels of sophistication and each has strengths and weaknesses.

Another important aspect of configuration management, which has received
less attention, is that of how management functions are scheduled, both in
response to specific events and as a general matter of the maintenance of the
system. Policy-based administration, employing agents or software robots, is an
administrative method which scales to large numbers of hosts in distributed
systems, precisely because every host is essentially responsible for its own state
of configuration. However, the interdependencies of such networked machines
mean that configuration management must reflect global properties of the network community, such as delegations and server functions. This presents special
challenges. It is thus important to have predictable scheduling properties.

Policy-based configuration languages associate the occurrence of specified
events or conditions, with responses to be carried out by an agent. Cfengine
accomplishes this by classifying the state of a host, at the time of invocation, into
a number of string identifiers. Some of these represent the time of invocation,
others the nature of the environment, and so on. For example:

```
files:

 (linux|solaris).Hr12::

   /etc/passwd mode=0644 action=fixall inform=true
```

The class membership is described in the second line. In this instance, it specifies the class of all hosts which are of type Linux or Solaris, during the time interval from 12:00 hours to 12:59 (Hr12). Tasks to be scheduled are placed in classes which determine the host(s) on which they should be executed, or the time at which they should be executed. Host-classes are essentially labels which document the attributes of different systems. They might be based on the physical attributes of the machine, such as its operating system type, architecture, or on some human attributes, such as geographical location or departmental affiliation. Actions are placed in such classes and are only performed if the agent executes the code in an environment which belongs to one of the relevant classes. Thus, by placing actions in judiciously chosen classes, one specifies actions to be carried out on either individual machines or on arbitrary groups of machines which have a common feature relating them. We thus have:

- Scheduling in time.

- Scheduling by host attribute (location, type etc).

Scheduling takes many forms, such as job-shop scheduling, production scheduling, multiprocessor scheduling, and so on. It can take place within any extent of time, space or other suitable covering-label.

The two main classes of scheduling are *dynamic* and *static* scheduling. Dynamic schedules can change their own execution pattern, while static ones are fully predetermined. In general, solving static scheduling problems is NP hard (i.e. there is no known algorithm that can do this in polynomial time). This involves assigning the vertices (tasks) of an acyclic, directed graph onto a set of resources, such that the total time to process all the tasks is minimized. The total time to process all the tasks is usually referred to as the *makespan*.

An additional objective is often to achieve a short makespan while minimizing the use of resources. Such multi-objective optimization problems involve complex trade-offs and compromises, and good scheduling strategies are based on a detailed and deep understanding of the specific problem domain. Most approaches belong to the family of priority-list scheduling algorithms, differentiated by the way in which task priorities are assigned to the set of resources. Traditionally, heuristic methods have been employed in the search for high-quality solutions [174]. Over the last decade, heuristics have been combined with modern search techniques such as simulated annealing and genetic algorithms [5].

In version 1 of cfengine, scheduling of tasks occurred in bulk, according to a sequence of simple list structures. This approach is extremely simple and works well enough, but it is unsatisfactory because it requires the author of a policy to understand the details of the scheduling of tasks and recursion properties. In cfengine 2, this is replaced by the methods described below.

7.7.4 Scheduling objectives and configuration management

The configuration management process can be understood as scheduling in several ways. The purpose of building a graphical representation is that it allows modeling of task management, and analysis that can be used to prove actual results, or to adapt results from well-known scheduling theory.

First of all, within a single policy there is often a set of classes or triggers which are interrelated by precedence relations. These relations constrain the order in which policies can be applied, and these graphs have to be parsed. A second way in which scheduling enters, is through the response of the configuration system to arriving events. Should the agents activate once every hour, in order to check for policy violations, or immediately; should they start at random times, or at predictable times? Should the policies scheduled for specific times of day, occur always at the same times of day, or at variable times, perhaps random. This decision affects the predictability of the system, and thus possibly its security in a hostile encounter. Finally, although scheduling is normally regarded as referring to extent over time, a distributed system also has two other degrees of 'spatial' extent: h and c. Scheduling tasks over different hosts, or changing the details of software components is also a possibility. It is possible to confound the predictability of software component configuration to present a 'moving target' to would-be attackers. The challenge is to accomplish this without making the system nonsensical to legitimate users. These are the issues we wish to discuss below.

A set of precedence relations can be represented by a directed graph, $G = (V, E)$, containing a finite, nonempty set of vertices, V, and a finite set of directed edges, E, connecting the vertices. The collection of vertices, $V = \{v_1, v_2, ..., v_n\}$, represents the set of n policies to be applied and the directed edges, $E = \{e_{ij}\}$, define the precedence relations that exist between these policies (e_{ij} denotes a directed edge from policy v_i to v_j).

This graph can be cyclic or acyclic. Cyclic graphs consist of *inter-cycle* and *intra-cycle* edges, where the inter-cycle edges are dependencies within a cycle and intra-cycle edges represent dependencies across cycles. When confronted with a cyclic graph then a set of transformations needs to be applied such that *intra-cycle* edges can be removed and the graph can be converted into an acyclic graph.

Configuration management is a mixture of a *dynamic* and *static* scheduling. It is dynamic in the sense that it is an ongoing real-time process where policies are triggered as a result of the environment. It is static in the sense that all policies are known *a priori*. Policies can be added, changed and removed arbitrarily in a dynamic fashion. However, this does not interfere with the static model because such changes would typically be made during a time-interval in which the configuration tools were idle or offline (in a quiescent state). The hierarchal policy model remains static in the reference frame of each configuration, but may change dynamically between successive frames of configuration.

7.7.5 Security and variable configurations

The predictability of a configuration is both an advantage and a disadvantage to the security of the system. While one would like the policy objectives to be constant, the details of implementation could legitimately vary without unacceptable loss. Predictability is often exploited by hostile users, as a means of circumventing policy. For instance, at Oslo University College, policy includes forced deletion of MP3 files older than one day, allowing users to download files for transfer to another medium, but disallowing prolonged storage. Hostile users quickly learn the time at which this tidying takes place and set up their own counter-measures in order to consume maximum resources. One way around this problem is to employ the methods of Game Theory [225, 48, 13, 33] to randomize behavior.

Randomization, or at least ad hoc variation, can occur and even be encouraged at a number of levels. The use of mobile technologies is one example. The use of changeable IP addresses with DHCP is another. The timing of important events, such as backups or resource-consuming activities is another aspect that can be varied unpredictably. In each case, such a variation makes it harder for potential weaknesses to be exploited by attackers, and similarly it prevents extensive maintenance operations from affecting the same users all of the time. In scheduling terms, this is a kind of load balancing. In configuration terms, it is a way of using unpredictability to our advantage in a controlled way.

Of course, events cannot be completely random. Some tasks must be performed before others. In all scheduling problems involving precedence relations, the graph is traversed using topological sorting. Topological sorting is based around the concept of a freelist. One starts by filling the freelist with the entry nodes, i.e. nodes with no parents. At any time one can freely select, or schedule, any element in the freelist. Once all the parents of a node have been scheduled the node can be added to the freelist. Different scheduling strategies and problems differ in the way elements are selected from the freelist. Most scheduling problems involve executing a set of tasks in the shortest possible time. A popular heuristic for achieving short schedules is the Critical Path/Most Immediate Successor First (CP/MISF) [174]. Tasks are scheduled with respect to their levels in the graph. Whenever there is a tie between tasks (when tasks are on the same level) the tasks with the largest number of successors are given the highest priority. The critical path is defined as the longest path from an entry node to an exit node.

In configuration management, the selection of nodes from the freelist is often viewed as a trivial problem, and the freelist may, for instance, be processed from left to right, then updated, in an iterative manner. If instead one employs a strategy such as the CP/MISF, one can make modifications to a system more efficiently in a shorter time than by a trivial strategy.

A system can be prone to attacks when it is configured in a deterministic manner. By introducing randomness into the system, it becomes significantly harder to execute repetitive attacks on the system. One can therefore use a random policy implementation when selecting elements from the freelist. The randomized topological sorting algorithms can be expressed as:

```
freelist := all_entry_nodes;
unscheduled := all_nodes;
while (not unscheduled.empty())
  begin
    node := freelist[random];
    delay(random);
    process(node);           // do whatever
    scheduled.add(node);
    freelist.remove(node);
    for all nodes in unscheduled whose parents are all scheduled
```

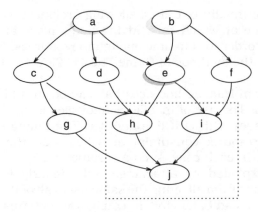

Figure 7.1: Random scheduling of precedence constrained policies.

```
        begin
          freelist.add(nodes);
          unscheduled.remove(nodes);
        end
    end
```

For example, figure 7.1 illustrates a policy dependence graph. In this example, policy *e* is triggering a management response. Clearly, only policies *h*, *i* and *j* depend on *e* and consequently need to be applied. Since policy *j* depends on both *h* and *i*, policy *h* and *i* must be applied prior to *j*. Therefore, the freelist is first filled with policies *h* and *i*. Policies *h* and *i* are then applied in the sequences *h*, *i* or *i*, *h*, both with a probability of 0.5.

Scheduling in a distributed environment is a powerful idea which extends in both time and 'space' (h, c, t). The main message of this discussion is that scheduling can be used to place reasonable limits on the behavior of configuration systems: ensuring that policy checks are carried out often enough, but not so often that they can be exploited to overwork the system. It should neither be possible to exploit the action of the configuration system, nor prevent its action. Either of these would be regarded as a breach of policy and security.

7.8   Automation of host configuration

The need for automation has become progressively clearer as sites grow and the complexity of administration increases. Some advocates have gone in for a distributed object model [157, 298, 84]. Others have criticized a reliance on network services [44].

7.8.1   Tools for automation

Most system administration tools developed and sold today (insofar as they exist) are based either on the idea of *control interfaces* (interaction between administrator and machine to make manual changes) or on the cloning of existing reference systems (mirroring) [14]. One sees graphical user interfaces of increasing complexity, but seldom any serious attention to autonomous behavior.

Many ideas for automating system administration have been reported; see refs. [138, 114, 180, 194, 21, 191, 10, 116, 259, 113, 84, 258, 249, 76, 229, 217, 92, 145, 173]. Most of these have been ways of generating or distributing simple shell or Perl scripts. Some provide ways of cloning machines by distributing files and binaries from a central repository. In spite of the creative effort spent developing the above systems, few if any of them can survive in their present form in the future. As indicated by Evard [108], analyzing many case studies, what is needed is a greater level of abstraction. Although developed independently, cfengine [38, 41, 55] satisfies Evard's requirements quite well.

Vendors have also built many system administration products. Their main focus in commercial system administration solutions has been the development of man–machine interfaces for system management. A selection of these projects are described below. They are mainly control-based systems which give responsibility to humans, but some can be used to implement partial immunity type schemes by instructing hosts to execute automatic scripts. However, they are not comparable to cfengine in their treatment of automation, they are essentially management frameworks which can be used to activate scripts.

Tivoli [298] is probably the most advanced and wide-ranging product available. It is a Local Area Network (LAN) management tool based on CORBA and X/Open standards; it is a commercial product, advertised as a complete management system to aid in both the logistics of network management and an array of configuration issues. As with most commercial system administration tools, it addresses the problems of system administration from the viewpoint of the business community, rather than the engineering or scientific community. Tivoli admits bidirectional communication between the various elements of a management system. In other words, feedback methods could be developed using this system. The apparent drawback of the system is its focus on application-level software rather than core system integrity. Also it lacks abstraction methods for coping with real-world variation in system setup.

Tivoli's strength is in its comprehensive approach to management. It relies on encrypted communications and client-server interrelationships to provide functionality including software distribution and script execution. Tivoli can activate scripts but the scripts themselves are a weak link. No special tools are provided here; the programs are essentially shell scripts with all of the usual problems. Client-server reliance could also be a problem: what happens if network communications are prevented?

Tivoli provides a variety of ways for activating scripts, rather like cfengine:

- Execute by hand when required.

- Schedule tasks with a cron-like feature.

- Execute an action (run a task on a set of hosts, copy a package out) in response to an event.

Tivoli's Enterprise Console includes a language Prolog for attaching actions to events. Tivoli is clearly impressive but also complex. This might also be a weakness. It requires a considerable infrastructure in order to operate, an infrastructure which is vulnerable to attack.

HP OpenView [232] is a commercial product based on SNMP network control protocols. Openview aims to provide a common configuration management system for printers, network devices, Windows and HPUX systems. From a central location, configuration data may be sent over the local area network using the SNMP protocol. The advantage of Openview is a consistent approach to the management of network services; its principal disadvantage, in the opinion of the author, is that the use of network communication opens the system to possible attack from hacker activity. Moreover, the communication is only used to alert a central administrator about perceived problems. Little automatic repair can be performed and thus the human administrator is simply overworked by the system.

Sun's Solstice [214] system is a series of shell scripts with a graphical user interface which assists the administrator of a centralized LAN, consisting of Solaris machines, to initially configure the sharing of printers, disks and other network resources. The system is basically old in concept, but it is moving towards the ideas in HP Openview.

Host Factory [110] is a third party software system, using a database combined with a revision control system [302] which keeps master versions of files for the purpose of distribution across a LAN. Host Factory attempts to keep track of changes in individual systems using a method of revision control. A typical Unix system might consist of thousands of files comprising software and data. All of the files (except for user data) are registered in a database and given a version number. If a host deviates from its registered version, then replacement files can be copied from the database. This behavior hints at the idea of an immune system, but the heavy-handed replacement of files with preconditioned images lacks the subtlety required to be flexible and effective in real networks. The blanket copying of files from a master source can often be a dangerous procedure. Host Factory could conceivably be combined with cfengine in order to simplify a number of the practical tasks associated with system configuration and introduce more subtlety into the way changes are made. Currently Host Factory uses shell and Perl scripts to customize master files where they cannot be used as direct images. Although this limited amount of customization is possible, Host Factory remains essentially an elaborate cloning system. Similar ideas for tracking network heterogeneity from a database model were discussed in refs. [301, 296, 113].

In recent years, the GNU/Linux community has been engaged in an effort to make GNU/Linux (indeed Unix) more user-friendly by developing any number of graphical user interfaces for the system administrator and user alike. These tools offer no particular innovation other than the novelty of a more attractive work environment. Most of the tools are aimed at configuring a single stand-alone host, perhaps attached to a network. Recently, several projects have been initiated to tackle clusters of Linux workstations [248]. A GUI for heterogeneous management was described in ref. [240].

7.8.2 Monitoring tools

Monitoring tools have been in proliferation for several years [144, 280, 178, 142, 150, 233, 262, 141]. They usually work by having a daemon collect some basic auditing information, setting a limit on a given parameter and raising an alarm if the value exceeds acceptable parameters. Alarms might be sent by mail, they might be routed to a GUI display or they may even be routed to a system administrator's pager [141].

Network monitoring advocates have done a substantial amount of work in perfecting techniques for the capture and decoding of network protocols. Programs such as `etherfind`, `snoop`, `tcpdump` and `bro` [236], as well as commercial solutions such as Network Flight Recorder [102], place computers in 'promiscuous mode', allowing them to follow the passing data-stream closely. The thrust of the effort here has been in designing systems for collecting data [9], rather than analyzing them extensively. The monitoring school advocates storing the huge amounts of data on removable media such as CD, to be examined by humans at a later date if attacks should be uncovered. The analysis of data is not a task for humans, however. The level of detail is more than any human can digest and the rate of its production and the attention span and continuity required are inhuman. Rather we should be looking at ways in which machine analysis and pattern detection could be employed to perform this analysis – and not merely after the fact. In the future, adaptive neural nets and semantic detection will likely be used to analyze these logs in real time, avoiding the need to even store the data in raw form.

Unfortunately there is currently no way of capturing the details of every action performed by the local host, analogous to promiscuous network monitoring, without drowning the host in excessive auditing. The best one can do currently is to watch system logs for conspicuous error messages. Programs like SWATCH [141] perform this task. Another approach which we have been experimenting with at Oslo college is the analysis of system logs at a statistical level. Rather than looking for individual occurrences of log messages, one looks for patterns of logging behavior. The idea is that logging behavior reflects (albeit imperfectly) the state of the host [100].

Visualization is now being recognized as an important tool in understanding the behavior of network systems [80, 162, 128]. This reinforces the importance of investing in a documentable understanding of host behavior, rather than merely relating experiences and beliefs [54]. Network traffic analysis has been considered in [16, 324, 228].

7.8.3 A generalized scripting language

Customization of the system requires us to write programs to perform special tasks. Perl was the first of a group of scripting languages including python, tcl and scheme, to gain acceptance in the Unix world. It has since been ported to Windows operating systems also. Perl programming has, to some extent, replaced much shell programming as the Free Software lingua franca of system administration. More recently Python, PHP and Tcl have been advocated also.

The Perl language (see appendix B.2) is a curious hybrid of C, Bourne shell and C-shell, together with a number of extra features which make it ideal for dealing with text files and databases. Since most system administration tasks deal with these issues, this places Perl squarely in the role of system programming. Perl is semi-compiled at runtime, rather than interpreted line-by-line like the shell, so it gains some of the advantages of compiled languages, such as syntax check before execution and so on. This makes it a safer and more robust language. It is also portable (something which shell scripts are not [19]). Although introduced as a scripting language, like all languages, Perl has been used for all manner of things for which it was never intended. Scripting languages have arrived on the computing scene with an alacrity which makes them a favorable choice to anyone wanting to get code running quickly. This is naturally a mixed blessing. What makes Perl a winner over many other special languages is that it is simply too convenient to ignore for a wide range of frequently required tasks. By adopting the programming idioms of well-known languages, as well as all the basic functions in the C library, Perl ingratiates itself to system administrators and becomes an essential tool.

7.9 Preventative host maintenance

In some countries, local doctors do not get paid if their patients get sick. This motivates them to practice preventative medicine, thus keeping the population healthy and functional at all times. A computer system which is healthy and functional is always equipped to perform the task it was intended for. A sick computer system is an expensive loss, in downtime and in human resources spent fixing the problem. It is surprising how effective a few simple measures can be toward stabilizing a system.

The key principle which we have to remember is that system behavior is a social phenomenon, an interaction between users' habits and resource availability. In any social or biological system, survival is usually tied to the ability of the system to respond to threats. In biology we have immunity and repair systems; in society we have emergency services like fire, police, paramedics and the garbage collection service, combined with routines and policy ('the law'). We scarely notice these services until something goes wrong, but without them our society would quickly decline into chaos.

7.9.1 Policy decisions

A policy of prevention requires system managers to make several important decisions. Let's return for a moment to the idea that users are the greatest danger to the stability of the system; we need to strike a balance between restricting their activities and allowing them freedom. Too many rules and restrictions leads to unrest and bad feelings, while too much freedom leads to anarchy. Finding a balance requires a policy decision to be made. The policy must be digested, understood and, not least, obeyed by users and system staff alike.

- *Determine the system policy.* This is the prerequisite for all system maintenance. Know what is right and wrong and know how to respond to a crisis.

Again, as we have reiterated throughout, no policy can cover every eventuality, nor should it be a substitute for thinking. A sensible policy will allow for sufficient flexibility (fault tolerance). A rigid policy is more likely to fail.

- *Sysadmin team agreement.* The team of system administrators needs to work together, not against one another. That means that everyone must agree on the policy and enforce it.

- *Expect the worst.* Be prepared for system failure and for rules to be broken. Some kind of police service is required to keep an eye on the system. We can use a script, or an integrated approach like cfengine for this.

- *Educate users in good and bad practice.* Ignorance is our worst enemy. If we educate users in good practice, we reduce the problem of policy transgressions to a few 'criminal' users, looking to try their luck. Most users are not evil, just uninformed.

- *Special users.* Do some users require special attention, extra resources or special assistance? An initial investment catering to their requirements can save time and effort in the long run.

7.9.2 General provisions

Damage and loss can come in many forms: by hardware failure, resource exhaustion (full disks, excessive load), by security breaches and by accidental error. General provisions for prevention mean planning ahead in order to prevent loss, but also minimizing the effects of inevitable loss.

- Do not rely exclusively on service or support contracts with vendors. They can be unreliable and unhelpful, particularly in an organization with little economic weight. Vendor support helpdesks usually cannot diagnose problems over the phone and a visit can take longer than is convenient, particularly if a larger customer also has a problem at the same time. Invest in local expertise.

- Educate users by posting information in a clear and friendly way.

- Make rules and structure as simple as possible, but no simpler.

- Keep valuable information about configuration securely, but readily, available.

- Document all changes and make sure that co-workers know about them, so that the system will survive, even if the person who made the change is not available.

- Do not make changes just before going away on holiday: there are almost always consequences which need to be smoothed out.

- Be aware of system limitations, hardware and software capacity. Do not rely on something to do a job it was not designed for.

- Work defensively and follow the pulse of the system. If something looks unusual, investigate and understand what is happening.

- Avoid gratuitous changes to things which already work adequately. 'If it ain't broke, don't fix it', but still aim for continuous but cautious improvement.

- Duplication of service and data gives us a fallback which can be brought to bear in a crisis.

Vendors often like to pressure sites into signing expensive service contracts. Today's computer hardware is quite reliable: for the cost of a service contract it might be possible to buy several new machines each year, so one can ask the question: should we write off seldom hardware failure as acceptable loss, or pay the one-off repair bill? If one chooses this option, it is important to have another host which can step in and take over the role of the old one, while a replacement is being procured. Again, this is the principle of redundancy. The economics of service contracts need to be considered carefully.

7.9.3 Garbage collection

Computer systems have no natural waste disposal system. If computers were biological life, they would have perished long ago, poisoned by their own waste. No system can continue to function without waste disposal. It is a thermodynamic impossibility to go on using resources forever, without releasing some of them again. That process must come to an end.

Garbage collection in a computer system refers to two things: disk files and processes. Users seldom clear garbage of their own accord, either because they are not really aware of it, or because they have an instinctive fear of throwing things away. Administrators have to enforce and usually automate garbage collection as a matter of policy. Cfengine can be used to automate this kind of garbage collection.

- *Disk tidying:* Many users are not even aware that they are building up junk files. Junk files are often the by-product of running a particular program. Ordinary users will often not even understand all of the files which they accumulate and will therefore be afraid to remove them. Moreover, few users are educated to think of their responsibilities as individuals to the system community of all users, when it comes to computer systems. It does not occur to them that they are doing anything wrong by filling the disk with every bit of scrap they take a shine to.

- *Process management:* Processes, or running programs, do not always complete in a timely fashion. Some buggy processes go amok and consume CPU cycles by executing infinite loops, others simply hang and fail to disappear. On multiuser systems, terminals sometimes fail to terminate their login processes properly and will leave whole hierarchies of idle processes which do not go away by themselves. This leads to a gradual filling of the process table. In the end, the accumulation of such processes will prevent new programs from being started. Processes are killed with the `kill` command on Unix-like systems, or with the Windows Resource Kit's `kill` command, or the Task Manager.

7.9.4 Productivity or throughput

Throughput is how much real work actually gets done by a computer system. How efficiently is the system fulfilling its purpose or doing its job? The policy decisions we make can have an important bearing on this. For instance, we might think that the use of disk quotas would be beneficial to the system community because then no user would be able to consume more than his or her fair share of disk space. However, this policy can be misguided. There are many instances (during compilation, for instance) where users have to create large temporary files which can later be removed. Rigid disk quotas can prevent a user from performing legitimate work; they can get in the way of the system throughput. Limiting users' resources can have exactly the opposite effect of that which was intended.

Another example is in process management. Some jobs require large amounts of CPU time and take a long time to run: intensive calculations are an example of this. Conventional wisdom is to reduce the process priority of such jobs so that they do not interfere with other users' interactive activities. On Unix-like systems this means using the `nice` command to lower the priority of the process. However, this procedure can also be misguided. Lowering the priority of a process can lead to process *starvation*. Lowering the priority means that the heavy job will take even longer, and might never complete at all. An alternative strategy is to do the reverse: increasing the priority of a heavy task will get rid of it more quickly. The work will be finished and the system will be cleared of a demanding job, at the cost of some inconvenience for other users over a shorter period of time. We can summarize this in a principle:

> **Principle 42 (Resource chokes and drains).** *Moderating resource availability to key processes can lead to poor performance and low productivity. Conversely, with free access to resources, resource usage needs to be monitored to avoid the problem of runaway consumption, or the exploitation of those resources by malicious users.*

7.10 SNMP tools

In spite of its limitations (see section 6.4.1), SNMP remains the protocol of choice for the management of most network hardware, and many tools have been written to query and manage SNMP enabled devices.

The fact that SNMP is a simple read/write protocol has motivated programmers to design simple tools that focus more on the SNMP protocol itself than on the semantics of the data structures described in MIBs. In other words, existing tools try to be generic instead of doing something specific and useful. Typical examples are so-called MIB browsers that help users to browse and manipulate raw MIB data. Such tools usually only understand the machine-parseable parts of a MIB module – which is just adequate to shield users from the bulk of the often arcane numbers used in the protocol. Other examples are scripting language APIs which provide a 'programmer-friendly' view on the SNMP protocol. However, in order to realize more useful management application, it is necessary to understand the semantics of and the relationships between MIB variables. Generic tools require that the users have this knowledge – which is however not always the case.

PHP

The PHP server-side web page language (an enhanced encapsulation of C) is perhaps the simplest way of extracting MIB data from devices, but it is just a generic, low-level interface. PHP makes use of the Net SNMP libraries. For example, here is a simple PHP web page that prints all of the SNMP variables for a device and allows the data to be viewed in a web browser:

```php
<?php

$a = snmpwalk("printer.example.org", "public", "");

for ($i=0; $i < count($a); $i++)
   {
   echo "$a[$i]<br>";
   }

?>
```

The community string is written here with its default values 'public', but it is assumed that this has been changed to something more private. PHP is well and freely documented online, in contrast with Perl. For monitoring small numbers of devices, and for demonstrating the principles of SNMP, this is an excellent tool. However, for production work, something more sophisticated will be required by most users.

Perl, Tcl etc.

There are several SNMP extensions for Perl; a widely used Perl SNMP API is based on the NET-SNMP implementation and supports SNMPv1, SNMPv2c and SNMPv3. The Perl script shown below is based on the NET-SNMP Perl extension and retrieves information from the routing table defined in the RFC1213-MIB module and displays them in a human-readable format.

The problem with Perl is that it only puts a brave face on the same problems that PHP has: namely, it provides only a low-level interface to the basic read/write operations of the protocol. There is no intelligence to the interface, and it requires a considerable amount of programming to do real management with this interface.

Another SNMP interface worthy of mention is the Tcl extension, Scotty.

SCLI

One of the most effective ways of interacting with any system is through a command language. With language tools a user can express his or her exact wishes, rather than filtering them through a graphical menu.

The `scli` package [268, 269] was written to address the need for rational command line utilities for monitoring and configuring network devices. It utilizes a MIB compiler called smidump to generate C stub code. It is easily extensible with a minimum of knowledge about SNMP.

The programs contained in the `scli` package are specific rather than generic. Generic SNMP tools such as MIB browsers or simple command line tools (e.g. snmpwalk) are hard to use since they expose too many protocol details for most users. Moreover, in most cases, they fail to present the information in a format that is easy to read and understand. A nice feature of `scli` is that it works like other familiar Unix commands, such as `netstat` and `top`, and generates a feeling of true investigative interaction.

```
host$ scli printer-XXX
100-scli version 0.2.12 (c) 2001-2002 Juergen Schoenwaelder
100-scli trying SNMPv2c ... timeout
100-scli trying SNMPv1  ... ok.
(printer-714) scli > show printer info
Device:            1
Description:       HP LaserJet 5M
Device Status:     running
Printer Status:    idle
Current Operator:
Service Person
Console Display:   1 line(s) a 40 chars
Console Language:  en/US
Console Access:    operatorConsoleEnabled
Default Input:     input #2
Default Output:    output #1
Default Marker:    marker #1
Default Path:      media path #1
Config Changes:    4
(printer-XXX) scli >
```

Similarly, a 'top'-like continuous monitoring can be obtained with

```
printer-XXX> monitor printer console display

Agent:   printer-XXX:161 up 61 days 01:13:49                     13:48:49
Descr:   HP ETHERNET MULTI-ENVIRONMENT,JETDIRECT,JD24,EEPROM A.08.32
IPv4:    7 pps in   5 pps out    0 pps fwd   0 pps rasm   0 pps frag
UDP:     5 pps in   5 pps out
TCP:     0 sps in   0 sps out    2 con est   0 con aopn   0 con popn
Command: monitor printer console display

PRINTER LINE = TEXT =============================================================
    1       1    Done: mark (STDIN):p
```

Now the fields are continuously updated. This is network traffic intensive, but useful for debugging devices over a short interval of time.

7.11 Cfengine

System maintenance involves a lot of jobs which are repetitive and menial. There are half a dozen languages and tools for writing programs which will automatically check the state of your system and perform a limited amount of routine maintenance automatically. Cfengine is an environment for turning system policy into automated action. It is a very high-level *language* (much higher level than shell or Perl) and a *robot* for interpreting your programs and implementing them. Cfengine is a general tool for structuring, organizing and maintaining information systems on a network. Because it is general, it does not try to solve every little problem you might come across, instead it provides you with a framework for solving all problems in a consistent and organized way. Cfengine's strength is that it encourages organization and consistency of practice – also it may easily be combined with other languages.

Cfengine is about (i) defining the way you want all hosts on your network to be set up (configured), (ii) writing this in a single 'program' which is read by every host on the network, (iii) running this program on every host in order to check and possibly fix the setup of the host. Cfengine programs make it easy to specify general rules for large groups of hosts and special rules for exceptional hosts. Here is a summary of cfengine's capabilities.

- Check and configure the network interface on network hosts.

- Edit textfiles for the system or for all users.

- Make and maintain symbolic links, including multiple links from a single command.

- Check and set the permissions and ownership of files.

- Tidy (delete) junk files which clutter the system.

- Systematic, automated (static) mounting of NFS filesystems.

- Checking for the presence or absence of important files and filesystems.

- Controlled execution of user scripts and shell commands.

- Process management.

By automating these procedures, you will save a lot of time and irritation, and make yourself available to do more interesting work.

A cfengine configuration policy is not in an imperative language like Perl, but in a declarative language that resembles Prolog. It is more like a Makefile. Instead of using low-level logic, it uses high-level classes to make decisions. Actions to be carried out are not written in the order in which they are to be carried out, but listed in bulk. The order in which commands are executed is specified in a special list called the *action-sequence*. A cfengine program is a free-format text file, usually called `cfagent.conf` and consisting of declarations of the form:

```
action-type:

    classes::

        list of actions
```

The action type tells cfengine what the commands which follow do. The action type can be from the following list.

```
binservers, broadcast, control, copy, defaultroute,
directories, disable, editfiles, files, groups, homeservers,
ignore, import, links, mailserver, miscmounts, mountables,
processes, required, resolve, shellcommands, tidy, unmount
```

You may run cfengine scripts/programs as often as you like. Each time you run a script, the engine determines whether anything needs to be done – if nothing needs to be done, nothing is done! If you use it to monitor and configure your entire network from a central file-base, then the natural thing is to run cfengine daily with the help of `cron`.

7.11.1 The simplest way to use cfengine

The simplest cfengine configuration you can have consists of a control section and a shellcommands section, in which you collect together scripts and programs which should run on different hosts or host-types. Cfengine allows you to collect them all together in one file and label them in such a way that the right programs will be run on the right machines.

```
control:

    domain = (  mydomain  )

    actionsequence = ( shellcommands )

shellcommands:

    # All GNU/Linux machines

    linux::
            "/usr/bin/updatedb"

    # Just one host

    myhost::

            "/bin/echo Hi there"
```

While this script does not make use of cfengine's special features, it shows you how you can control many machines from a single file. Cfengine reads the same file on every host and picks out only the commands which apply.

7.11.2   A simple file for one host

Although cfengine is designed to organize all hosts on a network, it can also be used on a single stand-alone host. In this case you don't need to know about classifying commands. Let's write a simple file for checking the setup of your system. Here are some key points:

- Every cfengine must have a `control:` section with an `actionsequence` list, which tells it what to do, and in which order.

- You need to declare basic information about the way your system is set up. Try to keep this simple.

```
#!/usr/local/sbin/cfagent -f
#
# Simple cfengine configuration file
#

control:

 actionsequence = ( checktimezone netconfig resolve files shellcommands )

 domain         = ( domain.country )
 netmask        = ( 255.255.255.0 )
 timezone       = ( MET )

##################################################################

broadcast:

  ones

defaultroute:

  my-gw

##################################################################

resolve:

  #
  # Add these name servers to the /etc/resolv.conf file
  #

  128.39.89.10  # nameserver 1
  158.36.85.10  # nameserver 2
  129.241.1.99
```

```
#####################################################################

files:

    /etc/passwd mode=644 owner=root action=fixall

#####################################################################

shellcommands:

    Wednesday||Sunday::

        "/usr/local/bin/DoBackupScript"
```

7.11.3 A file for multiple hosts

If you want to have just a single file which describes all the hosts on your network, then you need to tell cfengine which commands are intended for which hosts. Having to mention every host explicitly would be a tedious business. Usually though, we are trying to make hosts on a network basically the same as one another so we can make generic rules which cover many hosts at a time. Nonetheless there will still be a few obvious differences which need to be accounted for.

For example, the Solaris operating system is quite different from the GNU/Linux operating system, so some rules will apply to all hosts which run Solaris, whereas others will only apply to GNU/Linux. Cfengine uses classes like `solaris::` and `linux::` to label commands which apply only to these systems.

We might also want to make other differences, based not on operating system differences but on groups of hosts belonging to certain people, or with a special significance. We can therefore create classes using groups of hosts.

7.11.4 Classes

The idea of classes is central to the operation of cfengine. Saying that cfengine is 'class oriented' means that it doesn't make decisions using if...then...else constructions the way other languages do, but only carries out an action if the host running the program is in the same class as the action itself. To understand what this means, imagine sorting through a list of all the hosts at your site. Imagine also that you are looking for the *class* of hosts which belong to the computing department, which run the GNU/Linux operating system and which have yellow spots! To figure out whether a particular host satisfies all of these criteria, you first delete all of the hosts which are not GNU/Linux, then you delete all of the remaining ones which don't belong to the computing department, then you delete all the remaining ones which don't have yellow spots. If you are on the remaining list, then you are in the class of all computer-science-Linux-yellow-spotted hosts and you can carry out the action.

Cfengine works in this way, narrowing things down by asking if a host is in several classes at the same time. Although some information (like the kind of operating system you are running) can be obtained directly, clearly, to make this work, we need to have lists of which hosts belong to the computer department and which ones have yellow spots.

So how does this work in a cfengine program? A program or configuration script consists of a set of declarations for what we refer to as *actions* which are to be carried out only for certain classes of host. Any host can execute a particular program, but only certain action are extracted – namely those which refer to that particular host. This happens automatically because cfagent builds up a list of the classes to which it belongs as it goes along, so it avoids having to make many decisions over and over again.

By defining classes which classify the hosts on your network in some easy to understand way, you can make a single action apply to many hosts in one go – i.e. just the hosts you need. You can make generic rules for specific type of operating system, you can group together clusters of workstations according to who will be using them and you can paint yellow spots on them – whatever works for you.

A *cfengine action* looks like this:

```
action-type:

    single-or-compound-class::

        declaration
```

A single class can be one of several things:

- The name of an operating system architecture, e.g. ultrix, sun4 etc. This is referred to henceforth as a *hard class*.

- The (unqualified) name of a particular host. If your system returns a fully qualified domain name for your host, cfagent truncates it so as to un-qualify the name.

- The name of a user-defined group of hosts.

- A day of the week (in the form Monday, Tuesday, Wednesday, ...).

- An hour of the day (in the form Hr00, Hr01 ... Hr23).

- Minutes in the hour (in the form Min00, Min17 ... Min45).

- A five-minute interval in the hour (in the form Min00_05, Min05_10 ... Min55_00)

- A day of the month (in the form Day1 ... Day31).

- A month (in the form January, February, ... December).

- A year (in the form Yr1997, Yr2001).

- An arbitrary user-defined string.

A compound class is a sequence of simple classes connected by dots or 'pipe' symbols (vertical bars). For example:

```
myclass.sun4.Monday::
```

```
sun4|ultrix|osf::
```

A compound class evaluates to 'true' if all of the individual classes are separately true, thus in the above example the actions which follow compound_class:: are only carried out if the host concerned is in myclass, is of type sun4 and the day is Monday! In the second example, the host parsing the file must be either of type sun4 *or* ultrix *or* osf. In other words, compound classes support two operators: AND and OR, written . and | respectively. Cfagent doesn't care how many of these operators you use (since it skips over blank class names), so you could write either

```
solaris|irix::
```

or

```
solaris||irix::
```

depending on your taste. On the other hand, the order in which cfagent evaluates AND and OR operations *does* matter, and the rule is that AND takes priority over OR, so that . binds classes together tightly and all AND operations are evaluated before ORing the final results together. This is the usual behavior in programming languages. You can use round parentheses in cfengine classes to override these preferences.

Cfagent allows you to define switch on and off dummy classes so that you can use them to select certain subsets of action. In particular, note that by defining your own classes, using them to make compound rules of this type, and then switching them on and off, you can also switch on and off the corresponding actions in a controlled way. The command line options -D and -N can be used for this purpose.

A logical NOT operator has been added to allow you to exclude certain specific hosts in a more flexible way. The logical NOT operator is (as in C and C++) !. For instance, the following example would allow all hosts except for myhost:

```
action:

!myhost::

    command
```

and similarly, to allow all hosts in a user-defined group mygroup, *except* for myhost, you would write

```
action:

mygroup.!myhost::

    command
```

which reads 'mygroup AND NOT myhost'. The NOT operator can also be combined with OR. For instance

    class1|! class2

would select hosts which were either in class 1, or were not in class 2.

Finally, there is a number of reserved classes. The following are hard classes for various operating system architectures. They do not need to be defined because each host knows what operating system it is running. Thus the appropriate one of these will always be defined on each host. Similarly the day of the week is clearly not open to definition, unless you are running cfagent from outer space. The reserved classes are:

ultrix, sun4, sun3, hpux, hpux10, aix, solaris, osf, irix4, irix, irix64, freebsd, netbsd, openbsd, bsd4_3, newsos, solarisx86, aos, nextstep, bsdos, linux, debian, cray, unix_sv, GnU

If these classes are not sufficient to distinguish the hosts on your network, cfengine provides more specific classes which contain the name and release of the operating system. To find out what these look like for your systems, you can run cfagent in 'parse-only-verbose' mode:

    cfagent -p -v

and these will be displayed. For example, Solaris 2.4 systems generate the additional classes sunos_5_4 and sunos_sun4m, sunos_sun4m_5_4.

Cfagent uses both the unqualified and fully host names as classes. Some sites and operating systems use fully qualified names for their hosts, i.e. uname -n returns a full domain qualified hostname. This spoils the class-matching algorithms for cfagent, so cfagent automatically truncates names which contain a dot '.' at the first '.' it encounters. If your hostnames contain dots, they will be replaced by underscores in cfengine.

In summary, the operator ordering in cfengine classes is as follows:

- () Parentheses override everything.

- ! The NOT operator binds tightest.

- . The AND operator binds more tightly than OR.

- | OR is the weakest operator.

We may now label actions by these classes to restrict their scope:

editfiles:

solaris::

 /etc/motd

PrependIfNoSuchLine "Plan 9 was a better movie and a better OS!"

```
Rivals::

 /etc/motd

AppendIfNoSuchLine "Your rpc.spray is so last month"
```

Actions or commands which work under a class operator like `solaris::` are only executed on hosts which belong to the given class. This is the way one makes decisions in cfengine: by class assignment rather than by `if ... then ... else` clauses.

7.11.5 Using `cfagent` as a front-end to `cron`

One of cfengine's strengths is its use of classes to identify systems from a single file or set of files. Distributed resource administration would be much easier if the `cron` daemon also worked in this way. One way of setting this up is to use cfagent's time classes to work like a user interface for `cron`. This allows us to have a single, central file which contains all the `cron` jobs for the whole network without losing any of the fine control which cron affords us. All of the usual advantages apply:

- It is easier to keep track of what cron jobs are running on the system when they are all registered in one place.

- Groups and user-defined classes can be used to identify which host should run which programs.

The central idea behind this scheme is to set up a regular cron job on every system which executes cfagent at frequent intervals. Each time cfagent is started, it evaluates time classes and executes the shell commands defined in its configuration file. In this way we use cfagent as a wrapper for the cron scripts, so that we can use cfengine's classes to control jobs for multiple hosts. Cfengine's time classes are at least as powerful as `cron`'s time specification possibilities, so this does not restrict us in any way. The only price is the overhead of parsing the cfengine configuration file.

To be more concrete, imagine installing the following `crontab` file onto every host on the network:

```
#
# Global Cron file
#
0,15,30,45 * * * * /usr/local/sbin/cfexecd -F
```

This file contains just a single cron job, namely the cfengine scheduler cfexecd. Here we are assuming that it will not be necessary to execute any cron script more often than every fifteen minutes. If this is too restrictive, the above can be changed. We refer to the time interval between runs of the scheduler cfexecd.

Cfengine assumes that it will find a configuration file in

```
/var/cfengine/inputs/cfagent.conf
```

that looks something like this:

```
#
# Simple cfengine configuration file
#

control:

    actionsequence = ( checktimezone files )

    domain          = ( example.com )
    timezone        = ( MET )

    smtpserver      = ( smtphost.example.org )   # used by cfexecd
    sysadm          = ( me@example.com )          # where to mail output


##################################################################

files:

    # Check some important files

    /etc/passwd mode=644 owner=root action=fixall
    /etc/shadow mode=600 owner=root action=fixall

    # Do a tripwire check on binaries!

    /usr                    # Scan /usr dir

      owner=root,daemon  # all files must be owned by root or daemon
      checksum=md5       # use md5 or sha
      recurse=inf        # all subdirs
      ignore=tmp         # skip /usr/tmp
      action=fixall
```

7.11.6 Time classes

Each time cfengine is run, it reads the system clock and defines the following classes based on the time and date:

- *Yrxx*:: The current year, e.g. Yr1997, Yr2001. This class is probably not useful very often, but it might help us to turn on the new-year lights, or shine up your systems for the new millennium (1st Jan 2001)!

- *Month*:: The current month can be used for defining very long-term variations in the system configuration, e.g. January, February. These classes could be used to determine when students have their summer vacation, for instance, in order to perform extra tidying, or to specially maintain some administrative policy for the duration of a conference.

- *Day*:: The day of the week may be used as a class, e.g. `Monday`, `Sunday`.

- Day*xx*:: A day in the month (date) may be used to single out by date, e.g. the first day of each month defines `Day1`, the 21st `Day21` etc.

- Hr*xx*:: An hour of the day, in 24-hour clock notation: `Hr00...Hr23`.

- Min*xx*:: The precise minute at which cfengine was started: `Min0 ... Min59`. This is probably not useful alone, but these values may be combined to define arbitrary intervals of time.

- Min*xx_xx*:: The five-minute interval in the hour at which cfengine was executed, in the form `Min0_5`, `Min5_10 ... Min55_0`.

Time classes based on the precise minute at which cfengine started are unlikely to be useful, since it is improbable that we will want to ask cron to run cfengine every single minute of every day: there would be no time for anything to complete before it was started again. Moreover, many things could conspire to delay the precise time at which cfengine was started. The real purpose in being able to detect the precise start time is to define composite classes which refer to arbitrary intervals of time. To do this, we use the `group` or `classes` action to create an alias for a group of time values. Here are some creative examples:

```
classes:  # synonym groups:

  LunchAndTeaBreaks = ( Hr12 Hr10 Hr15 )

  NightShift        = ( Hr22 Hr23 Hr00 Hr01 Hr02 Hr03 Hr04 Hr05 Hr06 )

  ConferenceDays    = ( Day26 Day27 Day29 Day30 )

  QuarterHours      = ( Min00 Min15 Min30 Min45 )

  TimeSlices        = ( Min01 Min02 Min03 Min33 Min34 Min35)
```

In these examples, the left-hand sides of the assignments are effectively the OR-ed result of the right-hand side. Thus if any classes in the parentheses are defined, the left-hand side class will become defined. This provides an excellent and readable way of pinpointing intervals of time within a program, without having to use | and . operators everywhere.

7.11.7 Choosing a scheduling interval

How often should we call a global cron script? There are several things to think about:

- How much fine control do we need? Running cron jobs once each hour is usually enough for most tasks, but we might need to exercise finer control for a few special tasks.

- Are we going to run the entire cfengine configuration file or a special light-weight file?

- System latency. How long will it take to load, parse and run the cfengine script?

Cfengine has an intelligent locking and timeout policy which should be sufficient to handle hanging shell commands from previous crons so that no overlap can take place.

7.12 Database configuration management

A database is a framework for structured information storage. Databases are used for providing efficient storage and retrieval of data, using a data structure based on search-keys. Although it is correct to call the regular file system of a computer a hierarchical database, disk file systems are not optimized for storing special data in a way that can be searched and sorted. The criteria for storing and retrieving data are somewhat different in these cases.

Web services are increasingly reliant on databases and vice versa. Much of the content available in the web is now constructed on the fly by server-side technologies that assemble HTML pages from information stored in relational databases, using scripting languages such as Perl, PHP (Personal Homepage Tools), JSP (Java Server Pages) and ASP (Active Server pages). Online services, like web mail, often consist of a farm of PCs running FreeBSD Unix (this has retained the record for the most efficient network handling of all the operating systems to date), backed up by large multiprocessor database engines running on Unix hardware with a hundred processors. Search engines run fast database applications on huge farms of PC hardware, each host dedicated to a particular part of the database, with a small cluster of machines that dispatch incoming requests to them.

There are several kinds of database: relational databases, object databases, high- and low-level databases. Low-level databases are used by application programs like the Windows registry, cfengine checksum storage, LDAP data records, the Network Information Service (NIS), and so on. Low-level databases save data in 'structures', or chunks of memory that have no structure to the database itself. High-level relational databases build on low-level ones as 'middle-ware' and are used to represent more complex data structures, like personnel databases, company records, and so on. High-level databases use Structured Query Language (SQL) for submitting and retrieving data in the form of tables. They maintain the abstraction of tables, and use primary keys to maintain uniqueness.

Managing databases is like managing a filesystem within a filesystem. It involves managing usernames, passwords, creation and deletion of objects, garbage collection and planning security considerations. Since databases are user applications that run on top of a host operating system, often as an externally available service, they usually have their own independent usernames and passwords, separate from regular user accounts. Not all users of the host system need access to the database, and not all users of the database need access to the host operating system.

7.12.1 SQL relational databases

Structured Query Language (SQL) was created for building and searching within relational databases. It is now an essential part of virtually all production databases. These include open source databases such as MySQL, PostgresSQL, and commercial databases like DB2, Oracle and Microsoft SQL. We shall consider MySQL as an example of a free software SQL database.

An SQL database starts with a number of tables; tables are related to other tables by 'relations'. The structure of these tables is mainly of interest to the database designer. From the viewpoint of a system administrator, one only requires the schema for the database, i.e. a series of definitions. Here is a trivial example, of a database schema.

```
# schema.txt

USE mydatabase;

CREATE TABLE mytable
    (
    section char(64),
    title char(64),
    file char(64),
    keywords char(64),
    classes char(64)
    );
```

The file in the example above is written in SQL. We notice two things about this: there are two types of object within the system – databases and tables.

- *Database:* Within the multi-user database system (e.g. MySQL), there is a number of databases belonging to a variety of users. Each database has a unique name or identifier and may contain any number of tables.

- *Table:* Each table has a name or *classifier* that is unique to that database. A table declaration of this type is an abstract schema or 'blueprint' for an actual data record. All data records are *instances* of tables, i.e. they have the structure defined in the table definition, but contain real data. There can be any number of instances of a table (records), provided they are uniquely identifiable by a *key*.

- *Key:* Every table must have an element (or combination of elements) within it that is unique. This identifies the record to the database engine.

Database users must be users on the host system in order to gain access to the command tools, but database users are independent of login users, and have their own separate password system. This allows remote clients of a database to gain limited access to the data without having administrative access to other parts of the system.

```
mysqladmin -u root password  newpassword
```

```
mysqladmin -p create  mydatabase
```

The `-p` option asks for the root (administrator) password to be prompted for. This causes a new, blank database to be created, and is equivalent to logging in as root and giving direct SQL commands:

```
host# mysql -u root
```

```
mysql> CREATE DATABASE  mydatabase;
```

Similarly, a database can be deleted as follows:

```
mysqladmin -p drop  mydatabase
```

Once a database has been created, it is possible to see the list of all databases by logging into a MySQL root shell:

```
host# mysql -u root
```

```
mysql> SHOW DATABASES;
```

```
+----------+
| Database |
+----------+
| mysql    |
| test     |
| mydatab  |
+----------+
```

Note that all standard SQL commands must be terminated with a semicolon. The database called 'mysql' is a database containing security levels for users and databases, i.e. permissions for different tables and databases within the system.

By our principle of minimal privilege, we do not wish to continue to access this database with root privilege. Rather, we create a special user for a new database, with a password. The username and password can be used by local programs and users to 'log on' to the database. The contents of the permissions database can be set using regular SQL commands, but MySQL provides commands 'GRANT' and 'REVOKE' for manipulating it.

```
host$ mysql --user=root mysql
mysql> GRANT ALL PRIVILEGES ON mydatabase.table TO mark@localhost
    ->      IDENTIFIED BY 'password' WITH GRANT OPTION;
```

```
mysql> GRANT USAGE ON *.* TO dummy@localhost;
```

Programmers who write scripts and software that access the database must code the password explicitly in the program, and thus special precautions must be taken to ensure that the password is not visible to other users of the system. The script should be on a web server, where only administrators can log in, and should not be readable by any remote service on the server host. The following example adds a user who can connect from hosts localhost, example.org. The user wants to access the 'mydatabase' database only from localhost and the 'example' database only from example.org. He wants to use the password 'mysecret' from both hosts. Thus to set up this user's privileges using GRANT statements:

```
host$ mysql --user=root mysql

mysql> GRANT SELECT,INSERT,UPDATE,DELETE,CREATE,DROP
    ->     ON mydatabase.*
    ->     TO  user@localhost
    ->     IDENTIFIED BY 'mysecret';
mysql> GRANT SELECT,INSERT,UPDATE,DELETE,CREATE,DROP
    ->     ON example.*
    ->     TO  user@example.org
    ->     IDENTIFIED BY 'mysecret';
```

Note that access to localhost is given via Unix sockets and the remote machine 'example.org' over a TCP/IP connection. At this stage, the database has a foothold on the system, but no structure. Once we have designed a database schema, it can be loaded into the system as follows:

```
host# mysql -u dbuser -p < schema.txt
```

Again, the -p option asks for the password to be prompted. This loads the table structure, so that table entries can be added. To add, examine these, or debug manually, one uses standard SQL commands, e.g.

```
host$ mysql -p -u mark
password: ???????

mysql> USE mydatabase;
mysql> SHOW TABLES;

+----------------------+
| Tables in mydatabase |
+----------------------+
| mytable              |
+----------------------+

mysql> describe mytable;
+----------+----------+------+-----+---------+-------+
| Field    | Type     | Null | Key | Default | Extra |
+----------+----------+------+-----+---------+-------+
| section  | char(64) | YES  |     | NULL    |       |
| title    | char(64) | YES  |     | NULL    |       |
```

```
| file      | char(64)  | YES  |     | NULL     |       |
| keywords  | char(64)  | YES  |     | NULL     |       |
| classes   | char(64)  | YES  |     | NULL     |       |
+----------+----------+------+-----+---------+-------+
5 rows in set (0.01 sec)
```

```
mysql> INSERT INTO mytable
    -> VALUES ('mysection','mytitle','myfile','mykey','myclass');
```

```
mysql> SELECT * FROM mytable;
```

Other commands include search and delete commands, e.g.

```
SELECT * FROM someTable WHERE tableID='264';
```

```
SELECT * FROM otherTable WHERE name='SomeName';
```

```
SELECT weight FROM measuresTable WHERE measureID='264';
```

```
UPDATE testTab SET weight='10' WHERE measureID='264';
```

```
DELETE FROM otherTable WHERE name='SomeName';
```

7.12.2 LDAP directory service

The lightweight Directory Access Protocol (LDAP) uses a database to store frequently required information. Directories are databases that are optimized for lookup, rather than for update transactions. They are intended for serving more or less fixed data in large volumes. Often, only the system administrator will have write access to the data. See also section 9.8 about setting up an LDAP server.

7.12.3 Data entry administration

Data for a simple directory are entered in the form of the common file format. The LDIF (LDAP Data Interchange Format) is used to define and store source data. This data format is extremely fragile to extra spaces and lines, and offers little help for debugging. One day it will probably be rewritten in XML; until then, a certain care is required. Here is a definition of a simple database of people.

LDAP directories are defined using a *schema* of *classes* that can inherit other classes. Each class has its own attributes. One of the challenges of using LDAP is to find out which classes have which attributes and vice versa. Solving a directory problem is largely about getting these relationships to work. Some of the schema classes are defined by X.500, such as cn (common name), description, and postalAddress.

DN	Distinguished name	Primary key
CN	Common name	Typically an identifier
RDN	Relative Distinguished Name	Primary key of subobject
DIT	Directory Information Tree	LDAP hierarchy
DSA	Directory System Agent	X.500 name for LDAP server
DSE	DSA-specific Entry	Root node of a DIT naming context

Table 7.1: LDAP basic abbreviations and concepts.

	Distinguished name	Primary key
cn	Common name	Typically an identifier
dc	Domain component	Caseless 'dot' element in DNS name.

Table 7.2: LDAP schema object classes and attributes.

```
dn:dc=iu,dc=hio,dc=no
objectclass:organization
o:Oslo University College

dn: cn=Mark Burgess,dc=iu,dc=hio,dc=no
objectClass: person
cn: Mark Burgess
cn: Mark Sparc
sn: Burgess

dn: cn=Sigmund Straumsnes,dc=iu,dc=hio,dc=no
objectClass: person
cn: Sigmund Straumsnes
cn: Ziggy
sn: Straumsnes

dn: cn=Frode Sandnes,dc=iu,dc=hio,dc=no
objectClass: person
cn: Frode Sandnes
cn: Frodo
sn: Sandnes
```

To add entries from this file (example2.ldif):

```
daneel$ ldapadd -x -D "cn=Manager,dc=iu,dc=hio,dc=no" -W -f example2.ldif
Enter LDAP Password:
adding new entry "dc=iu,dc=hio,dc=no"
adding new entry "cn=Mark Burgess,dc=iu,dc=hio,dc=no"
```

```
adding new entry "cn=Sigmund Straumsnes,dc=iu,dc=hio,dc=no"
adding new entry "cn=Frode Sandnes,dc=iu,dc=hio,dc=no"
```

To check that this has been entered correctly, print all records as follows:

```
daneel$ ldapsearch -x -b 'dc=iu,dc=hio,dc=no' '(objectclass=*)'
```

This yields output of the form:

```
# extended LDIF
#
# LDAPv3
# filter: (objectclass=*)
# requesting: ALL
#

# iu.hio.no
dn: dc=iu,dc=hio,dc=no
objectClass: organization
o: Oslo University College

# Mark Burgess, iu.hio.no
dn: cn=Mark Burgess,dc=iu,dc=hio,dc=no
objectClass: person
cn: Mark Burgess
cn: Mark Sparc
sn: Burgess


# Sigmund Straumsnes, iu.hio.no
dn: cn=Sigmund Straumsnes,dc=iu,dc=hio,dc=no
objectClass: person
cn: Sigmund Straumsnes
cn: Ziggy
sn: Straumsnes

# Frode Sandnes, iu.hio.no
dn: cn=Frode Sandnes,dc=iu,dc=hio,dc=no
objectClass: person
cn: Frode Sandnes
cn: Frodo
sn: Sandnes

# search result
search: 2
result: 0 Success

# numResponses: 5
# numEntries: 4
```

Additional schema classes

The example above is a flat list, formed from the core class schema. What about adding additional classes and subtrees? To inherit extra schema attributes, one must include the schema in `slapd.conf`, after the default 'core' schema line:

```
include /usr/local/etc/openldap/schema/core.schema
include /usr/local/etc/openldap/schema/cosine.schema
include /usr/local/etc/openldap/schema/inetorgperson.schema
include /usr/local/etc/openldap/schema/nis.schema
```

Now we can add entries under 'organizationalPerson', for instance (see figure 7.2),

```
dn:dc=iu,dc=hio,dc=no
objectclass:organization
o:Oslo University College

dn: cn=Mark Burgess,dc=iu,dc=hio,dc=no
objectClass: person
objectClass: organizationalPerson
cn: Mark Burgess
cn: Mark Sparc
sn: Burgess
registeredAddress: Cort Adelers Gate 30
telephoneNumber: +47 22453272

dn: cn=Sigmund Straumsnes,dc=iu,dc=hio,dc=no
objectClass: person
cn: Sigmund Straumsnes
cn: Ziggy
sn: Straumsnes

dn: cn=Frode Sandnes,dc=iu,dc=hio,dc=no
objectClass: person
cn: Frode Sandnes
cn: Frodo
sn: Sandnes
```

The objectclass and attributeTypes configuration file directives can be used to define schema rules on entries in the directory. It is customary to create a file to contain definitions of custom schema items:

```
include /usr/local/etc/openldap/schema/local.schema
```

Different class schema cannot be mixed in records. For example, you cannot register information for schema 'person' in the same stanza as for 'posixAccount'. Thus, the following would be wrong:

```
dn: cn=Mark Burgess,dc=iu,dc=hio,dc=no
objectClass: person
```

```
objectClass: account
objectClass: posixAccount
cn: Mark Burgess
cn: Mark Sparc
sn: Burgess
uid: mark
userPassword: cryptX5/DBrWPOQQaI
gecos: Mark Burgess (staff)
loginShell: /bin/tcsh
uidNumber: 10
gidNumber: 10
homeDirectory: /site/host/mark
```

because account and person are mutually exclusive. However, by extending the Distinguished Names so as to split the tree into two sub-types, we can end up with the following:

```
dn:dc=iu,dc=hio,dc=no
objectclass: top
objectclass: organization
o:Oslo University College
description: Faculty of Engineering
streetAddress: Cort Adelers Gate 30
postalAddress: 0254 Oslo Norway

dn: cn=Mark Burgess,dc=iu,dc=hio,dc=no
objectclass: top
objectClass: person
objectClass: organizationalPerson
objectClass: inetOrgPerson
cn: Mark Burgess
cn: Mark Sparc
sn: Burgess
uid: mark
registeredAddress: Cort Adelers Gate 30
telephoneNumber: +47 22453272

dn: cn=Sigmund Straumsnes,dc=iu,dc=hio,dc=no
objectclass: top
objectClass: person
objectClass: organizationalPerson
objectClass: inetOrgPerson
cn: Sigmund Straumsnes
cn: Ziggy
sn: Straumsnes
uid: sigmunds
registeredAddress: Cort Adelers Gate 30
telephoneNumber: +47 22453273
```

```
dn: cn=Frode Sandnes,dc=iu,dc=hio,dc=no
objectclass: top
objectClass: person
objectClass: organizationalPerson
objectClass: inetOrgPerson
cn: Frode Sandnes
cn: Frodo
sn: Sandnes
uid: frodes
registeredAddress: Cort Adelers Gate 30
telephoneNumber: +47 22453274

dn: uid=mark,dc=iu,dc=hio,dc=no
cn: Mark Burgess
cn: Mark Sparc
objectClass: account
objectClass: posixAccount
uid: mark
userPassword: cryptX5/DBrWPOQQaI
gecos: Mark Burgess (staff)
loginShell: /bin/tcsh
uidNumber: 10
gidNumber: 10
homeDirectory: /site/host/mark

dn: uid=sigmunds,dc=iu,dc=hio,dc=no
cn: Sigmund Straumsnes
cn: Ziggy
objectClass: account
objectClass: posixAccount
uid: mark
userPassword: cryptX5/sdWPOQQaI
gecos: Sigmund Straumsnes (staff)
loginShell: /bin/zsh
uidNumber: 11
gidNumber: 11
homeDirectory: /site/host/sigmunds

dn: uid=frodes,dc=iu,dc=hio,dc=no
cn: Frode Sandnes
cn: Frodo
objectClass: account
objectClass: posixAccount
uid: frodes
userPassword: cryptX5/DBr111QaI
gecos: Frode Sandnes (staff)
loginShell: /bin/bash
```

```
uidNumber: 12
gidNumber: 12
homeDirectory: /site/host/frodes
```

We can now search for individual object classes and attributes:

```
ldapsearch -x -b 'dc=iu,dc=hio,dc=no' '(objectclass=account)'
ldapsearch -x -b 'dc=iu,dc=hio,dc=no' '(objectclass=person)'
ldapsearch -x -b 'dc=iu,dc=hio,dc=no' '(cn=Mark*)'
ldapsearch -x -b 'dc=iu,dc=hio,dc=no' '(uid=fr*)'
ldapsearch -x -b 'dc=iu,dc=hio,dc=no' '(loginShell=/bin/zsh)'
```

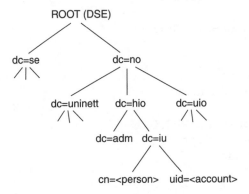

Figure 7.2: An example LDAP data model hierarchy for iu.hio.no Directory Information Tree (DIT).

Basic pitfalls

The LDAP data format is almost impossibly sensitive to trailing spaces on lines.

```
ldap_add: Invalid syntax (21)
        additional info: objectclass: value #0 invalid per syntax
```

Also, the schema definitions do not seem to be updated.

```
ldap_add: Object class violation (65)
        additional info: attribute 'c' not allowed
```

This means that a relevant part of the schema inheritance is missing. We need to add the correct chain to slapd.conf.

Applications have to keep track of what data are already in the directory. Data can be replaced rather than added. For example, suppose we have a file of data example.ldif:

```
daneel$ ldapadd -x -D "cn=Manager,dc=iu,dc=hio,dc=no" -W -f example.ldif
Enter LDAP Password:
adding new entry "dc=iu,dc=hio,dc=no"
ldapadd: update failed: dc=iu,dc=hio,dc=no
ldap_add: Already exists (68)
```

When adding data from a file `example.ldif` one can simply delete the database format and enter everything from scratch.

```
rm /usr/local/var/openldap-data/*
```

This is useful when the maintenance of the data is performed at source level, rather than using the data in the database as authoritative.

Exercises

Self-test objectives

1. What is meant by configuration management in the context of network and system administration?

2. How is configuration information stored by devices?

3. Explain why system configurations tend to fall into a state of disorder over time.

4. What is meant by the concept of a dynamic balance, or configuration equilibrium?

5. What is the role of policy in determining device configuration?

6. What is meant by root-cause maintenance and symptom maintenance?

7. What is meant by change management?

8. What is the role of clock synchronization in configuration management?

9. What role does task scheduling play in system maintenance?

10. Name the scheduling services for Windows and Unix-like operating systems.

11. Explain how randomized scheduling can be used as an alternative to a queue-based schedule.

12. Summarize the alternatives available for automating host management. What limitations does each of the alternatives have?

13. Explain when it is appropriate to supply more resources to a task, and when it is appropriate to limit the consumption of resources.

14. Explain how SNMP can be used to watch over and configure network devices. What are the limitations of SNMP?

15. Explain how cfengine can be used to watch over and configure network devices. What are the limitations of cfengine?

16. Database management is a common task for system administrators; explain why this is a natural extension of system administrative work.

17. How does an SQL database differ from a directory service such as LDAP?

Problems

1. Compare and contrast the shell, Perl, Python, PHP and Tcl as rival languages for scripting system administration tasks.

2. Imagine a busy organization, such as a newspaper, where users need constant access to software, and clients need constant access to news via a web server. Describe the precautions you would take in securing the continued functioning of a system during a major software change or upgrade. How would you involve the users in this procedure?

3. Find out about process priorities. How are process priorities changed on the computer systems on your network? Formulate a policy for handling processes which load the system heavily. Should they be left alone, killed, rescheduled etc?

4. Review the role of cfengine in system administration. What is it used for? What are its special strengths? What are its weaknesses? Review also the role of the Perl language. What are its special strengths? Is there any overlap between Perl and cfengine? Do the languages compete or supplement one another?

5. Collect and compile cfengine. Set up a simple cfengine script which you can build on. Make it run hourly.

6. Why are Unix shell scripts not portable? Is Perl portable? How can cfengine help in the issue of script portability?

7. Discuss the advantages of having all scripts which perform configuration and maintenance in one place, and of spreading them around the network on the hosts to which they apply.

8. Discuss the ethical issues associated with garbage collection of files and processes. Is it right to delete users' files? How would a garbage collection policy at a research laboratory differ from a policy at a high school? What is the risk associated with tidying files automatically?

9. Collect the SNMP software `scli` from the network and install it. Use it to query the attributes of printers attached to the network.

10. Create an LDAP directory for the students in your class. Begin with a simple directory and then expand it gradually to incorporate more data. Explain the strategy you use for extending information in the directory gradually, without having to start from scratch on each revision.

11. Discuss what kinds of tools a system administrator needs to maintain and use directory information effectively.

Chapter 8

Diagnostics, fault and change management

All complex systems behave unexpectedly some of the time. They fail to operate within the limits addressed by policy and the reason for this can be clearly understood by comparing information content. Policy is generally a set of simplistic, high level general rules that cannot capture the same level of detail as the true human–computer interaction in its real environment. One must therefore expect failure and plan for it. If a failure occurs in a manner that was expected, its effects can be controlled and mitigated.

> **Principle 43 (Predictable failure).** *Systems should fail predictably so that they can be recovered quickly. Predictability is encouraged by adopting standardized (or well-understood) protocols and procedures for quality assurance in design and maintenance.*

This chapter is about learning what to expect of a non-deterministic system: how to understand its flaws, and how to insure oneself against the unexpected.

8.1 Fault tolerance and propagation

How do errors penetrate a system? Faults travel from part to part as if in a network of interconnections. If errors can propagate freely, then a small error in one part of a system can have consequences for another part. By studying different kinds of network, we can learn about the likelihood of error propagation.

Networks come in a variety of forms. Figure 8.1 shows the progression from a highly ordered, centralized structure to a decentralized form, to a generalized mesh. This classification was originally discussed by Paul Baran of RAND corporation in 1964 as part of a project to develop a communications system that would be robust to failure in the case of a nuclear attack [36, 25].

The same argument applies to the propagation of errors though any set of interconnected parts.

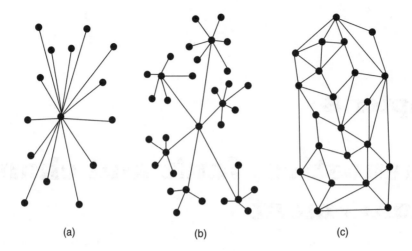

Figure 8.1: Network topologies: (a) centralized, (b) decentralized or hierarchical, and (c) distributed mesh.

Many complex systems exhibit a surprising degree of tolerance against errors. This is because they have in-built redundancy. Certain types of network also have this property in the routes between the nodes. If we think of networks not so much in the sense of communication lines between computers, but as abstract links between different dependent parts of the whole, then the importance of networks becomes apparent. The idea of a network is thus of more general importance than as a means of communication between computers and humans. Networks are *webs of influence*. If a system is tolerant to faults and security breaches, then we can look at it in one of two complementary ways:

- The access network that allows problems to propagate is poorly connected; i.e. connections (security breaches) between nodes (resources) are absent.

- The resource network is well connected and is resilient to removal of nodes (resources) and connections (supply channels).

The first of these viewpoints is useful for modeling intrusion or penetration by faults or intruders, while the latter is useful for securing a system against lack of access to critical resources.

A *tolerant network* is robust to node removal and connection removal. Node removal is usually more serious (see figure 8.2).

One type of network of special importance is the *random network*. A random network is formed by making random connections between nodes within a set. Randomness is a good strategy for covering a large number of possibilities without making exhaustive use of resources. In the absence of precise knowledge about a system, random 'shots in the dark' are an efficient way of hitting an unpredictable or moving target, such as a random fault [263]. Conversely, random links lead to a high probability of connecting together all of the elements in a set of nodes, provided their density is sufficient [6]. While this double dose of unpredictability

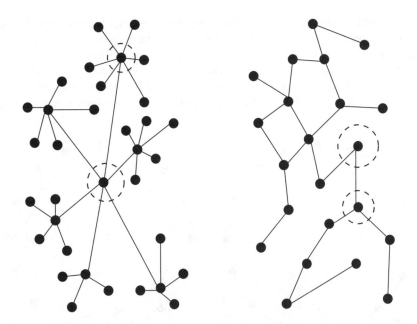

Figure 8.2: Network tolerance to node removal: nodes are more important than connectors.

sounds like an unlikely combination for success, it works and leads to highly robust networks.

Humans do not build technology at random so, apart from a robustness to failure, why should random networks be of interest to the study of human–computer systems? The answer lies in so-called *small-world* networks, that approximate random ones.

8.2 Networks and small worlds

You have probably heard the maxim that no two individuals in the world are more than six degrees of separation from one another. In other words, I know someone, who knows someone, who knows someone,... who knows you. In the world of system administration, the degree of separation is probably much less than six; but on average, the value is around six for arbitrary people on the planet. How could this possibly be?

This strange, almost counter-intuitive, idea is not a freak coincidence of human social structures; it is a property of a kind of network known as a small-world network [319].

> **Definition 6 (Small-world network).** *There is a class of highly clustered graphs that behave like random graphs. These are called small-world networks.*

Small-world networks have local clustering, i.e. they have a centralized structure at the level of small groups, but this is not the reason they are called small-world networks. The 'small world' phenomenon is rather the opposite of this, namely that someone in a small cluster will be closely connected to someone in a rather distant cluster. The reason for this is the existence of a few long-range or 'weak' links. In a small-world network, these weak links play a vital role in connecting distant parts of the network together. If we add a sufficient number of random, long-distance links something magical happens: suddenly a group of small clusters starts to achieve the connectivity of a random network (figure 8.3 and 8.4).

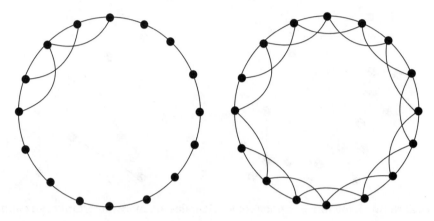

Figure 8.3: A network is built up by adding connections between neighbors. As more distant neighbors become connected, small, local clusters become connected over longer distances.

The study of networks reveals that networks with the small-world property also exhibit so-called 'scale-free' behavior, over a wide range of scales. In other words, over a wide range of scales, the networks appear to have the same properties regardless of how one zooms in or out and looks at different regions of the network.

Scale-free networks are formed spontaneously when there is some form of preferential attachment, i.e. when the likelihood of a new connection is determined by an already existing connection. This is observed, for instance, in the links to sites in the World Wide Web and is exploited by search engines like Google in order to rank the importance of sites. When someone sees that a site is well-connected, they tend to refer to it themselves, thus making it even more well-connected. This 'rich get richer' phenomenon leads to a form of connectivity that is not necessarily ordered, but which exhibits a form of ordering.

Why should this phenomenon be of more than passing interest to network and system administration? The small-world phenomenon is a sociological phenomenon, but it is mimicked in the deployment of technology. Studies of real networks, both of humans and of computers, reveal that the small-world property crops up in a wide range of circumstances in computer technologies. The effect that humans have on the systems we create is not negligible; it has some important consequences, because of the scale-free nature of the graphs. In particular, the lack of actual randomness leads to so-called 'heavy tailed' distributions in the properties that are associated with small-world configurations. This is leading technology designers to re-examine their strategies for handling traffic flow around networks.

To summarize, the reason why networks are important to human–computer systems is this: the ease with which information flows through a network depends on how well it is connected; this affects

- The propagation of faults

- Security breaches

- The likelihood of emergent properties (bugs).

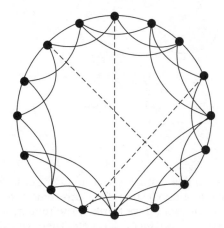

Figure 8.4: In a small-world network, weak links to distant neighbors provide important short-cuts that dramatically reduce the distance between random individuals.

8.3   Causality and dependency

We would like to be able to establish a causal connection between the change of a specific parameter and the resulting change in the system. This will be essential for fault analysis and in substantiating claims about the effectiveness of a program or policy. The principle of causality is simply stated:

> **Principle 44 (Causality).** *Every change or effect happens in response to a cause that precedes it.*

This principle sounds intuitive and even manifestly obvious, but the way in which cause and effect are related in a dynamical system is not always as clear as one might imagine. In this section, the aim is to show ways in which we can be deceived as to the true cause of observed behavior through inadequate analysis.

Suppose we want to consider the behavior of a small subsystem within the entirety of a networked computer system. First of all we have to define what we mean by the subsystem we are studying. This might be a straightforward conceptual partitioning of the total system, but conceptual decompositions do not necessarily preserve causal relationships (see figure 8.5).

In fact we might have to make special allowances for the fact that the subsystem might not be completely described by a closed set of variables. By treating a

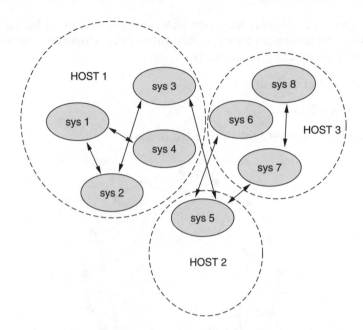

Figure 8.5: A complex system is a causal web or network of intercommunicating parts. It is only possible to truly isolate a subsystem if we can remove a piece of the network from the rest without cutting a connection. If we think of the total system as $S(x_1 \ldots x_n)$, and the individual subsystems as $s_1(x_1 \ldots x_p), s_2(x_p \ldots x_n)$ etc, then we can analyze a subsystem as an open system if the subsystems share any variables, or as a closed system if there are no shared variables.

subsystem as though it were operating in isolation, we might be ignoring important links in the causal web. If we ignore some of the causal influences to the subsystem, its behavior will seem confusing and unpredictable.

There is a simple mathematical expression of this idea. A total system $S(x_1 \ldots x_n)$ can be treated as two independent subsystems if and only if the system of variables can be factorized

$$S(x_1 \ldots x_n) \rightarrow s_1(x_1 \ldots x_p) \cdot s_2(x_p \ldots x_n).$$

In other words, there has to be a separation of variables. This is a precise statement of something which is intuitively obvious, but which might be practically impossible to achieve. The problem is this:

Most of the parts of the causal web in figure 8.5 are themselves closed to us. We do not know the state of all their internal variables, or how they are affected by other parts of the system. Indeed, the task of knowing all of this information is prohibitively difficult.

Interactions with third party systems can introduce behavior which would appear confusing or even impossible in a closed system. How many times have we cursed the computer for not behaving logically? Of course it always behaves causally and logically, the problem when it seems to make no sense is simply that it is behaving outside of our current conceptual model. That is a failure in our conceptual model. The principle of causality tells us that unpredictable behavior means that we have an *incomplete description* of the subsystem. There is another issue, however, by which confusing behavior can seem to arise. That is by *coarse graining* information. Whenever we simplify data by blurring distinctions, information is lost irretrievably. If we then trust the coarse-grained data, it is possible to obtain the illusion of non-causal behavior, since the true explanation of the data has been blurred into obscurity.

Causality is a mapping from cause to effect. The point of a complex system with many variables is that this mapping might not be one-to-one or even many-to-one. In general the mapping is many-to-many. There are knock-on effects. Experimentally, we must have a repeatable demonstration (this establishes a stable context), but we also need a theory about cause and effect (a description of the mapping, sometimes called the kernel of the mapping). We need to identify which variables play a relevant role and we need to factor out any irrelevant variables from the description.

8.4 Defining the system

Given that the many complex interactions in an open system result in effects that have far-reaching consequences, how shall we face up to the reality of taking all of this into account? Where do we place the boundary between the 'system' and its 'environment'? In other words, how do we make an informed decision about what is important and what is unimportant?

This step is the hard one in any analysis. One is usually guided by a desire for simplicity, balanced against a need for completeness. Exactly how one finds this equilibrium is not a task for logic or deduction, but for *induction* or inferral from experiment.

The most conscientious approach to the problem is to perform an analysis of risks from the system that goes beyond the limit that is actually of interest, and then to prune the analysis at a certain level of detail.

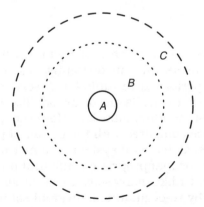

Figure 8.6: Looking for the boundary between system and environment. Region *A* consists of a physical computer boundary. Region *B* represents a region in which the failure cause probability is greater than 10^{-3}. Region *C* represents the radius for fault causes of greater than 10^{-4}.

In figure 8.6, we see a schematic representation of a computer connected to its environment (by temperature, by network, by users etc). The question is: do we choose the boundary of the hardware box that the computer lives in (*A*) as the boundary of the system? Or do we choose an abstract boundary that includes all of the devices and users that it is connected to that are likely to cause errors with some minimum level of probability? The second alternative is the most reasonable one from the systemic viewpoint. The physical boundary of a computing device is not really a relevant one – it is purely cosmetic. The real sphere of influence is wider than this. Indeed, computers are more likely to exhibit faults that result from usage than through any other source of errors.

8.5 Faults

The IEEE classification of software anomalies is [166],

- Operating system crash

- Program hang-up

- Program crash

- Input problem

- Output problem

- Failed required performance

- Perceived total failure

- System error message

- Service degraded

- Wrong output

- No output.

This classification touches on a variety of themes, all of which might plague the interaction between users and an operating system. Some of these issues encroach on the area of performance tuning, e.g. service degraded. Performance tuning is certainly related to the issue of availability of network services and thus this is a part of system administration. However, performance tuning is of only peripheral importance compared with the matter of possible complete failure. Many of the problems associated with system administration can be attributed to input problems (incorrect or inappropriate configuration) and failed performance through loss of resources. Unlike many software situations these are not problems which can be eliminated by re-evaluating individual software components.

Another source of error is found at the human edge of the system:

- Management error

- Miscommunication

- Forgetfulness

- Misunderstanding/miscommunication

- Misidentification

- Confusion/stress/intoxication

- Ignorance

- Carelessness

- Slowness of response

- Random procedural errors

- Systematic procedural errors

- Inability to deal with complexity

- Inability to cooperate with others.

In system administration the problems are partly social and partly due to the cooperative nature of the many interacting software components. The unpredictability of operating systems is dominated by these issues.

8.5.1 How are faults corrected?

Faults occur for a plethora of reasons, too complex to present in any summarial fashion. Sometimes diagnosing a fault can take days or even weeks. In spite of this, a working solution to the fault is often extremely simple. It might be as simple as restarting a process, killing a process, editing a file, changing the access rights (permissions) to a file object, and so on. The complexity of fault diagnosis originates from the same place as the complexity of the system: i.e. that operating systems are cooperative systems with intricate causal relationships. It is usually these causal relationships which are difficult to diagnose, not the measurable effects which they have on the system. Such causal relationships make useful studies to publish in journals, since they document important experience.

The root cause of a fault is often not important to the running of the system in practice. One may complain about buggy software, but system administrators are not always in a position to fix the software, nor is it rational for them to do so. While everyone agrees that the fault needs to be fixed at source, the system must continue to function in lieu of that time. Once a fault has been successfully diagnosed it is usually a straightforward matter to find a recipe for preventing the problem, or for curing it, if it should occur again. Problem diagnosis is way beyond the abilities of current software systems except in the simplest cases, so the best one could do would be to capture the experience of a human administrator using a knowledge-based expert system. In artificial intelligence studies expert systems are not the only approach to diagnosis. Another approach, for instance, is the use of genetic algorithms. Such algorithms can be fruitful when looking for trends in statistical data, but statistically meaningful data are seldom available in system administration. The nature of most problems is direct cause and effect, perhaps with a cascade or domino effect. That is not to say that statistical data cannot be used in the future. However, at present no such data exist and no one knows what such data are capable of revealing about system behavior.

Suppose we abstract an operating system by considering it as the sum of its interfaces and resources. There is only a handful of operations which can be performed on this collection of objects and so this set of basic primitives is the complete toolbox of a system administrator. One can provide helpful user interfaces to execute these primitives more easily but no greater functionality is possible. The basic primitives are:

- Examining files

- Creating files

- Aliasing files

- Replacing files

- Renaming files

- Removing files

- Editing files

- Changing access rights on files

- Starting and stopping processes or threads

- Signaling processes or threads

- Examining and configuring hardware devices.

From these primitives one may build more complex operations such as frequently required tasks for sharing resources. Note that the difference between a thread and a process is not usually relevant for the system administrator, so we shall speak mainly of processes and ignore the concept of a thread. The reason for this is that kernel-level threads are usually transparent or invisible to processes and user-level threads cannot normally be killed or restarted without restarting an entire process.

8.5.2 Fault report and diagnosis

When problems arise, one needs to develop a systematic approach to diagnosing the error and to getting the system on its feet again. As in the field of medicine, there is only a limited number of symptoms which a body or computer system can express (sore throat, headache, fever, system runs sluggishly, hangs etc). What makes diagnosis difficult is that virtually all ailments therefore lead to the same symptoms. Without further tests, it is thus virtually impossible to determine the cause of symptoms.

As mentioned in section 6.6, a distressing habit acquired from the home computer revolution is the tendency to give up before even attempting a diagnosis and simply reboot the computer. This might bypass an immediate problem but we learn nothing about why the problem arose. It is like killing a patient and replacing him with another. The act of rebooting a computer can have unforseen effects on what other users are doing, disrupting their work and perhaps placing the security of data in jeopardy. Rather we need to carefully examine the evidence on a process by process and file by file basis.

8.5.3 Error reporting

Reporting a health problem is the first step to recognizing its importance and solving it. Users tend to fall into the categories of active and passive users. Active users do not need encouraging to report problems. They will usually report even the smallest of problems; sometimes they will even determine the cause and report a fix. While they can often be wearisome in a stressful situation, active users of this type are our friends and go a long way to spreading the burden of problem solving. Remember the community principle of delegation: if we cannot make good use of resources, then the community is not working.

Active users are sometimes more enthusiastic than they are experienced, however, so the system administrator's job is not simply to accept on trust what they say. Their claims need to be verified and perhaps improved upon. Sometimes, users' proposed solutions cannot be implemented because they are in conflict with the system policy, or because the solution would break something else. Only the system administrator has that kind of bird's-eye view of the system to make the judgment.

In contrast to active users, passive users normally have to be encouraged to report errors. They will fumble around trying to make something work, without understanding that there is necessarily a problem. Help desk systems such as Rust, Gnats, Nearnet, Netlog, PTS, QueueMH and REQ can help in this way, but they can also encourage reports of problems which are only misunderstandings.

> **Suggestion 10 (FAQs).** *Providing users with a road-map for solving problems, starting with Frequently Asked Questions and ending with an error report, can help to rationalize error reporting.*

8.5.4 A diagnostic principle

Once an error has been reported, we must determine its cause. A good principle of diagnostics comes from an old medical adage: When you hear the sound of distant hooves, think horses not zebras, i.e.

> **Principle 45 (Diagnostics).** *Always eliminate the obvious first.*

What this means is that we should always look for the most likely explanation before toying with exotic ideas. It is embarrassing to admit how many times apparently impossible problems have resulted from a cable coming out, or forgetting to put in a plug after being distracted in the middle of a job. If the screen is dark, is it plugged in, is the brightness turned up, is the picture centered? Power failures, loose connections, and accidentally touching an important switch can all confuse us. Since these kinds of accident are common, it is logical to begin here. Nothing is too simple or menial to check. A systematic approach, starting with simple things and progressing through the numbers often makes light work of many problems. The urge to panic is often strong in novices, when there is no apparent explanation; with experience, however, we can quell the desire to run for help. A few tests will almost always reveal a problem. Experience allows us to expand our repertoire and recognize clues, but there is no reason why cold logic should not bring us home in every case.

Having eliminated the obvious avenues of error, we are led into the murkier waters of fault diagnosis. When a situation is confusing, it is of paramount importance to keep a clear head. Writing down a log of what we try and the effect it has on the problem prevents a forgetful mind from losing its way. Drawing a conceptual map of the problem, as a picture, is also a powerful way of persuading the human mind to do its magic.

Once of the most powerful features of the human mind (the thing which makes it, by far, the most powerful pattern-recognition agent in existence) is its ability to associate information input with conceptual models from previous experience. Even the most tenuous of resemblances can lead us to be amused at a likeness of a person or object, seen in an unusual context. We recognize human faces in clouds and old cars; we recognize a song from just a few notes. The ability to make connections leads us in circles of thought which sooner or later lead to 'inspiration'. As most professionals know, however, inspiration is seldom worth waiting for. A competent person knows how to work through these mental contortions systematically to come up with the same answer. While this might be a less romantic notion than waiting for inspired enlightenment, it is usually more efficient.

8.5.5 Establishing cause and effect

If a problem has arisen, then something in the system is different than it was before the error occurred. Our task then is to determine the source of that change and identify a chain of events which resulted in the unfortunate effect. The hope is that this will tell us whether or not we can prevent the problem from recurring and perhaps also whether or not we can fix it. It is not merely so that we can fill out a report in triplicate that we need to debug errors.

Problem diagnosis is one of the hardest problems in any field, be it system administration, medicine or anything else. Once a cause has been found, a cure can be simple, but finding the problem itself often requires experience, a large knowledge base and an active imagination. There is a three-stage process:

- Gather evidence from users and from other tests.

- Make an informed guess as to the probable cause.

- Try to reproduce (or perhaps just fix) the error.

It is only when we have shown that a particular change can switch the error on or off that we can say with certainty what the cause of the error was.

Sometimes it is not possible to directly identify the causal chain which led to an error with certainty. Trying to reproduce a problem on an unimportant host is one way of verifying a theory, but this will not always work. Computers are complex systems which are affected by the behavior of users, interactions between subsystems, network traffic, and any combination of these things. Any one of these factors can have changed in the meantime. Sometimes it can be a chance event which creates a unique set of conditions for an error to occur. Usually this is not the case though; most problems are reproducible with sufficient time and imagination.

Trying to establish probable cause in such a web of intrigue as a computer system is enough to challenge the best detectives. Indeed, we shall return to this point in chapter 13 and consider the nature of the problems in more detail. To employ a tried and tested strategy, in the spirit of Sherlock Holmes, we can gradually eliminate possibilities and therefore isolate the problem, little by little. This requires a certain inspiration for hypothesizing causes which can be found from any number of sources.

- One should pay attention to all the facts available about the problem. If users have reported it, then one should take seriously what they have to say, but always attempt to verify the facts before taking too much on trust.

- Reading documentation can sometimes reveal simple misunderstandings in configuration which would lead to the problem.

- Talking to others who might have seen the problem before can provide a short cut to the truth. They might have done the hard work of diagnosis before. Again, their solutions need to be verified before taking them on trust.

- Reading old bug and problem reports can provide important clues.

- Examining system log files will sometimes provide answers.

- Performing simple tests and experiments, based on a best-guess scenario, sharpens the perception of the problem and can even allow the cause to be pinpointed.

- If the system is merely running slower than it should, then some part of it is struggling to allocate resources. Is the disk nearing full, or the memory, or even the process table? Entertain the idea that it is choking in garbage. For instance, deleted files take up space on systems like Novell, since the files are stored in such a way that they can be undeleted. One needs to purge the filesystem every so often to remove these, or the system will spend much longer than it should looking for free blocks. Unix systems thrash when processes build up to unreasonable levels. Garbage collection is a powerful tool in system maintenance. Imagine how human health would suffer if we could never relieve ourselves of dead cells or the byproducts of a healthy consumption. All machines need to do this.

Ideally, one would have a control measurement ('baseline') of the system, so that one has a set of measurements when the system is working normally for comparison. This is beyond the scope of this book however.

8.5.6 Gathering evidence

From best guess to verification of fault can be a puzzling time in which one grapples with the possible explanations and seeks tests which can confirm or deny their plausibility. One could easily write a whole book exemplifying techniques for troubleshooting, but that would take us beyond the limits set for this book. Let us just provide two simplified examples of real cases which help to illustrate how the process of detection can proceed.

Example 6 (Network services become unavailable). *A common scenario is the sudden disappearance of a network service, like, say, the WWW from a site. If a network service fails to respond it can only be due to a few possibilities:*

- *The service has died on the server host.*

- *The line of communication has been broken.*

- *The latency of the connection is so long that the service has timed-out.*

A natural first step is to try to send a 'ping' to the server-host:

```
ping www.domain.country
```

to see whether it is alive. A ping signal will normally return with an answer within a couple of seconds, even for a machine halfway across the planet. If the request responds with

```
www.domain.country is alive
```

then we know immediately that there is an active line of communication between our host and the server hosts and we can eliminate the second possibility. If the ping request does not return, then there are two further possibilities:

- *The line of communication is broken.*

- *The DNS lookup service is not responding.*

The DNS service can hang a request for a long period of time if a DNS server is not responding. A simple way to check whether the DNS server is at fault or not is to bypass it, by typing the IP address of the WWW server directly:

```
ping -n 128.39.74.4
```

If this fails to respond then we know that the fault was not primarily due to the name service. It tends to suggest a broken line of communication. The traceroute *command on Unix-like operating systems, or* tracert *on Windows can be used to follow a net connection through various routers to its destination. This often allows us to narrow down the point of failure to a particular group of cables in the network. If a network break has persisted for more than a few minutes, a ping or traceroute will normally respond with the message*

```
ICMP error: No route to host
```

and this tells us immediately that there is a network connectivity problem.

But what if there is no DNS problem and the ping tells us that the host is alive? Then the natural next step is to verify that the WWW service is actually running on the server host. On a Unix-like OS we can simply log onto the server host (assuming it is ours) and check the process table for the `httpd` daemon which mediates the WWW service

```
ps waux | grep httpd
ps -elf | grep httpd
```

for BSD and Sys V Unices respectively. On a Windows machine, we would have to go to the host physically and check its status. If the WWW service is not running, then we would like to know why it stopped working. Checking log files to see what the server was doing when it stopped working can provide clues or even an answer. Sometimes a server will die because of a bug in the program. It is a simple matter to start the service again. If it starts and seems to work normally afterwards, then the problem was probably a bug in the program. If the service fails to start, then it will log an error message of some kind which will tell us more. One possibility is that someone has changed something in the WWW service's configuration file and has left an error behind. The server can no longer make sense of its configuration and it gives up. The error can be rectified and the server can be restarted.

What if the server process has not died? What if we cannot even log onto the server host? The latter would be a clear indication that there was something more fundamentally wrong with the server host. Resisting the temptation to simply reboot it, we could then try to test other services on the server host to see if they respond. We already know that the ping echo service is responding, so the host is not completely dead (it has power, at least). There are therefore several things which could be wrong:

- The host is unable to respond (e.g. it is overloaded).

- The host is unwilling to respond (e.g. a security check denying access to our host).

We can check that the host is overloaded by looking at the process table to see what is running. If there is nothing to see there, the host might be undergoing a denial of service attack (see chapter 11). A look at `netstat` will show how many external connections are directed towards the host and their nature. This might show something that would confirm or deny the attack theory. An effective attack would be difficult to prevent, so this could be the end of the line for this particular investigation and the start of a new one, to determine the attacker. If there is no attack, we could check that the DNS name service is working on the server-host. This could cause the server to hang for long periods of time. Finally, there are lots of reasons why the kernel itself might prevent the server from working correctly: the TCP connection close time in the kernel might be too long, leading to blocked connections; the kernel itself might have gone amok; a full disk might be causing errors which have a knock-on effect (the log files from the server might have filled up the disk), in which case the disk problem will have to be solved first. Notice how the DNS and disk problems are problems of dependency: a problem in one service having a knock-on effect in another.

Example 7 (Disks suddenly become full). *A second example, with a slightly surprising conclusion, begins with an error message from a program telling us that the system disk of a particular host has become full. The nature of this particular problem is not particularly ambiguous. A full disk is a disk with no space left on it. Our aim is to try to clear enough space to get the system working again, at least until a more permanent solution can be found. In order to do this, we need to know why the disk became full. Was it for legitimate reasons, or because of a lack of preventative garbage collection, or in this case a completely different reason? There are many reasons why a disk partition might become full. Here are some obvious ones:*

- *A user disk partition can become full if users download huge amounts of data from the Internet, or if they generate large numbers of temporary files. User disks can become full both for valid reasons and for mischievous reasons.*

- *The contents of the system disk only change for one of two reasons: log files which record system activity can grow and fill up a disk; temporary files written to public directories can grow and fill a disk.*

If a user disk becomes full, it is usually possible to find some unnecessary files which can be deleted in order to make space temporarily. The files we deem as unnecessary have to be defined as such as a matter of policy. It would be questionable ethically to make a habit of deleting files which users did not know could be removed, in advance. Some administrators follow the practice of keeping a large file on every disk partition which can be removed to make space. Of course, if we have done our preventative maintenance, then there should not be any junk files taking up space on the system. In the end, all user disk usage grows monotonically and new disks have to be bought, users can be moved to new disks to spread the load, and so on.

If a system disk becomes full, there are three main things to look for:

- core *files (Unix)*

- *Temporary files*

- *Log files.*

Core files are image files which are dumped when programs crash. They are meant to be used for debugging purposes; in practice they cause more problems than they solve. Core files are very large and one or two can easily fill a tight partition, though disk sizes are always growing and giving us more playing room. Preventative maintenance should delete such files regularly. Temporary files /tmp *and* /var/tmp *in Unix-like systems, or* C:\Temp *on Windows are publicly writable directories which usually take up space on the system disk. Temporary files can also be written elsewhere. These can be filled up either accidentally or maliciously. Again, these should be cleared regularly. The final source of trouble is log files. Log files need to be rotated on a regular basis so that they do not grow too large. Rotation means starting a new log and saving a small number of old log files. This means that old log data eventually get thrown away, rather than keeping it forever.*

In all of the above cases, we can identify the recent change in a filesystem by searching for files which have changed in the last 24 hours. On a Unix-like system,

*this is easily done by running a command to look at all subdirectories of the current
directory:*

```
find . -mtime -1 -print -xdev
```

*On other systems it is harder and requires special software. A GNU version of the
Unix* find *utility is available for Windows.*

*A third reason why a filesystem can become full is corruption. In one instance
a Unix disk continued to grow, despite verifying that no new files had been created
and after removing all old log files. The Unix* df *disk utility eventually reported
that the filesystem was 130% full (an impossibility) and it continued to grow. The
eventual cause of this problem was identified as a fault in the filesystem structure,
or inode corruption. This was brought about by the host concerned overheating
and causing memory errors (system log errors confirmed memory write errors). The
problem recurred twice before the host was moved to a cooler environment, after
which time it righted itself (though the filesystem had to be repaired with* fsck *on
each occasion).*

There are many tips for tracing the activity of programs. For instance, to trace
what files are read by a program, use strace or truss to watch for file descriptors

```
truss -t open,close  program
```

This runs the program concerned in a monitor which prints out all the listed
system calls. This can be a good way of finding out which libraries a program uses
(or tries and fails to use) or which configuration files it opens.

Complete your own list of troubleshooting tips. This is a list you will be building
for the rest of your life.

8.6 Cause trees

From the previous sections, we recognize that the causal relationships within
a system can form complex networks. Unraveling such networks is difficult. In
many cases we can simplify the causal structure by replacing part of the network
with an effective tree that more clearly describes the causal relationships. The
price for this simplification is that the events are non-deterministic; by hiding
details, we lose complete information about the system, but achieve a higher level
understanding. Cause trees were advocated before the topology of networks was
fully appreciated.

Charting cause trees is a systematic method used in fault diagnosis. The idea
is to begin by building lists of possible causes, then causes of those causes, and
so on, until one has covered an appropriate level of detail. Once a cause tree
has been constructed for a system, it becomes a road-map for fault finding for
the future also. The use of cause trees is sometimes called *Root Cause Analysis*
(RCA). A related method called *Event Tree Analysis* (ETA) maps out every single
eventuality as a true/false binary tree, where every possibility is documented but
only certain pathways actually occur. The latter is mainly a way of documenting
the extent of a system; it has little analytical value.

Many of the techniques described in this chapter were pioneered over the last half century by authorities working with nuclear power, where the risk of accidents takes on a whole different level of importance. The keyword in causal analyses is *dependencies*. All of the immediate causes of a phenomenon or event are called dependencies, i.e. the event depends on them for its existence. The cause tree for diagnostic example 6 is shown in figure 8.7. The structure is not completely hierarchical, but it is approximately so.

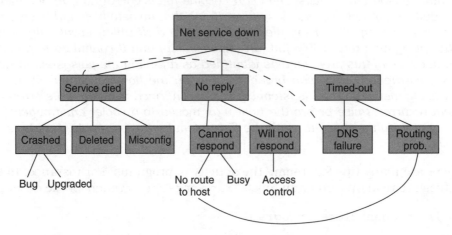

Figure 8.7: Attempt at cause tree for a missing network service.

The cause tree for diagnostic example 7 is shown in figure 8.8. This is a particularly simple example; it simply becomes a flat list. Causal analysis can be

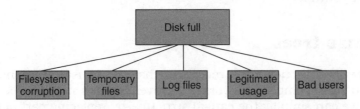

Figure 8.8: Attempt at cause tree for a full disk.

used at different levels. At the level of human management, it takes on a more heuristic role, e.g.

- Inadequate procedures

- Inadequate training

- Quality control

- Miscommunication

- Poor management

- Social/human engineering

- Supervision error

- Preventative maintenance lacking.

Information is collected about an incident or phenomenon and this is broken down into cause–effect relationships. Analysts must understand the systems they model thoroughly from the highest levels, down to the component level.

The construction of an event tree is just like the top-down analysis performed in programming. Breaking the event up into component causes is like breaking up a task into subroutines. The benefit is the same: a complex problem is reduced to a structured assembly of lesser problems.

8.7 Probabilistic fault trees

How can we go beyond the simple thinking aid of mapping of *possible* cause and effect to actually calculating the likely outcomes of the different pathways through a cause tree? To do that, we must acknowledge that not all of the possible pathways occur all of the time: some occur only infrequently, some are mutually exclusive, some are co-dependent and others are uncorrelated. To make serious headway in estimating likely cause, we thus need to add probabilities and combinatorics to the discussion. This is the contribution of fault tree analysis. The discussion here follows that of Apthorpe [17], based on ref. [227].

8.7.1 Faults

For the purposes of modeling, fault tree analysis distinguishes between:

- *Failures*: abnormal occurrences that do not prevent the system from functioning.

- *Faults*: systemic breakdowns within the system.

An important subset of faults is formed by *component faults*.
Component faults fall into three categories:

- *Primary faults*: occur when a component is working within its design limits, e.g. a web server that is rated at 50 transactions per second fails when it reaches 30 transactions per second.

- *Secondary faults*: occur when a fault is operating outside its design specification, e.g. a web server that is rated at 50 transactions per second fails when it reaches 90 transactions per second.

- *Command faults*: are faults that occur when a system performs its specified function, but at the wrong time or place, e.g. a Web server that begins querying a database persistently when no request is being made by an external agent.

Faults occur in response to events. The events are also categorized, this time depending on their position within the tree structure:

- *Top*: This is the top of the tree – the end phenomenon that we are trying to explain. It is analogous to the 'main' function in a computer program.

- *Intermediary*: This is a dependency within the tree, but not a root cause of the phenomenon. It is analogous to a subroutine of the main program, it has deeper dependencies that are subroutines of itself.

- *Primary*: This is an event that is either a root cause, or as deep an explanation as we can manage to determine. In a computer program analogy, it is like a basic library function, i.e. the lowest level of control available. Events that we cannot say much about are called *undeveloped events* because although we cannot dig any deeper, we know that there is more going on than we can say. Events that have no further explanation are called *basic events*. These are the primitive atoms of causality: the very root causes.

Events are drawn using the symbols in figure 8.9.

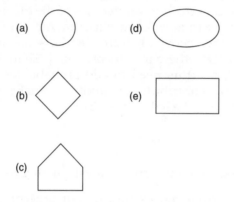

Figure 8.9: Basic symbols for fault trees.

8.7.2   Conditions and set logic

When several smaller causes lead to an intermediate event or phenomenon, there arises a question about how many of the sub-events were needed to trigger the higher level event – all of them? any of them? a certain number? Events thus combine in ways that can be represented by simple combinatoric set notation – with 'AND' and 'OR' or other conditions. These are best known to computer scientists in the form of *logic gates*. Figure 8.10 shows the standard symbols for the gate types. Although there are many gate types, in practice AND and OR suffice for most cases.

The properties of the gates in combining the probabilities are noted below. Note that it makes a difference whether or not events are independent, in the probabilistic sense: i.e. the occurrence of one event does not alter the probability of occurrence of another.

- In OR gates, probabilities combine so as to get *larger*.

$$P(A \text{ OR } B) = P(A) + P(B) - P(A \text{ AND } B). \tag{8.1}$$

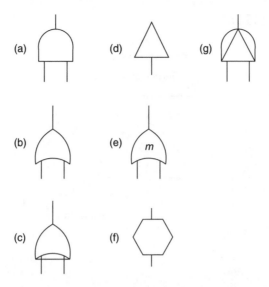

Figure 8.10: Basic gate types: (a) AND, (b) OR, (c) XOR, (d) transfer partial result to separate sub-tree, (e) voting gate (m of n), (f) inhibit conditional of 'if' gate, and (g) priority AND (inputs ordered from left to right) (see ref. [227]). Many simple cases can be modeled with just AND and OR.

In general,

$$P(A_1 \text{ OR } A_2 \text{ OR } \dots \text{ OR } A_n) = \sum_{i=1}^{n} P(A_i) - \sum_{i=1}^{n-1} n \sum_{j=i+1}^{n} P(A_i)P(A_j) + \dots \quad (8.2)$$

$$+(-1)^{n+1} P(A_1)P(A_2)\dots P(A_n).$$

- In AND gates, probabilities combine so as to get *smaller*:

$$P(A \text{ AND } B) = P(A)P(B|A), \quad (8.3)$$

or in general:

$$P(A_1 \text{ AND } A_2 \text{ AND } \dots \text{ AND } A_n) = \prod_{i=1}^{n} P(A_i). \quad (8.4)$$

If A and B are independent, then

$$P(A)P(B|A) = P(A)P(B), \quad (8.5)$$

which is smaller than $P(A)$ or $P(B)$; but if the events are not independent, the result can be much greater than this.

- XOR gates have no predictable effect on magnitudes.

$$P(A \text{ OR } B) = P(A) + P(B) - 2P(A \text{ AND } B). \quad (8.6)$$

Thus if we see many OR pathways, we should be scared. If we see many AND pathways, we should be pleased – the latter means that things are tied down quite tightly with redundancy or protections.

8.7.3 Construction

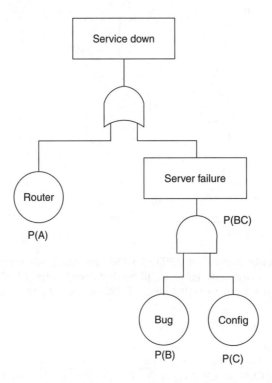

Figure 8.11: A simple fault tree for an unavailable service.

As a simple example, consider how to work out the probability of failure for a system attack, where an attacker tries the obvious pathways of failure: guessing the root password, or exploiting some known loopholes in services which have not been patched (see figure 8.11).

We split the tree into two main branches: first try the root password of the system, 'OR' try to attack any services which might contain bugs.

- The two main branches are 'independent' in the probabilistic sense, because guessing the root password does not change the sample space for attacking a service and vice versa (it's not like picking a card from a deck).

- On the service arm, we split (for convenience) this probability into two parts and say that hosts are vulnerable if they have a service which could be exploited AND the hosts have not been patched or configured to make them invulnerable.

- Note that these two arms of the AND gate are time-dependent. After a service vulnerability becomes known, the administrator has to try to patch/reconfigure the system. Attackers therefore have a *window of opportunity*. This adds a time dimension to the fault analysis which we might or might not wish to address.

Since all the events are independent, we have:

$$P(\text{breakin}) = P(A \text{ OR } (\text{NOT } A \text{ AND } (B \text{ AND } C))) \qquad (8.7)$$
$$= P(A) + (1 - P(A)) \times P(B)P(C) \qquad (8.8)$$

Suppose we have, from experience,

- Chance of router problem $P(A) = 5/1000 = 0.005$.

- Chance of server problem $P(B) = 50/1000 = 0.05$.

- Chance that server is misconfigured $P(C) = 10\% = 0.1$.

$$P(\text{breakin}) = 0.005 + 0.995 \times 0.05 \times 0.1$$
$$= 0.005 + 0.0049$$
$$= 0.01$$
$$= 1\% \qquad (8.9)$$

Notice how, even though the chance of guessing the root password is small, it becomes an equally likely avenue of attack, due to the chance that the host might have been upgraded. Thus we see that the chance of breakin is a competition between an attacker and a defender.

A *cutset* is a set of basic events that are essential for a top-level fault to occur. A *minimal cutset* is a cutset in which the removal of a single event no longer guarantees the occurrence of the top-level event. The aim of fault tree analysis is to identify these cutsets.

8.8 Change management revisited

Change management is about planning the timing and deployment of upgrades and overhauls to the system. One of the fears that makes system administrators reticent in changing anything is the maxim 'if it ain't broke, don't fix it'. We want to know what the knock-on effects of change will be. Perhaps upgrading an operating system will have significant repercussions for users. What will be the consequences of such change?

Dependencies in a graph show us the consequences of our actions. How will a change propagate into the rest of the system, for better or for worse? A change is no different to a fault: a change of policy makes what was once a feature become a bug that needs to be fixed. Managing change is therefore analogous to the fixing of bugs, except that it begins with an extra step: a policy decision.

A checklist for change management can be specified as follows:

1. Decide on the change.

2. Map out the repercussion network (dependencies) of the change, as far as possible.[1]

---

[1] Some dependencies might be hidden or be beyond your control, e.g. operating system upgrade changes.

3. Revise policy for each affected component in the system to reflect the change.

4. Inform users of the impending change and wait for comments.

5. Incorporate any user comments into the policy change.

6. Lock the system to prevent incomplete reconfiguration from being a hazard to the system.

7. Make the changes.

8. Unlock the system.

9. Inform users that the change has been implemented.

Notice that it is important to lock down the system during a major 'non-atomic' change. This secures the system against problems that can occur because a part of the system is not yet upgraded. Locking the system prevents policy conflicts from adversely affecting the reliable functioning of the system during the upgrade.

In change management we are interested in consistency, i.e. moving from a state of widespread predictability to a new state of widespread predictability.

8.9 Game-theoretical strategy selection

Game theory is a method of rational decision making. More specifically, it is a method for pitting a set of pre-emptive and defensive strategies against one another, and finding their point of balance in order to maximize gain and minimize loss (see figure 8.12).

Game theory is useful in cases where it is difficult to evaluate the rational gains of following particular policies without some calculational framework. This occurs whenever the number of choices is large and the effects are subtle. Contests which are caused by conflicts of interest between system policy and user wishes, unfold in this framework as environmental interactions which tend to oppose convergence and stability [225, 96]. Game theory is about introducing 'players', with goals and aims, into a scheme of rules and then analyzing how much each player can win, according to those restrictions. Each pair of strategies in a game affords the player a characteristic value, often referred to as the 'payoff'. Game theory has been applied to warfare, to economics (commercial warfare) and many other situations.

> **Principle 46 (Strategic administration).** *System administration can be viewed as a strategic game whose aim is to maintain a policy-conformant state [47]. A fault of the system, and its corresponding fault tree, is thus a strategy for driving the system off-policy, while an administrative maintenance strategy is a countermeasure that tends to restore conformance with policy.*

Games come in several forms. Some are trivial, one-person games of chance, and are not analyzable in terms of strategies (these are more suitable to 'flat' fault tree analysis), since the actions of the players are irrelevant to the outcome;

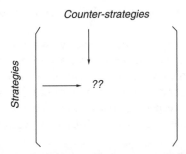

Figure 8.12: The payoff matrix for a two-person game is a table of strategies and counter-strategies for one of the players. Each player has a payoff matrix.

in this case, one has a rather simple fault tree. More interesting is the case in which the outcome of the game can be determined by a specific choice of strategy on the part of the players. The most basic model for such a game is that of a two-person zero-sum game, or a game in which there are two players, and where the losses of one player are the gains of the other. This model is simplistic, applied as users versus system, because it seems to say that all users must work contrary to system policy, which is clearly not true. However, experience shows that it is mainly those few users who do attempt to confound policy who need to be dealt with strategically. Thus, the real 'battle' for the ideal *error-free* state of the system, is between those factions who are for and those who are against policy. The majority of neutral users play only a background role (as chance noise) and do not need to be modeled explicitly.

The courses of action available to each party label the rows and columns of the matrix. Rows are strategies and columns are counter-strategies, or vice versa. The values within the matrix are the values gained by one of the players, in units of the arbitrary currency of the game when a given row-strategy and column-strategy are chosen. Once this 'payoff' matrix has been formulated, it contains information about the potential outcome of a game or scenario, using the strategies. This forms the basis for the theory of games [225, 96], whose methods and theorems make it possible to determine the optimal course or courses of action in order to maximize one's winnings. Obviously, any and all information which contributes to a judgment is useful, however one does not necessarily need a particularly detailed or accurate description to begin making simple value judgments about system behavior. Even a simple quantification is useful, if it can distinguish between two possible courses of action.

How much can a user or an attacker hope to win? What is the currency of this evaluation? In addition to work produced or resources gained by a user's strategy, other things might be deemed to be of value, such as privilege and status. In a community, wealth does not guarantee privilege or status unless that coincides with the politics of the community. Payoff can therefore be a complex issue to model. If one includes these ranking issues in calculations, one might allow for the possibility that a user plays the system rules in order to gain privileges for some later purpose. A user who accrues the goodwill of the system administrator might eventually gain trust or even special privileges, such as extra disk space, access to restricted data etc. Such problems are of special interest in connection with security [171, 327].

In a community, games are not necessarily two-player zero-sum engagements. What is lost by one player is not necessarily gained by an obvious opponent. Moreover, the information available to different sides in a conflict can affect their modes of play. In this case the theory of non-zero sum games becomes important; in particular, the idea of a Nash equilibrium arises. The so-called prisoner's dilemma leads to the famous example of Nash equilibrium [222] which is a trade-off:

> **Principle 47 (Nash dilemma).** *A user of the system who pursues solely private interests, does not necessarily promote the best interest of the community as a whole.*

Should strategies cooperate or 'fight' to maximize their winnings? See the example in section 10.9. The non-zero sum game is beyond the scope of this book, but interested readers are encouraged to find out more about this important method.

Many games can be stated in terms of a basic zero-sum model: it is, for example, the model taken by current system administration agents such as cfengine [41] and PIKT [231], as well as several commercial products, to good effect. Indeed, it is also the view taken by vertebrate immune systems, in detecting potential sickness or damage. Thus, while it might be a simplistic first step where intelligent humans are concerned, it provides a non-trivial example for introductory purposes without overly simplifying the issues. In a realistic situation, both parties in the two-person game would use *mixed strategies*. A strategy is any specified choice of action. It can involve:

- A schedule of operations,

- A specification of moves and counter-moves (rules).

In addition to simple short-term strategies (tactics), there can be meta-strategies, or long-term goals. For instance, a nominal community strategy might be to implement the stability criteria discussed earlier:

- Maintain the stability of the system

- Maximize total productivity or the generation of work,

- Gain the largest feasible share of resources,

but this might be implemented in the short term by a variety of tactics, such as policy cooperation, non-cooperation and so on. An attack strategy might be to

- Consume or destroy key resources

- Oppose system policy

- Denial of service.

Tactics for attaining intermediate goals might include covert strategies such as *bluffing* (falsely naming files or other deceptions), taking out an attacker, counter-attacking, or evasion (concealment), exploitation, trickery, antagonization, incessant complaint (spam), revenge etc. Security and privilege, levels of access, integrity and trust must be woven into algebraic measures for the payoff. Faced with a problem to the system, one may address it either by patching symptoms, or by seeking to root out the fundamental cause. Most successful strategies, including those used by biological life, employ both. A means of expressing all of these devices must be formulated within a model. For an example, see ref. [47].

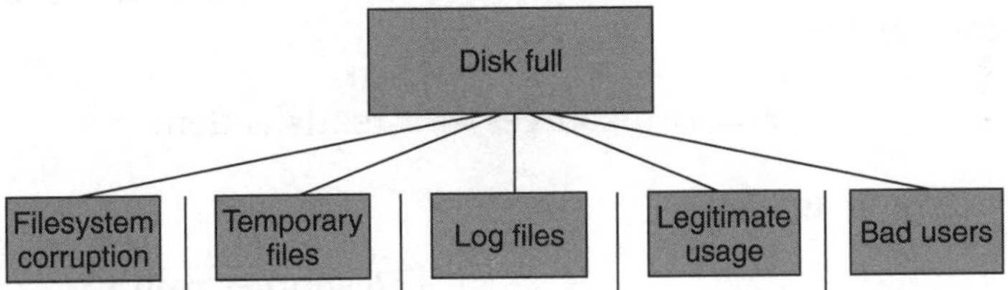

Counter-strategies	Filesystem corruption	Temporary files	Log files	Legitimate usage	Bad users
Force tidy	?	?	?	?	?
Ask users	?	?	—	?	?
Rotate logs	?	?	?	?	?
Check fs	?	?	?	?	?
Disk quotas	?	—	—	?	?

Figure 8.13: Payoff matrix and a fault tree showing how the fault tree feeds into the game as probabilities, and vice versa. The values in the matrix are probabilistic expressions expressing the likelihood of achieving each strategic goal, weighted by a currency scale for its relative importance. See ref. [48] for details of this game.

The rows and columns of a payoff matrix feed into the lowest level twigs of the fault tree (see figure 8.13). Each row and column represents a *pure strategy* of the game, but it is known that an optimal mixture of strategies is often the best solution, on average. In a situation where the failure modes are motivated by user actions, not merely random occurrences, this blend of game theory and fault tree analysis has a unique role to play.

Example 8 (Garbage collection). *The difficult part of a type II analysis is turning the high-level concepts and aims listed above into precise numerical values. To illustrate the procedure, consider an example of some importance, namely the filling of user disks. The need for forced garbage collection has been argued on several occasions [336, 41, 55], but the effectiveness of different strategies for preventing disks filling may now be analyzed theoretically. This analysis is inspired by the user environment at Oslo University College, and the expressions derived here are designed to model this situation, not an arbitrary system.*

The currency of this game must first be agreed upon. What value will be transferred from one player to the other in play? There are three relevant measurements to take into account: (i) the amount of resources consumed by the attacker (or freed by the defender); sociological rewards: (ii) 'goodwill' or (iii) 'privilege' which are conferred as a result of sticking to the policy rules. These latter rewards can most easily be combined into an effective variable 'satisfaction'. A 'satisfaction' measure is needed in order to set limits on individuals' rewards for cheating, or balance the situation in which the system administrator prevents users from using any resources at all. This is clearly not a defensible use of the system, thus the system defences should be penalized for restricting users too much. The characteristic matrix now has two contributions,

$$\pi = \pi_r(\text{resources}) + \pi_s(\text{satisfaction}). \tag{8.10}$$

It is convenient to define

$$\pi_r \equiv \pi(\text{resources}) = \frac{1}{2}\left(\frac{\text{Resources won}}{\text{Total resources}}\right). \tag{8.11}$$

Satisfaction π_s is assigned arbitrarily on a scale from plus to minus one half, such that,

$$-\frac{1}{2} \leq \pi_r \leq +\frac{1}{2}$$
$$-\frac{1}{2} \leq \pi_s \leq +\frac{1}{2}$$
$$-1 \leq \pi \leq +1. \tag{8.12}$$

The different strategies can now be regarded as duels, or games of timing.

Users/System	Ask to tidy	Tidy by date	Tidy above threshold	Quotas
Tidy when asked	$\pi(1,1)$	$\pi(1,2)$	$\pi(1,3)$	$\pi(1,4)$
Never tidy	$\pi(2,1)$	$\pi(2,2)$	$\pi(2,3)$	$\pi(2,4)$
Conceal files	$\pi(3,1)$	$\pi(3,2)$	$\pi(3,3)$	$\pi(3,4)$
Change timestamps	$\pi(4,1)$	$\pi(4,2)$	$\pi(4,3)$	$\pi(4,4)$

These elements of the characteristic matrix must now be filled, using a model and a policy. A general expression for the rate at which users produce files is approximated by:

$$r_u = \frac{n_b r_b + n_g r_g}{n_b + n_g}, \tag{8.13}$$

where r_b is the rate at which bad users (i.e. problem users) produce files, and r_g is the rate for good users. The total number of users is $n_u = n_b + n_g$. From experience, the ratio n_b/n_g is about one percent. The rate can be expressed as a scaled number between zero and one, for convenience, so that $r_b = 1 - r_g$.

The payoff in terms of the consumption of resources by users, to the users themselves, can then be modeled as a gradual accumulation of files, in daily waves, which are a maximum around midday:

$$\pi_u = \frac{1}{2} \int_0^T dt \, \frac{r_u \left(\sin(2\pi t/24) + 1\right)}{R_{\text{tot}}}, \tag{8.14}$$

where the factor of 24 is the human daily rhythm, measured in hours, and R_{tot} is the total amount of resources to be consumed. Note that, by considering only good users or bad users, one has a corresponding expression for π_g and π_b, with r_u replaced by r_g or r_b respectively. An automatic garbage collection system (cfengine) results in a negative payoff to users, i.e. a payoff to the system administrator. This may be written

$$\pi_a = -\frac{1}{2} \int_0^T dt \, \frac{r_a \left(\sin(2\pi t/T_p) + 1\right)}{R_{\text{tot}}}, \tag{8.15}$$

where T_p is the period of execution for the automatic system (in our case, cfengine). This is typically hourly or more often, so the frequency of the automatic cycle is some twenty times greater than that of the human cycle. The rate of resource-freeing r_a is also greater than r_u, since file deletion takes little time compared with file creation, and also an automated system will be faster than a human. The quota payoff yields a fixed allocation of resources, which are assumed to be distributed equally amongst users and thus each quota slice is assumed to be unavailable to other users. The users are nonchalant, so $\pi_s = 0$ here, but the quota yields

$$\pi_q = +\frac{1}{2} \left(\frac{1}{n_b + n_g} \right). \tag{8.16}$$

The matrix elements are expressed in terms of these.

$\pi(1, 1):$ *Here $\pi_s = -\frac{1}{2}$ since the system administrator is as satisfied as possible by the users' behavior. π_r is the rate of file creation by good users π_g, i.e. only legal files are produced. Comparing the strategies, it is clear that $\pi(1, 1) = \pi(1, 2) = \pi(1, 3)$.*

$\pi(1, 4):$ *Here $\pi_s = 0$, reflecting the users' dissatisfaction with the quotas, but the system administrator is penalized for restricting the freedom of the users. With fixed quotas, users cannot generate large temporary files. π_q is the fixed quota payoff, a fair slice of the resources. Clearly $\pi(4, 1) = \pi(4, 2) = \pi(4, 3) = \pi(4, 4)$. The game has a fixed value if this strategy is adopted by the system administrator. However, it does not mean that this is the best strategy, according to the rules of the game, since the system administrator loses points for restrictive practices, which are not in the best interest of the organization. This is yet to be determined.*

$\pi(2, 1):$ *Here $\pi_s = \frac{1}{2}$ since the system administrator is maximally dissatisfied with users' refusal to tidy their files. The payoff for users is also maximal in taking control of resources, since the system administrator does nothing to prevent this, thus $\pi_r = \pi_u$. Examining the strategies, one finds that $\pi(2, 1) = \pi(3, 1) = \pi(3, 2) = \pi(3, 3) = \pi(4, 1) = \pi(4, 2)$.*

$\pi(2,2)$: *Here $\pi_s = \frac{1}{2}$ since the system administrator is maximally dissatisfied with users' refusal to tidy their files. The payoff for users is now mitigated by the action of the automatic system which works in competition, thus $\pi_r = \pi_u - \pi_a$. The automatic system is invalidated by user bluffing (file concealment).*

$\pi(2,3)$: *Here $\pi_s = \frac{1}{2}$ since the system administrator is maximally dissatisfied with users' refusal to tidy their files. The payoff for users is mitigated by the automatic system, but this does not activate until some threshold time is reached, i.e. until $t > t_0$. Since changing the date cannot conceal files from the automatic system, when they are tidied above threshold, we have $\pi(2,3) = \pi(4,3)$.*

Thus, in summary, the characteristic matrix is given by:

$$\pi(u,s) = \begin{pmatrix} -\frac{1}{2} + \pi_g(t) & -\frac{1}{2} + \pi_g(t) & -\frac{1}{2} + \pi_g(t) & \pi_q \\ \frac{1}{2} + \pi_u(t) & \frac{1}{2} + \pi_u(t) + \pi_a(t) & \frac{1}{2} + \pi_u(t) + \pi_a(t)\,\theta(t_0 - t) & \pi_q \\ \frac{1}{2} + \pi_u(t) & \frac{1}{2} + \pi_u(t) & \frac{1}{2} + \pi_u(t) & \pi_q \\ \frac{1}{2} + \pi_u(t) & \frac{1}{2} + \pi_u(t) & \frac{1}{2} + \pi_u(t) + \pi_a(t)\,\theta(t_0 - t) & \pi_q \end{pmatrix}, \quad (8.17)$$

where the step function is defined by,

$$\theta(t_0 - t) = \begin{cases} 1 \ (t \geq t_0) \\ 0 \ (t < t_0) \end{cases}, \qquad (8.18)$$

and represents the time-delay in starting the automatic tidying system in the case of tidy-above-threshold. This was explained in more detail in ref. [47].

It is possible to say several things about the relative sizes of these contributions. The automatic system works at least as fast as any human so, by design, in this simple model we have

$$\frac{1}{2} \geq |\pi_a| \geq |\pi_u| \geq |\pi_g| \geq 0, \qquad (8.19)$$

for all times. For short times $\pi_q > \pi_u$, but users can quickly fill their quota and overtake this. In a zero-sum game, the automatic system can never tidy garbage faster than users can create it, so the first inequality is always saturated. From the nature of the cumulative payoffs, we can also say that

$$(\frac{1}{2} + \pi_u) \geq (\frac{1}{2} + \pi_u + \pi_a \theta(t_0 - t)) \geq (\frac{1}{2} + \pi_u + \pi_a), \qquad (8.20)$$

and

$$|\frac{1}{2} + \pi_u| \geq |\pi_g - \frac{1}{2}|. \qquad (8.21)$$

Applying these results to a modest strategy of automatic tidying of garbage, referring to figure 8.14, one sees that the automatic system can always match users' moves.

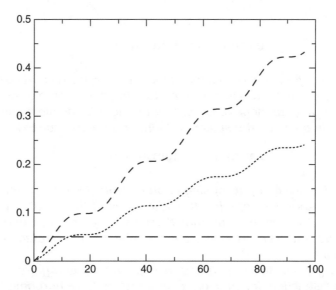

Figure 8.14: The absolute values of payoff contributions as a function of time (in hours), For daily tidying $T_p = 24$. User numbers are set in the ratio $(n_g, n_b) = (99, 1)$, based on rough ratios from the author's College environment, i.e. one percent of users are considered mischievous. The filling rates are in the same ratio: $r_b/R_{tot} = 0.99, r_g/R_{tot} = 0.01, r_a/R_{tot} = 0.1$. The flat dot-slashed line is $|\pi_q|$, the quota payoff. The lower wavy line is the cumulative payoff resulting from good users, while the upper line represents the payoff from bad users. The upper line doubles as the magnitude of the payoff $|\pi_a| \geq |\pi_u|$, if we apply the restriction that an automatic system can never win back more than users have already taken. Without this restriction, $|\pi_a|$ would be steeper.

As drawn, the daily ripples of the automatic system are in phase with the users' activity. This is not realistic, since tidying would normally be done at night when user activity is low, however such details need not concern us in this illustrative example.

The policy created in setting up the rules of play for the game penalizes the system administrator for employing strict quotas which restrict users' activities. Even so, users do not gain much from this, because quotas are constant for all time. A quota is a severe handicap to users in the game, except for very short times before users reach their quota limits. Quotas could be considered cheating by the system administrator, since they determine the final outcome even before play commences. There is no longer an adaptive allocation of resources. Users cannot create temporary files which exceed these hard and fast quotas. An immunity-type model which allows fluctuations is a more resource-efficient strategy in this respect, since it allows users to span all the available resources for short periods of time, without consuming them for ever.

According to the minimax theorem, proved by John von Neumann, any two-person zero-sum game has a solution, either in terms of a pair of optimal pure strategies or as a pair of optimal mixed strategies [225, 96]. The solution is found as the balance between one player's attempt to maximize his payoff and the other player's attempt to minimize the opponent's result. In general, one can say of the payoff matrix that

$$\max_{\downarrow} \min_{\rightarrow} \pi_{rc} \leq \min_{\rightarrow} \max_{\downarrow} \pi_{rc}, \tag{8.22}$$

where the arrows refer to the directions of increasing rows ($\downarrow$) and columns ($\rightarrow$). The left-hand side is the least users can hope to win (or conversely the most that the system administrator can hope to keep) and the right is the most users can hope to win (or conversely the least the system administrator can hope to keep). If we have

$$\max_{\downarrow} \min_{\rightarrow} \pi_{rc} = \min_{\rightarrow} \max_{\downarrow} \pi_{rc}, \tag{8.23}$$

it implies the existence of a pair of single, pure strategies (r^*, c^*) which are optimal for both players, regardless of what the other does. If the equality is not satisfied, then the minimax theorem tells us that there exist optimal mixtures of strategies, where each player selects at random from a number of pure strategies with a certain probability weight.

The situation for our time-dependent example matrix is different for small t and for large t. The distinction depends on whether users have had time to exceed fixed quotas or not; thus 'small t' refers to times when users are not impeded by the imposition of quotas. For small t, one has:

$$\max_{\downarrow} \min_{\rightarrow} \pi_{rc} = \max_{\downarrow} \begin{pmatrix} \pi_g - \frac{1}{2} \\ \frac{1}{2} + \pi_u + \pi_a \\ \frac{1}{2} + \pi_u \\ \frac{1}{2} + \pi_u + \pi_a \, \theta(t_0 - t) \end{pmatrix}$$

$$= \frac{1}{2} + \pi_u. \tag{8.24}$$

The ordering of sizes in the above minimum vector is:

$$\frac{1}{2} + \pi_u \geq \frac{1}{2} + \pi_u + \pi_a \theta(t_0 - t) \geq \pi_u + \pi_a \theta(t_0 - t) \geq \pi_g - \frac{1}{2}. \tag{8.25}$$

For the opponent's endeavors one has

$$\min_{\rightarrow} \max_{\downarrow} \pi_{rc} = \min_{\rightarrow}(\frac{1}{2} + \pi_u, \frac{1}{2} + \pi_u, \frac{1}{2} + \pi_u, \pi_q)$$

$$= \frac{1}{2} + \pi_u. \tag{8.26}$$

This indicates that the equality in eqn. (8.23) is satisfied and there exists at least one pair of pure strategies which is optimal for both players. In this case, the pair is for users to conceal files, regardless of how the system administrator tidies files (the system administrator's strategies all contribute the same weight in eqn (8.26)). Thus for small times, the users are always winning the game if one assumes that they are allowed to bluff by concealment. If the possibility of concealment or bluffing is removed (perhaps through an improved technology), then the next best strategy is for users to bluff by changing the date, assuming that the tidying looks at the date. In that case, the best system administrator strategy is to tidy indiscriminately at threshold.

For large times (when system resources are becoming or have become scarce), then the situation looks different. In this case one finds that

$$\max_{\downarrow} \min_{\rightarrow} \pi_{rc} = \min_{\rightarrow} \max_{\downarrow} \pi_{rc} = \pi_q. \tag{8.27}$$

In other words, the quota solution determines the outcome of the game for any user strategy. As already commented, this might be considered cheating or poor use of resources, at the very least. If one eliminates quotas from the game, then the results for small times hold also at large times.

8.10 Monitoring

Having set policy and implemented it to some degree, it is important to verify the success of this programme by measuring the state of the system. Various monitoring tools exist for this purpose, depending upon the level at which we wish to evaluate the system:

- Machine performance level

- Abstract policy level.

While these two levels are never unrelated, they pose somewhat different questions.

A very interesting idea which might be used both in fault diagnosis and security intrusion detection is the idea of *anomaly detection*. In anomaly detection we are looking for anything abnormal. That could come from abnormal traffic, patterns of kernel activity, or changes in the statistical profiles of usage. An anomaly can be responded to as a punishable offence, or as a correctable transgression that leads to regulation of behavior, depending on its nature and the policy of the system administrator (see figure 8.15).

Automated self-regulation in host management has been discussed in refs. [41, 42, 44, 48], as well as adaptive behavior [274] and network intrusion detection [102, 156]. In their insightful paper [159], Hoogenboom and Lepreau anticipated the need for monitoring time series data with feedback regulation in order to adjust policy automatically. Today much effort is aimed at detecting anomalies for security related intrusion detection rather than for general maintenance, or capacity planning. This has focused attention on mainly short-term changes; however, long-term changes can also be of interest in connection with maintenance of host state and its adaptability to changing demand.

SNMP tools such as MRTG, RRDtool and Cricket specialize in collecting data from SNMP devices like routers and switches. Cfengine's environment daemon adopts a less deterministic approach to anomaly detection over longer time scales, that can be used to trigger automated policy countermeasures [50]. For many, monitoring means feeding a graphical representation of the system to a human in order to provide an executive summary of its state.

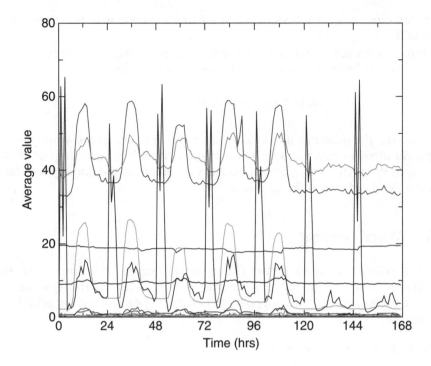

Figure 8.15: An average summary of system activity over the course of a week, as generated by cfengine's environment daemon.

8.11   System performance tuning

When is a fault not a fault? When it is an inefficiency. Sooner or later, user perception of system performance passes a threshold. Beyond that threshold we deem the performance of a computer to be unacceptably slow and we become irritated. Long before that happens, the system itself recognizes the symptoms of a lack of resources and takes action to try to counter the problem, but not always in the way we would like.

Efficiency and users' perception of efficiency are usually two separate things. The host operating system itself can be timesharing perfectly and performing real work at a break-neck pace, while one user sits and waits for minutes for something as simple as a window to refresh. For anyone who has been in this situation, it is painfully obvious that system performance is a highly subjective issue. If we aim to please one type of user, another will be disappointed. To extract maximal performance from a host, we must focus on specific issues and make particular compromises. Note that the system itself is already well adjusted to share resources: that is what a kernel is designed to do. The point of performance tuning is that what is good for one task is not necessarily good for another. Generic kernel configurations try to walk the line of being adequate for everyone, and in doing so they are not great at doing any of them in particular. The only way we can truly achieve maximal performance is to specialize. Ideally, we would have one host per task and optimize each host for that one task. Of course this is a huge waste of resources, which is why multitasking operating systems exist. The inevitability of sharing resources between many tasks is to strike compromise. This is the paradox of multitasking.

Whole books have been written on the subject of performance tuning, so we shall hardly be able to explore all of the avenues of the topic in a brief account. See for instance refs. [159, 97, 200, 307, 16, 318, 293, 266]. Our modest aim in this book is, as usual, to extract the essence of the topic, pointing fingers at the key performance bottlenecks. If we are to tune a system, we need to identify what it is we wish to optimize, i.e. what is most important to us. We cannot make everything optimal, so we must pick out a few things which are most important to us, and work on those.

System performance tuning is a complex subject, in which no part of the system is sacrosanct. Although it is quite easy to pin-point general performance problems, it is harder to make general recommendations to fix these. Most details are unique to each operating system. A few generic pointers can nonetheless offer the greatest and most obvious gains, while the tweaking of system-dependent parameters will put the icing on the cake.

In order to identify a problem, we must first measure the performance. Again there are the two issues: *user perception* of performance (interactive response time) and *system throughput* and we have to choose the criterion we wish to meet. When the system is running slowly, it is natural to look at what resources are being tested, i.e.

- What processes are running

- How much available memory the system has

- Whether disks are being used excessively

- Whether the network is being used heavily

- What software dependencies the system has (e.g. DNS, NFS).

The last point is easy to overlook. If we make one host dependent on another then the dependant host will always be limited by the host on which it depends. This is particularly true of file-servers (e.g. NFS, DFS, Netware distributed filesystems) and of the DNS service.

Principle 48 (Symptoms and cause). *Always try to fix problems at the root, rather than patching symptoms.*

8.11.1 Resources and dependencies

Since all resources are scheduled by processes, it is natural to check the process table first and then look at resource usage. On Windows, one has the process manager and performance monitor for this. On Unix-like systems, we check the process listing with `ps aux`, if a BSD compatible `ps` command exists, or `ps -efl` if the system is derived from System V. If the system has both, or a BSD compatible output mode, as in Solaris and Digital Unix (OSF1), for instance, then the BSD style output is recommended. This provides more useful information and orders the processes so that the heaviest process comes at the top. This saves time. Another useful Unix tool is top. A BSD process listing looks like this:

```
host% ps aux | more

USER      PID %CPU %MEM    SZ  RSS TT       S    START  TIME COMMAND
root        3  0.2  0.0     0    0 ?        S   Jun 15 55:38 fsflush
root    22112  0.1  0.5  1464 1112 pts/2    O 15:39:54  0:00 ps aux
mark    22113  0.1  0.3  1144  720 pts/2    O 15:39:54  0:00 more
root      340  0.1  0.4  1792  968 ?        S   Jun 15  3:13 /bin/fingerd
...
```

This one was taken on a quiet system, with no load. The columns show the user ID of the process, the process ID, an indication of the amount of CPU time used in executing the program (the percentage scale can be taken with a pinch of salt, since it means different things for different kernels), and an indication of the amount of memory allocated. The SZ post is the size of the process in total (code plus data plus stack), while RSS is the resident size, or how much of the program code is actually resident in RAM, as opposed to being paged out, or never even loaded. TIME shows the amount of CPU time accumulated by the process, while START indicates the amount of clock time which has elapsed since the process started. Problem processes are usually identified by:

- %CPU is large. A CPU-intensive process, or a process which has gone into an endless loop. TIME is large. A program which has been CPU intensive, or which has been stuck in a loop for a long period.

- %MEM is large. SZ is large. A large and steadily growing value can indicate a memory leak.

One thing we notice is that the ps command itself uses quite a lot of resources. If the system is low on resources, running constant process monitoring is an expensive intrusion.

Unix-like systems also tell us about memory performance through the virtual memory statistics, e.g. the vmstat command. This command gives a different output on each operating system, but summarizes the amount of free memory as well as paging performance etc. It can be used to get an idea of whether or not the system is paging a lot (a sign that memory is low). Another way of seeing this is to examine the amount of swap space which is in use:

OS	List virtual memory usage
AIX	lsps -a
HPUX	swapinfo -t -a -m
Digital Unix/OSF1	swapon -s
Solaris 1 or SunOS 3/4	pstat -s
Solaris 2 or SunOS 5	swap -l
GNU/Linux	free
Windows	Performance manager

Excessive network traffic is also a cause of impaired performance. We should try to eliminate unnecessary network traffic whenever possible. Before any complex analysis of network resources is undertaken, we can make sure that we have covered the basics:

- Make sure that there is a DNS server on each large subnet to avoid sending unnecessary queries through a router. (On small subnets this would be overkill.)

- Make sure that the nameservers themselves use the loopback address 127.0.0.1 as the primary nameserver on Unix-like hosts, so that we do not cause collisions by having the nameserver talk to itself on the public network.

- Try to avoid distributed file accesses on a different subnet. This loads the router. If possible, file-servers and clients should be on the same subnet.

- If we are running X-windows, make sure that each workstation has its DISPLAY variable set to :0.0 rather than hostname:0.0, to avoid sending data out onto the network, only to come back to the same host.

Some operating systems have nice graphical tools for viewing network statistics, while others have only netstat, with its varying options. Collision statistics can be seen with netstat -i for Unix-like OSs or netstat /S on Windows. DNS efficiency is an important consideration, since all hosts are more or less completely reliant on this service.

Measuring performance reliably, in a scientifically stringent fashion is a difficult problem (see chapter 13), but *adequate* measurements can be made, for the purpose of improving efficiency, using the process tables and virtual memory statistics. If we see frantic activity in the virtual memory system, it means that we are suffering from a lack of resources, or that some process has run amok.

Once a problem is identified, we need a strategy for solving it. Performance tuning can involve everything from changing hardware to tweaking software.

- Optimizing choice of hardware

- Optimizing chosen hardware

- Optimizing kernel behavior

- Optimizing software configurations

- (Optimizing service availability).

Hardware has *physical limitations*. For instance, the heads of a hard-disk can only be in one place at a time. If we want to share a hard-disk between two processes, the heads have to be moved around between two regions of the disk, back and forth. Moving the read heads over the disk platter is the slowest operation in disk access and perhaps the computer as a whole, and unfortunately something we can do nothing about. It is a fundamental limitation. Moreover, to get the data from disk into RAM, it is necessary to interrupt processes and involve the kernel.

Time spent executing kernel code is time not spent on executing user code, and so it is a performance burden. Resource sharing is about balancing *overheads*. We must look for the sources of overheads and try to minimize them, or mitigate their effects by cunning.

8.11.2 Hardware

The fundamental principle of any performance analysis is:

> **Principle 49 (Weakest link).** *The performance of any system is limited by the weakest link amongst its components. System optimization should begin with the* source. *If performance is weak at the source, nothing which follows can make it better.*

Obviously, any effect which is introduced after the source will only reduce the performance in a chain of data handling. A later component cannot 'suck' the data out of the source faster than the source wants to deliver it. This tells us that the logical place to begin is with the system hardware. A corollary to this principle follows from a straightforward observation about hardware. As Scotty said, we cannot change the laws of physics:

Corollary to principle (Performance). *A system is limited by its slowest moving parts. Resources with slowly moving parts, like disks, CD-ROMs and tapes, transfer data slowly and delay the system. Resources which work purely with electronics, like RAM memory and CPU calculation, are quick. However, electronic motion/communication over long distances takes much longer than communication over short distances (internally within a host) because of impedances and switching.*

Already, these principles tell us that RAM is one of the best investments we can make. Why? In order to avoid mechanical devices like disks as much as possible, we store things in RAM; in order to avoid sending unnecessary traffic over networks, we cache data in RAM. Hence RAM is the primary workhorse of any computer system. After we have exhausted the possibilities of RAM usage, we can go on to look at disk and network infrastructure.

- *Disks:* When assigning partitions to new disks, it pays to use the fastest disks for the data which are accessed most often, e.g. for user home directories. To improve disk performance, we can do two things. One is to buy faster disks and the other is to use *parallelism* to overcome the time it takes for physical motions to be executed. The mechanical problem which is inherent in disk drives is that the heads which read and write data have to move as a unit. If we need to collect two files concurrently which lie spread all over the disk, this has to be done *serially*. *Disk striping* is a technique whereby filesystems are spread over several disks. By spreading files over several disks, we have several sets of disk heads which can seek independently of one another, and work in parallel. This does not necessarily increase the transfer rate, but it does lower seek times, and thus performance improvement can approach as much as N times with N disks. RAID technologies employ striping techniques and are widely available commercially. GNU/Linux also has RAID support.

Spreading disks and files across multiple disk controllers will also increase parallelism.

- *Network:* To improve network performance, we need fast interfaces. All interfaces, whether they be Ethernet or some other technology, vary in quality and speed. This is particularly true in the PC world, where the number of competing products is huge. Network interfaces should not be trusted to give the performance they advertise. Some interfaces which are sold as 100Mbits/sec, Fast Ethernet, manage little more than 40Mbits/sec. Some network interfaces have intelligent behavior and try to detect the best available transmission rate. For instance, newer Sun machines use the *hme* fast Ethernet interface. This has the ability to detect the best transmission protocol for the line a host is connected to. The best transmission type is 100Mbits/sec, full duplex (simultaneous send and receive), but the interface will switch down to 10Mbits/sec, half duplex (send or receive, one direction at a time) if it detects a problem. This can have a huge performance effect. One problem with auto-detection is that, if both ends of the connection have auto-detection, it can become an unpredictable matter which speed we end up with. Sometimes it helps to try setting the rate explicitly, assuming that the network hardware supports that rate. There are other optimizations also, for TCP/IP tuning, which we shall return to below. Refs. [295, 312] are excellent references on this topic.

The sharing of resources between many users and processes is what networking is about. The competition for resources between several tasks leads to another performance issue.

> **Principle 50 (Contention/competition).** *When two processes compete for a resource, performance can be dramatically reduced as the processes fight over the right to use the resource. This is called contention. The benefits of sharing have to be weighed against the pitfalls.*

Contention could almost be called a strategy, in some situations, since there exist technologies for avoiding contention altogether. For example, Ethernet technology allows contention to take place, whereas Token Ring technology avoids it. We shall not go into the arguments for and against contention. Suffice it to say that many widely used technologies experience this problem.

- *Ethernet collisions:* Ethernet communication is like a television panel of politicians: many parties shouting at random, without waiting for others to finish. The Ethernet cable is a shared bus. When a host wishes to communicate with another host, it simply tries. If another host happens to be using the bus at that time, there is a collision and the host must try again at random until it is heard. This method naturally leads to contention for bandwidth. The system works quite well when traffic is low, but as the number of hosts competing for bandwidth increases, the probability of a collision increases in step. Contention can only be reduced by reducing the amount of traffic on the network segment. The illusion of many collisions can also be caused by incorrect wiring, or incorrectly terminated cable, which leads to reflections. If collision rates are high, a wiring check might also be in order.

- *Disk thrashing:* Thrashing[2] is a problem which occurs because of the slowness of disk head movements, compared with the speed of kernel time-sharing algorithms. If two processes attempt to take control of a resource simultaneously, the kernel and its device drivers attempt to minimize the motion of the heads by queuing requested blocks in a special order. The algorithms really try to make the disks traverse the disk platter uniformly, but the requests do not always come in a predictable or congenial order. The result is that the disk heads can be forced back and forth across the disk, driven by different processes and slowing the system to a virtual standstill. The time for disk heads to move is an eternity to the kernel, some hundreds of times slower than context switching times.

  An even worse situation can arise with the virtual memory system. If a host begins paging to disk because it is low on memory, then there can be simultaneous contention both for memory and for disk. Imagine, for instance, that there are many processes, each loading files into memory, when there is no free RAM. In order to use RAM, some has to be freed by paging to disk; but the disk is already busy seeking files. In order to load a file, memory has to be freed, but memory can't be freed until the disk is free to page, this drags the heads to another partition, then back again ... and so on. This nightmare brings the system to a virtual standstill as it fights both over free RAM and disk head placement. The system spends more time juggling its resources than it does performing real work, i.e. the overhead to work ratio blows up. The only cure for thrashing is to increase memory, or reduce the number of processes contending for resources.

A final point to mention in connection with disks is to do with standards. Disk transfer rates are limited by the protocols and hardware of the disk interfaces. This applies to the interfaces in the computer and to the interfaces in the disks. Most serious performance systems will use SCSI disks, for their speed (see section 2.2). However, there are many versions of the SCSI disk design. If we mix version numbers, the faster disks will be delayed by the slower disks while the bus is busy, i.e. the average transfer rate is limited by the weakest link or the slowest disk. If one needs to support legacy disks together with new disks, then it pays to collect like disks with a special host for each type, or alternatively buy a second disk controller rather than to mix disks on the same controller.

8.11.3 Software tuning and kernel configuration

It is true that software is constrained by the hardware on which it runs, but it is equally true that hardware can only follow the instructions it has received from software. If software asks hardware to be inefficient, hardware will be inefficient. Software introduces many inefficiencies of its own. Hardware and software tuning are inextricably intertwined.

---

[2]For non-native English speakers, note the difference between *thrash* and *trash*. Thrashing refers to a beating, or the futile fight for survival, e.g. when drowning.

Software performance tuning is a more complex problem than hardware performance tuning, simply because the options we have for tuning software depend on what the software is, how it is written and whether or not the designer made it easy for us to tune its performance. Some software is designed to be stable rather than efficient. Efficiency is not a fundamental requirement; there are other priorities, such as simplicity and robustness.

In software the potential number of variables is much greater than in hardware tuning. Some software systems can be tuned individually. For instance, high-availability server software such as WWW servers and SMTP (E-mail) servers can be tuned to handle traffic optimally for heavy loads. See, for instance, tips on tuning sendmail [62, 185], and other general tuning tips [307, 200, 303].

More often than not, performance tuning is related to the availability or sharing of system resources. This requires tuning the system kernel. The most configurable piece of software on the system is the kernel. All Unix-like systems kernel parameters can be altered and tuned. The most elegant approach to this is taken by Unix SVR4, and Solaris. Here, many kernel parameters can be set at run time using the kernel module configuration command ndd. Others can be configured in a single file /etc/system. The parameters in this file can be set with a reboot of the kernel, using the reconfigure flag

```
reboot -- -r
```

For instance, on a heavily loaded system which allows many users to run external logins, terminals, or X-terminal software, we need to increase many of the default system parameters. The maxusers parameter (actually in most Unix-like systems) is used as a guide to estimating the size of many tables and limits on resources. Its default value is based on the amount of available RAM, so one should be careful about changing its value in Solaris, though other OSs are less intelligent. Solaris also has a separate parameter pt_cnt for extending the number of virtual terminals (pty's). It is possible to run out if many users are logged in to the same host simultaneously. Many graphics-intensive programs use shared memory in large blocks. The default limit for shared memory segments is only a megabyte, so it can be increased to optimize for intensive graphics use, but should not be increased on heavily loaded file-servers, where memory for caching is more important. The file /etc/system, then looks like this:

```
set maxusers=100
set shmsys:shminfo_shmmax = 0x10000000
set pt_cnt=128
```

After a reboot, these parameters will be set. Some caution is needed in editing this file. If it is non-existent or unparsable, the host will not be able to boot (a questionable design feature). The ndd command in Solaris can be chosen to optimize its over-safe defaults set on TCP/IP connections.

For busy servers which handle many TCP connections, the time it takes an operating system to open and close connections is important. There is a limit on the number of available connections and open sockets (see chapter 9); if finished socket connections are not purged quickly from the kernel tables, new connections cannot be opened in their place. On non-tuned hosts, used sockets can hang around for five minutes or longer on a Solaris host. On a heavily loaded server, this is unacceptable. The close time on sockets can be shortened to half a minute so as to allow newer sockets to be opened sooner (though note that this contravenes RFC 793). The parameters can be set when the system boots, or patched at any later time. The times are measured in milliseconds. See refs. [312, 295] for excellent discussions of these values.

```
/usr/sbin/ndd -set /dev/tcp tcp_keepalive_interval 900000
/usr/sbin/ndd -set /dev/tcp tcp_time_wait_interval 30000
```

Prior to Solaris 2.7 (SunOS 5.7) the latter line would have read:

```
/usr/sbin/ndd -set /dev/tcp tcp_close_wait_interval 30000
```

which illustrates the futility of documenting these fickle parameters in a static medium like a book. Note that setting these parameters to ultra-short values could cause file transmissions to be terminated incorrectly. This might lead to corruption of data. On a web server, this is a nuisance for the client, but it is not mission-critical data. For security, longer close times are desirable, to ensure correct closure of sockets. After setting these values, the network interface needs to be restarted, by taking it down and up with `ifconfig`. Alternatively, the values can be configured in a startup script which is executed before the interface is brought up at boot time.

> **Suggestion 11.** *Do not change operating system defaults unless you have good cause, and really know what you are doing. Deviations from expert defaults must be on a case-by-case basis.*

Most Unix-like operating systems do not permit run-time configuration. New kernels have to be compiled and the values hard-coded into the kernel. This requires not just a reboot, but a recompilation of the kernel in order to make a change. This is not an optimal way to experiment with parameters. Modularity in kernel design can save us memory, since it means that static code does not have to take up valuable memory space. However, the downside of this is that modules take time to load from disk, on demand. Thus a modular kernel can be slower than a statically compiled kernel. For frequently used hardware, static compilation is a must, since it eliminates the load-time for the module, at the expense of extra memory consumption.

The GNU/Linux system kernel is a modular kernel, which can load drivers for special hardware at run time, in order to remain small in the memory. When we build a kernel, we have the option to compile in modules statically. See section 4.8. Tips for Linux kernel configuration can readily be found by searching the Internet, so we shall not reproduce these tips here, where they would quickly become stale. See, for instance ref. [97].

Windows performance tuning can be undertaken by perusing the multitudinous screens in the graphical performance monitor and editing the values. For once, this useful tool is a standard part of the Windows system.

8.11.4 Data efficiency

Efficiency of storage and transmission depends on the configuration parameters used to manage disks and networks, and also on the amount of traffic the devices see. We have already mentioned the problem of contention.

Some filesystem formatting programs on Unix-like systems allow us to reserve a certain percentage of disk space for privileged users. For instance, the default for BSD is to reserve ten percent of the size of a partition for use by privileged processes only. The idea here is to prevent the operating system from choking due to the activities of users. This practice goes back to the early times when disks were small and expensive and partition numbers were limited. Today, these limits are somewhat inappropriate. Ten percent of a gigabyte disk is a huge amount of space, which many users could live happily with for many weeks. If we have partitioned a host so as to separate users from the operating system, then there is no need to reserve space on user disks. Better to let users utilize the existing space until a real problem occurs. Preventative tidying helps to avoid full disks. Whether one regards this as maintenance or performance tuning is a moot point. The effect is to save us time and loss of resource availability. See section 4.4.3 about making filesystems.

Another issue with disk efficiency is the configuration of block sizes. This is a technical issue which one probably does not want to play with too liberally. Briefly, the standard unit of space which is allocated on a filesystem is a *block*. Blocks are quite large, usually around 8 kilobytes. Even if we allocate a file which is one byte long, it will be stored as a separate unit, in a block by itself, or in a *fragment*. Fragments are usually around 1 kilobyte. If we have many small files, this can clearly lead to a large wastage of space and it might be prudent to decrease the filesystem block size. If, conversely, we deal with mostly large files, then the block size could be increased to improve transfer efficiency. The filesystem parameters can, in other words, be tuned to balance file size and transfer-rate efficiency. Normally the default settings are a good compromise.

Tuning the network is a complex subject and few operating systems allow us to do it at all. Solaris' ndd command can be used to configure TCP/IP parameters which can lead to noticeable performance improvements. See the excellent discussion in refs. [312, 68]. As far as software tuning is concerned, we have few options. The time we wait for a service to reply to a query is called the *latency*. Latency clearly depends on many factors, so it is difficult to pin down, but it is a useful concept since it reflects users' perceptions of performance. Network performance can degrade for a variety of reasons. Latency can increase as a result of network collisions, making traffic congested, and it can be increased due to server load, making the server slow to respond. Network latencies clearly increase with distance from the server: the more routers, switches and cables a signal has to travel through, the slower it will be. Our options are to reduce traffic congestion, increase server performance, and increase parallelism (if possible) with fail-over servers [139]. Some network services are multi-threaded (using either light or heavyweight processes) and can be configured to spawn more server threads to handle a greater number of simultaneous connections (e.g. nfsd, httpd, cfservd). If traffic congestion is not the problem, then a larger number of servers might help in expediting multiple connections (many multi-threaded servers set limits on the number of threads allowed, so as not to run a machine into the ground in the event of spamming). These measures help to reduce the need for retransmission of TCP segments and timeouts on connection. Assuming that the network interface is working as fast as it can (see previous section), a server will then respond as quickly as it can.

8.12 Principles of quality assurance

Quality assurance in service provision is a topic that is increasingly discussed in the world of network services (see section 10.8), but quality assurance is a process that has far wider implications than the commercially motivated issue of value for money. A system administrator also performs a service for the system and for users. Quality assurance take up three related issues:

- Accuracy of service (result)

- Efficiency of service (time)

- Predictability (result/time).

8.12.1 ISO 9000 series

The ISO 9000 series of standards represent an international consensus on management practices that apply to any process or organization. The aim of the standards is to provide a schematic quality management system and a framework for continual assessment and improvement. ISO 9000 has become quite important in some sectors of industry, in the countries that have adopted it.

First published in 1987, the ISO 9000 standards are widely used and a quick search of the net reveals that they are also money-making enterprises. Courses in these methods are numerous and costly. The principles, however, are straightforward. The idea is that a standard approach to quality assurance leads to less uncertainty in the outcome. Quality is associated with certainty. Here, we shall not dwell on the issue of ISO 9000 certification, but rather on the guiding principles that the standard embodies.

8.12.2 Creating a quality control system

Quality is clearly a subjective criterion. It is a matter for *policy* to decide what quality means. Quality control is an iterative process, with a number of key elements. It is a process, rather than a one-off task, because the environment in which we execute our work is never static. Even as we plan our quality handbooks and verification forms, the world is changing and has made them partially obsolete.

> **Principle 51 (Rapid maintenance).** *The speed of response to a problem can be crucial to its success or failure, because the environment is constantly changing the conditions for work. If one procrastinates, procedures will be out of date, or inappropriate.*

ISO 9000 reiterates one of the central messages of system administration and security: namely that they are on-going, dynamical processes rather than achievable goals (see figure 8.16).

- *Determine quality goals*: One begins by determining policy: what is it that we wish to accomplish? Until we know this, we cannot set about devising a strategy to accomplish the goals.

- *Assess the current situation*: We need to know where we stand, in order to determine how to get where we are going. How much work will it take to carry out the plan?

- *Devise a strategy*: Strategy determination is a complex issue. Sometimes one needs to back-track in order to go forward. This is reminiscent of the story of the stranger who comes to a city and asks a local how to get to the post office. The local shakes his head and replies 'If I were going to the Post Office, I certainly wouldn't start from here'. Clearly, this is not a helpful observation. We must always find a way to achieve our goals, even if it means first back-tracking to a more useful starting point.

- *Project management*: How we carry out a process is at least as important as the process itself. If the process is faulty, the result will be faulty. Above all, there must be progress. Something has to happen in order for something good to happen. Often, several actors collaborate in the execution of a project. Projects cost resources to execute – how will this be budgeted? Are resources adequate for the goals specified?

- *Documentation and verification*: A key reason for system failure is when a system becomes so complex that its users can no longer understand it. Humans, moreover, are naturally lazy, and their performance with regard to a standard needs to be policed. Documentation can help prevent errors and misunderstandings, while verification procedures are essential for ensuring the conformance of the work to the quality guidelines.

- *Fault-handling procedure*: Quality implies a line between the acceptable and unacceptable. When we discover something that falls short of the mark, we need a procedure for putting the problem right. That procedure should itself be quality assured, hence we see that quality assurance has a feedback structure. It requires self-assessment.

In principle 40, we found that standardization leads to predictability. It can also lead to limitations, but we shall assume that this problem can also be dealt with by a quality assurance programme.

The formulation of a quality assurance scheme is not something that can be done generically; one needs expert insight into specific issues, in order to know and evaluate the limitations and likely avenues for error recovery. Quality Assurance involves:

1. A definition of quality.

2. A fault tree or cause tree analysis for the system quality.

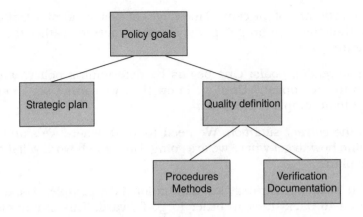

Figure 8.16: Elements of a quality assurance system.

3. Formulating a strategic remedial policy.

4. The formalization of remedies as a checklist.

5. Acknowledging and accepting inherent system limitations.

6. Checklists to document compliance with policy.

7. Examination of results and feedback into policy.

Measurements of tolerances, uncertainties and limitations need to be incorporated into this procedure in a continual feedback process. Quality is achieved through this continued process: it is not an achievable goal, but rather a never-ending journey.

Exercises

Self-test objectives

1. What is meant by the principle of predictable failure?

2. Explain the meaning of 'single point of failure'.

3. Explain how a meshed network can be both more robust and more susceptible to failure.

4. What is the 'small worlds' phenomenon and how does it apply to system administration?

5. Explain the principle of causality.

6. What is meant by an interaction?

7. How do interactions underline the importance of the principle of causality?

8. What is meant by the environment of a system?

9. How does one find the boundary between system and environment?

10. What kind of faults can occur in a human–computer system?

11. Describe some typical strategies for finding faults.

12. Describe some typical strategies for correcting faults.

13. Explain how a cause tree can be used help locate problems in a system. What are the limitations of cause-tree analysis?

14. Explain how fault trees can provide predictive power for the occurrence of faults. What are the limitations of this predictive power?

15. Explain the relationship between change management and cause-tree analysis.

16. Explain the role of game theory in system management. Comment on its limitations.

17. Explain how game theory reveals the principle of communities by finding optimal equilibria.

18. What role does monitoring the system play in a rational decision-making process?

19. Explain the weakest link principle in performance analysis.

20. Explain how competition for resources can lead to wasted resources.

21. What is ISO 9000?

22. Describe some of the issues in quality control.

23. Explain how the rate of maintenance affects the likely state of a system.

Problems

1. Find out about process priorities. How are process priorities changed on the computer systems on your network? Formulate a policy for handling processes which load the system heavily. Should they be left alone, killed, rescheduled etc?

2. Describe the process you would use to troubleshoot a slowly running host. Formalize this process as an algorithm.

3. Suppose you are performance tuning, trying to find out why one host is slower than another. Write a program which tests the efficiency of *CPU-intensive work only*. Write programs which test the speed of *memory-intensive work* and *disk-intensive* work. Would comparing the time it takes to compile a program on the hosts be a good way of comparing them?

4. Determine the network transmission speed on the servers on your network. Are they as high as possible? Do they have auto-detection of the interface transmission rates on their network connections (e.g. 10Mb/s or 100Mb/s)? If not, how are they configured? Find out how you can choose the assumed transmission rate.

5. What is meant by an Ethernet collision? How might doubling the speed of all hosts on an Ethernet segment make the total system slower?

6. Consider the fault tree in figure 8.17.

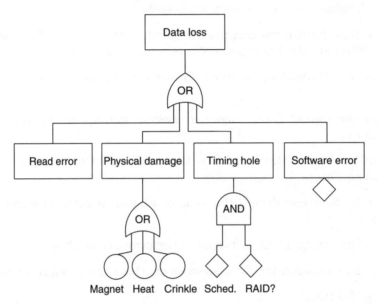

Figure 8.17: Partial fault tree for data loss due to backup failure.

(a) Given that the probability that data will be lost in a backup hole (data changed between scheduled backups) is approximately the same as the probability of physical media damage, what strategy would you suggest for improving security against data loss? Explain your answer.

(b) What security principle does RAID employ to protect data? Explain how RAID might be used at several places in this tree in order to help prevent data loss.

(c) Describe a fault tree for loss of service in a high availability web server placed in a server room. Describe how you would go about estimating the probabilities. Based on your analysis, concoct a number of long-term strategies for countering these failures; draw a provisional payoff matrix for these strategies versus the failure modes, and use this to estimate the most cost-effective long-term strategies.

(d) Design a change plan and schedule for upgrading 400 Windows hosts. Your plan should include a fault tree analysis for the upgrade and contingency plan for loss of some of the hosts.

7. Today CPU power is cheap, previously it was common for organizations to have to load users and services onto a single host with limited CPU.

   (a) Describe as many strategies as you can that you might use to prevent users from hogging CPU-intensive services.

   (b) Now imagine all of the possible strategies that selfish users might use to hog resources and describe these.

   (c) Would you say that CPU is a zero-sum resource, i.e. that what is lost by one user is gained by the others?

   (d) Estimate or argue the relative payoff to the selfish user for each of the pairs of strategies used by both parties, and thereby construct the payoff matrix for the system.

   (e) By inspection, find the defensive strategies that minimize the payoff to the user.

   (f) Use the minimax theorem to find the optimal strategy or strategies and compare your answer with the one you chose by inspection.

Chapter 9

Application-level services

Network services are the crux of network cooperation (see section 3.5). They distinguish a cooperative network from a loose association of hosts. A community is bound together by a web of delegation and sharing. We give this job to A and that job to B, and they carry out their specialized tasks, making the whole function. In a computer network, we assign specific functions to specific hosts, thereby consolidating effort while distributing functionality.

The way in which services are handled by most operating systems is to use the socket abstraction. A socket is, loosely speaking, a file-like interface with an IP address plus a TCP or UDP port number [165], where some kind of data are communicated. A server has a listening socket which responds to client requests by opening a new temporary socket at a random port number. Information is exchanged and then any connection is terminated.

The system administrator has the task of organizing and configuring network services. That includes installing, planning and implementing the daemons which carry out the services. For definiteness, the examples discussed in this chapter are based on Unix-like operating systems. In a network of Unix-like hosts, we have the freedom to locate a server on whatever host we wish. Although some services (e.g. remote login by ssh) normally run on every host, most are confined to one or two hosts, whose special function it is to perform the tasks on behalf of the network community.

Note also that although the details of the chapter will likely be out of date by the time the book comes to press, the principles should remain fairly constant. Readers are encouraged to verify the information using the latest information about the software concerned.

9.1 Application-level services

Internet networks use many high-level protocols to provide the distributed services which most users take for granted. Here are a few examples:

- FTP The File transfer protocol. Passwords are normally sent in clear text.

- HTTP The hypertext transfer protocol for the transmission of data on the World Wide Web. All data are sent in clear text.

- S-HTTP is a superset of HTTP, which allows messages to be encapsulated for increased security. Encapsulations include encryption, signing and MAC-based authentication. An S-HTTP message can have several security transformations applied to it. S-HTTP also includes support for key transfer, certificate transfer and similar administrative functions. It is generally regarded as being superior to HTTPS, but is now obsolete.

- HTTPS The secure World Wide Web protocol for exchanging hypertext and multimedia data. All data are encrypting using Netscape's Secure Socket Layer (SSL), now called Transmission Layer Security (TLS) by IETF standard.

- SSH The secure shell. A replacement for the remote shell (rsh) Unix protocol. The secure shell provides full encryption and forwarding of X11 display data through a secure pipe.

- LDAP The *Lightweight Directory Access Protocol* is a generalized protocol for looking up data in simple databases. It is a lightweight version of the Director Access Protocol originally written for X.500 and is currently at Version 3. LDAP can be used to register user information, passwords, telephone numbers etc. and interfaces through gateways to the NDS (Novell Directory Service), Microsoft's Exchange server and NIS (Sun's Network Information Service). The advantage of LDAP will be a uniform protocol for accessing table lookups. Currently the spread of LDAP is hindered by few up-to-date implementations of the protocol.

- NTP is the network time protocol, used for synchronizing clocks throughout the network.

- IMAP *Internet Mail Access Protocol* provides a number of network services for reading and transferring mail over the network. Other mail protocols include POP (Post Office Protocol).

- SMTP The *Simple Mail Transfer Protocol* is used to address and transfer E-mail over the network.

There is an almost endless list of services which are registered by the `/etc/services` file. These named services perform a wide range of functions.

9.2 Proxies and agents

A proxy is an agent which works on behalf of another. Proxies are used for two main reasons: for security and for caching (sometimes also for load-balancing). Some proxy agents collect information and cache it locally so that traffic over a slow network can be minimized. Web proxies can perform this kind of function. Rather than sending WWW requests out directly, they are sent to a proxy server which registers the requests and builds a list of popular requests. These requests are collected by the proxy and copied into local storage so that the next time the request is made, the data can be served from local storage. This improves both speed and traffic load, in principle. The proxy's agents make sure that its cached copies are up to date.

Another type of proxy is the firewall type. One of the advantages of asking another to do a job is that the original agent doesn't need to get its hands dirty. It is a little bit like the robots which bomb squads use to defuse bombs: better to send in a robot than get blown to bits yourself. Firewall proxies exist for most services to avoid handling potentially dangerous network connections directly. We shall return to the issue of proxy services in the discussion of firewalls in section 12.12.

9.3 Installing a new service

We need to configure the system to accept a new service by editing the file /etc/services. This file contains the names of services and their protocol types and port numbers.

The format of entries is like this:

```
     service         portnumber/protocol     aliases

     pop3            110/tcp                 postoffice
     bootp           67/udp
     cfinger         2003/tcp
```

There are two ways in which a service can run under Unix: one is that a daemon runs all the time in the background, handling connections. This method is used for services which are used often. Another way is to start the daemon only when an outside connection wishes to use it; this method is used for less frequently used services. In the second case, a master Internet daemon is used, which listens for connections for several services at once and starts the correct daemon only long enough to handle one connection. The aim is to save the overhead of running many daemons.

If we want to run a daemon all the time, then we just need to make sure that it is started in the appropriate rc startup files for the system. To add the service to the Internet daemon, on the other hand, we need to add a line of the following from the configuration file /etc/inetd.conf.

```
     service type    proto serial   user-id server-program      command

     pop3   stream   tcp nowait     root    /local/etc/pop3d     pop3d
```

The software installation instructions for the new network service tell us what we should add to this file.

Once we have configured a new service, it must be started by running the appropriate daemon, or by reinitializing inetd. Note that xinetd also exists, adding checks and controls to network service requests.

9.4 Summoning daemons

Network services are run by daemons. Having done the deed of configuring a network service, see section 9.3, by editing textfiles and ritually sacrificing a few doughnuts, we reach the point where we have to actually start the daemon in order to see the fruits of those labors. There are two ways to start network daemons:

- When the system boots, by adding an appropriate shell-command to one of the system's startup scripts. When we use this method, the daemon hangs around in the background all the time waiting for connections.

- On demand: that is, only when a network request arrives. We use the inetd daemon to monitor requests for a new service. It starts the daemon to handle requests on a one-off basis. Not all services should be started in this way. One should normally follow the guidelines in the documentation for the service concerned.

9.4.1 System 5 init

The SVR4 version of the init program is growing in popularity and is used by several GNU/Linux distributions. The idea with this program is to start the system in one of a number of run-levels. Run-levels decide how many services will be started when the system boots. The minimum level of operation is single-user mode, or run-level 's'. Full operation is usually run-level 2 or 3, depending on the type of system. (NB: be sure to check this!) When entering a run-level, init looks in a directory called /etc/rc?.d and executes scripts in this directory. For instance, if we are entering run-level 2, init would look in the directory /etc/rc2.d and execute scripts lying there in order to start necessary services for this run-level. All one has to do to add a new service is to make a new file here which conforms to init's simple rules. The files in these directories are usually labelled according to the following pattern:

```
S number- function

K number- function
```

Files beginning with S are for starting services and files beginning with K are for killing them again when the system is halted. The number is used to determine the order in which the scripts are read. It does not matter if two scripts have the same number, as long as it does not matter what order they are executed. Finally the function tells us what the script does.

Each script is supposed to accept a single argument, the word 'start' or the word 'stop', or 'restart' etc. Let's consider an example of how we might start the httpd daemon using init. Here is a checklist:

1. Determine the correct run-level for the service. Let us suppose that it is run-level 2.

2. Choose an unused filename, say S99http.

3. Create a script accepting a single argument:

```
#!/bin/sh

case $1 in

    start) /usr/local/bin/httpd -d /usr/local/lib/httpd ;;

    stop)  kill `cat /usr/local/lib/httpd/logs/httpd.pid` ;;

    *) echo Syntax error starting http

esac
```

The advantage of this system is that software packages can be added and removed transparently just by adding or removing a file. No special editing is required as is the case for BSD Unix.

9.4.2 BSD init

The BSD style is rather simple. It starts executing a shell script called /etc/rc which then generally calls other child-scripts. These scripts start important daemons and configure the system. To add our own local modifications, we have to edit the file /etc/rc.local. This is a Bourne shell script.

The BSD approach has a simpler structure than the system 5 inittab directories, but it is harder to manipulate package-wise.

9.4.3 inetd configuration

The Internet daemon is a *service demultiplexer*. In English, that means that it is a daemon which listens on the network for messages to several services simultaneously. When it receives a message intended for a specific port, it starts the relevant daemon to handle the request just long enough to handle one request. inetd saves the system some resources by starting daemons only when they are required, rather than having to clutter up the process table all the time.

The format of this file can differ slightly on older systems. The best way to glean its format is to look at the entries which are already there. Here is a common example of the format.

```
#
# Service|type|protocol|wait|user|daemon-file|command line
#
# NB wu-ftpd needs -a now
#
ftp     stream tcp nowait root   /usr/sbin/in.ftpd      in.ftpd -a
telnet  stream tcp nowait root   /usr/sbin/in.telnetd   in.telnetd
finger  stream tcp nowait finger /local/etc/in.fingerd  in.fingerd
cfinger stream tcp nowait finger /local/etc/in.cfingerd in.cfingerd
```

The first column is the name of the service from /etc/services. The next column is the type of connection (stream or dgram or tli), then comes the protocol type (tcp/udp etc). The wait column indicates whether the service is to be single or multi-transaction, i.e. whether new requests should wait for an existing request to complete or whether a new daemon should be started in parallel. The last two columns contain the location of the program which should handle the request and the actual command line (including options) which should be executed. Notice that the finger daemon runs as a special user with no privileges.

To add a new service, we edit the file /etc/inetd.conf and then send the inetd process the HUP signal. To do this, we find the process id:

```
ps aux | grep inetd
```

Then we type:

```
kill -HUP process-id
```

9.4.4 Binding to sockets

When a daemon is started, it creates a listening socket or *port* with a specific port number, which then gets 'bound' to the host running the service concerned. The act of binding a socket to a host's IP address identifies a fixed port service with that host. This has a specific consequence. It is only possible to bind a socket port to an address once. If we try to start another daemon, we will often see the error message

```
host: Couldn't bind to socket
bind: Address already in use
```

This means that another daemon is already running. This error can occur if two copies of inetd are started, or if we try to start a daemon twice, or indeed if we try to place a service in inetd and start a daemon at the same time. The error can also occur within a finite time-window after a service has crashed, but the problem should right itself within a few minutes.[1]

9.4.5 TCP wrapper security

One of the problems with inetd is that it accepts connections from any host and passes them to services registered in its configuration file without question. In today's network climate this is a dangerous step and it is usually desirable to limit the availability of certain services. For instance, services which are purely local (like RPC) should never be left open so that outside users could try to exploit them. In short, services should only be made available to those who need them. If they are left open to those who do not need them, we invite attacks on the system.

TCP wrappers is a solution to this problem for IPv4 connections only. In short, it gives us the possibility of adding Access Control Lists (ACLs) to network services. TCP wrappers exists in two forms: as the tcpd daemon, and as a library which stand-alone programs can link to, called libwrap.a. Services which are not

---

[1]Most network services set the SO_REUSEADDR socket option so that it can restart immediately and not have to wait for TIME_WAIT to time out.

explicitly compiled with the library can use the daemon as a wrapper, if the services can be started from `inetd`. TCP wrapper expects to find the daemons it proxies for in a special directory. It requires two configuration files, one which grants access to services and which denies access. If services are not listed explicitly TCP wrappers does nothing to prevent connection. The file to allow access to a service overrides the file to deny access, thus one normally denies access to all services as a default measure and opens specific services one by one (see below). The `hosts.allow` file contains the names of daemons followed by a list of hosts or IP addresses, or domains or network series. The word LOCAL matches any host which has an unqualified host name. If we are opening a service to our local domain, it is often necessary to have both the domain suffix and the word LOCAL, since different operating systems employ different name services in different ways. (LOCAL matches hostnames without any domain ending.)

```
# hosts.allow
in.fingerd: .domain.tld LOCAL
in.cfingerd: .domain.tld LOCAL
sendmail: ALL
cfd: .domain.tld LOCAL
sshd: 128.39.89. 128.39.74. 128.39.75. 127.0.0.1
[2001:700:700:3::] [2001:700:700:4::] [::1]
sshdfwd-X11: .domain.tld
# Portmapper doesn't understand DNS for security
portmap: 192.0.2.
rpc.mountd: 192.0.2.
rpc.nfsd: 192.0.2.
```

Note how IPv6 addresses must be bracketed. Be warned that not all programs understand IPv6 addressing, so these entries might cause services to crash (especially RPC). (See section 2.9.)

The TCP wrapper service works mainly for plain TCP streams, but in some operating systems (notably GNU/Linux) RPC services can also be placed under its umbrella. The portmapper and NFS mount daemons are also subject to TCP wrapper access controls. Note that we have to use IP addresses here. Hostnames are not accepted.

Apart from those explicitly mentioned above, all other services are denied access like this in `/etc/hosts.deny`:

```
ALL: ALL
```

9.5 Setting up the DNS nameservice

The Domain Name System (DNS) is that most important of Internet services which converts host names, such as `host.domain.tld`, into IP addresses, such as `192.0.2.10`, and vice versa. If a host name includes its complete domain name, it is said to be a Fully Qualified Host Name (FQHN). In the Unix world, the most popular implementation of the DNS client and server is called the Berkeley Internet Name Domain (BIND). The DNS client is called the 'resolver', and the DNS server is called the 'name server'.

Establishing a name service is not difficult, but BIND is complex and we shall only skim the surface in this book. More detailed accounts of DNS configuration can be found in refs. [7, 223]. A tool for managing domain naming and electronic mail has been described in ref. [267].

9.5.1 Master and slave servers

Each domain which is responsible for its own host registration requires at least one master name server. A master name server is a name server whose data lie in authoritative source files on the server-host, maintained by a local system administrator. A domain can also have a number of slave name servers which mirror the master data. A slave name server (or slave) does not use source file data, but downloads its data second-hand from a master server at regular intervals – thus its data are also considered authoritative for other domains. The purpose of a slave name server is to function as a backup to the master server or to spread the load of serving all the hosts in the domain. The only difference in setting up master and slave servers is one word in a configuration file and the location of the name data.

In practice, master and slave servers are identical, as seen from the outside. The only difference is in the source of the data: a master or master server knows that it should propagate changes to all slave servers, while a slave or slave server knows that it should accept updates.

The name server daemon is started once by `root`, since the DNS port is a privileged port. In order to function, the daemon needs to be told about its status within the DNS hierarchy and it needs to be told where to find the files of domain data. This requires us to set up a number of configuration files. The files can seem cryptic at first, but they are easy to maintain once we have a working configuration.

9.5.2 File structure on the master

Since the mapping of (even fully qualified) hostnames to IP addresses is not one-to-one (a host can have several aliases and a single hostname can point to multiple IP addresses), the DNS database needs information about conversion both from FQHN to IP address and the other way around. That requires two sets of data. To set up a master name server, we need to complete a checklist.

- We need to make a directory in our local or site-dependent files where the DNS domain data can be installed, called for instance `dns` or `named` and change to this directory.

- We then make subdirectories `master` and `slave` for master and slave data. We might not need both on the same host, but some servers can be master servers for a zone and slave servers for another zone. We shall only refer to the master data in this book, but we might want to add slave servers later, for whatever reason. Slave data are cached files which can be placed in this directory.

- Assuming that our domain name is *domain.tld*, we create a file `master/domain.tld`. We shall worry about its contents shortly. This file will contain data for converting names into addresses.

- Now we need files which will perform the reverse translation. It is convenient, but not essential, to keep different subnet addresses separate, for clarity. This is easy if we have a netmask which gives the subnets in our domain easily separable addresses. The domain `iu.hio.no`, for instance, has four networks: `128.39.89.0`, `128.39.73.0`, `128.39.74.0` which includes `128.38.75.*`. So we would create files `master/rev.128.39.89`, `master/rev.128.39.73` etc., one for each network. These files will contain data for converting addresses into 'canonical' names, or official hostnames (as opposed to aliases). We shall call these network files generically `master/subnet`. Of course, we can call any of the files anything we like, since the filenames must be declared in the configuration boot file.

- Dealing with the Unix loopback address requires some special attention. We handle this by creating a file for the loopback pseudo-network `master/rev.127.0.0`.

- Create a cache file `named.cache` which will contain the names of the Internet's master (root) name servers.

- Create a configuration file `named.conf`. We shall later link or synchronize this file to `/etc/named.conf` where the daemon expects to find it. We place it here, however, so that it doesn't get lost or destroyed if we should choose to upgrade or reinstall the operating system.

At this stage one should have the following directory structure in site-dependent files.

Names	Examples
`named/named.conf`	`dns/named.conf`
`named/named.cache`	`dns/named.cache`
`named/master/domain.tld`	`dns/master/domain.tld`
`named/master/subnet`	`dns/master/rev.192.0.2`
	`dns/master/rev.128.39.73`
	`dns/master/rev.128.39.89`

9.5.3 Sample `named.conf` for BIND 9.x

Using current BIND software, the file looks something like this:

```
options
   {
   directory "/local/site/dns";
```

```
  check-names master ignore;
  check-names response ignore;
  check-names slave warn;
  named-xfer "/local/site/bind/bin/named-xfer"; /* Location of daemon */
  fake-iquery no;                               /* security */
  notify yes;
  };


zone "."
  {
  type hint;
  file "named.cache";
  };

//
// Master and slave name/address zone files follow.
//

zone "0.0.127.in-addr.arpa"
  {
  type master;
  file "master/rev.127.0.0";
  };

zone "2.0.192.in-addr.arpa"
  {
  type master;
  file "master/rev.192.0.2";
  };


acl trustedhosts
  {
  ! 192.0.2.11;  // Not this host!
  192.0.2.0/24;  // Net with 24 bit netmask set. i.e. 255.255.255.0
  192.0.74.0/23; //           23                      . 255.255.254.0
  };


zone "domain.tld"
  {
  type master;
  file "master/domain.tld";

  allow-transfer   // Allows ls domain.tld in nslookup
      {            // and domain downloads
      trustedhosts; // Access Control List defined above
      }
  };
```

```
// dns.domain.tld server options

server 192.0.2.11
    {
    transfer-format many-answers;
    };

logging
    {
    channel admin_stuff
        {
        file "/local/site/logs/admin" versions 7;
        severity debug;
        print-time yes;
        print-category yes;
        print-severity yes;
        };

    channel xfers
        {
        file "/local/site/logs/xfer" versions 7;
        severity debug;
        print-time yes;
        print-category yes;
        print-severity yes;
        };

    channel updates
        {
        file "/local/site/logs/updates" versions 10;
        severity debug;
        print-time yes;
        print-category yes;
        print-severity yes;
        };

    channel security
        {
        file "/local/site/logs/security" versions 7;
        severity debug;
        print-time yes;
        print-category yes;
        print-severity yes;
        };

    category config
        {
        admin_stuff;
        };

    category parser
        {
```

```
            admin_stuff;
            };

    category update
            {
            updates;
            };

    category load
            {
            updates;
            };

    category security
            {
            security;
            };

    category xfer-in
            {
            xfers;
            };

    category xfer-out
            {
            xfers;
            };

    category db
            {
            updates;
            };

    category lame-servers
            {
            null;
            };

    category cname
            {
            null;
            };
    };
```

Note the `allow-transfer` statement which allows a user of `nslookup` to obtain
a dump of the local domain, using the 'ls' command within the `nslookup` shell. If
this is not present, version 8 and 9 BIND will not allow such a listing. BIND now
allows ACLs to control access to these data. In the example we have created an
ACL alias for all of the trusted hosts on our network. The ACLs use an increasingly
popular, if somewhat obscure, notation for groups of IP addresses. The 'slash'
notation is supposed to represent all of the hosts on a subnet. In order to fully

specify a subnet (which, in practice, might be part of a class A, B or C network), we need to specify the network address and the subnet mask. The slash notation does this by giving the network address followed by a slash, followed by the number of bits in the netmask which are set to one. So, for example, the address series

```
192.0.2.0/24
```

means all of the addresses from 192.0.2.0 to 192.0.2.255, since the netmask is 255.255.255.0. The example

```
192.0.74.0/23
```

is an example of a doubled-up subnet. This means all of the hosts from 192.0.74.0 to 192.0.74.255 and 192.0.75.0 to 192.0.75.255, since the netmask is 255.255.254.0, i.e. 23 non-zero bits. ACLs can contain any list of hosts. The pling (Am. bang) '!' operator negates an address, or entry. The important thing to remember about ACLs in general is that they work by taking each entry in turn. As soon as there is a match, the access algorithm quits. So if we were to write

```
acl test
    {
    192.0.2.11;
    !192.0.2.11;
    }
```

the result would always be to grant access to 192.0.2.11. Conversely, if we wrote

```
acl test
    {
    !192.0.2.11;
    192.0.2.11;
    }
```

the result would be to always deny access to this host, since the second instance of the address is never reached.

Note that for a slave, or slave server mirroring a master, we would replace the word master with slave, and `master` with `slave` for clarity.

There are many issues that we have not taken up here. This is only the beginning. You should read more about BIND. For instance, for IPv6 connections there is,

```
options
    {
    listen-on-v6  any; ;
    transfer-source-v6 2001:700:700:1::99;
    }
```

and for more security there is the `allow-recursion` directive.

9.5.4 Sample `named.cache` or `named.root`

The cache file (now often referred to as the root file) contains the names of root name servers. The data for the cache file were formerly maintained by the American military at `nic.ddn.mil`. Today they are retrieved by anonymous ftp from the INTERNIC `ftp.rs.internic.net`. The list of Internet root servers (which bind together all Internet domains) are listed in a file called `domain/named.root` The retrieved data are simply included in a file called `named.cache` or `named.root`. You should obtain an updated version of this file.

```
;             This file holds the information on root name servers needed to
;             initialize cache of Internet domain name servers
;             (e.g. reference this file in the "cache  .  <file>"
;             configuration file of BIND domain name servers).
;
;             This file is made available by InterNIC
;             under anonymous FTP as
;                 file                  /domain/named.root
;                 on server             FTP.INTERNIC.NET
;
;             last update:   Nov 5, 2002
;             related version of root zone:   2002110501
;
;
; formerly NS.INTERNIC.NET
;
.                             3600000   IN   NS    A.ROOT-SERVERS.NET.
A.ROOT-SERVERS.NET.           3600000        A     198.41.0.4
;
; formerly NS1.ISI.EDU
;
.                             3600000        NS    B.ROOT-SERVERS.NET.
B.ROOT-SERVERS.NET.           3600000        A     128.9.0.107
;
; formerly C.PSI.NET
;
.                             3600000        NS    C.ROOT-SERVERS.NET.
C.ROOT-SERVERS.NET.           3600000        A     192.33.4.12
;
; formerly TERP.UMD.EDU
;
.                             3600000        NS    D.ROOT-SERVERS.NET.
D.ROOT-SERVERS.NET.           3600000        A     128.8.10.90
;
; formerly NS.NASA.GOV
;
.                             3600000        NS    E.ROOT-SERVERS.NET.
E.ROOT-SERVERS.NET.           3600000        A     192.203.230.10
;
; formerly NS.ISC.ORG
;
```

```
.                         3600000      NS      F.ROOT-SERVERS.NET.
F.ROOT-SERVERS.NET.       3600000      A       192.5.5.241
;
; formerly NS.NIC.DDN.MIL
;
.                         3600000      NS      G.ROOT-SERVERS.NET.
G.ROOT-SERVERS.NET.       3600000      A       192.112.36.4
;
; formerly AOS.ARL.ARMY.MIL
;
.                         3600000      NS      H.ROOT-SERVERS.NET.
H.ROOT-SERVERS.NET.       3600000      A       128.63.2.53
;
; formerly NIC.NORDU.NET
;
.                         3600000      NS      I.ROOT-SERVERS.NET.
I.ROOT-SERVERS.NET.       3600000      A       192.36.148.17
;
; operated by VeriSign, Inc.
;
.                         3600000      NS      J.ROOT-SERVERS.NET.
J.ROOT-SERVERS.NET.       3600000      A       192.58.128.30
;
; housed in LINX, operated by RIPE NCC
;
.                         3600000      NS      K.ROOT-SERVERS.NET.
K.ROOT-SERVERS.NET.       3600000      A       193.0.14.129
;
; operated by IANA
;
.                         3600000      NS      L.ROOT-SERVERS.NET.
L.ROOT-SERVERS.NET.       3600000      A       198.32.64.12
;
; housed in Japan, operated by WIDE
;
.                         3600000      NS      M.ROOT-SERVERS.NET.
M.ROOT-SERVERS.NET.       3600000      A       202.12.27.33
; End of File
```

9.5.5 Sample `master/`*`domain.tld`*

The main domain file contains data identifying the IP addresses of hosts in
our domain; it defines possible aliases for those names and it also identifies
special servers such as mail-exchangers which mail-relay programs use to send
electronic mail to our domain. *Note that the IP addresses and hostnames used
here are examples. You should replace them with your own valid IP addresses.*

Each IP-configured network interface has a *canonical name* which is its official
name (the name that is returned by default in a reverse lookup). We may then
define any number of aliases to this canonical name (using the confusingly named
CNAME directive). For instance, it is common to create aliases for host-interfaces

that provide well-known services, like `www.domain.tld` and `ftp.domain.tld` to standardize access to services in our domain. Below is an abbreviated example file. There are several kinds of record here:

- `SOA` Indicates the Start Of Authority for this domain (referred to as `@`).

- `NS` Lists a nameserver for this domain or a sub-domain. NS records are not used for anything other than delegation. They exist only for convenience.

- `MX` Lists a mail exchanger for this domain (with priority).

- `A` Creates an A record, i.e. defines the canonical name of a host with a given IP address.

- `CNAME` Associates an alias with a canonical name.

- `HINFO` Advertises host information. No longer advisable for security reasons.

DNS database files contain *resource records* which refer to these different elements. The general form of such a record is

```
Name   [ttl]  [class]   assoc   data
```

The square brackets imply that the second and third fields are optional. The default class is `IN` for Internet. Other values for class refer to little-used nameservices which will not be considered here. Each resource record is an association of a name with an item of data. The type of association is identified by the *assoc* field, which is one of the set `A`, `PTR`, `NS` etc. For example

```
host1 86400 IN A          10.20.30.40
host1 86400 IN CNAME      host2
host1 86400 IN MX      10 mailhost
```

or simply

```
host1 A          10.20.30.40
host1 CNAME      host2
host1 MX      10 mailhost
```

A reverse lookup entry looks like this:

```
40      PTR    host1
```

In addition to mapping hostnames to addresses and vice versa, the DNS tables also tell E-mail services how to deliver mail. We will need to have a so-called 'mail-exchanger' record in the DNS tables in order to tell E-mail which host handles E-mail for the domain. An entry of the form

```
domain-name  MX  priority  mailhost
```

tells E-mail services that mail sent to *namedomain-name* should be routed to the host *mailhost*. For instance,

```
domain.tld. MX 10 mailhost
            MX 20 backup
```

tells our server that mail addresses of the form *name*@domain.tld should be handled by the host called mailhost (which is an alias for a host called mercury, as we shall see below). The priority number 10 is chosen at random. Several records can be added with backup servers if the first server does not respond.

Mail records are also possible on a per-host basis. If we want mail sent to host XXX handled by host YYY, we would add a record,

```
XXX MX 10 YYY
```

This would mean that mail sent to

```
XXX. domain-name
```

would be handled by YYY. For instance, mail addressed to

```
name@XXX.domain.tld
```

would be actually sent to

```
name@YYY.domain.tld
```

IPv6 registration in DNS looks like this, in the zone file:

```
daneel          A       192.0.2.230
                AAAA    2001:0700:0700:0003:0290:27ff:fea2:477b
```

The IETF also considered a record type called A6 records, but this has now been given experimental status and left on the shelf for the time being. The BIND documentation is somewhat out of date as of January 2003.

Here is an example file with all the elements in place. Note the meaning of the following special symbols

;	Comment
@	Stands for the local domain
()	Continue record over several lines

```
$ORIGIN domain.tld.     ; @ is an alias for this

@       IN  SOA   mercury.domain.tld.
                  sysadm.mercury.domain.tld.
                  (
                  1996111300 ; Serialnumber
                  3600     ; Refresh, 1 hr
                  600      ; Retry, 10 min
                  604800   ; Expire 1 week
                  86400    ; Minimum TTL, 1 day
                  )
```

```
            A        192.0.2.237  ; domain.tld points to
                                  ; this host by default

; Name servers:

        IN  NS      mercury.domain.tld.
        IN  NS      backup.domain.tld.
        IN  NS      dns.parent.co.

; Mail exchangers for whole domain

@                   MX      10      mercury

; Common aliases for well known services

www             CNAME   mercury    ; aliases
ftp             CNAME   mercury
mailhost        CNAME   mercury

; Router

domain-gw       A       192.0.2.1
                A       128.39.73.129 ; 2 addresses

iu-gw           CNAME   domain-gw

localhost       A       127.0.0.1


; example net

mercury         A       192.0.2.10
thistledown     A       192.0.2.233
jart            A       192.0.2.234
nostromo        A       192.0.2.235
daystrom        A       192.0.2.236
borg            A       192.0.2.237
backup          A       192.0.2.238
axis            A       192.0.2.239
```

Note that, as this file stands, mail exchanger data, described by the MX record are only described for the domain as a whole. If an external mailer attempts to send directly to a specific host, it is still allowed to do so. We can still override this by adding an explicit MX record for each A record also. For example:

```
mercury             A           192.0.2.10
                    MX      10 mailhost
                    MX      20 backup
```

```
thistledown      A                192.0.2.233
                 MX       10 mailhost
                 MX       20 backup
jart             A                192.0.2.234
                 MX       10 mailhost
                 MX       20 backup
```

This will tell an external mailer to send mail to each of these hosts to the mailhost
instead. Normally, this would not be a problem. One could simply configure the
non-mail-hosts as so-called null clients, meaning that they would just forward the
mail on to the mailhost. However, it can be important to avoid relying on client
forwarding if we are using a hub solution inside some kind of filtering router, since
the SMTP ports might be blocked to all the other hosts. Thus mail would not be
sendable to the other hosts unless these MX records were in place. See section 9.7
for more details of this.

9.5.6 Sample `master/network`

The network files are responsible for producing a fully qualified domain name
given an IP address. This is accomplished with so-called PTR records. In other
words, these records provide reverse lookup. *Note that the IP addresses used here
are examples. You should replace them with your own valid IP addresses.* The
reverse lookup-file looks like this:

```
$ORIGIN 89.39.128.in-addr.arpa.
@        IN      SOA     mercury.domain.tld.
                        sysadm.mercury.domain.tld.
                          (
                        1996111300 ; Serialnumber
                        3600      ; Refresh, 1 hr
                        600       ; Retry, 10 min
                        604800    ; Expire 1 week
                        86400     ; Minimum TTL, 1 day
                          )
; Name servers:

         IN      NS      mercury.domain.tld.
         IN      NS      dns.parent.co.
         IN      NS      backup.domain.tld.


;
; Domain data:
;

1        PTR     domain-gw.domain.tld.

; etc
```

```
10        PTR       mercury.domain.tld.

; etc

233       PTR       thistledown.domain.tld.
234       PTR       jart.domain.tld.
```

Note carefully how the names end with a dot. If we forget this, the name server appends the domain name to the end, resulting in something like lore.domain.tld. domain.tld.

9.5.7   Sample master/127.0.0

In order to avoid problems with the loopback address, all domains should define a fake 'loopback' network simply to register the Unix loopback address correctly within the DNS. Since 127.0.0 is not a physical network and the loopback address doesn't belong to anyone, it is acceptable for everyone to define this as part of the local name server. No name collisions will occur as a result.

```
; Zone file for "localhost" entry.

$ORIGIN 0.0.127.IN-ADDR.ARPA.
@   IN      SOA      mercury.domain.tld.
                     sysadm.mercury.domain.tld.
                       (
                       1995070300 ; Serialnumber
                       3600     ; Refresh
                       300      ; Retry
                       3600000 ; Expire
                       14400    ; Minimum
                       )

    IN      NS       mercury.domain.tld.

;
; Domain data
;


1   PTR    localhost.

0.0.127.in-addr.arpa. IN NS mercury.domain.tld.
0.0.127.in-addr.arpa  IN NS backup.domain.tld.

1.0.0.127.in-addr.arpa. IN PTR localhost.
```

9.5.8 Zone transfers

A zone is a portion of a complete domain which is self-contained (as a zone file). Responsibility for a zone is delegated to the administrators of that zone. A zone administrator keeps and maintains the files we have discussed above. When changes are made to the data in a domain, we need to update the serial number of the data in the source files. Slave name servers use this serial number to register when changes have occurred in the zone data, i.e. to determine when they should download new data.

9.5.9 Reverse IPv6 records

DNS and IPv6 make a study in confusion. The IETF has changed official policy on this issue more than once, leaving some documentation out of date and in a state of confusion. As of January 2003, the claim is that there is finally agreement that the forward records shall be called AAAA records (not A6) and that the reverse lookup domain will be called `.ip6.arpa` (not `.ip6.int` as previously held), but resolvers continue to look for both of these, so it is worth registering both. In `named.conf` one can make two entries

```
zone "3.0.0.0.0.0.7.0.0.0.7.0.1.0.0.2.ip6.int"

    type master;
    file "master/2001.700.700.3";
    ;


zone "3.0.0.0.0.0.7.0.0.0.7.0.1.0.0.2.ip6.arpa"

    type master;
    file "master/2001.700.700.3";
    ;
```

Note that this uses the same file for both zones. Now, in the reverse-lookup zone file, named as `master/2001.700.700.3`, we omit the ORIGIN directive and BIND 9 assumes that the names are relative to the zone in the configuration file. Thus:

```
$TTL 14400

@       IN      SOA     mercury.domain.tld.
                        sysadm.mercury.domain.tld.
                          (
                          1996111300 ; Serialnumber
                          3600     ; Refresh, 1 hr
                          600      ; Retry, 10 min
                          604800   ; Expire 1 week
                          86400    ; Minimum TTL, 1 day
                          )
; Name servers:

        IN      NS      mercury.domain.tld.
        IN      NS      dns.parent.co.
```

```
      IN      NS      backup.domain.tld.
```

```
; relative to 2001:700:700:3/64
```

```
1.0.0.0.0.0.0.0.0.0.0.0.0.0.0.0 PTR      ip6-gw.example.org.
b.7.7.4.2.a.e.f.f.f.7.2.0.9.2.0 PTR      daneel.example.org.
```

Note that this omission of origin works only in master servers, since slave servers that mirror primaries add the origin directive automatically.

9.5.10 Sub-domains and structure

Suppose we are in a DNS domain college.edu and would like to name hosts according to their departmental affiliation. We could use a naming scheme which made each department look like a sub-domain of the true domain college.edu. For instance, we might want the following hosts:

```
einstein.phys.college.edu
darwin.bio.college.edu
von-neumann.comp.college.edu
```

We can achieve this very simply, because having the extra 'dot' in the name makes no difference to the name service. We just assign the A record for the host accordingly. In the zone file for college.edu

```
$ORIGIN college.edu.     ; @ is an alias for this
```

```
@         IN  SOA    chomsky.college.edu. sysadm.chomsky.college.edu
                         (
                         1996111300 ; Serialnumber
                         3600     ; Refresh, 1 hr
                         600      ; Retry, 10 min
                         604800   ; Expire 1 week
                         86400    ; Minimum TTL, 1 day
                         )
```

```
; ...
```

```
einstein.phys    A   192.0.2.5
darwin.bio       A   192.0.2.6
von-neumann.comp A   192.0.2.7
```

It does not matter that we have dots in the names on the left-hand side of an A record assignment. DNS does not care about this. It still looks and behaves like a sub-domain. There is no need for an SOA record for these sub-domains, as written, since we are providing authoritative information about them here explicitly. But we could handle this differently. According to the principle of delegation, we would like to empower local units of a network community with the ability to organize their own affairs. Since the computer science department is growing fat on the funds it receives, it has many hosts and it starts to make sense to delegate this sub-domain to a local administrator. The emaciated physics and biology departments don't want this hassle, so we keep them under our wing in the parent zone records.

Delegating the sub-domain `comp.college.edu` means doing the following:

- Setting up a nameserver which will contain an authoritative SOA database for the sub-domain.

- Delegating responsibility for the sub-domain to that name server, using an NS record in our parent domain's zone data.

- Informing the parent organization about the changes required in the top-level `in-addr.arpa` domain, required for reverse lookups.

Normally the NS records for a zone are only present to remind local administrators which hosts are nameservers. Suppose we choose the host m5 to be the nameserver for the sub-domain. A pair of records like this:

```
comp                    86400   IN   NS m5.comp.college.edu

m5.comp.college.edu     86400   IN   A  192.0.2.200
```

creates a sub-domain called 'comp'. The first line tells us the name of a nameserver in the sub-domain which will be authoritative for the sub-domain. We give it a specific time to live, for definiteness. Notice, however, that this is a cyclic definition: we have defined the comp sub-domain using a member of the comp-subdomain. In order to break the infinite loop, we have to also provide a *glue record* (an A record, borrowed from the sub-domain) which tells the system the actual IP address of the name server which will contain information about the remainder of the domain.

To delegate a sub-domain, we also have to delegate the reverse pointer records. To do this we need to contact the parent organization which owns the network above our own. In the 'olden days' in-addr.arpa delegation was performed by the 'nic' military, then the 'INTERNIC'. Today, the logistics of this mapping has become too large a job for any one organization. For ISPs who delegate subnets, it is passed back up the line to the network owners. Each organization knows the organization above it, and so we contact these until someone has authority to modify the in-addr.arpa domain. An erroneous delegation is usually referred to as a lame delegation. . This means that a nameserver is listed as being authoritative for a domain, but in fact does not service that domain. Lame delegations and other problems can be diagnosed with programs such as dnswalk. See also ref. [28].

9.6 Setting up a WWW server

The World Wide Web (or W3) service is provided by the daemon `httpd`. This description is based on the freely available Apache daemon which is widely regarded as the best and most up-to-date. It can be obtained from `http://www.apache.org`.

Configuring `httpd` is a relatively simple matter, but it does involve a few subtleties which we need to examine, Most of these have to do with security. Some are linked to minor changes between versions of the server. This discussion is based on Apache version 1.3.*x*, but most of it applies to the later version 2 rewrite. An `httpd` server can be used for two purposes:

- *Extranet:* For publishing information which is intended to be open to the world. The more people who see this information, the better.

- *Intranet:* For publishing private information for internal use within an organization.

Unless we are going to operate within a firewall configuration, there is probably no need to separate these two services. They can run on the same server, with access control restricting information on a need-to-know basis. Special attention should be given to CGI programs however. These are particularly insecure and can compromise any access controls which we place on data. If we need restricted information access we should not allow arbitrary users to have accounts or CGI privileges on a server: CGI programs can always be written to circumvent server security.

The WWW service will also publish two different kinds of web pages:

- *Site data:* A site's official welcome page and subsequent official data (access by `http://www.domain.tld`).

- *Personal data:* The private web pages of registered, local users (access by `http://www.domain.tld/~user`).

Whether to allow local users private web pages at a given organization is a matter of policy.

The WWW is an open service: it gives access to file information, usually without requiring a password. For that reason it has the potential to be a security hazard: not with respect to itself, or the information which one intends to publish, but to the well-being of the host on which it runs. A typical configuration error in a large corporation's web server, a few years ago, allowed an attacker to delete all users' home directories from the comfort of his browser.

To start a WWW service we need some `html`-files containing information we wish to publish and a server-daemon. We then need to edit configuration files which tell the daemon where to find the web pages it will be publishing. Finally, we need to tell it what we do *not* want it to tell the outside world. The security of the whole system can depend on which files and directories outsiders have access to.

9.6.1 Choosing a server host

Personal data are accessed from users' home directories, usually under a subdirectory called *www*. It makes considerable sense for the WWW server to be on the host which has the physically mounted disks. Otherwise, the WWW server would first have to access the files via NFS and then transmit them back to the requester. This would lead to an unnecessary doubling of network traffic.

9.6.2 Installation

A survey which was carried out in 1998 revealed that about 70 percent of all WWW servers in the world were Apache WWW servers running on FreeBSD or GNU/Linux PCs. The Apache server is ubiquitous and versatile, and it is Free Software so we shall adopt it as our working model. Apache-`httpd` runs both on Unix-like OSes and NT.

The server is compiled in the usual way by unpacking a `.tar.gz` file and by running `configure` then `make`. This has support for many bells and whistles which enhance its performance. For instance, one can run an embedded language called PHP from within HTML pages to create 'active web pages'. The `httpd` daemon must then be configured with special PHP support. Debian GNU/Linux has a ready-made package for the Apache server, but it is old. It is always worth collecting the latest version of the server from an official mirror site (see the Apache web site for a list of mirrors).

Apache uses a GNU autoconf `configure` program to prepare the compilation. As always, we have to choose a prefix for the software installation. If none is specified, the directory `/usr/local` is the default.

There is no particular reason for installing the binaries elsewhere, however Apache does generate a convenient startup/shutdown script which compiles in the location of the configuration files. The configuration files are kept under the installation-prefix, in `etc/apache/*.conf`. On the principle of separating files which we maintain ourselves from files installed by other sources, we almost certainly do not want to keep the true configuration files there, but rather would like to keep them together with other site-dependent configuration files. We shall bear this in mind below.

To build a basic web server, then, we follow the usual sequence for compiling Free software:

```
% configure
% make
% make -n install
% su
# make install
```

9.6.3 Configuration

Having compiled the daemon, we have to prepare some infrastructure. First we make sure that we have the two lines

```
www   80/tcp    http
www   80/udp    http
```

in the `/etc/services` file on Unix-like systems. Next we must:

- Create a directory in our site-dependent files called, say, `www`, where HTML documents will be kept. In particular, we will need a file `www/index.html` which will be the root of the web site.

- Edit the files `httpd/conf/*.conf` with a text editor so that we configure in our site-specific data and requirements.

- Create a special user and a special group which will be used to restrict the privilege of the `httpd` service.

The daemon's configuration determines the behavior of the WWW service. It is decided by the contents of a set of files:

`httpd.conf`	Properties of the daemon itself
`access.conf`	Access control for documents and CGI
`srm.conf`	Server resource management
`mime.types`	Multimedia file extensions

This breakdown is a matter of convention. There is no longer a difference between the files as far as the configuration language is concerned. The Apache server provides example configuration files which we can use as an initial template. In recent versions, Apache has moved away from the idea of using several configuration files, towards keeping everything in one file. You may wish to form your own opinion about what is best policy here.

The `httpd` is started by root/Administrator, but the daemon immediately relinquishes its special privileges in order to run with the access rights of a www user for all operations. The `User` and `Group` directives specify which user the daemon should run as. The default here is usually the user `nobody`. This is the default because it is the only non-privileged username which most systems already have. However, the `nobody` user was introduced in order to create a safe mapping of privileges for the Unix NFS (Network File System), so to use it here could lead to confusion and possibly even accidents later. A better approach is to use a completely separate user ID for the service. In fact, in general:

> **Principle 52 (Separate user IDs for services).** *Each service which does not require privileged access to the system should be given a separate, non-privileged user ID. This restricts service privileges, preventing any potential abuse should the service be hijacked by system attackers; it also makes clear which service is responsible for which processes in the process table.*

Corollary to principle (Privileged ports). *Unix services which run on ports 1–1023 must be started with root privileges in order for the socket to be validated, but can switch internally to a safer level of privilege once communications have been established.*

9.6.4 The `httpd.conf` file

Here is a cut-down example file which points out some important parameters in the configuration of the server. The actual example files distributed with the server are more verbose and contain additional options. You should probably not delete anything from those files unless you have read the documentation carefully, but you will need to give the following points special attention.

```
# httpd.conf

ServerRoot          /local/site/httpd/

ServerAdmin         sysadm@domain.tld
User                www
Group               www

ServerType          standalone  # not inetd
HostnameLookups off              # save time

 # Several request-transfers per connection is efficient

KeepAlive           On
MaxKeepAliveRequests 100
KeepAliveTimeout     15

 # Looks like several servers, really only one ..

NameVirtualHost 192.0.2.220

<VirtualHost www.domain.tld>
ServerAdmin webmaster@domain.tld
DocumentRoot /site/host/local/www-data
ServerName www.domain.tld
</VirtualHost>

<VirtualHost project.domain.tld>
ServerAdmin webmaster@domain.tld
DocumentRoot /site/host/local/project-data
ServerName project.domain.tld
</VirtualHost>
```

The `ServerRoot` directive tells the daemon which directory is to be used to look for additional configuration files (see below) and to write logs of transactions. When the daemon is started, it normally has to be told the location of the server root, with the '-d' option:

```
httpd -d /local/site/httpd
```

The daemon then looks for configuration files under `conf`, for log files under `logs` and so on. The location of the server root does not have to have anything to do with the location of the binaries, as installed above. Indeed, since configuration files and log files can both be considered local, site-dependent data, we have placed them here amongst local, site-dependent files.

The `User` and `Group` directives tell the daemon which users' privileges it should use after connecting to the privileged port 80. A special user and group ID should be created for this purpose. The user ID should be an account which it is not possible to log on to, with no valid shell and a barred password (see section 5.3).

The `ServerType` variable indicates whether we are planning to run `httpd` on demand from `inetd` or whether it should run as a stand-alone daemon. Running as a stand-alone daemon can give a considerable saving of overhead in forking new processes. A stand-alone daemon can organize its own resources, rather than relying on a multiplexer like `inetd`.

`HostnameLookups` determines whether the DNS names of hosts connecting to the server will be looked up and written into the access log. DNS lookups can add a significant amount of delay to a connection, so this should be turned off on busy servers. In a similar efficiency vein, the `KeepAlive` variable tells the server not to close a connection after every transaction, but to allow multiple transactions up to a limit of `MaxKeepAliveRequests` on the same connection. Since the overhead of starting a new connection is quite high, and of shutting one down even higher, a considerable improvement in efficiency can be achieved by allowing persistent connections.

The final part of the file concerns the `VirtualHost` environment. This is a feature of Apache which is very useful. It enables one to maintain the appearance of separate web servers, with just one daemon. For instance, we might want to have a generic point of contact for our domain, called `www.domain.tld`, but we might also want to run a special project machine, whose data were maintained by a separate research group, called `project.domain.tld`. To do this we need to create a `VirtualHost` structure for each virtual hostname we would like to attach to the server.

We also need to register these alternative names as DNS aliases so that others will be able to use them in normal URLs in their web browsers. Suppose the actual canonical name of the host we are running on is `workhorse.domain.tld`. In the master zone of the domain `domain.tld`, we would make the following aliases:

```
www      CNAME workhorse
project CNAME workhorse

workhorse  A  192.0.2.220
```

The IP address of `workhorse` must also be declared in `httpd.conf` so that we have a reliable address to bind the socket to. The declarations as shown then create two virtual hosts `www` and `project`, each of which has a default data root-directory pointed to by the `DocumentRoot` variable.

9.6.5 The `access.conf` file

This file determines what rights various users will have when trying to access data on the server. It also implicitly determines whether `httpd` will search for `.htaccess` files in directories. Such files can be used to override the settings in the `access.conf` file.

The `Directory` structure works like an access control list, granting or denying access to directories (and implicitly all subdirectories). A good place to start is to make a general structure denying access to directories which are not, later, dealt with explicitly.

```
  # access.conf

AccessFileName .htaccess

<Directory />
 order allow,deny
 deny from all
 AllowOverride None
</Directory>
```

This initializer tells the daemon that it should neither grant rights to arbitrary directories on the disk, nor allow any overriding of access rights by .htaccess files. This simple precaution can yield a performance gain on a web server because the daemon will not search for .htaccess files in every directory from the top of the file tree to the directory mentioned in a Directory structure. This can consume many disk operations which, on a busy server, could waste valuable time. We then need to go through the independent sub-trees of the filesystem which we want to publish.

```
# Don't allow users to make symlinks to files
# they don't own, thus circumventing .htaccess


<Directory /home>
 order allow,deny
 allow from all
 AllowOverride All
 Options Indexes SymLinksIfOwnerMatch
</Directory>
```

In a Directory structure, we express rules which determine how httpd evaluates access rights. The ordering allow followed by deny means that files are allowed unless explicitly denied. The line which follows has the form allow from all, meaning that the data in /home (users' home directories) are open to every caller. The Options directive is quite important. Indexes means that a browser will be able to present a directory listing of .html files which can be accessed, if a user browses a directory which does not contain a standard index.html file. The option SymLinksIfOwnerMatch means that httpd will follow symbolic links only if the user who made the symbolic link is also the owner of the file it points to. The point of the conditional is to make sure that a user can't link to a system directory, such as /etc, and, thus, expose sensitive information to the world. AllowOverride means that we can override access controls for specific directories using .htaccess files (see section 9.6.9).

```
<Directory /local/site/www>
 order allow,deny
 allow from all
 AllowOverride All
 Options Indexes FollowSymLinks
</Directory>
```

In this stanza, things are almost the same. The files under /local/site/www are the site's main web pages. They are available to everyone, and symbolic links are followed regardless of owner. We can afford to be magnanimous here since the site's main pages are controlled by a trusted user (probably us), whom we assume would not deliberately circumvent any security mechanisms. The story is different for ordinary users, whom we do not necessarily have any reason to trust.

```
<Directory /local/site/www/private>
 order allow,deny
 deny from all
 allow from 192.0.2.
 AllowOverride All
 Options Indexes FollowSymLinks
</Directory>
```

In this example, we restrict access to the subdirectory private, to hosts originating from network addresses 192.0.2.x. This is useful for controlling access to certain documents within an organization. Another way of doing this would be to write

```
allow from .domain.tld
```

but we might have a special reason for restricting on the basis of subnets, or network IP series. This kind of access control is a way of making an *intranet* server.

Finally, as an extra check to prevent ordinary (untrusted) users from making symbolic links to the password file, we can add a FilesMatch structure which checks to see whether the actual file pointed to matches a regular expression. In the event of a match, access is denied to everyone.

```
# Don't allow anyone to download a copy of the passwd file
# even by symbolic link

<FilesMatch ".*passwd.*">
order allow,deny
deny from all
</FilesMatch>
```

This is not an absolute security. If local users really want to publish the password file they can simply copy it into an HTML document. However, it does help to close obvious avenues of abuse.

9.6.6 srm.conf **file**

The srm.conf file is the file where we define the remaining behavior of the server in response to requests from clients. The first issue to deal with is that of users' private web pages. These are searched for in a subdirectory of each user's home directory which we must specify. Normally, this is called public_html, or better www or www-data. The UserDir directive is used to set this. Using this directive, it is also possible to say that certain users will not have web pages. The obvious contender here is the administrator account root.

```
# srm.conf

UserDir www
UserDir disabled root

DirectoryIndex index.html
FancyIndexing on
```

The `DirectoryIndex` directive determines the default filename which `httpd` looks for if the URL provided by the client is the name of a directory. Using this arrangement the start home-page for a user becomes:

`~user/www/index.html`

which, using the file scheme */site/host/contents* becomes

`/site/server/home/user/www/index.html`

Next, it is useful to be able to specify the way in which the server responds to errors. The default behavior is to simply send the client a rather dull text string indicating the number and nature of the error. We can alter this by asking the daemon to send a specially customized page, tailored to our own special environment, perhaps with a personal logo etc. The `ErrorDocument` directive is used for this. It traps error numbers and maps them to special pages. For example, to map to a standard local file in the root of the server's pages one would add

```
ErrorDocument 500 /errorpage.html
ErrorDocument 401 /errorpage.html
ErrorDocument 402 /errorpage.html
```

Another possibility is to make a generic CGI script for handling error conditions. An example script is provided in section 9.6.8. In that case, we declare all error-codes to point to the generic CGI-script.

```
# Customizable error response (Apache style)

ErrorDocument 500 /cgi-bin/error.pl
ErrorDocument 404 /cgi-bin/error.pl
ErrorDocument 401 /cgi-bin/error.pl
ErrorDocument 403 /cgi-bin/error.pl
ErrorDocument 407 /cgi-bin/error.pl
```

The final issue to mention about the `srm.conf` file is that of script aliases. In order for `httpd` to allow the execution of a CGI-script on the server, it must be referred to with the help of a `ScriptAlias`. There are two purposes to this. The script alias points to a single directory, usually a directory called `cgi-bin` which lies under the user's own `www` directory. The script alias means that only programs placed in this directory will be executed. This helps to prevent the execution of arbitrary programs which were not intended for web use; it also hides the actual directory structure on the server host. It is necessary to add one script alias entry for each directory that we want to execute CGI-programs from. That usually means at least one directory for each user, plus one for general site scripts. Here are two examples:

```
ScriptAlias /cgi-bin/        /local/site/www/cgi-bin
ScriptAlias /cgi-bin-mark/   /home/mark/www/cgi-bin
```

The script alias is used in all references to the CGI programs. For instance, in an HTML form, we refer to

```
<FORM method="POST" action="/cgi-bin-mark/script.pl">
```

9.6.7 Perl script for generating script aliases

A convenient way of generating script aliases for all users is to write a short Perl script which rewrites the srm.conf file by looking through the password file and adding a ScriptAlias entry for every user. In addition, a general cgi-bin directory is often desirable, where it is possible to place scripts which anyone can use. In the example below we call this alias cgi-bin-public. Each user has a script alias called cgi-bin-*username*.

```perl
#!/local/bin/perl
#
# Build script aliases from password file
#

# Path to the template and real srm.conf files

$srmconf = "/local/httpd/conf/srm.conf";
$srmbase = "/local/httpd/conf/srm.conf.in";

open (OUT,">$srmconf") || die;

open (BASE,"$srm") || die;

  while (<BASE>)     # Copy base file to output
     {
     print OUT $_;
     }

close (BASE);

setpwent();

while (($name,$pw,$uid,$gid,$qu,$com,$full,$dir) = getpwent)
   {
   # SKip system accounts

   next if ($uid < 100);

   print OUT "ScriptAlias /cgi-bin-$name $dir/www/cgi-bin\n";
```

```
    last if ($name eq "");
    }

close OUT;
```

9.6.8 Perl script for handling errors

This Perl script can be used to generate customized or intelligent responses to error conditions.

```perl
#!/local/bin/perl

 #
 # Error handler
 #

# Environment variables set
#
# REDIRECT_STATUS contains the error type
# REDIRECT_URL contains the requested URL
# REDIRECT_REQUEST_METHOD e.g. GET
# REMOTE_ADDR : 192.0.2.238
# HTTP_USER_AGENT : Mozilla/4.05 [en] (X11; I; SunOS 5.6 sun4m)

if ($ENV{"REDIRECT_STATUS"} == 500)
    {
    $color = "#ff0000";
    $error_type = "Server error";
    $error_message = "An error occurred in the configuration of the server.<br>";
    }
elsif ($ENV{"REDIRECT_STATUS"} == 403)
    {
    $color = "#ffff67";
    $error_type = "Access restricted";
    $error_message = "Sorry, that file is not available to you.";
    }
elsif ($ENV{"REDIRECT_STATUS"} == 404)
    {
    $color = "#ffff67";
    $error_type = "File request error";
    $error_message = "The file which you accessed was not found.";
    }
else
    {
    $color = "#ffff67";
    $error_type = "Unknown error";
    $error_message = "Please try again";
    }


#
# Spit out a standard format page
#

print "Content-type: text/html\n\n";
print <<END;

<html>
  <head>
    <title>$error_type</title>
  </head>

  <body bgcolor="#eeeeee">
  <img src="image.gif">

<blockquote>
```

```
<br>
<h1>$error_type</h1>

<br>
<table>
<tr>
<td>
 <table border="0" cellpadding=4>
  <tr><td bgcolor=$color>
  <br>
   $error_message
  <br><br>
</td></tr>
</table>
</td></tr>
</table>
<br><br><br><br>
Make sure that the error is not a mistake on your part. If you continue to have<br>
trouble, please contact the <a href="mailto:webmaster\@domain">Webmaster\@domain</a>.
</blockquote>

<br>

END

print "<br></body></html>";
```

The error codes are in `http_protocol.c` of the Apache distribution.

9.6.9 `mime.types` file

This file tells the server how to respond to file requests containing special data. It consists of a list of protocol names followed by a list of file extensions. Unrecognized files are displayed in a browser as text/ascii files. If we see graphics files (like vrml files) displayed as text, then we need to add a line here to inform the server about the existence of such files. Here is a brief excerpt:

```
video/mpeg                mpeg mpg mpe
video/quicktime           qt mov
video/x-msvideo           avi
video/x-sgi-movie         movie
x-world/x-vrml            wrl
```

9.6.10 Private directories

In some cases we require certain information to be made available to local users of our domain but not to general outside users. This can be accomplished by using a `.htaccess` file to override the default access rights set in the server configuration files. The assumes that we have set `AllowOverride All` in an appropriate `<Directory>` structure.

Creating a directory that is only available from the local domain is a simple matter of creating the directory and creating a `.htaccess` file owned by the 'www' user (i.e. the user running the daemon) with read permission for 'www', containing the lines:

```
order deny,allow
deny from all
allow from   .local.domain
```

9.7 E-mail configuration

Configuration of E-mail is one of the most complex issues for the system administrator, because it involves both nagging policy decisions and technical acrobatics. For many system administrators, the phrase *Nightmares on ELM[2] Street* does not conjure up a vision of Freddie Kruger, but of dark nights spent with E-mail configuration. E-mail is used for so many crucial purposes; it is the de-facto form of communication in a network environment [202, 8, 177, 81, 87].

Why should E-mail be so complex? Part of the trouble is that, in the past, there were many different kinds of network protocol and many different ways of connecting up to different hosts. This made it quite a complex issue to relay messages all over the world. Today things are much simpler: most sites use the Internet protocols and some of the technical aspects of mail configuration can be simplified. Some operating systems provide a program which automatically helps set up E-mail for simple host configurations, but these are no substitute for a carefully considered E-mail system.

In this chapter we shall consider only the popular mail transfer agent `sendmail`. Sendmail changes so often that anything specific written about it is likely to be out of date by the time you read this, so this section will necessarily be of a schematic nature. The source code and documentation for `sendmail` are available from ref. [275]. No matter whether the majority of local users read mail on a PC or on a Unix workstation, every site requires a mail transfer agent like sendmail in order to handle incoming and outgoing transfers.

9.7.1 Models of mail receipt and delivery

E-mail comprises two separate challenges: the delivery of messages and user access to a mailbox. E-mail can be delivered either locally (where the sending host is the same as the destination host) or across a network (where the destination host is different from the sending host). Non-local delivery uses the SMTP (actually ESMTP) mail protocol.

User access to a mailbox uses one of three methods: direct (local) access, POP or IMAP. Regardless of whether local or network delivery is used, E-mail has to end up in a *mailbox system*. For Unix-like operating systems, there are several actual choices:

- *mbox*: (or Berkeley format) This can be used with POP or local access methods.

- *maildir*: (from Qmail) can be used with POP, IMAP or local access.

- *Cyrus*: part of the Cyrus implementation of POP and IMAP.

- *mbx*: (from UWash IMAP) is basically an indexed mbox format as in RFC 822.

- *MH*: (for use with the MH and XMH mailers).

Windows has its own mailbox formats:

- *PST*: MS Outlook

---

[2]ELM is a free mail reader written by an employee of Hewlett Packard which redefined the standard for E-mail interfaces in the 1980s.

- *DBX*: Outlook Express

- *SNM*: Netscape Messenger or Netscape Collabra

- *MBX*: Eudora Mail.

The mailbox formats fall into two categories: those, such as the Berkeley format, that put all messages in a single file, one after the other with 'From' lines to mark the start of a new message, and those, such as maildir or Cyrus, that keep directories of mail with a new file for each message. In the former case, a bad character in a file can confuse mail readers about where one message ends and the next one starts; in the latter case, the addition or removal of a message must be accompanied by the update of index files or else the mailbox becomes corrupted. All mailbox formats are vulnerable to corruption by ad hoc editing, so users and administrators should be discouraged from attempting this.

As soon as a network is involved in E-mail transmission, there are many choices to be made. Some of the basic choices involve deciding a logistic topology for the E-mail service: should we consolidate mail services to one host, or should we deliver mail to every host independently. The consequences of the latter are that users will have different E-mail on every host they have an account on. Usually, users require and desire only one mailbox per institution.

One way to avoid having different E-mail on every host is to share an mbox filesystem between all hosts, using NFS. The Berkeley mail spool system is kept in one of the directories

```
/var/spool/mail
/usr/spool/mail
/var/mail
/usr/mail
```

depending on the flavor of operating system. To do this, we pick a special host which has the physical disk and we force every other host to mount that disk so that users see the same mailbox, independently of which host they happen to be logged onto. This lends itself to a non-distributed solution to E-mail however: if all mail has to end up on one disk, then the host with the disk should get the mail. If independent hosts try to perform local mail delivery to the same NFS-mounted filesystem there can be mailbox corruption due to locking contentions across many hosts. Some sites report that this is not a problem, however it is generally not advisable to use NFS in this way. A centralized solution is preferable. For a discussion of scalable sendmail configurations see ref. [63].

9.7.2 Relaying

Another issue which has attracted focus in recent times is whether or not a site should relay mail from other hosts, and if so which hosts. In order to build a flexible local mail solution, we usually need to relay mail between machines within our local domain. However, relaying of E-mail from other sites has become a security and ethical issue in recent times, with the explosion of mail spamming. Hostile senders often attempt to cover their tracks by relaying E-mail via an intermediate domain. This has led mail exchangers to revise policy on relaying. Whereas mail relaying was allowed by default, it is now generally denied by default. In most cases this is correct and safe behavior; however, some sites, within particularly complex organizations, might find the need to relay E-mail from a limited number of other additional sites.

9.7.3 Consolidated and distributed mail solutions

There are two main models for handling electronic mail at a domain. One is that every host receives mail independently. Since users normally have the same password and account on all of the hosts on a network, this is not usually appropriate.

The second approach is to have a mail 'hub', or central mail processor. In this model, all incoming mail is diverted to the hub and all outgoing mail is sent via the hub. With this approach, we focus all our effort into optimizing E-mail configuration on the hub, and all other machines have a simple configuration which simply collects or forwards mail on to the hub.

In order for mail to be diverted to a hub, we have to arrange for the mail exchanger data in DNS to point to the hub, for every system, i.e. for every host in DNS we should have an MX record accompanying the A record:

```
hostname   A   xxx.yyy.zzx.mmm
           MX  mailhub
```

Without such an MX record, mail which is addressed to

```
user@hostname.domain
```

will be sent directly to hostname. With such a record the mail for hostname is sent to `mailhub` instead. It can later be forwarded to hostname if desired using a mailertable. This has several advantages: first of all it means that mail configuration can be centralized, spam filtering can be performed even for dumb hosts and aliases can be expanded here without the need for a distributed alias database like NIS. The second advantage concerns security. If all mail is forced to pass through this hub then a secure setup here will help prevent SMTP attacks on weaker hosts, thus this simplifies the security administration of mail also. A further precaution is then to configure the site router to accept SMTP traffic only for the mailhub since it is supposed to go there anyway. That way, if one forgets an MX record in DNS there will be no back-doors for would-be attackers.

9.7.4 Compiling and installing sendmail

In this section we shall look only at the mail agent called *sendmail*. Some alternatives to sendmail also now exist, such as `smail`, `exim` and `postfix`.

This section provides only an outline of the installation procedure for sendmail, which has changed considerably in recent years. Information about sendmail and the latest version can be obtained from ref. [275]. After unpacking the distribution, we need to compile it. Sendmail uses BIND and TCP-wrappers libraries; these should be in place. Consider searching for the latest versions of these libraries on the Internet before compiling. BIND is the resolver library. The official place to get BIND is ref. [31]. This also contains a library lib44bsd.a which might be necessary. The latest version of TCP wrappers may be obtained from ref. [311]. Many of the database-lookup features require the Berkeley db package. This is obtainable from ref. [89].

Using the principle of separation, we build sendmail and keep it in a separate directory, along with its attendant files.

```
myhost# mkdir -p /usr/local/mail/bin
```

Then, the simplest installation is found by

```
vger$ tar zxf sendmail.8.12.9.tar.gz
vger$ cd sendmail-8.12.9/
vger$ sh Build
Making all in:
/home/mark/sendmail-8.12.9/libsm
Configuration: pfx=, os=Linux,...
```

The script Build selects the operating system type and compiles the program and places it in a directory that has the form:

```
obj.Linux.2.4.10-4GB.i686
```

where the string after 'obj' represents your kernel version. The built executables are placed here. We can copy these to /usr/local/mail/bin.

Our operating system most likely expects to find the sendmail executable file in either the /usr/lib/ directory, or the /usr/sbin directory on newer systems. We must replace the old executable in these directories by making a link to the new executable. For example:

```
mv /usr/lib/sendmail /usr/lib/sendmail.old
ln -s /usr/local/mail/bin/sendmail /usr/lib/sendmail
```

Make sure that the old file is no longer setuid or setgid, in case it contains any security vulnerabilities.

9.7.5 Configuring sendmail

To finish the installation, we need to create configuration files for our mail domain. Begin by going back to the sendmail distribution and copying the cf directory to the mail directory, like this:

```
cp -r sendmail-x.y.z/cf /usr/local/mail
```

Next make a lib directory.

```
mkdir /usr/local/mail/lib
```

To create a `sendmail.cf` file, we need to create a so-called macro file containing configuration options `/usr/local/mail/lib/domain.mc`. Here is an example file for domain `domain.tld`. We should only need to change the domain name and the OS name of the mailhost in the first three lines. Using this file we will be able to build the sendmail configuration more or less automatically. This example is for sendmail x.y.z for a mail hub:

```
divert(-1)
include('/local/site/mail/cf/m4/cf.m4')

VERSIONID('$Id: mercury.mc,v 1.1 1997/04/08 08:52:28 mroot Exp mroot $')
OSTYPE(solaris2)dnl
DOMAIN(domain.tld)dnl

MASQUERADE_AS(domain.tld)
MASQUERADE_DOMAIN(sub.domain.tld)

FEATURE(use_cw_file)
FEATURE(use_ct_file)
FEATURE(redirect)
FEATURE(relay_entire_domain)
FEATURE(always_add_domain)
FEATURE(allmasquerade)
FEATURE(masquerade_envelope)
FEATURE(domaintable, 'hash -o /local/site/mail/lib/domaintable')
FEATURE(mailertable, 'hash -o /local/site/mail/lib/mailertable')
FEATURE(access_db, 'hash -o /local/site/mail/lib/access_db')
FEATURE(genericstable, 'hash -o /local/site/mail/lib/genericstable')
FEATURE(virtusertable, 'hash -o /local/site/mail/lib/virtusertable')

FEATURE(local_procmail,'/local/bin/procmail')

GENERICS_DOMAIN_FILE(/local/site/mail/lib/sendmail.cG)

EXPOSED_USER(root)

define('ALIAS_FILE', /local/site/mail/lib/aliases)dnl
define('HELP_FILE', /local/site/mail/lib/sendmail.hf)dnl
define('STATUS_FILE', /local/site/mail/etc/sendmail.st)dnl
define('QUEUE_DIR', /var/spool/mqueue)
define('LOCAL_MAILER_CHARSET', iso-8859-1)
define('SMTP_MAIL_CHARSET', iso-8859-1)
define('SMTP_MAIL_MAX','2000000')
define('confMAX_MESSAGE_SIZE', '20000000')
define('confHOST_STATUS_DIRECTORY', '.hoststat')
define('confPRIVACY_FLAGS', 'authwarnings,noexpn,novrfy')
define('confME_TOO', 'True')
define('confMIME_FORMAT_ERRORS', 'False')
define('confTIME_ZONE', 'MET-1METDST')
define('confDEF_CHAR_SET', 'iso-8859-1')
define('confEIGHT_BIT_HANDLING', 'm')
define('confCW_FILE', '/local/site/mail/lib/sendmail.cw')
```

```
define('confCT_FILE', '/local/site/mail/lib/sendmail.ct')
define('confUSERDB_SPEC', '/local/site/mail/lib/userdb.db')
define('LOCAL_SHELL_PATH','/local/site/mail/bin/smrsh')

MAILER(local)
MAILER(smtp)
```

Create a makefile in /usr/local/mail/Makefile

```
MAKEMAP=        bin/makemap
SENDMAIL=       bin/sendmail
PIDFILE=        /var/run/sendmail.pid
MAILTABLE=      lib/mailertable
MCFILE=         lib/domain.mc
SUBMIT=         lib/submit.mc
ALIASES=        lib/aliases
ACCESSDB=       lib/access_db
CF_DIR=         cf/

all: sendmail.cf $(ALIASES).db $(MAILTABLE).db $(ACCESSDB).db .restart

$(ALIASES).db: $(ALIASES)
        $(SENDMAIL) -bi

$(ACCESSDB).db: $(ACCESSDB)
        $(MAKEMAP) hash $(ACCESSDB) < $(ACCESSDB)

$(MAILTABLE).db: $(MAILTABLE)
        $(MAKEMAP) hash $(MAILTABLE) < $(MAILTABLE)

sendmail.cf: $(MCFILE)
        m4 -D_CF_DIR_=$(CF_DIR) cf/m4/cf.m4 $(MCFILE) > sendmail.cf

.restart: sendmail.cf lib/sendmail.cw lib/access_db.db lib/mailertable.db
        kill -1 `head -1 $(PIDFILE)`
        touch .restart
```

Typing make in the /usr/local/mail directory should now result in a configuration file /usr/local/mail/sendmail.cf. Read the next section before doing this.

We will need to create a file lib/sendmail.cw which contains a list of possible machines or domains for which the sendmail program will accept mail. It is, amongst other things, this file which allows us to send mail of the form mark@domain.tld, i.e. to an entire domain, without specifying a particular machine. This file should contain a list of all the valid addresses, like this:

```
domain.tld
mailhost.domain.tld
www.domain.tld
mercury.domain.tld
dax.domain.tld
borg.domain.tld
worf.domain.tld
```

```
daystrom.domain.tld
regula.domain.tld
ferengi.domain.tld
lore.domain.tld
```

Finally, we need to make the files readable for normal users. There is no harm in giving everyone read access to all the files and directories.

9.7.6 Spam and junk mail

Spam or junk mail is E-mail where a message is sent to a large number of recipients. The term 'spam' comes from the Monty Python spam song sketch. Spam mail is most often commercial in nature and unsolicited (and unwanted) by the intended recipient. Spam has become a major problem since it is very easy to send E-mail and very hard to pick out what is useful from what is useless. There are two approaches to the filtering of spam, both of which are needed together:

- Site rules for rejecting mail (ACLs)
- Private user-rules for rejecting mail.

The reason why both of these are needed is that what one user wants to reject, another user might be glad to receive. Users prospecting for financial opportunities or collecting the latest 'artwork' might live for the messages which most of us get annoyed with.

Sendmail has rules for filtering mail at the site level. These include the ability to deny access to connecting mailers from certain domains. At the time of writing they seem to be only partially successful in practice [143].

At the user level, users of procmail can use junkfilter to create their own rules for rejecting spam. Filters for mail transfer agents are also emerging now. Many of these use Bayesian learning and filtering methods. See ref. [246].

9.7.7 Policy decisions

In order to protect our site from E-mail attacks, even ones made in innocence, we might want to restrict mail by other criteria too. For example, multimedia attachments can now allow users to send huge files by E-mail. This is a very inefficient way of sending large amounts of data and it causes problems for mailbox storage space. A possibility is to limit the size of mail messages handled by sendmail so that mail which is too large will be rejected with an error message. For example, the following rules limit E-mail to approximately 20MB. Even with such a large reject size a handful of messages per month are rejected on the basis of this rule.

```
define('SMTP_MAIL_MAX','2000000')
define('confMAX_MESSAGE_SIZE', '20000000')
```

Again, this must be a policy decision like garbage collection of users' files. It is never desirable to restrict the personal freedom of users, but it becomes a matter of survival. If one provides an opening, it will be exploited either through ignorance or malice.

9.7.8   Filtering outgoing mail

An organization might want to prevent certain types of E-mail from being sent. For example, mail generated by CGI-scripts is impossible to trace to a specific user, but is stamped with the domain name of the WWW server which sent it. CGI mail is therefore readily abused, and many institutions would therefore disallow it. If ordinary users are allowed to write their own CGI-scripts, however, this can be a difficult problem to contain. One can *discard* such mail however, with a local rule of the form:

```
HReturn-Path: $>local_ret_path
D{SpamMessage}"553 You are a spammer. Go away."

Slocal_ret_path
R<www>                          $#error $@ $: ${SpamMessage}
```

This is not terribly sociable since no-one will be informed that the mail was discarded.

The Milter (http://www.milter.org) interface now allows filtering of messages by content, e.g. to perform virus scanning.

9.7.9   Mail aliases

One of the first things to locate on a system is the sendmail alias file. This is a file which contains E-mail aliases for users and system services. Common locations for this file are /etc/aliases and /etc/mail/aliases. On some systems, the mail aliases are in the NIS network database.

If this file actually lies in the /etc directory, or some other place amongst the system files, then we should move it to a special area for site-dependent files and make a symbolic link to /etc/aliases instead. Mail aliases are valuable and we want to make sure that nothing happens to them if we reinstall the OS.

The format of the mail aliases file is as follows:

```
# Alias for mailer daemon; returned messages from our MAILER-DAEMON
# should be routed to our local Postmaster.

postmaster: mark,otheruser

MAILER-DAEMON: postmaster

nobody: /dev/null

#
#   alias: list of addresses
#

sysadm:mark@domain.tld,toreo@domain.tld
root:sysadm

#
# Alias for distribution list, members specified elsewhere:
```

```
#   alias: :include: file of names
#

maillist: :include:/mercury/local/maillists

#
# Dump mail to a file
#

archive: /mercury/local/archive/email.archive
```

9.7.10 Changes and updates

Sendmail is changing and developing rapidly. The details above are rudimentary, and you will have to adapt them to the current release of the software. Since this chapter was written, various restructurings have been performed:

1. A new user is required, smmsp, with a corresponding group. Sendmail is now setgid smmsp, not setuid root.

2. The default invocation of sendmail is as a Mail Submitter Program (option '-Ac'). This contacts port 25 on localhost in order to deliver mail. If no contact is established, mail is written to /var/spool/clientmqueue, which is owned by the new user. There is support for several queues.

3. When the daemon starts (option '-bd'), it is run as root and processes the usual queue /var/spool/mqueue.

4. sendmail -Ac -q flushes the MSP queue.

9.8 OpenLDAP directory service

OpenLDAP is the open source implementation of the Lightweight Directory Access Protocol server (DSA) (see section 7.12.2). Installation is straightforward: after unpacking the distribution from www.openldap.org,

```
configure
make depend
make
make test
(su)
make install
```

The configuration file slapd.conf determines the local name space as well as the identity and password protection of the database manager. There is much that can be configured here, related to security and schema extensions. To begin with, it is important to set a password for the database manager. This password has to be encrypted manually and pasted into the configuration file.

The slappasswd command hashes passwords into ascii strings, so that they can be added to the slapd.conf file.

```
/usr/local/sbin/slappasswd
New Password:
Repeat New Password:
SSHAkDPIIA9KR5LVQthcv+zJmzpC+GVYQ4Jj
```

A sample configuration file thus looks like this:

```
# See slapd.conf(5) for details on configuration options.
# This file should NOT be world readable.
#
include         /usr/local/etc/openldap/schema/core.schema
pidfile         /usr/local/var/slapd.pid
argsfile        /usr/local/var/slapd.args

database        bdb
suffix          "dc=iu,dc=hio,dc=no"
rootdn          "cn=Manager,dc=iu,dc=hio,dc=no"

# Cleartext passwords, especially for the rootdn, should
# be avoid.  See slappasswd(8) and slapd.conf(5) for details.
# Use of strong authentication encouraged.

#rootpw         secret
rootpw          SSHAkDPIIA9KR5LVQthcv+zJmzpC+GVYQ4Jj

# The database directory MUST exist prior to running slapd AND
# should only be accessible by the slapd/tools. Mode 700 recommended.

directory       /usr/local/var/openldap-data

# Indices to maintain
index   objectClass     eq
```

Note that the password is checked when adding data to the database. Password credential errors are reported if either the password is incorrect, or the dc components in the suffix are incorrect. Everything in the specification has to be correct. Think of these as username and password.

Starting the server is a confusing business. At the time of writing, the OpenLDAP server did not behave as described by its documentation.

The server can now be started as follows:

```
daneel# /usr/local/libexec/slapd -h "ldap://0.0.0.0"
```

See section 7.12.2 for details about directory configuration and specialist references.

9.9 Mounting NFS disks

The sharing of disks over the network is the province of NFS (Network File System). Unix disks on one host may be accessed across the network by other Unix hosts, or by PCs running PC-NFS. A disk attached physically to a host called a *server* is said to be *mounted* on a client host. In order to maintain a certain level of security, the server must give other hosts permission to mount disks. This is called *exporting* or *sharing* disks.

9.9.1 Server-side exporting

In order to mount a disk on a server we must export the disk to the client (this is done on the server) and we must tell the client to mount the disk. Permission to mount disks is given on the server in a file which is called `/etc/exports` or on recent SVR4 hosts `/etc/dfs/dfstab`. The format for information in these files differs from system to system so one should always begin by looking at the manual page for these files. Here are two examples. The first is from GNU/Linux.

```
# See exports(5) for a description.
# This file contains a list of all dirs exported to other computers.
# It is used by rpc.nfsd and rpc.mountd.

/iu/borg/local daystrom(rw) worf(rw) nanite(rw)  *.domain.tld(ro)
```

In this example, a file system called `/iu/borg/local` is exported read–write explicitly to the client hosts `daystrom`, `worf`, and `nanite`. It is also exported read-only to any host in the domain `domain.tld`. This last feature is not available on most types of Unix.

On some brands of Unix (such as SunOS 4.1.*) one must run a command after editing this file in order to register the changes. The command is `exportfs -a` to export all filesystems. The command `exportfs` alone shows which filesystems are currently exported and to whom.

Our second example is from Solaris (SVR4). The file is called `/etc/dfs/dfstab`. Under Solaris, one can use the `share` command to export filesystems manually from the shell, using a command line of the form

```
share -F nfs -o rw= hostname   filesystem
```

The `/etc/dfs/dfstab` file is in fact a shell script which simply executes such a command for each filesystem of interest. This has several advantages over traditional export files, since one may define variables, as in the example below.

```
#   place share(1M) commands here for automatic execution
#   on entering init state 3.
#
#   share [-F fstype] [ -o options] [-d "<text>"] <pathname> [resource]
#   .e.g,
#   share  -F nfs  -o rw=engineering  -d "home dirs"  /export/home2

hostlist=starfleet:axis:ferengi:borg:worf:daystrom:worf.domain.tld\
:daystrom.domain.tld:nostromo:voyager:aud4:aud4.domain.tld\
:aud1:aud1.domain.tld:aud2:bajor:nostromo:galron:ds9:thistledown\
:rama

share -F nfs -o rw=$hostlist  /iu/mercury/local
share -F nfs -o rw=$hostlist,root=starfleet /iu/mercury/u1
```

```
share -F nfs -o rw=$hostlist,root=starfleet /iu/mercury/u2
share -F nfs -o rw=$hostlist,root=starfleet /iu/mercury/u3
share -F nfs -o rw=$hostlist,root=starfleet /iu/mercury/u4
share -F nfs -o rw=$hostlist /var/mail
```

This script exports the six named filesystems, read–write to the entire list of hosts named in the variable `hostlist`. The command `shareall` runs this script, or it can be run manually by typing `sh /etc/dfs/dfstab`. The command `share` without arguments shows the currently exported filesystems. Notice that the hostname `daystrom` is repeated, once unqualified and again with a fully qualified hostname. This is sometimes necessary in order to make the entry recognized. The mount daemon is not particularly intelligent when it verifies hostnames. Some systems send the fully qualified name to verify and others send the unqualified name. If in doubt, list both like this.

9.9.2 Client-side mounting

Clients may mount any subdirectory of the exported directory onto any local directory by becoming `root` and either executing a shell command of the form

```
mount   server: remote-directory  local-directory
```

or by adding a line to the filesystem table file, usually called `/etc/fstab`. On some brands of Unix, this file has been renamed as `/etc/checklist` or `/etc/filesystems`. On Solaris systems it is called `/etc/vfstab`. The advantage of writing the disks in the filesystem table is that the mount commands will not be lost when we reboot our system. The filesystems in the filesystem table file are mounted automatically when the system is booted. All the file systems in this file are mounted with the simple command `mount -a`.

We begin by looking at the manual page on the appropriate file for the system, or better still looking at examples which are already in the file. The form of a typical filesystem table is as below.[3]

```
/dev/sda2                   swap             swap   rw,bg  1   1
/dev/sda1                   /                ext2   rw,bg  1   1
/dev/sda3                   /iu/borg/local   ext2   rw,bg  1   1
mercury:/iu/mercury/u1      /iu/mercury/u1       nfs    rw,bg
mercury:/iu/mercury/u2      /iu/mercury/u2       nfs    rw,bg
mercury:/iu/mercury/u3      /iu/mercury/u3       nfs    rw,bg
mercury:/iu/mercury/local   /iu/mercury/local nfs    rw,bg
```

This example is from GNU/Linux. Notice the left-hand column. These are disks which are to be mounted. The first disks which begin with `/dev` are local disks, physically attached to the host concerned. Those which begin with a hostname followed by a colon (in this case host `mercury`) are NFS filesystems which lie physically on the named host. The second column in this table is the name of a directory on which the disk or remote filesystem is to be mounted – i.e. where the files are to appear in the local host's file-tree. The remaining columns are

---

[3]On older HPUX systems, there is a bug which causes mysterious numbers to appear in the `/etc/checklists` file. These have no meaning.

options and filesystem types: rw means mount for read and write access, bg means 'background' which tells mount to continue trying to mount a filesystem in the background if it fails on a first attempt.

Editing the /etc/fstab (or equivalent) file is a process which can be automated very nicely with the help of the system administration tool cfengine. We shall discuss this in the next chapter.

9.9.3 Trouble-shooting NFS

If you get a message telling you 'Permission denied' when you try to mount a remote filesystem, you may like to check the following:

- Did you remember to add the name of the client to the export or dfstab file on the server?

- Some systems require a fully qualified hostname (i.e. hostname with domain-name appended) in the export file. Try using this.

- Did you mis-spell the name of the client or the server?

- Are the correct network daemons running which support nfs? On the server side, you must be running mountd or rpc.mountd. This is an authentication daemon. The actual transfer of data is performed by nfsd or rpc.nfsd. On older systems there should be at least four of these daemons running to handle multiple requests. Modern systems use a multi-threaded version of the program, so that only one daemon is required.

  On the client side, some systems use the block input/output daemon to make transfers more efficient. This is not strictly necessary to get NFS working. This daemon is called biod on older systems and nfsiod on newer systems like FreeBSD. Solaris no longer makes use of this daemon, its activities are now integrated into a kernel thread.

- The portmapper (portmap or rpcbind) is a strange creature. On some Unix-like systems, particularly GNU/Linux, the portmapper requires an entry in the TCP wrapper file /etc/hosts.allow in order for it to accept connections. Otherwise, you might see the error

  ```
  RPC service not registered.
  ```

  The portmapper requires numerical IP addresses in the TCP wrapper configuration. Host names will not do, for security reasons (see section 9.4.5).

- The exports file on GNU/Linux hosts is also somewhat unusual. If you are using a non-standard netmask, it is necessary to tell the mount daemon:

  ```
  # /etc/exports: the access control list for filesystems
  # which may be exported to NFS clients.  See exports(5).

  /site/cube/local *.college.edu/255.255.255.0(rw)
  /site/cube/local 192.0.2./255.255.255.0(rw)
  ```

9.10 Samba

Samba is a free software solution to the problem of making Unix filesystems available to Windows operating systems. Windows NT uses a system of network file sharing based on their own SMB (Server message block) protocol. Samba is a Unix daemon-based service which makes Unix disks visible to Windows NT. Samba maps usernames, so to use Samba we need an account with the same name on the NT server and on the Unix server. It maps usernames textually, without much security. Samba configuration is in Unix style, by editing the text-file /etc/smb.conf. Here is an example file. Note carefully the 'hosts allow' line which restricts access to disks to specific IP addresses, like TCP wrappers.

```
[global]
  printing = bsd
  printcap name = /etc/printcap
  load printers = yes
  guest account = nobody
  invalid users = root
  workgroup = UNIX
  hosts allow = 128.39.

[homes]
  comment = Home Directories
  browseable = no
  read only = no
  create mode = 0644

[printers]
  comment = All Printers
  browseable = no
  path = /tmp
  printable = yes
  public = no
  writable = no
  create mode = 0644
```

Once the Samba server is active, the disks are available for use with the net use command, e.g.

```
C:\> net use F: \\host\directory
```

This example maps the named directory on the named host to NT drive letter F:. The reverse problem of mounting NT filesystems on a Unix host works only for GNU/Linux hosts at present:

```
gnulinux% smbmount //nthost/directory /mountpoint -U administrator
```

9.11 The printer service

Printing services vary from single printers coupled to private workstations to huge consolidated spooling services serving large organizations [329, 251].

Host print services need to be told about available printers by registering the printers in a local database. In BSD-like print servers this database is kept in a flat file called /etc/printcap. In System V print servers, a program called lpadmin is used to register printers and it's anyone's guess what happens to that information.

The way in which we register printers thus depends on

- What kind of operating system we are using

- Whether we are running any special network printer software.

The main difference is between BSD-like systems and System V. Recently a replacement print service was introduced for a generic heterogeneous network. Called LPRng, this package preserves the simplicity of the BSD system while providing superior functionality to both [243]. Another alternative is the Common Unix Printing System (CUPS).

In order to register a printer with a BSD-like printer service, we do the following:

- Think of a name for the printer.

- Decide whether it is going to be connected directly to a host or stand alone on the network.

- Register the printer with the printing system so that the daemons which provide the print service know how to talk to it. This can include manually making a 'spool' directory for its queue files. This normally lies under var/spool or /usr/spool.

  mkdir /var/spool/ printer-name

- Most Unix systems assume the existence of a *default* printer which is referred to by the name 'lp'. If you do not specify a particular printer when printing, your data are sent to the default printer. It is up to us to name or alias one of our printers 'lp'. Each printer may have several names or aliases.

With some print spoolers, we also need to decide whether to send all data to a common central server, or whether to let each host handle its own negotiations for printing. If we are interested in maintaining a record of how many pages each user has printed, then a centralized solution is a much simpler option. The downside of this is that, if there is a large user base, the traffic might present a considerable load for one host. A central print spooler must have sufficient disk space to temporarily store all the incoming print jobs.

9.11.1 CUPS/LPRng

The Common Unix Print System (CUPS) has emerged in the last few years as the favored printing solution on many desktops. It reads information from traditional Unix format files.

LPRng is a rival attempt that is configured quite simply in a manner very similar to (but not identical to) the old Berkeley printcap system.

> **Suggestion 12 (Unix printing).** *Install LPRng on all hosts in the network. Forget about trying to understand and manage the native printing systems on system V and BSD hosts. LPRng can replace them all with a system which is at least as good. Another alternative system is the Common Unix Printing System.*[a]
>
> ---
> [a]The author's experience with CUPs is that it is not yet a robust alternative.

If one follows this suggestion there is only a single printer system to worry about. Note that most GNU/Linux distributions (e.g. Debian) have packages for this system, so it will not need to be installed from scratch.

The software uses a printcap file and two other optional files called `lpd.conf` and `lpd.perms`. The printcap file is like a regular printcap file but without the backslash continuation characters. LPRng provides effectively both `lpr`, `lpd`, `lpq` and `lprm` commands from Berkeley and `lp`, `lpstat` and `cancel` commands from System V. The daemon reads the three configuration files and handles spooling. The configuration is challenging but straightforward and there is extensive documentation. Here is a simple example for a network printer (with its own IP address) which allows logged on users to start and delete their own printjobs:

```
# /etc/printcap (lprng)

myprinter|lp
     :if=/local/bin/lpf                # LF/CR filter
     :af=/var/spool/lpd/acctfil
     :lf=/var/spool/lpd/printlog
     :sd=/var/spool/myprinter
     :lp=xxx.yyy.zzz.mmm%9100
     :rw
     :sh
```

The IP address of the printer is *xxx.yyy.zzz.mmm* and it must be written in numerical form. The percent symbol marks the standard port 9100. The `lpd.conf` file is slightly mysterious but has a number of useful options. Most, if not all, of these can be set in the printcap file also, but options set here apply for all printers. One nice feature for instance is the ability to reject printouts of binary (non-printable) files. This can save a few rain forests if someone is kind enough to dump `/bin/ls` to the printer.

```
#
# lpd.conf
#

# Purpose: name of accounting file (see also la, ar)
af=/var/spool/lpd/acctfil

# Purpose: accounting at start (see also af, la, ar)
```

```
as=jobstart $H $n $P $k $b $t

# Purpose: check for nonprintable file
check_for_nonprintable

# Purpose: default printer
default_printer=local

# Purpose: error log file (servers, filters and prefilters)
lf=/var/adm/printlog

# Purpose: lpd lock file
lockfile=/var/spool/lpd/lpd.lock.%h

# Purpose: lpd log file
logfile=/var/spool/lpd/lpd.log.%h

# Purpose: /etc/printcap files
printcap_path=/etc/printcap

# Purpose: suppress headers and/or banner page
sh
```

The lpd.perms file sets limits on who can access the printers and from where, unlike the traditional services which are open to everyone.

```
#
# lpd.perms
#
# allow root on server to control jobs
ACCEPT SERVICE=C SERVER REMOTEUSER=root
# allow anybody to get status
ACCEPT SERVICE=S
# reject all others, including lpc commands permitted by user_lpc
REJECT SERVICE=CSU
#
# allow same user on originating host to remove a job
ACCEPT SERVICE=M SAMEHOST SAMEUSER
# allow root on server to remove a job
ACCEPT SERVICE=M SERVER REMOTEUSER=root
REJECT SERVICE=M
# All other operations disallowed
DEFAULT REJECT      # orACCEPT
```

LPRng claims to support Berkeley printcap files directly. However, in trials its behavior has been quirky, with some things working and others not. In any event, LPRng is a highly welcome piece of software which works supremely well, once configured.

9.11.2 Environment variable PRINTER

The BSD print command and some application programs read the environment variable PRINTER to determine which printer destination to send data to. The System V print command lp does not.

9.11.3 BSD print queue

- lpr -p *printer* file Send file to named print queue.

- lpq Show the printer queue for the default printer, or the printer specified in the environment variable PRINTER if this is set. This lists the queue-ids.

- lprm *queue-id* Remove a job from the print queue. Get the queue-id using lpq.

- lpd Start the print service. (Must be killed to stop again.)

- lpc An old and unreliable interface to the print service.

9.11.4 SysV print queue

- lp -d *printer file* Send a file to the named print queue.

- lpstat -o all Show the printer queue for the default printer. This lists the queue-ids.

- lpstat -a Tells lies about when the print service was started.

- lpsched Start the print service.

- lpshut Stop the print service.

- cancel *queue-id* Remove a job from the print queue. Get the queue-id using lpstat.

The Solaris operating system used to have an optional printing system called Newsprint in addition to the SVR4 printing commands.

9.12 Java web and enterprise services

Java services are becoming increasingly important in the world of the network. The most important services are those connected to the Web, but any Java program can, in principle, make use of Java services. Java Server Pages (JSP) are Java's dynamical web page framework. Accompanying this are Java Servlets (the server counterpart of Applets) that house JSP-based services, mediated by the Web on port 80 or 8080. Java servlets are applications, based on the standard Java libraries and a class/object approach to services, in which services are objects called by object invocation.

The naming service attaches objects to services and routes requests to dependent services, such as databases to the correct host and port number. Enterprise Beans are essentially wrappers that provide transaction locking and security of data transfer for Java services that employ them. They are the 'heavyweight' side of Java services and are mediated by an enterprise application server.

Java has a close relationship with XML, and the configuration files that configure Java software and services are generally written in this eclectic framework. In spite of what XML followers would have us believe, XML was designed to be parsed by machines, not humans, and some of the XML configuration files one finds strain the credibility of their claims.

Java services require the Java Runtime Environment in order to work. Java virtual machines are provided by several sources, including Sun Microsystems, IBM, Microsoft and others, so there is no single recipe for making Java work. However, the basic Java compiler and virtual machine have to be installed and working in order for the related services to work.

9.12.1 Java development kit

As an example, we consider the Java Development Kit from Sun Microsystems. It is collected as an archive from the net. Once installed in some location, e.g. /usr/local, it lives in a directory that needs to be pointed to by the environment variable JAVA_HOME. Java's libraries are called classes and they have a library path analogous to LD_LIBRARY_PATH. For example,

```
JAVA_HOME=/local/jdk1.3.1
CLASSPATH=/usr/local/mm.mysql.jdbc-1.2c: \
/usr/lib/jdk1.3.1/lib/classes.zip: \
/usr/local/iu/JSDK2.0/lib/jsdk.jar: \
/usr/local/jserv/lib/ApacheJServ.jar:.
```

Once these variables have been set, the compiler javac and runtime environment java can be tested with the following test-program:

```
// File has same name as class, i.e. JavaTest.java

public class JavaTest
   {
   // An application class must include a ''main'' method

   public static void main ( String args[] )
      {
      System.out.println("This is a compiler test program\n");
      }
   }
```

This program is compiled and run as follows:

```
host% /usr/lib/jdk1.3/bin/javac JavaTest.java

host% /usr/lib/jdk1.3/bin/java JavaTest
This is a compiler test program
```

9.12.2 Web containers: Jserv and Tomcat

A Java 'web container' is an executable environment for Java Server Pages (JSP). Java Server Pages are Java program elements that are embedded into HTML pages, in order to create dynamic content. These are stripped out and compiled on the fly as mini-servers or 'servlets', Java programs linked to HTML pages, allowing dynamic content in HTML pages, with 'custom tag'-technology. Tomcat is the reference Java example of such a container; another example container is Jserv.

Tomcat can be used 'stand-alone' or as a module for an Apache web server. The connection between Tomcat and Apache is managed by an Apache Dynamic Share Object (DSO).

The Tomcat server goes by the name of CATALINA and it has environment variables that correspond to the Java variables:

```
CATALINA_HOME=/usr/local/jakarta-tomcat
CATALINA_TMPDIR=/var/run/tomcat
```

Installing Tomcat is simply a matter of unpacking it under /usr/local, for instance, and starting the server. A non-privileged tomcat user should be created:

```
host% cd /usr/local/jakarta-tomcat/bin/
host% ./startup.sh
```

or on Windows:

```
host% ./startup.bat
```

Somewhat inconveniently, executable code for servlets is placed under the distribution itself:

```
host% ls webapps/examples/
total 4
drwxr-xr-x    4 root      root          1024 Feb 21  2002 WEB-INF
drwxr-xr-x    2 root      root          1024 Feb 21  2002 images
drwxr-xr-x   17 root      root          1024 Feb 21  2002 jsp
drwxr-xr-x    2 root      root          1024 Feb 21  2002 servlets
host% v webapps/examples/WEB-INF/
total 11
drwxr-xr-x   14 root      root          1024 Feb 21  2002 classes
drwxr-xr-x    3 root      root          1024 Feb 21  2002 jsp
-rw-r--r--    1 root      root          8767 Feb 12  2002 web.xml
```

The example structure must be reproduced for any additional startup-pages or users. Tomcat needs writable temporary workspace in its distribution, so file permissions need to be set like this when running in non-privileged mode:

```
drwxr-xr-x    2 root      root          1024 Feb 21  2002 bin
drwxr-xr-x    2 root      root          1024 Feb 12  2002 classes
drwxr-xr-x    4 root      root          1024 Feb 12  2002 common
drwxr-xr-x    2 root      root          1024 Apr 23 18:31 conf
```

```
drwxr-xr-x      2 root        root          1024 Feb 21   2002 lib
drwxr-xr-x      2 tomcat      root          6144 Aug 22 18:09 logs
drwxr-xr-x      4 root        root          1024 Feb 12   2002 server
drwxr-xr-x      7 root        root          1024 Apr 23 19:11 webapps
drwxrwxrwt      3 tomcat      root          1024 Feb 21 21:06 work
```

Here is an example cfengine script to manage some of these issues: The server needs to be restarted regularly, to notice updates.

```
#
# A configuration for tomcat -
# to be run on port 8080 (conf/server.xml)
# servlet server runs as user "tomcat"
#
# to call up:
#
# http://host.example.org:8080/mark/servlet/HelloWorldExample
#
# (note no s in servlets!!!)
#
# Server config is in conf/server.xml (careful here!)
#

control:

# editfilesize = ( 90000 )

# actionsequence = ( files links processes )

 catalina_base = ( /local/jakarta-tomcat-4.0.2 )

####################################################################

files:

 $(catalina_base)       mode=644   ignore=bin   r=inf action=fixall
 $(catalina_base)/bin   mode=755   ignore=bin   r=inf action=fixall
 $(catalina_base)/logs  mode=644   owner=tomcat r=inf action=fixall
 $(catalina_base)/work  mode=1777  owner=tomcat       action=fixall

 #
 #  For now copy -r webapps/examples to ~user/servlets
 #  to get started, and then link that area below
 #  to webapps/user
 #

####################################################################

links:

 $(catalina_base)/webapps/mark -> /iu/nexus/ud/mark/servlets
# $(catalina_base)/webapps/frodes -> /iu/nexus/uc/frodes/servlets
```

```
# $(catalina_base)/webapps/paulsep -> /iu/cube/u1/paulsep/servlets
# $(catalina_base)/webapps/gjertsa -> /iu/cube/u1/gjertsa/servlets
# $(catalina_base)/webapps/pettern -> /iu/cube/u1/pettern/servlets
# $(catalina_base)/webapps/leskovk -> /iu/cube/u1/leskovk/servlets

 $(catalina_base)/webapps/timeplan -> /iu/cube/local/iu/IUservlets
 $(catalina_base)/webapps/24 -> /var/www/hovedprosjekter/2002/data/24


# $(catalina_base)/webapps/haugerud -> /iu/nexus/ud/haugerud/servlets
# $(catalina_base)/webapps/sigmunds -> /iu/nexus/ud/sigmunds/servlets
# $(catalina_base)/webapps/kjetilg -> /iu/nexus/ub/kjetilg/servlets
# $(catalina_base)/webapps/ulfu -> /iu/nexus/ua/ulfu/servlets
# $(catalina_base)/webapps/geirs -> /iu/nexus/ub/geirs/servlets


####################################################################

processes:

"jakarta-tomcat-4"
    restart "$(catalina_base)/bin/startup.sh"
    owner=tomcat

####################################################################

editfiles:

# Edit the server.xml file and add a line for each user
#
#   <Context path="/mark" docBase="mark" debug="0"/>


 ignore_for_now::

 $(catalina_base)/conf/server.xml

# ReplaceAll "8080" With "9090" to change port

ReplaceAll "/manager" With "XXX-dangerous-no-manager-XXX"
ReplaceAll "privileged=$(dblquote)true$(dblquote)"
With "privileged=$(dblquote)false$(dblquote)"


####################################################################

shellcommands:

 Hr12.OnTheHour::

 "$(catalina_base)/bin/shutdown.sh > /dev/null 2>&1"
```

9.12.3 Enterprise Java Beans

JBoss, Websphere and Weblogic are examples of Enterprise Java Beans (EJB) containers, an execution environment for EJB. JBoss has attracted a lot of attention since it not only is free software, but also has a very simple deployment mechanism that avoids the need for extra XML configuration to be supplied. Once archived into a 'jar' file, the bean can be deployed simply, by placing it into the deployment directory. This contrasts with commercial rivals that need extra XML files and specialized tools for deploying software.

Some additional configuration is needed to couple the server to a database backend. Connection to a PostgreSQL database, for instance, takes place through Java Data Base Connectivity (JDBC). The basics of this are provided by a Java Archive ('jar' file) distributed with the PostgreSQL Database Management Software.

Dynamical HTML/JSP content first contacts a servlet in order to access methods written in Java. Servlets, employing Enterprise Beans, contact the Bean Container (e.g. JBoss) for code and service. The connection between Tomcat and JBoss takes the form of an EJB Client connecting to an EJB Server. Tomcat and JBoss can thus be separate and several Tomcat installations can feed into several JBoss installations. This allows the scheme to scale, by load-distribution, to the limitations of hardware and the database manager. In the default configuration available from JBoss web pages, however, both Tomcat and JBoss reside on the same machine with a single connection.

EJB Clients need to find a number of Java archive ('jar') files containing classes to allow them to function. They need to find the Java Class files which define the interface between Client and Server too. This is accomplished by placing them somewhere in the CLASSPATH environment.

The Tomcat based EJB Clients also need Java Naming and Directory Interface (JNDI) information to allow them to connect to their Servers. This is accomplished by having a properties file (jndi.properties) somewhere within CLASSPATH. The contents of this file specify a local address (e.g. localhost) for the JNDI service.

Installation of JBoss is simplicity itself. Assuming that the service will run as a non-privileged user jboss:

```
cd /usr/local
tar zxf jboss-3.0.tar.gz

ln -s /usr/local/jboss-3.0 /usr/local/jboss

/bin/su -s /bin/sh jboss --command="whoami"

/bin/su -s /bin/sh jboss --command="sh /usr/local/jboss/bin/run.sh"
```

The server can be tested by using a web browser to access the portals:

```
http://host.example.org:8080
http://host.example.org:8082
```

9.12.4   Multi-user deployment

The Tomcat servlet environment is set up to provide only for a single user. The presumed model is a production environment with a single web server per company – not a college environment, with many students, for example. Thus, on a multi-user system where every user has their own servlets and JSP files, it is awkward to allow them to add and delete servlets without causing problems for one another. A single error seems to be able to cause the whole server to fail inexplicably.

However, it is possible to coax the server to look in more than one location for servlet and JSP files, so it is, in principle, possible to create a directory for every user with the necessary environment; although an error by one user can easily affect all the others; also the server must be frequently restarted to register errors.

To the configuration file $CATALINA_HOME/conf/server.xml, we must add an additional document base, one for each user. These are analogous to the 'examples' area described above, and provided by the Tomcat distribution.

```
<Context path="/mark" docBase="mark" debug="0" reloadable="true" />
<Context path="/frode" docBase="frode" debug="0" reloadable="true" />
```

and then link the directory

```
mark -> ~mark/servlets/
frode -> ~frode/servlets/
```

The whole webapps directory structure of Tomcat must then be reproduced under each user's servlet directory.

An example applet is then referred to, for instance, as:

```
http://host.example.org:8080/mark/servlet/HelloWorldExample
```

Exercises

Self-test objectives

1. What is a network application service?

2. What is an application server?

3. What is an application proxy?

4. What issues are involved in installing a new service on Linux?

5. What issues are involved in installing a new service on Windows?

6. What role does inetd play for application services?

7. What is TCP wrappers? How is it used?

8. Create a checklist for setting up a nameserver.

9. Create a checklist for setting up a web server.

10. Explain the principle of using a private user ID for each application service.

11. What is a privileged port?

Problems

1. Compare the Berkeley mailbox format with the IMAP mailbox format. Discuss the advantages and disadvantages of each.

2. Set up an Apache web server.

3. Build a tree of documents, where some files are public and others are restricted to access by your local organization, using the .htaccess file capability.

4. Show that a CGI-script can always be written which reveals all of the files restricted using .htaccess. This shows that untrusted CGI-scripts are a security risk.

5. Write a Perl script for handling WWW errors at your site.

6. Estimate the number of megabytes transferred per week by the file-servers at your domain. Could any of this traffic be avoided by reorganizing the network?

7. Where are the default nameservers placed around your network? Is there a nameserver on each subnet, i.e. does DNS lookup traffic have to pass through a router?

8. Set up TCP wrappers on your system (Unix-like OSs only).

9. Install the Java Development kit from Sun Microsystems. Compile the test program above, and then install Tomcat. Test the example servlets and JSP pages using a web browser to access port 8080.

10. Delete the Tomcat distribution in the previous exercise and collect the JBoss–Tomcat combined distribution from www.jboss.org. Install this, and check that it is working by using a web-browser to access the main web pages at ports 8080 and 8082.

11. Discuss the role of Java and .NET services in consolidating network application services in the future. What is the difference between multiple services over many IP ports, and having multiple services brokered over a single port? Think of security, reliability and ease of management in your answer.

12. Java's reliance on XML for configuration information is typical of a trend in current practice. Discuss the advantages and disadvantages of XML for configuration information.

Chapter 10

Network-level services

Networks are usually presented as an invention of the post Second World War cold war climate, but the first wired communication networks were built by the Victorians in the 1800s. Sir Francis Ronald was the first person to appreciate the need for telegraphic communication. In the first publication on the subject in 1823, he proposed a method for locating faults on a telegraph line. W.F. Cooke and Charles Wheatstone, professor of Physics at King's College, London produced their first telegraph patent in June 1837 and tested it over the mile-long line between two London railway stations. Samuel Finley Breese Morse had the idea for electrical communication in 1832 but did not produce a working telegraph in the United States until 1836 [66].

The first attempt to lay an underwater cable was begun in 1850, when a steam tug drew a single copper wire from Dover out across the ocean to Cap Gris-Nez. Unfortunately after only a day the cable broke around the French coast. Politics and rivalry intervened until it was left to Lord Kelvin (William Thomson) to show how low-power signals could be transmitted effectively over huge distances. Many failures were encountered before finally, on the 27th of July 1866, the steamboat *Great Eastern* delivered a cable from England's Valentia Bay to Heart's Content in North America. On the first day of operation the cable earned one thousand pounds. This was the birth of Internet commerce.

10.1 The Internet

One of the false myths about the Internet was that it was developed by the American military as a communications system that could survive a nuclear attack. In 1964, a researcher at the RAND corporation, Paul Baran, wrote a paper describing how different network topologies would be robust to failure (see chapter 8). This included many ideas that would eventually be incorporated into current networking technologies, but the idea was not taken up. Later, the American Department of Defence's Advanced Research Project Agency (DARPA) began a project to find ways of gaining access to expensive computing machinery remotely; the cost of duplicating computing services, at the time, was insurmountable so the logical solution was to find a way of accessing the services remotely.

The invention of packet switching was key in allowing networks to share bandwidth between multiple computers. The strength of the Internet Protocol was in being able to integrate many existing technologies for point to point connections (like X.25) that were deployed in Europe. Unix was instrumental in the spread of the Internet Protocol suite (nowadays referred to as TCP/IP). The fact that the Internet has developed into many of the things that Baran foresaw is a testament to his foresight, rather than a feat of planning. Internet development has meandered through differing technologies, driven by commercial forces such as telecom companies and standardizing bodies such as the IETF.

10.2   A recap of networking concepts

Here is a summary of what we assume understood at the beginning of this chapter:

- Computers communicate by sending electrical or optical signals over wires or fibers.

- Short cables can only 'hold' one bit at a time. A bit floods a cable or fiber like signaling Morse code with a torch, and has a physical size normally equal to the fundamental wavelength of the binary signal. The signal spreads through the medium in all directions at anything up to the speed of light in the medium.

- Each computer has a hardware interface at layer 1 of the OSI model.

- Each interface has a Media Access Control (MAC) address at layer 2, e.g. an Ethernet address such as 00:90:27:A2:47:7B.

- All hosts connected to the same cable see all the signals passing through it, but messages are framed using a protocol that incorporates a MAC address, and only the host with the correct MAC address normally bothers to read a message with its address. (A computer that listens to all traffic is said to be in promiscuous mode.)

- MAC addresses are 'flat'; they have no structure, so the only way to find a host with a given MAC address is to either direct the message over a dedicated path, or send a message to every computer and wait for the right one to respond. This is impractical in large networks, so we need another layer of addressing: layer 3.

- A message sent to *one* computer from another is called a *unicast*.

- A message sent from one computer to all computers on a Local Area Network (LAN) is called a *broadcast*.

- When multiple cables are joined together as part of an Internetwork, they must be joined by a *router*. If the cables are part of the same logical IP network, they are joined by a *switch* (or a bridge, which is an old name for a primitive switch).

10.3 Getting traffic to its destination

How do data get 'here' from 'there' and from 'there' to 'here'? This is a complex question that flirts with a number of quite independent issues, making its answer seem often unnecessarily opaque. We shall try to approach the answer in a number of stages. Two particular problems lie at the heart of getting traffic to its destination:

1. Directing packets to their proper destination.

2. Scheduling packets for transmission over a shared channel.

These two, obviously independent, issues become entwined because the hardware and software that deal with delivery are also forced to deal with the sharing. System administrators are barraged with technical specifications and explanations of these issues when purchasing and installing network infrastructure. A basic understanding of the issues is important.

10.3.1 Multiplexing

As with many problems in computing, we begin with resource sharing. Cable technologies have in-built limitations: only one user can send data at a time, so we use a form of packet switching. A contiguous Ethernet, for instance, can only span a distance of, at most, 5000m with a minimum packet size of 64 bytes. This value is normally halved to 2500m to allow a wide margin for error (see section 10.4.3). If these limits are exceeded, the expected collision rate leads to thrashing of the scheduling algorithm and network gridlock.

Even if it were possible, it would never be practical to build such a network covering the world: with hosts broadcasting to every other machine in order to find one another, the number of collisions would be enormous – why should a host in Norway be prevented from using the network by a host in the United States, or vice versa? Clearly, one must devise a way of structuring the flow of traffic to avoid unnecessary contention.

This can be done by packet switching. Switching uses essentially two strategies to form multiple channels from a single resource:

- *Time Division Multiplexing*: interleaving packets in time-slots (scheduling).

- *Wave Division Multiplexing*: choosing different wavelengths or frequencies to encode signals. This is sometimes referred to as Lambda (λ) Switching in fiber optic networks.

10.3.2 From bridges to switches

Directing traffic in a Local Area Network (LAN) is simple. In older Ethernet networks, cables were simply spliced by hubs, and occasionally broken up by bridges that would stop traffic from crossing a boundary unless it needed to. Today, bridges and hubs have been combined into star-topology LAN switches (figure 10.1).

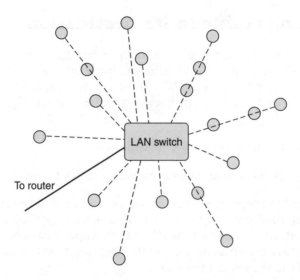

Figure 10.1: A LAN switch normally offers a separate channel to each host on the LAN, though it is still possible for a few hosts to share a channel using a cable splitter or hub. Traffic is switched from channel to channel and hosts that do not need to see it, do not see it. Switching is fast and efficient. The switch prevents a router from being exposed to LAN 'chit-chat'.

LAN switches are very successful in passing traffic from one host to another without creating unnecessary contention elsewhere in the network.

LAN switching is straightforward, but to cover a large area it is not enough to tap into a single cable, we must also have crossroads and intersections (see figure 10.2). At each junction, a decision has to be made about which way traffic will be forwarded. We thus have to multiplex not only single cables, but junctions. This traffic flow control at junctions is exactly what happens in a star topology, but what happens when two stars are connected?

Can packets now find their way to their destination? Can this model scale to any number of hosts? It can scale to some extent, but not indefinitely: the limitations of Ethernet prevent us from growing Ethernet indefinitely, but even with a better link layer, a flat address space would be extremely inefficient. One must therefore place something in between Ethernets that can span larger distances: Wide Area Networks (WAN). This now involves the IP address of hosts in a more important way, and we need a new kind of hardware: a router.

The terms *switch* and *router* are becoming increasingly mixed up as technologies evolve. These two devices seem to perform similar tasks, but at different layers of the puzzle.

- A *switch* is a device that forwards packets according to a forwarding table using MAC addresses of the interfaces that it is connected to as an index. Switching is so simple that it can be completely hardwired, if necessary, so it is quite efficient to switch packets. This lack of intelligence has a price however: a switch needs help in order to build a forwarding table – i.e. to

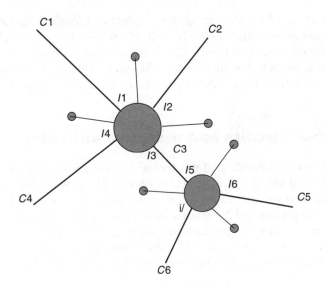

Figure 10.2: Junctions of cables are required to create a non-trivial network topology. The blobs represent 'forwarding agents' or switches that can receive data from a cable $C1\ldots C6$ attached to an incoming interface $I1\ldots I7$ and pass it to a different cable attached to a different interface. This is how traffic can be passed around a network with junctions.

find out how it can reach a particular computer MAC address along one of its interfaces. In some cases, this task is very simple: simple Ethernet star-formation networks attach each computer to a single interface of a switch, so it is easy to build a table of associations. Other technologies, such as ATM, Frame Relay and MPLS (see section 10.5) are less easily defined than this: they do not work in the same way as Ethernet, and they allow more complicated switching over wide areas, through several switches, but they help in order to assemble the information in their forwarding tables. This help can be manually added by a system administrator, or it can be automated by linking the layer 2 switching to a layer 3 routing algorithm. In the latter case, some manufacturers are starting to talk about 'layer 3 switches'.

- A *router* is a specialized computer, running on software, that probes and determines the global topology of the network and decides how to forward packets. It can replace, supplement or assist a switch in forwarding packets. In order to succeed at this, a router needs to understand OSI layer 3, or the IP layer, and sometimes has occasion to examine levels 4–7 in making decisions. The IP layer is based on an address structure that is hierarchical and can therefore be navigated automatically.

Confusion arises between routing and switching when one begins to discuss the methods and algorithms for forwarding packets. A router matches hierarchical IP address prefixes (layer 3) in order to determine the right forwarding path. A switch uses layer 2 addresses in a flat table for forward packets. Today, the market uses expressions like 'layer 3 switch' to talk about hybrid devices that optimize tasks by caching the information from a layer 3 router in the forwarding table of a layer 2 switch for improved efficiency. However, fully-blown routers perform functions other than forwarding, such as access control and filtering of packets.

10.3.3   Virtual circuits and wide area switching

In Wide Area Networks (WAN), and moderately sized areas, often called Metropolitan Area Networks (MAN), it is possible to direct traffic by switching alone. Although Ethernet is limited in its coverage, other transport technologies like Frame Relay and ATM can be transported by fibers over larger areas. Frame Relay and ATM lie somewhere in the gray area between layer 2 and layer 3 of the OSI Model, because they can be forwarded by switching alone using *virtual circuits*. (They do not 'need' the IP layer to get traffic from here to there, but they draw assistance from it.)

Virtual circuits have their origin in telephony and come in two forms: Permanent Virtual Circuits (PVC) and Switched Virtual Circuits (SVC). They are predetermined routes through a number of switches (see figure 10.3). The distinction refers to the way the circuits are administered. A permanent circuit is set up by an administrator for long-term usage; it is not expected to be rerouted. A switched circuit is established automatically by 'signaling'; this requires the assistance of a protocol that understands the topology of the network, such as IP routing.

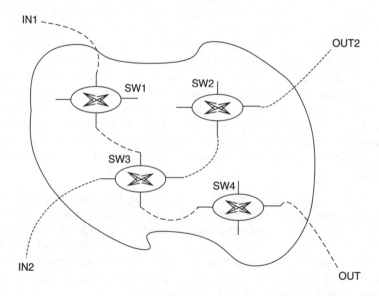

Figure 10.3: An assembly of switches, connected by semi-permanent internal wiring (not shown), can be used to establish virtual circuits (dotted lines). In simple regions, this can be managed manually, or with assistance from routing protocols. Each separate virtual circuit can be switched using simple labels, without having to bother with level 3 IP addresses.

Labels, or virtual circuit identifiers, are used by the switches to forward traffic along dedicated multiplexed channels. This technology is widely used in backbone networks, where routing is simple, but speed is of the essence. These interlinked switches are often represented as a 'network cloud' at the IP layer, concealing the details of transport that doesn't entirely fit the IP model.

10.4 Alternative network transport technologies

10.4.1 Medium sharing

There are two main strategies for sharing media.

- *Deterministic sharing*: every host is given a predictable chance to send data at a basic minimum rate, e.g. token rings. This concept is easy to predict and sell, and so has often been adopted in commercial technologies.

- *Non-deterministic sharing*: any host has only a finite chance of being able to send a message – there is no minimum rate, e.g. Ethernet. This method uses the assumption that most LANs are only lightly loaded, so that the probability of transmission is usually high.

These are reflected in the prevalent technologies and each has its usage. Being somewhat simplistic, one might say that well below capacity non-deterministic sharing is the most efficient way of sharing available resources, but as we approach saturation it fails badly and a deterministic approach is required. This is simply because it is easy to share when everyone has plenty; but when competition for resources gets tough, some kind of enforcement of sharing is required.

10.4.2 Token rings

There are several kinds of token rings, including the now defunct Fiber Distributed Data Interface (FDDI). Token ring LANs are widely used in IBM networks. The basic idea is that all hosts are arranged in a ring and that packets circulate uni-directionally around the ring. In order to avoid collisions, a control packet (called the token) is circulated around the ring and a host can only begin transmitting if it has received the token. The host can then transmit for a maximum amount of time and it must then pass on the token to the next host. As data are transmitted, all hosts look to see if the packets were intended for them, i.e. anyone can receive all of the time.

10.4.3 Ethernet

Ethernet technology was developed by Xerox, Intel and DEC in 1976, at the Palo Alto Research Center (PARC) [103]. In the Ethernet bus approach, every host is connected to a common cable or bus. Ethernet naturally supports broadcasting, since all hosts share the same channel, but it also means that packets can collide and must contend for transmission over each cable segment. This is called

CSMA/CD, or Carrier Sense Multiple Access/Collision Detect. A collision occurs when two hosts attempt to send signals simultaneously.

The naming convention for Ethernet is:

- 10Base-T = 10 Mbps, over two twisted-pair cables.

- 100Base-T2 = 100 Mbps, over two twisted-pair cables.

- 100Base-T4 = 100 Mbps, over four-twisted pair cables.

- 1000Base-LX/FX/SX = 1000 Mbps, long wavelength over optical fiber cable.

The latter is nicknamed Gigabit Ethernet.

Ethernet *collisions* occur when two hosts try to send data at the same time. To give all hosts an equal opportunity to use the shared line, there is a Maximum Transmission Unit (MTU) or Ethernet frame size of 1500 bytes, which limits the time that a host can use the line.

Before sending a frame, the interface checks to see if its receiver sees any existing transmission, if so it waits until the coast is clear. As the speed (bit rate) of Ethernet transmission increases and LANs grow in size, the finiteness of the speed of light becomes noticeable and it is increasingly likely for two hosts to start sending at the same time, at different parts of a cable, before detecting each others' signal. When this occurs, there is a 'collision' and a burst of noise is transmitted to inform all hosts of a collision: both hosts must stop and retry after a short wait.

- An interface can only detect a collision while it is transmitting itself, so we must be careful to prevent the sending of packets that are too short. (If incoming power is greater than outgoing power, there must be a collision.)

- Each bit is encoded by a single wavelenth λ of electromagnetic waves in Ethernet's Manchester bit-encoding. If packets are long enough then they *must* fill up the physical size of the cable, because the combined wavelength $N\lambda$ is larger than the cable size. Thus hosts will not be able to avoid seeing one another's transmissions at some time during the transmission. We should therefore use a minimum packet size to be certain of detecting all collisions.

Suppose we have a cable segment of length L. The worst case scenario is when two hosts A and B at opposite ends of the cable start transmitting, just as the signal arrives from A to B. In order to detect a collision, a signal must then have travelled a distance of L to the collision point, and then the noise burst must travel back the same distance to be detected by A, before the message finished transmitting. Thus:

$$N\lambda \geq 2L$$

or in terms of bit-rate (frequency) f,

$$Nc_{\text{copper}} \geq 2fL,$$

where c_{copper} is the speed of light in copper or fiber, which are both of the order 2×10^8 meters per second. The left-hand side is the distance occupied by N bits, or wavelengths of the bit signal, and the right-hand side is the distance of the round-trip. There are two variables to fix N or L. The Ethernet standard chooses to fix the minimum size of frames to be 512 bits (64 bytes), giving a maximum length of about 5000 meters for 10Mbs Ethernet; this is usually halved to 2500 meters to allow a wide margin for error. Any small data payloads are padded out with zeros. At gigabit speeds, even larger MTUs are required to extend the length limits of the cables; even so, they cannot be very long.

Other limits on the size of Ethernet segments come from the physical properties of cables, i.e. signal attenuation. The Ethernet standard allows for a maximum of four repeaters (amplifiers), so the average length of each segment above can be divided by the number of repeaters needed to get the signal across this maximum length.

10.4.4 Digital Subscriber Line (DSL)

DSL includes variations such as ADSL, RADSL, SDSL, HDSL, VDSL, and is a family of multiplexing transmission methods that uses the existing telecommunications infrastructure. Asymmetric DSL (ADSL) is asymmetric in that it has a higher download capacity than upload capacity. This is an arbitrary decision, derived from observed usage. SDSL is a symmetric version of this. RADSL is a Rate Adaptive DSL that adds some prioritization to traffic types.

DSL technologies employ improved transceiver technology to transmit data more efficiently over copper wires. They are sometimes referred to as last-mile technologies because they are used only for connections from a telephone exchange or cable television operator to the end user. They are not routable. DSL can transmit at rates limited only by the physical properties of the cable, whereas telephone modem channels are restricted by the bandwidth of filters designed to give a clear voice signal.

10.4.5 Integrated Services Digital Network (ISDN)

This is an international communications standard for sending voice, video and data over digital telephone lines or normal telephone wires. ISDN allows multiple devices to share a single line and supports data transfer rates of 64 Kbps and has never really taken off. ISDN was more widely deployed in Europe, but has quickly lost ground to cable and telephone DSL solutions.

10.4.6 Fiber: SONET/SDH

After the break up of AT&T, the newly formed Bellcore began to work on the Synchronous Optical Network (SONET). Later the International Telecommunications Union (ITU) joined the effort and renamed the standards slightly, calling the standard not SONET but the Synchronous Digital Hierarchy (SDH). In SDH-speak STM-n is a SONET optical carrier OC-$3n$ or Synchronous Transport Signal STS-$3n$ for the electrical (copper) version.

STS-1 / OC-1	–	51.84 Mbps
STS-3 / OC-3	STM-1	155.52 Mbps
STS-12 /OC-12	STM-4	622.08 Mbps

10.4.7   T1 and E1

The old U.S. designations for high speed telephone lines include T1 - 1.544 Mbps, T3 - 44.736 Mbps. Corresponding European standards are called E1, E3 etc. These lines are copper wire cables that can be used with various protocols, including ISDN and DSL. They are usually leased lines, owned by telecom companies.

10.5   Alternative network connection technologies

We have focused mainly on the Ethernet so far, because it is the most widely deployed networking technology (apart from the telephone system). A number of other technologies are in widespread use and warrant a brief description, if only for cultural or historical reasons.

10.5.1   X.25

X.25 is a nickname for a layered packet switching technology that was widely used in the 1970s and 1980s. In OSI layer 1, the physical layer, it employs several standards such as V.35, RS232 and X.21. At layer 2 it uses an implementation of the ISO HDLC standard called Link Access Procedure Balanced (LAPB) and provides error correction between two connected devices. Layer 3 is referred to as the X.25 Packet Layer Protocol (PLP) and is primarily concerned with network routing functions and the multiplexing of simultaneous logical connections over a single physical connection. X.25 offers virtual circuits. Today it has been replaced by lighter weight protocols such as Frame Relay.

10.5.2   Frame Relay

Frame Relay was designed in the 1980s and deployed in the 1990s as a second generation X.25. Like X.25 and ATM, it uses the idea of virtual circuits. Frame relay was designed for transmission over media with much lower error rates than before. Frame Relay implements a virtual circuit without flow control or error recovery. If errors are detected in a Frame Relay packet, the packet must simply be dropped. Frame Relay offers a rudimentary Quality of Service functionality.

10.5.3   Asynchronous Transfer Mode (ATM)

ATM is a technology introduced in the 1980s and embraced by the telephone companies as a way of creating a network infrastructure that resembled existing telephone infrastructure. It was thought that ATM might one day replace both telephony and computer networking in a single integrated solution. ATM was originally envisaged as a competitor to the TCP/IP that would work both at LAN and WAN scales, however it has lost out to IP in LANs due mainly to IP's ability to work across a variety of technologies. It was assumed that ATM would run over SONET, but this is not a necessity.

ATM offers Quality of Service (QoS), that enables it to offer guaranteed bandwidth to customers.

Rather than speaking of 'packets', ATM speaks of 'cells'. Cells have a fixed size, which makes multiplexing them extremely easy. In the 1980s this was seen as a great advantage over rival link layers such as Ethernet, since it allowed much higher speeds to be achieved. ATM is a hybrid of layer 2 and layer 3 technology. In order to 'route' ATM packets over a complex network of junctions, a 'virtual circuit' must be established. This is either routed 'by hand', i.e. programmed by an administrator, or established with the aid of routing protocol. In other words, ATM needs help in order to route traffic. In this respect it is like frame relay.

ATM is a switched technology – it does not support broadcast in the normal sense, however it has a LAN emulation mode (LANE) which admits the use of ATM for local networking; this has not received wide acceptance. ATM allows bandwidth allocation and Quality of Service (QoS) guarantees. ATM transmits only fixed-size frames, called cells, not variable-sized frames as with frame relay and packet switching. The standard for ATM cell relay is 53 byte cells. Frame relay will probably be used in the future as an inter-operable access protocol to higher speed ATM networks. Thus, frame relay and ATM are likely to be complementary rather than competitive technologies in the future.

10.6 IP routing and forwarding

Packet switches forward data from one cable to another, thus securing routes for end to end communication. There are two processes at work here:

- *Routing*: is the process of discovering network topology and selecting a viable path from one place to another.

- *Forwarding*: is what a packet switch does at each junction of a packet's journey: it is the selection of the next hop towards a final destination, based on the best available route (see figure 10.4). Forwarding is sometimes performed in hardware and sometimes in software.

With virtual circuits and purely layer 2 technology, forwarding tables have to be built up by hand. Above a certain level of complexity, however, it becomes impractical to manage the routes through a network by programming forwarding tables by hand. Global networks have a highly non-trivial structure that cannot be managed without computational assistance. Routing protocols are designed to provide this assistance, by 'signaling' between switches. Signaling is a process which requires a protocol that can discover network topology and program software-programmable switches with the necessary information to construct and

```
foreach interface attached to router
  {
  if (destination-network == interface-address)
    {
    Deliver packet to interface
    }
  else
    {
    foreach network in forwarding table
      {
      if (destination-network == network)
        {
        Deliver packet to neighbor router
        }
      else
        {
        Deliver packet to default route
        }
      }
    }
  }
```

Figure 10.4: A simplified, schematic forwarding algorithm, given a table of information about the structure of the network and the immediate neighbors. To take into account subnetting and CIDR masks, we must interpret the equals '==' sign to include a logical AND between the network and its mask.

maintain forwarding tables. The Internet Protocol family was designed for this purpose. It uses a routable packet format in which:

1. Every IP datagram contains the IP address of its destination host, and can thus be routed independently.

2. Each IP address contains a network part that identifies a unique destination network, somewhere on the Internet.

3. Every network is connected to the Internet by a router.

This arrangement leads to a fairly simple hierarchy that is, in principle, sufficient to send traffic to any destination. The datagram forwarding algorithm used by routers is straightforward, and uses a lookup table, called a *forwarding table*. The forwarding table lists network addresses and interfaces over which to send the packet, either to reach the next hop router or the final host (see figure 10.4).

Protocols that set up forwarding tables include Open Shortest Path First (OSPF) and the Routing Information Protocol (RIP) to name but two examples. Unfortunately, these protocols do not scale very well to very large numbers of networks, so they are only used within limited regions called *areas*, or groups of areas called *Autonomous Systems*.[1] Between such areas, a different system of forwarding is used. This is a deliberate strategy that has several benefits.

- The task of finding detailed routes can be delegated to small autonomous areas, which behave as closed containers with privacy policies. This is called *interior routing*.

- The task of locating the correct autonomous area can be handled separately, using an aggregate label for all of the networks within the container. This is called *exterior routing*.

- Another advantage of the container model is that, by assigning local route autonomy, one can build private networks. Today, this allows a business model for the Internet, in which passage through someone else's autonomous region can be charged for or otherwise made into a contractual agreement.

How do we progress from creating such a simple local algorithm to directing traffic over the entire globe? The answer to this lies in the hierarchy of the network structure. When a router does not know where to send a packet, it sends it to a generic *default route*: this normally takes the search up a level of the hierarchy to a router that knows about more subordinate networks.[2] The very top level routers (between Autonomous Systems) know implicitly about all of the networks on the Internet. This idea assumes that the network is a strict hierarchy, but it is only approximately a hierarchy. A suitable generalization of a tree structure is to form a top level super-network mesh, that connects multiple parallel tree/mesh structures (see figure 10.5).

Thus, rather than dealing with one huge mesh, there is a forcible break-up into routing domains, or Autonomous Systems.

> **Definition 7 (Autonomous System).** *An Autonomous System is an aggregate of networks that belongs to a single political entity on the net; often, it represents a large organization, such as an Internet Service Provider or company. The networks within an Autonomous System share a common external routing policy. More importantly for the scalability of the Internet, Autonomous Systems are black-box containers, somewhat analogous to file-directories that hide detail from the top-level view of locating networks within containers. They allow separation of responsibility for what happens inside from what happens in between. Each AS has a label or AS number. Inside an AS, traffic flows freely along optimal paths, without regard for politics. Between Autonomous Systems, the politics of organizations decide which routes are allowed to pass through neighboring ASs.*

To cope with the scaling issues, this extra hierarchical structure has been added to the Internet. The Autonomous System structure allows *aggregation* of networks

---

[1]The nomenclature of network region units is confused. Strictly speaking, only OSPF speaks of areas, and only BGP defines true autonomous systems. However, Cisco OSPF refers to autonomous systems as groups of related areas. We use these terms in their intended spirit, but loosely.

[2]This is like typing cd ... when one is navigating a file system. If we do not know the location of a file, it makes sense to just go up a level to get a better overview.

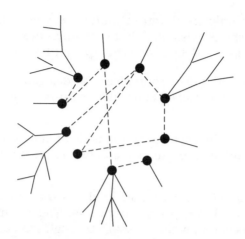

Figure 10.5: A simplified view of the approximately two-level hierarchy of the Internet. If we arrange the Autonomous Systems in a circle, we see a spatial distinction between the lower level network (radiating from the center) and the interconnections between the tops of each 'tree'. The dark spots represent the Border Gateways or top-level routers in these Autonomous Systems. Traffic that crosses from one AS to another is passed along these 'exterior routes' (dashed lines). The BGP protocol acts as a directory service for locating networks in the Autonomous Systems, somewhat like finding files in directories. Once traffic arrives at the correct AS, it is up to the local AS to get the packets to their destination through the low-level network. Note that few low-level networks are really tree-like, but they are often approximately so, somewhat like a file system with extra symbolic links.

into families that are referred to by collective labels or prefixes, thus reducing the number of forwarding table entries that have to be placed in top-level routers.

10.6.1 Static routing

We have already considered static routing in section 2.7.5, in connection with setting up a host in a LAN. Since most LANs are connected by only a single router, it suffices to delegate the task of 'getting there from here' to that router. One does this by sending all traffic to the default location: the LAN router. This is just a single entry in a routing table. On Unix-like systems this table looks something like this:

```
Routing Table: IPv4
   Destination              Gateway              Flags   Ref    Use    Interface
-------------------    -------------------    -----   -----  ------   ---------
128.39.89.0            128.39.89.4               U      1       8     le0
224.0.0.0             128.39.89.4               U      1       0     le0
default               128.39.89.1               UG     1      67
127.0.0.1             127.0.0.1                 UH     1       0     lo0

Routing Table: IPv6
   Destination/Mask         Gateway                      Flags Ref Use    If
-------------------    ------------------------    ----- --- ---  -----
2001:700:700:3::/64    2001:700:700:3:a00:20ff:fe85:bb11 U 1    0 le0:1
```

```
fe80::/10           fe80::a00:20ff:fe85:bb11    U      1    0 le0
ff00::/8            fe80::a00:20ff:fe85:bb11    U      1    0 le0
default             fe80::2a0:c9ff:fe28:2489    UG     1    0 le0
::1                 ::1                         UH     1    9 lo0
```

It is a list of interfaces, and networks that can be reached from them. The table contains a default route for 'all other traffic'. One can easily extend this idea over a larger network, and configure routes manually by knowing all of the interfaces and networks available to them. This would be a huge job, however, prone to error.

10.6.2 Source routing

Source routing is like creating a Permanent Virtual Circuit. The source host must have knowledge of all the network hardware and its topology. It then specifies the exact route that a packet must take through the network. In other words, the path through the network is predetermined. Normally, this is not the case: changing topology and errors mean that one cannot guarantee the same route, so adaptive routing is used, in which routes are not fixed at the outset; packets are sent by the best available route at the time, hop by hop.

10.6.3 Routing protocols

Automated, adaptive routing protocols fall into two classes:

- *Distance Vector (DV) algorithms*: e.g. RIP or (E)IGRP. These use the Bellman–Ford shortest path algorithm, which is approximately as follows: each router begins by announcing its own beliefs about network topology. As it receives messages from other neighboring routers, it revises this belief and re-announces. A cost or *metric* is assigned to reaching a particular network from each router. The cost is usually the number of hops required to reach the destination, so a network attached to a neighboring router would have a hop-count of 1 from its origin. The algorithm then reasons: if router A is one hop away from router B, who believes that it is 4 hops away from network X, then A must be 5 hops away from network X. As all of the messages are sent and resent, the numbers get adjusted and the path costs (metrics) stabilize. A router then picks the cheapest available route to forward packets to a given destination.

  A metric of 'infinity' (an arbitrary large number) is used to indicate no available route. If some routers go down, or metrics suddenly increase, the updating algorithm can become confused and distant routers do not receive correct information. It is possible then for *routing loops* to occur, in which a packet is sent one way, as a result of new data about the shortest path, only to be sent back again as a result of old data about the shortest path. Packets can ping-pong back and forth, and routing table updates count slowly upward to 'infinity' before things right themselves. Distance vector algorithms send route announcements every 30 seconds or so, between adjacent pairs, so counting to infinity can take a long time.

The computational complexity of the distance vector algorithm's convergence is of order LN where L is the number of links or adjacencies and $N \sim L$ is the number of nodes. This is quite expensive for large N.

- *Link State (LS) algorithms*: e.g. OSPF. These use the Dijkstra shortest path algorithm. Link state algorithms attempt to construct a map of an entire network area, by sending messages of the form: 'router A is adjacent to router B and the link is up', which allows the construction of an adjacency matrix representing the network. Routers then send their information to all their neighbors, who – in turn – pass on the information to others, only if it is new. Link state algorithms are less 'chatty' because they send only differential information (updates), not a complete copy of everything each time. Each router creates a link state packet (LSP) containing the ID of the router node, a list of directly connected neighbors and a link cost for each one, a sequence number and a time to live. Sequence numbers ensure updates take precedence, and node ID ensures that a copy is not flooded back to the original sender in a loop. Once a complete map is known, a router can compute the shortest path from the adjacency matrix. The link state algorithm scales like $L \log L$ for L links, which is significantly better than the distance vector scaling of L^2; thus for large networks, it has a bright future.

RIP

RIP (versions 1 and 2) is a distance vector routing protocol that is still found in some networks, but its largely considered to be obsolete. RIP sends UDP packets containing routing updates based on hop-count to neighbors. RIP was made popular by its inclusion as part of Unix (in the `routed` daemon). The RIP protocol has various limitations on size: the maximum hop count is only 15, so it can only be used in small networks.

OSPF

The Open Shortest Path First (OSPF) was originally developed to defend the idea of distributed routing from those who believed that centralized management was the answer to routing. OSFP is designed to work within an Autonomous System, i.e. it is an *Interior Routing Protocol*. OSPF attempts to scale by introducing its own layers or hierarchy called *areas*. Area 0 is normally an organizational backbone, running an efficient point-to-point protocol, such as Frame Relay. Other areas are connected to this backbone by Area Border Routers (ABR), and the backbone of the Autonomous System is connected to others by an Autonomous System Border Router (ASBR) running BGP.

IS-IS

The Intermediate System to Intermediate System (IS-IS) protocol was designed in competition with OSPF in order to implement the OSI model for routing. It has similar functionality to OSFP and is also a link state protocol. Although OSPF is more widely implemented, IS-IS has its share of followers. One of the criticisms of IS-IS is that it was developed to politicize adherence to the OSI routing model, while being somewhat removed from the real needs and wishes of users. IS-IS was early in having support for IPv6.

BGP

The Border Gateway Protocol (BGP) is an *Exterior Routing Protocol*, designed to route top-level traffic between Autonomous Systems (sometimes called Routing Domains). BGP is neither a Distance Vector nor a Link State protocol in the normal sense. Instead it may be called a *Path Vector Protocol*, since it stores not only hop metrics but entire pathways through Autonomous System maps. In a sense, it automatically performs source routing. This is to account for policy decisions: who says that just anyone should be able to send traffic over just any Autonomous System? BGP tries to find the best route, only after finding an 'authorized route'.

BGP's support for Classless InterDomain Routing (CIDR) has made it possible to rescue IPv4 from an early demise during the 1990s. Top-level routers need to know paths to all networks, the table of network numbers must be stored on each inter-domain router. Storing and parsing this table places great demands on these backbone routers.

BGP works over TCP, which makes it predictable, but this has also led to routing problems associated with traffic congestion.

> **Principle 53 (Routing policy).** *At the level of Autonomous Systems, policy (access controls) plays the major role in determining routes; efficiency is of secondary importance. Lower down within each AS, routes are calculated based on availability and distance metrics.*

In a real sense, BGP is not a routing protocol at all, but a directory service, telling top-level routers in which general direction they must send packets in order to get closer to their final destination; i.e. it is a database of hints. A BGP route cannot be guaranteed to be true. The assumptions on which it is built are that the underlying transport routing will be correctly performed by something like OSPF or IS-IS, and that no policies will change as packets are following their suggested routes. BGP tells a packet: I cannot send you to your destination, but if you go to this Autonomous System, they should be able to help you.

Note, however, that Autonomous Systems are literally autonomous: they can decide not to cooperate with their neighbors, at their own option. BGP is literally peer-to-peer cooperation. The consistency of global routing mechanisms depends entirely on trusting neighbors to play their part and keep responsible policy practices. A simple misconfiguration of BGP could lead to widespread routing confusion.

10.7 Multi-Protocol Label Switching (MPLS)

The argument over IP or ATM has condensed down to an effort to combine the best of both worlds. Multi-Protocol Label Switching (MPLS) is a hybrid layer 2–3 technology that uses IP to guide switched technologies of all kinds. It is about the separation of control and forwarding mechanisms.

Layer 2 switches provide high-speed connectivity, while the IP routers at the edge – interconnected by a mesh of layer 2 virtual circuits – provide the intelligence to forward IP datagrams. The difficulty with this approach lies in the complexity of mapping between two distinct architectures that require the definition and maintenance of separate topologies, address spaces, routing protocols, signaling protocols and resource allocation schemes. The emergence of the multilayer switching solutions and MPLS is part of the evolution of the Internet to decrease complexity by combining layer 2 switching and layer 3 routing into a fully integrated solution.

Another goal of MPLS is to integrate Quality of Service (QoS) functionality into IP. ATM has QoS functionality, but IP has no true support for this. Today the best one can do is to simulate long-term average Quality of Service (see section 10.8).

The forwarding component of virtually all multilayer switching solutions and MPLS is based on a label-swapping forwarding algorithm. This is the same algorithm used to forward data in ATM and Frame Relay switches; it is based on signaling and label distribution. A label is a short, fixed-length value carried in the packet's header to identify a Forwarding Equivalence Class (FEC). A label is analogous to a Virtual Circuit Identifier, but an FEC also distinguishes between differentiated services, analogous to IP service port numbers.

An FEC is a set of packets that is forwarded over the same path through a network even if their ultimate destinations are different. For example, in conventional longest-match IP routing, the set of unicast packets whose destination addresses map to a given IP address prefix is an example of an FEC.

10.8   Quality of Service

The commercialization of the network has seen the arrival of Internet Service Providers (ISP), Application Service Providers (ASP), Web Hotels, outsourcing and hosting companies. The desire to sell these services to other organizations and companies has placed deliverability at center stage. Customers will not pay for a service that they cannot be certain will be delivered; there are many ways in which one might choose to deal with this challenge:

- A cheaper price for living with uncertainty – but this might not be acceptable.

- A planned over-capacity to guarantee a level of service – but this might be considered wasteful.

- Precision technology that can deliver and regulate exactly what is needed – but this requires investment in infrastructure.

Sorting out the details of a solution to these issues is the job of a Service Level Agreement (SLA) between the service provider and the service client (see section 10.10). Clearly, technology is at the heart of this; one cannot promise what cannot be delivered.

There are many levels at which one can discuss 'service'. In the most general case, one can simply talk about quality assurance of an entire business process, but the expression Quality of Service in networking terms generally refers to *delivery rate assurance* and *value for money*. Traditionally one has referred to networked services as the *application-level services* of the previous chapter, because the network was not for sale – it simply existed as a non-commercial service to academia and the military. Today, the connectivity itself is being sold and it must be included in the list of services that companies want to buy or charge for. Service providers are thus interested in being able to sell connectivity with bandwidth guarantees. Different kinds of applications require different levels of lower level service guarantees. For instance, voice and video traffic are time critical and data intensive, whereas Web traffic and E-mail are not. All quality of service guarantees rely on the basic transport guarantee; thus Quality of Service must be defined *bottom up* in terms of the OSI-layers.

Today, some are discussing QoS (Quality of Service), QoD (Quality of Devices), QoE (Quality of Experience), QoB (Quality of Business), and any number of variations of the issue of service provision. Each of these is trying to capture the essence of a usable measure that can be sold like 'kilos of sugar' to customers, and be used to gauge a provider's own performance. So how does one define Quality of Service more rigorously? It has been suggested that it must be a function of 'Quality of Devices'.

$$QoS = f(QoD) \tag{10.1}$$

This is clearly sensible, from the laws of causality; the higher OSI levels can make demands for service but if the lower levels are not willing, they will not be successful. What kind of function should this be? Is it linear, non-linear, stochastic, chaotic? Some principles for Quality of Service for management are discussed in ref. [255]. This discussion is based on ref. [51].

The basic Internet protocol family (TCP/IP) has no provision for securing quality of service guarantees at the protocol level; a limited form of quality of service can be simulated at the router level by prioritizing packet delivery. To do this, a router must open up packets and look at the higher OSI layers 4–7. This incurs an additional cost that adds to the delivery time:

```
Total = Latency + Transport Round-Time + Query-Response Processing
```

Other transport agents, like Frame Relay, ATM and MPLS, on the other hand, are designed with Quality of Service in mind. These, however, are rarely deployed end to end for the normal user, so some compromise is required.

When one speaks of Quality of Service in networking, one really means Quality of Service *Rate*, i.e. timing guarantees, but this poses an important question: over what time scale can quality assurance be provided? Data rates are never constant; at some level, one will begin to see the graininess of traffic and see variations in the amount of data delivered per second. It is only the average rate, over several seconds, minutes or hours that can be regulated and thus be predicted. Thus the issue of quality of service is one of what the time scale is over which guarantees are required.

Principle 54 (Rate guarantees). *The maximum rate at which any service can be provided is limited by the weakest link in the chain of communication (see principle 49). The variability of the rate is limited by random errors at the shortest time scale Δt of any component in the chain. In a steady state service, the average rate, over a time $T \gg \Delta t$ is:*

$$\langle R \rangle = \frac{1}{T} \int_0^T R(t)dt, \tag{10.2}$$

where $dt = \Delta t$ in practice. If one assumes that the average transmission rate is constant, up to a variable amount of random noise, one may write

$$R(t) = \langle R(t) \rangle + \delta R(t), \tag{10.3}$$

where $\delta R(t)$ is a random source with time granularity Δt, then the variability over time T is

$$\Delta R(T) = \sqrt{\frac{1}{T} \int_0^T (R(t) - \langle R \rangle)^2 dt}. \tag{10.4}$$

If the system is in a steady state (not a state of growth or decay), then this tends towards a small constant value (approximately zero) as $T \gg \Delta t$.

Thus, the longer the time scale over which a rate guarantee is defined, the less control is needed through technology, and the smaller the overhead to manage it; i.e. $\Delta t/T \to 0$ is the goal of devices (small packet size or granularity).

Example 9. *A service guarantee of 10MB per day is entirely believable for UUCP (a modem, dial-up protocol), but a rate of 10MB per minute is not. A rate of 350 kilobits per second is reasonable for a Digital Subscriber Line (DSL) service provider, but a rate of 3 kilobits per hundredth of a second is not.*

This agrees with intuition. Indeed, ATM uses small fixed cell sizes; MPLS allows variable packet sizes, with a fine granularity.

It is important to note the difference between determinism (i.e. explicit control over information) and predictability. Quality of Service demands predictability over a given time scale, but this does not imply deterministic behavior along the way.

Principle 55 (Predictability vs determinism). *Predictability always has limits or tolerances. Predictability does not imply precise determinism, but determinism provides predictability. Predictability requires only a deterministic average behavior.*

Example 10. *The Ethernet is a non-deterministic protocol, but within a reasonable margin for error, it is possible to calculate the average data rate, on a time scale of minutes, that is fairly constant. Thus the Ethernet can be predictable, without requiring deterministic control.*

Diffserv is a way of defining routing policy for *differentiated services* (see RFC 2475), i.e. of setting priorities on routed packets. Since the router is performing packet forwarding regulation, the average packet size along the journey is the limit of granularity for Quality Assurance. RSVP is a QoS signaling service, proposed by the Internet Engineering Task Force (IETF), that is used by hosts to signal resource requests. These must be negotiated between hosts and routers between end points.

10.8.1 Uncertainty

The term *service guarantee* seems to imply determinism of service mechanisms, but this need not be the case. All we require is predictability over an appropriate time scale.

It is important to understand that service is about changes occurring in time, and thus time is an essential element of any service-level agreement. If we focus on shorter and shorter intervals of time, it becomes impossible to guarantee what will happen. It is only over longer intervals that we can say, on average, what has been the level of service and what is likely to be the level of service in the future. We must therefore specify the *time scale* on which we shall measure service levels.

Example 11. *A Service Level Agreement for UUCP network connectivity could agree to transfer up to 10 MB of data per day. This is an easy goal, by modern standards, and it hardly seems worth including any margin for error in this. On the other hand, a Digital Subscription Line (DSL) network provider might offer a guaranteed rate of 350 kbps (kilobits per second). This is a common level of service at the time of writing. But what are the margins for error now? If each customer has a private network telephone line, we might think that there is no uncertainty here, but this would be wrong. There might be noise on the line, causing a reduction in error-free transmission rate. When the signal reaches the Service Provider's switching center, customers are suddenly expected to share common resources, and this sharing must maintain the guarantees. It now becomes realistic to assess the margin for error in the figure 350 kbps, since resources are tighter.*

Example 12. *A University Professor can agree to grade 10 examination papers per day. It is not clear that the level of interruptions and other duties will not make this goal unreasonable. The level of uncertainty is much higher than in a mechanistic network switch. We might estimate it to be 10 ± 3 exam papers per day. In this case, the Professor should include this margin for error in the contract of service.*

Uncertainty is an important concern in discussing Quality of Service.

Uncertainty is calculated using the 'theory of errors'. This assumes that errors or uncertainties occur at random, according to a Gaussian profile, about some true value. The Gaussian assumption basically ensures that errors are small or do not grow to an arbitrarily large size, compared with the rate of change of the average. Whether or not a phenomenon really has a Gaussian profile or not, error handling techniques can be used to estimate uncertainties provided there is a suitable separation of time scales.

Example 13. *Consider the rate of arrival of data R, in bytes, from the viewpoint of a network switch or router. The measurables are typically the packet size P and the number of packets per second r. These are independent quantities, with independent* *uncertainties: packet sizes are distributed according to network protocol and traffic types, whereas packet rates are dictated by router/switch performance and queue lengths. The total rate is expressed as:*

$$\lambda = r P. \tag{10.5}$$

Using the method of combining independent uncertainties, we write:

$$\lambda = \langle \lambda \rangle + \Delta \lambda$$
$$r = \langle r \rangle + \Delta r$$
$$P = \langle P \rangle + \Delta P,$$

and

$$\Delta \lambda \;\; = \;\; \sqrt{\left(\frac{\partial \lambda}{\partial P}\right)^2 \Delta P^2 + \left(\frac{\partial \lambda}{\partial r}\right)^2 \Delta r^2}. \tag{10.6}$$

Now, ATM packets have a fixed size of 53 bytes, thus $\Delta P_{\text{ATM}} = 0$, but Ethernet or Frame Relay packets have varying sizes. An average uncertainty needs to be measured over time. Let us suppose that it might be 1kB, or something of that order of magnitude.

For a Service Provider, the uncertainty in r also requires measurement; r represents the aggregated traffic from multiple customers. A Service Provider could hope that the aggregation of traffic load from several customers would even out, allowing the capacity of a channel to be used evenly at all times. Alas, traffic in the same geographical region tends to peak at the same times, not different times, so channels must be idle most of the time and inundated for brief periods. To find r and Δr, we aggregate the separate sources into the total packet-rate:

$$r(t) = \sum_i r_i(t). \tag{10.7}$$

The aggregated uncertainty in r is the Pythagoran sum:

$$\Delta r = \sqrt{\sum_i \Delta r_i^2}. \tag{10.8}$$

The estimated uncertainty is

$$\Delta \lambda \;\; = \;\; \sqrt{r^2 (\Delta P)^2 + \langle P \rangle^2 (\Delta r)^2}. \tag{10.9}$$

Since r and Δr are likely to be of similar orders of magnitude for many customers, whereas $\Delta P < P$, this indicates that uncertainty is dominated by demand uncertainty, i.e.

$$\Delta \lambda \simeq \langle P \rangle \Delta r. \tag{10.10}$$

This uncertainty can now be used in queuing estimates.

Now that we are able to quantify uncertainty, we can create a sensible service-level agreement on the following kind of assertion:

> *'We, the provider, promise to provide a service of $S \pm \Delta S$, measured over time intervals ΔT, at the price ...'*

10.9 Competition or cooperation for service?

Consider, for simplicity, just two customers or users A and B who wish to share a service resource. We shall assume that the service 'market' is a free-for-all; i.e. no one player has any *a priori* advantage over the other, and that both parties behave rationally.

The users could try to cooperate and obtain a 'fair' share of the resource, or they could let selfish interest guide them into a competitive battle for the largest share. The cooperation or collaboration might, in turn, be voluntary or it might be enforced by a service provider.

These two strategies of competition and collaboration are manifestly reflected in technologies for networking, for instance:

- *Voluntary sharing*: The Ethernet is an example of voluntary sharing, in which any user can grab as much of a share as is available. There is a maximum service rate that can be shared, but it is not necessarily true that what one user loses is automatically gained by the other. It is not a zero-sum game.

- *Forced sharing*: Virtual circuits (like ATM or Frame Relay) are examples of forced sharing over parallel circuits. There are thus fixed quotas that enforce users' cooperation. These quotas could be allocated unevenly to prioritize certain users, but for now we shall assume that each user receives an equal share of the resource pot.

We analyze this situation, in a very simple way, using a classic game-theoretical approach. The customers can 'win' a certain amount of the total service rate R (e.g. bytes per second, in the case of network service), and must choose strategies for maximizing their interests. We can therefore construct a 'payoff' matrix for each of the two users (see tables 10.1, 10.2 and 10.3). We see that when both customers collaborate (either willingly or by forced quota), they obtain equal shares. If one of them competes greedily, it can obtain an extra δR that is then subtracted from the other's share. However, if both users compete, the result is generally worse (R_c) than an equal share.

Thus, we assume that each of the users assumes an equal share $R/2$ when they cooperate with one another. The relative sizes of the payoff are important. We have:

$$\delta R \leq \frac{R}{2} \tag{10.11}$$

$$\left(\frac{R}{2} - \delta R\right) \leq \frac{R}{2} \leq \left(\frac{R}{2} + \delta R\right). \tag{10.12}$$

In other words, by competing, a selfish user might be able to gain an additional amount of the service capacity δR to the other's detriment. The sum of both users' shares cannot exceed R. If both users choose to compete, the resulting competition might lead to an amount of waste that goes to neither of the users. This is the case in Ethernet, for instance, where collisions reduce the efficiency of transmission for all parties equally. We model this by assuming that both users then obtain a share of $R_c < R/2$.

Table 10.1: A's payoff matrix in two-customer sharing.

A	B Cooperate	B Compete
A Cooperate	$\frac{R}{2}$	$\frac{R}{2} - \delta R$
A Compete	$\frac{R}{2} + \delta R$	R_c

Table 10.2: B's payoff matrix in two-customer sharing.

B	B Cooperate	B Compete
A Cooperate	$\frac{R}{2}$	$\frac{R}{2} + \delta R$
A Compete	$\frac{R}{2} - \delta R$	R_c

Table 10.3: A, B combined payoff matrix in two-customer sharing.

A, B	B Cooperate	B Compete
A Cooperate	$\left(\frac{R}{2}, \frac{R}{2}\right)$	$\left(\frac{R}{2} - \delta R, \frac{R}{2} + \delta R\right)$
A Compete	$\left(\frac{R}{2} + \delta R, \frac{R}{2} - \delta R\right)$	(R_c, R_c)

This leaves us with two separate cases to analyze:

1. $R_c > R/2 - \delta R$: If the result from competitive 'attacks' against one another is greater than the result that can be obtained by passively accepting the other customer's aggressiveness, then we are inclined to retaliate. This becomes an instance of the Prisoner's Dilemma game. It has a solution in terms of Nash equilibria by dominant strategies (see figure 10.6).

2. $R_c < R/2 - \delta R$: If the payoff for mutual competition is less than the penalty for collaborating, then the situation becomes equivalent to another classic game: the Maynard-Smith dove–hawk game [206]. Both players see that they can win an important share by being greedy, but if the other player retaliates they both stand to win less. Thus one player can afford to be aggressive (hawkish) but then the other must be peaceful (dove-like). This is the case with the Ethernet, for instance. If there is excessive contention, there is an exponential 'backoff' from collisions leading to significantly worsened performance (see figure 10.7).

We can ask if there is a mixed strategy of partial cooperation that would succeed in countering the poor result from mutual competition, but which would yield slightly more. To show that this is not the case, let us pick B's strategy and then allow A to choose cooperation with probability p:

(a) *B cooperates*: compare the payoffs for A and B and ask, is there a value of p such that

$$p\frac{R}{2} + (1 - p)\left(\frac{R}{2} + \delta R\right) > p\frac{R}{2} + (1 - p)\left(\frac{R}{2} - \delta R\right)? \qquad (10.13)$$

Either we must have $\delta R = 0$ or $p = 0$, so the answer is no: there is no way to improve on this strategy as long as there is something to gain from competition.

(b) *B competes*: compare the payoffs for A and B and ask, is there a value of p such that

$$p\left(\frac{R}{2} - \delta R\right) + (1 - p)R_c > p\left(\frac{R}{2} + \delta R\right) + (1 - p)R_c? \qquad (10.14)$$

Again, consistency forces us to take $p = 0$ or $\delta R = 0$.

These simple games approximate the essence of the issues involved in sharing. They reflect both human strategies for competition and technological ones. We see that there is no clear answer as to whether Ethernet (hawkish) or fixed quota virtual circuit (dove-like) behavior is preferable, it depends on the level of traffic.

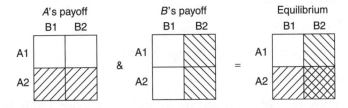

Figure 10.6: With $R_c > R/2 - \delta R$, the game becomes a classic game-theoretical problem of 'Prisoner's Dilemma' [222]. The dominant Nash equilibrium is where both players decide to compete with one another. If the customers are altruistic and decide to collaborate (or are forced to collaborate) with one another, they can win the maximum amount. However, if they know nothing about each other's intentions then they realize, rationally, that they can increase their own share by δR by choosing a competitive strategy. However, if both choose to be competitive, they cannot achieve exactly this much: the balance point for mutual competition is R_c. This value is determined by the technology used by the service provider.

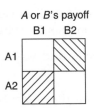

Figure 10.7: With $R_c < R/2 - \delta R$ the game becomes another classic game of dove–hawk. If both players are 'hawkish' and attack greedily, they both lose out. The stable equilibria are that one player is greedy and the other is submissive.

10.10 Service Level Agreements

Network connectivity and data transfer rates are now saleable commodities. To sell them, we must be able to measure the quantity and 'quality' of services levels, so that guarantees can be provided to customers. Quality is clearly a heuristic value with no clear definition, yet the buzzword of network service provision is 'Quality of Service' (QoS). There is much current research devoted to defining this elusive metric.

Service Level Agreements (SLA) are contracts between clients and service providers that set expectations, and specify levels of resources and costs in a service. Increased interest in 'outsourcing' or sub-contracting services and work has placed these agreements center stage. In some cases, they fuel expectations that technology cannot match.

In service centers, system administration is shifting away from device management, where relatively little has been accomplished, towards service management which is more the domain of marketing and contractual law. However, to really define a service level quality factor, we must translate this heuristic 'quality' into a hard-nosed measurable such as data-rate. The basic principles involved are no mystery, if we think scientifically:

1. Predictability (determinism)

2. Cause–effect (dependence)

3. Strategy for resource sharing amongst clients

4. Uncertainty management.

Putting these items together enables us to address service levels in quantitative terms. The details of this are beyond the scope of the present book.[3]

Example 14. *The simplest kind of SLA is that offered by Internet Service Providers, using ADSL lines, who might offer a home user a bit rate of 512 kbps downstream and 128 kbps upstream. A home user could, in principle, use* ping *or* ftp *or some other method to test this transfer rate and verify that the bit rate is at least as good as that advertised. Similarly, the service provider might say that any downtime will be corrected within a period no longer than 48 hours, or else give a money back guarantee.*

An agreement for mission-critical services would need to be more comprehensive than this. There are two approaches to writing SLAs:

- *Top down:* examine user needs and wishes and try to translate these into low-level device performance.

- *Bottom up:* examine the limitations of technology and build up possible services.

A basic checklist for top-down SLAs should include:

1. What service is being offered?

2. What are the users' responsibilities?

3. Plan for mapping quality of experience onto physical measurables.

---

[3]For a discussion of this point, see the follow-up book by the author: *Scientific Principles of Network and System Administration*, J. Wiley & Sons, 2004.

4. How will the measurables be monitored?

5. How will errors be fixed, within a predictable time-frame?

6. How often will service levels be evaluated and revised?

7. What are maximum response times?

8. What is the security of operations (integrity, authenticity of parties etc)?

9. Intellectual property rights.

Of the more legal aspects of contractual agreement, one must have:

1. A clause defining when a service agreement has been broken.

2. What liability is agreed to (financial reparation)?

3. When does the agreement terminate?

Security is an essential aspect of SLAs (see chapter 11): a company's livelihood can depend on a service. While it makes sense for any company to secure its assets by using redundant service providers, it is important to cover the possible damage that loss of service could result in, or simply to follow up on a breach of contract.

Today, SLAs are being suggested for outsourced Web services based on SOAP and XML-RPC. SLAs are even being defined as XML Document Type Definitions (DTD). Rodosek suggests the need for a language to describe SLAs in terms of quality of service parameters at all levels [255]. This is a matter of continuing research. Two approaches to mechanizing service regulation have been explored by policy-based feedback using cfengine [42, 50] and, more recently, fuzzy controllers with more specific service-based knowledge [95].

Exercises

Self-test objectives

1. What is meant by multiplexing?

2. Recall the difference between a bridge and a switch.

3. What is the difference between a switch and a router?

4. What is meant by a layer 3 switch?

5. What is a virtual circuit?

6. Explain the difference between deterministic and non-deterministic network protocols.

7. Give examples of deterministic and non-deterministic layer 2 technologies.

8. Give examples of deterministic and non-deterministic layer 3 technologies.

9. Is there a limit to the length of cable that can be used to connect two computers together with:

    (a) Ethernet?

    (b) ATM over fiber?

    (c) Token ring?

    If so explain how the length limitation arises.

10. What does the wavelength of an electromagnetic signal have to do with the rate at which data can be transmitted?

11. How does the wavelength of an electromagnetic signal affect the distance a signal can travel (through cable or by wireless means)?

12. Why can DSL technology transmit higher data rates over telephone lines than modems?

13. What is meant by a T1 line? What is meant by an E1 line?

14. Explain the difference between Frame Relay and Asynchronous Transfer Mode (ATM). Can these technologies carry Internet Protocol traffic?

15. Explain the difference between routing and forwarding.

16. What is meant by a default route?

17. What is an Autonomous System in the context of routing?

18. Explain what static routing is and how it is configured.

19. Explain what dynamical routing is and how one would go about configuring it.

20. What is a Distance Vector routing protocol? Give an example and explain why this method of routing is little used.

21. What is a Link State routing algorithm? Give an example of this and explain its advantages over Distance Vector algorithms.

22. Which so-called routing algorithm uses a Path Vector algorithm?

23. Explain the function of BGP in global routing.

24. Explain why BGP, alone, cannot route packets from source to destination.

25. What is MPLS and how does it differ from ATM?

26. What is meant by quality of service?

27. Explain how the principle of causality limits the attainable service rate of a network service. (Hint: what devices are involved in providing the service?)

28. What does game theory tell us about the usefulness of strategies for cooperative (shared) and non-cooperative (private) media for quality of service?

29. Explain the purpose of a Service Level Agreement.

Problems

1. Use the `ping` and `ping6` commands to ping different IP addresses on your network (note that these differ somewhat on different platforms – the examples here are from GNU/Linux). Pinging the addresses repeatedly with a large packet size (9064 bytes) yields something like this:

```
cube$ ping -s 9064 daneel
PING daneel (128.39.89.230) from 128.39.74.16 : 9064(9092) bytes
9072 bytes from daneel (128.39.89.230): icmp_seq=1 ttl=63 time=17.1 ms
9072 bytes from daneel (128.39.89.230): icmp_seq=2 ttl=63 time=16.8 ms
9072 bytes from daneel (128.39.89.230): icmp_seq=3 ttl=63 time=17.9 ms
9072 bytes from daneel (128.39.89.230): icmp_seq=4 ttl=63 time=17.9 ms
--- daneel ping statistics ---
4 packets transmitted, 4 received, 0% loss, time 3030ms
rtt min/avg/max/mdev = 16.858/17.462/17.945/0.475 ms

host$ ping6 -s 9064 2001:700:700:3:290:27ff:fea2:477b
PING 2001:700:700:3:290:27ff:fea2:477b
from 2001:700:700:4:290:27ff:fe93:6723 : 9064 data bytes
9072 bytes from 2001:700:700:3:290:27ff:fea2:477b: icmp_seq=1 ttl=63
time=25.0 ms
9072 bytes from 2001:700:700:3:290:27ff:fea2:477b: icmp_seq=2 ttl=63
time=22.4 ms
9072 bytes from 2001:700:700:3:290:27ff:fea2:477b: icmp_seq=3 ttl=63
time=26.0 ms
9072 bytes from 2001:700:700:3:290:27ff:fea2:477b: icmp_seq=4 ttl=63
time=21.3 ms
9072 bytes from 2001:700:700:3:290:27ff:fea2:477b: icmp_seq=5 ttl=63
time=21.3 ms
--- 2001:700:700:3:290:27ff:fea2:477b ping statistics ---
6 packets transmitted, 5 received, 16% loss, time 5047ms
rtt min/avg/max/mdev = 21.376/23.268/26.096/1.956 ms
```

Explain what the `icmp_seq` numbers are and why the time in milliseconds is not constant.

2. Collect the test tcp program `ttcp` (e.g. `ttcpw` for Windows or `ttcp_linux`) for traffic testing between hosts. Choose pairs of hosts on your local network and test the transmission rates between them. On the receiver host, use:

```
ttcp_linux -s -r
```

to receive and discard a standard source transmission, and on the transmitting host, use:

```
ttcp_linux -s -t  receiver-IP
```

   (a) Write a script to repeat this standard test every five minutes over the course of a day. Plot the transmission rate as a function of time throughout the day. Explain why the measured value varies as a function of time.

(b) Work out the average transmission rate and the standard deviation of the values in the previous part. What is the meaning of (what interpretation do you offer for) the average and standard deviation values for the whole day?

(c) Now pick ten hosts from a variety of locations on your LAN; make ten measurements of the transmission rate between each host and a single reference host. Work out the average and standard deviation in each case. Make a table of the results. Can you explain the differences between different hosts? Hint: think about the different hardware of hosts, what hardware connects them, and environmental factors.

3. Explain the difference between a switch and a router. Can switching alone be used to forward packets over a Wide Area Network?

4. Make a table of equivalences between switched networks with virtual circuits and IP services; include the following in your table: Forwarding Equivalence Classes (FEC), Virtual Circuit Identifiers, Labels, IP port numbers, IP addresses (network part and host part). Be sure to find analogues between routed IP data and switched data in all possible cases.

5. Use the traceroute program on Unix or tracert on Windows to compare routes. If you have a commercial Internet connection at home and a university Internet connection, repeat this from both locations and compare the results.

   (a) Determine your hosts IP address and subnet mask.

   (b) Trace the route to a host on the same subnet as your own.

   (c) Trace the route to your nearest gateway router.

   (d) Trace the route to a host on the next subnet above yours (e.g. try guessing a number).

   (e) Trace the routes to www.gnu.org, www.iu.hio.no, www.cisco.com.

6. A router has the following CIDR entries in its routing table:

```
Network               Next hop
192.0.16.0/22         Interface 0
192.0.20.0/22         Interface 1
2001:700:700:3/64     Interface 3
192.0.40.0/23         Router 1
default               Router 2
```

What happens to packets with the following destination addresses?

   (a) 192.0.23.10

   (b) 192.0.17.5

   (c) 192.0.41.7

   (d) 192.0.42.99

   (e) 192.0.41.255

(f) 2001:700:700:3:290:27ff:fea2:477b

(g) fe80::220:e0ff:fe6c:5877

7. Look at the search algorithm for finding data in a binary tree. Compare this with the way that Internet packets are routed. What are the similarities and differences?

8. Explain the main reason why Link State routing protocols generate less gratuitous traffic than Distance Vector Protocols.

9. Quality of Service assumes that it is possible to build up a stable average service level from a minimum level of granularity. Suppose we are switching packets at a rate of ω bits per second. We can model a stream of switches as a function that changes in time between 1 and 0 at this frequency. The simplest signal function with these properties is:

$$S(t) = \frac{1}{2}(1 + \sin(\omega t)), \qquad (10.15)$$

where t is time.

(a) Sketch this function and draw on it the time scale $\Delta t = \omega^{-1}$.

(b) Sketch this function over a period $T \gg \omega^{-1}$.

(c) Prove that the average bit rate of eqn. (10.3), over long times $T \to \infty$ does not depend on ω and is approximately constant, thus showing that quality can be assured only *on average* over times T that are long compared with $\Delta t = \omega^{-1}$.

10. You are going to buy an Internet connection from a local ISP that you know owns a 2 megabit per second wireless connection. The ISP has an aggressive marketing policy for recruiting new customers. The standard Service Level Agreement you receive offers you a symmetrical transfer rate of 640kb. Does this sound like a reliable service? Explain your thoughts on this.

11. You rent space within a building that has its own network infrastructure, based on switched Ethernet. Upon investigation, you find that the building has an external Frame Relay service, with a gigabit connection rate, and a single gateway router. The computing services management offers a guaranteed connection rate of 10mb/s to all its customers. Does this sound like a reasonable agreement? Explain your reasoning. Can the company guarantee you this level of service at all times?

12. The speed of light in copper wire is measured to be of the order of $2 \times 10^8 \text{ms}^{-1}$. Use the conditional formula $N\lambda \geq 2L$ for predictable collision behavior in Ethernet frames to work out the maximum length of a cable, for the three Ethernet types: 1) $f = 10\text{Mbps}$, 2) $f = 100\text{Mbps}$, 3) $f = 1000\text{Mbps}$, given that the minimum packet size is fixed at 512 bits.

Chapter 11

Principles of security

The need for an integrated view of security has been emphasized throughout this book: security management cannot be separated from network and system administration because security requires a fully systemic approach. However, it is important to identify some principles of security management in isolation, in order to better understand them and underline their importance. In this and the next chapter, we dissect security into its constituent parts.

Security is about protecting things of value to an organization, in relation to the possible risks. This includes material and intellectual assets; it includes the very assumptions that are the foundation of an organization or human–computer system. Anything that can cause a failure of those assumptions can result in loss, and must therefore be considered a threat. In system administration terms this often means a loss of data or availability in the computing system, but that is really just the tip of the iceberg. The number of ways in which this can occur is vast – making security a difficult problem.

In order to have security, we must sacrifice a certain level of convenience [171] for a measure of discipline. This promotes systems with predictable behavior, where one can arrange to safeguard the system from unpleasant occurrences. To develop computer security by assuring predictability, we have to understand the interrelationships between all of the hosts and services on our networks as well as the ways in which those hosts can be accessed. A system can be compromised by:

- *Physical threats*: weather, natural disaster, bombs, power failures etc.

- *Human threats*: cracking, stealing, trickery, bribery, spying, sabotage, accidents.

- *Software threats*: viruses, Trojan horses, logic bombs, denial of service.

Protecting against these issues requires both pro-active (preventative) measures and damage control after breaches. Our task is roughly as follows:

- Identify what we are trying to protect.

- Evaluate the main sources of risk and where trust is placed.

- Work out possible or cost-effective counter-measures to attacks.

Security is an increasingly important problem. In recent years the number of attacks and break-ins to computer systems has risen to millions of cases a year. Crackers or hackers[1] have found their way inside the computers of the Pentagon, the world's security services, warships, fighter plane command computers, banks and major services such as electrical power grids. With this kind of access the potential for causing damage is great. Computer warfare is the next major battlefield to subdue; it is going on now, as you read these words: it is here, like it or not. It is estimated that the banks lose millions of dollars a year to computer crime.

Security embraces other issues such as reliability. For instance, many computers are used in mission-critical systems, such as aircraft controls and machinery, where human lives are at stake. Thus reliability and safety are also concerns. *Real-time systems* are computer systems which are guaranteed to respond within a well-defined time limit when a request is made of them. This is a kind of quality of service (see section 10.8). That means that a real-time system must always be fast enough to cope with any demand which is made of it. Real-time systems are required in cases where human lives and huge sums of money are involved. For instance, in a flight control system it would be unacceptable to give a command 'Oh my goodness, we're going to crash, flaps NOW!' and have the computer reply with 'Processing, please wait...'.

Security is a huge subject, because modern computer systems are complex and the connectivity of the Internet means that millions of people can try to break into networked systems. In this chapter we consider the basic principles of security. Having studied this, you might wish to read more about security in refs. [131, 126, 61, 45, 279].

11.1 Four independent issues

For many, security is regrettably perceived as being synonymous with network privacy or network intrusion. Privacy and intrusion are two particular aspects of security, but the network is not our particular enemy. Many breaches of security happen from within, or by accident. If we focus exclusively on network connectivity we ignore the threats from internal employees (e.g. the janitor who is a computer expert and has an axe to grind, or the mischievous son of the director who was left waiting to play in mom's office, or perhaps the unthinkable: a disgruntled employee who feels as though his/her talents go unappreciated).

Software security is a vast subject, because modern computer systems are complex. It is only exacerbated by the connectivity of the Internet which allows millions of people to have a go at breaking into networked systems. What this points to is the fact that a secure environment requires the control of all parts of a system, not merely at specific access points like login terminals or firewalls.

---

[1]It is sometimes considered incorrect to call intruders hackers, since hacker has several meanings; in computer communities, hackers are usually thought of as legitimate programmers.

Principle 56 (Security is a property of systems). *Security is a property of entire systems, not an appendage that can be added in any one place, or be applied at any one time. It relies on the constant appraisal and re-appraisal (the integrity) of our assumptions about a system. There are usually many routes through a system that permit theft or destruction. If we try to 'add security' in one place, an attacker or random chance will simply take a different route.*

If we stretch our powers of abstraction even to include loss by natural disaster, then system security can be summarized by a basic principle.

Principle 57 (Access and privilege). *A fundamental prerequisite for security is the ability to restrict access to data. This leads directly to a notion of privilege for certain users.*

The word privilege does not apply to loss by accident or natural disaster, but the word access does. If accidental actions or natural disasters do not have access to data, then they cannot cause them any harm. Any attempt to run a secure system where restriction of access is not possible is fundamentally flawed.

There are four basic elements in security:

- *Privacy or confidentiality*: restriction of access.

- *Authentication*: verification of presumed identity.

- *Integrity*: protection against corruption or loss (redundancy).

- *Trust*: underlies every assumption.

Some authors include the following as independent points:

- *Availability*: preventing disruption of a service.

- *Non-repudiation*: preventing deniability of actions.

They can also be considered simply as issues of *integrity* of a service (availability) and the imperviousness of accountability logs (non-repudiation).

The most important issue to understand about security is a basic tenet that is widely unappreciated:

Principle 58 (Security is about trust). *Every security problem boils down to a question of whom or what do we trust?*

Once we have understood this, the topic of security is reduced to a litany of examples of how trust may be exploited and how it may be improved using certain technological aids. Failure to understand this point can lead to embarrassing mistakes being made.

We introduce the somewhat ill-defined notion of 'security' to describe protecting ourselves against parties whom we do not trust. But how do we solve this problem? Usually, we introduce some kind of technology to move trust from a risky place to a safer place. For example, if we do not trust our neighbors not to steal our possessions, we might put a lock on our door. We no longer have to trust our neighbors, but we have to trust that the lock will do its job in the way we expect. This is easier to trust, because a simple mechanical device is more *predictable* than complicated human beings, but it can still fail. If we don't entirely trust the lock, we could install an alarm system which rings the police if someone breaks in. Now we are trusting the lock a little, the alarm system and the police. After all, who says that the police will not be the ones to steal your possessions? In some parts of the world, this idea is not so absurd.

Trust is based on assumption. It can be bolstered with evidence but, just as science can never prove something is true, we can never trust something with absolute certainty. We only know when trust is broken. This is the real insight of security – not the technologies that help us to build trust.

Example 15. *One of the big problems with security mechanisms is that they hinder people sometimes from taking part in legitimate activities. They are then frequently turned off out of misunderstanding or annoyance, leaving a system unprotected. It is therefore important to educate the managers of security systems about procedures and practices surrounding a secured system. If there is a way to proceed, it should be by an approved channel; if a pathway is blocked, then it should be for a good reason that is understood by all parties.*

11.2   Physical security

For a computer to be secure it must be physically secure. If we can get our hands on a host then we are never more than a screwdriver away from all of its assets. Disks can be removed. Sophisticated users can tap network lines and listen to traffic. The radiation from monitor screens can be captured and recorded, showing an exact image of what a user is looking at on his/her screen. Or one can simply look over the shoulder of a colleague while he or she types a password. The level of physical security one requires depends on the sophistication of the potential intruder, and therefore in the value of the assets which one is protecting.

Cleaning staff frequently dust monitors and keyboards, switch off monitors and computers by accident and even pull plugs on computers to plug in their machinery. If a computer serves a valuable purpose, or is vulnerable to accidental input, it is not only attackers we have to protect against. Cleaning staff have keys to the building, so locking an office door will not help here.

Assuming that hosts are physically secure, we still have to deal with the issues of software security which is a much more difficult topic. Software security is about access control and software reliability. No single tool can make computer systems secure. Major blunders have been made out of the belief that a single product (e.g. a 'firewall') would solve the security problem. The bottom line is that there is no such thing as a secure operating system. What is required is a persistent mixture of vigilance and adaptability.

11.3 Trust relationships

There are many implicit trust relationships in computer systems. It is crucial to understand them. If we do not understand where we are placing our trust, that trust can be exploited by attackers who have thought more carefully than we have.

For example, any host that shares users' home-directories (such as an NFS server or DFS server) trusts the identities and personal integrity of the users on the hosts which mount those directories. Some accidents are prevented by mapping administrator privileges (root) to the user nobody on remote Unix systems, but this is not security, only a trivial obstacle. The Unix root user can always use 'su' to become any user in its password file and access/change any data within those filesystems; similarly for Windows. The .rhosts and hosts.equiv files on Unix machines grant root (or other user) privileges to other hosts without the need for authentication; these are very hazardous.

When collecting software from remote servers, we should also make sure that it comes from a machine that is trustworthy, particularly if the files could lead to privileged access to the system. For example, it would be fool-hardy to copy a privileged program such as the Unix program /bin/ps from a host one knows nothing about. This program runs with root privileges. If someone were to replace that version of ps with a Trojan horse command, the system would have effectively been opened to attack at the heart of the system.

Most users trust anonymous FTP servers where they collect free software. In any remote copy we are setting up an implicit trust relationship. First of all we trust integrity of the host we are collecting files from. Secondly we trust that they have the same username database with regard to access control (i.e there are not two different users with identical user IDs on the two systems). The root user on the collecting host has the same rights to read files as the root user on the server. The same applies to any matched username.

In any remote file transfer one is also forced to trust the integrity of the data received. No matter how hard a program may work to authenticate the identity of the host, even once the host's identity is verified, the accuracy or trustworthiness of unknown data is still in doubt. This has nothing to do with encryption as users sometimes believe: encrypted connections do not change these trust relationships; they improve the privacy of the data being transmitted but neither their accuracy nor their trustworthiness.

Implicit trust relationships lie at the heart of so many software systems which grant access to services or resources that it would be impossible to list them all here. Trust relationships are important to grasp because they can lead to security holes.

11.4 Security policy and definition of security

Security only has meaning when we have defined a frame of reference. It is intrinsically connected to our own appreciation of risks. It must be based on a thorough *risk analysis*.

> **Principle 59 (Risk).** *There is always a non-zero level of risk associated with any system.*

Clearly, there is a finite chance that a dinosaur-killer asteroid will strike your computer and destroy it. This risk is not very high, but it is real. Few organizations would care to try to protect themselves against this eventuality and would consider themselves secure if this were the only remaining threat, but this parodic example makes an important point. Security is intrinsically related to a threat assessment. An acceptable definition of a secure system is:

> **Definition 8 (Secure system).** *A secure system is one in which every possible threat has been analyzed and where all the risks have been assessed and accepted as policy.*

Clearly this is a tall order, and it is probably impossible to realize, but we should be clear about what this means: it is a definition that tells us that security is determined by policy – as *acceptable risk*.

Defining what *we*, a local community, mean by security is essential. Only then will we know when security has been breached, and what to do about it. Some sites, which contain sensitive data, require strict security and spend a lot of time enforcing it, others do not particularly care about their data and would rather not waste their time on pointless measures to protect them. Security must be balanced against convenience [171]. How secure must we be

- From outside the organization?

- From inside the organization (different host)?

- From inside the organization (same host)?

- Against the interruption of services?

- From user error?

Finally, how much inconvenience are the users of the system willing to endure in order to uphold this level of security? This point should not be underestimated: if users consider security to be a nuisance, they try to circumvent it.

> **Suggestion 13 (Work defensively).** *Expect the worst, do your best, preferably in advance of a problem.*

Visible security can be a problem in itself. Systems which do not implement high-level security tend to attract only low-level crackers – and those who manage to break in tend to use the systems only as a springboard to go to other places. The more security one implements, and the more visible it is, the more of a challenge it is for a cracker. So spending a lot of time on security might only have the effect of asking for trouble.

> **Suggestion 14 (Network security).** *Extremely sensitive data should not be placed on a computer which is attached in any way to a public network.*

What resources are we trying to protect?

- *Secrets:* Some sites have secrets they wish to protect. They might be government or trade secrets or the solutions to a college exam.

- *Personnel data:* In your country there are probably rules about what you must do to safeguard sensitive personal information. This goes for any information about employees, patients, customers or anyone else we deal with. Information about people is private.

- *CPU usage/System downtime:* We might not have any data that we are afraid will fall into the wrong hands. It might simply be that the system is so important to us that we cannot afford the loss of time incurred by having someone screw it up. If the system is down, everything stops.

- *Abuse of the system:* It might simply be that we do not want anyone using our system to do something for which they are not authorized, like breaking into other systems.

Who are we trying to protect them from?

- *Competitors*, who might gain an advantage by learning your secrets.

- *Malicious intruders.* Note that people with malicious intent might come from inside or outside our organization. It is wrong to think that the enemy is simply everyone outside of our domain. Too many organizations think 'inside/outside' instead of dealing with proper access control. If one *always ensures that systems and data are protected* on a need-to-know basis, then there is no reason to discriminate between inside or outside of an organization.

- *Old employees with a grudge* against the organization.

Next: what will happen if the system is compromised?

- Loss of money

- Threat of legal action against you

- Missed deadlines

- Loss of reputation.

How much work will we need to put into protecting the system? Who are the people trying to break in?

- Sophisticated spies

- Tourists, just poking around

- Braggers, trying to impress.

Finally: *what risk is acceptable?* If we have a secret which is worth 4 lira, would we be interested in spending 5 lira to secure it? Where does one draw the line? How much is security worth?

The social term in the security equation should never be forgotten. One can spend a hundred thousand dollars on the top of the range firewall to protect data from network intrusion, but someone could walk into the building and look over an unsuspecting shoulder to obtain it instead, or use a receiver to collect the stray radiation from your monitors. Are employees leaving sensitive printouts lying around? Are we willing to place our entire building in a Faraday cage to avoid remote detection of the radiation expelled by monitors? In the final instance, someone could just point a gun at someone's head and ask nicely for their secrets. An example of security policies can be found at RFC 1244 and British Standard/ISO17799.

11.5   RFC 2196 and BS/ISO 17799

Security standards are attempts at capturing the essence of security management. Rather than focusing on the technologies that can be used to implement security, as most texts do, these standards attempt to capture the more important points of how these technologies and methods can be used in concert to address the actual risks. There are two main standards to consider; both are worth careful study.

RFC 2196 (Site Security Handbook, 1997) replaces an older RFC, 1244, and is a guide to producing a site security policy that is addressed at system administrators. It emphasizes that a policy must be closely tied to administrative practice, as we have iterated in this book. The document correctly points out that:

- It must be implementable through system administration procedures, publishing of acceptable use guidelines, or other appropriate methods.

- It must be enforceable with security tools, where appropriate, and with sanctions, where actual prevention is not technically feasible.

- It must clearly define the areas of responsibility for the users, administrators and management.

The standard goes on to describe the elements of such a policy, including purchasing guidelines, privacy policy, access policy, accountability policy, authentication policy, a statement of availability requirements, a maintenance policy and a reporting policy in case of security breach. It also iterates the importance of documentation and supporting information for users and staff.

The RFC describes the protection of infrastructure and network services and discusses specific technologies (DNS, NIS, FTP etc), mainly related to Unix milieux.

ISO 17799 (Information Technology – Code of Practice for Security Management) is a recently recognized security standard that is based upon the British Standard BS7799, published in 1999. ISO 17799 was published in 2000 and accepted as a British Standard in 2001. It is an excellent starting place for formulating an organization's security policy. It is less technical than RFC 2196, but goes into greater detail from a logistic viewpoint. It has been constructed with great care and expertise. Compliance with ISO 17799 is far from trivial, even for the most security conscious of organizations.

As with all ISO standards, one can obtain a certificate of compliance in the final instance. It is almost certainly too early to recommend such a certification, since it is both costly and of limited value to an organization; nevertheless, the standard is a fine summary of basic security ideas that reiterates many of the ideas explored in this book. Copyright prevents us from detailing the standard here, or quoting from its many interesting guidelines, but we can describe its layout. The document describes ten points:

1. **Security policy**: The standard iterates the importance of a security policy that sets clear goals, and demonstrates a commitment by an organization to the seriousness of its security. The policy should ensure that legal and contractual commitments are met, and that the economic ramifications of a security breach are understood. The policy itself must be maintained and updated by a responsible party.

2. **Organizational security**: A security team should be assembled that sets policy and provides multi-disciplinary advice. The team should allocate responsibilities within the organization for maintaining security of assets at all levels. Levels of authorization to assets must be determined. Contact with law-enforcement organizations and regulatory bodies should be secured and policies and procedures should be peer-reviewed for quality assurance. Any 'outsourcing', i.e. third party contracts, must address the risks associated with opening the organization's security borders.

3. **Asset classification and control**: Organizations should have an inventory of their assets, which classifies each asset according to its appropriate level of security. Procedures for labelling and handling different levels of information, including electronic and paper transmission (post, fax, E-mail etc.) and speech (telephone or conversation over dinner) must be determined.

4. **Personnel security**: In order to reduce the risks of human error, malicious attacks by theft, fraud or vandalism, staff should be screened and given security responsibilities. Confidentiality (non-disclosure (NDA)) agreements, as well as terms and conditions of employment may be used as a binding agreement of responsibility. Most importantly, training of staff (users) in the possible threats and their combative procedures is needed to ensure compliance with policy. A response contingency plan should be drawn up and familiarized to the staff, so that security breaches and weaknesses are reported immediately.

5. **Physical and environmental security**: All systems must have physical security; this usually involves a 'security perimeter' with physical constraints against theft and intrusion detection systems, as well as a controlled, safe environment. Secure areas can provide extra levels of security for special tasks. Equipment should be protected from physical threats (including fire, coffee, food etc.) and have uninterruptible power supplies where appropriate. Cables must be secured from damage and wire-tapping. Desks and screens

and refuse/trash should be cleared when not in use, to avoid accidental disclosure of confidential information.

6. **Communications and operations management**: The processing and handling of information must be specified with appropriate procedures for the level of information. Change management should include appropriate authorizations and significant documentation of changes to allow analysis in the case of problems. Procedures must be documented for responding to all kinds of threat. Analysis (causality) and audit trails should be planned for breaches. Housekeeping, backups, safe disposal of information and materials and other regular maintenance should be in place and be integrated into the scheme. System administration features heavily here: security and administration go hand in hand; they are not separate issues. This part of the standard covers many miscellaneous issues.

7. **Access control**: User management, password and key management, access rights, securing unattended equipment. Enforced pathways to assets that prevent 'back-doors'. Segregation of independent assets and authentication for access. Use of securable operating systems, restriction of privilege. Clock synchronization. Mobile computing issues.

8. **Systems development and maintenance**: Security should be built into systems from the start. Input–output validation. Policy on cryptographic controls, including signatures and certificates. Interestingly, the standard recommends against open source software. Covert channels (secret channels that bypass security controls) must be avoided.

9. **Business continuity management**: Each organization should estimate the impact of catastrophes and security breaches on its business. Will the organization be able to continue after such a breach? What will be the impact? The standard suggests the testing of this continuity plan.

10. **Compliance**: Laws and regulations must be obeyed, with regard to each country and contractual obligation. Regulation of personal information and cryptographic methods must be taken into account in different parts of the world. Compliance with the organization's own policy must be secured by auditing.

The ISO standard is a good introduction to human–computer security that can be recommended for any organization.

11.6 System failure modes

Since the explosion of interest in the Internet, the possibility of hosts being attacked from outside sources has become a significant problem. With literally millions of users on the net, the tiny percentage of malicious users becomes a large number. The number of ways in which a system can fail are thus many and varied.

11.6.1 Social engineering

Network attackers, i.e. system crackers, are people. It is easy to become so fascinated by the network that we forget that people can just walk into a building and steal something. If one can avoid complex technical expertise in order to break in to a system, then why not do it? There is more than one way to crack a system.

The only secure computer is a computer which is locked into a room, not connected to a network, shielded from all electromagnetic radiation. In social studies of large companies, it has been demonstrated that – in spite of expensive firewall software and sophisticated anti-cracking technology – all most crackers had to do to break into the system was to make a phone call to an unwary employee of the company and ask for their username and password [327]. Some crackers posed as system administrators trying to fix a bug, others simply questioned them as in a marketing survey until they gave away information which allowed the crackers to guess their passwords. Some crackers will go one step further and visit the building they are trying to break into, going through the garbage/refuse to look for documents which would give clues about security. Most people do not understand the lengths that people will go to to break into systems if they really want to. For example, consider this conversation between a cracker and a student user at a university.

```
"Hello - I am calling from the student finance office to tell you that your
term grant has been deposited directly in your K-Bank account, as you
requested."
```

```
"What?! I didn't ask for that! I don't even have an account at
K-Bank!?"
```

```
"Oh really? Are you sure? What is your student number?"
```

```
"s123456" (Attacker now has a user name)
```

```
"Okay, here it is, strange...looks legitimate. Well look, if you like
I could make an exception and push this through quickly."
```

```
"That would be great - I really need that money!"
```

```
"Okay, I could get in trouble for this, but if you give me your
password, I can fix this straight away."
```

Notice how the attacker builds trust by claiming to be in a difficult situation himself (or herself).

A few things can be done to counteract social threats:

- Train all staff and make them aware of the threat of social engineering.

- Keep a clean desks policy, so that no information can be picked up by cleaning staff or people who wander into the building after hours.

- Never leave 'live' equipment unattended or unlocked.

- Always be suspicious of a caller whom you do not know. Ask for ID. Some social engineers might build up trust over time, so be suspicious of unusual requests too.

- Always have two persons verify requests for information or access.

- Never disclose information over the telephone, especially through a voice-mail system. Phone calls can be spoofed.

- Warn others about suspicious callers.

- Examine system logs, check the system regularly, run checks to ensure consistency to look for other signs of attack.

- Make hard-copies of messages sent with all the headers printed out. Many people don't know how to hide their true identity on the Internet.

- Log all calls and visits.

- Make proper backups of computers.

- Inform the whole system of attacks so that anyone who knows something can help you.

- Do not assume that what someone tells you is true.

- Have a clear security policy.

- Threats of serious crimes should probably be reported to the company responsible for sending the message, and perhaps even the police.

11.6.2   Security through obscurity

'Security through obscurity' have become the dirty words of the computing industry – a chant of ridicule to scorn flawed systems. The idea is that making something difficult to find or awkward to use does not prevent a determined attacker or an insidious threat.

In the mid-1990s, when security first came to the general public's attention, it was felt that the general apathy towards security made it important to underline this fact. There was a commonly held belief that, if one made it difficult for intruders to find out information, they would not bother to try. This, of course, is completely wrong. Sometimes the reverse is even true; it acts as a red rag to a bull. If determined attackers can see that there is nothing worth finding they might leave systems alone. If everything is concealed they will assume that there must be something interesting worth breaking in for.

However, there is another side to the coin with obscurity that is generally suppressed. The scorn has gone perhaps too far. Obscurity, i.e. hiding things, does provide a low-level filter against casual threats. If this were not the case, why would anyone be interested in encryption for privacy, or bother to keep passwords in a secret location? Sometimes obscurity is the only possible security. It only depends on how likely the obscurity is to work. There is always a non-zero risk. The question is only how likely the strategy is to work.

In a careful risk analysis, obscuring data or assets *can* reduce the risk of low-level attacks, and thereby reduce the total risk, but it rarely reduces the risk of the most insidious or persistent threats; these are the threats that security experts like to emphasize, since they are usually trying to determine any and every point of failure. Thus, the likelihood of obscurity to work as a strategy depends on the likelihood of persistent attacks to a system. The Queen of England does not hide the crown jewels under her bed – while this might prevent her staff from finding them, a more reliable security is needed against thieves. The same applies to any system.

Security through obscurity is a naive form of security which at best delays break-ins.

Example 16. *Shadow passwords are an example of this. By making the encrypted password list inaccessible to normal users, one makes it harder for them to automate the search for poor passwords, but one does not prevent it! It is still possible to guess passwords in exactly the same way as before, but it takes much longer. The NT password database is not in a readable format. Some people have claimed that this makes it more secure than the Unix password file. Since then tools have been written which rewrite the NT password file in Unix format with visible encrypted passwords. In other words, making it difficult for people to break in does not make it impossible.*

Example 17. *NFS export access control lists make it harder for an arbitrary machine on the same network to get access to an exported filesystem, but not impossible. They can sniff the network or guess root filehandles. Despite this largely being security by obscurity, we should still bother to limit the list of systems that can gain easy access to this information.*

Clearly there is no need to give away information to potential intruders. Information should be available to *everyone* on a need-to-know basis, whether they be local users or people from outside the organization. But at the same time, obscurity is no real protection. Even the invisible man could get shot. Time spent securing systems is better than time spent obscuring them. Obscurity might attract more attention than we want and make the system as obscure to us as to a potential intruder.

11.6.3 Honey pots and sacrificial lambs

A *honey pot* is a host which is made to look attractive to attackers. It is usually placed on a network with the intention of catching an intruder or distracting them from more important systems. A *sacrificial lamb* host is one which is not considered to be particularly important to the domain. If it is compromised by an attacker then that is an acceptable loss and no real harm is done.

Some network administrators believe that the use of such machines contributes to security. For example, WWW servers are often placed on sacrificial lamb machines which are placed outside firewalls. If the machine is compromised then it can simply be reinstalled and the data reloaded from a secure backup.

This practice might seem rather dubious. There is certainly no evidence to support the idea that either honey pot havens or sacrificial lamb chops actually improve security, by any definition, but they provide management options.

11.6.4 Security holes

One way that outside users can attack a system is by exploiting security holes in software. Classic examples usually involve *setuid-root* programs, which give normal users temporary superuser access to the system. Typical examples are programs like `sendmail` and `finger`. These programs are constantly being fixed, but even so, new security holes are found with alarming regularity. Faults in software leave back-doors open to intruders. The premier way of limiting such attacks is to build a so-called *firewall* around your network, see section 12.12.

The computer emergency response team (CERT) was established in the wake of the Internet Worm incident to monitor potential security threats. CERT publish warnings to a mailing list about known security holes. This is also available on the newsgroup *comp.security.announce*. Several other organizations, often run by staff who work as security consultants, are now involved in computer security monitoring. For instance, the SANS organization performs an admirable job of keeping the community informed about security developments, both technical and political. Moreover, old phreaker organizations like Phrack and the l0pht (pronounced loft) now apply their extensive knowledge of system vulnerabilities for the good of the network community. See refs. [4, 300, 72, 279, 239, 189].

11.6.5 System homogeneity

In a site with a lot of different kinds of platforms, perhaps several Unix variants, NT and Windows 9x, the job of closing security holes is much harder. Inhomogeneity often provides the determined intruder with more possibilities for bug-finding. It also increases the system's unpredictability. You might ask yourself whether you need so many different kinds of platform. If you do, then perhaps a firewall solution would provide an extra level of protection, giving you a better chance of being able to upgrade your systems before something serious happens. The converse of this viewpoint is that systems with a variety of operating systems can provide a backup if one type of system becomes compromised; e.g. if an important NT server is compromised, it might be good to have a Unix backup.

11.6.6 Modem pools

Some companies expend considerable effort to secure their network connections, but forget that they have dial-in modems. Modem pools are a prime target for attackers because they are often easy targets. There are many problems associated with modem pools. Sometimes they are quite unexpected. For example, if one has network access to Windows systems using the same modem then those systems are automatically on a shared segment and can use one another's resources, regardless of whether they have any logical relationship. Modems can also succumb to denial of service attacks by repetitive dialing.

Modems should never allow users to gain access to a part of the network which needs to be secure. Modems should never be allowed to be back-doors into firewalled networks by being placed on the secure side of a firewall.

11.6.7 Laptops and mobile devices

Laptop computers and Personal Digital Assistants (PDA) are increasingly popular and they are popular targets for thieves. There have been cases of laptop computers containing sensitive information being stolen, often enough to give crackers access to further systems, or simply to give competitors the information they wanted!

11.6.8 Backups

If you make backups of important data (private data) then you must take steps to secure the backups also. If an intruder can steal your backups, then he or she does not need to steal the originals.

11.6.9 TCP/IP security

On top of the hardware, there are many levels of protocol which make network communication work. Many of these layers are invisible or are irrelevant to us, but there are two layers in the protocol stack which are particularly relevant to network security, namely the IP layer and the TCP/UDP layer.

11.6.10 The Internet protocol (IPv4)

The Internet protocol was conceived in the 1970s as a military project. The aim was to produce a routable network protocol. The version of this protocol in use today is version 4, with a few patches. Let's review some of the basics of IPv4. TCP/IP is a transmission protocol which builds on lower level protocols like Ethernet and gives it extra features like 'streams' or virtual circuits, with automatic handshaking. UDP is a cheaper version of this protocol which is used for services which do not require connection-based communication. The TCP/IP protocol stack consists of several layers (see figure 2.6).

At the application level we have text-based protocols like telnet and FTP etc. Under these lies the TCP (Transmission Control Protocol) which provides reliable connection-based handshaking, in a virtual circuit. TCP and UDP introduce the concept of the port and the socket (=port+IP address). We base our communications on these, and thus we also base the security of our communications on these. Under TCP/UDP is the IP transport layer, then Ethernet or token ring etc. ICMP is a small protocol which is used by network hardware to send control and error messages as a part of the IP protocol set, e.g. ping uses ICMP.

With all of its encapsulation packaging, a TCP/IP packet looks like figure 11.1. TCP packets are 'reliable', connection-oriented data. They form *streams* or continuous data-flows with handshaking. This is accomplished by using a three-way handshake based on so-called SYN (synchronize) and ACK (acknowledge) bits in the TCP header. Suppose host A wishes to set up a connection with host B. Host A

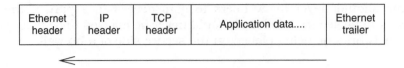

Figure 11.1: Encapsulation with Ethernet and TCP/IP.

sends a TCP segment to host B with its SYN bit set and a sequence number X which will be used to keep track of the order of the segments. Host B replies to this with its SYN and ACK bits set, with Acknowledgement=X+1 and a new sequence number Y. Host A then replies to host B with the first data and the Acknowledge field=Y+1. The reason why each side acknowledges every segment with a sequence number which is one greater than the previous number sent is that the Acknowledgement field actually determines the next sequence number expected. This sequence is actually a weakness which network attackers have been able to exploit through different connections, in 'sequence number guessing' attacks. Now many implementations of TCP allow random initial sequence numbers.

The purpose of this circuit connection is to ensure that both hosts know about every packet which is sent from source to destination. Because TCP guarantees delivery, it retransmits any segment for which it has not received an ACK after a certain period of time (the TCP timeout).

At the end of a transmission the sender sends a FIN (finished) bit, which is replied to with FIN/ACK. In fact closing connections is quite complex since both sides must close their end of the connection reliably. See the reference literature for further details of this.

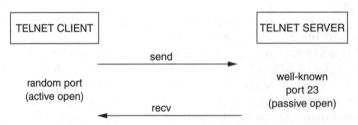

Figure 11.2: A telnet connection.

Let us consider telnet as an example and see how the telnet connection looks at the TCP level (see figure 11.2). Telnet opens a socket from a random port address (e.g. 54657) to a standard well-known port (23) where the telnet service lives. The combination of a port number at an IP address over a communication channel is called a socket. The only security in the telnet service lies in the fact that port 23 is a reserved port which only root can use. (Ports 0–1023 are reserved.)

The TCP protocol guarantees to deliver data to their destination in the right order, without losing anything. In order to do this it breaks up a message into segments and numbers the parts of the message according to a sequence. It then confirms that every part of that sequence has been received. If no confirmation of receipt is received, the source retransmits the data after a timeout. The TCP header contains handshaking bits. Reliable delivery is achieved through a three-way handshake. Host A begins by sending host B a packet with a SYN (synchronize) bit set and a sequence number. This provides a starting reference for the sequence of communication. Host B replies to this message with a SYN/ACK which confirms receipt of an open-connection request and provides a new sequence number which confirms identity. Host A acknowledges this and makes a request. Then host B replies with actual data. We can see this in an actual example (see figure 11.3). This handshaking method of sending sequence numbers with acknowledgement allows the TCP protocol to guarantee and order every piece of a transmission. The ACK return values are incremented by one because in earlier implementations this would be the next packet required in the sequence. This predictability in the sequence is unfortunately a weakness which can be exploited by so-called sequence guessing attacks. Today, in modern implementations, sequence numbers are randomized to avoid this form of attack. Older operating systems still suffer from this problem. Future implementations of TCP/IP will be able to solve this problem by obscuring the sequence numbers entirely through encryption.

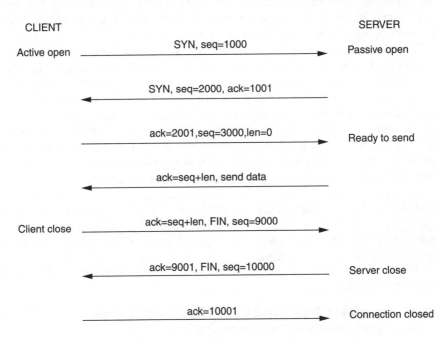

Figure 11.3: The TCP three-way handshake.

The TCP handshake is useful for filtering traffic at the router level, since it gives us something concrete to latch onto. TCP would rather drop a connection than break one of its promises about data integrity, so if we want to block telnet connections, say, we only have to break one part of this fragile loop. The usual strategy is to filter all incoming connections which do not have their ACK bit set, using router filtering rules. This will prevent any new connections from being established by outside machines contacting servers inside the network. This rule, however, does not prevent packets from entering the network that belong to connections that were initiated within the network itself. This provides a simple router-level firewall protection. It is useful for stopping IP spoofing attempts. The UDP protocol does not have SYN, ACK bits and so it is more difficult to filter.

11.6.11 Example telnet session

An example telnet packet trace is provided in Appendix C.

11.7 Preventing and minimizing failure modes

Prevention of loss is usually cheaper than recovery after the fact. Any reasonable preventative measures we can take are worth the investment.

11.7.1 Loss of data: backup

The data collected and produced by an organization are usually the primary reason for them owning a computer installation. The loss of those data, for whatever reason, would be a catastrophe, second to none.

Data can be lost by accident, by fire or natural catastrophe, by disk failure, or even vandalism. If you live in a war-zone or police state, you might also have to protect data from bombs or brutal incursions onto your premises. Once destroyed, data cannot be recovered. The laws of thermodynamics dictate this. So, to avoid complete data-loss, you need to employ a policy of *redundancy*, i.e. you need to make several copies of data, and make sure that they do not befall the same fate. Of course, no matter how many copies of data you make, it is possible that they might all be destroyed simultaneously, no matter what you do to protect them, but we are aiming to minimize the likelihood of that occurrence.

> **Principle 60 (Data invulnerability).** *The purpose of a backup copy is to provide an image of data which is unlikely to be destroyed by the same act that destroys the original, i.e. the backup and the original should not have any common dependencies that can be attacked.*

There is an obvious corollary,

Corollary to principle (Data invulnerability). *Backup copies should be stored at a different physical location than the originals.*

The economics of backup has changed in recent times for several reasons: first of all, storage media are far more reliable than they once were. Component failures tend to follow exponential distributions. If a disk does not show signs of a problem within a few months then it might stand a good chance of effectively never failing of its own accord, before you change the whole machine on other grounds. Disks often tolerate continuous usage for perhaps five years, after which time you will almost certainly want to replace them for other reasons, e.g. performance. The other important change is the almost universal access to networks. Networks can be used to transport data simply and cheaply from one physical location to another.

Traditionally backups have been made to tape, since tape is relatively cheap and mobile. This is still the case at many sites, particularly larger ones; but tapes usually need to be dealt with manually, by a human or by an expensive robot. This adds a price tag to tape-backup which smaller institutions can find difficult to manage. By way of contrast, the price of disks and networking has fallen dramatically. For an organization with few resources, a cheap solution to the backup problem is to mirror disks across a network [244], using well-known tools like `rdump`, `rdist` or `cfengine`. This solves the problems of redundancy and location; and, for what it costs to employ a human or tape robot, one can purchase quite a lot of disk space.

Another change is the development of fast, reliable media like CD-ROM. In earlier times, it was normal to backup the operating system partitions of hosts to tape. Today that practice is largely unnecessary: the operating system is readily available on some straightforward medium (e.g. CD-ROM or DVD) which is at least as fast as a tape streamer and consumes a fraction of the space. It is only necessary to make backups of whatever special configuration files have been modified locally. Sites which use cfengine can simply allow cfengine to reconstruct local modifications after an OS installation. In any event, if we have followed the principle of separating the operating system from local modifications, this is no problem at all.

Similar remarks can be made about other software. Commercial software is now sold on CD-ROM and is trivial to reinstall (remember to keep a backup of license keys). For freely available software, there are already many copies and mirrors at remote locations by virtue of the Internet. For convenience, a local source repository can also be kept, to speed up recovery in the case of an accident. In the unlikely event of every host being destroyed simultaneously, downloading the software again from the network is the least of your worries!

Reconstructing a system from source rather than from backup has never been easier than now. Moreover, a policy of not backing up software which is easily accessible from source, can make a considerable saving in the volume of backup space required, at the price of more work in the event of accident. In the end this is a matter of policy.

It should be clear that user-data must have maximum priority for backup. This is where local creativity manifests itself; these are the data which form your assets.

11.7.2 Loss of service

Loss of service might be less permanent than the loss of data, but it can be just as debilitating. Downtime costs money for businesses and wastes valuable time in academia.

The basic source of all computing power is electricity. Loss of electrical power can be protected against, to a limited extent, with an *un-interruptible power supply* (UPS). This is not an infallible security, but it helps to avoid problems due to short breaks in the power. UPS solutions use a battery backup to keep the power going for a few hours when power has failed. When the battery begins to run down, they can signal the host so as to take it down in a controlled fashion, thus minimizing damage to disks and data. Investing in a UPS for an important server could be the best thing one ever does. Electrical spike protectors are another important accessory for anyone living in a region where lightning strikes are frequent, or where the power supply is of variable quality. No fuse will protect a computer from a surge of electricity: microelectronics burn out much quicker than any fuse.

Service can also be interrupted by a breach of the network infrastructure: a failed router or broken cable, or even a blown fuse. It can be interrupted by cleaning staff, or carelessness. A backup or stand-by replacement is the only option for hardware failure. It helps to have the telephone number of those responsible for network hardware when physical breaches occur.

Software can be abused in a *denial of service attack*. Denial of service attacks are usually initiated by sending information to a host which confuses it into inactivity. There are as many variations on this theme as there are vandals on the network. Some attacks exploit bugs, while others are simply spamming episodes, repeatedly sending a deluge of service requests to the host, so that it spends all of its resources on handling the attack.

11.7.3 Protocols

What is the solution to uncertainty? An amount of uncertainty is inevitable in any complex system. Where humans are concerned, uncertainty is always significant. A strict mode of behavior is the usual way of counteracting this uncertainty. Protocols are ways of eliminating unnecessary uncertainty by reducing the freedom of the participants.

> **Principle 61 (Protocols offer predictability).** *A well-designed protocol, either for human behavior or machine behavior, standardizes behavior and offers predictability.*

11.7.4 Authentication

In order to provide basic security for individuals, we need to keep track of the identity of users who make requests of the system. Authentication means determining whether the claim of identity is authentic. Usually we mean verifying somebody's identity. There are two reasons for authenticating users:

- User-based access control of files and programs requires users to be distinguished by an identity.

- Accountability: attaching actions to users for recording in logs.

All authentication is based on the idea of comparing unique attributes of individuals with some database. Often ownership of a shared secret is used for this purpose, such as a password or encryption key, known only to the individual and the authenticator.

There is much confusion surrounding authentication. Much of this stems from the many claims made by cryptographic methods to provide secure methods for authenticating user identities. While this is not incorrect, it misses a crucial point.

> **Principle 62 (Identification requires trust).** *Establishing identity is 'impossible'. Identification requires an initial introduction, based on trust.*

Corollary to principle (Authentication is re-identification). *Authentication is the confirmation of a previously trusted identity.*

The first time we meet a person or contact a host on a network, we know nothing about them. When a previously unknown person or host claims their identity we must accept this information on trust. No matter how many detailed measurements we make (DNA test, processor serial number, secure exchange of keys etc.), there is no basis for matching those identifying marks to the identity claimed – since we cannot mind-read, we simply have to trust it. Once an initial identity has been accepted as true, one can then use unique properties to identify the individual again in the future, in a variety of ways, some more secure than others. The special markers or unique properties can only confirm that a person or host is the same person or host as we met previously. If the original introduction was faked, the accuracy of recognition cannot detect this.

Password login

The provision of a username claims our identity and a password verifies that claim. If this authentication succeeds, we are granted access to the system, and all of our activities then occur within the scope of an identifier which represents that user. On Unix-like systems, the username is converted into a global unique user-id number (UID). On Windows systems, the username is converted into a security-id (SID) which is only unique on a local host.

There are obvious problems with password authentication: passwords can be guessed and they can be leaked. Users with only weak passwords are vulnerable to dictionary and other brute-force attacks.

This type of login is called unilateral authentication, that is, it identifies the user to the computer. It does not verify the identity of the computer to the user. Thus a malicious party could fake a login dialogue on a computer, using this to collect passwords and account information.

Unix does not attempt to solve this problem, but NT and its successors provide a 'secure attention sequence'. If the user types CTRL+ALT+DEL, they are guaranteed to be directed to the operating system, rather than any user programs which might be trying to look like the OS.

Authentication types

The OSI security architecture (ISO 7498-2) makes a distinction between different kinds of authentication:

- *Entity authentication*: checking the identity of an individual or entity.

- *Origin authentication*: checking the location of an individual or entity.

- *Unilateral authentication*: verifying the entity to the authenticator.

- *Mutual authentication*: verifying both parties to one another.

Authentication is usually performed at the start of a session between client and system. Once one stops checking, an attacker could subsequently sneak in and change places with an authenticated user. Thus to ensure security in an on-going conversation, we have to verify identity and then use some kind of secret key to ensure that the identity cannot be changed, e.g. by encrypting the conversation. The key is only known by the authenticated parties, such as a secret that has been exchanged.

Challenge response protocols

Consider two parties A and B, who need to open a dialogue and verify a previously trusted identity.

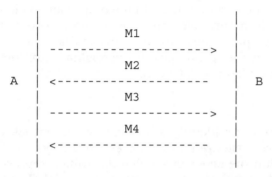

A starts the protocol by sending a message to B, M1. B replies with M2, etc. We assume that message $N + 1$ is not sent until message N has been received and understood.

During or after the exchange of the messages we need to be sure of the following:

- That the messages were received (unaltered) from the hosts which were supposed to send them.

- That the messages are fresh, i.e. not replays of old messages.

- That message $N + 1$ is a correct reply to message N, not a misleading reply to a different question.

The first of these assurances can be made by using cryptographic checksums (message digests such as MD5 or SHA-1) or Message Authentication Code (MAC) that verifies both the identity of the sender and the integrity of the message, using a cryptographic key.

The second could be assured by the use of a time-stamp, though this would be vulnerable to errors of clock synchronization. A better approach is to use a random *challenge* or *nonce* (from the medieval English for 'once only').

A nonce is usually a long random number that is encrypted with a key that can only be decrypted by the receiver. The receiver then replies to the sender of the nonce by decrypting it and sending it back. Only the keeper of the secret could do this, and thus this confirms the identity of the receiver as well as the freshness of the reply. To achieve a mutual authentication, both parties send challenges to one another.

11.7.5 Integrity

Trust is the pernicious problem of security. How are we able to trust files and data which others send? Programs that we download could contain viruses or Trojan horses. Assuming that we trust the person who wrote the program, how can we be sure that no one else has tampered with it in between?

There are some things we can do to increase our confidence in data we receive from a foreign source. One is to compare message digests.

Message digests or hashes are cryptographic checksums which quickly summarize the contents of a file. The idea is to create an algorithm which digests the contents of a file and produces a single value which uniquely summarizes its contents. If we change one bit of a file, then the value of the message digest also changes. Popular algorithms include:

```
MD4
MD5    (Stronger than md4)
SHA1
```

```
host$ md5 .cshrc
MD5 (.cshrc) = 519ab7d30dba4a2d16b86328e025ec72
```

MD5 signatures are often quoted at security software repositories so that it is possible to verify the authenticity of software (assuming the MD5 signature is authentic!).

11.8 Some well-known attacks

There are many ways to attack a networked computer in order to gain access to it, or simply disable it. Some well-known examples are listed below. The actual attack mechanisms used by attackers are often intricate and ingenious, but the common theme in all of them is to exploit naive limitations in the way network services are implemented. Time and again one sees crackers make use of software systems which were written in good faith, by forcing them into unnatural situations where the software fails through inadequate checking.

11.8.1 Ping attacks

The RFC 791 specifies that Internet datagrams shall not exceed 64kB. Some implementations of the protocol can send packets which are larger than this, but not all implementations can receive them.

```
ping -s 65510 targethost
```

Some older network interfaces can be made to crash certain operating systems by sending them a 'ping' request like this with a very large packet size. Most modern operating systems are now immune to this problem (e.g. NT 3.51 is vulnerable, but NT 4 is not). If not, it can be combatted with a packet filtering router. See http://www.sophist.demon.co.uk/ping/.

11.8.2 Denial of service (DoS) attacks

Another type of attack is to overload a system with so many service requests that it grinds to a halt. One example is mail spamming,[2] in which an attacker sends large numbers of repetitive E-mail messages, filling up the server's disk and causing the `sendmail` daemon to spawn rapidly and slow the system to a standstill.

Denial of service attacks are almost impossible to protect against. It is the responsibility of local administrators to prevent their users from initiating such attacks wherever possible.

11.8.3 TCP/IP spoofing

Most network resources are protected on the basis of the host IP addresses of those resources. Access is granted by a server to a client if the IP address is contained in an access control list (ACL). Since the operating system kernel itself declares its own identity when packets are sent, it has not been common to verify whether packets actually do arrive from the hosts which they claim to arrive from. Ordinary users have not traditionally had access to privileges which allow them to alter network protocols. Today everyone can run a PC with privileged access to the networking hardware.

Normally an IP datagram passing from host A to host B has a destination address 'host B' and source address 'host A' (see figure 11.4). IP spoofing is the act of forging IP datagrams in such a way that they appear to come from a third party host, i.e. an attacker at host A creates a packet with destination address 'host B' and source address 'host C'. The reasons for this are various. Sometimes an attacker wants to appear to be host C in order to gain access to a special resource which host C has privileged access to. Another reason might be to attack host C, as part of a more elaborate attack. Usually it is not quite this simple however, since the forgery is quickly detected. The TCP handshake is such that host A sends a packet to host B and then replies to the source address with a sequence number which has to match the next number of an agreed sequence. If another packet is not received with an agreed sequence number the connection will be reset and abandoned. Indeed, if host C received the confirmation reply for a message which it never sent, it would send a reset signal back immediately, saying effectively 'I know nothing about this'. To prevent this from happening it is common to take out host C first by attacking it with some kind of Denial of Service method, or simply choosing an address which is not used by any host. This prevents it from sending a reset message. The advantage of choosing a real host C is that the blame for the attack is placed on host C.

11.8.4 SYN flooding

IP spoofing can also be used as a denial of service attack. By choosing an address for host C which is not in use so that it cannot reply with a reset, host A can send SYN packets (new connections) on the same and other ports repeatedly. The

---

[2]From the Monty Python song 'Spam spam spam spam...'.

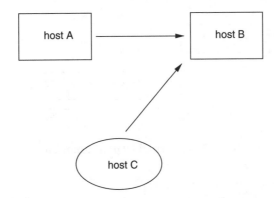

Figure 11.4: IP spoofing. A third party host C assumes the role of host A.

RECV queue quickly fills up and cannot be emptied since the connections cannot be completed. Because the queues are filled the services are effectively cut off.

These attacks could be prevented if routers can be configured so as to disallow packets with forged source addresses.

11.8.5 TCP sequence guessing

This attack allows an attacker to make a TCP connection to a host by guessing the initial TCP sequence number used by the other end of the connection. This is a form of IP spoofing by a man in the middle. The attack was made famous by the break in to Tsutomo Shinomura's computers which led to the arrest of Kevin Mitnick. This attack is used to impersonate other hosts for trusted access [29, 220]. This approach can now be combatted by using random initial sequence numbers (using the strategy expounded in section 7.7.5), though many operating systems require special configuration to enable such measures.

11.8.6 IP/UDP fragmentation (Teardrop)

A Teardrop attack was responsible for the now famous twelve-hour attack which 'blue-screened' thousands of NT machines all over the world. This attack uses the idea of datagram fragmentation. Fragmentation is something which happens as a datagram passes through a router from one network to another network where the Minimum Transfer Unit (MTU) is lower. Large packets can be split up into smaller packets for more efficient network performance. In a Teardrop attack, the attacker forges two UDP datagrams which appear to be fragments of a larger packet, but with data offsets which overlap.

When fragmentation occurs it is always the end host which reassembles the packets. In order to allocate memory for the data, the kernel calculates the difference between the end of the datagram and the offset at which the datagram fragment started. In a normal situation that would look like that in figure 11.5. In a Teardrop attack the packets are forged so that they overlap, as shown in figure 11.6. The assumption that the next fragment would follow on from the

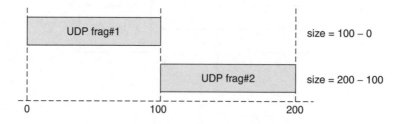

Figure 11.5: Normal UDP fragmentation.

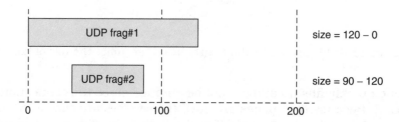

Figure 11.6: Spoofed UDP fragmentation, generates a negative size.

previous one leads to a negative number for the size of the fragment. As the kernel tries to allocate memory for this it calls `malloc(size)` where the size is now a negative number. The kernel panics and the system crashes on implementations which did not properly check the bounds.

11.8.7   ICMP flooding (Smurf)

ICMP flooding is another denial of service attack. The ICMP protocol is the part of TCP/IP which is used to transmit error messages and control information between hosts. Well-known services like `ping` and `echo` use ICMP. Normally all hosts respond to ping and echo requests without question, since they are useful for debugging. In an ICMP flooding attack, the attacker sends a spoofed ICMP packet to the broadcast address of a large network. The source address of the packet is forged so that it appears to come from the host which the attacker wishes to attack. Every host on the large network receives the ping/echo request and replies to the same host simultaneously. The host is then flooded with requests. The requests consume all the system resources.

11.8.8   DNS cache poisoning

This attack is an example of the exploitation of a trusted service in order to gain access to a foreign host. Again it uses a common theme, that of forging a network service request. This time, however, the idea is to ask a server to cache some information which is incorrect so that future look-ups will result in incorrect information being given instead of the correct information [29].

DNS is a hierarchical service which attempts to answer queries about IP names and addresses locally. If a local server does not have the information requested it asks an authoritative server for that information. Having received the information from the authoritative server it caches it locally to avoid having to contact the other server again; after all, since the information was required once, it is likely that the same information will be required again soon. The information is thus placed in the cache for a period of time called the TTL (*Time To Live*). After that time has expired it has to be obtained again from the authoritative server.

In a cache poisoning attack, the aim is to insert incorrect information into the cache of a server. Once it is there it will be there for the TTL period. In order to arrange this an attacker does the following.

1. The attacker launches his/her attack from the authoritative nameserver for his/her network. This gives him/her the chance to send information to another nameserver which will be trusted.

2. The attacker sends a query for the IP address of the victim host to the victim's default DNS server in order to obtain a DNS query ID. This provides a point of reference for guessing, i.e. forging, the next few query IDs from that server.

3. The attacker then sends a query asking for the address of a host which the victim machine trusts, i.e. the host which the attacker would like to impersonate.

4. The attacker hopes that the victim host will soon need to look up the IP address of the host it trusts; he/she sends a fake 'reply' to such a DNS lookup request, forged with the query ID to look as though it comes from a lookup of the trusted host's address. The answer for the IP address of the trusted host is altered so that it is the IP address of the attacker's host.

5. Later when the victim host actually sends such a DNS request it finds that it has already received a UDP reply to that request (this is the nature of UDP) and it ignores the real reply because it arrives later. Now the victim's DNS cache has been poisoned.

6. The attacker now attempts to connect directly to the victim host, posing as the trusted host. The victim host tries to verify the IP address of the host by looking up the address in its DNS server. This now responds from its cache with the forged address.

7. The attacker's system is accepted.

This kind of attack requires the notion of external login based on trust, e.g. with Unix .rhosts files. This doesn't help with NT because NT doesn't have trusted hosts in the same way. On the other hand, NT is much easier to gain access to through NULL sessions.

Exercises

Self-test objectives

1. Describe the nature of possible threats to the security of a human–computer system.

2. What is meant by 'security is a property of systems'?

3. What are the four main themes in computer security?

4. What role does trust play in setting the ground rules for security?

5. Explain how security relates to risk assessment.

6. What are the main threats to human–computer security?

7. Who present the main threats to human–computer security?

8. What is ISO17799?

9. What is RFC 2196?

10. What is meant by social engineering?

11. List some ways of countering social engineering.

12. What is meant by a honey pot?

13. What is meant by a sacrificial lamb?

14. What are the pros and cons of system homogeneity in security?

15. Explain how laptops and mobile devices can compromise security.

16. What are the problems with the security of the Internet Protocol?

17. State the ways of minimizing the likelihood of a serious security breach.

18. How does economy play a role in security?

19. What is the point of strict protocols in human–computer systems?

20. Explain why it is not possible to ever really identify someone – only to re-identify someone whose identity we have already trusted.

21. What is mutual authentication?

22. What is a challenge–response system?

23. What is meant by a nonce?

24. What is a cryptographic hash or checksum?

25. What is a message authentication code?

26. What is meant by a Denial of Service (DoS) attack?

27. What is meant by cache poisoning?

Problems

1. What are the basic requirements for computer security? Look around your network. Which hosts satisfy these basic requirements?

2. Devise a checklist for securing a PC attached to a network in your organization. How would you secure a PC in a bank? Are there any differences in security requirement between your organization and a bank? If so, what are they and how do you justify them?

3. Determine what password format is used on your own system. Are shadow password files used? Does your site use NIS (i.e. can you see the password database by typing `ypcat passwd`)?

4. Assume that passwords may consist of only the 26 letters of the alphabet. How many different passwords can be constructed if the number of characters in the password is 1, 2, 3, 4, 5, 6, 7 or 8 characters?

5. Suppose a password has four characters, and it takes approximately a millisecond (10^{-3} s) to check a password. How long would a brute-force attack take to determine the password?

6. Discuss how you can really determine the identity of another person. Is it enough to see the person? Is a DNA test sufficient? How do you know that a person's body has not been taken over by aliens, or they have not been brainwashed by a mad scientist? This problem is meant to make you think carefully about the problem of *authentication*.

7. Password authentication works by knowing a shared secret. What other methods of authentication are used?

8. The secure shell uses a Virtual Private Network (VPN) or encrypted channel between hosts to transfer data. Does this offer complete security? What does encryption not protect against?

9. Explain the significance of redundancy in a secure environment.

10. When the current TCP/IP technology was devised, ordinary users did not have personal computers or access to network listening devices. Explain how encryption of TCP/IP links can help to restore the security of the TCP/IP protocol.

11. Explain the purpose of a sacrificial lamb.

12. Discuss the point of making a honey pot. Would this attract anyone other than bears of little brain?

13. Answer true or false to the following (you might have to read ahead to answer some of these):

    (a) Current DNS implementations have no strong authentication.

(b) DNSSec can use digital signatures to solve the problem of authenticity for zone transfers between redundant servers.

(c) DNSSec can use symmetric shared secrets to solve the authenticity problem for zone transfers.

(d) Current implementations of DNS have no way of restricting access and are thus completely vulnerable to integrity attacks.

(e) Current DNS implementations use unreliable connections.

(f) SSL/TLS uses Kerberos to authenticate secure sockets.

(g) SSL/TLS use trust management based on a signing authority, like a trusted third party.

(h) IPSec was designed for and only works with IPv6, so it will not be available for some years.

(i) IPSec has solved the problem of contradictory policy rules.

(j) IPSec permits packet filtering based on Mandatory Access Control.

(k) IPSec's use of encrypted tunnels allows it to function like a VPN, provided that end devices themselves support IPSec.

(l) Wireless IP security does not support end to end encryption, only encryption between wireless device and receiving station.

14. Explain why encryption can be used as a form of authentication.

15. What is meant by masquerading or spoofing?

16. Describe the issues to consider in finding a backup scheme for a large and a small organization. Your answer should address tactical, economic and ethical issues.

Chapter 12

Security implementation

In the previous chapter we looked at the meaning of security in the context of a computer system. Now we apply the basic principles and consider what practical steps can be taken to provide a basic level of security.

12.1   System design and normalization

Security is a property of systems; to address security, we must speak of the system as a whole:

- Identify what assets we are trying to protect.

- Evaluate the main sources of risk and where trust is placed.

- Work out possible counter-measures to attacks.

Counter-measures can be both preventative and reactive. They consist of:

- Rules

- Codified responses.

The foundation of security is policy. We must agree on what is valuable and acceptable in the system. Without such an assessment, we cannot speak of the risk to those assets, and determine what level of risk is acceptable. Policy is decided by social groups.

A system consists of an assembly of parts that exhibit three main activities:

- Input

- Rules

- Output.

Each of these must be addressed and poses different threats. Input exposes a part of the system to its outside environment. Output exposes the environment to the system part. The rules determine whether the part fulfills its role in the system. Security of a system requires the safe and predictable functioning of all parts within a system, and the safe and predictable functioning of the sum of those parts.

Protecting ourselves against threat also involves a limited number of themes:

- Applying safeguards (shields)

- Access control (selective shields)

- Protocols (specification of and limitation to safe behavior)

- Feedback regulation (continuous assessment)

- Redundancy (parallelism instead of serialism) detection and correction

- Monitoring the system

- Regulation.

We need to apply these to environments which utilize computer systems. *Normalization* of a system is a concept from the theory of databases.

- Avoid unnecessary dependencies and inconsistencies.

- Validate assumptions.

12.2 The recovery plan

When devising a security scheme, think of the post-disaster scenario. When disaster strikes, how will the recovery proceed? How long is this likely to take? How much money or time will be lost as a result?

The network is a jigsaw puzzle in which every piece has its place and plays its part. Recall the principle of redundancy: the more dependent we are on one particular piece of the puzzle, the more fragile the set up. Recovery will occur more quickly if we have backups of all key hardware, software and data.

In formulating a recovery plan, then, we need a scheme for replacing key components either temporarily or permanently, and we should also bear in mind that we do rely on many things which are outside of our immediate control. What happens, for instance, if a digger (back-hoe) goes through the net cable, our only link to the outside world? Whom should we call? Less fundamental but more insidious, what if the network managers above us decide to decouple us from the network without informing us in advance? In a large organization, different people have responsibility for different maintenance tasks. It has happened on more than one occasion that the power has been shut down without warning – a potentially lethal act for a computer.

12.3 Data integrity and protection

As part of any infrastructure plan, we need to apply the principles of redundancy and protection to the system's data. Although backup copies will not protect us against loss, they do provide minimal insurance against accidents, intentional damage and natural disasters, and make the business of *recovery* less painful. There are several general strategies:

Encryption	Prevention of access on theft or tampering
Integrity checksums	Detection of error or tampering
Redundancy	Recovery from loss

12.3.1 Preventing error, tampering and loss

Data must be protected both when standing still (in storage) and when passing from place to place (in transport).

Encryption is a strategy for prevention of theft and tampering, particularly in the transmission of data over networks, though it can also be used to protect disk data from theft and backups from tampering. Encryption is only effective if the encryption keys are managed properly.

Disk information is a separate concern. Once a file is deleted in Unix-like operating systems, it is not directly recoverable. Unlike DOS and its successors, there is no way to undelete a file. Some system administrators like to protect inexperienced users by making an alias (in C-shell)

```
alias rm    rm -i
```

which causes the rm command to ask whether it really should delete files before actually doing so. This is a simple idea and it is not foolproof, but it is an example of the kind of small details which make systems safer. On the other hand, some believe that relying on such tactics only prolongs the inevitable, and that learning to be careful is a better approach. The only real security against deletion is to keep extensive backups of user disks. In Windows environments, it is not uncommon to hear screams of anguish as users lose two hours' work because they didn't save before the system crashed, or reformatted their text according to some arbitrary template. Sensible software defaults can go a long way to preventing loss of data.

Loss against physical disk failure can be mitigated by using RAID solutions which offer real redundancy. RAID stands for Redundant Array of Inexpensive Disks.[1] The idea is that, since disks are relatively cheap, compared with human time and labor, we can build a system which uses extra disks in order to secure increased performance and redundancy. RAID disks systems are sold by most manufacturers and come in a variety of levels. Not all of the RAID levels have anything at all to do with redundancy. Indeed some are more concerned with striping disks to increase performance and are more insecure than using single disks. There are currently more than seven levels of RAID from 0 to 6 or 7 depending on where you look; these incorporate a number of themes:

- *Disk striping:* This is a reorganization of filesystem structure amongst a group of disks. Data are spread across disks, using parallelism to increase data throughput and improved search rate. This can improve performance dramatically, but reduces security by an equal amount, since if one disk fails, all the data are lost from the other disks.

---

[1]Nowadays, the RAID advisory board use Independent for the 'I'.

- *Real-time mirroring:* When data are written to one disk, they are simultaneously written to a second disk, rather than mirroring as a batch job performed once per day (see next section). This increases security. This protects against random disk failure, but not necessarily against natural disasters etc., since RAID disks are usually located all in one place.

- *Hamming code parity protection:* Data are split across several disks to utilize parallelism, and a special parity disk enables data to be reconstructed provided no more than one disk fails randomly. Again, this does not help us against loss due to wide-scale influences like natural disasters.

New RAID solutions appear frequently and the correspondence between manufacturers' solutions and RAID levels is not completely standardized. RAID provides enhancements for performance and fault tolerance, but it cannot protect us against deliberate vandalism or widespread failure.

12.3.2 Backup schemes

We can lose information in many ways: by accident, technical failure, natural disaster or even sabotage. We must make sure that there are several copies of the data so that everything may be recovered from a secure backup. Backups are one of the favorite topics of the system administration community. Everyone has their own local tricks. Many schemes for backup have been described; most of them resemble one another apart from cosmetic differences. Descriptions of backup schemes are manifold. Regular incremental style backups with site customizations can be found in refs. [310, 158, 169, 241, 148, 234, 335, 218, 257, 213]. A forward-looking backup scheme with a broad generality in its ability to use different services and devices for remote backups is described in ref. [284] and backup to optical disks is discussed in refs. [65, 320]. Automated tape backup and restore is discussed in ref. [184] and in the Amanda system [283]; the AFS backup system is discussed in ref. [151]. A review of how well backup systems deal with special Unix sparse files was conducted in ref. [338].

Backup applies to individual changes, to system setup and to user data alike. In backing up data according to a regular pattern, we are assuming that no major changes occur in the structure of data [281]. If major changes occur, we need to start backups afresh. The network has completely changed the way we have to think about backup. Transmitting copies of files to secondary locations is now much simpler. The basics of backup are these:

- *Physical location:* A backup should be kept at a different physical location than the original. If data were lost because of fire or natural disaster, then copies will also be lost if they are stored nearby. On the other hand, they should not be too far away, or restoration time will suffer.

- *How often?:* How often do the data change significantly, i.e. how often do we need to make a backup? Every day? Do you need to archive several different versions of files, or just the latest version? The cost of making a backup is a relevant factor here.

- *Relevant and irrelevant files:* There is no longer much point in making a backup of parts of the operating system distribution itself. Today it is usually just as quick to reinstall the operating system from source, using the original CD-ROM. If we have followed the principle of separating local modifications from the system files, then it should be trivial to backup only the files which cannot be recovered from the CD-ROM, without having to backup everything.

- *Backup policy:* Some sites might have rules for defining what is regarded as valid information, i.e. what it is worth making a backup of. Files like `prog.tar.gz` might not need to be kept on backup media since they can be recovered from the network just as easily. Also one might not want to make backups of teen 'artwork' which certain users collect from the network, nor temporary data, such as browser cache files.

Medium

Traditionally backups have been made from disk to tape (which is relatively cheap and mobile), but tape backup is awkward and difficult to automate unless one can afford a specialized robot to change and manage the tapes. For small sites it is also possible to perform disk mirroring. Disk is cheap, while human operators are expensive. Many modern filesystems (e.g. DFS) are capable of automatic disk mirroring in real-time. A cheap approach to mirroring is to use cfengine:

```
# cfengine.conf on backup host

copy:

    /home dest=/backup/home
          recurse=inf
          server=myhost
          exclude=core
```

When run on the backup host, this makes a backup of all the files under the directory /home on the host myhost, apart from core files. RAID disks also have inbuilt redundancy which allows data to be recovered in the event of a single disk crash. Another advantage with a simple mirroring scheme is that users can recover their files themselves, immediately without having to bother a system administrator.

Of course, as the size of an institution grows, the economics of backup change. If one part of an organization has the responsibility for making backups for the entire remainder, then disk mirroring suddenly looks expensive. If each department of the organization invests in its own mirror disks, then the cost is spread. Economics has a lot to do with appearance as well as reality. One criticism of disk mirroring is that it is not always possible to keep the disk mirrors far enough away from the original to be completely safe. An additional tape backup as a last resort is probably a good idea anyway.

A backup schedule

How often we need to make backups depends on two competing rates of change:

- The rate at which new data are produced.

- The expected rate of loss or failure.

For most sites, a daily backup is sufficient. In a war-zone, where risk of bombing is a threat at any moment, it might be necessary to back up more often. Most organizations do not produce huge amounts of data every day; there are limits to human creativity. However, other organizations, such as research laboratories collect data automatically from instruments which would be impractically expensive to re-acquire. In that case, the importance of backup would be even greater. Of course, there are limits to how often it is possible to make a backup. Backup is a resource-intensive process.

Suggestion 15 (Static data). *When new data are acquired and do not change, they should be backed up to permanent write-once media at once. CD-ROM is an excellent medium for storing permanent data.*

For a single, un-networked host used only occasionally, the need for backup might be as little as once per week or less.

The options we have for creating backup schemes depend on the tools we have available for the job. On Windows we have NTBackup. On Unix-like systems there is a variety of tools which can be used to copy files and filesystems.

Backup	Restore
cp -ar	cp -ar
tar cf	tar xpf
GNU tar zcf	tar zxpf
dd	dd
cpio	cpio
dump	restore
ufsdump	restore
rdump	rrestore
NTBackup	NTBackup

Of course, commercial backup solutions exist for all operating systems, but they are often costly.

On both Unix and Windows, it is possible to backup filesystems either *fully* or *differentially*, also called *incrementally*. A full dump is a copy of every file. An incremental backup is a copy of only those files which have changed since the last backup was taken. Incremental backups rely on dump timestamps and a consistent and reliable system clock to avoid files being missed. For instance, the Unix dump utility records the dates of its dumps in a file /etc/dumpdates. Incremental dumps work on a scheme of levels, as we shall see in the examples below.

There are many schemes for performing system dumps:

- *Mirroring:* By far the simplest backup scheme is to mirror data on a daily basis. A tool like cfengine or rsync (Unix) can be used for this, copying only the files which have changed since the previous backup. Cfengine is capable of retaining the last two versions of a file, if disk space permits. A disadvantage with this approach is that it places the onus of keeping old versions of files on the user. Old versions will be mercilessly overwritten by new ones.

- *Simple tape backup:* Tape backups are made at different *levels*. A level 0 dump is a complete dump of a filesystem. A level 1 dump is a dump of only those files which have changed since the last level 0 dump; a level 2 dump backs up files which have changed since the last level 1 dump and so on, *incrementally*. There are commonly nine levels of dumps using the Unix dump commands. NTBackup also allows incremental dumps.

  The point of making incremental backups is that they allow us to capture changes in rapidly changing files without having to copy an entire filesystem every time. The vast majority of files on a filesystem do not change appreciably over the space of a few weeks, but the few files which we are working on specifically do change often. By pin-pointing these for special treatment we save both time and tapes.

So how do we choose a backup scheme? There are many approaches, but the key principle to have in mind is that of *redundancy*. The more copies of a file we have, the less likely we are to lose the file. A dump sequence should always begin with a level 0 dump, i.e. the whole filesystem. This initializes the sequence of incremental dumps. Monday evening, Tuesday morning or Saturday are good days to make a level 0 dump, since that will capture most large changes to the filesystem that occur during the week or weekend, in the level 0 dump rather than in the subsequent incremental ones. Studies show that users download large amounts of data on Mondays (after the weekend break) and it stands to reason that after a week of work, large changes will have taken place by Saturday. So we can take our pick. Here is a simple backup sequence for user home-directories, then, assuming that the backups are taken at the end of each day:

Day	Dump level
Mon	0
Tue	1
Wed	2
Thu	3
Fri	4
Sat	1

Notice how this sequence works. We start with a full dump on Monday evening, collecting all files on the filesystem. Then on subsequent days we add only those files which have changed since the previous day. Finally on Saturday we go back to a level 1 dump which captures all the changes from the whole week (since the Monday dump) in one go. By doing this, we have two backups of the changes, not just one. If we do not expect much to happen over the weekend, we might want to drop the dump on Saturday.

A variation on this scheme, which captures several copies of every file over multiple tapes, is the so-called *Towers of Hanoi* sequence. The idea here is to switch the order of the dump levels every other day. This has the effect of capturing not only the files which have changed since the last dump, but also all of the files from the previous dump as well. Here is a sample for Monday to Saturday:

Towers of Hanoi sequence over 4 weeks
$0 \rightarrow 3 \rightarrow 2 \rightarrow 5 \rightarrow 4 \rightarrow 6$
$1 \rightarrow 3 \rightarrow 2 \rightarrow 5 \rightarrow 4 \rightarrow 6$
$1 \rightarrow 3 \rightarrow 2 \rightarrow 5 \rightarrow 4 \rightarrow 6$
$1 \rightarrow 3 \rightarrow 2 \rightarrow 5 \rightarrow 4 \rightarrow 6$

There are several things to notice here. First of all, we begin with a level 0 dump at the beginning of the month. This captures primarily all of the static files. Next we begin our first week with a level 3 dump which captures all changes since the level 0 dump. Then, instead of stepping up, we step down and capture all of the changes since the level 0 dump again (since 3 is higher than 2). This means that we get everything from the level 3 dump and all the changes since then too. On day 4 we go for a level 5 dump which captures everything since the last level 3, and so on. Each backup captures not only new changes, but all of the previous backup also. This provides double the amount of redundancy as would be gained by a simple incremental sequence. When it comes to Monday again, we begin with a level 1 backup which grabs the changes from the whole of the previous week. Then once a month, a level 0 backup grabs the whole thing again.

The Towers of Hanoi sequence is clever and very secure, in the sense that it provides a high level of redundancy, but it is also expensive since it requires time and attention. Robotic automation can help here.

The level of redundancy which is appropriate for a given site has to be a question of economics based on four factors:

1. The cost of the backup (in time and media).

2. The expected rate of loss.

3. The rate of data production.

4. Media reliability.

These factors vary for different kinds of data, so the calculation needs to be thought out for each filesystem independently. The final point can hardly be emphasized enough. It helps us nothing to make ten copies of a file, if none of those copies are readable when we need them.

Suggestion 16 (Tape backup). *Tapes are notoriously unreliable media, and tape streamers are mechanical nightmares, with complex moving parts which frequently go wrong. Verify the integrity of each substantial backup tape backup once you have made it. Never trust a tape. If the tape streamer gets serviced or repaired, check old tapes again afterwards. Head alignment changes can make old tapes unreadable.*

Needless to say, backups should be made when the system is virtually quiescent: at night, usually. The most obvious reason for this is that, if files are being changed while the backup is progressing, then data can be corrupted or backed up incorrectly. The other reason is one of load: traversing a filesystem is a highly disk-intensive operation. If the disk is being used extensively for other purposes at the same time, both backup and system will proceed at a snail's pace.

Enterprise backup

Special requirements for the backup of data at very large institutions are beyond the scope of this book. Readers are referred to ref. [245] for more information.

File separation

The principle of keeping independent files separate was not merely to satisfy any high-flying academic aesthetic, it also has a concrete practical advantage, particularly when it comes to backing up the system. There is little sense in backing up the static operating system distribution. It can be reinstalled just as quickly from the original CD-ROM (a non-perishable medium). However, operating system files that change often such as /etc/passwd or /etc/shadow which need to be at special locations within largely quiescent filesystems, can be copied to another filesystem which is backed up often. This follows automatically from our principle of keeping local changes separate from the OS files.

The same thing applies to other files like /etc/fstab or /etc/group and crontab which have been modified since the operating system was installed. However, here one can reverse the policy for the sake of a rational approach. While the password and shadow files have to be at a fixed place, so that they will be correctly modified when users change their passwords, none of the other files have to be kept in their operating system recommended locations.

> **Suggestion 17 (OS configuration files).** *Keep master versions of all configuration files like /etc/fstab, /etc/group or crontabs/ in a directory under site-dependent files, and use a tool which synchronizes the contents of the master files with the operating system files (e.g. cfengine). This also allows the files to be distributed easily to other hosts which share a common configuration, and provides us with one place to make modifications, rather than having to hunt around the system for long-forgotten modifications. Site-dependent files should be on a partition which is backed up. Do not use symbolic links for synchronizing master files with the OS: only the root filesystem is mounted when the system boots, and cross-partition links will be invalid. You might render the system unbootable.*

12.3.3 Recovery from loss

The ability to recover from loss presupposes that we have enough pieces of the system from which to reconstruct it, should disaster strike. This is where the principle of redundancy comes in. If we have done an adequate job of backing up the system, including special information about its hardware configuration, then we will not lose data, but we can still lose valuable time.

Recovery plans can be useful provided they are not merely bureaucratic exercises. Usually a checklist is sufficient, provided the system administration team are all familiar with the details of the local configuration. A common mistake in a large organization, which is guaranteed to lead to friction, is to make unwarranted assumptions about a local department. Delegation can be a valuable strategy in the fight against time. If there are sufficient local system administrators who know the details of each part of the network, then it will take such people less time to make the appropriate decisions and implement the recovery plan. However, delegation also opens us up to the possibility of inconsistency – we must make sure that those we delegate to are well trained. (Remember to set the write-protect tab on tapes and have someone check this afterwards.)

When loss occurs, we have to recover files from the backups. One of the great advantages of a disk mirroring scheme is that users can find backups of their own files without having to involve an administrator. For larger file recoveries, it is more efficient for a system administrator to deal with the task. Restoring from tape backup is a much more involved task. Unfortunately, it is not merely a matter of donkey work. First of all we have to locate the correct tape (or tapes) which contain the appropriate versions of backed up files. This involves having a system for storage, reading labels and understanding any incremental sequence which was used to perform the dump. It is a time-consuming business. One of the awkwardnesses of incremental backups is that backing up files can involve changing several tapes to gather all of the files. Also, imagine what would happen if the tapes were not properly labeled, or if they are overwritten by accident.

> **Suggestion 18 (URL filesystem names).** *Use a global URL naming scheme for all filesystems, so that the filename contains the true location of the file, and you will never lose a file on a tape, even if the label falls off. (See section 3.8.7.) Each file will be sufficiently labeled by its time-stamp and its name.*

We have two choices in recovery: reconstruction from backup or from source. Recovery from source is not an attractive option for local data. It would involve typing in every document from scratch. For software which is imported from external sources (CD-ROMs or ftp repositories), it is possible to reconstruct software repositories like /usr/local or Windows' software directories. Whether or not this is a realistic option depends on how much money one has to spend. For a particularly impoverished department, reconstruction from source is a cheap option.

ACLs present an awkward problem for Windows filesystems. Whereas Unix's root account always has permission to change the ownership and access rights of a file, Windows's Administrator account does not. On Windows systems, it is important not to reinstate files with permissions intact if there is a risk of them belonging to a foreign domain. If we did that, the files would be unreadable to everyone, with no possibility of changing their permissions.

Data directory loss is one thing, but what if the system disk becomes corrupted? Then it might not even be possible to start the system. In that case it is necessary to boot from floppy disk, CD-ROM or network. For instance, a PC with GNU/Linux can be booted from a 'rescue disk' or boot disk, in single-user mode (see section 4.3.1), just by inserting a disk into the floppy drive. This will allow full access to the system disk by mounting it on a spare directory:

```
mount /dev/hda1 /mnt
```

On Sun Sparc systems, we can boot from CD-ROM, from the monitor:

```
boot cdrom
```

or `boot sd(0,6,2)` with very old PROMs.[2] Then, assuming we know which is the root partition, it can be mounted and examined:

```
mount /dev/dsk/c0t0d0t3 /mnt
```

Recovery also involves some soul searching. We have to consider the reason for the loss of the data. Could the loss of data have been prevented? Could it be prevented at a later time? If the loss was due to a security breach or some other form of vandalism, then it is prudent to consider other security measures at the same time as we reconstruct the system from the pieces.

12.3.4 Checksum or hash verification

Every time we use the privileged system account, we are at risk of installing a virus or a Trojan horse, or of editing the contents of important files which define system security. The list of ingenious ploys for tricking root privileged processes into working on the behalf of attackers makes an impressive ream. The seeming inevitability of it, sooner or later, implores us to verify the integrity of programs and data by comparing them with a trusted source. A popular way to do this is to use a checksum comparison. To all intents and purposes, an MD5 checksum cannot be forged by any known procedure. An MD5 checksum or hash is a numerical value that summarizes the contents of a file. Any small change in a file changes its cryptographic checksum, with virtually complete certainty. A checksum can therefore be used to determine whether a file has changed. First we must compile a database of checksums for all important files on the system, in a trusted state. Then we check the actual files against this database over time. Assuming that the database itself is secure, this enables us to detect changes in the files and programs. The Tripwire program was the original program written to perform this function. Tripwire can be configured to cross-check several types of checksum, just on the off-chance that someone manages to find a way to forge an MD5 checksum. Cfengine can also perform this task routinely, while doing other file operations. Cfengine currently uses only MD5 checksums (see figure 12.1).

12.4 Authentication methods

Authentication methods are techniques for re-identifying users. They are based on matching attributes that uniquely identify individuals. Traditionally authentication has been based on shared secrets used in conjunction with cryptographic

---

[2]The SunOS CD player traditionally has to be on controller 0 with SCSI id 6.

```
control:

 actionsequence = ( files )

files:

 /usr owner=root, bin mode=o-w checksum=md5 recurse=inf
```

Figure 12.1: A cfengine program to gather and check MD5 checksums of the /usr file tree.

algorithms. There are two main approaches to the use of encryption: the use of symmetric encryption algorithms and the use of public key algorithms. Recently, related techniques such as smart cards (used in mobile phones) and biometrics (fingerprints and iris scans) have been experimented with.

12.4.1   Symmetric and asymmetric key methods

A shared secret identifies two parties to one another. With a symmetric key algorithm both parties must have explicit knowledge of the same secret key; one then has the problem of agreeing secrets with all of the individuals we want to talk to. If N parties need to communicate privately with a unique key, then one needs $N(N-1)/2$ secrets in total. Trust is established between each pair of individuals during the mutual agreement of the key. This is a simple and effective model, but its great overhead is the work required to establish and remember all of the keys.

With a public (or asymmetric) key algorithm, each party has two keys: a public key and a private key; thus there are $2N$ keys in total. The key-pair belonging to a given party consists of two related keys. A message that is encrypted with one of them can only be decrypted with the other. Each user can now keep one key completely secret and make the other key known to everyone. To send a secret message to the owner of the private key, someone only needs to encrypt a message with their public key. Only the owner of the matching private key can decrypt the message again (not even the person who encrypted it). This makes the problem of key distribution very straightforward. However, it has a price: since it obviates the need for a trusted meeting between the parties to agree on a secret, it makes the issue of trusting keys much harder. If you find a key, supposedly belonging to X on a particular web-site, you have only the word of the web-site owner that the key really is the key belonging to X. If you send a secret message to X using this key, it will only be readable by the owner of the private key that matches this key, but that could be anyone. Thus one has no idea, in general, whether or not to trust the identity associated with a public key. This issue is explored further below.

Public key algorithms are now widely used in authentication for their great convenience and flexibility.

12.4.2   Trust models and signing

Having chosen an encryption scheme for authentication, there is still the issue of what trust model to choose. This is particularly important in cases where authentication is required by non-interactive programs such as client-server mechanisms, where human intelligence is not available to make a value judgment (see principle 62 in section 11.7.4).

A caveat to public key methods is that they make possible the creation of *digital signatures*. Since the two keys in a key-pair both work in the same way (one merely makes an arbitrary choice about which is to be public and which is to be private), the owner of a private key can also encrypt messages with his or her private key that only the owner of the public key can decrypt. This does not help with privacy now, because everyone knows the public key. However, since only the matching public key can decrypt the message, it is possible for the receiver to verify which key was used to encrypt the message, i.e. the identity of the sender. This is the essence of digital signatures. It has the same trust problems as the encryption mentioned above; however, if one has somehow learned to trust who is the true originator of a public key, then one can also trust the signature.

The problem of trusting public keys is solved in one of three ways, all of which are certified by *signing* keys:

1. *Persona grata*: a key can be transferred 'in person' from a person that we already know. On accepting the key we sign it with our own digital signature as a certification of its authenticity.

2. *Peer review*: a key that has been accepted and signed by 'friends' whom we also trust is also acceptable if we see our friends' signature(s) on the public key. Once we have accepted and trusted the key, we sign it also and pass it on to others. The more signatures on a key from people we trust, the more likely it is that we can trust the key. This is also called the 'web of trust'. It is the model used by the encryption software PGP.

3. *Trusted third party*: we can authorize an entity to take responsibility for validating the identity of parties. This trusted entity is called a Trusted Third Party (TTP) and it has a signature that we trust implicitly. When we see a key that has been signed by a trusted third party, we take it to be a valid identity. Companies like Verisign sell this service for secure (HTTPS) web sites that use the Secure Socket Layer.

Principle 63 (Trusted third parties). *A trusted third party reduces the number of trust interactions from order N^2 to order N, by acting as a trusted repository for information about the N individuals. This is only possible because the TTP is trusted itself.*

Corollary to principle (Trusted third parties). *A trusted third party is a single point of failure within an authentication system.*

Schemes that are based on trusted third parties have a single point of failure and one is therefore completely dependent upon the security and reliability of their services. This makes them vulnerable to Denial of Service attacks.

Symmetric keys need not be signed, because they are private by definition. Peer review is therefore not applicable as a trust method. We are left with two possibilities: personal hand-off or verification by trusted third parties. Kerberos uses such a third party scheme for symmetric keys (see section 12.4.6).

12.4.3   SSH and cfengine

The secure shell, SSH, and cfengine share a similar trust model and authentication mechanisms. Cfengine's authentication dialogue is essentially a simplification of the SSH method, adapted to non-interactive use.

Much of the sophistication in SSH concerns the negotiation of an available encryption method, given the uncertain environment of connecting to potentially widely different sites. Cfengine has a much simpler task in this regard, since it is used primarily within a single organization with access to the same set of cryptographic tools and algorithms.

The user end of SSH is normally an interactive shell, in which a user can answer a direct question about whether or not to accept a new key. Cfengine, on the other hand, normally works non-interactively and must therefore make a decision internally about the acceptance of new keys.

Neither of these tools uses a trusted third party approach by default, though SSH can use multiple authentication methods. It is a Swiss army knife of authenticators. Cfengine does not allow a trusted third party model, since this kind of centralization is contrary to the spirit of a distributed system where one would like to make each player self-sufficient and independent of any single point of failure.

SSH uses a 'trusted port', i.e. port 22, which – in principle – prevents an untrusted user from setting up a service that looks like SSH and checks IP origin, like TCP wrappers.[3] However, it must accept client keys on trust, since no one is available on the server side to make a decision manually.

Cfengine checks IP origin and treats both server and client as untrusted: it requires a trust window to be opened for the acceptance of a new key, by requiring an administrator to 'switch-on' trust to a given IP address just before a trusted exchange. Once the key exchange is completed, the potential for subversion is passed. Both SSH and cfengine are, in principle, vulnerable to client identification races; however, secure shell has a backup in that it also demands a interactive backup authentication (such as password), so this does not necessarily matter.

It should be said that the likelihood of being able to exploit such a race is very small. It places the onus on the system administrator to secure the trusted environment for the key exchange. The payoff is the autonomy of the clients and the clear isolation of risk.

12.4.4   Transport Layer Security

The secure socket layer (SSL) was originally introduced by Netscape communications in order to allow private web transactions based on X.509 certificates. (HTTPS is SSL encoded HTTP). Version 3 of the protocol was extended with experiences and suggestions from other companies in the industry and was published as an Internet draft document standard. Transport layer security (TLS) is essentially an outgrowth of SSLv3, and it is intended that this will become a network industry standard.

---

[3]In reality, the trusted ports can no longer be trusted since every PC owner is a trusted user on their own system. The threshold for trust has been lowered considerably by the proliferation of computing.

SSL and TLS use public key methods to authenticate sites and establish a session key for communications. The protocol authenticates both parties and negotiates a computationally 'cheaper' encryption algorithm and message digest to sign the message.

SSL is designed to be a drop-in replacement for standard socket communication, easily implemented, with minimal investment on the part of the programmer. Roughly speaking, one simply replaces some system calls with library functions from SSL and the encryption should be transparent. In order to achieve this level of simplicity, a Trusted Third Party Trust model is used, since this avoids an interaction.

Keys are referred to as certificates and are only accepted on trust if they are signed by a signing authority (normally Verisign). Any keys that are not signed by a known authority are presented to users so that they can make a manual decision.

In a system administration context, SSL has both advantages and disadvantages. Clearly, one does not want to pay a signing authority a hundred dollars or more to authenticate each host at a site, but this applies mainly to the Web and could be circumvented with custom software. A larger problem is the centralization of the model: each new communication requires a verification with the central authority, thus there is a single point of failure. Administratively speaking, forced centralization is either a convenience or a curse depending on how centralized administrative practices are.

12.4.5 Sign and encrypt attacks

The belief that signing and public key encryption give strong security, especially in combination, is only partially true. It is still possible to construct attacks against the naive use of these encryption methods [88]. These attacks apply to a number of security infrastructures, including S/MIME and IPSec. They are easily curable with administrative care. We define first some notation for representing encryption and signing:

- Public keys: capital letters.

- Private keys: small letters.

- Encryption with public key A: {"message"}$_A$.

- Signing with private key b: ("message")$_b$.

Notice that a small letter denotes both signing and the use of a private key, and a capital letter denotes both encryption and the use of a public key. We now consider the two attacks on the sign-encrypt trust model.

Sign then encrypt attack

Alice signs and encrypts a message for her heart's desire, Bob:

$$A \rightarrow B : \{(\text{"I love you!!"})_a\}_B \qquad (12.1)$$

Alas, Bob does not like Alice and wants to embarrass her. He decrypts Alice's message, leaving her signed message,

$$\{(\text{"I love you!!"})_a\}_B \rightarrow (\text{"I love you!!"})_a \qquad (12.2)$$

and re-encrypts the message for Charlie to read:

$$B \rightarrow C : \{(\text{"I love you!!"})_a\}_C \qquad (12.3)$$

Now, when Charlie decrypts the message, he sees Alice's signature and believes that Alice loves him. The very security assured by signing will now incriminate Alice. This is more serious if the message is "I.O.U. 1,000,000".

Encrypt then sign attack

Inventor Alice encrypts a document describing her secret biotechnology patent, worth millions, for Bob, the patent lawyer. She signs the message so that Bob knows it is authentic. Unfortunately, her so-called friend Charlie (still angry about her falsified affections) intercepts the message along the way:

$$A \rightarrow C : (\{\text{"My patent...."}\}_B)_a \qquad (12.4)$$

Charlie laughs, knowing he is now rich. He strips off Alice's signature and signs the message himself.

$$(\{\text{"My patent"}\}_B)_a \rightarrow \{\text{"My patent"}\}_B \qquad (12.5)$$
$$\{\text{"My patent"}\}_B \rightarrow (\{\text{"My patent"}\}_B)_c \qquad (12.6)$$

He then sends it to Bob, the patent lawyer:

$$C \rightarrow B : (\{\text{"My patent...."}\}_B)_c \qquad (12.7)$$

It now appears that the idea comes from Charlie.

The solution to both of these attacks is to SIGN, ENCRYPT and SIGN again messages. Note that protocols using symmetrical ciphers are not susceptible to these attacks. We see that encryption mechanisms, while useful, are not an assurance of security.

12.4.6 Kerberos

Another protocol for establishing identity and exchanging a session key was devised in 1978 by R. Needham and M. Schroeder. It uses the idea of a trusted third party or key-broker and uses *symmetric* encryption keys to pass messages, and forms the backbone of the Kerberos system. In practice, the Needham–Schroeder protocol simulates the idea of public keys by sending all requests through a trusted third party or mediator.

Suppose A wishes to send a private message to B. Both A and B have already registered a secret key with a trusted key server S, and they assume that everyone else in their local domain has done the same. In order to talk privately to someone else, the trick is to establish an encryption key K_{ab} from A to B, given keys known only to themselves and S, without an attacker being able to understand the messages. Essentially Alice asks Sam to encrypt a message to Bob for her, without giving away Bob's key.

$$A \rightarrow S : A, B, N_a \tag{12.8}$$
$$S \rightarrow A : \{N_a, B, K_{ab}, \{K_{ab}\}_{K_{bs}}\}_{K_{as}} \tag{12.9}$$
$$A \rightarrow B : \{K_{ab}\}_{K_{bs}} \tag{12.10}$$
$$B \rightarrow A : \{N_b\}_{K_{ab}} \tag{12.11}$$
$$A \rightarrow B : \{N_b\}_{K_{ab}} \tag{12.12}$$

Curly braces indicate a message that is encrypted, using the key in the subscript. In words, this says the following:

1. A says to S: "I am A, I want to talk to B and I'm giving you a random nonce N_a."

2. S replies, quoting her nonce to show that the reply is not a replay, confirms that the message is about a key with B, and provides a key for encrypting messages between A and B. He also provides a message for Bob, already encrypted with the secret key that B and S share (K_{bs}). This message contains Alice's name and the session key (K_{ab}) for talking to A privately. All of this is encrypted with the common key that A and S share (K_{as}).

3. Alice simply sends the message which S encrypted to B. This is already encrypted so that B can read it.

4. B decrypts the message and replies using the session key (K_{ab}) with a nonce of its own to make sure that A's request is fresh, i.e. that this is not a replay.

5. A responds that it has received the nonce.

A and B are now ready to talk, using the secret session key K_{ab}. This protocol is the basis of the Kerberos system, which is used in many Unix and Windows 2000 systems.

Note that A and B could be two hosts, or two users on the same host. By routing communication through a trusted third party, they avoid having to agree more than one private key (the trusted party's key), in advance. Otherwise they would have to verify the $N(N-1)/2$ individual keys that are required to communicate privately between N individuals.

12.5 Analyzing network security

In order to assess the potential risks to a site, we must gain some kind of overview of how the site works. We have to place ourselves in the role of an outsider: how would someone approach the network from outside? Then we have to consider the system from the viewpoint of an insider: how do local users approach the system? To begin the analysis, we form a list:

- What hosts exist on our site?

- What OS types are used?

- What services are running?

- What bug patches are installed?

- Run special tools, nmap, SATAN, SAINT, TITAN to automate the examination procedure and find obvious holes.

- Examine trust relationships between hosts.

This list is hardly a trivial undertaking. Simply building the list can be a lesson to many administrators. It is so easy to lose control over a computer network, so difficult to keep track of changes and the work of others in a team, that one can easily find oneself surprised by the results of such a survey. Having made the list, it should become clear as to where potential security weaknesses lie. Network services are a common target for exploitation. FTP servers and Windows's commercial WWW servers have had a particularly hard time with bugs which have been exploited by attackers.

Correct host configuration is one of the prerequisites for network security. Even if we have a firewall shielding us from outside intrusion, an incorrectly configured host is a security risk. Firewalls do not protect us from the contents of data which are relayed to a host. If a bug can be exploited by sending a hidden message, then it will get through a firewall. Some form of automated configuration checking should be installed on hosts. Manual checking of hosts is impractical even with a single host; a site which has hundreds requires an automated procedure for integrity checking. On Unix and Windows one has cfengine and Perl for these tasks.

Trust relationships are amongst the hardest issues to debug. A trust relationship is an implicit *dependency*. Any host which relies on a network service, implicitly trusts that service to be reliable and correct. This can be the cause of many stumbling blocks. The complexity of interactions between host services makes many trust relationships opaque. Trust relationships occur in any instance in which there is an external source of information: remote copying, hostname lookup, directory services etc. The most important trust relationship of all is the Domain Name Service (DNS). Many access control systems rely on an accurate identification of the host name. If the DNS service is compromised, hosts can be persuaded to do almost anything. For instance, access controls which assign special privileges to a name, can be spoofed if the DNS lookups are corrupted or intercepted. DNS servers are therefore a very important pit-stop in a security analysis.

Access control is the fundamental requirement for security. Without access controls there can be no security. Access controls apply to files on a filesystem and to services provided by remote servers. Access should be provided on a need-to-know basis. If we are too lax in our treatment of access rights, we can fall foul of intrusion. For example: a common error in the configuration of Unix file-servers is to grant arbitrary hosts the right to mount filesystems which contain the personal files of users. If one exports filesystems which contain users' personal data to Unix-like hosts, it should be done on a host-by-host basis, with strict controls.

If a user, who is root on their own host (e.g. a portable PC running GNU/Linux), can mount a user filesystem (with files belonging to a non-root user), that person owns the data there. The privileged account can read any file on a mounted file system by changing its user ID to whatever it likes. That means that anyone with a laptop could read any user's mail or change any user's files. This is a huge security problem. Hosts which are allowed to mount NFS filesystems containing users' private data should be secured and should be active at all times to prevent IP spoofing; otherwise it is trivial to gain access to a user's files.

There are many tools written for Unix-like operating systems which can check the security of a site, literally by trying every conceivable security exploit. Tools like SPY [292], COPS, SATAN, SAINT, TITAN [111], Nessus [224] are aimed at Unix-like hosts. Port scanners such as nmap will detect services on any host with any operating system. These tools can be instrumental in finding problems. Recent and frightening statistics from the Computer Emergency Response Team indicated that only a pitiful number of sites actually upgrade or install patches and review their security, even after successful network intrusions [160].

Having mapped out an overview of a network site, and used the opportunity both to learn more about the specifics of the system, as well as fix any obvious flaws, we can turn our attention to more specific issues at the level of hosts.

12.5.1 Password security

Perhaps the most important issue for network security, beyond the realm of accidents, is the consistent use of strong passwords. Unix-like operating systems which allow remote logins from the network are particularly vulnerable to password attacks. The `.rhosts` and `hosts.equiv` files which allowed login without password challenge via `rsh` and `rlogin` were acceptable risks in bygone times, but these days one cannot afford to be lax about security. The problem with this mechanism is that `.rhosts` and `hosts.equiv` use hostnames as effective passwords. This mechanism trusts DNS name service lookups which can be spoofed in elaborate attacks. Moreover, if a cracker gets into one host, he/she will then be able to log in on every host in these files without a password. This greatly broadens the possibilities for effective attack. Typing a password is not such a hardship for users and there are alternative ways of performing remote execution for administrators, without giving up password protection (e.g. use of cfengine).

Password security is the first line of defence against intruders. Once a malicious user has gained access to an account, it is very much easier to exploit other weaknesses in security. Experience, indeed empirical evidence [219], shows that many users have little or no idea about the importance of using a good password. Consider some examples from a survey of passwords at a university. About 40 physicists had the password 'Einstein', around 10 had 'Newton' and several had 'Kepler'. Hundreds of users used their login-name as their password, some of them really went to town and added '123' to the end. Many girls chose 'horse' as their passwords. Even after extensive campaigns encouraging good passwords, users have a shocking tendency to trivialize this matter. User education is clearly an important weapon against weak passwords.

Some sites use schemes such as password aging in order to force users to change passwords regularly. This helps to combat password familiarity gained over time by local peer users, but it has an unfortunate side-effect. Users who tend to set poor passwords will not appreciate having to change their passwords repeatedly and will tend to rebel by setting trivial passwords if they can. Once a user has a good password, it is often advantageous to leave it alone. The problems of password aging are insignificant compared with the problem of weak passwords. Finding the correct balance of changing and leaving alone is a challenge.

Passwords are not visible to ordinary users, but their encrypted form is often visible. Even on Windows systems, where a binary file format is used, a freely available program like PwDump can be used to decode the binary format into ASCII. There are many publicly available programs which can guess passwords and compare them with the encrypted forms, e.g. crack, which is available both for Unix and for Windows. No one with an easy password is safe. Passwords should never be any word in a dictionary or a simple variation of such a word or name. It takes just a few seconds to guess these.

Modern operating systems have *shadow password files* or databases that are not readable by normal users. For instance, the Unix password file contains an 'x' instead of a password, and the encrypted password is kept in an unreadable file. This makes it much harder to scan the password file for weak passwords.

Tools for password cracking (e.g. Alec Muffet's crack program) can help administrators find weak passwords before crackers do. Other tools can be obtained from security sites to prevent users from typing in weak passwords. See refs. [300, 72, 4, 153].

12.5.2 Password sniffing

Many communication protocols (telnet, ftp etc.) were introduced before security was a concern amongst those on the Internet, so many of these protocols are very insecure. Passwords are often sent over the network as plain text. This means that a sophisticated cracker could find out passwords simply by listening to everything happening on the network and waiting for passwords to go by. If a cracker has privileged access to at least one machine with a network interface on the same network he/she can use tcpdump to capture all network traffic. Normal users do not have this privilege for precisely this reason. These days however, anyone with a laptop, an Ethernet card and a GNU/Linux installation could do this. Switched networks used to be immune to this problem since traffic is routed directly from host to host. However, now there exist tools that can poison the ARP cache and cause packets to be rerouted; thus switching is now only a low-level hindrance to password sniffing. In principle, any mildly determined user could do this.

Programs which dump all network traffic include tcpdump, etherfind, snoop and ethereal. Here is a sample of the output from Solaris' snoop program showing the Ethernet traffic from a segment of cable. Snoop recognizes common high-level protocols (SMTP/FTP/ARP etc.) and lists them explicitly. Unknown protocol types (in this case IPX) are simply listed as ETHER. In the right-hand column is the information which an intruder would try to use to sniff passwords.

```
Using device /dev/hme (promiscuous mode)
 post.eet.no -> nexus          SMTP C port=4552 oJyhnJycoZyhnKCcnGCc
torget.drammensnett.no -> nexus        SMTP C port=54621 AGoHRPVU9VT3
      nexus -> torget.drammensnett.no SMTP R port=54621
pc111-75.iu.hioslo.no -> nexus        FTP C port=1093
      nexus -> pc111-75 FTP R port=1093 226 Transfer complet
      nexus -> post.eet.no  SMTP R port=4552
 post.eet.no -> nexus          SMTP C port=4546 UHAQcBB/UB9QcBBwH1AQ
      nexus -> post.eet.no  SMTP R port=4546
 post.eet.no -> nexus          SMTP C port=4546 H2AQcBBwH1AfYBAQH1Af
   fw.nki.no -> nexus          SMTP C port=11424 O3Jw+XF7cMFCCweEQ/
      nexus -> fw.nki.no     SMTP R port=11424
 post.eet.no -> nexus          SMTP C port=4552 niYmJgomChomChoaChoK

      nexus -> post.eet.no  SMTP R port=4546
      nexus -> (broadcast)   ARP C Who is 128.39.89.230, takpeh ?
      nexus -> post.eet.no  SMTP R port=4552

      ? -> *                ETHER Type=0000 (LLC/802.3), size = 86 bytes
      ? -> *                ETHER Type=0000 (LLC/802.3), size = 128 bytes
      ? -> *                ETHER Type=0000 (LLC/802.3), size = 80 bytes
```

One way to avoid the problem of password sniffing is to use fully encrypted links such as ssh [332] and SSL (Secure Socket Layer) enabled services which replace the standard services. Another is to use a system of one-time passwords. One-time passwords are designed to eliminate the need for users to send their passwords over the network at all. Instead of typing an actual password, one types the remote password for a host into a program on a local machine, in order to generate a sequence of throw-away passwords which can be used in place of the actual remote password. The passwords are used only once so, even if someone gets to overhear them, it will already be too late: the password will have expired. Also the system is ingeniously designed so that the actual remote password (which is used to generate the one-time passwords) never gets sent over the network at all. S/KEY is such a system. Here is an example of how it works:

1. We want to make a connection from host A to host B.

2. We have earlier set a password on host B.

3. We telnet to host B from host A.

4. Host B prompts us with a code string: 659 ta55095 and asks for our username. We type the username and host B asks for the one-time password.

5. We now need to find the one-time password by running a local program on host A with the code string as an argument:

```
key 659 ta55095
passwd: *******
```

The key program prompts us for the secret password on host B. When we type this it does not go across the network. The key program returns a clear text, one-time password valid for one session: 'EASE FREY WRY NUN ANTE POT'.

6. We type 'EASE FREY WRY NUN ANTE POT'on host B (sent over the network) and the password is accepted.

7. Next time we follow the same procedure and get a different password.

12.5.3 Network services

When installing a new service which is available to more than one user it is appropriate to ask the questions:

- Do I need this service?

- Whom or what information do I have to trust in order to use this?

- What will happen if someone abuses that trust?

For example, the `rlogin` feature of Unix has a file called `.rhosts` in which a user can add a list of trusted hosts. That user can log in to the host with the `.rhosts` file from any one of those trusted hosts without giving a password. The user is clearly willing to trust this list of hosts. But that is not the only trust relationship here. Unix uses DNS (the Domain Name Service) in order to verify the identity of connecting machines, so the rlogin service *implicitly* trusts the DNS service. If someone could corrupt that service, there would be a potential security problem, see section 11.8.8.

Another example is in software distribution, both for Unix and Windows. In order to distribute software from a central server to many clients, the clients have to trust the information being sent to them from the server. They have to give the server permission to install unknown files which might be security hazards.

SNMP control systems accept information from a controller, based only on a fairly weak password (community string). The password has a default value of 'public' which many sites forget to change (a potentially huge security risk). This information can be used to read or even change control functions of key network components and is even used for performing remote system administration in certain products. Usually a second password is required to actually change data. Its default value is 'private'.

Cfengine places all of its trust in the correctness of its input file, it does not accept unsolicited input from the network at all. In software distribution it will trust files from a software server of its own choosing, but arbitrary servers cannot send data to it uninvited.

12.5.4 Protecting against attacks

- Look out for users with weak or non-existent passwords. This is the easiest way for an attacker to enter the system.

- Train all staff in basic security procedures, and pay special attention to those who are highly privileged.

- Do not give trusted access to other hosts unless absolutely necessary. Make sure there are no NIS wildcards + in /etc/hosts.equiv. Avoid using .rhosts files altogether, and replace all of the old Berkeley 'r'-commands (rlogin, rsh etc.) with a version of secure shell (ssh).[4]

- Attempts at initiating ping attack have been identified by large numbers of persistent ping processes.

- Disable unused services, e.g. in /etc/inetd.conf, which might contain security leaks, like UUCP, TFTP.

- Make sure that each active service runs in its own sandbox, with non-overlapping privileges.

- Make sure the router filters all unnecessary traffic. Usually there is no reason to permit RPC or SNMP, NetBEUI, or NFS traffic outside of the local domain for instance. Anti-spoof filtering of IP addresses is also a must: e.g. a packet with a source address from a network on the other side of the planet cannot originate from inside the local network, so filter it.

- Make sure that the latest security patches are installed on all systems.

- Monitor connections using netstat -a to show all listening connections. Use tcpd logging.

- Monitor processes running on the system. How many copies of important processes are running? How many should be running? Often it is possible to see that one is under attack by looking at what processes are running and who is running them. For instance an attempt at port sniffing or spamming might be seen with a bunch of processes like this:

```
nobody   .... /usr/sbin/inetd
nobody   .... /usr/sbin/inetd
nobody   .... /usr/sbin/inetd
nobody   .... /usr/sbin/inetd
nobody   .... /usr/sbin/inetd
```

  inetd is a multiplexer which starts Internet services on many ports. Normally it is only root who runs this. The above indicates that a user is trying to use the well-known account nobody to start services, or to overload the system with requests.

- Check filesystems for suspicious looking hidden files, i.e. files with names like .. . These are often used to hide dangerous programs or shells which users can use to gain root privileges. Cfengine performs this task automatically when it examines filesystems.

---

[4]As the reviewer of this book put it: 'They're done. Stick a fork in them.'

- Check file integrity of static files and program code using MD5, SHA-1 or other checksums.

- Make sure that . is not in root's path. It is possible to inadvertently execute a Trojan horse program.

- Make sure that log and audit files like /var/adm/utmp are not world writable, if possible, hence allowing crackers to cover their tracks. Modern Unices do not have this problem.

12.5.5 Port scanning

In order to find back-doors into vulnerable systems, many network attackers scan ports on network hosts in order to find out which services are running on them. Programs for performing such scans (e.g. nmap or queso) can be obtained freely from the network, as can many other intrusion tools, so crackers require little or no intelligence in order to carry out these simple attacks these days. Most intrusion tools can also be used to help secure systems.

In a poorly configured system a cracker might find active services which even the system owner did not realize were running. UUCP and TFTP are typical examples. These services can often be exploited to install files in illegal places. Known faults in services can be exploited if one knows about the services which are running. TCP/IP fingerprinting is the process by which port scanners determine the type of operating system from the quirks of a host's TCP stack. If a telnet to a host does not immediately reveal a banner with the OS type (it usually does on any operating system):

```
nomad% telnet 127.0.0.1
Trying 127.0.0.1...
Connected to 127.0.0.1.
Escape character is '^]'.

Red Hat Linux release 4.2 (Biltmore)
Kernel 2.0.30 on an i586
login:
```

then more intricate signatures can be combed for tell-tale signs.

Primitive port scanning attempts are detectable if network activity is followed closely. Strings of attempted 'connect' requests to one port after the other are easily spotted. Recently, however, the trend has expanded to include 'stealth scanning' in which scans are performed at random over long periods of time to avoid attracting attention. Port scanning is only dangerous if there are poorly configured hosts on the network. Perhaps the most important issue is the consistent use of strong passwords. The .rhosts and hosts.equiv files which allow login without password challenge via rsh/rlogin were okay in bygone times, but these days we cannot afford to be lax about security. The problem with this mechanism is that .rhosts and hosts.equiv use hostnames as effective passwords. This mechanism trusts DNS lookups which can be spoofed in elaborate attacks in order to mislead a host about the identity of a connecting host. Moreover, if a hacker gets into one host, he/she will then be able to log in on every host in these files without a password. This greatly broadens the possibilities for effective attack.

There are similar, but somewhat different issues with ssh and .shosts. The key-per-host scheme makes it possible to thwart these kinds of attacks, but ssh and sshd are rarely set up this securely, since the default implementation just leaves it up to the client to worry about spoofing.

12.5.6 X11 security

Although many users are not aware of it, it is often possible to download the screen image of another user who is using the X-windows system. While this might occasionally be a useful opportunity to help remote users with a specific problem [337], in general it must be considered a grave security risk. It is equally possible to 'bug' the keyboard and listen to all the key-presses. The problem is an out-dated security mechanism which has long since been replaced, but which is still used by very many users. The problem is the xhost program. This is used to grant other hosts permission to draw on your X server – in other words, if you are remotely logged on to a host other than the one you are using as a display, you must grant the remote host access to write on your screen.

In the old X-windows system, prior to release 5, one had to grant access to a particular host. Once this was done, *anyone* on that host had access to your server, not just you. This was later replaced by the xauth magic-cookie mechanism which works on a user basis. Some users still insist on using xhost however, with a command like this:

```
xhost +
```

Any user writing this, opens their display to everyone in the world. The antidote, of course is the command xhost -. Users of the secure shell ssh, see section 12.6, can now have automatic X11 forwarding with authentication cookies. Everyone should therefore execute xhost - once and never use the xhost mechanism again.

12.6 VPNs: secure shell and FreeS/WAN

VPN stands for a Virtual Private Network. This is simply an encrypted tunnel (like an armored pipe) connecting two locations. It is a line of communication which is reinforced by encryption and authentication. Privacy is obtained through encryption and the line is virtual because it sits on top of regular TCP/IP communication. VPNs are sometimes uses to connect together branches of organizations that are located at geographically diverse locations; traffic can be kept 'internal', even though the packets travel over public media. Of course, an armored pipe is no stronger than its weakest end-point.

Secure shell software can be used to build VPNs for many services. The secure shell [332] is a secure replacement for the rsh commands. It protects against IP spoofing where a remote host pretends to be a trusted host by faking IP datagrams; DNS spoofing where an attacker forges name entries in the name-service; the interception of passwords in network packets and several other kinds of attack.

FreeS/WAN is another project [247] started for GNU/Linux systems which will provide encrypted tunnels. See also the Virtual Private Network Consortium [74].

12.7 Role-based security and capabilities

In a dynamic, interactive situation we could generalize the notion of access to allow users different permissions depending on what they are doing. This can be done in different ways:

- Define roles for users (e.g. by membership in privileged groups with access to special systems, like man in Unix).

- By asking a service to carry out an operation, whose abilities have the appropriate privileges for the task (e.g. WWW, telnet, Java).

- By setting some attribute which determines the allowed permissions for a given task (e.g Unix setuid programs).

- Use of abstract ownership (e.g. polymorphic methods in object-oriented languages).

Unix setuid programs are an example where the activities of a program can be changed (by the superuser) so as to grant a specific program the right to operate with a different user-identity and thus privileges (without authentication). The setgid is a corresponding mechanism for setting the group ownership of a process. Note that setuid programs often give more privilege than is necessary and such programs have been a major cause of security problems on Unix platforms.

POSIX 'Capabilities' have recently been implemented in the Linux kernel [57]. These 'Capabilities' are an additional form of privilege control to enable more specific control over what privileged processes can do by giving them a direct line to the kernel. Rather than making a program 'setuid root', one could give a program privilege to perform a specific task and nothing more. Other examples are Rule Set Based Access Control (RSBAC), and LIDS (Secure Linux Project) which implement Mandatory Access Control in the kernel for all kinds of operations on files and processes. This presents some administrative difficulties for software, since there is no longer any user with complete privilege.

12.8 WWW security

The concept of World Wide Web (WWW) security sounds like a contradiction in terms. The WWW is designed to publish information to the masses. Security has to do with restricting access. What has the WWW got to do with security?

Web security has to do with:

- Protecting the published data from corruption.

- Granting access only to those files we wish to publish.

- Preventing users from tricking the WWW server into executing unauthorized commands on the server host.

- Protecting against a protocol that opens the system to all manner of attacks through abuses of the protocol.

Although there have been many security problems with the feature over-laden Internet Information Server for Windows [300], there is nothing principally insecure about the WWW service. Any file-server can, in principle, compromise the security of a host by making information about that host available to others. If a server provides access to unauthorized files, this will clearly be the case. All we need to do is to ensure that proper access controls are maintained.

The Free Apache WWW server (see section 9.6) has all of the features one requires to operate a secure web service. It can be run without special privilege, and it has quite sophisticated mechanisms for restricting access to data. It is nevertheless possible to configure the server in an insecure fashion, so one needs to be cautious. There are three distinct categories for web use:

- External web service for organization.

- Internal web service for organization.

- Private users' web pages.

The last of these is arguably the greatest potential security risk for the Web: we usually trust the files and programs which we write ourselves in the name of our organization, but we have no reason to trust the integrity of private or guest users. There are two areas where a security breach can occur:

- File ownership and access rights.

- CGI-scripts.

CGI-scripts can be used to execute commands on the server-host with the user-privileges of the WWW user. Although the WWW user is introduced precisely to isolate the powers of the WWW service, we can still do quite a bit of damage – not to the host directly, but to other users and to the web server access controls. It is an inevitable consequence of running a public service with a private ID that any file which gets written by a CGI-script can also be overwritten by another CGI-script, regardless of which user is responsible for that script. Thus users could wage war on one another with CGI-scripts such as guest-books, corrupting or even deleting one another's data freely. This is a fundamental weakness in the WWW service: if we allow the existence of arbitrary CGI-scripts on the system, then we can carry out arbitrary operations with the privileges of the WWW user. Users can:

- Send anonymous, untraceable mail which appears to come from the WWW user at the organization hosting the CGI program.

- Circumvent .htaccess access controls to certain files on most types of operating system, by executing the command /bin/cat filename as part of a CGI-script.

The first principle of server security is thus:

Principle 64 (Service corruption). *If a server runs with the privileges of a non-privileged user, then none of the data or configuration files of the system should be owned by, or be writable by the* www *user, otherwise it is often trivial to alter the contents of the data using the service.*

Example 18. *The WWW server usually runs under a user ID of* www. *If any of the data files or configuration files are owned by this user, it is trivial to write a CGI-script that gives complete control of the service to any outside user.*

If we violate this principle, any local user can overwrite and corrupt web pages simply by writing a CGI-script. Of course, the WWW server does not have any special privileges. It is just an ordinary, non-privileged user who has to obey normal file permissions, nevertheless this is not enough to prevent a few accidents. This brings us to the fundamental flaw in WWW security.

Any files which are to be served by a WWW server have to be readable by the WWW user. All CGI-scripts run with the rights of the WWW user. It therefore follows that any CGI-script can read any file which is capable of being served by the daemon. To put it bluntly: *Any user can write a CGI-script to circumvent* .htaccess *security barriers.* The solution to this problem is to either disallow CGI-scripts, or to move sensitive (non-public) documents to a separate host, which regular users do not have access to.

CGI-scripts which send mail are a conundrum. If a user decides to write a CGI-script which sends E-mail, it executes the mail program with the user identity of the WWW user. The identity of the true sender is irrelevant, since the actual sender is the WWW server. This could be an unfortunate situation for an organization. If private users can send E-mail anonymously, but which can be traced back to the WWW server of our organization, we clearly stand in the firing line for all kinds of trouble. A user could harass anyone with impunity, and only the organization would be responsible.

12.9   IPSec – secure IP

Many problems in network communication would be easily solved if there were transport layer encryption of Internet traffic. Spoofing would be impossible, because attackers would have access to cryptographic checksums of the packets (spoofing could be easily detected). Similarly sniffing the net for passwords, leaked by old protocols, would be impossible, since no plaintext data would be sent.

IPSec is a security system developed for use with IPv6, but it has also been implemented for IPv4 (RFC1636). It offers encryption at the IP level (below the TCP/UDP layer). This means that common TCP attacks, such as sequence guessing or spoofing attacks, cannot occur since attackers could never see the contents of travelling packets.

IPSec allows hosts to set security *policies* on routed packets. It includes access control lists for encryption, integrity checks and point-to-point private tunnels. This all sounds like the perfect solution to the problem, however IPSec is not without problems: it is not fully implemented by network hardware and software today. This could take some time.

IPSec supports both session encryption and strong authentication, based on either public or secret keys. It consists approximately of two protocols:

- *Authentication Header (AH)*: this describes the initial negotiation of identity and encryption methods.

- *Encapsulation Security Payload (ESP)*: this describes the encryption schemes and also relates to the strong authentication of data.

These provide the following services:

- Access control

- Connectionless integrity

- Data origin authentication

- Replay protection

- Privacy (encryption).

12.9.1 Security Associations (SA)

IPSec maintains a security context known as a Security Association (SA), which is a *policy* decision that times out after a specified lifetime. A Security Association is uniquely defined by three parameters:

- *Security Parameters Index*: This is a context identifier.

- *IP destination address*: A unicast address that is to be the endpoint for the SA (but not necessarily the endpoint of a packet/datagram).

- *Security Protocol Identifier*: Indicates whether an AH or ESP security method is to be used.

Decisions based on these parameters are collected into a Security Policy Database (SPD), where they are examined for each packet or datagram that is forwarded by a router, firewall or host. IPSec is designed to offer great flexibility to administrators; however, with such power comes the possibility of great error as we shall see in section 12.10. IPSec offers the possibility to distinguish between a variety of security options for traffic routed along different paths, using selectors.

12.9.2 Selectors

An IPSec Security Association policy is built up from *selectors*, or matching parameter sets that are compared with high-level packet header fields. Selectors are used to filter outgoing traffic from a router or firewall. Each packet is processed as follows:

1. Compare header field values with the values stored in the policy database and select zero or more Security Associations determining the packet's outcome.

2. Determine which SAs apply to the current packet.

3. Process according to AH or ESP protocols.

The selectors match on a number of values. The most important of these are:

- *Destination IP address*: This can be a single unicast address, or a list or range of IP addresses.

- *Source IP address*: This can be a single IP address, or a list or range of values, thus allowing single rules to cover traffic from a group of collaborating hosts.

- *Data Sensitivity Level*: A user security classifier that identifies the degree of security required for the information.

- *IPSec protocol*: Either AH, ESP or AH/ESP combined.

- *Source and destination ports*: The port numbers of the services for the TCP and UDP layer.

12.9.3 Modes

IPSec defines two modes for traffic. In *transport mode*, IPSec provides protection of the upper layers of the protocol headers, e.g. TCP and UDP. This prevents replay attacks such as sequence guessing and address spoofing. ESP in transport mode encrypts and authenticates the IP packet contents, but not the IP header, which might still be observed or rerouted by an eavesdropper or middle-man. AH in transport mode authenticates the IP packet contents and sensitive parts of the IP header.

In *tunnel mode*, the entire original IP packet becomes private. New fields are added to encapsulate the IP packet – hence the whole data stream – in a 'tunnel'. No routers along the way are able to examine the contents of the packets. Thus, in principle, this encapsulation could be used to send packets on a secret journey that is not detectable by eavesdropping at a single location.

Tunnels can be nested; indeed, this is required as traffic might pass through a variety of routers, under the administration of different organizations each with their own policies. We expect therefore:

- Host-to-host encryption: by agreed secret session key.

- Point-to-point encryption: between gateways, on route.

12.9.4 Rule ordering

Like any rule-based system, IPSec is susceptible to authentication–encryption ordering exploits. Because authentication (like signing) and encryption are two separate operations, different orderings lead to different results. If authentication data are applied only after encryption, then they can be altered by a middle-man, leading to authentication spoofing (see section 12.4.5). Similarly, if encryption is applied after authentication, then the destination host can reroute data under false pretences.

The policy manager searches for the first network object that matches from the top of the list, and continues down through all the policy rules in turn, generating rule lists from the policy rules until all instances of that network object are added to the rule list. Therefore, rules appearing first can prevent subsequent rules from being enforced. For example, assume you create the following two policy rules:

```
Policy Rule 1:

 src= host1 dest=host2 serv=all IP action=Permit and IPSec

Policy Rule 2:

 src=network1 dest=network2 serv=all IP action=Permit
```

where host1 is assumed to be on network1 and host2 is on network2. Policy Rule 1 is a more specific rule; therefore, it should appear first in the Policy Rule table so that traffic from host1 to host2 is routed through an IPSec tunnel. If Policy Rule 2 appeared first, it would take precedence and non-tunneled IP traffic would be permitted from host1 to host2.

12.10 Ordered access control and policy conflicts

Access control lists are the basis of access control in most computer security systems. They are irreplaceable, and yet they have a basic flaw: they are order dependent.

> **Principle 65 (Conflicting rules).** *In any situation where conflicting rules can arise, the result will be sensitive to the order in which the rules are evaluated.*

Example 19 (Ordering in list-based policies). *List-based policy decisions are sensitive to ordering issues. Lists usually satisfy a 'first match wins' rule, or an 'evaluate all rules in order' rule.*

If the ordering of two rules is reversed, valuable protection can be lost. An example of this was mentioned in section 12.4.5 for signing and encryption. Encryption is often a problem here, because it hides rules that might be evaluated, preventing any 'corrective measures' that might have been applied to eliminate conflicts. Consider three examples of IPSec security polices [124], where inconsistencies can lead to unfortunate and incorrect behavior.

Example 20 (IPSec 1). *Consider a scenario between two domains (figure 12.2), one of which has a firewall and one of which has a gateway supporting IPSec security policies. The users of H1 are concerned about the privacy of data, so they arrange for the traffic to be encrypted.*

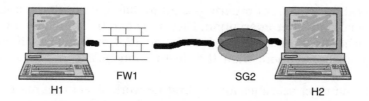

Figure 12.2: IPSec configuration 1.

Using IPSec policy rules, an encrypted tunnel is built between H1 and the secure gateway SG2 in order to protect the traffic. However, the IPSec policy rules on the firewall are set by a different authority, and they can be specified so that encrypted packets can be denied access. If the firewall FW1 has such a rule, either intentionally or unintentionally, then all packets will be dropped and communication will be mysteriously impossible.

Example 21 (IPSec 2). *Suppose that H1 is still trying to encrypt traffic to SG2, with the same tunnel rule. Suppose the firewall FW1 now has the rules:*

```
Allow: source=H1, destination=H2
Deny:  all others
```

However, since the encryption tunnel changes the destination to be SG2 in the outer encapsulation header, the firewall will mistakenly drop all traffic from H1 to H2 that should be allowed. Even though the traffic has the correct source and destination addresses, the overlapping rules cause problems.

In the following example, encryption plays a role in fixing a strong ordering of rules that can lead to unfortunate mis-communications.

Example 22. (IPSec 3). *Consider two separate sites (figure 12.3), each with their own IPSec gateways (SG1 and SG2). Suppose that the administrator from department D1 who is in charge of SG1 decides that all traffic from D1 to site O2 should be encrypted by a tunnel from SG1 to SG3. In a different building, another administrator who controls SG2 decides that traffic from site O1 to site O2 should be encrypted through a tunnel from SG2 to SG4.*

What happens now, when someone in department D1 attempts to send a message to someone in department D2? The traffic between the sites is now governed by two

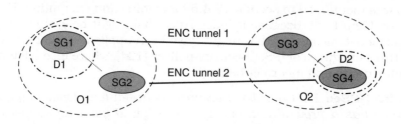

Figure 12.3: IPSec configuration 2.

policies that do not agree, and either tunnel could be chosen. Part of the journey is unencrypted, either in the first organization, or in the second.

If the administrator in D1 does not add a selector for traffic specifically to D2 (via SG4) that allows it to pass via SG2, then it could take the upper tunnel and be unencrypted within the second organization (between SG3 and SG4). If the communication is between an employee of organization O1 and the organization itself, this might be a breach of security.

On the other hand, if the rules are adjusted so as to direct traffic to the lower tunnel for all traffic destined for site O2, then there would be two overlapping rules to SG4 (from SG1 and SG2) and the traffic could pass by either one of two routes.

Suppose someone in department D1 now wishes to send data to a host outside of department D2. If the traffic takes the upper tunnel 1, there is no problem. However, if the traffic chooses the lower tunnel in the diagram, via a new tunnel between SG1 and SG2, then some strange effects can occur. With this configuration, traffic is encapsulated with a secure header from SG1 and then encapsulated by a new header from SG2 to send to SG4. When SG4 decrypts and removes the packaging, it finds that the destination is SG3, SG4 sends the traffic back to SG3 unencrypted, which finally delivers the packet to its actual destination.

```
SG1: (dest=H2)_SG4, send SG2
SG2: ((dest=H2)_SG4)_SG4, send SG4
SG4: (dest=H2), send SG3
SG3: send destination
```

Although the intention was to encrypt all the traffic, the traffic ends up passing from SG4 to SG3 unencrypted.

The problem over overlapping rules can thus lead to security problems, unless a careful site-wide management assures the' consistency of policy throughout. The alternative to using multiple encapsulation rules is use point-to-point encryption, but this has its own problems. All points along a route must be trusted to deny access to eavesdroppers. This is not enforceable.

12.11 IP filtering for firewalls

Filtering of TCP/IP data can be accomplished in numerous ways, both at routers and at the host level. Filters can exact access control on datagrams, where the attributes are, amongst other things,

- Source port

- Destination port (service type)

- Source IP address

- Destination IP address

- TCP protocol attributes (SYN/ACK).

A firewall blocks access at the network level. For instance, Cisco IOS rules:

```
ip access-group 100 in
access-list 100 permit tcp any host 128.39.74.16 eq http
access-list 100 permit tcp any host 128.39.74.16 eq smtp
access-list 100 deny   ip  any any
```

Modern versions of operating systems can filter IP packets in the kernel too, giving hosts effectively a host-based firewall. For instance, Linux and FreeBSD have IP tables, formerly known as 'IP chains':

```
iptables -N newchain                               # new ACL/chain
iptables -A newchain -p tcp -s 0/0 smtp -j ACCEPT  # -s source address
iptables -A newchain -p tcp -s 0/0  www -j ACCEPT
iptables -A newchain -j DENY                       # all else
```

The CIDR notation 0/0 is the same as 0.0.0.0 255.255.255.255, or any. A default policy for any packets that are not ACCEPTed is set as follows:

```
iptables -P INPUT DROP
iptables -P OUTPUT DROP
```

Windows 2000 has corresponding 'IPSec filters' and the local security policy has an IP filter list.

12.12   Firewalls

A firewall is a network configuration which isolates some machines from the rest of the network. It is a gate-keeper which limits access to and from a network. Our human bodies are relatively immune to attack by bacteria and viruses because we have a barrier: skin. The skin contains layers of various fatty acids in which bacteria and viruses cannot normally survive. If we lose the skin from a part of the body, wounds become quickly infected; indeed, prior to antibiotics, many people died from infected wounds. A firewall is like a skin for a local area network.

The idea is this: if we could make a barrier between our local network and the Internet which is impenetrable, then we would be safe from network attacks. But if there is an impenetrable barrier so that no one can get into the network, then no one can get out either. Why pay for a firewall when we could just pull out the network cable? Think of the body again: we have to put food and air into our bodies and we have to let stuff out, so we need a hole in the skin (preferably several). We do not usually die of the food we eat because the body has filters which screen out and break down dangerous organisms (stomach acid and layers of mucus etc.). These then hand us the 'input' by proxy. We do the same thing with computer networks. A firewall is not an impenetrable barrier: it has holes in it with passport checks. We demand that only network data with appropriate credentials should be allowed to pass.

12.12.1   A firewall concept

A firewall is a concept. It is not a thing; there is no single firewall solution. The name 'firewall' is a collective description for a variety of methods which restrict

access to a network. They all involve placing restrictions on the way in which
network packets are routed. A firewall might be a computer which is programmed
to act like a router, or it might be a dedicated router or a combination of routers
and software systems. The idea with a firewall is to keep important data behind
a barrier which has some kind of passport-control and can examine and restrict
network packets, allowing only 'harmless' packets to pass.

- All traffic from inside to outside or vice versa must pass through the firewall.

- Only authorized traffic is allowed to pass.

- Potentially risky network services (like mail) are rendered safer using intermediary systems.

- The firewall itself should be immune to attack.

A firewall cannot help with the following:

- Badly configured hosts or mis-configured networks.

- Data-based attacks (where the attack involves sending some harmful information, like the code word which makes you take your own life, or an E-mail
  which bolts a Trojan horse).

There are two firewall philosophies: *block everything unless we make an explicit
exception* and *pass everything unless we make a specific exception*. The first of
these is clearly the most secure or at least the more paranoid of the two.

Here are a few concepts which get bandied around in firewall-speak:

- *Screening router or 'choke'*: A router which can be programmed to filter or
  reject packets directed at certain IP ports.

- *Bastion host*: A computer, specially modified to be secure but available.

- *Dual-homed host*: A computer with two net-cards, which can be used to link
  an isolated network to a larger network.

- *Application gateway*: A filter, usually run on a bastion host, which has the
  ability to reject or forward packets at a high level (i.e. at the application level).

- *Screened subnet/DMZ*: An isolated subnet, between the Internet and the
  private network. Also called a DMZ (de-militarized zone). A DMZ is the bit
  between a screening router and the firewall, bastion host. This is a good
  place for external WWW services.

The firewall philosophy builds on the idea that it is easier to secure one host
(the bastion host) than it is to secure hundreds or thousands of hosts on a local
network. One focuses on a single machine and ensures that it is the only one
effectively coupled directly to the network. One forces all network traffic to stop at
the bastion host, so if someone tries to attack the system by sending some kind of
IP attack there can be little damage to the rest of the network because the private
network will never see the attack. This is of course a simplification. It is important

to realize that installing a firewall does not give absolute protection and it does not remove the importance of configuring and securing the hosts on the inside of the firewall.

It should also be noted that a firewall is usually a *single point of failure* for a network. It is vulnerable to Denial of Service attacks.

12.12.2 Firewall proxies

Of course we do not want all traffic to stop; some services like E-mail and maybe HTTP should be able to pass through. To allow this, one uses a so-called 'proxy' service or a 'gateway'.[5] A common solution is to give the bastion host two network interfaces (one is then connected to the unsafe part of the network and the other is connected to the safe part), though the same effect can be obtained with a single interface. A service is said to be *proxied* if the bastion host forwards the packets from the unsafe network to the safe one. It only does this for packets which meet the requirements of the security policy. For instance, you might decide that the services you require to cross the firewall are inbound/outbound telnet, inbound/outbound SMTP (mail), DNS, HTTP and FTP but no others.

> **Principle 66 (Community borders).** *Proxying is about protecting against breaches to the fundamental principle of communities. A firewall proxy provides us with a buffer against violations of our own community rights from outside, and also provides others with a buffer against what we choose to do in our own home.*

Proxying requires some special software, often at the level of the kernel where the validity of connections can be established. For instance, packets with forged addresses can be blocked. Data arriving at ports where there was no registered connection can be discarded. Connections can be discarded if they do not relate to a known user-account.

12.12.3 Example: dual-homed bastion host

A simple firewall configuration is shown in figure 12.4.

In this example we have effectively two routers, a DMZ and a protected network. The first packet-filtering router will route packets between the Internet and one of three hosts. FTP is routed directly to a special FTP server. The same applies to HTTP packets. These services are dealt with by separate hosts, so that (if something should go wrong and the machines are broken into) it is no worse than having to restore these single hosts from backup. None of the servers in the DMZ have normal user accounts, so there would be no help to crackers trying to crack password files there, if they managed to break in. The bastion host gets all packets which are not for the other services. The bastion host forwards okay-looking packets to the internal router which is really just a further packet filter (a backup in case of failure of the bastion host). The internal router accepts only packets passing between the safe network and the bastion host, all others are rejected.

---

[5]This should not be confused with a WWW caching proxy, which is a kind of cache for frequently used HTML pages.

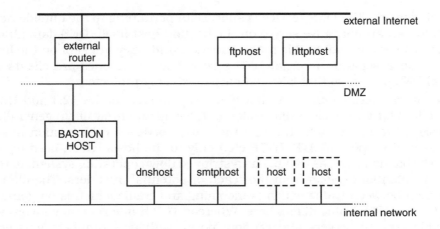

Figure 12.4: A simple firewall with a dual-homed bastion host.

The bastion host proxies all of the appropriate protocols including FTP and HTTP between the safe network and the DMZ.

12.12.4 Example: two routers

A second example, in which there is no dual-homed host, is shown in figure 12.5.

In this configuration we use two routers to allow increased protection. An exterior router connects the site to the Internet, or the untrusted 'outside' network. The interior router protects the internal network from the bastion host and from the DMZ. Although the bastion host does not physically separate the exterior and interior networks, it still separates them through proxy software, by forcing packets to be routed through the bastion host's proxy services.

In order to illustrate router filtering tables more explicitly, let us assume that we have a WWW server and FTP server in the DMZ, and an SMTP server on the

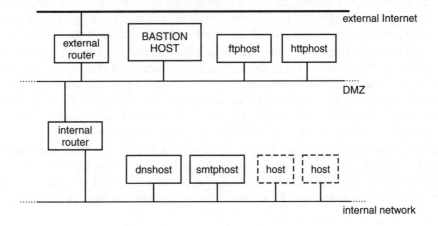

Figure 12.5: Firewall with no dual-homed host, but two routers.

internal network. The DNS service is split. Data pertaining to the outside network are kept in an authoritative server on the bastion host itself. DNS data about the internal network are not visible to the outside world; they are kept on the internal network, on a separate internal DNS server. Local machines are clients of the internal DNS server, so that DNS data are maximally protected.

The router filtering tables are shown and explained in tables 12.1 and 12.2 (see also ref. [61] for an excellent discussion of filtering and firewalls in general). They are designed to route traffic through the proxy servers on the bastion host, and direct special services (SMTP, HTTP etc.) only to the hosts which need to receive them. The bastion host, as usual, has a stripped down operating system, to remove as many potential exploits from the reach of potential intruders. The filter rules distinguish between traffic which is incoming and traffic which is outgoing. Note that TCP and UDP traffic differs here. Whereas TCP traffic generally involves fixed port addresses on servers and random ports (with port numbers greater than 1023, actually usually much higher than this) on clients, we have to be careful about filtering possible traffic based on port numbers. In practice, 1023 is probably far too low a port number to set here, but it is difficult to make generic rules for random port numbers, so we use this number as a mnemonic. Some spoofing attempts are prevented by requiring the ACK bit to be set on TCP connection requests. The ACK bit is not set on SYN packets which initiate connections, only on replies, so requiring the ACK bit to be set is a way of saying that these rules require traffic to be part of an already established dialogue between legitimate ports. This prevents a remote attacker from using a well-known port externally to attempt to bypass the filter rules to attack a server living at a port number over 1023.[6] The corresponding outgoing rule can be considered a service to other sites, which stifles local spoofing attempts.

12.12.5 A warning

The foregoing configurations are just examples. In practice we might not have all the hardware we need to separate things as cleanly as shown here. Although there is a public domain firewall toolkit [115], most firewall software is commercial in nature because it needs to live in the kernel and make use of code which is proprietary.

Firewall management is a complex issue. We cannot set up a firewall and then forget about it. Firewalls need constant maintenance and they are susceptible to bugs just like any other software. It is best to build up a firewall system slowly, understanding each step. A good place to start is with packet-filtering routers to eliminate the most offensive or least secure service requests from outside your local network. These include NFS (RPC), IRC, ping, finger etc.

Today, many consider firewalls to be an outdated idea, one that is no substitute for host-based security. Network services are evolving so quickly that it is difficult for any 'patch it up' technology to keep up. What is needed is fundamentally secure services. For instance, many services today are implemented via the World

---

[6]Attackers are devious. We should not imagine that, simply because a filtering rule was intended for, say, SMTP traffic, it could not be manipulated for some other purpose.

Rule	I/O	Src addr	Dest addr	Proto	Src port	Dest port	ACK set	Action
spoof	in	intern	any	any	any	any	any	deny
ssh1	in	bastion	intern	TCP	22	> 1023	yes	permit
ssh2	in	bastion	intern	TCP	> 1023	22	any	permit
ssh3	out	intern	bastion	TCP	> 1023	22	any	permit
ssh4	out	intern	bastion	TCP	22	> 1023	yes	permit
ftp1	out	intern	bastion	TCP	> 1023	21	any	permit
ftp2	in	bastion	intern	TCP	21	> 1023	yes	permit
ftp3	in	bastion	intern	TCP	20	> 1023	any	permit
ftp4	out	intern	bastion	TCP	> 1023	20	yes	permit
smtp1	out	intern	bastion	TCP	> 1023	25	any	permit
smtp2	in	bastion	smtphost	TCP	25	> 1023	any	permit
smtp3	out	smtphost	bastion	TCP	25	> 1023	yes	permit
smtpX	in	bastion	intern	TCP	25	> 1023	yes	permit
http1	out	intern	bastion	TCP	> 1023	80	any	permit
http2	in	bastion	intern	TCP	80	> 1023	yes	permit
dns1	out	dnshost	bastion	UDP	53	53	N/A	permit
dns2	in	bastion	dnshost	UDP	53	53	N/A	permit
dns3	out	dnshost	bastion	TCP	> 1023	53	any	permit
dns4	in	bastion	dnshost	TCP	53	> 1023	yes	permit
dns5	in	bastion	dnshost	TCP	> 1023	53	any	permit
dns6	out	dnshost	bastion	TCP	53	> 1023	yes	permit
default1	out	any	any	any	any	any	any	deny
default1	in	any	any	any	any	any	any	deny

Table 12.1: Internal router filter table. *Incoming ssh traffic is allowed from the bastion host ssh proxy to the internal hosts, but not to the DMZ. Outgoing traffic is channeled through the bastion host proxy, which avoids the origin IP address being seen by outsiders. FTP, HTTP and SMTP traffic is allowed between the respective server-hosts and the bastion hosts proxies. Note how WWW and FTP servers are special 'sacrificial lamb' hosts in the DMZ, with data backed up on internal hosts. Note that FTP uses two channels, a transmission channel and a control channel on ports 20 and 21. An SMTP mail hub is used. DNS MX records should be set to point to the bastion host proxy. DNS filters are slightly complex, since the DNS services uses both UDP for lookup and TCP for bulk transfer and forwarding.*

Rule	I/O	Src addr	Dest addr	Proto	Src port	Dest port	ACK set	Action
spoof1	in	intern	any	any	any	any	any	deny
spoof2	in	outside	any	any	any	any	any	deny
ssh1	in	any	bastion	TCP	22	> 1023	yes	permit
ssh2	in	any	bastion	TCP	> 1023	22	any	permit
ssh3	out	bastion	any	TCP	> 1023	22	any	permit
ssh4	out	bastion	any	TCP	22	> 1023	yes	permit
ftp1	out	bastion	any	TCP	> 1023	21	any	permit
ftp2	in	any	bastion	TCP	21	> 1023	yes	permit
ftp3	in	any	bastion	TCP	20	> 1023	any	permit
ftp4	out	bastion	any	TCP	> 1023	20	yes	permit
smtp1	out	bastion	any	TCP	> 1023	25	any	permit
smtp2	in	any	bastion	TCP	25	> 1023	yes	permit
smtp3	in	any	bastion	TCP	> 1023	25	any	permit
smtp4	out	bastion	any	TCP	25	> 1023	yes	permit
http1	out	bastion	any	TCP	> 1023	80	any	permit
http2	in	any	bastion	TCP	80	> 1023	yes	permit
http3	in	any	httphost	TCP	> 1023	80	any	permit
http4	out	httphost	any	TCP	80	> 1023	yes	permit
dns1	out	bastion	any	UDP	53	53	N/A	permit
dns2	in	any	bastion	UDP	53	any	N/A	permit
dns3	in	any	bastion	UDP	any	53	N/A	permit
dns4	out	bastion	any	UDP	53	any	N/A	permit
dns5	out	bastion	any	TCP	53	> 1023	any	permit
dns6	in	any	bastion	TCP	53	> 1023	yes	permit
dns7	in	any	bastion	TCP	> 1023	53	any	permit
dns8	out	bastion	any	TCP	53	> 1023	yes	permit
default1	out	any	any	any	any	any	any	deny
default1	in	any	any	any	any	any	any	deny

Table 12.2: External router filter table. *External connections are forced to go through the bastion host proxies.*

Wide Web, tunneled over port 80 requests. Such requests cannot be filtered by a firewall in the traditional sense.

12.13 Intrusion detection and forensics

In the last few years the reality of network intrusion has led to several attempts to build systems which can detect break-ins, either while they are in progress or afterwards.

There are several ways in which we can gather evidence about intrusions. Evidence can be direct and indirect. Direct evidence might come from audits and log files, smoking guns, user observations, records of actions conducted by intruders, and so on. Checksums of important files can detect unauthorized changes, for instance. Indirect evidence can be obtained by looking at system activity and trying to infer unusual activity. Changes in the behavior of programs can signal changes in the patterns of usage of a system, perhaps flagging the exploit of a vulnerability in software.

Intrusion detection by process monitoring is a relatively new idea. The idea is to gather a profile of what is normal and compare it with software behavior over time. This idea is a little like the idea of an immune system which tolerates 'self' and reacts against 'non-self'. Forrest et al. have pioneered system call profiling, inspired by vertebrate immune systems [119, 156] in order to detect hostile patterns of activity in special software processes. They build a database of short patterns of system call usage and then perform direct pattern search on subsequent data to detect anomalous patterns. The rationale for this approach is that intrusions are often caused by exploits of system calls which do not follow intended patterns. The beauty of this approach is its natural simplicity; its disadvantage is that it incurs a high overhead in resources to implement pattern searching in real-time; also the system needs to be taught what is normal in advance. Unfortunately 'normal' is a rather fickle concept [54], so in spite of its appealing simplicity, this is unlikely to be a complete, workable solution to the problem.

Another approach is to go to the network level and examine the totality of traffic arriving at a host. In order to detect an intrusion in progress, programs like *Network Flight Recorder* [102] (NFR) and *Big Brother* [236] (Bro) attempt to examine every packet on the network in order to look for tell-tale signatures of network break-in activity. This is an extremely resource-consuming task and it is beset with a number of problems. Few organizations have the resources to actually analyze the volumes of data they collect.

Network monitors look for packets containing data which might represent an attack, as they arrive. Network monitoring has its problems, however. One problem is that of *fragmentation*. Fragmentation is something which occurs to IP datagrams which pass between networks with different transmission rates. Larger packets can be broken up into smaller packets in order to optimize transmission. These fragments are reassembled at the final destination. This presents a problem for intrusion detection systems because the fragmented packets might not contain enough data to identify them as hostile. This would allow them to get past the detection system. An intruder might be able to generate packets which were fragmented in such as way as to confound the attempts at detection. Another problem is that switches and routers limit the spread of traffic to specific cables. An intrusion detection system needs to see all packets in order to cover every attack. In spite of the difficulties, network intrusion detection is a hot research topic. A number of conferences on intrusion detection methods have sprung up to explore this problem in depth.

Network forensics is what one does after an intrusion. The idea is to examine logs and system audits in order to name the intruder and determine the damage. Network forensics is perhaps most important for the purpose of possible legal action against intruders. The cost of keeping the necessary logs and audits is very great and the work required after a break-in is far from trivial. This topic is beyond the scope of this book. See ref. [321] for an introduction, and the coroner's toolkit (search the Internet for the nearest repository).

12.14 Compromised machines

Once an intrusion has been detected, one should not necessarily give away knowledge of the intrusion until all possible information about the intrusion has been collected. One should judge the risk of allowing the hack to continue: if the risk is acceptable, then important clues can be gathered by observing activity for a time. Keep a set of basic program tools on a read-only medium like a CD-ROM so that you are certain that you are not using Trojans. This should include a trusted shutdown command (halt).

1. Do not shut down the system, or pull the network plug until you have attempted to secure the volatile information in the system (process table, open port table).

2. Check that programs such as `netstat`, `ps` and `halt` are trusted, i.e. have not been replaced with modified programs. (If you are prepared, you will have an integrity check in advance.) If not, copy trusted versions from another system to `/tmp`, or use a diskette or CD-ROM containing trusted versions. Do not try to replace them while the system is running.

3. We want to avoid the activation of planted booby-traps, or logic bombs.

   (a) Look for open ports with `netstat` – are there any open connections that can lead you to attackers? If you have a packet-based IDS, you might be able to see this information elsewhere.

   (b) Look at all running processes and dump this information to a file for later examination. Do several dumps with different options.

   (c) Hit the reset switch (if it exists) or pull the power plug or suspend the operating system: on Windows or Unix, a controlled shutdown using a trusted program is probably best, in order to ensure synchronization of caches with disks. On Windows 95, 98, ME and MacOS prior to version X, pulling the plug is good enough. Do not try a controlled shutdown unless you have a trusted copy of the `halt` program – you might set off a logic bomb planted by the cracker.

4. Look for files planted in user directories and packet sniffers. Script-kiddy software often leaves known filenames that can be searched for. Hackers will often try to divert attention from themselves by placing files in another user's home directory – often several copies in case one is found.

5. The system should not be rebooted until necessary evidence has been secured. Indeed, the compromised machine should not be returned to normal service without a complete overhaul. Investigation should normally proceed by connecting the disk to a different, trusted computer. Note that some operating systems write data to disks when the OS starts, so disks should be isolated, write protected and *copied* before analysis is attempted. Special tools can be obtained for forensic work on IDE disks; SCSI disks can be protected by hardware jumpers.

A recovery policy should be in place as to what to do with forensic data. Will it be followed up by reporting to the police and then prosecution? The system should not be rebooted or the disk altered in any way.

Exercises

Self-test objectives

1. What elements should you have in a security and recovery plan?

2. Suggest some simple safeguards to protect inexperienced users from themselves.

3. What is meant by a file integrity check?

4. What is meant by a public-private key pair?

5. What is meant by a digital signature? Can such a signature be trusted?

6. Explain the significance of a trusted third party.

7. Give an example of an alternative to the use of trusted third parties.

8. Explain the assumptions that lie behind the security of the HTTPS Web protocol.

9. Is Kerberos a public-private key system?

10. Is Kerberos as secure as, say, SSL?

11. Describe how you would go about gauging security at a site.

12. What is meant by password sniffing?

13. How do one-time passwords work?

14. What is port scanning?

15. Explain the idea behind a virtual private network.

16. What is meant by role-based security?

17. What is meant by Unix capabilities?

18. What is meant by a sandbox?

19. Why should a network service never be given privileges to change its own configuration?

20. What is IPSec and why is it not in widespread use?

21. How can the ordering of access rules in a rule-based security scheme affect the degree of protection afforded by an access monitor?

22. What is IP filtering and where is it normally implemented?

23. Explain the purpose of a firewall.

24. Explain the limitations of firewalls.

25. Explain the purpose of intrusion detection.

26. How would you deal with a host that you knew to be compromised by crackers?

Problems

1. Research the appropriate commands for making filesystem backups at your site. Consider backups to disk and backups to tape.

2. Determine how many copies of each file are made in the Towers of Hanoi backup sequence.

3. Design two backup plans: one for a small organization such as a school of fifty pupils with one file-server and three workstations, and one for a large organization with many thousands of computers. Compare and contrast these plans.

4. Collect and compile a version of secure shell. (Note that this software is a commercial product. You are allowed to download for strictly educational purposes, but commercial organizations must pay. OpenSSH is also a good alternative.)

5. Explain why a switched network reduces the risk of password sniffing. Explain why it does not offer absolute protection against it.

6. Consider the two schematic access control lists for file security below.

```
ACL 1:                              ACL 2:

grant:                              grant:

www/                    anyone      private/                    mark
```

private/	mark	www/	anyone
work/	mark	work/	mark
work/group1	mark,group1	work/group1/markonly	mark
work/group1/markonly	mark	work/group1	mark,group1

You see two attempts at protecting the directories for user 'mark'. The order of the entries is slightly different. Do these ACLs yield the same protection? Are Mark's private files properly protected in both cases?

7. Which of the following are software for file change detection?

    (a) Tripwire or cfengine

    (b) Snort

    (c) Network Flight Recorder

    (d) LIDS

    (e) Trustix

8. Imagine that you were recommending a security strategy to a company. Which of the following priority lists would you recommend for the most cost-effective security?

    (a)   i. Security consultant service contract (outsourcing)
         ii. Network Intrusion Detection Systems
        iii. A firewall (network access control)
         iv. Encrypted Virtual Private Networks
          v. Strong authentication and access controls
         vi. Smart cards for employees

    (b)   i. A firewall (network access control)
         ii. Network Intrusion Detection Systems
        iii. Strong authentication and access controls
         iv. A security policy for prevention and response
          v. Penetration testing
         vi. Personnel security training

    (c)   i. A security policy for prevention and response
         ii. File integrity checks on all machines
        iii. Strong authentication and access controls
         iv. Personnel security training
          v. A firewall (network access control)
         vi. Encrypted Virtual Private Networks

9. Try port scanning a part of your network. Be sure to inform the local system administrator of this in advance – it might be viewed as a hostile act.

10. Set up cfengine to perform a file integrity check on important system files on any hosts that you have privileged access to.

11. Are there any security risks associated with network printers? If so, what are they and how can they be removed?

12. Suggest ways of protecting against denial of service attacks from outside your company network.

Chapter 13

Analytical system administration

System administration has always involved a high degree of experimentation. Inadequate documentation, combined with a steep learning curve, had made that a necessity. As the curve continues to steepen and the scope of the problem only increases, the belief has gradually deepened that system administration is not merely a mechanic's job, but a scientific discipline.

A research community has grown up, led by a mixture of academics and working administrators, encouraged by organizations such as USENIX and SAGE, mainly in the US though increasingly in Europe and Australasia. The work has often been dominated by the development of software tools, since tools for the trade have been most desperately required. Now that many good tools exist, at least for Unix-based networks, the focus is changing towards more careful analyses of system administration [41, 42, 108, 44], with case studies and simple experiments.

This chapter provides a brief introduction to a larger field of theoretical system administration [52].

13.1 Science vs technology

Most of the research which is presently undertaken in system administration is of an applied nature. In most cases, it involves the construction of a tool which solves a specific local problem, a one-off solution to a general problem, i.e. a demonstration of possibility. A minority of authors has attempted to collate the lessons learned from these pursuits and distill their essence into a general technology of more permanent value. This is partly the nature of technological research. Science, on the other hand, deals in abstraction. The aim of science is to regard the full horror of reality and condense it into a few themes which capture its essence, without undue complication. We say that scientific knowledge has increased if we are able to perform this extraction of the foundations in some study and if that knowledge empowers with some increased understanding of the problem.

In science, knowledge advances by undertaking a series of studies, in order to either verify or falsify a hypothesis. Sometimes these studies are theoretical, sometimes they are empirical and frequently they are a mixture of the two. The aim of a study is to contribute to a larger discussion, which will eventually lead to progress in the field. A single piece of work is rarely, if ever, an end in itself. Once a piece of work is published, it needs to be verified or shown to be false by others also. *Reproducibility* is an important criterion for any result, otherwise it is worthless.

How we measure progress in a field is often a contentious issue, but it can involve several themes. In order to test an idea it is often necessary to develop a suitable 'technology' for the investigation. That technology might be mathematical, computational or mechanical. It does not relate directly to the study itself, but it makes it possible for the study to take place. In system administration, software tools form this technology. For example, the author's management system cfengine [41] is a tool which was created in order to implement and refine a conceptual scheme, namely the immunity model of system maintenance [44]. There is a distinction between the tool which makes the idea possible, and the idea itself.

Having produced the tool, it is still necessary to test whether or not the original idea was a good one, better or worse than other ideas, or simply unworkable in practice. Scientific progress is made, with the assistance of the tool only if the results of previous work can be improved upon, or if an increased understanding of the problem can be achieved, perhaps leading to greater predictive power or a more efficient solution to the original problem.

All problems are pieces of a larger puzzle. A complete scientific study begins with a *motivation*, followed by an *appraisal* of the problems, the construction of a *theoretical model* for understanding or solving the problems, and finally an *evaluation* or *verification* of the *approach used* and the *results obtained*. Recently much discussion has been directed towards finding suitable methods for evaluating technological innovations in computer science as well as encouraging researchers to use them. Nowadays many computing systems are of comparable complexity to phenomena found in the natural world and our understanding of them is not always complete, in spite of the fact that they were designed to fulfill a specific task. In short, technology might not be completely predictable, hence there is a need for experimental verification.

13.2 Studying complex systems

There are many issues to be studied in system administration. Some issues are of a technical nature, while others are of a human nature. System administration confronts the human–machine interaction as few other branches of computer science do. Here are some examples:

- *Reliability studies* (e.g. failure rate of hardware/software, evaluation of policies and strategies)

- *Determining and evaluating methods for ensuring system integrity* (e.g. automation, cooperation between humans, formalization of policy etc.)

- *Observations which reveal aspects of system behavior that are difficult to predict* (e.g. strange phenomena, periodic cycles)

- *Issues of strategy and planning.*

Science proceeds as a dialogue between theory and experiment. We need theory to interpret results of observations and we need observations to back up theory. Any conclusions must be a consistent mixture of the two.

To date, very little theory has been applied to the problems of system administration. Most studies have been empirical, or anecdotal. Very few of the studies made, in the references of this book, attempt to quantify their findings. In a subject which is complex, like system administration, it is easy to fall back on *qualitative* claims. This is dangerous, however, since one is more easily fooled by qualitative descriptions than by hard numbers. At the same time, one must not believe that it is sensible to demand hard-nosed falsification of claims (à la Karl Popper) in such a complex environment. Any numbers which we can measure must be considered valuable, provided they actually have a sensible interpretation.

> Computers are *complex systems*. Complexity in a system means that there is a large number of variables to be considered, probably too many to deal with in detail. Many issues are hidden directly from view and have to be discovered with some ingenuity.

A liberal attitude is usually the most constructive in making the best of a difficult lot. Any study will be worthwhile if it has something to tell us, however little. However, it is preferable if studies are authoritative, i.e. if they are able to tell us something of deeper value than mere here-say. Still, we have to judge studies for what they are worth, and no more. Authors should try to avoid marketing language which is prevalent in the commercial world, and also pointless tool-building without regard for any well thought-out model. The following questions are useful:

- What am I trying to study?

- Has it been done before? Can it be improved?

- What are the criteria for improvement?

- Can I formulate my study as a hypothesis which can be verified or falsified to some degree?

- If not, how can I clearly state the aims of my work? What are the available methods for gauging success/failure?

- How general is my study? What is the scope of its validity?

- How can my study be generalized?

- How can I ensure objectivity?

Then afterwards check:

- Is my result unambiguously true or merely a matter of interpretation?

- Are there alternative viewpoints which lead to the same conclusion?

- Is the result worth reporting to others?

Case studies are often used in fields of research where metrics are few and far between. Case studies, or anecdotal evidence, are a poor-man's approach to the truth, but in system administration we suffer from a general poverty of available avenues for investigation. Case studies, made as objectively as possible, are often the best one can do.

13.3 The purpose of observation

In technology the act of observation has two objective goals: i) to gather information about a problem in order to motivate the design and construction of a technology which solves it, and ii) to determine whether or not the resulting technology fulfills its design goals. If the latter is not fulfilled in a technological context, the system may be described as faulty, whereas in natural science there is no right or wrong. In between these two empirical book marks lies a theoretical model which hopefully connects the two.

The problem with technological disciplines is that what constitutes an evaluation of success or failure is often far from clear. This is because both goals and assisting technologies can be dominated by invested interests and dogged by the difficulty of constructing objective experiments with clear metrics. System administration is an example where these problems are particularly acute.

System administration is a mixture of technology and sociology. The users of computer systems are constantly changing the conditions for observations. If the conditions under which observations are made are not constant, then the data lose their meaning: the message we are trying to extract from the data is supplemented by several other messages which are difficult to separate from one another. Let us call the message we are trying to extract *signal* and the other messages which we are not interested in *noise*. Complex systems are often characterized by very noisy environments.

In most disciplines one would attempt to reduce or eliminate the noise in order to isolate the signal. However, in system administration, it would be no good to eliminate the users from an experiment, since it is they who cause most of the problems that one is trying to solve. In principle this kind of noise in data could be eliminated by statistical sampling over very long periods of time, but in the case of real computer systems this might not be possible since seasonal variations in patterns of use often lead to several qualitatively different types of behavior which should not be mixed. The collection of reliable data might therefore take many years, even if one can agree on what constitutes a reasonable experiment. This is often impractical, given the pace of technological change in the field.

13.4 Evaluation methods and problems

The simplest and potentially most objective way to test a model of system administration is to combine heuristic experience with repeatable simulations.

Experienced system administrators have the pulse of their system and can evaluate their performance in a way that only humans can. Their knowledge can be used to define *repeatable* benchmarks or criteria for different aspects of the problem. But even this approach is not without its difficulties. Many of the administrators' impressions would be very difficult to gauge numerically. For example: a common theme is research which is designed to relieve administrators of tedious work, leaving them to work on more important tasks. Can such a claim be verified? Here are some of the difficulties.

Measure the time spent working on the system	The administrator has so much to do that he/she can work full time no matter how much one automates 'tedious tasks'.
Record the actions taken by the automatic system, which a human administrator would have been required to do by hand and compare.	There is no unique way to solve a problem. Some administrators fix problems by hand, while others will write a script for each new problem. The time/approach taken depends on the person.

In this case the issue was too broad to be able to quantify. Choosing the appropriate question to ask is often the most difficult aspect of an experimental study. If we restrict the scope of the question to a very specific point, we can end up with an artificial study; if the question is too broad in its scope, we risk not being able to test it convincingly.

To further clarify this point it is useful to refer to an analogy. Imagine two researchers who create vehicles for the future, one based on renewable solar power and another based on coal. The two vehicles have identical functionality; the solar powered vehicle seems cleaner than the coal powered one, but in fact the level of pollution required to make the solar cells equals the harmful output of the coal vehicle throughout its lifetime. The laws of thermodynamics tell us that there is potential for improving this situation for the electric car but probably not for the coal powered one. The solar vehicle is lighter and more efficient, but it cannot do anything that the coal powered car cannot. All in all, one suspects that the solar powered system is a better solution, since one does not have to refuel it frequently and it is based on a technology which is universally useful, whereas the coal system is quite restricted. So what are the numbers which we should measure to distinguish one from the other, to verify the hypothesis that the solar powered vehicle is better? Is one solution really better than the other? Regardless of whether either solution is optimal, is one of them going in a sustainable direction for future development? It might seem clear that the electric vehicle is a sounder technology since it is both sustainable in its power source and in its potential for future development, whereas the coal vehicle is something of a dead end. The solution can be ideologically correct, but this is a matter of opinion. Anyone can claim to prefer the coal powered vehicle, whether others would deem that belief to be rational or not. One can attempt to evaluate their basic principles on the basis of anecdotal evidence. One can produce numbers for many small contributing factors (such as the weight of the vehicles, or their power efficiency), but when it comes down to it anyone can claim that those numbers do not matter because both vehicles fulfill their purpose identically.

This example is not entirely contrived. System administration requires tools. Often such tools acquire a following of users who grow to like them, regardless of what the tools allow them to achieve. Also, the marketing skills of one software producer might be better than those of another. Thus one cannot rely on counting the numbers of users of a specific tool as an indication of its power or usefulness. On the other hand, one has to rely on the evaluations of the tools by their users.

In some cases one technology might be better than another only in a certain context. There might be room for several different solutions. For example, are transistors better than thermionic valve devices for building computers? Most people think so, because valve technology is large and cumbersome. But advances in Russian military aerospace technology developed miniature valves because they were robust against electromagnetic pulse interference. One can think of many examples of technologies which have clear advantages, but which cannot be proved numerically, because it boils down to what people prefer to believe about them. This last case also indicates that there is not necessarily a single universal solution to a problem.

Although questionnaires and verbal evaluations which examine experienced users' impressions can be amongst the best methods of evaluating a hypothesis with many interacting components, the problems in making such a study objective are great. Questionnaires, in particular, can give misleading results, since they are often only returned by users who are already basically satisfied. Completely dissatisfied users will usually waste no time on what they consider to be a worthless pursuit, by filling out a questionnaire.

13.5 Evaluating a hierarchical system

Evaluating a model of system administration is a little bit like evaluating the concept of a bridge. Clearly a bridge is a structure with many components each of which contributes to the whole. The bridge either fulfills its purpose in carrying traffic past obstacles or it does not. In evaluating the bridge, should one then consider the performance of each brick and wire individually? Should one consider the aesthetic qualities of the bridge? There might be many different designs each with slightly different goals. Can one bridge be deemed better than another on the basis of objective measurement? Perhaps only the bridge's maintainer is in a position to gain a feeling for which bridge is the most successful, but the success criterion might be rather vague: a collection of small differences which make the perceptible performance of the bridge optimal, but with no measurably significant data to support the conclusion. These are the dilemmas of evaluating a complex technology.

In references [69, 334] and many others it is clear that computer scientists are embarrassed by this difficulty in bringing respectability to the field of study. In fact the difficulty is general to all fields of technology. In order to evaluate an approach to the solution of a problem it is helpful to create a model. A model is comprised of a principle of operation, a collection of rules and the implementation of these rules through specific algorithms. It involves a conceptual decomposition of the problem and a number of assertions or hypotheses. System administration is full of intangibles; this restricts model building to those aspects of the problem which can be addressed in schematic terms. It is also sufficiently complex that it must be addressed at several different levels in an approximately hierarchical fashion.

In brief, the options we have for performing experimental studies are,

- Measurements

- Simulations

- Case studies

- User surveys

with all of the incumbent difficulties which these entail.

13.5.1 Evaluation of the conceptual decomposition

It is a general principle in analysis that the details of lower level structure, insofar as they function, do not change the structural organization of higher levels. In physics this is called the separation of scales; in computer science it is called procedural structure or object orientation. The structure of lower levels does not affect the optimal structure of higher levels, for example. An important part of a meaningful evaluation is to sort out the conceptual hierarchy. Is the separation between high-level abstractions and low-level primitives sufficient, flexible, restrictive etc?

13.5.2 Simplicity

Conceptual and practical simplicity are often deemed to be positive attributes of software systems and procedures. User surveys can be used to collect evidence of what users believe about this. The system designer's belief about the relative simplicity of his/her creation is a scientific irrelevancy.

13.5.3 Efficiency

The efficiency of a program or procedure might be an interesting way to evaluate it. Efficiency can mean many things, so the first step is to establish precisely what is meant by efficiency in context.

Most system administration tasks are not resource intensive for individual hosts. The efficiency with which they are carried out is less important than the care with which they are carried out. The reason is simple: the time required to complete most system administration tasks is very short compared with the time most users are prepared to wait.

Efficiency in terms of the consumption of human time is a much more pertinent factor. An automatic system which aims to avoid human interaction is by definition more efficient in man hours than one which places humans in the driving seat. This presupposes, of course, that the setup and maintenance of the automatic system is not so time-consuming in itself as to outweigh the advantages provided by such an approach.

13.5.4 Evaluation of system administration as a collective effort

Few system administrators work alone. In most cases they are part of a team who all need to keep abreast of the behavior of the system and the changes made in administration policy. Automation of system administration issues does not alter this. One issue for human administrators is how well a model for administration allows them to achieve this cooperation in practice. Does the automatic system make it easier for them to follow the development of the system in i) theory and ii) practice? Here theory refers to the conceptual design of the system as a whole, and practice refers to the extent to which the theoretical design has been implemented in practice. How is the task distributed between people, systems, procedures and tools? How is responsibility delegated and how does this affect individuals? Is time saved, are accuracy and consistency improved? These issues can be evaluated in a heuristic way from the experiences of administrators. Longer-term, more objective studies could also be performed by analyzing the behavior of system administrators in action. Such studies will not be performed here.

13.5.5 Cooperative software: dependency

The fragile tower of components in any functional system is the fundament of its operation. If one component fails, how resilient is the remainder of the system to this failure? This is a relevant question to pose in the evaluation of a system administration model. How do software systems depend on one another for their operation? If one system fails, will this have a knock-on effect for other systems? What are the core systems which form the basis of system operation? In the present work it is relevant to ask how the model continues to work in the event of the failure of DNS, NFS and other network services which provide infrastructure. Is it possible to immobilize an automatic system administration model?

13.5.6 Evaluation of individual mechanisms

For individual pieces of software, it is sometimes possible to evaluate the efficiency and correctness of the components. Efficiency is a relative concept and, if used, it must be placed in a context. For example, efficiency of low-level algorithms is conceptually irrelevant to the higher levels of a program, but it might be practically relevant, i.e. one must say what is meant by efficiency before quoting results. The correctness of the results yielded by a mechanism/algorithm can be measured in relation to its design specifications. Without a clear mapping of input/output the correctness of any result produced by a mechanism is a heuristic quality. Heuristics can only be evaluated by experienced users expressing their informed opinions.

13.5.7 Evidence of bugs in the software

Occasionally bugs significantly affect the performance of software. Strictly speaking an evaluation of bugs is not part of the software evaluation itself, but of the process of software development, so while bugs should probably be mentioned they may or may not be relevant to the issues surrounding the software itself. In this work software bugs have not played any appreciable role in either the development or the effectiveness of the results so they will not be discussed in any detail.

13.5.8 Evidence of design faults

In the course of developing a program one occasionally discovers faults which are of a fundamental nature, faults which cause one to rethink the whole operation of the program. Sometimes these are fatal flaws, but that need not be the case. Cataloguing design faults is important for future reference to avoid making similar mistakes again. Design faults may be caused by faults in the model itself or merely in its implementation. Legacy issues might also be relevant here: how do outdated features or methods affect software by placing demands on onward compatibility, or by restricting optimal design or performance?

13.5.9 Evaluation of system policies

System administration does not exist without human attitudes, behaviors and policies. These three fit together inseparably. Policies are adjusted to fit behavioral patterns; behavioral patterns are local phenomena. The evaluation of a system policy has only limited relevance for the wider community then: normally only relative changes are of interest, i.e. how changes in policy can move one closer to a desirable solution.

Evaluating the effectiveness of a policy in relation to the applicable social boundary conditions presents practical problems which sociologists have wrestled with for decades. The problems lie in obtaining statistically significant samples of data to support or refute the policy. Controlled experiments are not usually feasible since they would tie up resources over long periods. No one can afford this in practice. In order to test a policy in a real situation the best one can do is to rely on heuristic information from an experienced observer (in this case the system administrator). Only an experienced observer would be able to judge the value of a policy on the basis of incomplete data. Such information is difficult to trust however unless it comes from several independent sources. A better approach might be to test the policy with simulated data spanning the range from best to worst case. The advantage with simulated data is that the results are reproducible from those data and thus one has something concrete to show for the effort.

13.5.10 Reliability

Reliability cannot be measured until we define what we mean by it. One common definition uses the *average (mean) time before failure* as a measure of system reliability. This is quite simply the average amount of time we expect to elapse between serious failures of the system. Another way of expressing this is to use the *average uptime*, or the amount of time for which the system is responsive (waiting no more than a fixed length of time for a response). Another complementary figure is then, the *average downtime*, which is the average amount of time the system is unavailable for work (a kind of informational entropy). We can define the reliability as the probability that the system is available:

$$\rho = \frac{\text{Mean uptime}}{\text{Total elapsed time}}$$

Some like to define this in terms of the Mean Time Before Failure (MTBF) and the Mean Time To Repair (MTTR), i.e.

$$\rho = \frac{\text{MTBF}}{\text{MTBF} + \text{MTTR}}.$$

This is clearly a number between 0 and 1. Many network device vendors quote these values with the number of 9's it yields, e.g. 0.99999.

The effect of parallelism or redundancy on reliability can be treated as a facsimile of the Ohm's law problem, by noting that service provision is just like a flow of work (see also section 6.3 for examples of this).

Rate of service (delivery) = rate of change in information / failure fraction

This is directly analogous to Ohm's law for the flow of current through a resistance:

$$I = V/R$$

The analogy is captured in this table:

Potential difference V	Change in information
Current I	Rate of service (flow of information)
Resistance R	Rate of failure

This relation is simplistic. For one thing it does not take into account variable latencies (although these could be defined as failure to respond). It should be clear that this simplistic equation is full of unwarranted assumptions, and yet its simplicity justifies its use for simple hand-waving. If we consider figure 6.10, it is clear that a flow of service can continue, when servers work in parallel, even if one or more of them fails. In figure 6.11 it is clear that systems which are dependent on other systems are coupled in series and a failure prevents the flow of service. Because of the linear relationship, we can use the usual Ohm's law expressions for combining failure rates:

$$R_{\text{series}} = R_1 + R_2 + R_3 + \dots$$

and

$$\frac{1}{R_{\text{parallel}}} = \frac{1}{R_1} + \frac{1}{R_2} + \frac{1}{R_3} \cdots$$

These simple expressions can be used to hand-wave about the reliability of combinations of hosts. For instance, let us define the rate of failure to be a probability of failure, with a value between 0 and 1. Suppose we find that the rate of failure of a particular kind of server is 0.1. If we couple two in parallel (a double redundancy) then we obtain an effective failure rate of

$$\frac{1}{R} = \frac{1}{0.1} + \frac{1}{0.1}$$

i.e. $R = 0.05$, the failure rate is halved. This estimate is clearly naive. It assumes, for instance, that both servers work all the time in parallel. This is seldom the case. If we run parallel servers, normally a default server will be tried first, and, if there is no response, only then will the second backup server be contacted. Thus, in a fail-over model, this is not really applicable. Still, we use this picture for what it is worth, as a crude hand-waving tool.

The Mean Time Before Failure (MTBF) is used by electrical engineers, who find that its values for the failures of many similar components (say light bulbs) has an exponential distribution. In other words, over large numbers of similar component failures, it is found that the probability of failure has the form

$$P(t) = \exp(-t/\tau)$$

or that the probability of a component lasting time t is the exponential, where τ is the mean time before failure and t is the failure time of a given component. There are many reasons why a computer system would not be expected to have this simple form. One is *dependency*. Computer systems are formed from many interacting components. The interactions with third party components mean that the environmental factors are always different. Again, the issue of fail-over and service latencies arises, spoiling the simple independent component picture. Mean time before failure doesn't mean anything unless we define the conditions under which the quantity was measured. In one test at Oslo College, the following values were measured for various operating systems, averaged over several hosts of the same type.

Solaris 2.5	86 days
GNU/Linux	36 days
Windows 95	0.5 days

While we might feel that these numbers agree with our general intuition of how these operating systems perform in practice, this is not a fair comparison since the patterns of *usage* are different in each case. An insider could tell us that the users treat the PCs with a casual disregard, switching them on and off at will: and in spite of efforts to prevent it, the same users tend to pull the plug on GNU/Linux hosts also. The Solaris hosts, on the other hand, live in glass cages where prying fingers cannot reach. Of course, we then need to ask: what is the reason why users reboot and pull the plug on the PCs? The numbers above cannot have any meaning until this has been determined; i.e. the software components of a computer system are not atomic; they are composed of many parts whose behavior is difficult to catalogue.

Thus the problem with these measures of system reliability is that they are almost impossible to quantify and assigning any real meaning to them is fraught with subtlety. Unless the system fails regularly, the number of points over which it is possible to average is rather small. Moreover, the number of external factors which can lead to failure makes the comparison of any two values at different sites meaningless. In short, this quantity cannot be used for anything other than illustrative purposes. Changes in the reliability, for constant external conditions, can be used as a measure to show the effect of a single parameter from the environment. This is perhaps the only instance in which this can be made meaningful, i.e. as a means of quantitative comparison within a single experiment.

13.5.11 Metrics generally

The quantifiers which can be usefully measured or recorded on operating systems are the variables which can be used to provide quantitative support for or against a hypothesis about system behavior. System auditing functionality can be used to record just about every operation which passes through the kernel of an operating system, but most hosts do not perform system auditing because of the huge negative effect it has on performance. Here we consider only metrics which do not require extensive auditing beyond what is normally available.

Operating system metrics are normally used for operating system performance tuning. System performance tuning requires data about the efficiency of an operating system. This is not necessarily compatible with the kinds of measurement required for evaluating the effectiveness of a system administration model. System administration is concerned with maintaining resource availability over time in a secure and fair manner. It is not about optimizing specific performance criteria.

Operating system metrics fall into two main classes: current values and average values for stable and drifting variables respectively. Current (immediate) values are not usually directly useful, unless the values are basically constant, since they seldom accurately reflect any changing property of an operating system adequately. They can be used for fluctuation analysis, however, over some coarse-graining period. An averaging procedure over some time interval is the main approach of interest. The Nyquist law for sampling of a continuous signal is that the sampling rate needs to be twice the rate of the fastest peak cycle in the data if one is to resolve the data accurately. This includes data which are intended for averaging since this rule is not about accuracy of resolution but about the possible complete loss of data. The granularity required for measurement in current operating systems is summarized in the following table.

0 − 5 secs	Fine grain work
10 − 30 secs	For peak measurement
10 − 30 mins	For coarse-grain work
Hourly average	Software activity
Daily average	User activity
Weekly average	User activity

Although kernel switching times are of the order of microseconds, this time scale is not relevant to users' perceptions of the system. Inter-system cooperating requires many context switch cycles and I/O waits. These compound themselves into intervals of the order of seconds in practice. Users themselves spend long periods of time idle, i.e. not interacting with the system on an immediate basis. An interval of seconds is therefore sufficient. Peaks of activity can happen quickly by user perceptions but they often last for protracted periods, thus ten to thirty seconds is appropriate here. Coarse-grained behavior requires lower resolution, but as long as one is looking for peaks a faster rate of sampling will always include the lower rate. There is also the issue of how quickly the data can be collected. Since the measurement process itself affects the performance of the system and uses its resources, measurement needs to be kept to a level where it does not play a significant role in loading the system or consuming disk and memory resources.

The variables which characterize resource usage fall into various categories. Some variables are devoid of any apparent periodicity, while others are strongly periodic in the daily and weekly rhythms of the system. The amount of periodicity in a variable depends on how strongly it is coupled to a periodic driving force, such as the user community's daily and weekly rhythms, and also how strong that driving force is (users' behavior also has seasonal variations, vacations and deadlines etc). Since our aim is to find a sufficiently complete set of variables which characterize a macrostate of the system, we must be aware of which variables are ignorable, which variables are periodic (and can therefore be averaged over a periodic interval) and which variables are not periodic (and therefore have no unique average).

Studies of total network traffic have shown an allegedly self-similar (fractal) structure to network traffic when viewed in its entirety [192, 324]. This is in contrast to telephonic voice traffic on traditional phone networks which is bursty, the bursts following a random (Poisson) distribution in arrival time. This almost certainly precludes total network traffic from a characterization of host state, but it does not preclude the use of numbers of connections/conversations between different protocols, which one would still expect to have a Poissonian profile. A value of none means that any apparent peak is much smaller than the error bars (standard deviation of the mean) of the measurements when averaged over the presumed trial period. The periodic quantities are plotted on a periodic time scale, with each covering adding to the averages and variances. Non-periodic data are plotted on a straightforward, unbounded real line as an absolute value. A running average can also be computed, and an entropy, if a suitable division of the vertical axis into cells is defined [42]. We shall return to the definition of entropy later.

The *average type* referred to below divides into two categories: pseudo-continuous and discrete. In point of fact, virtually all of the measurements made have discrete results (excepting only those which are already system averages). This categorization refers to the extent to which it is sensible to treat the average value of the variable as a continuous quantity. In some cases, it is utterly meaningless. For the reasons already indicated, there are advantages to treating measured values as continuous, so it is with this motivation that we claim a pseudo-continuity to the averaged data.

In this initial instance, the data are all collected from Oslo College's own computer network which is an academic environment with moderate resources. One might expect our data to lie somewhere in the middle of the extreme cases which might be found amongst the sites of the world, but one should be cognizant of the limited validity of a single set of such data. We re-emphasize that the purpose of the present work is to gauge *possibilities* rather than to extract actualities.

Net

- *Total number of packets:* Characterizes the totality of traffic, incoming and outgoing on the subnet. This could have a bearing on latencies and thus influence all hosts on a local subnet.

- *Amount of IP fragmentation:* This is a function of the protocols in use in the local environment. It should be fairly constant, unless packets are being fragmented for scurrilous reasons.

- *Density of broadcast messages:* This is a function of local network services. This would not be expected to have a direct bearing on the state of a host (other than the host transmitting the broadcast), unless it became so high as to cause a traffic problem.

- *Number of collisions:* This is a function of the network community traffic. Collision numbers can significantly affect the performance of hosts wishing to communicate, thus adding to latencies. It can be brought on by sheer amount of traffic, i.e. a threshold transition and by errors in the physical network, or in software. In a well-configured site, the number of collisions should be random. A strong periodic signal would tend to indicate a burdened network with too low a capacity for its users.

- *Number of sockets (TCP) in and out:* This gives an indication of service usage. Measurements should be separated so as to distinguish incoming and outgoing connections. We would expect outgoing connections to follow the periodicities of the local site, where as incoming connections would be a superposition of weak periodicities from many sites, with no net result. See figure 13.1.

- *Number of malformed packets:* This should be zero, i.e. a non-zero value here specifies a problem in some networked host, or an attack on the system.

Storage

- *Disk usage in bytes:* This indicates the actual amount of data generated and downloaded by users, or the system. Periodicities here will be affected by whatever policy one has for garbage collection. Assuming that users do not produce only garbage, there should be a periodicity superposed on top of a steady rise.

- *Disk operations per second:* This is an indication of the physical activity of the disk on the local host. It is a measure of load and a significant contribution to latency both locally and for remote hosts. The level of periodicity in this signal must depend on the relative magnitude of forces driving the host. If a

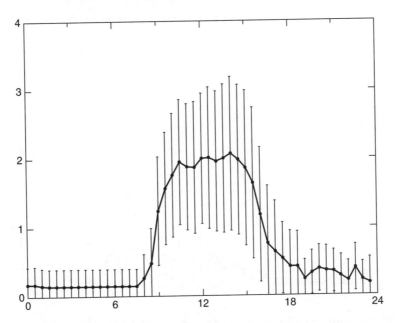

Figure 13.1: The daily rhythm of the external logins shows a strong unambiguous peak during work hours.

host runs no network services, then it is driven mainly by users, yielding a strong periodicity. If system services dominate, these could be either random or periodic. The values are thus likely to be periodic, but not necessarily strong.

- *Paging (out) rate (free memory and thrashing):* These variables measure the activity of the virtual memory subsystem. In principle they can reveal problems with load. In our tests, they have proved singularly irrelevant, though we realize that we might be spoiled with the quality of our resources here. See figures 13.2 and 13.3.

Processes

- *Number of privileged processes:* The number of processes running the system provides an indication of the number of forked processes or active threads which are carrying out the work of the system. This should be relatively constant, with a weak periodicity indicating responses to local users' requests. This is separated from the processes of ordinary users, since one expects the behavior of privileged (root/Administrator) processes to follow a different pattern. See figure 13.4.

- *Number of non-privileged processes:* This measure counts not only the number of processes but provides an indication of the range of tasks being performed by users, and the number of users by implication. This measure has a strong periodic quality, relatively quiescent during weekends, rising sharply

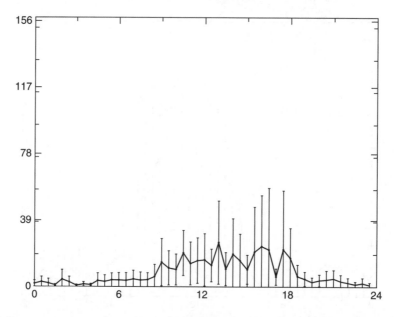

Figure 13.2: The daily rhythm of the paging data illustrates the problems one faces in attaching meaning directly to measurements. Here we see that the error bars (signifying the standard deviation) are much larger than the variation of the graph itself. Nonetheless, there is a marginal rise in the paging activity during daytime hours, and a corresponding increase in the error bars, indicating that there is a real effect, albeit of little analytical value.

on Monday to a peak on Tuesday, followed by a gradual decline towards the weekend again. See figures 13.5 and 13.6.

- *Maximum percentage CPU used in processes:* This is an experimental measure which characterizes the most CPU expensive process running on the host at a given moment. The significance of this result is not clear. It seems to have a marginally periodic behavior, but is basically inconclusive. The error bars are much larger than the variation of the average, but the magnitude of the errors increases also with the increasing average, thus, while for all intents and purposes this measure's average must be considered irrelevant, a weak signal can be surmised. The peak value of the data might be important however, since a high max-cpu task will significantly load the system. See figure 13.7.

Users

- *Number logged on:* This follows the classic pattern of low activity during the weekends, followed by a sharp rise on Monday, peaking on Tuesday and declining steadily towards the weekend again.

- *Total number:* This value should clearly be constant except when new user accounts are added. The average value has no meaning, but any change in this value can be significant from a security perspective.

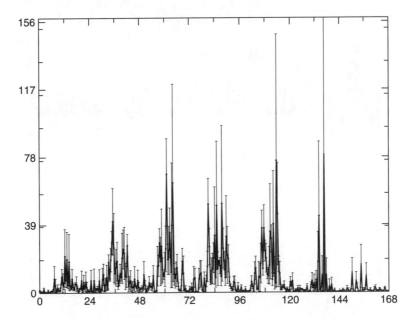

Figure 13.3: The weekly rhythm of the paging data show that there is a definite daily rhythm, but again, it is drowned in the huge variances due to random influences on the system, and is therefore of no use in an analytical context.

- *Average time spent logged on per user:* Can signify patterns of behavior, but has a questionable relevance to the behavior of the system.

- *Load average:* This is the system's own back-of-the-envelope calculation of resource usage. It provides a continuous indication of load, but on an exaggerated scale. It remains to be seen whether any useful information can be obtained from this value; its value can be quite disordered (high entropy).

- *Disk usage rise per session per user per hour:* The average amount of increase of disk space per user per session, indicates the way in which the system is becoming loaded. This can be used to diagnose problems caused by a single user downloading a huge amount of data from the network. During normal behavior, if users have an even productivity, this might be periodic.

- *Latency of services:* The latency is the amount of time we wait for an answer to a specific request. This value only becomes significant when the system passes a certain threshold (a kind of phase transition). Once latency begins to restrict the practices of users, we can expect it to feed back and exacerbate latencies. Thus the periodicity of latencies would only be expected in a phase of the system in which user activity was in competition with the cause of the latency itself.

Part of what one wishes to identify in looking at such variables is patterns of change. These are classifiable but not usually quantifiable. They can be relevant to policy decisions as well as in fine tuning of the parameters of an automatic response. Patterns of behavior include

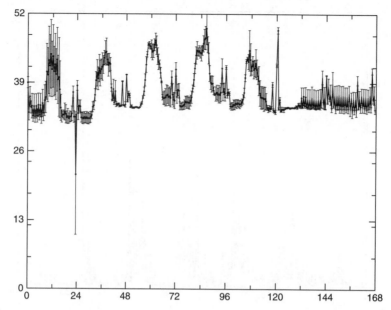

Figure 13.4: The weekly average of privileged (root) processes shows a constant daily pulse, steady on week days. During weekends, there is far less activity, but wider variance. This might be explained by assuming that root process activity is dominated by service requests from users.

- Social patterns of the users
- Systematic patterns caused by software systems.

Identifying such patterns in the variation of the metrics listed above is not an easy task, but it is the closest one can expect to come to a measurable effect in a system administration context.

In addition to measurable quantities, humans have the ability to form value judgments in a way that formal statistical analyses cannot. Human judgment is based on compounded experience and associative thinking and while it lacks scientific rigor it can be intuitively correct in a way that is difficult to quantify. The down side of human perception is that prejudice is also a factor which is difficult to eliminate. Also not everyone is in a position to offer useful evidence in every judgment:

- *User satisfaction*: software, system-availability, personal freedom
- *Sysadmin satisfaction*: time-saving, accuracy, simplifying, power, ease of use, utility of tools, security, adaptability.

Other heuristic impressions include the amount of dependency of a software component on other software systems, hosts or processes; also the dependency of a software system on the presence of a human being. In ref. [186] Kubicki discusses metrics for measuring customer satisfaction. These involve validated questionnaires, system availability, system response time, availability of tools, failure analysis, and time before reboot measurements.

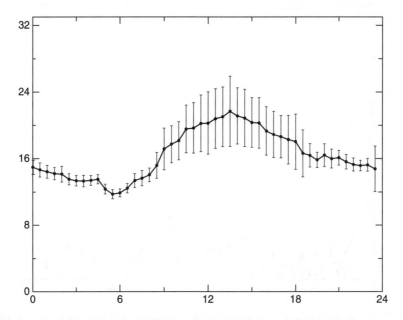

Figure 13.5: The daily average of non-privileged (user) processes shows an indisputable, strong daily rhythm. The variation of the graph is now greater than the uncertainty reflected in the error bars.

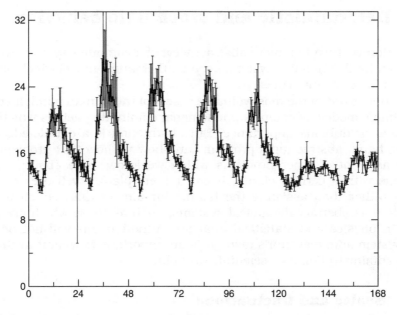

Figure 13.6: The weekly average of non-privileged (user) processes shows a constant daily pulse, quiet at the weekends, strong on Monday, rising to a peak on Tuesday and falling off again towards the weekend.

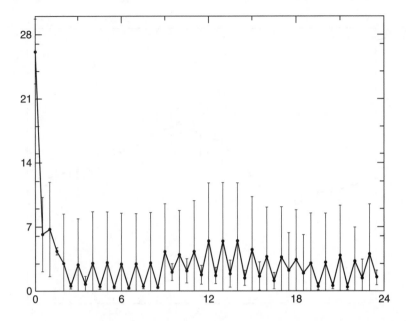

Figure 13.7: The daily average of maximal CPU percentage shows no visible rhythm, if we remove the initial anomalous point then there is no variation, either in the average or its standard deviation (error bars) which justifies the claim of a periodicity.

13.6   Deterministic and stochastic behavior

In this section we turn to a more abstract view of a computer system: we think of it as a generalized dynamical system, i.e. a mathematical model which develops in time, according to certain rules.

Abstraction is one of the most valuable assets of the human mind: it enables us to build simple models of complex phenomena, eliminating details which are only of peripheral or dubious importance. But abstraction is a double-edged sword: on the one hand, abstracting a problem can show us how that problem is really the same as a lot of other problems which we know more about; conversely, unless done with a certain clarity, it can merely plant a veil over our senses, obscuring rather than assisting the truth. Our aim in this section is to think of computers as abstract dynamical systems, such as those which are routinely analyzed in physics and statistical analysis. Although this will not be to every working system administrator's taste, it is an important viewpoint in the pursuit of system administration as a scientific discipline.

13.6.1   Scales and fluctuations

Complex systems are characterized by behavior at many levels or scales. In order to extract information from a complex system it is necessary to focus on the appropriate scale for that information. In physics, three scales are usually distinguished in many-component systems: the *microscopic, mesoscopic* and *macroscopic* scales. We can borrow this terminology for convenience.

- *Microscopic* behavior details exact mechanisms at the level of atomic operations.

- *Mesoscopic* behavior looks at small clusters of microscopic processes and examines them in isolation.

- *Macroscopic* processes concern the long-term average behavior of the whole system.

These three scales can also be discerned in operating systems and they must usually be considered separately. At the microscopic level we have individual system calls and other atomic transactions (on the order of microseconds to milliseconds). At the mesoscopic level we have clusters and patterns of system calls and other process behavior, including algorithms and procedures, possibly arising from single processes or groups of processes. Finally, there is the macroscopic level at which one views all the activities of all the users over scales at which they typically work and consume resources (minutes, hours, days, weeks). There is clearly a measure of arbitrariness in drawing these distinctions. The point is that there are typically three scales which can usefully be distinguished in a relatively stable dynamical system.

13.6.2 Principle of superposition

In any dynamical system where several microscopic processes can coexist, there are two possible scenarios:

- Every process is completely independent of every other. System resources change linearly (additively) in response to new processes.

- The addition of each new process affects the behavior of the others in a non-additive (non-linear) fashion.

The first of these is called the principle of superposition. It is a generic property of *linear* systems (actually this is a defining tautology). In the second case, the system is said to be non-linear because the result of adding lots of processes is not merely the sum of those processes: the processes interact and complicate matters. Owing to the complexity of interactions between subsystems in a network, it is likely that there is at least some degree of non-linearity in the measurements we are looking for. That means that a change in one part of the system will have communicable, knock-on effects on another part of the system, with possible feedback, and so on.

This is one of the things which needs to be examined, since it has a bearing on the shape of the distribution one can expect to find. Empirically one often finds that the probability of a deviation Δx from the expected behavior is [130]

$$P(\Delta x) = \frac{1}{2\sigma} \exp\left(-\frac{|\Delta x|}{\sigma}\right)$$

for large jumps. This is much broader than a Gaussian measure for a random sample

$$P(\Delta x) = \frac{1}{(2\pi)^{1/2}\sigma} \exp\left(-\frac{\Delta x^2}{2\sigma^2}\right)$$

which one might normally expect of random behavior [34].

13.6.3 The idea of convergence

In order to converge to a stable equilibrium one needs to provide counter-measures to change that are switched off when the system has reached its desired state. In order for this to happen, a policy of checking-before-doing is required. This is actually a difficult issue which becomes increasingly difficult with the complexity of the task involved. Fortunately most system configuration issues are solved by simple means (file permissions, missing files etc.) and thus, in practice, it can be a simple matter to test whether the system is in its desired state before modifying it.

In mathematics a random perturbation in time is represented by Gaussian noise, or a function whose expectation value, averaged over a representative time interval, is zero

$$\langle f \rangle = \frac{1}{T} \int_0^T dt \; f(t) = 0.$$

The simplest model of random change is the driven harmonic oscillator.

$$\frac{d^2s}{dt^2} + \gamma \frac{ds}{dt} + \omega_0^2 = f(t),$$

where s is the state of the system and γ is the rate at which it converges to a steady state. In order to make oscillations converge, they are damped by a frictional or counter force γ (in the present case the immune system is the frictional force which will damp down unwanted changes). In order to have any chance of stopping the oscillations the counter force must be able to change direction in time with the oscillations so that it is always opposing the changes at the same rate as the changes themselves. Formally this is ensured by having the frictional force proportional to the rate of change of the system as in the differential representation above. The solutions to this kind of motion are *damped oscillations* of the form

$$s(t) \sim e^{-\gamma t} \sin(\omega t + \phi),$$

for some frequency ω and damping rate γ. In the theory of harmonic motion, three cases are distinguished: under-damped motion, damped and over-damped motion. In under-damped motion $\gamma \ll \omega$, there is never sufficient counter force to make the oscillations converge to any degree. In damped motion the oscillations do converge quite quickly $\gamma \sim \omega$. Finally with over-damped motion $\gamma \gg \omega$ the counter force is so strong as to never allow any change at all.

Under-damped	Inefficient: the system can never quite keep errors in check.
Damped	System converges in a time scale of the order of the rate of fluctuation.
Over-damped	Too draconian: processes killed frequently while still in use.

Clearly an over-damped solution to system management is unacceptable. This would mean that the system could not change at all. If one does not want any changes then it is easy to place the machine in a museum and switch it off. Also an under-damped solution will not be able to keep up with the changes to the system made by users or attackers.

The *slew rate* is the rate at which a device can dissipate changes in order to keep them in check. If immune response ran continuously then the rate at which it completed its tasks would be the approximate slew rate. In the body it takes two or three days to develop an immune response, approximately the length of time it takes to become infected, so that minor episodes last about a week. In a computer system there are many mechanisms which work at different time scales and need to be treated with greater or lesser haste. What is of central importance here is the underlying assumption that an immune response will be timely. The time scales for perturbation and response must match. Convergence is not a useful concept in itself, unless it is a dynamical one. Systems must be allowed to change, but they must not be allowed to become damaged. Presently there are few objective criteria for making this judgment so it falls to humans to define such criteria, often arbitrarily.

In addition to random changes, there is also the possibility of systematic error. Systematic change would lead to a constant unidirectional drift (clock drift, disk space usage etc). These changes must be cropped sufficiently frequently (producing a sawtooth pattern) to prevent serious problems from occurring. A serious problem would be defined as a problem which prevented the system from functioning effectively. In the case of disk usage, there is a clear limit beyond which the system cannot add more files, thus corrective systems need to be invoked more frequently when this limit is approached, but also in advance of this limit with less frequency to slow the drift to a minimum. In the case of clock drift, the effects are more subtle.

13.6.4 Parameterizing a dynamical system

If we wish to describe the behavior of a computer system from an analytical viewpoint, we need to be able to write down a number of variables which capture its behavior. Ideally, this characterization would be numerical since quantitative descriptions are more reliable than qualitative ones, though this might not always be feasible. In order to properly characterize a system, we need a theoretical understanding of the system or subsystem which we intend to describe. Dynamical systems fall into two categories, depending on how we choose our problem to analyze. These are called *open systems* and *closed systems*.

- *Open system:* This is a *subsystem* of some greater whole. An open system can be thought of as a black box which takes in input and generates output, i.e. it communicates with its environment. The names *source* and *sink* are traditionally used for the input and output routes. What happens in the black box depends on the state of the environment around it. The system is open because input changes the state of the system's internal variables and output changes the state of the environment. Every piece of computer software is an open system. Even an isolated total computer system is an open system as long as any user is using it. If we wish to describe what happens inside the black box, then the source and the sink must be modeled by two variables which represent the essential behavior of the environment. Since one cannot normally predict the exact behavior of what goes on outside of a black box (it might itself depend on many complicated variables), any study of an open system tends to be incomplete. The source and sink are essentially unknown quantities. Normally one would choose to analyze such a system by choosing some special input and consider a number of special cases. An open system is internally *deterministic*, meaning that it follows strict rules and algorithms, but its behavior is not necessarily determined, since the environment is an unknown.

- *Closed system:* This is a system which is complete, in the sense of being isolated from its environment. A closed system receives no input and normally produces no output. Computer systems can only be approximately closed for short periods of time. The essential point is that a closed system is neither affected by, nor affects its environment. In thermodynamics, a closed system always tends to a steady state. Over short periods, under controlled conditions, this might be a useful concept in analyzing computer subsystems, but only as an idealization. In order to speak of a closed system, we have to know the behavior of all the variables which characterize the system. A closed system is said to be completely *determined*.[1]

An important difference between an open system and a closed system is that an open system is not always in a steady state. New input changes the system. The internal variables in the open system are altered by external perturbations from the source, and the sum state of all the internal variables (which can be called the system's *macrostate*) reflect the history of changes which have occurred from outside. For example, suppose we are analyzing a word processor. This is clearly an open system: it receives input and its output is simply a window on its data to the user. The buffer containing the text reflects the history of all that was inputted by the user and the output causes the user to think and change the input again. If we were to characterize the behavior of a word processor, we would describe it by its internal variables: the text buffer, any special control modes or switches etc.

---

[1]This does not mean that it is exactly calculable. Non-linear, chaotic systems are deterministic but inevitably inexact over any length of time.

Normally we are interested in components of the operating system which have more to do with the overall functioning of the machine, but the principle is the same. The difficulty with such a characterization is that there is no unique way of keeping track of a system's history over time, quantitatively. That is not to say that no such measures exist. Let us consider one simple cumulative quantifier of the system's history, which was introduced by Burgess in ref. [42], namely its entropy or disorder. Entropy has certain qualitative, intuitive features which are easily understood. Disorder in a system measures the extent to which it is occupied by files and processes which prevent useful work. If there is a high level of disorder, then – depending on the context – one might either feel satisfied that the system is being used to the full, or one might be worried that its capacity is nearing saturation.

There are many definitions of entropy in statistical studies. Let us choose Shannon's traditional informational entropy as an example [277]. In order for the informational entropy to work usefully as a measure, we need to be selective in the type of data which are collected.

In ref. [42], the concept of an informational entropy was used to gauge the stability of a system over time. In any feedback system there is the possibility of instability: either wild oscillation or exponential growth. Stability can only be achieved if the state of the system is checked often enough to adequately detect the resolution of the changes taking place. If the checking rate is too slow, or the response to a given problem is not strong enough to contain it, then control is lost.

In order to define an entropy we must change from dealing with a continuous measurement, to a classification of ranges. Instead of measuring a value exactly, we count the amount of time a value lies within a certain range and say that all of those values represent a single state. Entropy is closely associated with the amount of granularity or roughness in our perception of information, since it depends on how we group the values into classes or states. Indeed all statistical quantifiers are related to some procedure for coarse-graining information, or eliminating detail. In order to define an entropy one needs, essentially, to distinguish between signal and noise. This is done by blurring the criteria for the system to be in a certain state. As Shannon put it, we introduce redundancy into the states so that a range of input values (rather than a unique value) triggers a particular state. If we consider every single jitter of the system to be an important quantity, to be distinguished by a separate state, then nothing is defined as noise and chaos must be embraced as the natural law. However, if one decides that certain changes in the system are too insignificant to distinguish between, such that they can be lumped together and categorized as a single state, then one immediately has a distinction between useful signal and error margins for useless noise. In physics this distinction is thought of in terms of order and disorder.

Let us represent a single quantifier of system resources as a function of time $f(t)$. This function could be the amount of CPU usage, or the changing capacity of system disks, or some other variable. We wish to analyze the behavior of system resources by computing the amount of entropy in the signal $f(t)$. This can be done by coarse-graining the range of $f(t)$ into N cells:

$$F_-^i < f(t) < F_+^i,$$

where $i = 1, \ldots, N$,

$$F_+^i = F_-^{i+1}$$

and the constants $F_\pm^i$ are the boundaries of the ranges. The probability that the signal lies in cell i, during the time interval from zero to T is the fraction of time the function spends in each cell i:

$$p_i(T) = \frac{1}{T} \int_0^T dt \left[\theta \left(f(t) - F_-^i \right) - \theta \left(f(t) - F_+^i \right) \right],$$

where $\theta(t)$ is the step function, defined by

$$\theta(t - t') = \begin{cases} 1 & t - t' > 0 \\ \frac{1}{2} & t = t' \\ 0 & t - t' < 0. \end{cases}$$

Now, let the statistical degradation of the system be given by the Shannon entropy [277]

$$E(T) = - \sum_{i=1}^N p_i(T) \log p_i(T),$$

where p_i is the probability of seeing event i on average. i runs over an alphabet of all possible events from 1 to N, which is the number of independent cells in which we have chosen to coarse-grain the range of the function $f(t)$. The entropy, as defined, is always a positive quantity, since p_i is a number between 0 and 1.

Entropy is lowest if the signal spends most of its time in the same cell $F_\pm^i$. This means that the system is in a relatively quiescent state and it is therefore easy to predict the probability that it will remain in that state, based on past behavior. Other conclusions can be drawn from the entropy of a given quantifier. For example, if the quantifier is disk usage, then a state of low entropy or stable disk usage implies little usage which in turn implies low power consumption. This might also be useful knowledge for a network; it is easy to forget that computer systems are reliant on physical constraints. If entropy is high it means that the system is being used very fully: files are appearing and disappearing rapidly: this makes it difficult to predict what will happen in the future and the high activity means that the system is consuming a lot of power. The entropy and entropy gradient of sample disk behavior is plotted in figure 13.8.

Another way of thinking about the entropy is that it measures the amount of noise or random activity on the system. If all possibilities occur equally on average, then the entropy is maximal, i.e. there is no pattern to the data. In that case all of the p_i are equal to $1/N$ and the maximum entropy is $(\log N)$. If every message is of the same type then the entropy is minimal. Then all the p_i are zero except for one, where $p_x = 1$. Then the entropy is zero. This tells us that, if $f(t)$ lies predominantly in one cell, then the entropy will lie in the lower end of the range $0 < E < \log N$. When the distribution of messages is random, it will be in the higher part of the range.

Entropy can be a useful quantity to plot, in order to gauge the cumulative behavior of a system, within a fixed number of states. It is one of many possibilities

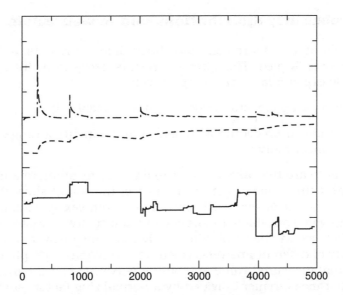

Figure 13.8: Disk usage as a function of time over the course of a week, beginning with Saturday. The lower solid line shows actual disk usage. The middle line shows the calculated entropy of the activity and the top line shows the entropy gradient. Since only relative magnitudes are of interest, the vertical scale has been suppressed. The relatively large spike at the start of the upper line is due mainly to initial transient effects. These even out as the number of measurements increases. From ref. [42].

for explaining the behavior of an open system over time, experimentally. Like all cumulative, approximate quantifiers it has a limited value however, so it needs to be backed up by a description of system behavior.

13.6.5 Stochastic (random) variables

A stochastic or random variable is a variable whose value depends on the outcome of some underlying random process. The range of values of the variable is not at issue, but which particular value the variable has at a given moment is random. We say that a stochastic variable X will have a certain value x with a probability $P(x)$. Examples are:

- Choices made by large numbers of users.

- Measurements collected over long periods of time.

- Cause and effect are not clearly related.

Certain measurements can often appear random, because we do not know all of the underlying mechanisms. We say that there are *hidden variables*. If we sample data from independent sources for long enough, they will fall into a stable type of distribution, by virtue of the *central limit theorem* (see for instance ref. [136]).

13.6.6 Probability distributions and measurement

Whenever we repeat a measurement and obtain different results, a distribution of different answers is formed. The spread of results needs to be interpreted. There are two possible explanations for a range of values:

- The quantity being measured does not have a fixed value.

- The measurement procedure is imperfect and a incurs a range of values due to error or uncertainty.

Often both of these are the case. In order to give any meaning to a measurement, we have to repeat the measurement a number of times and show that we obtain approximately the same answer each time. In any complex system, in which there are many things going on which are beyond our control (read: just about anywhere in the real world), we will never obtain exactly the same answer twice. Instead we will get a variety of different answers which we can plot as a graph: on the x-axis, we plot the actual measured value and on the y-axis we plot the number of times we obtained that measurement divided by a normalizing factor, such as the total number of measurements. By drawing a curve through the points, we obtain an idealized picture which shows the probability of measuring the different values. The normalization factor is usually chosen so that the area under the curve is unity.

There are two extremes of distribution: complete certainty (figure 13.9) and complete uncertainty (figure 13.10). If a measurement always gives precisely the

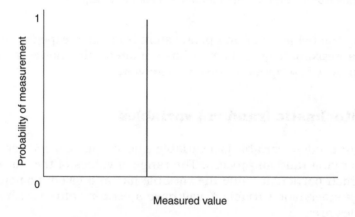

Figure 13.9: The delta distribution represents complete certainty. The distribution has a value of 1 at the measured value.

same answer, then we say that there is no error. This is never the case with real measurements. Then the curve is just a sharp spike at the particular measured value. If we obtain a different answer each time we measure a quantity, then there is a spread of results. Normally that spread of results will be concentrated around some more or less stable value (figure 13.11). This indicates that the probability of measuring that value is biased, or tends to lead to a particular range of values. The smaller the range of values, the closer we approach figure 13.9. But the converse might also happen: in a completely random system, there might be no fixed value

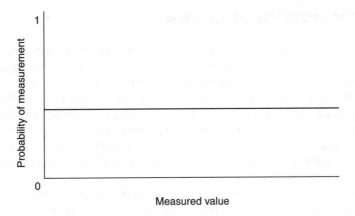

Figure 13.10: The flat distribution is a horizontal line indicating that all measured values, within the shown interval, occur with equal probability.

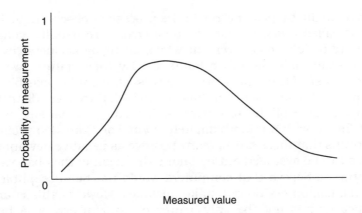

Figure 13.11: Most distributions peak at some value, indicating that there is an expected value (expectation value) which is more probable than all the others.

of the quantity we are measuring. In that case, the measured value is completely uncertain, as in figure 13.10. To summarize, a flat distribution is unbiased, or completely random. A non-flat distribution is biased, or has an expectation value, or probable outcome. In the limit of complete certainty, the distribution becomes a spike, called the *delta distribution*.

We are interested in determining the shape of the distribution of values on repeated measurement for the following reason. If the variation of the values is symmetrical about some preferred value, i.e. if the distribution peaks close to its mean value, then we can likely infer that the value of the peak or of the mean is the true value of the measurement and that the variation we measured was due to random external influences. If, on the other hand, we find that the distribution is very asymmetrical, some other explanation is required and we are most likely observing some actual physical phenomenon which requires explanation.

13.7   Observational errors

All measurements involve certain errors. One might be tempted to believe that, where computers are involved, there would be no error in collecting data, but this is false. Errors are not only a human failing, they occur because of unpredictability in the measurement process, and we have already established throughout this book that computer systems are nothing if not unpredictable. We are thus forced to make estimates of the extent to which our measurements can be in error. This is a difficult matter, but approximate statistical methods are well known in the natural sciences, methods which become increasingly accurate with the amount of data in an experimental sample.

The ability to estimate and treat errors should not be viewed as an excuse for constructing a poor experiment. Errors can only be minimized by design.

13.7.1   Random, personal and systematic errors

There are three distinct types of error in the process of observation. The simplest type of error is called *random error*. Random errors are usually small deviations from the 'true value' of a measurement which occur by accident, by unforeseen jitter in the system, or some other influence. By their nature, we are usually ignorant of the cause of random errors, otherwise it might be possible to eliminate them. The important point about random errors is that they are distributed evenly about the mean value of the observation. Indeed, it is usually assumed that they are distributed with an approximately *normal* or *Gaussian* profile about the mean. This means that there are as many positive as negative deviations and thus random errors can be averaged out by taking the mean of the observations.

It is tempting to believe that computers would not be susceptible to random errors. After all, computers do not make mistakes. However this is an erroneous belief. The measurer is not the only source of random errors. A better way of expressing this is to say that random errors are a measure of the unpredictability of the measuring process. Computer systems are also unpredictable, since they are constantly influenced by outside agents such as users and network requests.

The second type of error is a *personal error*. This is an error which a particular experimenter adds to the data unwittingly. There are many instances of this kind of error in the history of science. In a computer-controlled measurement process, this corresponds to any particular bias introduced through the use of specific software, or through the interpretation of the measurements.

The final and most insidious type of error is the *systematic error*. This is an error which runs throughout all of the data. It is a systematic shift in the true value of the data, in one direction, and thus it cannot be eliminated by averaging. A systematic error leads also to an error in the mean value of the measurement. The sources of systematic error are often difficult to find, since they are often a result of misunderstandings, or of the specific behavior of the measuring apparatus.

In a system with finite resources, the act of measurement itself leads to a change in the value of the quantity one is measuring. In order to measure the CPU usage of a computer system, for instance, we have to start a new program which collects that information, but that program inevitably also uses the CPU and therefore changes the conditions of the measurement. These issues are well known in the physical sciences and are captured in principles such as Heisenberg's Uncertainty Principle, Schrödinger's cat and the use of infinite idealized heat baths in thermodynamics. We can formulate our own verbal expression of this for computer systems:

Principle 67 (Uncertainty). *The act of measuring a given quantity in a system with finite resources, always changes the conditions under which the measurement is made, i.e. the act of measurement changes the system.*

For instance, in order to measure the pressure in a tyre, you have to let some of the air out, which reduces the pressure slightly. This is not noticeable on a car tyre, but it can be noticeable on a bicycle. The larger the available resources of the system, compared with the resources required to make the measurement, the smaller the effect on the measurement will be.

13.7.2 Adding up independent causes

Suppose we want to measure the value of a quantity v whose value has been altered by a series of independent random changes or perturbations Δv_1, Δv_2, ... etc. By how much does that series of perturbations alter the value of v? Our first instinct might be to add up the perturbations to get the total:

$$\text{Actual deviation} = \Delta v_1 + \Delta v_2 + \dots$$

This estimate is not useful, however, because we do not usually know the exact values of Δv_i, we can only guess them. In other words, we are working with a set of guesses Δg_i, whose sign we do not know. Moreover, we do not know the signs of the perturbations, so we do not know whether they add or cancel each other out. In short, we are not in a position to know the actual value of the deviation from the true value. Instead, we have to estimate the limits of the possible deviation from the true value v. To do this, we add the perturbations together as though they were independent vectors.

Independent influences are added together using Pythagoras' theorem, because they are independent vectors. This is easy to understand geometrically. If we think of each change as being independent, then one perturbation Δv_1 cannot affect the value of another perturbation Δv_2. But the only way that it is possible to have two changes which do not have any effect on one another is if they are movements at right angles to one another, i.e. they are orthogonal. Another way of saying this is that the independent changes are like the coordinates $x, y, z, \dots$ of a point which is at a distance from the origin in some set of coordinate axes. The total distance of the point from the origin is, by Pythagoras' theorem,

$$d = \sqrt{x^2 + y^2 + z^2 + \dots}$$

The formula we are looking for, for any number of independent changes, is just the root mean square N-dimensional generalization of this, usually written σ. It is the standard deviation.

13.7.3   The mean and standard deviation

In the theory of errors, we use the ideas above to define two quantities for a set of data: the mean and the standard deviation. Now the situation is reversed: we have made a number of observations of values $v_1, v_2, v_3, \ldots$ which have a certain scatter, and we are trying to find out the actual value v. Assuming that there are no systematic errors, i.e. assuming that all of the deviations have independent random causes, we define the value $\bar{v}$ to be the arithmetic mean of the data:

$$\bar{v} = \frac{v_1 + v_2 + \cdots + v_N}{N} = \frac{1}{N} \sum_{i=1}^{N} v_i.$$

Next we treat the deviations of the actual measurements as our guesses for the error in the measurements:

$$\begin{aligned}
\Delta g_1 &= \bar{v} - v_1 \\
\Delta g_2 &= \bar{v} - v_2 \\
&\vdots \\
\Delta g_N &= \bar{v} - v_N
\end{aligned}$$

and define the *standard deviation* of the data by

$$\sigma = \sqrt{\frac{1}{N} \sum_{i=0}^{N} \Delta g_i^2}.$$

This is clearly a measure of the scatter in the data due to random influences. σ is the root mean square (RMS) of the assumed errors. These definitions are a way of interpreting measurements, from the assumption that one really is measuring the true value, affected by random interference.

An example of the use of standard deviation can be seen in the error bars of the figures in this chapter. Whenever one quotes an average value, the number of data and the standard deviation should also be quoted in order to give meaning to the value. In system administration, one is interested in the average values of any system metric which fluctuates with time.

13.7.4   The normal error distribution

It has been stated that 'Everyone believes in the exponential law of errors; the experimenters because they think it can be proved by mathematics; and the mathematicians because they believe it has been established by observation' [323]. Some observational data in science satisfy closely the normal law of error, but this is by no means universally true. The main purpose of the normal error law is to provide an adequate idealization of error treatment which is simple to deal with, and which becomes increasingly accurate with the size of the data sample.

The normal distribution was first derived by DeMoivre in 1733, while dealing with problems involving the tossing of coins; the law of errors was deduced theoretically in 1783 by Laplace. He started with the assumption that the total error in an observation was the sum of a large number of independent deviations, which could be either positive or negative with equal probability, and could therefore be added according to the rule explained in the previous sections. Subsequently Gauss gave a proof of the error law based on the postulate that the most probable value of any number of equally good observations is their arithmetic mean. The distribution is thus sometimes called the Gaussian distribution, or the bell curve.

The Gaussian normal distribution is a smooth curve which is used to model the distribution of discrete points distributed around a mean. The probability density function $P(x)$ tells us with what probability we would expect measurements to be distributed about the mean value $\bar{x}$ (see figure 13.12).

$$P(x_i) = \frac{1}{(2\pi\sigma^2)^{1/2}} \exp\left(-\frac{(x_i - \bar{x})^2}{2\sigma^2}\right).$$

It is based on the idealized limit of an infinite number of points. No experiments have an infinite number of points though, so we need to fit a finite number of points to a normal distribution as best we can. It can be shown that the most probable choice is to take the mean of the finite set to be our estimate of mean

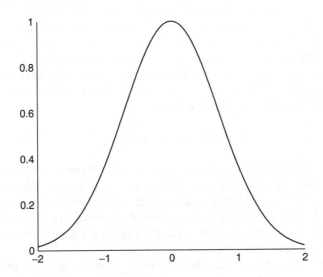

Figure 13.12: The Gaussian normal distribution, or bell curve, peaks at the arithmetic mean. Its width characterizes the standard deviation. It is therefore the generic model for all measurement distributions.

of the ideal set. Of course, if we select at random a sample of N values from the idealized infinite set, it is not clear that they will have the same mean as the full set of data. If the number in the sample N is large, the two will not differ by much, but if N is small, they might. In fact, it can be shown that if we take many random samples of the ideal set, each of size N, they will have mean values which are themselves normally distributed, with a standard deviation equal to $\sigma/\sqrt{N}$. The quantity

$$\alpha = \frac{\sigma}{\sqrt{N}}$$

is therefore called the *standard error of the mean*. This is clearly a measure of the accuracy with which we can claim that our finite sample mean agrees with the actual mean. In quoting a measured value *which we believe has a unique or correct value*, it is therefore normal to write the mean value, plus or minus the standard error of the mean:

$$\text{Result} = \bar{x} \pm \sigma/\sqrt{N} \text{ (for } N \text{ observations),}$$

where N is the number of measurements. Otherwise, if we believe that the measured value should have a distribution of values, we use the standard deviation as a measure of the error. Many transactional operations in a computer system do not have a fixed value (see next section).

The law of errors is not universally applicable, but it is still almost universally applied, for it serves as a convenient fiction which is mathematically simple.[2]

13.7.5 The Planck distribution

Another distribution which appears in the periodic rhythms of system behavior is the Planck radiation distribution, so named for its origins in the physics of blackbody radiation and quantum theory. This distribution can be derived theoretically as the most likely distribution to arise from an assembly of fluctuations in equilibrium with an indefatigable reservoir or source [54]. The precise reason for its appearance in computer systems is subtle, but has to do with the periodicity imposed by users' behaviors, as well as the interpretation of transactions as fluctuations. The distribution has the form

$$D(\lambda) = \frac{\lambda^{-m}}{e^{1/\lambda T} - 1},$$

where T is a scale, actually a temperature in the theory of blackbody radiation, and m is a number greater than 2. When $m = 3$, a single degree of freedom is represented. In ref. [54], Burgess et al. found that a single degree of freedom was sufficient to fit the data measured for a single variable, as one might expect. The shape of the graph is shown in figure 13.13. Figures 13.14 and 13.15 show fits of real data to Planck distributions.

A number of transactions take this form: typically this includes network services that do not stress the performance of a server significantly. Indeed, it was shown in ref. [54] that many transactions on a computing system can be modeled as a linear superposition of a Gaussian distribution and a Planckian distribution, shifted from the origin:

$$D(\lambda) = A\, e^{-\left(\frac{(\lambda - \bar{\lambda})^2}{4\sigma}\right)} + \frac{B}{(\lambda - \lambda_0)^3 (e^{1/(\lambda - \lambda_0)T} - 1)}.$$

---

[2]The applicability of the normal distribution can, in principle, be tested with a χ^2 test, but this is seldom used in physical sciences, since the number of observations is usually so small as to make it meaningless.

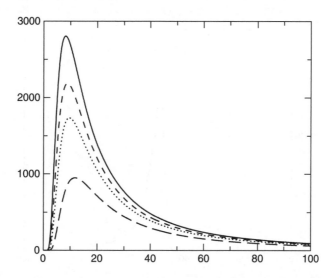

Figure 13.13: The Planck distribution for several temperatures. This distribution is the shape generated by random fluctuations from a source which is unchanged by the fluctuations. Here, a fluctuation is a computing transaction, a service request or new process.

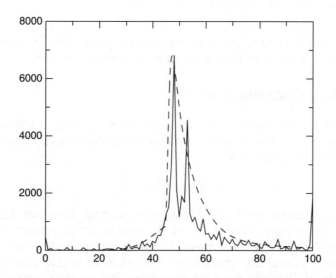

Figure 13.14: The distribution of system processes averaged over a few daily periods. The dotted line shows the theoretical Planck curve, while the solid line shows actual data. The jaggedness comes from the small amount of data (see next graph). The x-axis shows the deviation about the scaled mean value of 50 and the y-axis shows the number of points measured in class intervals of a half σ. The distribution of values about the mean is a mixture of Gaussian noise and a Planckian blackbody distribution.

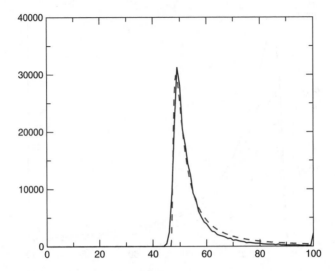

Figure 13.15: The distribution of WWW socket sessions averaged over many daily periods. The dotted line shows the theoretical Planck curve, while the solid line shows actual data. The smooth fit for large numbers of data can be contrasted with the previous graph. The x-axis shows the deviation about the scaled mean value of 50 and the y-axis shows the number of points measured in class intervals of a half σ. The distribution of values about the mean is a pure Planckian blackbody distribution.

This is a remarkable result, since it implies the possibility of using methods of statistical physics to analyze the behavior of computer systems.

13.7.6   Other distributions

Internet network traffic analysis studies [237, 325] show that the arrival times of data packets within a stream has a long-tailed distribution, often modeled as a Pareto distribution (a power law)

$$f(\omega) = \beta\, a^{\beta}\, \omega^{-\beta-1}.$$

This can be contrasted with the Poissonian arrival times of telephonic data traffic. It is an important consideration to designers of routers and switching hardware. It implies that a fundamental change in the nature of network traffic has taken place. A partial explanation for this behavior is that packet arrival times consist not only of Poisson random processes for session arrivals, but also of internal correlations within a session. Thus it is important to distinguish between measurements of packet traffic and measurements of numbers of sockets (or tcp sessions).

13.7.7   Fourier analysis: periodic behavior

As we have already commented, many aspects of computer system behavior have a strong periodic quality, driven by the human perturbations introduced by users' daily rhythms. Other natural periods follow from the largest influences on the system from outside. This must be the case since there are no natural periodic sources internal to the system.[3] Apart from the largest sources of perturbation, i.e. the users themselves, there might be other lesser software systems which can generate periodic activity, for instance hourly updates or automated backups. The source might not even be known: for instance, a potential network intruder attempting a stealthy port scan might have programmed a script to test the ports periodically, over a length of time. Analysis of system behavior can sometimes benefit from knowing these periods, e.g. if one is trying to determine a causal relationship between one part of a system and another, it is sometimes possible to observe the signature of a process which is periodic and thus obtain direct evidence for its effect on another part of the system.

Periods in data are in the realm of Fourier analysis. What a Fourier analysis does is to assume that a data set is built up from the superposition of many periodic processes. This might sound like a strange assumption but, in fact, this is always possible. If we draw any curve, we can always represent it as a sum of sinusoidal-waves with different frequencies and amplitudes. This is the complex Fourier theorem:

$$f(t) = \int d\omega \, f(\omega) e^{-i\omega t},$$

where $f(\omega)$ is a series of coefficients. For strictly periodic functions, we can represent this as an infinite sum:

$$f(t) = \sum_{n=0}^{\infty} c_n e^{-2\pi i n t/T},$$

where T is some time scale over which the function $f(t)$ is measured. What we are interested in determining is the function $f(\omega)$, or equivalently the set of coefficients c_n which represent the function. These tell us how much of which frequencies are present in the signal $f(t)$, or its *spectrum*. It is a kind of data prism, or spectral analyzer, like the graphical displays one finds on some music players. In other words, if we feed in a measured sequence of data and Fourier analyze it, the spectral function shows the frequency content of the data which we have measured.

We shall not go into the whys and wherefores of Fourier analysis, since there are standard programs and techniques for determining the series of coefficients. What is more important is to appreciate its utility. If we are looking for periodic behavior in system characteristics, we can use Fourier analysis to find it. If we analyze a signal and find a spectrum such as the one in figure 13.16, then the peaks in the spectrum show the strong periodic content of the signal.

To discover these smaller signals, it will be necessary to remove the louder ones (it is difficult to hear a pin drop when a bomb explodes nearby).

---

[3]Of course there is the CPU clock cycle and the revolution of disks, but these occur on a time scale which is smaller than the software operations and so cannot affect system behavior.

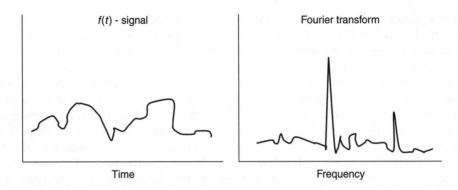

Figure 13.16: Fourier analysis is like a prism, showing us the separate frequencies of which a signal is composed. The sharp peaks in this figure illustrate how we can identify periodic behavior which might otherwise be difficult to identify. The two peaks show that the input source conceals two periodic signals.

13.8 Strategic analyses

The use of formal mathematics to analyze system administration has so far been absent from the discussion. There are two reasons why such analyses are of interest: i) a formal description of a subject often reveals expectations and limitations which were invisible prior to the systematic model, and ii) optimal solutions to problems can be explored, avoiding unnecessary prejudice.

The languages of Game Theory [47] and Dynamical Systems [46] will enable us to formulate and model assertions about the behavior of systems under certain administrative strategies. At some level, the development of a computer system is a problem in economics: it is a mixed game of opposition and cooperation between users and the system. The aims of the game are several: to win resources, to produce work, to gain control of the system, and so on. A proper understanding of the issues should lead to better software and better strategies from human administrators. For instance, is greed a good strategy for a user? How could one optimally counter such a strategy? In some cases it might even be possible to solve system administration games, determining the maximum possible 'win' available in the conflict between users and administrators. These topics are somewhat beyond the scope of this book.

13.9 Summary

Finding a rigorous experimental and theoretical basis for system administration is not an easy task. It involves many entwined issues, both technological and sociological. A systematic discussion of theoretical ideas may be found in ref. [52]. The sociological factors in system administration cannot be ignored, since the goal of system administration is, amongst other things, user satisfaction. In this respect one is forced to pay attention to *heuristic* evidence, as rigorous statistical analysis of a specific effect is not always practical or adequately separable from whatever else is going on in the system. The study of computers is a study of *complexity*.

Exercises

Self-test objectives

1. What is meant by a scientific approach to system administration?

2. What does complexity really mean?

3. Explain the role of observation in making judgments about systems.

4. How can one formulate criteria for the evaluation of system policies?

5. How is reliability defined?

6. What principles contribute to increased reliability?

7. Describe heuristically how you would expect key variables, such as numbers of processes and network transactions, to vary over time. Comment on what this means for the detection of anomalies in these variables.

8. What is a stochastic system? Explain why human–computer systems are stochastic.

9. What is meant by convergence in the context of system administration?

10. What is meant by regulation?

11. Explain how errors of measurement can occur in a computer.

12. Explain how errors of measurement should be dealt with.

Problems

1. Consider the following data which represent a measurement of CPU usage for a process over time:

   ```
   2.1
   2.0
   2.1
   2.2
   2.2
   1.9
   2.2
   2.2
   2.1
   2.2
   2.2
   ```

   Now answer the following:

   (a) To the eye, what appears to be the correct value for the measurement?

   (b) Is there a correct value for the measurement?

    (c) What is the mean value?

    (d) What is the standard deviation?

    (e) If you were to quote these data as one value, how would you quote the
result of the measurement?

2. What is meant by random errors? Explain why computers are not immune
to random errors.

3. Explain what is meant by Mean Time Before Failure. How is this quantity
measured? Can sufficient measurements be made to make its value credible?

4. If a piece of software has a MTBF of two hours and an average downtime of
15 seconds, does it matter that it is unstable?

5. Explain why one would expect measurements of local SMTP traffic to show
a strong daily rhythm, while measurements of incoming traffic would not
necessarily have such a pronounced daily rhythm.

6. Discuss whether one would expect to see a daily rhythm in WWW traffic. If
such a rhythm were found, what would it tell us about the source of the
traffic?

7. Describe a procedure for determining causality in a computer network.
Explain any assumptions and limitations which are relevant to this.

8. Explain why problems with quite different causes often lead to the same
symptoms.

Chapter 14

Summary and outlook

The aim of this book has been to present an overview of the field of system administration for active system administrators, university courses and computer scientists everywhere. For a long time, system administration has been passed on by word of mouth and has resisted formalization. Only in recent times has the need for a formalization of the field been acknowledged, through courses and certifications: determined, if not always ideal, attempts to crystallize something definite from the fluid and fickle body of knowledge which system administrators operate.

Compared with many other books on system administration, which are excellent how-to references, this book is quite theoretical. It might disappoint those who hold tradition as an authority. I have gone out of my way to be logical rather than conventional, to ignore redundant quirks where appropriate and to make suggested improvements (with accompanying justifications). History has seldom been the servant for logic and I believe that it is time to abandon some old practices for the good of the field. That is not to say that I claim to have any ultimate answers, but the main message of this book is to make you, the reader, think and judge for yourself. There are, after all, no questions which should not be asked; there is no authority which should not be questioned.

System administration is about putting together a network of computers (workstations, PCs and supercomputers), getting them running and then *keeping* them running in spite of the activities of *users* who tend to cause the systems to fail. The failure of an operating system can be caused by one of several things. Most operating systems do not fail by themselves: it is users perturbing the system which causes problems to occur. Even in the cases where a problem can be attributed to a bug in a software component, it normally takes a user to provoke the bug. The fact that users play an important role in the behavior of computer systems is far from doubt. At universities students rush to the terminal rooms to surf on the Web during lunch breaks. This can result in the sudden caching of hundreds of megabytes of temporary files which can prevent legitimate work from being carried out. In offices, the workers probably run from their desks giving the opposite pattern of behavior. The *time scale* involved here is just a matter of minutes, perhaps an hour. In that short space of time, user behavior (Web surfing) can cause a general failure of the system for all users (disk full). System administration is therefore a mixture of technical expertise and sociology. Patterns of user behavior need to be taken into account in any serious discussion of this problem. As a consequence, it is necessary to monitor the state of the system and its resources and react swiftly (on the time scale of human behavior) to correct problems.

14.1 Information management in the future

The future is almost upon us and no branch of technology has exploded with such a lack of planning and critical review as information technology. The state of our world knowledge is already well beyond our ability to cope with it. We currently have no way of searching and accessing *most* of the scientific and cultural resources which have been produced in the untold years of human endeavor of our history. In short, in our present state, most of our scientific knowledge has gone to waste. This is clearly an unacceptable situation and it is probably one which will be solved by new information retrieval technology in the future, but the ability to retrieve information is critically dependent on its being organized into an easily parsable structure. This is the basis of programming algorithms in computer software and the same thing applies to conglomerations of different software systems. The same principle applies to the storage of any kind of information. If information is not organized by a clear principle, it will get lost or muddled.

Structure and organization are the unsung heroes of science and of society. While scientists and computer hackers are frequently portrayed in the popular press as absent-minded muddlers, subject to fits of divine inspiration, the random element plays only a minor role in the true development of knowledge. Contrary to the popular affectation, it is not cool to have a relaxed attitude to organization. Claims to the effect that system administration is a 'dirty' business, not for academics, that we fly by the seats of our pants and so on, only serve to demean the system administration profession. If there is one service we can do for the future it is to think critically and carefully about the information structures of our network communities.

14.2 Collaboration with software engineering

Every computer programmer should have to do service as a network administrator. If computer programs were written together with system administrators they would be efficient at resource usage, they would log useful information, they would be more reliable and more secure. In the future, every piece of software running on a computer system will need to take responsibility for system security and intrusion detection. There is no better way to build reliable and secure software, since every program knows its own internal state better than any external agent can. This is not how software is written today, and we suffer the consequences of this.

14.3 Pervasive computing

In only a few years' time, computers will be everywhere in our lives. Embedded computers are already built into cars, kitchen appliances, media and telecommunications equipment; soon we will have smart walls with built in audiovisual equipment, smart buildings that can respond to those within it, cities wired with sensors that regulate traffic, and many other computing applications. Today many of these devices are running specialized operating systems, but increasingly Windows and Linux based kernels are being used. Such high-level operating systems have the advantage of being well known and highly adaptable, but they present the specter of complexity to tasks that are relatively simple. This presents a significant management challenge that will have to be addressed. Today, very few organizations face a challenge of this magnitude and very few technologies exist to cope with this level of complexity.

One clue about how this might be tackled lies in the Internet and the network of routers. Originally it was thought that routers might be controlled by a central authority; it did not take long to realize that the scale of the Internet (which rapidly outgrew expectations) was far greater than a centralized model could cope with. Bottleneck designs, like central SNMP management, are quickly falling from favor. Routing succeeded because routers were made able to communicate and cooperate in building up their routing paths automatically, while satisfying broad criteria set by policy. This type of collaborative ordering is sometimes referred to as *swarm intelligence*, after the phenomenon observed in collaborating insects. This gives us a clue as to how the future of system administration is likely to evolve.

14.4 The future of system administration

We are approaching a new generation of operating systems, with the capacity for self-analysis and self-correction. It is no longer a question of whether they will arrive, but of when they will arrive. When it happens, the nature of system administration will change.

The day to day tasks of system administration change constantly and we pay these changes little attention. However, improvements in technology always lead to changing work practices, as humans are replaced by machinery in those jobs which are menial and repetitive. The core principles of system administration will remain the same, but the job description of the system manager will be rather different. In many ways, the day to day business of system administration consists of just a few recipes which slowly evolve over time. However, underneath the veneer of cookery, there is a depth of understanding about computer systems which has a more permanent value. Even when software systems take over many of the tasks which are now performed manually, there will be new challenges to meet.

For understandable reasons, the imaginations and attentions of our college generations have been captured, not by the intrigue of learning machines and intelligent systems, but by the glamour of multimedia. The computer has matured from a mere machine to a creative palette. It is difficult to articulate just why the administration of computer communities is an exciting challenge, but if we are to succeed in pushing through programmes of research which will bring about the level of automation we require, then it will be necessary to attract willing researchers. Fortunately, today there is a high proportion of system administrators with scientific backgrounds with the will and training to undertake such work. However, only the surface has been scratched. The tendency has been to produce tools rather than to investigate concepts, and while the tools are necessary, they must not become an end in themselves. A clearer understanding of the problems we face, looking forward, will only be achieved with more analytical work.

It is on this canvas that we attempt to congeal the discipline of system administration. We began this book by asking whether system administration was indeed a discipline. I hope that it is now clear that it is – for a long time a diffuse one, but nevertheless real. In many ways system administration is like biology. Animals are machines, just billions of times more complex than our own creations, but the gap is closing and will continue to close as we enter into an era of quantum and biological computing techniques. The essence of experimental observation, and of the complex phenomena and interrelationships between hosts is directly analogous to what one does in biology. We may have created computers, but that does not mean that we understand them implicitly. In our field, we are still watching the animals do their thing, trying to learn.

Exercise

1. Now that we are done, compare your impressions of system administration with those you had at the end of chapter 1.

Appendix A

Some useful Unix commands

This book is not specifically about Unix system administration, but Free, Open Source incarnations of Unix make system administration easy for anyone to develop into a class with a minimum of resources. The following commands will be particularly useful. Always check the manual page (Unix *man* command) on your local system before trying these commands. Versions, options and even names differ, especially on older systems.

Who am I?

- whoami: Prints your user name.

- who am i: Prints your real and effective user id, and terminal.

- id: GNU program which prints all your user ids and groups.

Remote logins

The ssh command is the most reliable way of logging onto a remote Unix host. The telnet, rlogin or rsh commands should not be used. The secure shell ssh is a secure replacement for the rsh command. It is recommended in its place. The rlogin command can be used to login without a password using the .rhosts authority file for trusted hosts and users. Using secure shell, one may use public/private key pairs to obtain a much stronger authentication.

Monitoring disk usage

- df: Displays the usage of all mounted disk partitions if no argument is given. If a directory is named, the state of the disk partition on which the given directory resides is displayed. On SVR4 systems the output of this command seems unfamiliar unless the -k option is used.

- du: Shows disk usage on a per-file basis. The file sizes are either in kilobytes or in 512 byte blocks. The -k option forces output to be in kilobytes. The -s option prevents du from outputting information about every file and yields a summary of the named directory instead.

- `swap -s`: System 5 program to show swap space.

- `pstat`: BSD program to show swap space.

Disk backups

- `dump`: Raw dump of a disk partition to a file or to tape.

- `rdump`: Same as dump, but this can be done over the network, remotely without the need for physical contact with the host.

- `ufsdump`: Solaris/SVR4 replaces `dump` with this command.

- `restore`: Restores a disk partition from a filesystem dump.

- `cp -r`: Copies a directory and all files recursively to a new location. This does not preserve symbolic links but makes multiple copies of the file instead. See `tar` below.

- `tar`: A simple way to copy an entire filesystem, preserving symbolic links, is to do the following:

```
cd source-dir; tar cf - . | (cd destination-dir; tar xf - )
```

This pipes the output directly to the new directory using the streams interface for standard IO.

Mounting filesystems

- `mount`: Mounts a local or remote disk.

- `umount`: Unmounts a local or remote disk. Note the peculiar spelling.

- `showmount`: Shows all hosts who are mounting filesystems from this server.

Packing and unpacking archives

- `tar cf tarfile.tar source-dir`: Packs all the files and subdirectories in the directory *source-dir* into a single 'tape-archive' file. If the `-f` argument is missing, `tar` expects to be able to write data to a default tape-streamer device and will complain with an error message.

- `tar zcf tarfile.tar.gz source-dir`: Same as above, but piped through `gzip` to compress the data. This only works with GNU tar.

- `tar xf tarfile.tar`: Unpacks the contents of a tar-file into the current directory.

- `tar zxf tarfile.tar.gz`: Same as above, but pipes through `gzip` to uncompress data. This only works with GNU tar.

Shared libraries

- `ldd`: Displays the shared libraries used by a compiled executable file (some Unices only).

- `ldconfig`: Some systems require this command to be run after installing or upgrading shared libraries. It updates symbolic links to the latest version of the library and in some cases generates a cache file of library names. Especially GNU/Linux and SunOS prior to Solaris.

Handling binaries

- `strings`: This command lists all of the strings in a binary file. It is useful for finding out information which is compiled into software.

- `file`: Prints the type of data a file contains.

- `strip`: Removes debugging information from a compiled program. This can reduce the size of the program substantially.

Files and databases

- `locate`: GNU fast-find command, part of the GNU `find` package. Locates the names of files matching the argument string in part, by reading from a database. See `updatedb` below.

- `find`: Locates by searching through every directory. Slow but powerful search facilities.

- `which`: Locates an executable file by searching through directories in the `PATH` or `path` variable lists.

- `whatis`: Gives a one-line summary of a command from the manual page (see `catman`).

- `catman -M`: This program builds the `apropos` or `man -k` 'whatis' databases.

- `updatedb`: This shell script updates the `locate` fast-find database.

Process management

- `ps aux`: Shows all processes on the system (BSD).

- `ps -ef` Shows all processes on the system (SysV).

- `kill`: Sends a signal to the named process (pid), not necessarily to kill it. The process ID is the one listed by the `ps` command. Typical options are `-HUP` to send the hangup signal. This is used by many system daemons like `inetd` and `cron` as a signal which tells them to reread their configuration files. Another option is `-9` which is a non-ignorable kill instruction.

- `nice`: Runs a program with a non-default scheduling priority. This exists both as a shell command and as a C-shell builtin. The two versions use different syntax. Normal users can only reduce the priority of their processes (make them 'nicer'). Only the superuser can increase the priority of a process. The priority values differ between BSD and SysV systems. Under BSD, the nice values run from -20 (highest priority) to 20 (lowest priority), with 0 being the default. Under SysV, priorities run from 0 to 39, with 20 being the default. The C-shell builtin priorities are always from -20 to 20 for consistency.

- `renice` *new-priority* `-p` *pid*: Resets the scheduling priority of a process to a new value. The priority values used by the system (not C-shell) apply here.

- `crontab`: Modern releases of Unix use the crontab command to schedule commands or scripts which are to be run at a specified time, or at regular intervals. The `crontab -l` command lists currently registered jobs. The `crontab -e` command is used to edit the crontab file. Each user has his or her own crontab file on every host. On older BSD systems, only root could alter the crontab file, which was typically a single file `/etc/crontab` or `/usr/lib/crontab` containing usernames and jobs to be performed.

Mail management

Sometimes mail gets stuck and cannot be delivered for some reason. This might be because the receiving mailhost is down, or because there is insufficient disk space to transfer the message, or many other reasons. In that case, incoming and outgoing mail gets placed in a queue which usually lies under the Unix directory `/var/spool/mail`, `/var/mail` or one of these with `/var` replaced by `/usr`.

- `mailq`: Displays any messages waiting in the mail queue. Same as `sendmail -bp`.

- `sendmail -q -v`: Manually processes the mail queue in verbose mode.

Disk management

- `fsck`: The filesystem check program. A disk doctor that should not be run on an active filesystem. This checks the consistency of the filesystem (superblock consistency etc.) and repairs simple problems.

- `newfs`: Creates a new filesystem on a disk partition, erasing any previous data. This is analogous to formatting a diskette.

- `swapon`: This command causes the system to begin using a disk partition or swap file for system swapping/paging. `swapon -a` starts swapping on all devices registered in the filesystem table `/etc/fstab` or equivalent.

- `mkfile`: Creates a special file for swapping inside a filesystem. The file has a fixed size, it cannot grow or shrink, or be edited directly. Normally swapping should be to a raw partition. Swapping to this kind of file is inefficient, but is used by (for instance) diskless clients.

Name service lookups

- `nslookup`: An interactive query program for reading domain data from the Domain Name Service (DNS/BIND) that is now falling from favor.

- `host`: DNS lookup tool.

- `dig`: DNS lookup tool.

- `dnsquery`: A non-interactive query program for reading domain data from the Domain Name Service (DNS/BIND).

- `whois`: Displays information about who is responsible for the listed domain.

System statistics

- `iostat`: Displays I/O summary from the disks at an interval of *time-in-seconds*.

- `vmstat`: Displays virtual-memory summary info at an interval of *time-in-seconds*.

- `netstat`: Shows all current network socket connections.

- `netstat -i`: Shows statistics from all network interfaces.

- `netstat -r`: Shows the static routing table.

- `nfsstat`: Shows NFS statistics. The `-c` option shows client-side data, while the `-s` option shows server-side data, where appropriate.

Networks

- `ping`: Sends a 'ping' to see if a host is alive. The `-s` option sends multiple pings on some types of Unix.

- `traceroute`: Shows the route, passing through all gateways to the named host. This command normally has to be made setuid-root in order to open the network kernel structures. Here is an example:

```
traceroute to wombat.gnu.ai.mit.edu (128.52.46.26), 30 hops max,
40 byte packets
 1   ca30-gw (128.39.89.1)  3 ms  1 ms  2 ms
 2   hioslo-gw.uninett.no (158.36.84.17)  5 ms  4 ms  5 ms
 3   oslo-gw2.uninett.no (158.36.84.1)  15 ms  15 ms  19 ms
 4   no-gw2.nordu.net (128.39.0.177)  43 ms  34 ms  32 ms
 5   nord-gw.nordu.net (192.36.148.57)  40 ms  31 ms  38 ms
 6   icm-gw.nordu.net (192.36.148.193)  37 ms  21 ms  29 ms
 7   icm-uk-1-H1/0-E3.icp.net (198.67.131.41)  58 ms  57 ms
 8   icm-pen-1-H2/0-T3.icp.net (198.67.131.25)  162 ms  136 ms
 9   icm-pen-10-P4/0-OC3C.icp.net (198.67.142.69)  198 ms  134
10   bbnplanet1.sprintnap.net (192.157.69.51)  146 ms  297 ms
```

```
11  * nyc2-br2.bbnplanet.net (4.0.1.25)   144 ms   120 ms
12  nyc1-br1.bbnplanet.net (4.0.1.153)   116 ms   116 ms   123
13  cambridge1-br1.bbnplanet.net (4.0.1.122)   131 ms   136 ms
14  cambridge1-br1.bbnplanet.net (4.0.1.122)   133 ms   124 ms
15  cambridge1-cr1.bbnplanet.net (206.34.78.23)   138 ms   129
16  cambridge2-cr2.bbnplanet.net (192.233.149.202)   128 ms
17  ihtfp.mit.edu (192.233.33.3)   129 ms   170 ms   143 ms
18  B24-RTR-FDDI.MIT.EDU (18.168.0.6)   129 ms   147 ms   148
19  radole.lcs.mit.edu (18.10.0.1)   149 ms *   130 ms
20  net-chex.ai.mit.edu (18.10.0.2)   134 ms   129 ms   134 ms
21  * * *
22  * * *   <--- routing problem here or blocked
```

- `tcpdump`: Dumps Ethernet packet activity to console, showing traffic etc.

- `snoop`: Newer version of tcpdump in Solaris.

- `ifconfig`: Configures or summarizes the setup of the a network interface, e.g. `ifconfig -a` shows all interfaces. Used to set the broadcast address, netmask and Internet address of the host.

- `route`: Makes an entry in the static routing table. Hosts which do not act as routers need only a default route, e.g.

```
route add default  xxx.xxx.xxx.1 1
```

or in GNU/Linux

```
route add default gw  xxx.xxx.xxx.1
```

Appendix B

Programming and compiling

A system administrator is frequently called on to make minor fixes to compiled software, improvise short programs to fill a need and correct errors in the compilation process. A few facts are collected here to avoid referring to too many text-books.

B.1 Make

Make is a *declarative* language which was designed for building software. In fact, its usefulness far outshines this meager goal. Make is, in reality, a generalized hierarchical organizer for instructions which generate file objects.

Nowadays compilers are often sold with fancy user environments driven by menus which make it easier to compile programs. Make was originally written so that Unix programmers could write huge source trees of code, occupying many directories and subdirectories and assemble them efficiently and effortlessly.

Building programs

Typing lines like

```
cc -c file1.c file2.c ...
cc -o target file1.o ....
```

repeatedly to compile a complicated program can be a real nuisance. One possibility would therefore be to keep all the commands in a script. This could waste a lot of time though. Suppose you are working on a big project which consists of many lines of source code – but are editing only one file. You really only want to recompile the file you are working on and then re-link the resulting object file with all of the other object files. Recompiling the other files which hadn't changed would be a waste of time. But that would mean that you would have to change the script each time you change what you need to compile.

A better solution is to use the make command. make was designed for precisely this purpose. To use make, we create a file called Makefile in the same directory as our program. make is a quite general program for building software. It is not specifically tied to the C programming language – it can be used in any programming language.

A `make` configuration file, called a `Makefile`, contains rules which describe how to compile or build all of the pieces of a program. For example, even without telling it specifically, `make` knows that in order to go from `prog.c` to `prog.o` the command `cc -c prog.c` must be executed. A Makefile works by making such associations. The Makefile contains a list of all of the files which compose the program and rules as to how to get to the finished product from the source.

The idea is that, to compile a program, we just have to type `make`. The program `make` then reads a configuration file called a `Makefile` and compiles only the parts which need compiling. It does not recompile files which have not changed since the last compilation! How does it do this? `make` works by comparing the time-stamp on the file it needs to create with the time-stamp on the file which is to be compiled. If the compiled version exists and is newer than its source then the source does not need to be recompiled.

To make this idea work in practice, `make` has to know how to go through the steps of compiling a program. Some default rules are defined in a global configuration file, e.g.

`/usr/include/make/default.mk`

Let's consider an example of what happens for the three files `a.c`, `b.c` and `c.c` in the example above – and let's not worry about what the Makefile looks like yet.

The first time we compile, only the '.c' files exist. When we type `make`, the program looks at its rules and finds that it has to make a file called 'myprog'. To make this it needs to execute the command

    gcc -o myprog   a.o b.o c.o

So it looks for 'a.o' etc. and doesn't find them. It now goes to a kind of subroutine and looks to see if it has any rules for making files called '.o' and it discovers that these are made by compiling with the `gcc  -c` option. Since the files do not exist, it does this. Now the files 'a.o b.o c.o' exist and it jumps back to the original problem of trying to make 'myprog'. All the files it needs now exist and so it executes the command and builds 'myprog'.

If we now edit 'a.c', and type `make` once again – it goes through the same procedure as before but now it finds all of the files. So it compares the dates on the files – if the source is newer than the result, it recompiles.

By using this recursive method, `make` only compiles those parts of a program which need compiling.

Makefiles

To write a Makefile, we have to tell `make` about *dependencies*. The dependencies of a file are all of those files which are required to build it. In a strong sense, dependencies are like subroutines which are carried out by `make` in the course of building the final target. The dependencies of `myprog` are `a.o`, `b.o` and @fiec.o. The dependencies of `a.o` are simply `a.c`, the dependencies of `b.o` are `b.c` and so on.

A Makefile consists of rules of the form:

```
target : dependencies
[ TAB]                        rule;
```

The target is the thing we eventually want to build, the dependencies are like subroutines to be executed first if they do not exist. Finally the rule is some code which is to be executed if all of the dependencies exist; it takes the dependencies and turns them into the current target. Notice how dependencies are like subroutines, so each sub-rule makes a sub-target. In the end, the aim is to combine all of the sub-targets into one final target. There are two important things to remember:

- The file names must start on the first character of a line.

- There must be a TAB character at the beginning of every rule or action. If there are spaces instead of tabs, or no tab at all, make will signal an error. This bizarre feature can cause a lot of confusion.

Let's look at an example Makefile for a program which consists of two course files main.c and other.c and which makes use of a library called libdb which lies in the directory /usr/local/lib. Our aim is to build a program called database:

```
#
# Simple Makefile for 'database'
#

# First define a macro

OBJ = main.o other.o

CC = gcc
CFLAGS = -I/usr/local/include
LDFLAGS = -L/usr/local/lib -ldb
INSTALLDIR = /usr/local/bin

#
# Rules start here. Note that the $@ variable becomes the name of the
# executable file. In this case it is taken from the $OBJ variable
#

database: $OBJ
        $CC -o $@ $OBJ $LDFLAGS

#
# If a header file changes, normally we need to recompile everything.
# There is no way that make can know this unless we write a rule which
# forces it to rebuild all .o files if the header file changes...
#

$OBJ: $HEADERS

#
# As well as special rules for special files we can also define a
# "suffix rule". This is a rule which tells us how to build all files
# of a certain type. Here is a rule to get .o files from .c files.
```

```
# The $< variable is like $? but is only used in suffix rules.
#

.c.o:
        $CC -c $CFLAGS $<


####################################################################
# Clean up
####################################################################

 #
 # Make can also perform ordinary shell command jobs
 # "make tidy" here performs a cleanup operation
 #

clean:
        rm -f $OBJ
        rm -f y.tab.c lex.yy.c y.tab.h
        rm -f y.tab lex.yy
        rm -f *% *~ *.o
        make tidy

install: $INSTALLDIR/database
        cp database $INSTALLDIR/database
```

The Makefile above can be invoked in several ways.

```
make
make database
make clean
make install
```

If we simple type make, i.e. the first of these choices, make takes the first of the rules it finds as the object to build. In this case the rule is 'database', so the first two forms above are equivalent.

On the other hand, if we type

```
make clean
```

then execution starts at the rule for 'clean', which is normally used to remove all files except the original source code. Make 'install' causes the compiled program to be installed at its intended destination.

make uses some special variables (which resemble the special variables used in Perl – but don't confuse them). The most useful one is $ which represents the current *target* – or the object which make would like to compile, i.e. as make checks each file it would like to compile, $ is set to the current filename.

- $@ This evaluates to the current target, i.e. the name of the object you are currently trying to build. It is normal to use this as the final name of the program when compiling.

- $? This is used only outside of suffix rules and means the name of all the files which must be compiled in order to build the current target.

```
target: file1.o file2.o
TAB cc -o $@ $?
```

- $< This is only used in suffix rules. It has the same meaning as $? but only in suffix rules. It stands for the prerequisite, or the file which must be compiled in order to make a given object.

Note that, because make has some default rules defined in its configuration file, a single-file C program can be compiled very easily by typing

```
make filename.c
```

This is equivalent to

```
cc -c filename.c
cc -o filename filename.o
```

B.2 Perl

To summarize Perl [316], we need to know about the structure of a Perl program, the conditional constructs it has, its loops and its variables. In the latest versions of Perl, you can write object-oriented programs of great complexity. We shall not go into this depth, for the simple reason that Perl's strength is not as a general programming language but as a specialized language for textfile handling. The syntax of Perl is in many ways like the C programming language, but there are important differences.

- Variables do not have *types*. They are interpreted in a context-sensitive way. The operators which act upon variables determine whether a variable is to be considered a string or as an integer etc.

- Although there are no types, Perl defines *arrays* of different kinds. There are three different kinds of array, labelled by the symbols $, @ and %.

- Perl keeps a number of standard variables with special names, e.g. $_ @ARGV and %ENV. Special attention should be paid to these. They are very important!

- The shell reverse apostrophe notation `command` can be used to execute Unix programs and get the result into a Perl variable.

Here is a simple 'structured hello world' program in Perl. Notice that subroutines are called using the & symbol. There is no special way of marking the main program – it is simply that part of the program which starts at line 1.

```
#!/local/bin/perl
#
```

```perl
# Comments
#

&Hello();
&World;

# end of main

sub Hello
    {
    print "Hello ";
    }


sub World
    {
    print "World\n";
    }
```

The parentheses on subroutines are optional if there are no parameters passed. Notice that each line must end in a semi-colon.

Scalar variables

In Perl, variables do not have to be declared before they are used. Whenever you use a new symbol, Perl automatically adds the symbol to its symbol table and initializes the variable to the empty string.

It is important to understand that there is no practical difference between zero and the empty string in Perl – except in the way that you, the user, choose to use it. Perl makes no distinction between strings and integers or any other types of data – except when it wants to interpret them. For instance, to compare two variables as strings is not the same as comparing them as integers, even if the string contains a textual representation of an integer. Take a look at the following program.

```perl
#!/local/bin/perl
#
# Nothing!
#

print "Nothing == $nothing\n";

print "Nothing is zero!\n" if ($nothing == 0);

if ($nothing eq "")
    {
    print STDERR "Nothing is really nothing!\n";
    }
```

```
$nothing = 0;

print "Nothing is now $nothing\n";
```

The output from this program is:

```
Nothing ==
Nothing is zero!
Nothing is really nothing!
Nothing is now 0
```

There are several important things to note here. First of all, we never declare the variable 'nothing'. When we try to write its value, Perl creates the name and associates a NULL value to it, i.e. the empty string. There is no error. Perl knows it is a variable because of the $ symbol in front of it. All *scalar* variables are identified by using the dollar symbol.

Next, we compare the value of $nothing with the integer '0' using the integer comparison symbol ==, and then we compare it with the empty string using the string comparison symbol eq. Both tests are true! That means that the empty string is interpreted as having a numerical value of zero. In fact *any string* which does not form a valid integer number has a numerical value of zero.

Finally we can set $nothing explicitly to a valid integer string zero, which would now pass the first test, but fail the second.

As extra spice, this program also demonstrates two different ways of writing the if command in Perl.

The default scalar variable

The special variable $_ is used for many purposes in Perl. It is used as a buffer to contain the result of the last operation, the last line read in from a file etc. It is so general that many functions which act on scalar variables work by default on $_ if no other argument is specified. For example,

```
print;
```

is the same as

```
print $_;
```

Array (vector) variables

The complement of scalar variables is arrays. In Perl, an array is identified by the @ symbol and, like scalar variables, is allocated and initialized dynamically.

```
@array[0] = "This little piggy went to market";
@array[2] = "This little piggy stayed at home";

print "@array[0] @array[1] @array[2]";
```

The index of an array is always understood to be a number, not a string, so if you use a non-numerical string to refer to an array element, you will always get the zeroth element, since a non-numerical string has an integer value of zero.

An important array which every program defines is

```
@ARGV
```

This is the argument vector array, and contains the commands line arguments by analogy with the C-shell variable `$argv[]`.

Given an array, we can find the last element by using the `$#` operator. For example,

```
$last_element = $ARGV[$#ARGV];
```

Notice that each element in an array is a scalar variable. The `$#` cannot be interpreted directly as the number of elements in the array, as it can in the C-shell. You should experiment with the value of this quantity – it is often necessary to add 1 or 2 to its value in order to get the behavior one is used to in the C-shell.

Perl does not support multiple-dimension arrays directly, but it is possible to simulate them yourself. (See the Perl book [316].)

Special array commands

The `shift` command acts on arrays and returns and removes the first element of the array. Afterwards, all of the elements are shifted down one place. So one way to read the elements of an array in order is to repeatedly call `shift`.

```
$next_element=shift(@myarray);
```

Note that, if the array argument is omitted, then `shift` works on `@ARGV` by default.

Another useful function is `split`, which takes a string and turns it into an array of strings. `split` works by choosing a character (usually a space) to delimit the array elements, so a string containing a sentence separated by spaces would be turned into an array of words. The syntax is

```
@array = split;                      # works with spaces on $_
@array = split(pattern,string);      # Breaks on pattern
($v1,$v2...) = split(pattern,string); # Name array elements with scalars
```

In the first of these cases, it is assumed that the variable `$_` is to be split on whitespace characters. In the second case, we decide on what character the split is to take place and on what string the function is to act. For instance

```
@new_array = split(":","name:passwd:uid:gid:gcos:home:shell");
```

The result is a seven-element array called `@new_array`, where `$new_array[0]` is name etc.

In the final example, the left-hand side shows that we wish to capture elements of the array in a named set of scalar variables. If the number of variables on the left-hand side is fewer than the number of strings which are generated on the right-hand side, they are discarded. If the number on the left-hand side is greater, then the remainder variables are empty.

Associated arrays

One of the useful features of Perl is the ability to use one string as an index to another string in an array. For example, we can make a short encyclopedia of zoo animals by constructing an associative array in which the keys (or indices) of the array are the names of animals, and the contents of the array are the information about them.

```perl
$animals{"Penguin"} = "Suspicious animal, good with cheese crackers...\n";
$animals{"dog"} = "Plays stupid, but could be a cover...\n";

if ($index eq "fish")
    {
    $animals$index = "Often comes in square boxes. Very cold.\n";
    }
```

An entire associated array is written %array, while the elements are $array{$key}.

Perl provides a special associative array for every program called %ENV. This contains the *environment variables* defined in the parent shell which is running the Perl program. For example

```perl
print "Username = $ENV{"USER"}\n";

$ld = "LD_LIBRARY_PATH";
print "The link editor path is $ENV{$ld}\n";
```

To get the current path into an ordinary array, one could write,

```perl
@path_array= split(":",$ENV"PATH");
```

Array example program

Here is an example which prints out a list of files in a specified directory, in order of their Unix protection bits. The *least* protected file comes first.

```perl
#!/local/bin/perl
#
# Demonstration of arrays and associated arrays.
# Print out a list of files, sorted by protection,
# so that the least secure files come first.
#
# e.g.     arrays <list of words>
#          arrays *.C
#
############################################################

print "You typed in ",$#ARGV+1," arguments to command\n";

if ($#ARGV < 1)
    {
    print "That's not enough to do anything with!\n";
    }
```

```perl
while ($next_arg = shift(@ARGV))
   {
   if ( ! ( -f $next_arg || -d $next_arg))
      {
      print "No such file: $next_arg\n";
      next;
      }

   ($dev,$ino,$mode,$nlink,$uid,$gid,$rdev,$size) = stat($next_arg);
   $octalmode = sprintf("%o",$mode & 0777);

   $assoc_array{$octalmode} .= $next_arg.
           " : size (".$size."), mode (".$octalmode.")\n";
   }

print "In order: LEAST secure first!\n\n";

foreach $i (reverse sort keys(%assoc_array))
   {
   print $assoc_array{$i};
   }
```

Loops and conditionals

Here are some of the most commonly used decision-making constructions and loops in Perl. The following is not a comprehensive list – for that, you will have to look in the Perl bible: *Programming Perl*, by Larry Wall and Randal Schwartz [316]. The basic pattern follows the C programming language quite closely. In the case of the `for` loop, Perl has both the C-like version, called `for` and a `foreach` command which is like the C-shell implementation.

```perl
if ( expression )
   {
   block;
   }
else
   {
   block;
   }


command if ( expression );

unless ( expression )
   {
   block;
   }
else
   {
   block;
   }
```

```
while ( expression )
   {
   block;
   }

do
   {
   block;
   }
while ( expression);

for ( initializer;  expression;  statement )
   {
   block;
   }

foreach  variable( array )
   {
   block;
   }
```

In all cases, the else clauses may be omitted. Strangely, Perl does not have a switch statement, but the Perl book describes how to make one using the features provided.

The for loop

The for loop is exactly like that in C or C++ and is used to iterate over a numerical index, like this:

```
for ($i = 0; $i < 10; $i++)
   {
   print $i, "\n";
   }
```

The foreach loop

The foreach loop is like its counterpart in the C-shell. It is used for reading elements one by one from a regular array. For example,

```
foreach $i ( @array )
   {
   print $i, "\n";
   }
```

Iterating over elements in arrays

One of the main uses for `for` type loops is to iterate over successive values in an array. This can be done in two ways which show the essential difference between `for` and `foreach`.

If we want to fetch each value in an array in turn, without caring about numerical indices, then it is simplest to use the `foreach` loop.

```
@array = split(" ","a b c d e f g");

foreach $var ( @array )
   {
   print $var, "\n";
   }
```

This example prints each letter on a separate line. If, on the other hand, we are interested in the index for the purposes of some calculation, then the `for` loop is preferable.

```
@array = split(" ","a b c d e f g");

for ($i = 0; $i <= $#array; $i++)
   {
   print $array[$i], "\n";
   }
```

Notice that, unlike the for-loop idiom in C/C++, the limit is `$i <= $#array`, i.e. 'less than or equal to' rather than 'less than'. This is because the `$#` operator does not return the number of elements in the array but rather the last element.

Associated arrays are slightly different, since they do not use numerical keys. Instead they use a set of strings, like in a database, so that you can use one string to look up another. In order to iterate over the values in the array we need to get a list of these strings. The `keys` command is used for this.

```
$assoc{"mark"} = "cool";
$assoc{"GNU"} = "brave";
$assoc{"zebra"} = "stripy";

foreach $var ( keys %assoc )
   {
   print "$var , $assoc{$var} \n";
   }
```

The order of the keys is not defined in the above example, but you can choose to sort them alphabetically by writing

```
foreach $var ( sort keys %assoc )
```

instead.

Iterating over lines in a file

Since Perl is about file handling we are very interested in reading files. Unlike C and C++, Perl likes to read files line by line. Angle brackets are used for this. Assuming that we have some file handle <file>, for instance <STDIN>, we can always read the file line by line with a while-loop like this.

```
while ($line = <file>)

    print $line;
```

Note that $line includes the end of line character on the end of each line. If you want to remove it, you should add a chomp command:

```
while ($line = <file>)
    {
    chomp $line;
    print "line = ($line)\n";
    }
```

Files in perl

Opening files is straightforward in Perl. Files must be opened and closed using – wait for it – the commands open and close. You should be careful to close files after you have finished with them – especially if you are writing *to* a file. Files are buffered and often large parts of a file are not actually written until the close command is received.

Three files are, of course, always open for every program, namely STDIN, STDOUT and STDERR.

Formally, to open a file, we must obtain a file descriptor or file handle. This is done using open;

```
open (file_descrip,"Filename");
```

Angle brackets <..> are used to read from the file. For example,

```
$line = <file_descrip>;
```

reads one line from the file associated with file_descrip.

Let's look at some examples of filing opening. Here is how we can implement Unix's cut and paste commands in Perl:

```
#!/local/bin/perl
#
# Cut in perl
#


    # Cut second column
```

```
while (<>)
   {
   @cut_array = split;

   print "$cut_array[1]\n";
   }
```

This is the simplest way to open a file. The empty file descriptor `<>` tells Perl to take the argument of the command as a filename and open that file for reading. This is really short for `while($_=<STDIN>)` with the standard input redirected to the named file.

The `paste` program can be written as follows:

```
#!/local/bin/perl
#
# Paste in perl
#
# Two files only, syntax : paste file 1file2
#

open (file1,"@ARGV[0]") || die "Can't open @ARGV[0]\n";
open (file2,"@ARGV[1]") || die "Can't open @ARGV[1]\n";

while (($line1 = <file1>) || ($line2 = <file2>))
   {
   chop $line1;
   chop $line2;

   print "$line1 $line2\n";     # tab character between
   }
```

Here we see more formally how to read from two separate files at the same time. Notice that, by putting the read commands into the test-expression for the `while` loop, we are using the fact that `<..>` returns a non-zero (true) value unless we have reached the end of the file.

To write and append to files, we use the shell redirection symbols inside the `open` command.

```
open(fd,"> filename");    # open file for writing
open(fd,">> filename");   # open file for appending
```

We can also open a pipe from an arbitrary Unix command and receive the output of that command as our input:

```
open (fd,"/bin/ps aux | ");
```

A simple Perl program

Let us now write the simplest Perl program which illustrates the way in which Perl can save time. We shall write it in three different ways to show what the short cuts mean. Let us implement the cat command, which copies files to the standard output. The simplest way to write this in Perl is the following:

```
#!/local/bin/perl

while (<>)
   {
   print;
   }
```

Here we have made heavy use of the many default assumptions which Perl makes. The program is simple, but difficult to understand for novices. First of all we use the default file handle <> which means 'take one line of input from a default file'. This object returns true as long as it has not reached the end of the file, so this loop continues to read lines until it reaches the end of file. The default file is standard input, unless this script is invoked with a command line argument, in which case the argument is treated as a filename and Perl attempts to open the argument-filename for reading. The print statement has no argument telling it what to print, but Perl takes this to mean 'print the default variable $_'.

We can therefore write this more explicitly as follows:

```
#!/local/bin/perl

open (HANDLE,"$ARGV[1]");

while (<HANDLE>)
   {
   print $_;
   }
```

Here we have simply filled in the assumptions explicitly. The command <HANDLE> now reads a single line from the named file-handle into the default variable $_. To make this program more general, we can eliminate the defaults entirely.

```
#!/local/bin/perl

open (HANDLE,"$ARGV[1]");

while ($line=<HANDLE>)
   {
   print $line;
   }
```

== **and** eq

Be careful to distinguish between the comparison operator for integers == and the corresponding operator for strings eq. These do not work in each other's places so if you get the wrong comparison operator your program might not work and it is quite difficult to find the error.

chop **and** chomp

The command chop cuts off the last character of a string. This is useful for removing newline characters when reading files etc. The syntax is

```
chop;            # chop $_;

chop $scalar; # remove last character in $scalar
```

A slightly more refined version which only chops off whitespace and end of line characters is the chomp function.

Perl subroutines

Subroutines are indicated, as in the example above, by the ampersand & symbol. When parameters are passed to a Perl subroutine, they are handed over as an array called @_, which is analogous to the $_ variable. Here is a simple example:

```
#!/local/bin/perl

$a="silver";
$b="gold";

&PrintArgs($a,$b);

# end of main

sub PrintArgs

    {
    ($local_a,$local_b) = @_;

    print "$local_a, $local_b\n";
    }
```

die – exit on error

When a program has to quit and give a message, the die command is normally used. If called without an argument, Perl generates its own message including a line number at which the error occurred. To include your own message, you write

```
die "My message....";
```

If the string is terminated with a \n newline character, the line number of the error is not printed, otherwise Perl appends the line number to your string.

When opening files, it is common to see the syntax:

```
open (filehandle,"Filename") || die "Can't open...";
```

The logical OR symbol is used, because open returns true if all goes well, in which case the right-hand side is never evaluated. If open is false, then die is executed. You can decide for yourself whether or not you think this is good programming style – we mention it here because it is common practice.

The stat() idiom

The Unix library function stat() is used to find out information about a given file. This function is available both in C and in Perl. In Perl, it returns an array of values. Usually we are interested in knowing the access permissions of a file. stat() is called using the syntax

```
@array = stat ("filename");
```

or alternatively, using a named array

```
($device,$inode,$mode) = stat("filename");
```

The value returned in the *mode* variable is a bit pattern. The most useful way of treating these bit patterns is to use octal numbers to interpret their meaning.

To find out whether a file is readable or writable to a group of users, we use a programming idiom which is very common for dealing with bit patterns: first we define a mask which zeros out all of the bits in the mode string except those which we are specifically interested in. This is done by defining a mask value in which the bits we want are set to 1 and all others are set to zero. Then we AND the mask with the mode string. If the result is different from zero then we know that all of the bits were also set in the mode string. As in C, the bitwise AND operator in Perl is called &.

For example, to test whether a file is writable to other users in the same group as the file, we would write the following.

```
$mask = 020;    # Leading 0 means octal number

($device,$inode,$mode) = stat(" file");

if ($mode & $mask)

   print "File is writable by the group";
```

Here the 2 in the second octal number means 'write', the fact that it is the second octal number from the right means that it refers to 'group'. Thus the result of the if-test is only true if that particular bit is true. We shall see this idiom in action below.

Perl example programs

The passwd program and `crypt()` function

Here is a simple implementation of the Unix `passwd` program in Perl.

```perl
#!/local/bin/perl
#
# A perl version of the passwd program.
#
# Note - the real passwd program needs to be much more
# secure than this one. This is just to demonstrate the
# use of the crypt() function.
#
##########################################################

print "Changing passwd for $ENV{'USER'} on $ENV{'HOST'}\n";

system 'stty','-echo';
print "Old passwd: ";

$oldpwd = <STDIN>;
chop $oldpwd;

($name,$coded_pwd,$uid,$gid,$x,$y,$z,$gcos,$home,$shell)
                              = getpwnam($ENV{"USER"});

if (crypt($oldpwd,$coded_pwd) ne $coded_pwd)
   {
   print "\nPasswd incorrect\n";
   exit (1);
   }

$oldpwd = "";                            # Destroy the evidence!

print "\nNew passwd: ";

$newpwd = <STDIN>;

print "\nRepeat new passwd: ";

$rnewpwd = <STDIN>;

chop $newpwd;
chop $rnewpwd;

if ($newpwd ne $rnewpwd)
   {
   print "\n Incorrectly typed. Password unchanged.\n";
```

```
     exit (1);
     }

\index{{\code rand()}}
$salt = rand();
$new_coded_pwd = crypt($newpwd,$salt);

print "\n\n$name:$new_coded_pwd:$uid:$gid:$gcos:$home:$shell\n";
```

Example with `fork()`

The following example uses the `fork` function to start a daemon which goes into
the background and watches the system to find out which process is using the
greatest amount of CPU time each minute. A pipe is opened from the BSD `ps`
command.

```
#!/local/bin/perl
#
# A fork() demo. This program will sit in the background and
# make a list of the process which uses the maximum CPU average
# at 1 minute intervals. On a quiet BSD like system this will
# normally be the swapper (long term scheduler).
#

$true = 1;
$logfile="perl.cpu.logfile";

print "Max CPU logfile, forking daemon...\n";

if (fork())
    {
    exit(0);
    }

while ($true)
    {
    open (logfile,">> $logfile") || die "Can't open $logfile\n";
    open (ps,"/bin/ps aux |") || die "Couldn't open a pipe from ps !!\n";

    $skip_first_line = <ps>;
    $max_process = <ps>;
    close(ps);

    print logfile $max_process;
    close(logfile);
    sleep 60;

    ($a,$b,$c,$d,$e,$f,$g,$size) = stat($logfile);

    if ($size > 500)
        {
```

```
        print STDERR "Log file getting big, better quit!\n";
        exit(0);
        }
    }
```

Pattern matching and extraction

Perl has regular expression operators for identifying patterns. The operator

```
/ regular expression/
```

returns true or false depending on whether the regular expression matches the contents of $_. For example

```
if (/perl/)

    print "String contains perl as a substring";
```

```
if (/(Sat|Sun)day/)

    print "Weekend day....";
```

The effect is rather like the grep command. To use this operator on other variables you would write

```
$variable =~ / regexp/
```

Regular expression can contain parenthetic sub-expressions, e.g.

```
if (/(Sat|Sun)day (..)th (.*)/)

    $first = $1;
    $second = $2;
    $third = $3;
```

in which case Perl places the objects matched by such sub-expressions in the variables $1, $2 etc.

Searching and replacing text

The sed-like function for replacing all occurrences of a string is easily implemented in Perl using

```
while (<input>)

    s/$search/$replace/g;
    print output;
```

This example replaces the string inside the default variable. To replace in a general variable we use the operator = , with syntax:

```
$variable =~ s/ search/ replace/
```

Here is an example of this operator in use. The following is a program which searches and replaces a string in several files. This is a useful program for making a change globally in a group of files. The program is called 'file-replace'.

```
#!/local/bin/perl
############################################################
#
# Look through files for findstring and change to newstring
# in all files.

# Define a temporary file and check it doesn't exist

$outputfile = "/tmp/file";
unlink $outputfile;

#
# Check command line for list of files
#

if ($#ARGV < 0)
   {
   die "Syntax: file-replace [file list]\n";
   }

print "Enter the string you want to find (Don't use quotes):\n\n:";
$findstring=<STDIN>;
chop $findstring;

print "Enter the string you want to replace with (Don't use quotes):\n\n:";
$replacestring=<STDIN>;
chop $replacestring;

#

print "\nFind: $findstring\n";
print "Replace: $replacestring\n";
print "\nConfirm (y/n)   ";
$y = <STDIN>;
chop $y;

if ( $y ne "y")
   {
   die "Aborted -- nothing done.\n";
   }
else
   {
   print "Use CTRL-C to interrupt...\n";
   }
```

```perl
#
# Now shift default array @ARGV to get arguments 1 by 1
#

while ($file = shift)
    {
    if ($file eq "file-replace")
        {
        print "Findmark will not operate on itself!";
        next;
        }

    #
    # Save existing mode of file for later
    #

    ($dev,$ino,$mode)=stat($file);

    open (INPUT,$file) || warn "Couldn't open $file\n";
    open (OUTPUT,"> $outputfile") || warn "Can't open tmp";

    $notify = 1;

    while (<INPUT>)
        {
        if (/$findstring/ && $notify)
            {
            print "Fixing $file...\n";
            $notify = 0;
            }
        s/$findstring/$replacestring/g;
        print OUTPUT;
        }

    close (OUTPUT);

    #
    # If nothing went wrong (if outfile not empty)
    # move temp file to original and reset the
    # file mode saved above
    #

    if (! -z $outputfile)
        {
        rename ($outputfile,$file);
        chmod ($mode,$file);
        }
    else
        {
        print "Warning: file empty!\n.";
        }
    }
```

Similarly we can search for lines containing a string. Here is the grep program written in Perl

```
#!/local/bin/perl
#
# grep as a perl program
#

# Check arguments etc

while (<>)

    print if (/$ARGV[1]/);
```

The operator `/search-string/` returns true if the search string is a substring of the default variable `$_`. To search an arbitrary string, we write

```
.... if (teststring =~ /search-string/);
```

Here *teststring* is searched for occurrences of *search-string* and the result is true if one is found.

In Perl you can use regular expressions to search for text patterns. Note however that, like all regular expression dialects, Perl has its own conventions. For example the dollar sign does not mean 'match the end of line' in Perl, instead one uses the \n symbol. Here is an example program which illustrates the use of regular expressions in Perl:

```
#!/local/bin/perl
#
# Test regular expressions in perl
#
# NB - careful with  $ * symbols etc. Use '' quotes since
#      the shell interprets these!
#

open (FILE,"regex_test");

$regex = $ARGV[$#ARGV];

# Looking for $ARGV[$#ARGV] in file...

while (<FILE>)

    if (/$regex/)

        print;
```

This can be tested with the following patterns:

`.*`	prints every line (matches everything)
`.`	all lines except those containing only blanks (. doesn't match ws/white-space)
`[a-z]`	matches any line containing lowercase
`[^a-z]`	matches any line containing something which is not lowercase a–z
`[A-Za-z]`	matches any line containing letters of any kind
`[0-9]`	match any line containing numbers
`#.*`	line containing a hash symbol followed by anything
`^#.*`	line starting with hash symbol (first char)
`;\n`	match line ending in a semi-colon

Try running this program with the test data on the following file which is called `regex_test` in the example program.

```
# A line beginning with a hash symbol

JUST UPPERCASE LETTERS

just lowercase letters

Letters and numbers 123456

123456

A line ending with a semi-colon;

Line with a comment # COMMENT...
```

Generate WWW pages auto-magically

The following program scans through the password database and builds a stan-dardized html-page for each user it finds there. It fills in the name of the user in each case. Note the use of the `<<` operator for extended input, already used in the context of the shell. This allows us to format a whole passage of text, inserting variables at strategic places, and avoid having to `print` over many lines.

```
#!/local/bin/perl
#
# Build a default home page for each user in /etc/passwd
#
#
```

```
$true = 1;
$false = 0;

# First build an associated array of users and full names

setpwent();

while ($true)
    {
    ($name,$passwd,$uid,$gid,$quota,$comment,$fullname) = getpwent;
    $FullName{$name} = $fullname;
    print "$name - $FullName{$name}\n";
    last if ($name eq "");
    }

print "\n";

# Now make a unique filename for each page and open a file

foreach $user (sort keys(%FullName))
    {
    next if ($user eq "");

    print "Making page for $user\n";
    $outputfile = "$user.html";

    open (OUT,"> $outputfile") || die "Can't open $outputfile\n";

    &MakePage;

    close (OUT);
    }

##################################################################

sub MakePage

{
print OUT <<ENDMARKER;

<HTML>
<BODY>
<HEAD><TITLE>$FullName{$user}'s Home Page</TITLE></HEAD>
<H1>$FullName{$user}'s Home Page</H1>

Hi welcome to my home page. In case you hadn't
got it yet my name is: $FullName{$user}...

I study at <a href=http://www.iu.hioslo.no>Oslo College</a>.

</BODY>
```

```
</HTML>

ENDMARKER
}
```

Summary

Perl is a superior alternative to the shell which has much of the power of C and is therefore ideal for simple and even more complex system programming tasks. A Perl program is more efficient than a shell script since it avoids large overheads associated with forking new processes and setting up pipes. The resident memory image of a Perl program is often smaller than that of a shell script when all of the sub-programs of a shell script are taken into account. We have barely scratched the surface of Perl here. If you intend to be a system administrator for Unix or NT systems, you could do much worse than to read the Perl book [316] and learn Perl inside out.

B.3 WWW and CGI programming

CGI stands for the Common Gateway Interface. It is the name given to scripts which can be executed from within pages of the World Wide Web. Although it is possible to use any language in CGI programs (hence the word 'common'), the usual choice is Perl, because of the ease with which Perl can handle text.

The CGI interface is pretty unintelligent, in order to be as general as possible, so we need to do a bit of work in order to make scripts work.

Permissions

The key thing about the WWW which often causes a lot of confusion is that the WWW service runs with a user ID of nobody or www. The purpose of this is to ensure that no web user has the right to read or write files unless they are opened very explicitly to the world by the user who owns them.

In order for files to be readable on the WWW, they must have file mode 644 and they must lie in a directory which has mode 755. In order for a CGI program to be executable, it must have permission 755 and in order for such a program to write to a file in a user's directory, it must be possible for the file to be created (if necessary) and everyone must be able to write to it. That means that files which are written to by the WWW must have mode 666 and must either exist already or lie in a directory with permission 777.[1]

Protocols

CGI script programs communicate with WWW browsers using a very simple protocol. It goes like this:

- A web page sends data to a script using the 'forms' interface. Those data are concatenated into *a single line*. The data in separate fields of a form are

---

[1]You could also set the sticky bit 1777 in order to prevent malicious users from deleting your file.

separated by & signs. New lines are replaced by the text %0D%0A, which is the DOS ASCII representation of a newline, and spaces are replaced by + symbols.

- A CGI script reads this single line of text on the standard input.

- The CGI script replies to the web browser. The first line of the reply *must* be a line which tells the browser what mime-type the data are sent in. Usually, a CGI script replies in HTML code, in which case the first line in the reply must be:

```
Content-type: text/html
```

This must be followed by a blank line.

HTML coding of forms

To start a CGI program from a web page we use a *form* which is a part of the HTML code enclosed with the parentheses

```
<FORM method="POST" ACTION="/cgi-script-alias/program.pl">
  ...
</FORM>
```

The method 'post' means that the data which get typed into this form will be piped into the CGI program via its standard input. The 'action' specifies which program you want to start. Note that you cannot simply use the absolute path of the file, for security reasons. You must use something called a 'script alias' to tell the web browser where to find the program. If you do not have a script alias defined for you personally, then you need to get one from your system administrator. By using a script alias, no one from outside your site can see where your files are located, only that you have a 'cgi-bin' area somewhere on your system.

Within these parentheses, you can arrange to collect different kinds of input. The simplest kind of input is just a button which starts the CGI program. This has the form

```
<INPUT TYPE="submit" VALUE="Start my program">
```

This code creates a button. When you click on it the program in your 'action' string gets started. More generally, you will want to create input boxes where you can type in data. To create a single-line input field, you use the following syntax:

```
<INPUT NAME="variable-name" SIZE=40>
```

This creates a single-line text field of width 40 characters. This is not the limit on the length of the string which can be typed into the field, only a limit on the amount which is visible at any time. It is for visual formatting only. The NAME field is used to identify the data in the CGI script. The string you enter here will be sent to the CGI script in the form variable-name=value of input.... Another type of input is a text area. This is a larger box where one can type in text on several lines. The syntax is

```
<TEXTAREA NAME="variable-name" ROW=50 COLS=50>
```

which means 'create a text area of fifty rows by fifty columns with a prompt to the left of the box'. Again, the size has only to do with the visual formatting, not to do with limits on the amount of text which can be entered.

As an example, let's create a WWW page with a complete form which can be used to make a guest book, or order form.

```
<HTML>
<HEAD>
<TITLE>Example form</TITLE>
<!-- Comment: Mark Burgess, 27-Jan-1997 -->
<LINK REV="made" HREF="mailto:mark@iu.hioslo.no">
</HEAD>
<BODY>
<CENTER><H1>Write in my guest book...</H1></CENTER>
<HR>

<CENTER><H2>Please leave a comment using the form below.</H2><P>
<FORM method="POST" ACTION="/cgi-bin-mark/comment.pl">

Your Name/E-mail: <INPUT NAME="variable1" SIZE=40> <BR><BR>

<P>
<TEXTAREA NAME="variable2" cols=50 rows=8></TEXTAREA>
<P>

<INPUT TYPE=submit VALUE="Add message to book">
<INPUT TYPE=reset VALUE="Clear message">
</FORM>

<P>

</BODY>
</HTML>
```

The reset button clears the form. When the submit button is pressed, the CGI program is activated.

Interpreting data from forms

To interpret and respond to the data in a form, we must write a program which satisfies the protocol above, see section 2.6.5. We use Perl as a script language. The simplest valid CGI script is the following.

```
#!/local/bin/perl

 #
 # Reply with proper protocol
 #
```

```
print "Content-type: text/html\n\n";

 #
 # Get the data from the form ...
 #

$input = <STDIN>;

 #
 # ... and echo them back
 #

print $input, "\n Done! \n";
```

Although rather banal, this script is a useful starting point for CGI programming, because it shows you just how the input arrives at the script from the HTML form. The data arrive all in a single, enormously long line, full of funny characters. The first job of any script is to decode this line.

Before looking at how to decode the data, we should make an important point about the protocol line. If a web browser does not get this 'content-type' line from the CGI script it returns with an error:

```
500 Server Error

The server encountered an internal error or misconfiguration and was
unable to complete your request.

Please contact the server administrator, and inform them of the time
the error occurred, and anything you might have done that may have
caused the error.

Error: HTTPd: malformed header from script www/cgi-bin/comment.pl
```

Before finishing your CGI script, you will probably encounter this error several times. A common reason for getting the error is a syntax error in your script. If your program contains an error, the first thing a browser gets in return is not the 'content-type' line, but an error message. The browser does not pass on this error message, it just prints the uninformative message above.

If you can get the above script to work, then you are ready to decode the data which are sent to the script. The first thing is to use Perl to split the long line into an array of lines, by splitting on &. We can also convert all of the + symbols back into spaces. The script now looks like this:

```
#!/local/bin/perl

 #
 # Reply with proper protocol
 #
```

```
print "Content-type: text/html\n\n";

 #
 # Get the data from the form ...
 #

$input = <STDIN>;

 #
 # ... and echo them back
 #

print "$input\n\n\n";

$input =~ s/\+/ /g;

 #
 # Now split the lines and convert
 #

@array = split('&',$input);

foreach $var ( @array )
   {
   print "$var\n";
   }

print "Done! \n";
```

We now have a series of elements in our array. The output from this script is
something like this:

```
variable1=Mark+Burgess&variable2=%0D%0AI+just+called+to+say+    (wrap)
....%0D%0A...hey+pig%2C+nothing%27s+working+out+the+way+I+planned
variable1=Mark Burgess variable2=%0D%0AI just called to say    (wrap)
....%0D%0A...hey pig%2Cnothing%27s working out the way I planned Done!
```

As you can see, all control characters are converted into the form %XX. We should
now try to do something with these. Since we are usually not interested in keeping
new lines, or any other control codes, we can simply null-out these with a line of
the form

```
$input =~ s/%..//g;
```

The regular expression %.. matches anything beginning with a percent symbol
followed by two characters. The resulting output is then free of these symbols. We
can then separate the variable contents from their names by splitting the input.
Here is the complete code:

```
#!/local/bin/perl

 #
 # Reply with proper protocol
 #

print "Content-type: text/html\n\n";

 #
 # Get the data from the form ...
 #

$input = <STDIN>;

 #
 # ... and echo them back
 #

print "$input\n\n\n";

$input =~ s/%..//g;

$input =~ s/\+/ /g;

@array = split('&',$input);

foreach $var ( @array )
    {
    print "$var<br>";
    }

print "<hr>\n";

($name,$variable1) = split("variable1=",$array[0]);
($name,$variable2) = split("variable2=",$array[1]);

print "<br>var1 = $variable1<br>";
print "<br>var2 = $variable2<br>";

print "<br>Done! \n";
```

and the output

```
variable1=Mark+Burgess&variable2=%0D%0AI+just+called+to+say    (wrap)
+....%0D%0A...hey+pig%2C+nothing%27s+working+out+the+way+I+planned
variable1=Mark Burgess
variable2=I just called to say .......hey pig nothings working    (wrap)
 out the way I planned
```

```
var1 = Mark Burgess

var2 = I just called to say .......hey pig nothings working out    (wrap)
the way I planned

Done!
```

Appendix C

Example telnet session

The Transmission Control Protocol (RFC 793) is used to transport most high-level protocols today. One of these is the telnet protocol, which has been a general workhorse for many years, but is now replaced with more secure or robust alternatives. As a login service, telnet is no longer deemed suitable, since it transmits secret information in plain text over the network. RFC 845 details the telnet protocol.

As an exercise to the reader, it is helpful to see a real example of how password information is sent in plain text by reproducing the TCP/IP packets and their contents in hard copy. Although slightly cumbersome, it is very informative to see how the communication actually takes place. The retransmission of a packet also demonstrates the reliable property of TCP. Readers are encouraged to research the behavior of the TCP/IP protocol and study this transfer.

This dump was made with the Solaris snoop program, using snoop -v for verbose output. The trace as provided is all the data transmitted over the network in the time it takes to telnet the 'to' host from the 'from' host, get the login banner, type a username and a password and end up with a command prompt.

The first thing we see is how inefficient the telnet protocol is, how passwords are transmitted in clear text over the network and how fragmentation and retransmission of IP fragments is performed in order to guarantee transmission. Notice also how the sequence numbers are randomized.

```
from% telnet to.domain.country
Trying 192.0.2.238...
Connected to to.domain.country
Escape character is '^]'.

SunOS 5.6

login: mark
Password:
SunOS Release 5.6 Version Generic [UNIX(R) System V Release 4.0]

  [/etc/motd]

to% echo hei
to% exit
```

Send Syn to establish connection, + random Seq

```
from -> to ETHER Type=0800 (IP), size = 58 bytes
from -> to IP   D=192.0.2.238 S=192.0.2.10 LEN=44, ID=53498
from -> to TCP D=23 S=54657 Syn Seq=4095044366 Len=0 Win=8760
from -> to TELNET C port=54657
```

Reply with Syn,Ack and Ack=prev Seq+1

```
to -> from        ETHER Type=0800 (IP), size = 60 bytes
to -> from        IP   D=192.0.2.10 S=192.0.2.238 LEN=44, ID=43390
to -> from        TCP D=54657 S=23 Syn Ack=4095044367 Seq=826419455 Len=0 Win=8760
to -> from        TELNET R port=54657
```

Reply with Ack = prev Seq+1

```
from -> to ETHER Type=0800 (IP), size = 54 bytes
from -> to IP   D=192.0.2.238 S=192.0.2.10 LEN=40, ID=53499
from -> to TCP D=23 S=54657      Ack=826419456 Seq=4095044367 Len=0 Win=8760
from -> to TELNET C port=54657
```

Retransmit:

```
from -> to ETHER Type=0800 (IP), size = 81 bytes
from -> to IP   D=192.0.2.238 S=192.0.2.10 LEN=67, ID=53500
from -> to TCP D=23 S=54657      Ack=826419456 Seq=4095044367 Len=27 Win=8760
from -> to TELNET C port=54657
```

Now send data: ack = seq + Len each time until Fin

```
to -> from        ETHER Type=0800 (IP), size = 60 bytes
to -> from        IP   D=192.0.2.10 S=192.0.2.238 LEN=40, ID=43391
to -> from        TCP D=54657 S=23      Ack=4095044394 Seq=826419456 Len=0 Win=8760
to -> from        TELNET R port=54657

to -> from        ETHER Type=0800 (IP), size = 69 bytes
to -> from        IP   D=192.0.2.10 S=192.0.2.238 LEN=55, ID=43396
to -> from        TCP D=54657 S=23      Ack=4095044394 Seq=826419456 Len=15 Win=8760
to -> from        TELNET R port=54657
```

```
from -> to ETHER Type=0800 (IP), size = 54 bytes
from -> to IP   D=192.0.2.238 S=192.0.2.10 LEN=40, ID=53504
from -> to TCP D=23 S=54657      Ack=826419471 Seq=4095044394 Len=0 Win=8760
from -> to TELNET C port=54657
```

Retransmit with different Len no fragmentation, same Ack

```
from -> to ETHER Type=0800 (IP), size = 66 bytes
from -> to IP   D=192.0.2.238 S=192.0.2.10 LEN=52, ID=53505
from -> to TCP D=23 S=54657      Ack=826419471 Seq=4095044394 Len=12 Win=8760
from -> to TELNET C port=54657
```

```
to -> from        ETHER Type=0800 (IP), size = 69 bytes
to -> from        IP   D=192.0.2.10 S=192.0.2.238 LEN=55, ID=43397
to -> from        TCP D=54657 S=23      Ack=4095044394 Seq=826419471 Len=15 Win=8760
to -> from        TELNET R port=54657
```

```
      from -> to ETHER Type=0800 (IP), size = 54 bytes
      from -> to IP  D=192.0.2.238 S=192.0.2.10 LEN=40, ID=53506
      from -> to TCP D=23 S=54657     Ack=826419486 Seq=4095044406 Len=0 Win=8760
      from -> to TELNET C port=54657
```

```
to -> from          ETHER Type=0800 (IP), size = 75 bytes
to -> from          IP  D=192.0.2.10 S=192.0.2.238 LEN=61, ID=43398
to -> from          TCP D=54657 S=23     Ack=4095044406 Seq=826419486 Len=21 Win=8760
to -> from          TELNET R port=54657
```

```
      from -> to ETHER Type=0800 (IP), size = 120 bytes
      from -> to IP  D=192.0.2.238 S=192.0.2.10 LEN=106, ID=53507
      from -> to TCP D=23 S=54657     Ack=826419507 Seq=4095044406 Len=66 Win=8760
      from -> to TELNET C port=54657 \377\372\30\0VT100\377\360\377\372#\0from
```

Transfers TERM variable - VT100:

```
to -> from          ETHER Type=0800 (IP), size = 75 bytes
to -> from          IP  D=192.0.2.10 S=192.0.2.238 LEN=61, ID=43399
to -> from          TCP D=54657 S=23     Ack=4095044472 Seq=826419507 Len=21 Win=8760
to -> from          TELNET R port=54657
```

```
      from -> to ETHER Type=0800 (IP), size = 54 bytes
      from -> to IP  D=192.0.2.238 S=192.0.2.10 LEN=40, ID=53508
      from -> to TCP D=23 S=54657     Ack=826419528 Seq=4095044472 Len=0 Win=8760
      from -> to TELNET C port=54657
```

```
to -> from          ETHER Type=0800 (IP), size = 60 bytes
to -> from          IP  D=192.0.2.10 S=192.0.2.238 LEN=46, ID=43400
to -> from          TCP D=54657 S=23     Ack=4095044472 Seq=826419528 Len=6 Win=8760
to -> from          TELNET R port=54657
```

```
      from -> to ETHER Type=0800 (IP), size = 60 bytes
      from -> to IP  D=192.0.2.238 S=192.0.2.10 LEN=46, ID=53509
      from -> to TCP D=23 S=54657     Ack=826419534 Seq=4095044472 Len=6 Win=8760
      from -> to TELNET C port=54657
```

```
to -> from          ETHER Type=0800 (IP), size = 60 bytes
to -> from          IP  D=192.0.2.10 S=192.0.2.238 LEN=43, ID=43401
to -> from          TCP D=54657 S=23     Ack=4095044478 Seq=826419534 Len=3 Win=8760
to -> from          TELNET R port=54657
```

```
      from -> to ETHER Type=0800 (IP), size = 54 bytes
      from -> to IP  D=192.0.2.238 S=192.0.2.10 LEN=40, ID=53510
      from -> to TCP D=23 S=54657     Ack=826419537 Seq=4095044478 Len=0 Win=8760
      from -> to TELNET C port=54657
```

```
to -> from          ETHER Type=0800 (IP), size = 61 bytes
to -> from          IP  D=192.0.2.10 S=192.0.2.238 LEN=47, ID=43402
to -> from          TCP D=54657 S=23     Ack=4095044478 Seq=826419537 Len=7 Win=8760
to -> from          TELNET R port=54657 login:
```

Here comes the login name

```
      from -> to ETHER Type=0800 (IP), size = 54 bytes
      from -> to IP  D=192.0.2.238 S=192.0.2.10 LEN=40, ID=53511
      from -> to TCP D=23 S=54657     Ack=826419544 Seq=4095044478 Len=0 Win=8760
      from -> to TELNET C port=54657
```

Retransmit, bad Len:

```
      from -> to ETHER Type=0800 (IP), size = 55 bytes
      from -> to IP  D=192.0.2.238 S=192.0.2.10 LEN=41, ID=53512
      from -> to TCP D=23 S=54657     Ack=826419544 Seq=4095044478 Len=1 Win=8760
      from -> to TELNET C port=54657 m
```

```
to -> from         ETHER Type=0800 (IP), size = 60 bytes
to -> from         IP   D=192.0.2.10 S=192.0.2.238 LEN=41, ID=43403
to -> from         TCP D=54657 S=23     Ack=4095044479 Seq=826419544 Len=1 Win=8760
to -> from         TELNET R port=54657 m

        from -> to ETHER Type=0800 (IP), size = 54 bytes
        from -> to IP  D=192.0.2.238 S=192.0.2.10 LEN=40, ID=53513
        from -> to TCP D=23 S=54657    Ack=826419545 Seq=4095044479 Len=0 Win=8760
        from -> to TELNET C port=54657

        from -> to ETHER Type=0800 (IP), size = 55 bytes
        from -> to IP  D=192.0.2.238 S=192.0.2.10 LEN=41, ID=53514
        from -> to TCP D=23 S=54657    Ack=826419545 Seq=4095044479 Len=1 Win=8760
        from -> to TELNET C port=54657 a

to -> from         ETHER Type=0800 (IP), size = 60 bytes
to -> from         IP  D=192.0.2.10 S=192.0.2.238 LEN=41, ID=43404
to -> from         TCP D=54657 S=23     Ack=4095044480 Seq=826419545 Len=1 Win=8760
to -> from         TELNET R port=54657 a

        from -> to ETHER Type=0800 (IP), size = 54 bytes
        from -> to IP  D=192.0.2.238 S=192.0.2.10 LEN=40, ID=53515
        from -> to TCP D=23 S=54657    Ack=826419546 Seq=4095044480 Len=0 Win=8760
        from -> to TELNET C port=54657

        from -> to ETHER Type=0800 (IP), size = 55 bytes
        from -> to IP  D=192.0.2.238 S=192.0.2.10 LEN=41, ID=53516
        from -> to TCP D=23 S=54657    Ack=826419546 Seq=4095044480 Len=1 Win=8760
        from -> to TELNET C port=54657 r

to -> from         ETHER Type=0800 (IP), size = 60 bytes
to -> from         IP  D=192.0.2.10 S=192.0.2.238 LEN=41, ID=43405
to -> from         TCP D=54657 S=23     Ack=4095044481 Seq=826419546 Len=1 Win=8760
to -> from         TELNET R port=54657 r

        from -> to ETHER Type=0800 (IP), size = 54 bytes
        from -> to IP  D=192.0.2.238 S=192.0.2.10 LEN=40, ID=53517
        from -> to TCP D=23 S=54657    Ack=826419547 Seq=4095044481 Len=0 Win=8760
        from -> to TELNET C port=54657
```

Retransmit:

```
        from -> to ETHER Type=0800 (IP), size = 55 bytes
        from -> to IP  D=192.0.2.238 S=192.0.2.10 LEN=41, ID=53518
        from -> to TCP D=23 S=54657    Ack=826419547 Seq=4095044481 Len=1 Win=8760
        from -> to TELNET C port=54657 k

to -> from         ETHER Type=0800 (IP), size = 60 bytes
to -> from         IP  D=192.0.2.10 S=192.0.2.238 LEN=41, ID=43406
to -> from         TCP D=54657 S=23     Ack=4095044482 Seq=826419547 Len=1 Win=8760
to -> from         TELNET R port=54657 k

        from -> to ETHER Type=0800 (IP), size = 54 bytes
        from -> to IP  D=192.0.2.238 S=192.0.2.10 LEN=40, ID=53519
        from -> to TCP D=23 S=54657    Ack=826419548 Seq=4095044482 Len=0 Win=8760
        from -> to TELNET C port=54657
  (retrans)
        from -> to ETHER Type=0800 (IP), size = 56 bytes
        from -> to IP  D=192.0.2.238 S=192.0.2.10 LEN=42, ID=53520
        from -> to TCP D=23 S=54657    Ack=826419548 Seq=4095044482 Len=2 Win=8760
        from -> to TELNET C port=54657

to -> from         ETHER Type=0800 (IP), size = 60 bytes
to -> from         IP  D=192.0.2.10 S=192.0.2.238 LEN=42, ID=43407
to -> from         TCP D=54657 S=23     Ack=4095044484 Seq=826419548 Len=2 Win=8760
to -> from         TELNET R port=54657

        from -> to ETHER Type=0800 (IP), size = 54 bytes
        from -> to IP  D=192.0.2.238 S=192.0.2.10 LEN=40, ID=53521
        from -> to TCP D=23 S=54657    Ack=826419550 Seq=4095044484 Len=0 Win=8760
        from -> to TELNET C port=54657
```

```
to -> from          ETHER Type=0800 (IP), size = 64 bytes
to -> from          IP  D=192.0.2.10 S=192.0.2.238 LEN=50, ID=43408
to -> from          TCP D=54657 S=23     Ack=4095044484 Seq=826419550 Len=10 Win=8760
to -> from          TELNET R port=54657 Password:
```

Here comes the password, in plain text, for all to see!

```
from -> to ETHER Type=0800 (IP), size = 54 bytes
from -> to IP  D=192.0.2.238 S=192.0.2.10 LEN=40, ID=53522
from -> to TCP D=23 S=54657     Ack=826419560 Seq=4095044484 Len=0 Win=8760
from -> to TELNET C port=54657
```

Retransmit:

```
from -> to ETHER Type=0800 (IP), size = 55 bytes
from -> to IP  D=192.0.2.238 S=192.0.2.10 LEN=41, ID=53523
from -> to TCP D=23 S=54657     Ack=826419560 Seq=4095044484 Len=1 Win=8760
from -> to TELNET C port=54657 p
```

```
to -> from          ETHER Type=0800 (IP), size = 60 bytes
to -> from          IP  D=192.0.2.10 S=192.0.2.238 LEN=40, ID=43409
to -> from          TCP D=54657 S=23     Ack=4095044485 Seq=826419560 Len=0 Win=8760
to -> from          TELNET R port=54657 p
```

```
from -> to ETHER Type=0800 (IP), size = 55 bytes
from -> to IP  D=192.0.2.238 S=192.0.2.10 LEN=41, ID=53524
from -> to TCP D=23 S=54657     Ack=826419560 Seq=4095044485 Len=1 Win=8760
from -> to TELNET C port=54657 a
```

```
to -> from          ETHER Type=0800 (IP), size = 60 bytes
to -> from          IP  D=192.0.2.10 S=192.0.2.238 LEN=40, ID=43410
to -> from          TCP D=54657 S=23     Ack=4095044486 Seq=826419560 Len=0 Win=8760
to -> from          TELNET R port=54657 a
```

```
from -> to ETHER Type=0800 (IP), size = 55 bytes
from -> to IP  D=192.0.2.238 S=192.0.2.10 LEN=41, ID=53525
from -> to TCP D=23 S=54657     Ack=826419560 Seq=4095044486 Len=1 Win=8760
from -> to TELNET C port=54657 s
```

```
to -> from          ETHER Type=0800 (IP), size = 60 bytes
to -> from          IP  D=192.0.2.10 S=192.0.2.238 LEN=40, ID=43411
to -> from          TCP D=54657 S=23     Ack=4095044487 Seq=826419560 Len=0 Win=8760
to -> from          TELNET R port=54657 s
```

```
from -> to ETHER Type=0800 (IP), size = 55 bytes
from -> to IP  D=192.0.2.238 S=192.0.2.10 LEN=41, ID=53526
from -> to TCP D=23 S=54657     Ack=826419560 Seq=4095044487 Len=1 Win=8760
from -> to TELNET C port=54657 w
```

```
to -> from          ETHER Type=0800 (IP), size = 60 bytes
to -> from          IP  D=192.0.2.10 S=192.0.2.238 LEN=40, ID=43412
to -> from          TCP D=54657 S=23     Ack=4095044488 Seq=826419560 Len=0 Win=8760
to -> from          TELNET R port=54657 w
```

```
from -> to ETHER Type=0800 (IP), size = 55 bytes
from -> to IP  D=192.0.2.238 S=192.0.2.10 LEN=41, ID=53530
from -> to TCP D=23 S=54657     Ack=826419560 Seq=4095044491 Len=1 Win=8760
from -> to TELNET C port=54657 d
```

```
to -> from          ETHER Type=0800 (IP), size = 60 bytes
to -> from          IP  D=192.0.2.10 S=192.0.2.238 LEN=40, ID=43416
to -> from          TCP D=54657 S=23     Ack=4095044492 Seq=826419560 Len=0 Win=8760
to -> from          TELNET R port=54657 d
```

```
from -> to ETHER Type=0800 (IP), size = 56 bytes
from -> to IP  D=192.0.2.238 S=192.0.2.10 LEN=42, ID=53531
from -> to TCP D=23 S=54657     Ack=826419560 Seq=4095044492 Len=2 Win=8760
from -> to TELNET C port=54657 \n
```

```
to -> from        ETHER Type=0800 (IP), size = 60 bytes
to -> from        IP   D=192.0.2.10 S=192.0.2.238 LEN=42, ID=43417
to -> from        TCP D=54657 S=23     Ack=4095044494 Seq=826419560 Len=2 Win=8760
to -> from        TELNET R port=54657
  (fragment)
to -> from        ETHER Type=0800 (IP), size = 357 bytes
to -> from        IP   D=192.0.2.10 S=192.0.2.238 LEN=343, ID=43484
to -> from        TCP D=54657 S=23     Ack=4095044494 Seq=826419562 Len=303 Win=8760
to -> from        TELNET R port=54657 SunOS Release 5.6 Ve
```

```
      from -> to ETHER Type=0800 (IP), size = 54 bytes
      from -> to IP   D=192.0.2.238 S=192.0.2.10 LEN=40, ID=53599
      from -> to TCP D=23 S=54657     Ack=826419865 Seq=4095044494 Len=0 Win=8760
      from -> to TELNET C port=54657
```

```
to -> from        ETHER Type=0800 (IP), size = 130 bytes
to -> from        IP   D=192.0.2.10 S=192.0.2.238 LEN=116, ID=43487
to -> from        TCP D=54657 S=23     Ack=4095044494 Seq=826419865 Len=76 Win=8760
to -> from        TELNET R port=54657   1:33pm  up 2 day(s
```

Fragment:

```
to -> from        ETHER Type=0800 (IP), size = 60 bytes
to -> from        IP   D=192.0.2.10 S=192.0.2.238 LEN=42, ID=43882
to -> from        TCP D=54657 S=23     Ack=4095044494 Seq=826419941 Len=2 Win=8760
to -> from        TELNET R port=54657
```

```
      from -> to ETHER Type=0800 (IP), size = 54 bytes
      from -> to IP   D=192.0.2.238 S=192.0.2.10 LEN=40, ID=54316
      from -> to TCP D=23 S=54657     Ack=826419943 Seq=4095044494 Len=0 Win=8760
      from -> to TELNET C port=54657
```

```
to -> from        ETHER Type=0800 (IP), size = 101 bytes
to -> from        IP   D=192.0.2.10 S=192.0.2.238 LEN=87, ID=43887
to -> from        TCP D=54657 S=23     Ack=4095044494 Seq=826419943 Len=47 Win=8760
to -> from        TELNET R port=54657 You have mail (total
```

```
      from -> to ETHER Type=0800 (IP), size = 54 bytes
      from -> to IP   D=192.0.2.238 S=192.0.2.10 LEN=40, ID=54319
      from -> to TCP D=23 S=54657     Ack=826419990 Seq=4095044494 Len=0 Win=8760
      from -> to TELNET C port=54657
```

```
to -> from        ETHER Type=0800 (IP), size = 60 bytes
to -> from        IP   D=192.0.2.10 S=192.0.2.238 LEN=45, ID=43890
to -> from        TCP D=54657 S=23     Ack=4095044494 Seq=826419990 Len=5 Win=8760
to -> from        TELNET R port=54657 prompt\%
```

```
to -> from        ETHER Type=0800 (IP), size = 60 bytes
to -> from        IP   D=192.0.2.10 S=192.0.2.238 LEN=40, ID=43891
to -> from        TCP D=2049 S=1023    Ack=4258218482 Seq=1642166507 Len=0 Win=8760
```

```
      from -> to ETHER Type=0800 (IP), size = 54 bytes
      from -> to IP   D=192.0.2.238 S=192.0.2.10 LEN=40, ID=54320
      from -> to TCP D=23 S=54657     Ack=826419995 Seq=4095044494 Len=0 Win=8760
      from -> to TELNET C port=54657
```

```
      from -> to ETHER Type=0800 (IP), size = 55 bytes
      from -> to IP   D=192.0.2.238 S=192.0.2.10 LEN=41, ID=54321
      from -> to TCP D=23 S=54657     Ack=826419995 Seq=4095044494 Len=1 Win=8760
      from -> to TELNET C port=54657 e
```

```
to -> from        ETHER Type=0800 (IP), size = 60 bytes
to -> from        IP   D=192.0.2.10 S=192.0.2.238 LEN=41, ID=43892
to -> from        TCP D=54657 S=23     Ack=4095044495 Seq=826419995 Len=1 Win=8760
to -> from        TELNET R port=54657 e
```

```
      from -> to ETHER Type=0800 (IP), size = 54 bytes
      from -> to IP   D=192.0.2.238 S=192.0.2.10 LEN=40, ID=54322
      from -> to TCP D=23 S=54657     Ack=826419996 Seq=4095044495 Len=0 Win=8760
      from -> to TELNET C port=54657
```

Retransmit:

```
        from -> to ETHER Type=0800 (IP), size = 55 bytes
        from -> to IP   D=192.0.2.238 S=192.0.2.10 LEN=41, ID=54323
        from -> to TCP D=23 S=54657     Ack=826419996 Seq=4095044495 Len=1 Win=8760
        from -> to TELNET C port=54657 c
```

```
to -> from      ETHER Type=0800 (IP), size = 60 bytes
to -> from      IP   D=192.0.2.10 S=192.0.2.238 LEN=41, ID=43893
to -> from      TCP D=54657 S=23    Ack=4095044496 Seq=826419996 Len=1 Win=8760
to -> from      TELNET R port=54657 c
```

```
        from -> to ETHER Type=0800 (IP), size = 54 bytes
        from -> to IP   D=192.0.2.238 S=192.0.2.10 LEN=40, ID=54324
        from -> to TCP D=23 S=54657     Ack=826419997 Seq=4095044496 Len=0 Win=8760
        from -> to TELNET C port=54657
```

Retransmit:

```
        from -> to ETHER Type=0800 (IP), size = 55 bytes
        from -> to IP   D=192.0.2.238 S=192.0.2.10 LEN=41, ID=54325
        from -> to TCP D=23 S=54657     Ack=826419997 Seq=4095044496 Len=1 Win=8760
        from -> to TELNET C port=54657 h
```

```
to -> from      ETHER Type=0800 (IP), size = 60 bytes
to -> from      IP   D=192.0.2.10 S=192.0.2.238 LEN=41, ID=43894
to -> from      TCP D=54657 S=23    Ack=4095044497 Seq=826419997 Len=1 Win=8760
to -> from      TELNET R port=54657 h
```

```
        from -> to ETHER Type=0800 (IP), size = 54 bytes
        from -> to IP   D=192.0.2.238 S=192.0.2.10 LEN=40, ID=54326
        from -> to TCP D=23 S=54657     Ack=826419998 Seq=4095044497 Len=0 Win=8760
        from -> to TELNET C port=54657
```

Retransmit

```
        from -> to ETHER Type=0800 (IP), size = 55 bytes
        from -> to IP   D=192.0.2.238 S=192.0.2.10 LEN=41, ID=54327
        from -> to TCP D=23 S=54657     Ack=826419998 Seq=4095044497 Len=1 Win=8760
        from -> to TELNET C port=54657 o
```

```
to -> from      ETHER Type=0800 (IP), size = 60 bytes
to -> from      IP   D=192.0.2.10 S=192.0.2.238 LEN=41, ID=43895
to -> from      TCP D=54657 S=23    Ack=4095044498 Seq=826419998 Len=1 Win=8760
to -> from      TELNET R port=54657 o
```

```
        from -> to ETHER Type=0800 (IP), size = 54 bytes
        from -> to IP   D=192.0.2.238 S=192.0.2.10 LEN=40, ID=54328
        from -> to TCP D=23 S=54657     Ack=826419999 Seq=4095044498 Len=0 Win=8760
        from -> to TELNET C port=54657
    (retrans)
        from -> to ETHER Type=0800 (IP), size = 55 bytes
        from -> to IP   D=192.0.2.238 S=192.0.2.10 LEN=41, ID=54329
        from -> to TCP D=23 S=54657     Ack=826419999 Seq=4095044498 Len=1 Win=8760
        from -> to TELNET C port=54657
```

```
to -> from      ETHER Type=0800 (IP), size = 60 bytes
to -> from      IP   D=192.0.2.10 S=192.0.2.238 LEN=41, ID=43896
to -> from      TCP D=54657 S=23    Ack=4095044499 Seq=826419999 Len=1 Win=8760
to -> from      TELNET R port=54657
```

```
        from -> to ETHER Type=0800 (IP), size = 56 bytes
        from -> to IP   D=192.0.2.238 S=192.0.2.10 LEN=42, ID=54333
        from -> to TCP D=23 S=54657     Ack=826420001 Seq=4095044500 Len=2 Win=8760
        from -> to TELNET C port=54657 ei
```

```
to -> from      ETHER Type=0800 (IP), size = 60 bytes
to -> from      IP   D=192.0.2.10 S=192.0.2.238 LEN=41, ID=43898
to -> from      TCP D=54657 S=23    Ack=4095044502 Seq=826420001 Len=1 Win=8760
to -> from      TELNET R port=54657 e
```

```
        from -> to ETHER Type=0800 (IP), size = 54 bytes
        from -> to IP   D=192.0.2.238 S=192.0.2.10 LEN=40, ID=54334
        from -> to TCP D=23 S=54657     Ack=826420002 Seq=4095044502 Len=0 Win=8760
        from -> to TELNET C port=54657

to -> from        ETHER Type=0800 (IP), size = 60 bytes
to -> from        IP   D=192.0.2.10 S=192.0.2.238 LEN=41, ID=43899
to -> from        TCP D=54657 S=23     Ack=4095044502 Seq=826420002 Len=1 Win=8760
to -> from        TELNET R port=54657 i

        from -> to ETHER Type=0800 (IP), size = 54 bytes
        from -> to IP   D=192.0.2.238 S=192.0.2.10 LEN=40, ID=54335
        from -> to TCP D=23 S=54657     Ack=826420003 Seq=4095044502 Len=0 Win=8760
        from -> to TELNET C port=54657
```

Retransmit:

```
        from -> to ETHER Type=0800 (IP), size = 56 bytes
        from -> to IP   D=192.0.2.238 S=192.0.2.10 LEN=42, ID=54336
        from -> to TCP D=23 S=54657     Ack=826420003 Seq=4095044502 Len=2 Win=8760
        from -> to TELNET C port=54657

to -> from        ETHER Type=0800 (IP), size = 60 bytes
to -> from        IP   D=192.0.2.10 S=192.0.2.238 LEN=44, ID=43900
to -> from        TCP D=54657 S=23     Ack=4095044504 Seq=826420003 Len=4 Win=8760
to -> from        TELNET R port=54657

        from -> to ETHER Type=0800 (IP), size = 54 bytes
        from -> to IP   D=192.0.2.238 S=192.0.2.10 LEN=40, ID=54337
        from -> to TCP D=23 S=54657     Ack=826420007 Seq=4095044504 Len=0 Win=8760
        from -> to TELNET C port=54657

to -> from        ETHER Type=0800 (IP), size = 64 bytes
to -> from        IP   D=192.0.2.10 S=192.0.2.238 LEN=50, ID=43901
to -> from        TCP D=54657 S=23     Ack=4095044504 Seq=826420007 Len=10 Win=8760
to -> from        TELNET R port=54657 hei\r\nprompt\%

        from -> to ETHER Type=0800 (IP), size = 54 bytes
        from -> to IP   D=192.0.2.238 S=192.0.2.10 LEN=40, ID=54338
        from -> to TCP D=23 S=54657     Ack=826420017 Seq=4095044504 Len=0 Win=8760
        from -> to TELNET C port=54657
```

Retransmit:

```
        from -> to ETHER Type=0800 (IP), size = 55 bytes
        from -> to IP   D=192.0.2.238 S=192.0.2.10 LEN=41, ID=54339
        from -> to TCP D=23 S=54657     Ack=826420017 Seq=4095044504 Len=1 Win=8760
        from -> to TELNET C port=54657

to -> from        ETHER Type=0800 (IP), size = 60 bytes
to -> from        IP   D=192.0.2.10 S=192.0.2.238 LEN=44, ID=43902
to -> from        TCP D=54657 S=23     Ack=4095044505 Seq=826420017 Len=4 Win=8760
to -> from        TELNET R port=54657

        from -> to ETHER Type=0800 (IP), size = 54 bytes
        from -> to IP   D=192.0.2.238 S=192.0.2.10 LEN=40, ID=54343
        from -> to TCP D=23 S=54657     Ack=826420021 Seq=4095044505 Len=0 Win=8760
        from -> to TELNET C port=54657

to -> from        ETHER Type=0800 (IP), size = 62 bytes
to -> from        IP   D=192.0.2.10 S=192.0.2.238 LEN=48, ID=43907
to -> from        TCP D=54657 S=23     Ack=4095044505 Seq=826420021 Len=8 Win=8760
to -> from        TELNET R port=54657 logout\r\n

        from -> to ETHER Type=0800 (IP), size = 54 bytes
        from -> to IP   D=192.0.2.238 S=192.0.2.10 LEN=40, ID=54348
        from -> to TCP D=23 S=54657     Ack=826420029 Seq=4095044505 Len=0 Win=8760
        from -> to TELNET C port=54657
```

Send Fin, end of connection:

```
to -> from      ETHER Type=0800 (IP), size = 60 bytes
to -> from      IP   D=192.0.2.10 S=192.0.2.238 LEN=40, ID=43911
to -> from      TCP D=54657 S=23 Fin Ack=4095044505 Seq=826420029 Len=0 Win=8760
to -> from      TELNET R port=54657
```

Send Fin,Ack with Ack=previous Seq+1:

```
from -> to ETHER Type=0800 (IP), size = 54 bytes
from -> to IP   D=192.0.2.238 S=192.0.2.10 LEN=40, ID=54349
from -> to TCP D=23 S=54657      Ack=826420030 Seq=4095044505 Len=0 Win=8760
from -> to TELNET C port=54657

from -> to ETHER Type=0800 (IP), size = 54 bytes
from -> to IP   D=192.0.2.238 S=192.0.2.10 LEN=40, ID=54350
from -> to TCP D=23 S=54657 Fin Ack=826420030 Seq=4095044505 Len=0 Win=8760
from -> to TELNET C port=54657
```

Send Ack+1 to end:

```
to -> from      ETHER Type=0800 (IP), size = 60 bytes
to -> from      IP   D=192.0.2.10 S=192.0.2.238 LEN=40, ID=43912
to -> from      TCP D=54657 S=23      Ack=4095044506 Seq=826420030 Len=0 Win=8760
to -> from      TELNET R port=54657
```

Appendix D

Glossary

- *ACL:* Access control list, a list of access rights to an object.

- *Anycast:* A type of message introduced in IPv6. An anycast message is like a cross between a unicast and a broadcast. It is a message to the 'nearest available' host, and is used to find servers for particular services. The first host that responds to an anycast becomes the recipient.

- *ASN-1:* Abstract Syntax Notation number One (ASN.1) is an international standard that aims at specifying data used in communication protocols. It is used in protocols like SNMP and LDAP, and technologies such as mobile phones and even Internet Explorer.

- *ATM:* Asynchronous Transfer Mode. A network protocol that provides Quality of Service guarantees and competes with Frame Relay for wide area point to point links. It can also be switched for Local Area traffic, but since it does not support broadcast, it is difficult to use for IPv4 traffic. IPv6 offers workaround support for ATM.

- *Atomic operation:* A basic, primitive operation which cannot be subdivided into smaller pieces, e.g. reading a block from a file.

- *Binaries:* Files of compiled software in executable form. A compiler takes program sources and turns them into binaries.

- *Binary server:* A file-server which makes available executable binaries for a given type of platform. A binary server is operating system specific, since software compiled on one type of system cannot be used on another. (See also *Home server.*)

- *BIND:* Berkeley Internet Name Domain. An implementation of the Domain Name Service protocol suite, including both a client library (called the resolver) and the name server daemon.

- *Booting:* Bootstrapping a machine. This comes from the expression 'to lift yourself by your bootstraps', which is supposed to reflect the way computers are able to start running from scratch, when they are powered up.

- *Broadcast:* A message sent by flooding, that is directed to all hosts within a region of a network. Broadcasts are typically blocked by IP routers, but not by layer 2 switches.

- *C/MOS:* Complementary Metal Oxide Semiconductor. p-n back-to-back transistor technology, low dissipation.

- *COM:* Refers to the communications port on a PC. Also stands for Microsoft's Common Object Model.

- *Consolidated:* Grouping resources in one place. A centralized type of solution for concentrating computing power in one place. This kind of solution makes sense for heavy calculations, performed in engineering of computer graphics.

- *Context switching:* Time-sharing between processes. When the kernel switches between processes quickly in order to give the illusion of concurrency or multitasking.

- *Cracker:* A system intruder. Someone who cracks the system. A trespasser.

- *DAC:* Discretionary access control, i.e. optional rather than forced. (See *MAC*.)

- *DAP:* Directory Access Protocol (X.500).

- *Dataless client:* A client which has a disk and its own root partition, so it can boot by itself. Other data are mounted over NFS.

- *DIB:* Directory Information Base (X.500).

- *DIMM:* Memory chip.

- *Diskless client:* A client which has no disk at all but which shares the root and /usr file trees using the NFS from a server.

- *DISP:* Directory Information Shadowing Protocol (X.500).

- *Distributed:* A decentralized solution, in which many workstations spread the computing power evenly throughout the network.

- *DIT:* Directory Information Tree.

- *DLL:* Dynamic Link Library (Windows).

- *DN:* Distinguished Name (X.500), a primary key in a DAP database.

- *DNS:* The Domain Name Service, which converts Internet names into IP addresses and vice versa.

- *Domains:* A domain is a logical group of hosts. This word is used with several different meanings in connection with different software systems. The most common meaning is connected with DNS, the Domain Name Service. Here a domain refers to an Internet suffix, like .domain.country, or .nasa.gov. Internet domains denote organizations. Domain is also used in NT to refer to a group of hosts sharing the attributes of a common file-server. Try not to confuse Domain nameserver (DNS) server with NT Domain server.

- *DSA:* Directory System Agent (X.500), DAP or LDAP server.

- *DSE:* DSA specific entry, i.e. root name space point for a local directory (X.500).

- *Enterprise:* A small business network environment. Enterprise management is a popular concept today because NT has been aimed at this market. Enterprise management typically involves running a web server, a database, a disk server and a group of workstations and common resources like printers, and so on. Many magazines think of enterprise management as the network model, but when people talk about enterprise management they are really thinking of small businesses with fairly uniform systems.

- *FQHN:* Fully qualified host name. The name of a host which is a sum of its unqualified name and its domain name, e.g. `host.domain.country`, of which `host` is the unqualified name and `domain.country` is the domain name.

- *Free software:* This usually refers to software published under the GNU Public License, Artistic License or derivative of these. Free software is not about money, but about the freedom to use, modify and redistribute software without restrictions over and above what normal courtesy to the author demands. Free software must always include human readable source code. Recently people choose to distinguish between this and Open Source software, i.e. code whose source is open but which may or may not be free.

- *GUI:* Graphical user interface.

- *Heterogeneous:* Non-uniform. In a network context, a heterogeneous network is one which is composed of hosts with many different operating systems.

- *Home server:* A file-server which makes available users' home directories. A home server need not be operating system specific, provided it uses a commonly supported protocol, e.g. NFS, Samba. (See also *Binary server.*)

- *Homogeneous:* Uniform. In a network context, a homogeneous network is one in which all of the hosts have the same operating system.

- *IETF:* Internet Engineering Task Force. A working group that defines Internet standards.

- *IMAP:* Internet Message Access Protocol. A modern approach to distributed E-mail services.

- *Index node (inode):* Unix's method of indexing files on a disk partition.

- *Inhomogeneous:* The opposite of homogeneous. See also *Heterogeneous.*

- *Internetworking protocol:* A protocol which can send messages across quite different physical networks, binding them together into a unified communications base.

- *IP address:* Internet address. Something like `128.39.89.10` or now `2001:700:700:3:290:27ff:fea2:477b`

- *ISO:* International Standards Organization.

- *JNDI:* Java Naming and Directory Interface. Part of Java Enterprise services for distributed computing.

- *Latency:* The time you wait before receiving a reply during a transaction.

- *Legacy system:* An old computer or software package which a site has come to rely on, but which is otherwise outdated.

- *LISA:* Large Installation System Administration. This refers to environments with many (hundreds or thousands of) computers. The environments typically consist of many different kinds of system from multiple vendors. These systems are usually owned by huge companies, organizations like NASA or universities.

- *MAC:* Mandatory access control. (See *DAC*.)

- *MAC address:* Media access control address (e.g. Ethernet address). This is the hardware address which is typically burned into the network interface.

- *Memory image:* A copy of some software in the actual RAM of the system. Often used to refer to the *resident size* of a program, or the amount of memory actually consumed by a program as it runs.

- *Middleware:* A layer of software super-structure above the transport layer of network communications that adds additional services and abstractions, e.g. CORBA, DCOM, Jini, Java RMI.

- *MFT:* Master file table. NTFS's system of indexing files on a disk partition.

- *Multicast:* An IP message sent from a host to a number of other hosts. A multicast is typically used to distribute multimedia (video streams etc.) to a number of subscribers.

- *NAT:* Network address translator. A device which translates concealed, private IP addresses into public IP addresses. NAT allows an organization to have multiple distinct internal hosts appear as a smaller number of hosts to the Internet at large, as well as to hide the structure of the organization's internal network.

- *NDS:* Novell Directory Services.

- *NIS:* Network Information Services (Sun Microsystems' yellow pages service).

- *Open source:* A software 'trademark' for software whose source files are made available to users. This is similar to the idea of Free Software, but it does not necessarily license users the ability to use and distribute the software with complete freedom. See `http://www.OpenSource.com`

- *Open standards:* Inter-operability standards that are published freely and adopted as industry standards.

- *Open systems:* A concept promoted originally by Sun Microsystems for Unix. It is about software systems being compatible through the use of freely available standards. Competitors are not prevented from knowing how to implement and include a technology in their products or from selling it under license.

- *PC:* An Intel-based personal computer, used by a single user.

- *PID:* Process identity number.

- *Point to point:* A direct physical cable from one location to another, with no routing required. Protocols and transport mechanisms for such links are especially important in Wide Area Networks, where a point to point link might cross an ocean or half a country.

- *Proprietary systems:* The opposite of open systems. These systems are secret and the details of their operation are not disclosed to competitors.

- *RAID:* Redundant array of inexpensive (sometimes cited as independent) disks. A disk array with automatic redundancy and error correction. RAID 6 can tolerate 2 disk failures, and RAID 0,1 (though not an official RAID classification) can tolerate one or more concurrent disk failures, depending on which disks go.

- *RDN:* Relative Distinguished Name (X.500).

- *SASL:* Simple Authentication and Security Layer. See RFC 2222.

- *SCSI:* Small Computer Systems Interface. Used mainly for disks on multiuser systems and musical instruments.

- *Server:* A process (a daemon) which implements a particular service. Services can be local to one host, or net-wide.

- *Server-host:* The host on which a server process runs. This is often abbreviated simply to 'server', causing much confusion.

- *SID:* Security identity number (NT).

- *SIMM:* Memory chip arrays. See also *DIMM*.

- *SMS:* Short Message Service, a method of sending text messages that are up to 160 characters long, usually by mobile (cell) phone.

- *SNMP:* Simple Network Management Protocol, an application-layer protocol from the IETF for retrieving and setting simple configuration variables on network hardware.

- *Spoofing:* Impersonation, faking, posing as a false identity.

- *SSL:* Secure socket layer. A security wrapper which makes use of public-private key encryption in order to create a virtual private network link (VPN) between two hosts. The SSL, developed by Netscape, has become the standard for secure communication.

- *Striping:* A way of spreading data over several disk controllers to increase throughput. Striping can be dangerous on disk failure, since files are stored over several disks, meaning that if one disk fails, all data are lost.

- *Superuser:* The root or Administrator or privileged user account.

- *SVR4:* System 5 release 4 Unix. AT&T's code release.

- *TLD:* Top Level Domain. This is the topmost level of domain name resolution, e.g. .org, .com, .net, or country domains like .uk or .no

- *TLS:* Transport Layer Security (version 3 of SSL). See RFC 2246.

- *TTL:* Time to live or Transistor–Transistor Logic.

- *UID:* User identity number (Unix).

- *Unicast:* An IP message sent from a single host to another single host. Contrast this to a multicast, anycast and broadcast.

- *Unqualified name:* See *FQHN.*

- *URL:* Uniform resource locator. A network 'filename' including the name of the host on which the resource resides and the network service (port number) which provides it.

- *Vendor:* A company which sells hardware or software. This is common American parlance for a manufacturer or supplier.

- *Workstation:* A desktop computer which might be used by several users. Workstations can be based on, for example, SPARC (Sun Microsystems) or Alpha (Digital/Compaq) chip sets.

- *X11:* The Unix windows system.

Appendix E

Recommended reading

1. *The Practice of System Administration*, T. Limoncelli and C. Hogan, Addison Wesley, 2002.

2. *Unix System Administration Handbook*, E. Nemeth, G. Synder, S. Seebass and T.R. Hein, Prentice Hall, 2001.

3. *Essential System Administration*, Æ. Frisch, O'Reilly & Assoc, 2002.

4. *Windows NT: User Administration*, A.J. Meggitt and T.D. Ritchey, O'Reilly & Assoc, 1997.

5. *Computer Networks, A Systems Approach, Second Edition*, L.L. Peterson and B.S. Davie, Morgan Kaufman, 2000.

6. *Computer Networks, 4th edition*, A.S. Tannenbaum, Prentice Hall, 2003.

7. *Data Communications and Networking, 2nd edition*, B.A. Forouzan, McGraw-Hill, 2001.

8. *DNS and BIND*, Paul Albitz and Cricket Liu, O'Reilly & Assoc, 1992.

9. *Sendmail Performance Tuning*, N. Christenson, Addison Wesley, 2002.

10. *The Unix Programming Environment*, Brian W. Kernighan and Rob Pike, Prentice Hall, 1984.

11. *The Hacker Crackdown*, B. Sterling. Bantam, 1992.

12. *Computer Security: Art and Science*, M. Bishop, Addison-Wesley, 2002.

13. *Building Internet Firewalls, 2nd edition*, D.B. Chapman and E.D. Zwicky, O'Reilly & Assoc.

Bibliography

[1] J. Abbate. User account administration at project athena. *Proceedings of the Large Installation System Administration Workshop (USENIX Association: Berkeley, CA, 1987)*, page 28, 1987.

[2] J. Abbey. The group administration shell and the gash network computing environment. *Proceedings of the Eighth Systems Administration Conference (LISA VIII) (USENIX Association: Berkeley, CA)*, page 191, 1994.

[3] H. Abdu, H. Lutfiya, and M. Bauer. A model for adaptive monitoring configurations. *Proceedings of the VI IFIP/IEEE IM Conference on Network Management*, page 371, 1999.

[4] System administration and network security organization. http://www.sans.org.

[5] Imtiaz Ahmad and Muhammed K. Dhodhi. Multiprocessor scheduling in a genetic paradigm. *Parallel Computing*, 22:395–406, 1996.

[6] R. Albert and A. Barabási. Statistical mechanics of complex networks. *Rev. Mod. Phys*, 74, 2002.

[7] P. Albitz and C. Liu. *DNS and BIND*. O'Reilley & Assoc., California, 1992.

[8] D. Alter. Electronic mail gone wild. *Proceedings of the Large Installation System Administration Workshop (USENIX Association: Berkeley, CA, 1987)*, page 24, 1987.

[9] E. Anderson and D. Patterson. Extensible, scalable monitoring for clusters of computers. *Proceedings of the Eleventh Systems Administration Conference (LISA XI) (USENIX Association: Berkeley, CA)*, page 9, 1997.

[10] P. Anderson. Managing program binaries in a heterogeneous unix network. *Proceedings of the Fifth Large Installation Systems Administration Conference (LISA V) (USENIX Association: Berkeley, CA)*, page 1, 1991.

[11] P. Anderson. Effective use of personal workstation disks in an nfs network. *Proceedings of the Sixth Systems Administration Conference (LISA VI) (USENIX Association: Berkeley, CA)*, page 1, 1992.

[12] P. Anderson. Towards a high level machine configuration system. *Proceedings of the Eighth Systems Administration Conference (LISA VIII) (USENIX Association: Berkeley, CA)*, page 19, 1994.

[13] S.P. Anderson, J.K. Goeree, and C.A. Holt. Stochastic game theory: Adjustment to equilibrium under noisy directional learning. *Working paper, University of Virginia*, 1999.

[14] G.M. Jones and S.M. Romig. Cloning customized hosts (or customizing cloned hosts). *Proceedings of the Fifth Large Installation Systems Administration Conference (LISA V) (USENIX Association: Berkeley, CA)*, page 233, 1991.

[15] S.P. Schaefer and S.R. Vemulakonda. newu: Multi-host user setup. *Proceedings of the Fourth Large Installation System Administrator's Conference (LISA IV) (USENIX Association: Berkeley, CA, 1990)*, page 23, 1990.

[16] J. Apisdort, K. Claffy, K. Thompson, and R. Wilder. Oc3mon: Flexible, affordable, high performance statistics collection. *Proceedings of the Tenth Systems Administration Conference (LISA X) (USENIX Association: Berkeley, CA)*, page 97, 1996.

[17] R. Apthorpe. A probabilistic approach to estimating computer system reliability. *Proceedings of the Fifteenth Systems Administration Conference (LISA XV) (USENIX Association: Berkeley, CA)*, page 31, 2001.

[18] B. Archer. Towards a posix standard for software administration. *Proceedings of the Seventh Systems Administration Conference (LISA VII) (USENIX Association: Berkeley, CA)*, page 67, 1993.

[19] B. Arnold. If you've seen one unix, you've seen them all. *Proceedings of the Fifth Large Installation Systems Administration Conference (LISA V) (USENIX Association: Berkeley, CA)*, page 11, 1991.

[20] B. Arnold. Accountworks: users create accounts on sql, notes, nt and unix. *Proceedings of the Twelfth Systems Administration Conference (LISA XII) (USENIX Association: Berkeley, CA)*, page 49, 1998.

[21] E. Arnold and C. Ruff. Configuration control and management. *Proceedings of the Fifth Large Installation Systems Administration Conference (LISA V) (USENIX Association: Berkeley, CA)*, page 195, 1991.

[22] SAGE/Usenix association. *http://www.usenix.org*.

[23] ATM. Asychronous transfer mode. *http://www.atmforum.com*.

[24] AT&T. Virtual network computing. *http://www.uk.research.att.com/vnc*.

[25] A.L. Barabási. *Linked*. (Perseus, Cambridge, MA), 2002.

[26] M.R. Barber. Increased server availability and flexibility through failover capability. *Proceedings of the Eleventh Systems Administration Conference (LISA XI) (USENIX Association: Berkeley, CA)*, page 89, 1997.

[27] J. Becker-Berlin. Software synchronization at the federal judicial center. *Proceedings of the Large Installation System Administration Workshop (USENIX Association: Berkeley, CA, 1987)*, page 12, 1987.

[28] B. Beecher. Dealing with lame delegations. *Proceedings of the Sixth Systems Administration Conference (LISA VI) (USENIX Association: Berkeley, CA)*, page 127, 1992.

[29] S.M. Bellovin. Security problems in the tcp/ip protocol suite. *Computer Communications Review*, 19:2:32–48, http://www.research.att.com/s̃mb/papers/ipext.pdf, 1989.

[30] BGP. Global routing table statistics. *http://bgp.potaroo.net*.

[31] BIND. *http://www.isc.org*.

[32] M. Bishop. Sharing accounts. *Proceedings of the Large Installation System Administration Workshop (USENIX Association: Berkeley, CA)*, page 36, 1987.

[33] J. Brandts and C.A. Holt. Naive bayesian learning and adjustment to equilibrium in signaling games. *Working paper, University of Virginia*, 1995.

[34] A.M. Breipohl. *Probabilistic Systems Analysis*. J. Wiley & Sons, New York, 1970.

[35] D.R. Brownbridge and L.F. Marshall. The newcastle connection or unixes of the world unite. *Software Practice and Experience*, 12:1147, 1982.

[36] M. Buchanan. *Nexus: Small Worlds and the Groundbreaking Science of Networks*. W.W.Norton & Co., New York, 2002.

[37] P. Bumbulis, D. Cowan, E. Giguère, and T. Stepien. Integrating unix within a microcomputer oriented development environment. *Proceedings of the Fifth Large Installation Systems Administration Conference (LISA V) (USENIX Association: Berkeley, CA)*, page 29, 1991.

[38] M. Burgess. Cfengine www site. *http://www.iu.hio.no/cfengine*.

[39] M. Burgess. Talk at the cern hepix meeting, France. 1994.

[40] M. Burgess. Lecture notes. *http://www.iu.hio.no/ mark/lectures*, 1995.

[41] M. Burgess. A site configuration engine. *Computing Systems*. MIT Press: Cambridge, MA, 8:309, 1995.

[42] M. Burgess. Automated system administration with feedback regulation. *Software Practice and Experience*, 28:1519, 1998.

[43] M. Burgess. Cfengine as a component of computer immune-systems. *Proceedings of the Norwegian Conference on Informatics*, 1998.

[44] M. Burgess. Computer immunology. *Proceedings of the Twelfth Systems Administration Conference (LISA XII) (USENIX Association: Berkeley, CA)*, page 283, 1998.

[45] M. Burgess. Managing os security with cfengine. *;login:*, 1999.

[46] M. Burgess. The kinematics of distributed computer transactions. *International Journal of Modern Physics*, **C**12:759–789, 2000.

[47] M. Burgess. On the theory of system administration. Submitted to *Science of Computer Programming*, 2000.

[48] M. Burgess. Theoretical system administration. *Proceedings of the Fourteenth Systems Administration Conference (LISA XIV) (USENIX Association: Berkeley, CA)*, page 1, 2000.

[49] M. Burgess. Cfengine's immunity model of evolving configuration management. Submitted to *Science of Computer Programming*, 2002.

[50] M. Burgess. Two dimensional time-series for anomaly detection and regulation in adaptive systems. *IFIP/IEEE 13th International Workshop on Distributed Systems: Operations and Management (DSOM 2002)*, page 169, 2002.

[51] M. Burgess. A rational approach to the predictability of quality of service for service level agreements. *IFIP/IEEE 14th International Workshop on Distributed Systems: Operations and Management (DSOM 2003)*, 2003.

[52] M. Burgess. *Theory of Network and System Administration*. J. Wiley & Sons, Chichester, 2004.

[53] M. Burgess and G. Canright. Scalability of peer configuration management in partially reliable and ad hoc networks. *Proceedings of the VII IFIP/IEEE IM Conference on Network Management*, page 293, 2003.

[54] M. Burgess, H. Haugerud, T. Reitan, and S. Straumsnes. Measuring host normality. *ACM Transactions on Computing Systems*, 20:125–160, 2001.

[55] M. Burgess and R. Ralston. Distributed resource administration using cfengine. *Software Practice and Experience*, 27:1083, 1997.

[56] M. Burgess and F.E. Sandnes. Predictable configuration management in a randomized scheduling framework. *IFIP/IEEE 12th International Workshop on Distributed Systems: Operations and Management (DSOM 2001)*, page 293, 2001.

[57] Linux Capabilities. Linux privs project. *http://www.kernel.org/pub/linux/libs/security/linux-privs*.

[58] S. Carter. Standards and guidelines for unix workstation installations. *Proceedings of the Workshop on Large Installation Systems Administration (USENIX Association: Berkeley, CA)*, page 51, 1988.

[59] J. Case, M. Fedor, M. Schoffstall, and J. Davin. The simple network management protocol. *RFC1155*, STD 16, 1990.

[60] R. Chahley. Next generation planning tool. *Proceedings of the Large Installation System Administration Workshop (USENIX Association: Berkeley, CA)*, page 19, 1987.

[61] D.B. Chapman and E.D. Zwicky. *Building Internet Firewalls*. O'Reilly & Assoc., California, 1995.

[62] N. Christenson. *Sendmail performance tuning*. Addison-Wesley, New York, 2002.

[63] N. Christenson, T. Bosserman, and D. Beckemeyer. A highly scalable electronic mail service using open systems. *Proceedings of the USENIX Symposium on Internet Technologies and Systems, (USENIX Association: Berkeley, CA)*, page 1, 1997.

[64] T. Christiansen. Op: a flexible tool for restricted superuser access. *Proceedings of the Workshop on Large Installation Systems Administration III (USENIX Association: Berkeley, CA)*, page 89, 1989.

[65] T. Kovacs, C.J. Yashinovitz, and J. Kalucki. An optical disk backup/restore system. *Proceedings of the Workshop on Large Installation Systems Administration III (USENIX Association: Berkeley, CA)*, page 123, 1989.

[66] A.C. Clarke. *How the World was One: Beyond the Global Village*. Bantam, Doubleday Dell, 1992.

[67] NTP client software. Clock synchronization software. *http://www.eecis.udel.edu/ ntp/software.html*.

[68] Cockroft and Pettit. *Sun Performance and Tuning*. Prentice Hall, New York, 1998.

[69] P. R. Cohen. *Empirical Methods for Artificial Intelligence*. MIT Press, Cambridge, MA, 1995.

[70] W. Colyer and W. Wong. Depot: a tool for managing software environments. *Proceedings of the Sixth Systems Administration Conference (LISA VI) (USENIX Association: Berkeley, CA)*, page 151, 1992.

[71] D.E. Comer and L.L. Peterson. Understanding naming in distributed systems. *Distributed Computing*, 3:51, 1989.

[72] The computer incident center. *http://www.ciac.llnl.gov*.

[73] W.C. Connelly. Unix login administration at bellcore. *Proceedings of the Workshop on Large Installation Systems Administration (USENIX Association: Berkeley, CA)*, page 13, 1988.

[74] Virtual Private Network Consortium. *http://www.vpnc.org*.

[75] M.A. Cooper. Spm: system for password management. *Proceedings of the Ninth Systems Administration Conference (LISA IX) (USENIX Association: Berkeley, CA)*, page 149, 1995.

[76] P. Coq and S. Jean. Sysview: a user-friendly environment for administration of distributed unix systems. *Proceedings of the Sixth Systems Administration Conference (LISA VI) (USENIX Association: Berkeley, CA)*, page 143, 1992.

[77] B. Corbridge, R. Henig, and C. Slater. Packet filtering in an ip router. *Proceedings of the Fifth Large Installation Systems Administration Conference (LISA V) (USENIX Association: Berkeley, CA)*, page 227, 1991.

[78] P. Cottrell. Password management at the University of Maryland. *Proceedings of the Large Installation System Administration Workshop (USENIX Association: Berkeley, CA, 1987)*, page 32, 1987.

[79] A. Couch and M. Gilfix. It's elementary, dear Watson: Applying logic programming to convergent system management processes. *Proceedings of the Thirteenth Systems Administration Conference (LISA XIII) (USENIX Association: Berkeley, CA)*, page 123, 1999.

[80] A.L. Couch. Visualizing huge tracefiles with xscal. *Proceedings of the Tenth Systems Administration Conference (LISA X) (USENIX Association: Berkeley, CA)*, page 51, 1996.

[81] N.H. Cuccia. The design and implementation of a mailhub electronic mail environment. *Proceedings of the Fifth Large Installation Systems Administration Conference (LISA V) (USENIX Association: Berkeley, CA)*, page 37, 1991.

[82] D.A. Curry, S.D. Kimery, K.C. De La Croix, and J.R. Schwab. Acmaint: an account creation and maintenance system for distributed unix systems. *Proceedings of the Fourth Large Installation System Administrator's Conference (LISA IV) (USENIX Association: Berkeley, CA, 1990)*, page 1, 1990.

[83] M.S. Cyganik. System administration in the andrew file system. *Proceedings of the Workshop on Large Installation Systems Administration (USENIX Association: Berkeley, CA)*, page 67, 1988.

[84] G.E. da Silveria. A configuration distribution system for heterogeneous networks. *Proceedings of the Twelfth Systems Administration Conference (LISA XII) (USENIX Association: Berkeley, CA)*, page 109, 1998.

[85] M. Dagenais, S. Boucher, R. Gérin-Lajoie, P. Laplante, and P. Mailhot. Lude: a distributed software library. *Proceedings of the Seventh Systems Administration Conference (LISA VII) (USENIX Association: Berkeley, CA)*, page 25, 1993.

[86] N. Damianou, N. Dulay, E.C. Lupu, and M. Sloman. Ponder: a language for specifying security and management policies for distributed systems. *Imperial College Research Report DoC 2000/1*, 2000.

[87] T. Darmohray. A sendmail.cf scheme for a large network. *Proceedings of the Fifth Large Installation Systems Administration Conference (LISA V) (USENIX Association: Berkeley, CA)*, page 45, 1991.

[88] D. Davis. Defective sign & encrypt in s/mime, pkcs#7, moss, pem, pgp, and xml. *Proceedings of the USENIX Technical Conference (USENIX Association: Berkeley, CA)*, page 65, 2001.

[89] Sleepcat Berkeley db project. *http://www.sleepycat.com*.

[90] A. de Leon. From thinnet to 10base-t from sys admin to network manager. *Proceedings of the Ninth Systems Administration Conference (LISA IX) (USENIX Association: Berkeley, CA)*, page 229, 1995.

[91] L. de Leon, M. Rodriquez, and B. Thompson. Our users have root! *Proceedings of the Seventh Systems Administration Conference (LISA VII) (USENIX Association: Berkeley, CA)*, page 17, 1993.

[92] S. DeSimone and C. Lombardi. Sysctl:a distributed control package. *Proceedings of the Seventh Systems Administration Conference (LISA VII) (USENIX Association: Berkeley, CA)*, page 131, 1993.

[93] P. D'haeseleer. An immunological approach to change detection: Theoretical results. In *9th IEEE Computer Security Foundations Workshop (1996)*.

[94] P. D'haeseleer, S. Forrest, and P. Helman. Submitted to *ACM Transactions on Information System Security*, 1997.

[95] Y. Diao, J.L. Hellerstein, and S. Parekh. Optimizing quality of service using fuzzy control. *IFIP/IEEE 13th International Workshop on Distributed Systems: Operations and Management (DSOM 2002)*, page 42, 2002.

[96] M. Dresher. *The Mathematics of Games of Strategy*. Dover, New York, 1961.

[97] D. Eadline. Extreme linux performance tuning. *Proceedings of the second workshop on extreme linux*. http://www.extremelinux.org.

[98] T. Eirich. Beam: a tool for flexible software update. *Proceedings of the Eighth Systems Administration Conference (LISA VIII) (USENIX Association: Berkeley, CA)*, page 75, 1994.

[99] R. Elling and M. Long. User-setup: a system for custom configuration of user environments, or helping users help themselves. *Proceedings of the Sixth Systems Administration Conference (LISA VI) (USENIX Association: Berkeley, CA)*, page 215, 1992.

[100] R. Emmaus, T.V. Erlandsen, and G.J. Kristiansen. *Network log analysis*. Oslo College dissertation, Oslo, 1998.

[101] K. Chan et al. Cops usage for policy provisioning (cops-pr). *RFC3084*, 2001.

[102] M.J. Ranum et al. Implementing a generalized tool for network monitoring. *Proceedings of the Eleventh Systems Administration Conference (LISA XI) (USENIX Association: Berkeley, CA)*, page 1, 1997.

[103] Ethernet. *http://www.gigabit-ethernet.org.*

[104] Ethics. *http://www.acm.org/constitution/code.html.*

[105] Ethics. *http://www4.ncsu.edu/unity/users/j/jherkert/ethics.html.*

[106] R. Evard. Managing the ever growing to-do list. *Proceedings of the Eighth Systems Administration Conference (LISA VIII) (USENIX Association: Berkeley, CA)*, page 111, 1994.

[107] R. Evard. Tenwen: the re-engineering of a computing environment. *Proceedings of the Eighth Systems Administration Conference (LISA VIII) (USENIX Association: Berkeley, CA)*, page 37, 1994.

[108] R. Evard. An analysis of unix system configuration. *Proceedings of the Eleventh Systems Administration Conference (LISA XI) (USENIX Association: Berkeley, CA)*, page 179, 1997.

[109] R. Evard and R. Leslie. Soft: a software environment abstraction mechanism. *Proceedings of the Eighth Systems Administration Conference (LISA VIII) (USENIX Association: Berkeley, CA)*, page 65, 1994.

[110] Host factory. software system. *URL: http://www.wv.com.*

[111] Dan Farmer, Brad Powell, and Matthew Archibald. Titan. *Proceedings of the Twelfth Systems Administration Conference (LISA XII) (USENIX Association: Berkeley, CA)*, 1998.

[112] M.K. Fenlon. A case study of network management. *Proceedings of the Large Installation System Administration Workshop (USENIX Association: Berkeley, CA)*, page 2, 1987.

[113] J. Finke. Monitoring usage of workstations with a relational database. *Proceedings of the Eighth Systems Administration Conference (LISA VIII) (USENIX Association: Berkeley, CA)*, page 149, 1994.

[114] R. Finkel and B. Sturgill. Tools for system administration in a heterogeneous environment. *Proceedings of the Workshop on Large Installation Systems Administration III (USENIX Association: Berkeley, CA)*, page 15, 1989.

[115] TIS firewall toolkit. *http://www.tis.com.*

[116] M. Fisk. Automating the administration of heterogeneous lans. *Proceedings of the Tenth Systems Administration Conference (LISA X) (USENIX Association: Berkeley, CA)*, page 181, 1996.

[117] M. Fletcher. Doit: a network software management tool. *Proceedings of the Sixth Systems Administration Conference (LISA VI) (USENIX Association: Berkeley, CA)*, page 189, 1992.

[118] S. Forrest, S. Hofmeyr, and A. Somayaji. *Communications of the ACM*, 40:88, 1997.

[119] S. Forrest, S. A. Hofmeyr, A. Somayaji, and T. A. Longstaff. In *Proceedings of 1996 IEEE Symposium on Computer Security and Privacy (1996)*.

[120] S. Forrest, A.S. Perelson, L. Allen, and R. Cherukuri. In *Proceedings of the 1994 IEEE Symposium on Research in Security and Privacy, Los Alamitos, CA, IEEE Computer Society Press (1994)*.

[121] S. Forrest, A. Somayaji, and D. Ackley. In *Proceedings of the Sixth Workshop on Hot Topics in Operating Systems*, Computer Society Press, Los Alamitos, CA:67–72 (1997).

[122] Æ. Frisch. *Essential Windows NT System Administration.* O' Reilly, 1998.

[123] Æ. Frisch. *Essential System Administration, Second Edition.* O' Reilly, 1995.

[124] Z. Fu and S.F. Wu. Automatic generation of ipsec/vpn security policies in an intra-domain environment. *Proceedings of the 12th International Workshop on Distributed System Operation and Management (IFIP/IEEE),* INRIA Press:279, 2001.

[125] J.L. Furlani. Modules: providing a flexible user environment. *Proceedings of the Fifth Large Installation Systems Administration Conference (LISA V) (USENIX Association: Berkeley, CA),* page 141, 1991.

[126] S. Garfinkel and G. Spafford. *Practical UNIX Security (2nd Edition).* O'Reilley & Assoc., California, 1998.

[127] J.E. Gaskin. *Mastering Netware 5.* Sybex, Network Press, Alameda, 1999.

[128] L. Girardin and D. Brodbeck. A visual approach for monitoring logs. *Proceedings of the Twelfth Systems Administration Conference (LISA XII) (USENIX Association: Berkeley, CA),* page 299, 1998.

[129] X. Gittler, W.P. Moore, and J. Rambhaskar. Morgan Stanley's aurora system. *Proceedings of the Ninth Systems Administration Conference (LISA IX) (USENIX Association: Berkeley, CA),* page 47, 1995.

[130] N. Goldenfeld and N.P. Kadanoff. Lessons from complexity. *Science,* 284:87, 1999.

[131] D. Gollmann. *Computer Security.* J. Wiley & Sons, Chichester, 1999.

[132] M. Gomberg, R. Evard, and C. Stacey. A comparison of large-scale software installation methods on nt and unix. *Proceedings of the Large Installation System Administration of Windows NT Conference (SAGE/USENIX),* page 37, 1998.

[133] W.H. Gray and A.K. Powers. Project accounting on a large-scale unix system. *Proceedings of the Workshop on Large Installation Systems Administration (USENIX Association: Berkeley, CA),* page 7, 1988.

[134] J. Greely. A flexible filesystem cleanup utility. *Proceedings of the Fifth Large Installation Systems Administration Conference (LISA V) (USENIX Association: Berkeley, CA),* page 105, 1991.

[135] J-C Grégoire. Delegation: uniformity in heterogeneous distributed administration. *Proceedings of the Seventh Systems Administration Conference (LISA VII) (USENIX Association: Berkeley, CA),* page 113, 1993.

[136] G.R. Grimmett and D.R. Stirzaker. *Probability and Random Processes (3rd edition).* Oxford Scientific Publications, Oxford, 2001.

[137] P. Gupta and P.R. Kumar. The capacity of wireless networks. *IEEE Trans. Info. Theory,* 46(2):388–404, 2000.

[138] B. Hagemark and K. Zadeck. Site: a language and system for configuring many computers as one computer site. *Proceedings of the Workshop on Large Installation Systems Administration III (USENIX Association: Berkeley, CA)*, page 1, 1989.

[139] P. Hall. Resource duplication for 100 percent uptime. *Proceedings of the Large Installation System Administration Workshop (USENIX Association: Berkeley, CA)*, page 43, 1987.

[140] S. Hambridge and J.C. Sedayao. Horses and barn doors: evolution of corporate guidelines for internet usage. *Proceedings of the Seventh Systems Administration Conference (LISA VII) (USENIX Association: Berkeley, CA)*, page 9, 1993.

[141] S.E. Hansen and E.T. Atkins. Automated system monitoring and notification with swatch. *Proceedings of the Seventh Systems Administration Conference (LISA VII) (USENIX Association: Berkeley, CA)*, page 145, 1993.

[142] D.R. Hardy and H.M. Morreale. Buzzerd: automated system monitoring with notification in a network environment. *Proceedings of the Sixth Systems Administration Conference (LISA VI) (USENIX Association: Berkeley, CA)*, page 203, 1992.

[143] R. Harker. Selectively rejecting spam using sendmail. *Proceedings of the Eleventh Systems Administration Conference (LISA XI) (USENIX Association: Berkeley, CA)*, page 205, 1997.

[144] K. Harkness. A centralized multi-system problem tracking system. *Proceedings of the Large Installation System Administration Workshop (USENIX Association: Berkeley, CA)*, page 40, 1987.

[145] M. Harlander. Central system administration in a heterogeneous unix environmental genuadmin. *Proceedings of the Eighth Systems Administration Conference (LISA VIII) (USENIX Association: Berkeley, CA)*, page 1, 1994.

[146] J.A. Harris. The design and implementation of a network account management system. *Proceedings of the Tenth Systems Administration Conference (LISA X) (USENIX Association: Berkeley, CA)*, page 33, 1996.

[147] H.E. Harrison. Maintaining a consistent software environment. *Proceedings of the Large Installation System Administration Workshop (USENIX Association: Berkeley, CA)*, page 16, 1987.

[148] H.E. Harrison. A flexible backup system for large disk farms, or what to do with 20 gigabytes. *Proceedings of the Workshop on Large Installation Systems Administration (USENIX Association: Berkeley, CA)*, page 33, 1988.

[149] H.E. Harrison. So many workstations, so little time. *Proceedings of the Sixth Systems Administration Conference (LISA VI) (USENIX Association: Berkeley, CA)*, page 79, 1992.

[150] H.E. Harrison, M.C. Mitchell, and M.E. Shaddock. Pong: a flexible network services monitoring system. *Proceedings of the Eighth Systems Administration Conference (LISA VIII) (USENIX Association: Berkeley, CA)*, page 167, 1994.

[151] S. Hecht. The andrew backup system. *Proceedings of the Workshop on Large Installation Systems Administration (USENIX Association: Berkeley, CA)*, page 35, 1988.

[152] E. Heilman. Priv: an exercise in administrative expansion. *Proceedings of the Large Installation System Administration Workshop (USENIX Association: Berkeley, CA)*, page 38, 1987.

[153] J. Hietaniemi. ipasswd: Proactive password security. *Proceedings of the Sixth Systems Administration Conference (LISA VI) (USENIX Association: Berkeley, CA)*, page 105, 1992.

[154] N. Hillary. Implementing a consistent system over many hosts. *Proceedings of the Workshop on Large Installation Systems Administration III (USENIX Association: Berkeley, CA)*, page 69, 1989.

[155] S. A. Hofmeyr and S. Forrest. Immunizing computer networks: Getting all the machines in your network to fight the hacker disease. *1999 IEEE Symposium on Security and Privacy, 9–12* May.

[156] S. A. Hofmeyr, A. Somayaji, and S. Forrest. Intrusion detection using sequences of system calls. *Journal of Computer Security*, 6:151–180, 1998.

[157] C. Hogan. Decentralising distributed systems administration. *Proceedings of the Ninth Systems Administration Conference (LISA IX) (USENIX Association: Berkeley, CA)*, page 139, 1995.

[158] C.B. Hommel. System backup in a distributed responsibility environment. *Proceedings of the Large Installation System Administration Workshop (USENIX Association: Berkeley, CA)*, page 8, 1987.

[159] P. Hoogenboom and J. Lepreau. Computer system performance problem detection using time series models. *Proceedings of the USENIX Technical Conference (USENIX Association: Berkeley, CA)*, page 15, 1993.

[160] J.D. Howard. An analysis of security incidents on the internet. *http://www.cert.org/research/JHThesis/Start.html*, 1997.

[161] B. Howell and B. Satdeva. We have met the enemy. An informal survey of policy practices in the internetworked community. *Proceedings of the Fifth Large Installation Systems Administration Conference (LISA V) (USENIX Association: Berkeley, CA)*, page 159, 1991.

[162] D. Hughes. Using visualization in system administration. *Proceedings of the Tenth Systems Administration Conference (LISA X) (USENIX Association: Berkeley, CA)*, page 59, 1996.

[163] B.H. Hunter. Password administration for multiple large scale systems. *Proceedings of the Workshop on Large Installation Systems Administration (USENIX Association: Berkeley, CA)*, page 1, 1988.

[164] T. Hunter and S. Wanatabe. Guerilla system administration: scaling small group administration to a larger installed base. *Proceedings of the Seventh Systems Administration Conference (LISA VII) (USENIX Association: Berkeley, CA)*, page 99, 1993.

[165] IANA. Internet assigned numbers authority (port number delegation). *http://www.iana.org*.

[166] IEEE. A standard classification for software anomalies. *IEEE Computer Society Press*, 1992.

[167] ITU-T. *Open Systems Interconnection – The Directory: Overview of Concepts, models and service. Recommendation X.500.* International Telecommunications Union, Geneva, 1993.

[168] B. Jacob and N. Shoemaker. The Myer-Briggs type indicator: an interpersonal tool for system administrators. *Proceedings of the 7th Systems Administration Conference LISA (supplement), (SAGE/USENIX)*, page 7, 1993.

[169] H. Jaffee. Restoring from multiple tape dumps. *Proceedings of the Large Installation System Administration Workshop (USENIX Association: Berkeley, CA)*, page 9, 1987.

[170] D. Joiret. Administration of a unix machine network. *Proceedings of the Large Installation System Administration Workshop (USENIX Association: Berkeley, CA)*, page 1, 1987.

[171] V. Jones and D. Schrodel. Balancing security and convenience. *Proceedings of the Large Installation System Administration Workshop (USENIX Association: Berkeley, CA)*, page 5, 1987.

[172] W.H. Bent Jr. System administration as a user interface: an extended metaphor. *Proceedings of the Seventh Systems Administration Conference (LISA VII) (USENIX Association: Berkeley, CA)*, page 209, 1993.

[173] H. Kaplan. Highly automated low personnel system administration in a Wall Street environment. *Proceedings of the Eighth Systems Administration Conference (LISA VIII) (USENIX Association: Berkeley, CA)*, page 185, 1994.

[174] Hironori Kasahara and Seinosuke Narita. Practical multiprocessor scheduling algorithms for efficient parallel processing. *IEEE Transactions on Computers*, C-33 (11):1023–1029, 1984.

[175] J.O. Kephart. A biologically inspired immune system for computers. *Proceedings of the Fourth International Workshop on the Synthesis and Simulation of Living Systems (MIT Press. Cambridge, MA)*, page 130, 1994.

[176] Linux kernel site. http://www.linux.org.

[177] Y.W. Kim. Electronic mail maintenance/distribution. *Proceedings of the Large Installation System Administration Workshop (USENIX Association: Berkeley, CA)*, page 27, 1987.

[178] R.W. Kint. Scrape: System configuration resource and process exception. *Proceedings of the Fifth Large Installation Systems Administration Conference (LISA V) (USENIX Association: Berkeley, CA)*, page 217, 1991.

[179] R.W. Kint, C.V. Gale, and A.B. Liwen. Administration of a dynamic heterogeneous network. *Proceedings of the Workshop on Large Installation Systems Administration III (USENIX Association: Berkeley, CA)*, page 59, 1989.

[180] K. Kistlitzin. Network monitoring by scripts. *Proceedings of the Fourth Large Installation System Administrator's Conference (LISA IV) (USENIX Association: Berkeley, CA)*, page 101, 1990.

[181] N. Klasen. *Directory Services for Linux, in Comparison with Novell NDS and Microsoft Active Directory*. Department of Computer Science MSc Thesis, Rheinisch-Westfälische Technische Hochschule, Aachen, Germany, 2001.

[182] D. Koblas and P.M. Moriarty. Pits: a request management system. *Proceedings of the Sixth Systems Administration Conference (LISA VI) (USENIX Association: Berkeley, CA)*, page 197, 1992.

[183] C. Koenigsberg. Release of replicated software in the vice file system. *Proceedings of the Large Installation System Administration Workshop (USENIX Association: Berkeley, CA)*, page 14, 1987.

[184] R. Kolstad. A next step in backup and restore technology. *Proceedings of the Fifth Large Installation Systems Administration Conference (LISA V) (USENIX Association: Berkeley, CA)*, page 73, 1991.

[185] R. Kolstad. Tuning sendmail for large mailing lists. *Proceedings of the Eleventh Systems Administration Conference (LISA XI) (USENIX Association: Berkeley, CA)*, page 195, 1997.

[186] C. Kubicki. Customer satisfaction metrics and measurement. *Proceedings of the Sixth Systems Administration Conference (LISA VI) (USENIX Association: Berkeley, CA)*, page 63, 1992.

[187] C. Kubicki. The system administration maturity model: Samm. *Proceedings of the Seventh Systems Administration Conference (LISA VII) (USENIX Association: Berkeley, CA)*, page 213, 1993.

[188] D. Kuncicky and B.A. Wynn. *Educating and Training System Administrators: a survey*. SAGE, Short Topics in System Administration, 1998.

[189] The l0pht. *http://www.l0pht.com*.

[190] E.C. Leeper. Login management for large installations. *Proceedings of the Large Installation System Administration Workshop (USENIX Association: Berkeley, CA)*, page 35, 1987.

[191] R. Lehman, G. Carpenter, and N. Hien. Concurrent network management with a distributed management tool. *Proceedings of the Sixth Systems Administration Conference (LISA VI) (USENIX Association: Berkeley, CA)*, page 235, 1992.

[192] W.E. Leland, M. Taqqu, W. Willinger, and D. Wilson. On the self-similar nature of ethernet traffic. *IEEE/ACM Transactions on Networking*, pages 1–15, 1994.

[193] J. Li, C. Blake, D.S.J. DeCouto, H.I. Lee, and R. Morris. Capacity of ad hoc wireless networks. *Proc. 7th ACM Intl. Conf. on Mobile Computing and Networking*, pages 61–69, 2001.

[194] D. Libes. Using *expect* to automate system administration tasks. *Proceedings of the Fourth Large Installation System Administrator's Conference (LISA IV) (USENIX Association: Berkeley, CA)*, page 107, 1990.

[195] D. Lilly. Administration of network passwd files and nfs file access. *Proceedings of the Workshop on Large Installation Systems Administration (USENIX Association: Berkeley, CA)*, page 3, 1988.

[196] T. Limoncelli, T. Reingold, R. Narayan, and R. Loura. Creating a network for lucent bell labs south. *Proceedings of the Eleventh Systems Administration Conference (LISA XI) (USENIX Association: Berkeley, CA)*, page 123, 1997.

[197] T.A. Limoncelli. Deconstructing user requests and the nine step model. *Proceedings of the Thirteenth Systems Administration Conference (LISA XIII) (USENIX Association: Berkeley, CA)*, page 35, 1999.

[198] L.K.C. Leighton. Nt domains for unix. *Proceedings of the Large Installation System Administration of Windows NT Conference (SAGE/USENIX)*, page 85, 1998.

[199] S.W. Lodin. The corporate software bank. *Proceedings of the Seventh Systems Administration Conference (LISA VII) (USENIX Association: Berkeley, CA)*, page 33, 1993.

[200] M. Loukides. *System Performance Tuning (2nd edition)*. O'Reilley, California, 2002.

[201] K. Manheimer, B.A. Warsaw, S.N. Clark, and W. Rowe. The depot: a framework for sharing software installation across organizational and unix platform boundaries. *Proceedings of the Fourth Large Installation System Administrator's Conference (LISA IV) (USENIX Association: Berkeley, CA)*, page 37, 1990.

[202] P. Maniago. Consulting via mail at andrew. *Proceedings of the Large Installation System Administration Workshop (USENIX Association: Berkeley, CA)*, page 22, 1987.

[203] C. Manning and T. Irvin. Upgrading 150 workstations in a single sitting. *Proceedings of the 7th Systems Administration Conference LISA (supplement), (SAGE/USENIX)*, page 17, 1993.

[204] J.P. Martin-Flatin. Push vs. pull in web-based network management. *Proceedings of the VI IFIP/IEEE IM Conference on Network Management*, page 3, 1999.

[205] M. Matsushita. Telecommunication management network. *NTT Review*, 3:117–122, 1991.

[206] J. Maynard-Smith. *Evolution and the Theory of Games*. Cambridge University Press, Cambridge, 1981.

[207] D. McNutt. Role based system administration or who, what, where, how. *Proceedings of the Seventh Systems Administration Conference (LISA VII) (USENIX Association: Berkeley, CA)*, page 107, 1993.

[208] D. McNutt. Where did all the bytes go? *Proceedings of the Seventh Systems Administration Conference (LISA VII) (USENIX Association: Berkeley, CA)*, page 157, 1993.

[209] S. McRobert. From twisting country lanes to multi-lane ethernet superhighways. *Proceedings of the Ninth Systems Administration Conference (LISA IX) (USENIX Association: Berkeley, CA)*, page 221, 1995.

[210] J.T. Meek, E.S. Eichert, and K. Takayama. Wide area network ecology. *Proceedings of the Twelfth Systems Administration Conference (LISA XII) (USENIX Association: Berkeley, CA)*, page 149, 1998.

[211] A.J. Meggitt and T.D. Ritchey. *Windows NT User Administration*. O' Reilly, 1997.

[212] E.S. Menter. Managing the mission critical environment. *Proceedings of the Seventh Systems Administration Conference (LISA VII) (USENIX Association: Berkeley, CA)*, page 81, 1993.

[213] M. Metz and H. Kaye. Deejay: The dump jockey: a heterogeneous network backup system. *Proceedings of the Sixth Systems Administration Conference (LISA VI) (USENIX Association: Berkeley, CA)*, page 115, 1992.

[214] Sun Microsystems. *Solstice system documentation*. http://www.sun.com.

[215] M.M. Midden. Academic computing services and systems (acss). *Proceedings of the Large Installation System Administration Workshop (USENIX Association: Berkeley, CA)*, page 30, 1987.

[216] J.E. Miller. Managing an ever-changing user database. *Proceedings of the 7th Systems Administration Conference LISA (supplement), (SAGE/USENIX)*, page 1, 1993.

[217] T. Miller, C. Stirlen, and E. Nemeth. Satool: A system administrator's cockpit, an implementation. *Proceedings of the Seventh Systems Administration Conference (LISA VII) (USENIX Association: Berkeley, CA)*, page 119, 1993.

[218] K. Montgomery and D. Reynolds. Filesystem backups in a heterogeneous environment. *Proceedings of the Workshop on Large Installation Systems Administration III (USENIX Association: Berkeley, CA)*, page 95, 1989.

[219] R. Morris and K. Thompson. Password security: A case history. *Communication of the ACM*, 22:594, 1979.

[220] R.T. Morris. A weakness in the 4.2 bsd unix tcp/ip software. *Computer Science Technical Report*, 117:ftp://ftp.research.att.com/dist/internet_security/117.ps.Z.

[221] A. Mott. Link globally, act locally: a centrally maintained database of symlinks. *Proceedings of the Fifth Large Installation Systems Administration Conference (LISA V) (USENIX Association: Berkeley, CA)*, page 127, 1991.

[222] J.F. Nash. *Essays on Game Theory*. Edward Elgar, Cheltenham, 1996.

[223] E. Nemeth, G. Synder, S. Seebass, and T.R. Hein. *Unix System Administration Handbook, third edition*. Prentice Hall, 2000.

[224] Nessus. Nessus. *http://www.nessus.org*.

[225] J.V. Neumann and O. Morgenstern. *Theory of Games and Economic Behaviour*. Princeton University Press, Princeton, 1944.

[226] E.W. Norwood. Transitioning users to a supported environment. *Proceedings of the Workshop on Large Installation Systems Administration (USENIX Association: Berkeley, CA)*, page 45, 1988.

[227] U.S. Nuclear Regulatory Commission NRC. *Fault Tree Handbook*. NUREG-0492, Springfield, 1981.

[228] T. Oetiker. Mrtg–the multi router traffic grapher. *Proceedings of the Twelfth Systems Administration Conference (LISA XII) (USENIX Association: Berkeley, CA)*, page 141, 1998.

[229] J. Okamoto. Nightly: how to handle multiple scripts on multiple machines with one configuration file. *Proceedings of the Sixth Systems Administration Conference (LISA VI) (USENIX Association: Berkeley, CA)*, page 171, 1992.

[230] S. Omari, R. Boutaba, and O. Cherakaoui. Policies in snmpv3-based management. *Proceedings of the VI IFIP/IEEE IM Conference on Network Management*, page 797, 1999.

[231] R. Osterlund. Pikt: Problem informant/killer tool. *Proceedings of the Fourteenth Systems Administration Conference (LISA XIV) (USENIX Association: Berkeley, CA)*, page 147, 2000.

[232] Hewlett Packard. *Openview*.

[233] Palantir. The palantir was a project run by the University of Oslo Centre for Information Technology (usit). Details can be obtained from *palantirusit.uio.no*. and *http://www.palantir.uio.no*. I am informed that this project is now terminated.

[234] P.E. Pareseghian. A simple incremental file backup system. *Proceedings of the Workshop on Large Installation Systems Administration (USENIX Association: Berkeley, CA)*, page 41, 1988.

[235] D.A. Patterson and J.L. Hennessy. *Computer Organization and Design.* Morgan-Kaufmann, San Franciso, 1998.

[236] V. Paxson. Bro: A system for detecting network intruders in real time. *Proceedings of the 7th Security Symposium. (USENIX Association: Berkeley, CA)*, 1998.

[237] V. Paxson and S. Floyd. Wide area traffic: the failure of poisson modelling. *IEEE/ACM Transactions on Networking*, 3(3):226, 1995.

[238] P.D'haeseleer, S. Forrest, and P. Helman. An immunological approach to change detection: algorithms, analysis, and implications. In *Proceedings of the 1996 IEEE Symposium on Computer Security and Privacy* (1996).

[239] PHRACK. *http://www.phrack.com.*

[240] C. Pierce. The igor system administration tool. *Proceedings of the Tenth Systems Administration Conference (LISA X) (USENIX Association: Berkeley, CA)*, page 9, 1996.

[241] M. Poepping. Backup and restore for unix system. *Proceedings of the Large Installation System Administration Workshop (USENIX Association: Berkeley, CA)*, page 10, 1987.

[242] H. Pomeranz. Plod: keep track of what you are doing. *Proceedings of the Seventh Systems Administration Conference (LISA VII) (USENIX Association: Berkeley, CA)*, page 183, 1993.

[243] P. Powell and J. Mason. Lprng–an enhanced print spooler system. *Proceedings of the Ninth Systems Administration Conference (LISA IX) (USENIX Association: Berkeley, CA)*, page 13, 1995.

[244] W. Curtis Preston. Using gigabyte ethernet to backup six terabytes. *Proceedings of the Twelfth Systems Administration Conference (LISA XII) (USENIX Association: Berkeley, CA)*, page 87, 1998.

[245] W.C. Preston. *Unix Backup and Recovery.* O'Reilly, London, 1999.

[246] Spam prevention. *http://www.pobox.com/ gsutter/junkfilter/* for details.

[247] FreeS/WAN project. *http://www.xs4all.nl/ freeswan.*

[248] Webmin project. *http://www.webmin.com.*

[249] D. Pukatzki and J. Schumann. Autoload: the network management system. *Proceedings of the Sixth Systems Administration Conference (LISA VI) (USENIX Association: Berkeley, CA)*, page 97, 1992.

[250] R. Walters. Tracking hardware configurations in a heterogeneous network with syslogd. *Proceedings of the Ninth Systems Administration Conference (LISA IX) (USENIX Association: Berkeley, CA)*, page 241, 1995.

[251] I. Reguero, D. Foster, and I. Deloose. Large scale print spool service. *Proceedings of the Twelfth Systems Administration Conference (LISA XII) (USENIX Association: Berkeley, CA)*, page 229, 1998.

[252] P. Riddle, P. Danckeart, and M. Metaferia. Agus: an automatic multiplatform account generation system. *Proceedings of the Ninth Systems Administration Conference (LISA IX) (USENIX Association: Berkeley, CA)*, page 171, 1995.

[253] Token ring. *http://www.data.com/tutorials/tokenring.html.*

[254] M.F. Ringel and T.A. Limoncelli. Adverse termination procedures or how to fire a system administrator. *Proceedings of the Thirteenth Systems Administration Conference (LISA XIII) (USENIX Association: Berkeley, CA)*, page 45, 1999.

[255] G.B. Rodosek. Quality aspects in IT service management. *IFIP/IEEE 13th International Workshop on Distributed Systems: Operations and Management (DSOM 2002)*, page 82, 2002.

[256] M. Rodriquez. Software distribution in a network environment. *Proceedings of the Large Installation System Administration Workshop (USENIX Association: Berkeley, CA)*, page 20, 1987.

[257] S.M. Romig. Backup at Ohio State, take 2. *Proceedings of the Fourth Large Installation System Administrator's Conference (LISA IV) (USENIX Association: Berkeley, CA)*, page 137, 1990.

[258] M. Rosenstein and E. Peisach. Mkserv: workstation customization and privatization. *Proceedings of the Sixth Systems Administration Conference (LISA VI) (USENIX Association: Berkeley, CA)*, page 89, 1992.

[259] J.P. Rouillard and R.B. Martin. Config: a mechanism for installing and tracking system configurations. *Proceedings of the Eighth Systems Administration Conference (LISA VIII) (USENIX Association: Berkeley, CA)*, page 9, 1994.

[260] J.P. Rouillard and R.B. Martin. Depot-lite: a mechanism for managing software. *Proceedings of the Eighth Systems Administration Conference (LISA VIII) (USENIX Association: Berkeley, CA)*, page 83, 1994.

[261] G. Rudorfer. Managing pc operating systems a revision control system. *Proceedings of the Eleventh Systems Administration Conference (LISA XI) (USENIX Association: Berkeley, CA)*, page 79, 1997.

[262] N. Sammons. Multi-platform interrogation and reporting with rscan. *Proceedings of the Ninth Systems Administration Conference (LISA IX) (USENIX Association: Berkeley, CA)*, 1995.

[263] F.E. Sandnes. Scheduling partially ordered events in a randomized framework–empirical results and implications for automatic configuration management. *Proceedings of the Fifteenth Systems Administration Conference (LISA XV) (USENIX Association: Berkeley, CA)*, page 47, 2001.

[264] B. Satdeva and P.M. Moriarty. Fdist: A domain based file distribution system for a heterogeneous environment. *Proceedings of the Fifth Large Installation Systems Administration Conference (LISA V) (USENIX Association: Berkeley, CA)*, page 109, 1991.

[265] P. Schafer. Is centralized system administration the answer? *Proceedings of the Sixth Systems Administration Conference (LISA VI) (USENIX Association: Berkeley, CA)*, page 55, 1992.

[266] G.L. Schaps and P. Bishop. A practical approach to nfs response time monitoring. *Proceedings of the Seventh Systems Administration Conference (LISA VII) (USENIX Association: Berkeley, CA)*, page 165, 1993.

[267] J. Scharf and P. Vixie. Sends: a tool for managing domain naming and electronic mail in a large organization. *Proceedings of the Eighth Systems Administration Conference (LISA VIII) (USENIX Association: Berkeley, CA)*, page 93, 1994.

[268] J. Schönwälder. Specific simple network management tools. *Proceedings of the Fifteenth Systems Administration Conference (LISA XV) (USENIX Association: Berkeley, CA)*, page 109, 2001.

[269] J. Schönwälder. Evolution of open source snmp tools. *Proceedings of the 3rd International System Administration and Networking Conference (SANE2002)*, page 84, 2002.

[270] J. Schönwälder and H. Langendörfer. How to keep track of your network configuration. *Proceedings of the Seventh Systems Administration Conference (LISA VII) (USENIX Association: Berkeley, CA)*, page 189, 1993.

[271] K. Schwartz, L. Cottrell, and M. Dart. Adventures in evolution of a high-bandwidth network for central servers. *Proceedings of the Eighth Systems Administration Conference (LISA VIII) (USENIX Association: Berkeley, CA)*, page 159, 1994.

[272] K.L. Schwartz. Optimal routing of ip packets to multi-homed hosts. *Proceedings of the Sixth Systems Administration Conference (LISA VI) (USENIX Association: Berkeley, CA)*, page 9, 1992.

[273] J. Sellens. Software maintenance in a campus environment: the xhier approach. *Proceedings of the Fifth Large Installation Systems Administration Conference (LISA V) (USENIX Association: Berkeley, CA)*, page 21, 1991.

[274] M.I. Seltzer and C. Small. Self-monitoring and self-adapting operating systems. *Proceedings of the Sixth Workshop on Hot Topics in Operating Systems*, 1997.

[275] Sendmail. *http://www.sendmail.org*.

[276] M.E. Shaddock, M.C. Mitchell, and H.E. Harrison. How to upgrade 1500 workstations on Saturday and still have time to mow the yard on Sunday. *Proceedings of the Ninth Systems Administration Conference (LISA IX) (USENIX Association: Berkeley, CA)*, page 59, 1995.

[277] C.E. Shannon and W. Weaver. *The mathematical theory of communication.* University of Illinois Press, Urbana, 1949.

[278] J.M. Sharp. Request: a tool for training new sys admins and managing old ones. *Proceedings of the Sixth Systems Administration Conference (LISA VI) (USENIX Association: Berkeley, CA)*, page 69, 1992.

[279] Root shell security site. *http://www.rootshell.com*.

[280] C. Shipley and C. Wang. Monitoring activity on a large unix network with perl and syslogd. *Proceedings of the Fifth Large Installation Systems Administration Conference (LISA V) (USENIX Association: Berkeley, CA)*, page 209, 1991.

[281] S. Shumway. Issues in on-line backup. *Proceedings of the Fifth Large Installation Systems Administration Conference (LISA V) (USENIX Association: Berkeley, CA)*, page 81, 1991.

[282] T. Sigmon. Automatic software distribution. *Proceedings of the Large Installation System Administration Workshop (USENIX Association: Berkeley, CA)*, page 21, 1987.

[283] J. Da Silva and Ólafur Guðmundsson. The amanda network backup manager. *Proceedings of the Seventh Systems Administration Conference (LISA VII) (USENIX Association: Berkeley, CA)*, page 171, 1993.

[284] N. Simicich. Yabs. *Proceedings of the Workshop on Large Installation Systems Administration III (USENIX Association: Berkeley, CA)*, page 109, 1989.

[285] S. Simmons. Making a large network reliable. *Proceedings of the Workshop on Large Installation Systems Administration (USENIX Association: Berkeley, CA, 1988)*, page 47, 1988.

[286] S. Simmons. Life without root. *Proceedings of the Fourth Large Installation System Administrator's Conference (LISA IV) (USENIX Association: Berkeley, CA)*, page 89, 1990.

[287] K.C. Smallwood. Guidelines and tools for software maintenance. *Proceedings of the Fourth Large Installation System Administrator's Conference (LISA IV) (USENIX Association: Berkeley, CA)*, page 47, 1990.

[288] J.M. Smith. Creating an environment for novice users. *Proceedings of the Large Installation System Administration Workshop (USENIX Association: Berkeley, CA)*, page 37, 1987.

[289] T. Smith. Excelan administration. *Proceedings of the Large Installation System Administration Workshop (USENIX Association: Berkeley, CA)*, page 4, 1987.

[290] A. Somayaji and S. Forrest. Automated response using system-call delays. *Proceedings of the 9th USENIX Security Symposium (USENIX Association; Berkeley, CA)*, page 185, 2000.

[291] A. Somayaji, S. Hofmeyr, and S. Forrest. Principles of a computer immune system. *New Security Paradigms Workshop, ACM*, September 1997:75–82.

[292] B. Spence. Spy: a unix file systemsecurity monitor. *Proceedings of the Workshop on Large Installation Systems Administration III (USENIX Association: Berkeley, CA)*, page 75, 1989.

[293] H.L. Stern and B.L. Wong. Nfs performance and network loading. *Proceedings of the Sixth Systems Administration Conference (LISA VI) (USENIX Association: Berkeley, CA)*, page 33, 1992.

[294] R. Stevens. *Advanced Programming in the UNIX Environment*. Addison-Wesley, Reading, 1992.

[295] R. Stevens. *TCP/IP Illustrated Vols 1–3*. Addison-Wesley, Reading, 1994–6.

[296] R.J. Stolfa. Simplifying system administration tasks: the uams approach. *Proceedings of the Seventh Systems Administration Conference (LISA VII) (USENIX Association: Berkeley, CA)*, page 203, 1993.

[297] K. Stone. System cloning at hp-sdd. *Proceedings of the Large Installation System Administration Workshop (USENIX Association: Berkeley, CA)*, page 18, 1987.

[298] Tivoli systems/IBM. *Tivoli software products. http://www.tivoli.com.*

[299] L.W. Taylor and J.R. Hayes. An automated student account system. *Proceedings of the Large Installation System Administration Workshop (USENIX Association: Berkeley, CA)*, page 29, 1987.

[300] The Computer Emergency Response Team. *http://www.cert.org.*

[301] G.S. Thomas, J.O. Schroeder, M.E. Orcutt, D.C. Johnson, J.T. Simmelink, and J.P. Moore. Unix host administration in a heterogeneous distributed computing environment. *Proceedings of the Tenth Systems Administration Conference (LISA X) (USENIX Association: Berkeley, CA)*, page 43, 1996.

[302] W.F. Tichy. Rcs: a system for version control. *Software Practice and Experience*, 15:637, 1985.

[303] Tuning tips. *http://ps-ax.com.*

[304] S. Traugott. Why order matters: Turing equivalence in automated systems administration. *Proceedings of the Sixteenth Systems Administration Conference (LISA XVI) (USENIX Association: Berkeley, CA)*, page 99, 2002.

[305] S. Traugott and J. Huddleston. Bootstrapping an infrastructure. *Proceedings of the Twelfth Systems Administration Conference (LISA XII) (USENIX Association: Berkeley, CA)*, page 181, 1998.

[306] M. Urban. Udb: Rand's group and user database. *Proceedings of the Fourth Large Installation System Administrator's Conference (LISA IV) (USENIX Association: Berkeley, CA)*, page 11, 1990.

[307] D.L. Urner. Pinpointing system performance issues. *Proceedings of the Eleventh Systems Administration Conference (LISA XI) (USENIX Association: Berkeley, CA)*, page 141, 1997.

[308] P. van Epp and B. Baines. Dropping the mainframe without crushing the users: mainframe to distributed unix in nine months. *Proceedings of the Sixth Systems Administration Conference (LISA VI) (USENIX Association: Berkeley, CA)*, page 39, 1992.

[309] R.R. Vangala, M.J. Cripps, and R.G. Varadarajan. Software distribution and management in a networked environment. *Proceedings of the Sixth Systems Administration Conference (LISA VI) (USENIX Association: Berkeley, CA)*, page 163, 1992.

[310] A. Vasilatos. Automated dumping at project athena. *Proceedings of the Large Installation System Administration Workshop (USENIX Association: Berkeley, CA)*, page 7, 1987.

[311] Wietse Venema. Tcp wrappers. *http://ciac.llnl.gov/ciac/ToolsUnixNetSec.html*.

[312] J.S. Vöckler. *http://www.rvs.uni-hannover.de/people/voeckler/tune/en/tune.html*.

[313] J. von Neumann. The general and logical theory of automata. Reprinted in vol 5 of his *Collected Works*, 1948.

[314] J. von Neumann. Probabilistic logics and the synthesis of reliable organisms from unreliable components. Reprinted in vol 5 of his *Collected Works*, 1952.

[315] W.A.Doster, Y.-H. Leong, and S.J. Matteson. Uniqname overview. *Proceedings of the Fourth Large Installation System Administrator's Conference (LISA IV) (USENIX Association: Berkeley, CA)*, page 27, 1990.

[316] L. Wall and R. Schwarz. *Programming perl.* O'Reilly & Assoc., California, 1990.

[317] C. Warrender, S. Forrest, and B. Pearlmutter. Detecting intrusions using system calls: Alternative data models. Submitted to the *1999 IEEE Symposium on Security and Privacy*, 1999.

[318] A. Watson and B. Nelson. Laddis: A multi-vendor and vendor-neutral spec nfs benchmark. *Proceedings of the Sixth Systems Administration Conference (LISA VI) (USENIX Association: Berkeley, CA)*, page 17, 1992.

[319] D.J. Watts. *Small Worlds*. Princeton University Press, Princeton, 1999.

[320] L.Y. Weissler. Backup without tapes. *Proceedings of the Fifth Large Installation Systems Administration Conference (LISA V) (USENIX Association: Berkeley, CA)*, page 191, 1991.

[321] J. Heiser and W.G. Kruse. *Computer Forensics Essentials*. Addison-Wesley, New York, 2001.

[322] B. White, W.T. Ng, and B.K. Hillyer. Performance comparison of ide and scsi disks. *Technical report, Bell Labs*, 2001.

[323] E.T. Whittaker and G. Robinson. *Calculus of observations*. Blackie and Son Ltd., London, 1929.

[324] W. Willinger and V. Paxson. Where mathematics meets the internet. *Notices of the Am. Math. Soc.*, 45(8):961, 1998.

[325] W. Willinger, V. Paxson, and M.S. Taqqu. Self-similarity and heavy tails: structural modelling of network traffic. In *A Practical Guide to Heavy Tails: Statistical Techniques and Applications*, pages 27–53, 1996.

[326] C.E. Wills, K. Cadwell, and W. Marrs. Customizing in a unix computing environment. *Proceedings of the Seventh Systems Administration Conference (LISA VII) (USENIX Association: Berkeley, CA)*, page 43, 1993.

[327] I.S. Winkler and B. Dealy. Information security technology? Don't rely on it. A case study in social engineering. *Proceedings of the 5th Security Symposium. (USENIX Association: Berkeley, CA)*, page 1, 1995.

[328] W.C. Wong. Local disk depot: customizing the software environment. *Proceedings of the Seventh Systems Administration Conference (LISA VII) (USENIX Association: Berkeley, CA)*, page 51, 1993.

[329] B. Woodard. Building an enterprise printing system. *Proceedings of the Twelfth Systems Administration Conference (LISA XII) (USENIX Association: Berkeley, CA)*, page 219, 1998.

[330] M. Wyers and S. Eisenbach. Lexis exam invigilation system. *Proceedings of the Fifteenth Systems Administration Conference (LISA XV) (USENIX Association: Berkeley, CA)*, page 199, 2001.

[331] H.Y. Yeom, J. Ha, and I. Kim. Ip multiplexing by transparent port-address translator. *Proceedings of the Tenth Systems Administration Conference (LISA X) (USENIX Association: Berkeley, CA)*, page 113, 1996.

[332] T. Ylonen. Ssh–secure login connections over the internet. *Proceedings of the 6th Security Symposium (USENIX Association: Berkeley, CA)*, page 37, 1996.

[333] M. Zapf, K. Herrmann, K. Geihs, and J. Wolfang. Decentralized snmp management with mobile agents. *Proceedings of the VI IFIP/IEEE IM Conference on Network Management*, page 623, 1999.

[334] M.V. Zelkowitz and D.R. Wallace. Experimental models for validating technology. *IEEE Computer*, May, 23, 1998.

[335] E. Zwicky. Backup at Ohio State. *Proceedings of the Workshop on Large Installation Systems Administration (USENIX Association: Berkeley, CA)*, page 43, 1988.

[336] E.D. Zwicky. Disk space management without quotas. *Proceedings of the Workshop on Large Installation Systems Administration III (USENIX Association: Berkeley, CA)*, page 41, 1989.

[337] E.D. Zwicky. Enhancing your apparent psychic abilities. *Proceedings of the Fifth Large Installation Systems Administration Conference (LISA V) (USENIX Association: Berkeley, CA)*, page 171, 1991.

[338] E.D. Zwicky. Torture testing backup and archive programs: things you ought to know but probably would rather not. *Proceedings of the Fifth Large Installation Systems Administration Conference (LISA V) (USENIX Association: Berkeley, CA)*, page 181, 1991.

[339] E.D. Zwicky. Typecast: beyond cloned hosts. *Proceedings of the Sixth Systems Administration Conference (LISA VI) (USENIX Association: Berkeley, CA)*, page 73, 1992.

[340] E.D. Zwicky. Getting more work out of work tracking systems. *Proceedings of the Eighth Systems Administration Conference (LISA VIII) (USENIX Association: Berkeley, CA)*, page 105, 1994.

[341] E.D. Zwicky, S. Simmons, and R. Dalton. Policy as a system administration tool. *Proceedings of the Fourth Large Installation System Administrator's Conference (LISA IV) (USENIX Association: Berkeley, CA)*, page 115, 1990.

Index